Macroeconomics

Canadian Edition

R. Glenn Hubbard
Columbia University

Anthony Patrick O'Brien
Lehigh University

Apostolos Serletis
University of Calgary

Jason Childs
University of Regina

PEARSON

Toronto

Vice-President, Editorial Director: Gary Bennett
Acquisitions Editor: Claudine O'Donnell
Marketing Manager: Leigh-Anne Graham
Developmental Editor: Mary Watt
Project Manager: Rachel Thompson
Manufacturing Coordinator: Jane Schell
Production Editor: Sapna Rastogi, Cenveo® Publisher Services
Copy Editor: Claudia Forgas
Proofreader: Audrey Dorsch
Compositor: Cenveo Publisher Services
Photo Researcher: Zoe Milgram
Permissions Researcher : Khalid Shakhshir, Electronic Publishing Services
Art Director: Zena Denchik
Cover Designer: Anthony Leung
Interior Designer: Julia Hall
Cover Image: © Izabela Habur / Getty Images

Credits and acknowledgments for material borrowed from other sources and reproduced, with permission, in this textbook appear on the appropriate page within the text.

Original edition published by Pearson Education, Inc., Upper Saddle River, New Jersey, USA. Copyright © 2013 Pearson Education, Inc. This edition is authorized for sale only in Canada.

If you purchased this book outside the United States or Canada, you should be aware that it has been imported without the approval of the publisher or the author.

Library and Archives Canada Cataloguing in Publication

Hubbard, R. Glenn, author
        Macroeconomics / R. Glenn Hubbard, Anthony Patrick
O'Brien, Apostolos Serletis, Jason Childs.   First Canadian
edition

Includes index.
ISBN 978-0-13-702210-6 (pbk.)

        1. Macroeconomics. II. O'Brien, Anthony Patrick, author
III. Serletis, Apostolos, 1954-, author IV. Childs, Jason, 1974-,
author IV. Title.

HB172.5.H86 2013   339   C2013-903971-6

5 16

ISBN 978-0-13-702210-6

Glenn Hubbard, policymaker, professor, and researcher. R. Glenn Hubbard is the dean and Russell L. Carson Professor of Finance and Economics in the Graduate School of Business at Columbia University and professor of economics in Columbia's Faculty of Arts and Sciences. He is also a research associate of the National Bureau of Economic Research and a director of Automatic Data Processing, Black Rock Closed-End Funds, KKR Financial Corporation, and MetLife. He received his Ph.D. in economics from Harvard University in 1983. From 2001 to 2003, he served as chairman of the White House Council of Economic Advisers and chairman of the OECD Economy Policy Committee, and from 1991 to 1993, he was deputy assistant secretary of the U.S. Treasury Department. He currently serves as co-chair of the nonpartisan Committee on Capital Markets Regulation. Hubbard's fields of specialization are public economics, financial markets and institutions, corporate finance, macroeconomics, industrial organization, and public policy. He is the author of more than 100 articles in leading journals, including *American Economic Review, Brookings Papers on Economic Activity, Journal of Finance, Journal of Financial Economics, Journal of Money, Credit, and Banking, Journal of Political Economy, Journal of Public Economics, Quarterly Journal of Economics, RAND Journal of Economics,* and *Review of Economics and Statistics*. His research has been supported by grants from the National Science Foundation, the National Bureau of Economic Research, and numerous private foundations.

Tony O'Brien, award-winning professor and researcher. Anthony Patrick O'Brien is a professor of economics at Lehigh University. He received his Ph.D. from the University of California, Berkeley, in 1987. He has taught principles of economics for more than 15 years, in both large sections and small honors classes. He received the Lehigh University Award for Distinguished Teaching. He was formerly the director of the Diamond Center for Economic Education and was named a Dana Foundation Faculty Fellow and Lehigh Class of 1961 Professor of Economics. He has been a visiting professor at the University of California, Santa Barbara, and the Graduate School of Industrial Administration at Carnegie Mellon University. O'Brien's research has dealt with such issues as the evolution of the U.S. automobile industry, sources of U.S. economic competitiveness, the development of U.S. trade policy, the causes of the Great Depression, and the causes of black-white income differences. His research has been published in leading journals, including *American Economic Review, Quarterly Journal of Economics, Journal of Money, Credit, and Banking, Industrial Relations, Journal of Economic History,* and *Explorations in Economic History*. His research has been supported by grants from government agencies and private foundations. In addition to teaching and writing, O'Brien also serves on the editorial board of the *Journal of Socio-Economics*.

Apostolos Serletis is Professor of Economics at the University of Calgary. Since receiving his Ph.D. from McMaster University in 1984, he has held visiting appointments at the University of Texas at Austin, the Athens University of Economics and Business, and the Research Department of the Federal Reserve Bank of St. Louis.

Professor Serletis' teaching and research interest focus on monetary and financial economics, macroeconometrics, and nonlinear and complex dynamics. He is the author of 12 books, including *The Economics of Money, Banking, and Financial Markets: Fifth Canadian Edition,* with Frederic S. Mishkin (Pearson, 2014); *Macroeconomics: A Modern Approach: First Canadian Edition,* with Robert J. Barro (Nelson, 2010); *The Demand for Money: Theoretical and Empirical Approaches* (Springer, 2007); *Financial Markets and Institutions: Canadian Edition,* with Frederic S. Mishkin and Stanley G. Eakins (Addison-Wesley, 2004); and *The Theory of Monetary Aggregation,* co-edited with William A. Barnett (Elsevier, 2000).

In addition, he has published more than 200 articles in such journals as the *Journal of Economic Literature, Journal of Monetary Economics, Journal of Money, Credit, and Banking, Journal of Econometrics, Journal of Applied Econometrics, Journal of Business and Economic Statistics, Macroeconomic Dynamics, Journal of Banking and Finance, Journal of Economic Dynamics and Control, Economic Inquiry, Canadian Journal of Economics, Econometric Reviews,* and *Studies in Nonlinear Dynamics and Econometrics.*

Professor Serletis is currently an Associate Editor of two academic journals, *Macroeconomic Dynamics* and *Energy Economics,* and a member of the Editorial Board at the *Journal of Economic Asymmetries* and the *Journal of Economic Studies.* He has also served as Guest Editor of the *Journal of Econometrics, Econometric Reviews,* and *Macroeconomic Dynamics.*

Jason Childs is an Associate Professor of Economics at the University of Regina. He received his PhD from McMaster University in 2003. He has taught introductory economics (both microeconomics and macroeconomics) his entire career. He began his teaching career with the McCain Postdoctoral Fellowship at Mount Allison University. After this fellowship he spent six years at the University of New Brunswick, where he received one teaching award and was nominated for two others. Since joining the University of Regina, he has continued to teach introductory-level economics courses and was instrumental in designing a graduate-level program applying economics to problems of public policy. While in Saskatchewan, he has also consulted for the Ministry of Education on the social science curriculum. Professor Childs' research has dealt with a wide variety of issues ranging from the voluntary provision of public services, uncovered interest rate parity, rent controls, to lying. His work has been published in leading journals, including the *Journal of Public Economics, Review of International Economics, Computational Economics,* and *Economics Letters.*

BRIEF CONTENTS

Preface   xv

PART 1: Introduction

Chapter 1: Economics: Foundations and Models   2

　　Appendix A: Using Graphs and Formulas   22

Chapter 2: Trade-offs, Comparative Advantage,
and the Market System   34

Chapter 3: Where Prices Come From: The Interaction of
Supply and Demand   60

　　Appendix B: Quantitative Demand and Supply Analysis   90

PART 2: Macroeconomic Foundations and Long-Run Growth

Chapter 4: GDP: Measuring Total Production
and Income   94

Chapter 5: Unemployment and Inflation   120

Chapter 6: Economic Growth, the Financial
System, and Business Cycles   146

Chapter 7: Long-Run Economic Growth:
Sources and Policies   174

PART 3: Short-Run Fluctuations

Chapter 8: Aggregate Expenditure and
Output in the Short Run   212

Appendix C: The Algebra of Macroeconomic
Equilibrium   250

Chapter 9: Aggregate Demand and Aggregate Supply
Analysis   252

　　Appendix D: Macroeconomic Schools of Thought   287

PART 4: Monetary and Fiscal Policy

Chapter 10 Money, Banks, and the Bank of Canada   290

Chapter 11 Monetary Policy   324

Chapter 12 Fiscal Policy   362

　　Appendix E: A Closer Look at the Multiplier Formula   400

Chapter 13 Inflation, Unemployment, and Bank of
Canada Policy   406

PART 5: The International Economy

Chapter 14: Macroeconomics in an Open Economy   434

Chapter 15: The International Financial System   462

Glossary   G-1
Company Index   I-2
Subject Index   I-3

CONTENTS

Preface   xv
A Word of Thanks   xxvi

PART 1: Introduction

Chapter 1: Economics: Foundations and Models   2
You versus Caffeine   3
1.1 Three Key Economic Ideas   4
  People are Rational   4
  People Respond to Incentives   5
  Making the Connection Will Women in Quebec have
    More Babies if the Government Pays them to?   5
  Optimal Decisions are Made at the Margin   6
  Solved Problem 1.1 McCain Foods Makes a Decision
    at the Margin   6
1.2 The Economic Problems all Societies must Solve   7
  What Goods and Services will be Produced?   7
  How will the Goods and Services be Produced?   8
  Who will Receive the Goods and Services Produced? 8
  Centrally Planned Economies versus Market Economies 8
  The Modern Mixed Economy   9
  Efficiency and Equity   9
1.3 Economic Models   10
  The Role of Assumptions in Economic Models   10
  Forming and Testing Hypotheses in Economic Models 10
  Normative and Positive Analysis   11
  Don't Let This Happen to You Don't Confuse Positive
    Analysis with Normative Analysis   12
  Economics as a Social Science   12
  Making the Connection Should the Government of
    Ontario Increase its Minimum Wage?   12
1.4 Microeconomics and Macroeconomics   13
1.5 The Language of Economics   13
Conclusion   15
  An Inside Look Coffee Prices Set to Soar   16
*Chapter Summary and Problems   18
  Key Terms, Summary, Review Questions, Problems
  and Applications
Appendix A: Using Graphs and Formulas   22
  Graphs of One Variable   23
  Graphs of Two Variables   24
  Slopes of Lines   24
  Taking into Account More Than Two Variables
  on a Graph   25
  Positive and Negative Relationships   26
  Determining Cause and Effect   26
  Are Graphs of Economic Relationships Always
  Straight Lines?   29
  Slopes of Nonlinear Curves   29

Formulas   30
  Formula for a Percentage Change   30
  Formulas for the Areas of a Rectangle and a Triangle 31
  Summary of Using Formulas   31
  Problems and Applications   32

Chapter 2: Trade-offs, Comparative Advantage, and the Market System   34
Managers Make Choices at Toyota   35
2.1 Production Possibilities Frontiers and Opportunity
Costs   36
  Graphing the Production Possibilities Frontier   36
  Solved Problem 2.1 Drawing a Production
    Possibilities Frontier for Pat's Pizza Pit   38
  Making the Connection Facing the Trade-offs of
    Health Care Spending   40
  Increasing Marginal Opportunity Costs   40
  Economic Growth   41
2.2 Comparative Advantage and Trade   42
  Specialization and Gains from Trade   42
  Absolute Advantage versus Comparative Advantage   44
  Comparative Advantage and the Gains from Trade   45
  Don't Let This Happen to You Don't Confuse Absolute
    Advantage and Comparative Advantage   46
  Solved Problem 2.2 Comparative Advantage and the
    Gains from Trade   46
2.3 The Market System   48
  The Circular Flow of Income   48
  The Gains from Free Markets   50
  Making the Connection A Story of the Market
    System in Action: How Do you Make a
    PlayBook?   50
  The Legal Basis of a Successful Market System   51
Conclusion   53
  An Inside Look Toyota Faces a Trade-off   54

Chapter 3: Where Prices Come From: The Interaction of Supply and Demand   60
Red Bull and the Market for Energy Drinks   61
3.1 The Demand Side of the Market   62
  Demand Schedules and Demand Curves   62
  The Law of Demand   63
  What Explains the Law of Demand?   63
  That Magic Latin Phrase Ceteris Paribus   64
  Variables That Shift Market Demand   64
  Making the Connection Is Beer an Inferior Good?   65
  Making the Connection The Aging Baby Boomers   66
  A Change in Demand versus a Change in Quantity
  Demanded   68

*These end-of-chapter resource materials repeat in all chapters.

3.2 The Supply Side of the Market   **69**
Supply Schedules and Supply Curves   69
The Law of Supply   70
Variables That Shift Market Supply   71
A Change in Supply versus a Change in Quantity
Supplied   72
**3.3 Market Equilibrium: Putting Buyers and
Sellers Together**   **73**
How Markets Eliminate Surpluses and Shortages:
Getting to Equilibrium   74
Demand and Supply Both Count   74
Solved Problem 3.1 Demand and Supply Both Count:
A Tale of Two Cards   75
**3.4 The Effect of Demand and Supply Shifts on
Equilibrium**   **77**
The Effect of Shifts in Supply on Equilibrium   77
Making the Connection The Falling Price of
LCD TVs   77
The Effect of Shifts in Demand on Equilibrium   78
The Effect of Shifts in Demand and Supply over Time   79
Solved Problem 3.2 High Demand and Low
Prices in the Lobster Market   80
Don't Let This Happen to You Remember:
A Change in a Good's Price Does *Not* Cause
the Demand or Supply Curve to Shift   81
Shifts in a Curve versus Movements along a Curve   82
Conclusion   **83**
An Inside Look PepsiCo Tries to Create a New
Category of Drinks That Promises
Energy and Health Benefits   84
Appendix B: Quantitative Demand and Supply Analysis   90
Demand and Supply Equations   **90**
Review Questions   93
Problems and Applications   93

PART 2: Macroeconomic Foundations and
Long-Run Growth

Chapter 4: GDP: Measuring Total Production
and Income   94

The Health of the Canadian Economy   95
4.1 Gross Domestic Product Measures Total Production 96
Measuring Total Production: Gross Domestic Product   96
Solved Problem 4.1 Calculating GDP   97
Production, Income, and the Circular-Flow Diagram   98
Components of GDP   100
Don't Let This Happen to You Remember What
Economists Mean by *Investment*   100
An Equation for GDP and Some Actual Values   101
Making the Connection Do Canadians Spend
Too Much?   102
Measuring GDP Using the Value-Added Method   103
4.2 Does GDP Measure What We Want It to Measure?   104
Shortcomings of GDP as a Measure of Total
Production   104

Shortcomings of GDP as a Measure of Well-Being   105
Making the Connection GDP and Happiness   106
4.3 Real GDP versus Nominal GDP   **107**
Calculating Real GDP   107
Solved Problem 4.2 Calculating Real GDP   108
Comparing Real GDP and Nominal GDP   108
The GDP Deflator   109
**4.4 Other Measures of Total Production
and Total Income**   **110**
Gross National Product (GNP)   110
National Income   110
Household Income   111
Household Disposable Income   111
The Division of Income   111
Conclusion   **113**
An Inside Look A Slowdown in the Export of Goods
and Services Shrinks the Canadian Economy
in 2011   114

Chapter 5: Unemployment and Inflation   120

Canadian Manufacturers Grow While Others Shrink   121
**5.1 Measuring the Unemployment Rate and the
Labour Force Participation Rate**   **122**
The Labour Force Survey   122
Problems with Measuring the Unemployment Rate   124
Trends in Labour Force Participation   124
How Long Are People Typically Unemployed?   125
Job Creation and Job Destruction over Time   125
5.2 Types of Unemployment   **126**
Frictional Unemployment and Job Search   126
Structural Unemployment   127
Cyclical Unemployment   127
Seasonal Unemployment   127
Full Employment   128
Making the Connection How Should We
Categorize the Unemployment of Laid-off
Canada Post Employees?   128
5.3 Explaining Unemployment   **129**
Government Policies and the Unemployment Rate   129
Labour Unions   130
Efficiency Wages   130
Making the Connection Why Does Costco Pay Its
Workers More than Walmart?   131
5.4 Measuring Inflation   **131**
The Consumer Price Index   132
Is the CPI Accurate?   133
Don't Let This Happen to You Don't Miscalculate
the Inflation Rate   134
The Producer Price Index   134
**5.5 Using Price Indexes to Adjust for the Effects of
Inflation**   **135**
Solved Problem 5.1 Calculating Real Hourly Wages   135
5.6 Real versus Nominal Interest Rates   **136**
5.7 Does Inflation Impose Costs on the Economy?   **137**

Inflation Affects the Distribution of Income   138
The Problem with Anticipated Inflation   138
The Problem with Unanticipated Inflation   139
Conclusion   **139**
An Inside Look The Link between the Demand for
Manufactured Products and Employment   140

Chapter 6: Economic Growth, the Financial System,
and Business Cycles   **146**

Economic Growth and the Business
Cycle at Bombardier   147
6.1 Long-Run Economic Growth   **148**
Making the Connection Economic Prosperity and
Health   149
Calculating Growth Rates and the Rule of 70   150
What Determines the Rate of Long-Run Growth?   151
Solved Problem 6.1 The Role of Technological
Change in Economic Growth   152
Making the Connection Rapid Economic
Growth in Botswana   153
Potential GDP   154
6.2 Saving, Investment, and the Financial System   **155**
An Overview of the Financial System   155
The Macroeconomics of Saving and Investment   **156**
The Market for Loanable Funds   158
Solved Problem 6.2 How Does a Consumption
Tax Affect Saving, Investment, the Interest
Rate, and Economic Growth?   161
6.3 The Business Cycle   **162**
Some Basic Business Cycle Definitions   162
How Do We Know When the Economy
Is in a Recession?   163
What Happens during the Business Cycle   163
Don't Let This Happen to You Don't Confuse the
Price Level with the Inflation Rate   165
Conclusion   **167**
An Inside Look Bombardier and the Global Recession 168

Chapter 7: Long-Run Economic Growth:
Sources and Policies   **174**

Google's Dilemma in China   175
7.1 Economic Growth over Time and around
the World   **176**
Economic Growth from 1 000 000 BCE to the Present 176
Making the Connection Why Did the Industrial
Revolution Begin in England?   177
Small Differences in Growth Rates Are Important   178
Why Do Growth Rates Matter?   178
Don't Let This Happen to You Don't Confuse
the Average Annual Percentage Change with
the Total Percentage Change   179
"The Rich Get Richer and…"   179
Making the Connection Is Income All That Matters? 180
7.2 What Determines How Fast Economies Grow?   **181**
The Per-Worker Production Function   182

Which Is More Important for Economic Growth:
More Capital or Technological Change?   183
Technological Change: The Key to Sustaining
Economic Growth   184
Making the Connection What Explains the Economic
Failure of the Soviet Union?   184
Solved Problem 7.1 Using the Economic Growth
Model to Analyze the Failure of the Soviet
Economy   185
New Growth Theory   186
Joseph Schumpeter and Creative Destruction   188
Thomas Malthus and Endogenous Population
Growth   188
7.3 Economic Growth in Canada   **189**
Economic Growth in Canada since 1950   189
What Caused the Productivity Slowdown from
1973 to 1994?   190
Can Canada Maintain High Rates of Productivity
Growth?   190
7.4 Why Isn't the Whole World Rich?   **191**
Catch-up: Sometimes but Not Always   191
Solved Problem 7.2 The Economic Growth Model's
Prediction of Catch-up   192
Why Haven't Most Western European Countries,
Canada, and Japan Caught Up to the United States?   194
Why Don't More Low-Income Countries Experience
Rapid Growth?   196
Making the Connection What Do Parking Tickets
in New York City Tell Us about Poverty in the
Developing World?   197
The Benefits of Globalization   199
7.5 Growth Policies   **200**
Enhancing Property Rights and the Rule of Law   200
Making the Connection Will China's Standard of
Living Ever Exceed That of Canada?   200
Improving Health and Education   201
Policies That Promote Technological Change   202
Policies That Promote Saving and Investment   202
Is Economic Growth Good or Bad?   202
Conclusion   **203**
An Inside Look Despite a Plan for Change,
Investment Still Spurs China's Growth   204

PART 3: Short-Run Fluctuations

Chapter 8: Aggregate Expenditure and Output in
the Short Run   **212**

Fluctuating Demand at Tim Hortons   213
8.1 The Aggregate Expenditure Model   **214**
Aggregate Expenditure   214
The Difference between Planned Investment and
Actual Investment   215
Macroeconomic Equilibrium   215
Getting to Macroeconomic Equilibrium   216

8.2 Determining the Level of Aggregate Expenditure in the Economy   **217**
Consumption   218
Making the Connection Do Changes in Consumer Confidence Affect Consumption Spending?   219
The Relationship between Consumption and National Income   222
Income, Consumption, and Saving   223
Solved Problem 8.1 Calculating the Marginal Propensity to Consume and the Marginal Propensity to Save   224
Planned Investment   225
Making the Connection The Hills and Valleys of Snowmobile Purchases   227
Government Purchases   228
Net Exports   228
8.3 Graphing Macroeconomic Equilibrium   **230**
Showing a Recession on the 45°-Line Diagram   233
The Important Role of Inventories   234
A Numerical Example of Macroeconomic Equilibrium   235
8.4 The Multiplier Effect   **235**
A Formula for the Multiplier   237
Summarizing the Multiplier Effect   239
Solved Problem 8.2 Using the Multiplier Formula   239
Don't Let This Happen to You Understand Why Protectionism Doesn't Raise the Multiplier   240
The Paradox of Thrift   241
8.5 The Aggregate Demand Curve   **241**
Conclusion   **243**
An Inside Look Tim Hortons Depends on the Broader Economy   244
Appendix C: The Algebra of Macroeconomic Equilibrium   **250**
Review Questions   251

Chapter 9: Aggregate Demand and Aggregate Supply Analysis   **252**
Canadian National Railway and the Business Cycle   253
9.1 Aggregate Demand   **254**
Why Is the Aggregate Demand Curve Downward Sloping?   254
Shifts of the Aggregate Demand Curve versus Movements along It   256
Variables That Shift the Aggregate Demand Curve   256
Don't Let This Happen to You Understand Why the Aggregate Demand Curve Is Downward Sloping   256
Making the Connection The Role of Exports in Aggregate Demand   258
Solved Problem 9.1 Movements along the Aggregate Demand Curve versus Shifts of the Aggregate Demand Curve   259
Making the Connection Predicting Shifts of the Aggregate Demand Curve   261
9.2 Aggregate Supply   **262**

The Long-Run Aggregate Supply Curve   262
The Short-Run Aggregate Supply Curve   263
Shifts of the Short-Run Aggregate Supply Curve versus Movements along It   264
Variables That Shift the Short-Run Aggregate Supply Curve   264
9.3 Macroeconomic Equilibrium in the Long Run and the Short Run   **267**
Recessions, Expansions, and Supply Shocks   267
Making the Connection Does the Canadian Economy Import Recessions?   269
Making the Connection Does Government Intervention Help Fight a Recession?   271
9.4 A Dynamic Aggregate Demand and Aggregate Supply Model   **272**
What Is the Usual Cause of Inflation?   275
The Canadian Recession of 2008–2009   275
Solved Problem 9.2 Showing the Millennium Economic Boom on a Dynamic Aggregate Demand and Aggregate Supply Graph   277
Conclusion   **279**
An Inside Look Higher Freight Volumes Signal Good News for the Canadian Economy   280
Appendix D: Macroeconomic Schools of Thought   **287**
The Monetarist Model   287
The New Classical Model   288
The Real Business Cycle Model   288
Making the Connection Karl Marx: Capitalism's Severest Critic   289

Part 4: Monetary and Fiscal Policy

Chapter 10 Money, Banks, and the Bank of Canada   **290**
Coca-Cola Dries Up as Money Floods Zimbabwe   291
10.1 What Is Money, and Why Do We Need It?   **292**
Barter and the Invention of Money   292
The Functions of Money   293
What Can Serve as Money?   294
Making the Connection The Pokémon Currency System   295
10.2 How Is Money Measured in Canada Today?   **295**
The M1+ and M1++ Definitions of the Money Supply   297
The M2, M2+, and M2++ Definitions of the Money Supply   297
The M3 Definition of the Money Supply   297
Making the Connection Canada Drops the Penny   297
Don't Let This Happen to You Don't Confuse Money with Income or Wealth   298
Solved Problem 10.1 The Definitions of M1+ and M1++   298
What about Credit Cards and Debit Cards?   299

10.3 How Do Banks Create Money?   299
Bank Balance Sheets   299
Using T-Accounts to Show How a Bank Can
Create Money   300
The Simple Deposit Multiplier   302
Don't Let This Happen to You Don't Confuse
Assets and Liabilities   303
Solved Problem 10.2 Showing How Banks
Create Money   304
The Simple Deposit Multiplier versus the
Real-World Deposit Multiplier   306
10.4 The Bank of Canada   306
The Establishment of the Bank of Canada   307
The Bank of Canada's Operating Band for the
Overnight Interest Rate   307
How the Bank of Canada Implements
Monetary Policy   308
The Bank of Canada's Approach to Monetary Policy   310
The "Shadow Banking System" and the Global
Financial Crisis of 2007–2009   310
10.5 The Quantity Theory of Money   313
Connecting Money and Prices: The Quantity
Equation   313
The Quantity Theory Explanation of Inflation   314
How Accurate Are Estimates of Inflation
Based on the Quantity Theory?   314
High Rates of Inflation   315
Making the Connection The German
Hyperinflation of the Early 1920s   316
Conclusion   317
An Inside Look Price-Level Targeting versus
Inflation-Rate Targeting   318

Chapter 11: Monetary Policy   324

Monetary Policy and the Canadian Housing Market   325
11.1 What Is Monetary Policy?   326
The Goals of Monetary Policy   326
**11.2 The Money Market and the Bank of Canada's
Choice of Monetary Policy Targets**   328
Monetary Policy Targets   328
The Demand for Money   328
Shifts in the Money Demand Curve   329
How the Bank of Canada Manages the Money Supply:
A Quick Review   329
Equilibrium in the Money Market   330
A Tale of Two Interest Rates   331
Choosing a Monetary Policy Target   332
The Importance of the Overnight Interest Rate   332
11.3 Monetary Policy and Economic Activity   333
How Interest Rates Affect Aggregate Demand   333
The Effects of Monetary Policy on Real GDP
and the Price Level   334
Making the Connection Too Low for Zero:
Central Banks Try "Quantitative Easing"   335
Can the Bank of Canada Eliminate Recessions?   337

A Summary of How Monetary Policy Works   338
Don't Let This Happen to You Remember that with
Monetary Policy, It's the Interest Rates—Not the
Money—that Counts   338
**11.4 Monetary Policy in the Dynamic Aggregate
Demand and Aggregate Supply Model**   339
The Effects of Monetary Policy on Real GDP and the
Price Level: A More Complete Account   339
Using Monetary Policy to Fight Inflation   340
Solved Problem 11.1 The Effects of Monetary Policy   341
**11.5 A Closer Look at the Bank of Canada's Setting of
Monetary Policy Targets**   343
Should the Bank of Canada Target the Money Supply?   343
Why Doesn't the Bank of Canada Target Both the Money
Supply and the Interest Rate?   344
The Taylor Rule   344
Making the Connection How Does the Bank of
Canada Measure Inflation?   345
**11.6 Central Bank Policies during the 2007–2009
Global Financial Crisis**   346
The Inflation and Deflation of the Housing Market
Bubble in the United States   346
The Changing Mortgage Market in the United States   348
The Role of Investment Banks in the United States   348
Why Didn't Canada Have a Housing Bubble and
Banking Crisis in 2008?   349
Making the Connection The Wonderful World of
Leverage   349
The US Federal Reserve and the US Treasury
Department Respond   350
The US Federal Reserve Adopts Flexible
Inflation Targeting   352
Conclusion   353
An Inside Look The Bank of Canada's Response to a
Developing Housing Price Bubble   354

Chapter 12: Fiscal Policy   362

Canadian Fiscal Policy during and after the 2008–2009
Recession   363
12.1 What Is Fiscal Policy?   364
What Fiscal Policy Is and What It Isn't   364
Automatic Stabilizers versus Discretionary
Fiscal Policy   364
An Overview of Government Spending and Taxes   364
Where Does the Money Go?   366
Where Does the Money Come From?   367
Making the Connection The Exploding
Costs of Health Care   367
**12.2 The Effects of Fiscal Policy on Real GDP and
the Price Level**   369
Expansionary and Contractionary Fiscal Policy   369
A Summary of How Fiscal Policy Affects
Aggregate Demand   371
**12.3 Fiscal Policy in the Dynamic Aggregate Demand
and Aggregate Supply Model**   371
12.4 The Government Purchases and Tax Multipliers   373

The Effect of Changes in Tax Rates   375
Taking into Account the Effects of Aggregate Supply   375
The Multipliers Work in Both Directions   376
Don't Let This Happen to You Don't Overestimate
    the Size of the Multiplier   376
Making the Connection Fiscal Policy in Action:
    The Federal Government Responds to the
    Global Recession of 2007–2009   377
Solved Problem 12.1 Fiscal Policy Multipliers   378
12.5 The Limits of Fiscal Policy as a Stimulus   379
Does Government Spending Reduce
Private Spending   379
Crowding Out in the Short Run   380
Crowding Out in the Long Run   381
Making the Connection Is Losing Your Job
    Good for Your Health?   382
12.6 Deficits, Surpluses, and Federal
Government Debt   382
How the Federal Budget Can Serve as an Automatic
Stabilizer   383
Making the Connection The Greek Debt Crisis and
    Austerity   384
Solved Problem 12.2 The Effect of Economic
    Fluctuations on the Budget Deficit   385
Should the Federal Budget Always Be Balanced?   385
The Federal Government Debt   386
Is Government Debt a Problem?   386
12.7 The Effects of Fiscal Policy in the Long Run   387
The Long-Run Effects of Tax Policy   387
Tax Simplification   388
Making the Connection Should Canada Adopt the
    "Flat Tax"?   389
The Economic Effect of Tax Reform   390
How Big Are Supply-Side Effects?   391
Conclusion   393
An Inside Look Austerity Measures Aren't Always the
    Answer in Tough Economic Times   394
Appendix E: A Closer Look at the Multiplier Formula   400
An Expression for Equilibrium Real GDP   400
A Formula for the Government Purchases Multiplier   401
A Formula for the Tax Multiplier   402
The "Balanced Budget" Multiplier   402
The Effects of Changes in Tax Rates on the Multiplier   403
The Multiplier in an Open Economy   403

Chapter 13: Inflation, Unemployment, and Bank of
Canada Policy   406

Leverage, Bubbles, Bank of Canada Policies, and
Macroprudential Regulation   407
13.1 The Discovery of the Short-Run Trade-off between
Unemployment and Inflation   408
Explaining the Phillips Curve with Aggregate
Demand and Aggregate Supply Curves   409
Is the Phillips Curve a Policy Menu?   410
Is the Short-Run Phillips Curve Stable?   410
The Long-Run Phillips Curve   411

The Role of Expectations of Future Inflation   411
Making the Connection Do Workers Understand
    Inflation?   412
13.2 The Short-Run and Long-Run Phillips Curves   413
Shifts in the Short-Run Phillips Curve   414
How Does a Vertical Long-Run Phillips Curve Affect
Monetary Policy?   415
Making the Connection Does the Natural Rate of
    Unemployment Ever Change?   416
Solved Problem 13.1 Changing Views of the
    Phillips Curve   417
13.3 Expectations of the Inflation Rate and
Monetary Policy   418
The Effect of Rational Expectations on
Monetary Policy   418
Is the Short-Run Phillips Curve Really Vertical?   419
Real Business Cycle Models   420
13.4 Bank of Canada Policy from the 1970s to the
Present   420
The Effect of a Supply Shock on the Phillips Curve   421
The Canadian Disinflation, 1989–1993   422
Don't Let This Happen to You Don't Confuse
    Disinflation with Deflation   423
Inflation Targeting, 1989–Present   423
Solved Problem 13.2 Using Monetary Policy to
    Lower the Inflation Rate   424
The 2007–2009 Global Recession and the Crisis in
Monetary Policy   425
Conclusion   427
An Inside Look Can the Federal Reserve Balance the
    Trade-off between Unemployment and Inflation
    in the United States?   428

PART 5: The International Economy

Chapter 14: Macroeconomics in an Open
Economy   434

A Strong US Dollar Hurts McDonald's Profits   435
14.1 The Balance of Payments: Linking Canada to the
International Economy   436
The Current Account   437
The Financial Account   438
The Capital Account   438
Why Is the Balance of Payments Always Zero?   438
Don't Let This Happen to You Don't Confuse the
    Balance of Trade, the Current Account Balance,
    and the Balance of Payments   439
Solved Problem 14.1 Understanding the
    Arithmetic of Open Economies   439
14.2 The Foreign Exchange Market and
Exchange Rates   440
Making the Connection Exchange Rate Listings   441
Equilibrium in the Market for Foreign Exchange   442
How Do Shifts in Demand and Supply Affect the
Exchange Rate?   443

Making the Connection What Explains the
    Fall and Rise and Fall of the Canadian Dollar?   444
Some Exchange Rates Are Not Determined by
the Market   446
How Movements in the Exchange Rate Affect
Exports and Imports   446
Don't Let This Happen to You Don't Confuse
    What Happens When a Currency Appreciates
    with What Happens When It Depreciates   446
Solved Problem 14.2 The Effect of Changing
    Exchange Rates on the Prices of Imports
    and Exports   447
The Real Exchange Rate   447

14.3 The International Sector and National
Saving and Investment   **448**
Net Exports Equal Net Foreign Investment   448
Domestic Saving, Domestic Investment, and Net
Foreign Investment   449
Solved Problem 14.3 Arriving at the Saving and
    Investment Equation   450

14.4 The Effect of a Government Budget Deficit on
Investment   **451**
Making the Connection Why Is the United States
    Called the "World's Largest Debtor"?   452

14.5 Monetary Policy and Fiscal Policy in an Open
Economy   **453**
Monetary Policy in an Open Economy   453
Fiscal Policy in an Open Economy   454

Conclusion   **455**
An Inside Look The Canadian Dollar and the Effects of
    Economic Interdependence   456

Chapter 15: The International Financial System   **462**
Airbus Deals with Fluctuating Exchange Rates   463
15.1 Exchange Rate Systems   **464**
Don't Let This Happen to You Remember
    That Modern Currencies Are Fiat Money   465
15.2 The Current Exchange Rate System   **465**
The Floating Canadian Dollar   465
Making the Connection The Canadian
    Province of ... Arizona?   466
What Determines Exchange Rates in the Long Run?   467
Making the Connection The Big Mac Theory of
    Exchange Rates   468
Solved Problem 15.1 Calculating Purchasing Power
    Parity Exchange Rates Using Big Macs   469
The Euro   471
Making the Connection Can the Euro Survive?   472
Pegging against Another Currency   474
Making the Connection Crisis and Recovery in
    South Korea   477
15.3 International Capital Markets   **478**
Conclusion   **481**
An Inside Look Can Tariffs Offset the
    Effect of Overvaluation?   482

Glossary   **G-1**

Company Index   **I-1**

Subject Index   **I-2**

There have been dramatic advances in macroeconomics over the past 40 years, and the field is changing rapidly. Today, macroeconomics assumes that economic agents (i.e., people) have rational expectations and are forward-looking, relies on market-clearing conditions for households and firms, and relies on financial shocks and mechanisms that amplify and propagate those shocks over time. Yet, in the aftermath of the global financial crisis of 2007–2009, a number of economists, the media, and policymakers have argued that modern macroeconomics can't capture the complexity of the world that is to be explained.

We believe that with the increasing complexity and interdependence of real economies, macroeconomics must be relevant and applicable. However, most first-year books do not help students understand a number of contemporary issues and economic events and the policy responses to them. We realized that the 4th US edition of R. Glenn Hubbard and Anthony P. O'Brien's *Principles of Macroeconomics* is the kind of textbook that makes modern macroeconomics valuable and applicable. It is the textbook that we always wanted to use in our classes and decided to work on the Canadian edition of the book.

The Canadian edition of *Principles of Macroeconomics* is completely widget-free. It delivers economics coverage using many fresh, lively, real-world examples from newspapers, magazines, websites, and professional journals from around the world. By building from the specific example to the general case, this text fosters student engagement. In our testing of early drafts of the text in the classroom, we found that the degree of student engagement improved substantially when real-world examples and applications were placed at the forefront rather than treated as add-ons or afterthoughts. This approach is appealing to both instructors and students, because it captures the richness and interactions of the real world while demonstrating the value and applicability of modern macroeconomics.

Highlights of This Edition

The severe global financial crisis that began in 2007 when the housing bubble burst in the United States and the "Great Recession" and European debt crisis that followed still affect the world economy today. In many countries, unemployment has risen to levels not seen in decades. The crisis in the financial system was the worst since the Great Depression of the 1930s. Policy debates intensified as governments around the world introduced the largest packages of spending increases and tax cuts in history. Central banks, including the Bank of Canada, sailed into uncharted waters as they developed new policy tools to deal with the unprecedented financial turmoil. Other long-running policy debates continued as well, as huge long-run budget deficits, environmental problems, income inequality, and changes to the tax system all received attention from economists, policymakers, and the public.

The Canadian edition helps students understand recent economic events and the policy responses to them. It places applications at the forefront of the discussion. We believe that students find the study of economics more interesting and easier to master when they see economic analysis applied to real-world issues that concern them.

The Foundation: Contextual Learning and Modern Organization

Students come to study macroeconomics with a strong interest in understanding events and developments in the economy. We try to capture that interest and develop students' economic intuition and understanding in this text. We present macroeconomics in a way that is modern and based in the real world of business and economic policy. And we believe that we do so without making the analysis more difficult. We avoid the recent trend of using simplified versions of intermediate models, which are often more detailed and more complex than what students need to understand the basic macroeconomic issues. Instead, we use a more realistic version of the familiar aggregate demand and aggregate supply model to analyze short-run fluctuations and monetary and fiscal policy. We also avoid the "duelling schools of thought" approach often used to teach macroeconomics at the principles level. We emphasize the many areas of macroeconomics where most economists agree. We also present real business and policy situations throughout to develop students' intuition.

This edition includes the following:

- **A broad discussion of macro statistics.** Many students pay at least some attention to the financial news and know that the release of statistics by government agencies can cause movements in stock and bond prices. A background in macroeconomic statistics helps clarify some of the policy issues encountered in later chapters. In Chapter 4, "GDP: Measuring Total Production and Income," and Chapter 5, "Unemployment and Inflation," we provide students with an understanding of the uses and potential shortcomings of the key macroeconomic statistics, without getting bogged down in the minutiae of how the statistics are constructed.

- **Early coverage of long-run topics.** We place key macroeconomic issues in their long-run context in Chapter 6, "Economic Growth, the Financial System, and Business Cycles," and Chapter 7, "Long-Run Economic Growth: Sources and Policies." Chapter 6 puts the business cycle in the context of underlying long-run growth and discusses what actually happens during the phases of the business cycle. We believe that this material is important if students are to have the understanding of business cycles they will need to interpret economic events; this material is often discussed only briefly or omitted entirely in other textbooks. We know that many instructors prefer to have a short-run orientation to their macro courses, with a strong emphasis on policy. Accordingly, we have structured Chapter 6 so that its discussion of long-run growth would be sufficient for instructors who want to move quickly to short-run analysis. Chapter 7 uses a simple neoclassical growth model to explain important economic growth issues. We apply the model to topics such as the decline of the Soviet economy, the surprisingly strong growth performance of Botswana, and the failure of many developing countries to sustain high growth rates. And we challenge students with the discussion "Why Isn't the Whole World Rich?"

- **A dynamic model of aggregate demand and aggregate supply.** We take a fresh approach to the standard aggregate demand and aggregate supply (*AD–AS*) model. We realize there is no good, simple alternative to using the *AD–AS* model when explaining movements in the price level and in real GDP. But we know that more instructors are dissatisfied with the *AD–AS* model than with any other aspect of the macro principles course. The key problem, of course, is that *AD–AS* is a static model that attempts to account for dynamic changes in real GDP and the price level. Our approach retains the basics of the *AD–AS* model but makes it more accurate and useful by making it more dynamic. We emphasize two points: First, changes in the position of the short-run (upward-sloping) aggregate supply curve depend mainly on the state of expectations of the inflation rate. Second, the existence of growth in the economy means that the long-run (vertical) aggregate supply curve shifts to the right every year. This "dynamic" *AD–AS* model provides students with a more accurate understanding of the causes and consequences of fluctuations in real GDP and the price level. We introduce this model in Chapter 9, "Aggregate Demand and Aggregate Supply Analysis," and use it to discuss monetary policy in Chapter 11, "Monetary Policy," and fiscal policy in Chapter 12, "Fiscal Policy." Instructors may safely omit the sections on the dynamic *AD–AS* model without any loss in continuity to the discussion of macroeconomic theory and policy.

- **Extensive coverage of monetary policy.** Because of the central role monetary policy plays in the economy and in students' curiosity about business and financial news, we devote two chapters—Chapters 11, "Monetary Policy," and 13, "Inflation, Unemployment, and Bank of Canada Policy"—to the topic. We emphasize the issues involved in the Bank of Canada's choice of monetary policy targets, and we include coverage of the

Taylor rule. We also cover the Bank of Canada's new policies aimed at dealing with the bubble in the Canadian housing market and its effects on financial markets.

- **Coverage of both the demand-side and supply-side effects of fiscal policy.** Our discussion of fiscal policy in Chapter 12, "Fiscal Policy," carefully distinguishes between automatic stabilizers and discretionary fiscal policy. We also provide significant coverage of the supply-side effects of fiscal policy.

- **A self-contained but thorough discussion of the Keynesian income-expenditure approach.** The Keynesian income-expenditure approach (the "45°-line diagram," or "Keynesian cross") is useful for introducing students to the short-run relationship between spending and production. Many instructors, however, prefer to omit this material. Therefore, we use the 45°-line diagram only in Chapter 8, "Aggregate Expenditure and Output in the Short Run." The discussion of monetary and fiscal policy in later chapters uses only the *AD–AS* model, which makes it possible to omit Chapter 8.

- **Extensive international coverage.** We include two chapters devoted to international topics: Chapter 14, "Macroeconomics in an Open Economy," and Chapter 15, "The International Financial System." Having a good understanding of the international trading and financial systems is essential to understanding the macroeconomy and to satisfying students' curiosity about the economic world around them. In addition to the material in our two international chapters, we weave international comparisons into the narratives of several other chapters, including our discussion of labour market policies in Chapter 13, "Inflation, Unemployment, and Bank of Canada Policy," and central banking in Chapter 10, "Money, Banks, and the Bank of Canada."

- **Flexible chapter organization.** Because we realize that there are a variety of approaches to teaching principles of macroeconomics, we have structured our chapters for maximum flexibility. For example, our discussion of long-run economic growth in Chapter 6, "Economic Growth, the Financial System, and Business Cycles," makes it possible for instructors to omit the more thorough discussion of these issues in Chapter 7, "Long-Run Economic Growth: Sources and Policies." Our discussion of the Keynesian 45°-line diagram is confined to Chapter 8, "Aggregate Expenditure and Output in the Short Run," so that instructors who do not use this approach can proceed directly to aggregate demand and aggregate supply analysis in Chapter 9, "Aggregate Demand and Aggregate Supply Analysis." While we devote two chapters to monetary policy, the first of these—Chapter 11, "Monetary Policy"—is a self-contained discussion, so instructors may safely omit the material in Chapter 13, "Inflation, Unemployment, and Bank of Canada Policy," if they choose to. Finally, instructors may choose to omit both of the international chapters (Chapter 14, "Macroeconomics in an Open Economy," and Chapter 15, "The International Financial System"), cover just Chapter 14; or cover Chapter 14 and Chapter 15.

Special Features: A Real-World, Hands-on Approach to Learning Macroeconomics

Chapter-Opening Cases and *An Inside Look* News Articles

Each chapter-opening case provides a real-world context for learning, sparks students' interest in economics, and helps to unify the chapter. Each chapter-opening case describes a real situation that students can relate to. Here are a few examples of the topics we explore in the chapter openers in this new edition:

- Red Bull and the market for energy drinks (Chapter 3)
- Economic growth and the business cycle at Bombardier (Chapter 6)
- The effect of the business cycle on Canadian National Railways (Chapter 9)
- Monetary policy and the Canadian housing market (Chapter 11)
- Leverage, bubbles, and central bank policies (Chapter 13)

An Inside Look is a two-page feature that shows students how to apply the concepts from the chapter to the analysis of a news article. The articles selected deal with policy issues and are titled *An Inside Look*. Articles are from sources such as the *Hamilton Spectator*, the *Economist*, *National Post*, the *Toronto Star*, and the *Montreal Gazette*. *An Inside Look* presents an excerpt from an article, an analysis of the article, and critical thinking questions.

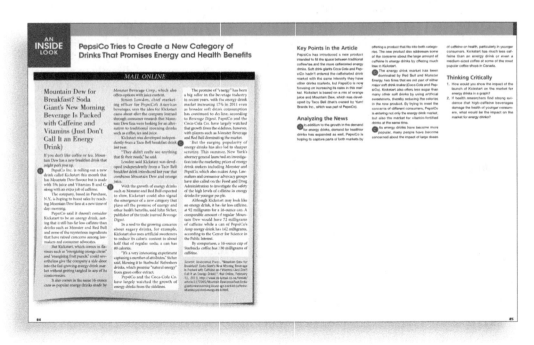

Here are a few examples of the articles featured in *An Inside Look*:

- "Coffee Prices Soar" (Chapter 1)
- "Canada's Economy Shrinks for First Time in Two Years" (Chapter 4)
- "Bombardier Cuts Regional Jet Production" (Chapter 6)
- "Tim Hortons Earnings Fall Short of Forecasts" (Chapter 8)
- "Canada's Housing Market: Look Out Below" (Chapter 11)

Economics in Your Life

After the chapter-opening real-world business case, we have added a personal dimension to the chapter opener, with a feature titled *Economics in Your Life*, which asks students to consider how economics affects their own lives. The feature piques the interest of students and emphasizes the connection between the material they are learning and their own experiences.

Economics in Your Life

Red Bull or Beaver Buzz Energy: What's Your Beverage?

Suppose you are about to buy an energy drink and you are choosing between a Red Bull and a Beaver Buzz Energy. As the more established, well-known brand, Red Bull has many advantages over a recent entrant like Beaver Buzz Energy. One strategy DD Beverage Company can use to overcome Red Bull's advantages is to have Beaver Buzz Energy compete based on price and value. Would you choose to buy a can of Beaver Buzz Energy if it had a lower price than a can of Red Bull? Would you be less likely to drink Beaver Buzz Energy if your income dropped? As you read this chapter, see if you can answer these questions. You can check your answers against those we provide on page 82 at the end of this chapter.

At the end of the chapter, we use the chapter concepts to answer the questions asked at the beginning of the chapter.

Economics in Your Life

Red Bull or Beaver Buzz Energy: What's Your Beverage?

At the beginning of the chapter, we asked you to consider two questions: Would you choose to buy a can of Beaver Buzz Energy if it had a lower price than a can of Red Bull? Would you be less likely to drink Beaver Buzz Energy if your income dropped? To determine the answer to the first question, you have to recognize that Beaver Buzz Energy and Red Bull are substitutes. If you consider the two drinks to be very close substitutes, then you are likely to buy the one with the lower price. In the market, if consumers generally believe that Beaver Buzz Energy and Red Bull are close substitutes, a fall in the price of Beaver Buzz Energy will increase the quantity of Beaver Buzz Energy demanded and decrease the demand for Red Bull. Suppose that you are currently leaning toward buying Red Bull because you believe that it is better tasting than Beaver Buzz Energy. If a decrease in your income made you more likely to buy Beaver Buzz Energy, then you consider Beaver Buzz Energy as an inferior good.

Here are a few examples of the topics featured in *Economics in Your Life*:

- Red Bull or Beaver Buzz Energy: what's your beverage? (Chapter 3)
- What's the best country for you to work in? (Chapter 4)
- Do you help the economy more if you spend or if you save? (Chapter 6)
- When consumer confidence falls, is your job at risk? (Chapter 8)
- Should you buy a house during a recession? (Chapter 11)

Solved Problems

Many students have great difficulty handling applied economics problems. We help students overcome this hurdle by including two or three worked-out problems tied to select chapter-opening learning objectives. Our goals are to keep students focused on the main ideas of each chapter and to give students a model of how to solve an economic problem by breaking it down step by step. Additional exercises in the end-of-chapter Problems and Applications section are tied to every *Solved Problem*. Additional *Solved Problems* appear in the Instructor's Manual and the print Study Guide. In addition, the Test Item Files include problems tied to the *Solved Problems* in the main book.

Table 3.3		Supply Curve Unchanged	Supply Curve Shifts Right	Supply Curve Shifts to the Left
How Shifts in Demand and Supply Affect Equilibrium Price (P) and Quantity (Q)	Demand curve unchanged	Q unchanged	Q increases	Q decreases
		P unchanged	P decreases	P increases
	Demand curve shifts right	Q increases	Q increases	Q increases or decreases
		P increases	P increases or decreases	P increases
	Demand curve shifts left	Q decreases	Q increases or decreases	Q decreases
		P decreases	P decreases	P increases or decreases

Solved Problem 3.2

High Demand and Low Prices in the Lobster Market

For many communities in the Maritimes, the lobster fishery is an essential part of the local economy. Lobster is fished only in season, and different communities are allowed to fish at different times of the year. For example, the fishing season for the area of Yarmouth, Nova Scotia, is from late November to the end of May. It isn't uncommon for the price of lobster to fluctuate during the season. In some cases, it can change from below $5 per pound to $8 or $9 per pound. A patch of really bad weather can drive up the price quickly, but so does Christmas (lobster tends to be a popular part of winter festivities in Canada, Europe, and other parts of the world).

What would happen if the weather just before Christmas was particularly good, allowing fishers to spend more time on the water and catch more lobster?

Solving the Problem

Step 1: Review the chapter material. This problem is about how shifts in demand and supply curves affect the equilibrium price, so you may want to review the section "The Effect of Shifts in Demand and Supply over Time."

Step 2: Draw the demand and supply graph. Draw a demand and supply graph,

Step 3: Add a demand and supply curve. Add a demand curve to account for the increase in the demand for lobster from Europe. Add a supply curve to account for the nicer-than-usual weather.

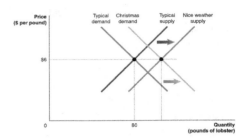

Step 4: Explain the graph. After studying the graph, you should see how the two events of increased demand from Europe and the nicer-than-usual weather combine to move the equilibrium price. The increase in supply due to the nicer-than-usual weather is offset by some of the increase in demand from Europeans. We can't say for sure which way the price will go. The price of lobster will rise if the shift in demand is greater than the shift in supply. If the shift in supply is greater than the shift in demand, prices will actually fall. All that we can say for certain is that the quantity of lobster sold (and eaten) will go up.

Source: Province of Nova Scotia, "Lobster Fishing Seasons in Atlantic Canada," *Nova Scotia Fisheries and Aquaculture,* May 17, 2012, http://www.gov.ns.ca/fish/marine/map/lobarea.shtml.

Your Turn: For more practice, do related problems 4.3 and 4.4 on page 88 at the end of this chapter.

Don't Let This Happen to You

We know from many years of teaching which concepts students find most difficult. Each chapter contains a box feature called *Don't Let This Happen to You* that alerts students to the most common pitfalls in that chapter's material. We follow up with a related question in the end-of-chapter Problems and Applications section.

Don't Let This Happen to You

Remember: A Change in a Good's Price Does *Not* Cause the Demand or Supply Curve to Shift

Suppose a student is asked to draw a demand and supply graph to illustrate how an increase in the price of oranges would affect the market for apples, other variables being constant. He draws the graph on the left below and explains it as follows: "Because apples and oranges are substitutes, an increase in the price of oranges will cause an initial shift to the right in the demand curve for apples, from D_1 to D_2. However, because this initial shift in the demand curve for apples results in a higher price for apples, P_2, consumers will find apples less desirable, and the demand curve will shift to the left, from D_2 to D_3, resulting in a final equilibrium price of P_3." Do you agree or disagree with the student's analysis?

You should disagree. The student has correctly understood that an increase in the price of oranges will cause the demand curve for apples to shift to the right. But the second demand curve shift the student describes, from D_2 to D_3, will not take place. Changes in the price of a product do not result in shifts in the product's demand curve. Changes in the price of a product result only in movements along a demand curve.

Making the Connection

Each chapter includes two or more *Making the Connection* features that provide real-world reinforcement of key concepts and help students learn how to interpret what they read on the Web and in newspapers. Most *Making the Connection* features use relevant, stimulating, and provocative news stories focused on businesses and policy issues. Each *Making the Connection* has at least one supporting end-of-chapter problem to allow students to test their understanding of the topic discussed. Here are a few examples of *Making the Connection* features:

- Will China's Standard of Living Ever Exceed That of Canada? (Chapter 7)
- Does the Canadian Economy Import Recessions? (Chapter 9)
- Too Low for Zero: Central Banks Try "Quantitative Easing" (Chapter 11)
- Why Is the United States Called the "World's Largest Debtor"? (Chapter 14)
- Can the Euro Survive? (Chapter 15)

Graphs and Summary Tables

Graphs are an indispensable part of a principles of economics course but are a major stumbling block for many students. Every chapter except Chapter 1 includes end-of-chapter problems that require students to draw, read, and interpret graphs. Interactive graphing exercises appear on the book's supporting website. We use four devices to help students read and interpret graphs:

1. Detailed captions
2. Notes in the graphs

Making the Connection

Is Beer an Inferior Good?

For most Canadians, a beverage on a hot summer afternoon is part of the culture. In 2012, Canadians drank 8.1 litres of alcohol in various forms per person, including 80.3 litres of beer. This is a profitable industry with the LCBO (Liquor Control Board of Ontario) paying a dividend to the Government of Ontario of $1.63 billion.

How does income affect the choices Canadians make at the liquor store? As Canadians have gotten wealthier, they have changed their drinking habits. There is an underlying trend: Instead of buying beer at the lowest possible price, more and more Canadians are opting for local micro-brewery beer or local wine. In 2009, New Brunswick's alcohol retailer (Alcool NB Liquor) launched its own brand of beer, which provided New Brunswickers with a low-cost alternative, but in July 2011, that brand was discontinued due to lack of sales. During the 2011 fiscal year, the LCBO noticed that the sales of its premium products recovered from the slump that started around the same time as the financial crisis; in Ontario, the volume of sales of alcoholic beverages changed little.

Alcool NB Liquor discontinued its low cost brand of beer as the economy recovered from recession.

What we're seeing from beer sales in particular is that Canadians have begun to treat mainstream beer as an inferior good. As the average income of Canadians rises, they switch from low-cost beverages to more expensive ones. Recall that when economists describe a product as inferior, they aren't necessarily saying it is of poor quality, they're just saying that consumers buy less of it when their incomes rise.

Sources: Statistics Canada – CANSIM Table 183-0019 Series v28463248; David Pett and Jared Lindzon, Financial Post-Jun. 3, 2011; Cigdem Iltan on Thursday, July 7, 2011, MacLean's Magazine.

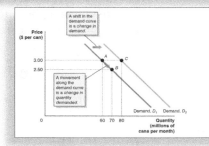

Figure 3.3

A Change in Demand versus a Change in Quantity Demanded

If the price of energy drinks falls from $3.00 to $2.50, the result will be a movement along the demand curve from point A to point B—an increase in quantity demanded from 60 million cans to 70 million cans. If consumers' incomes increase, or if another factor changes that makes consumers want more energy drinks at every price, the demand curve will shift to the right—an increase in demand. In this case, the increase in demand from D_1 to D_2 causes the quantity of energy drinks demanded at a price of $3.00 to increase from 60 million cans at point A to 80 million cans at point C.

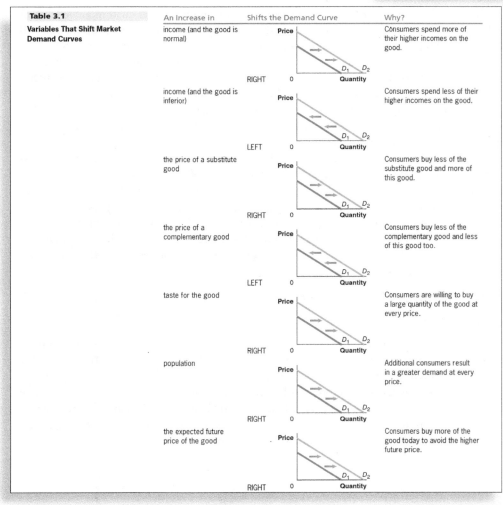

Table 3.1

Variables That Shift Market Demand Curves

An Increase in	Shifts the Demand Curve	Why?
income (and the good is normal)	RIGHT	Consumers spend more of their higher incomes on the good.
income (and the good is inferior)	LEFT	Consumers spend less of their higher incomes on the good.
the price of a substitute good	RIGHT	Consumers buy less of the substitute good and more of this good.
the price of a complementary good	LEFT	Consumers buy less of the complementary good and less of this good too.
taste for the good	RIGHT	Consumers are willing to buy a large quantity of the good at every price.
population	RIGHT	Additional consumers result in a greater demand at every price.
the expected future price of the good	RIGHT	Consumers buy more of the good today to avoid the higher future price.

3. Colour-coded curves
4. Summary tables with graphs (see pages 68, 72, and 260 for examples)

Review Questions and Problems and Applications

Every exercise in a chapter's Review Questions and Problems and Applications sections are available in MyEconLab. Using MyEconLab, students can complete these and many other exercises online, get tutorial help, and receive instant feedback and assistance on exercises they answer incorrectly. Also, student learning is enhanced by having the summary material and problems grouped together by learning objective, which will allow students to focus on the parts of the chapter they found most challenging. Each major section of the chapter, paired with a learning objective, has at least two review questions and three problems.

We include one or more end-of-chapter problems that test students' understanding of the content presented in the *Solved Problem*, *Making the Connection*, and *Don't Let This Happen to You* features in the chapter. Instructors can cover a feature in class and assign the corresponding problem for homework. The Test Item Files also include test questions that pertain to these special features.

Integrated Supplements

The authors and Pearson Canada have worked together to integrate the text, print, and media resources to make teaching and learning easier.

MyEconLab

MyLab and Mastering, our leading online learning products, deliver customizable content and highly personalized study paths, responsive learning tools, and real-time evaluation and diagnostics. MyLab and Mastering products give educators the ability to move each student toward the moment that matters most—the moment of true understanding and learning.

MyEconLab for Hubbard, Canadian Edition, can be used as a powerful out-of-the-box resource for students who need extra help, or instructors can take full advantage of its advanced customization options. Students can also benefit from MyEconLab's Study Play, now powered by a sophisticated adaptive learning engine that tailors learning material to meet their unique learning needs.

Pearson eText gives students access to the text whenever and wherever they have access to the Internet. eText pages look exactly like the printed text, offering powerful new functionality for students and instructors. Users can create notes, highlight text in different colours, create bookmarks, zoom, click hyperlinked words and phrases to view definitions, and view in single-page or two-page view. Pearson eText allows for quick navigation to key parts of the eText using a table of contents and provides full-text search. The eText may also offer links to associated media files, enabling users to access videos, animations, or other activities as they read the text.

Other Resources for the Instructor

Instructor's Manual

The Instructor's Manual includes chapter-by-chapter summaries grouped by learning objectives, teaching outlines incorporating key terms and definitions, teaching tips, topics for class discussion, new *Solved Problems*, new *Making the Connection* features, new *Economics in Your Life* scenarios, and solutions to all review questions and problems in the book. The Instructor's Manual is available for download from the Instructor's Resource Centre (www.pearsoned.ca/highered). The authors, Jason Childs and Apostolos Serletis, prepared the solutions to the end-of-chapter review questions and problems.

Two Test Item Files

This edition is accompanied by two Test Item Files. Each Test Item File includes 2000 class-tested multiple-choice, true/false, short-answer, and graphing questions. The first Test Item File will be available upon publication of the text; the second Test Item File of 2000 questions will be added a year following publication in order to incorporate market feedback and to provide a fresh and updated store of questions. There are questions to support each key feature in the book. The Test Item Files are available in print and for download from the Instructor's Resource Centre (www.pearsonhighered.com/hubbard). Test questions are annotated with the following information:

- **Difficulty:** 1 for straight recall, 2 for some analysis, 3 for complex analysis
- **Type:** multiple-choice, true/false, short-answer, essay
- **Topic:** the term or concept the question supports
- **Learning outcome**
- **AACSB** (see description that follows)
- **Page number**
- **Special feature in the main book:** chapter-opening case example, *Economics in Your Life*, *Solved Problem*, *Making the Connection*, *Don't Let This Happen to You*, and *An Inside Look*

The Association to Advance Collegiate Schools of Business (AACSB)

The Test Item File author has connected select questions to the general knowledge and skill guidelines found in the AACSB Assurance of Learning Standards.

TestGen

The computerized TestGen package allows instructors to customize, save, and generate classroom tests. The test program permits instructors to edit, add, or delete questions from the Test Item Files; analyze test results; and organize a database of tests and student results. This software allows for extensive flexibility and ease of use. It provides many options for organizing and displaying tests, along with search and sort features. The software and the Test Item Files can be downloaded from the Instructor's Resource Center (www.pearsonhighered.com/hubbard).

PowerPoint Lecture Presentation

Two sets of PowerPoint slides are available:

1. A comprehensive set of animated PowerPoint slides can be used by instructors for class presentations or by students for lecture preview or review. These animated slides include all the graphs, tables, and equations in the textbook.
2. A second set of PowerPoint slides without animations is available for those who prefer a more streamlined presentation for class use.

CourseSmart for Instructors

CourseSmart goes beyond traditional expectations—providing instant, online access to the textbooks and course materials you need at a lower cost for students. And even as students save money, you can save time and hassle with a digital eTextbook that allows you to search for the most relevant content at the very moment you need it. Whether it's evaluating textbooks or creating lecture notes to help students with difficult concepts, CourseSmart can make life a little easier. See how when you visit www.coursesmart.com/instructors.

Learning Solution Consultants

Pearson's Technology Specialists work with faculty and campus course designers to ensure that Pearson technology products, assessment tools, and online course materials are tailored to meet your specific needs. This highly qualified team is dedicated to helping students take full advantage of a wide range of educational resources by assisting in the integration of a variety of instructional materials and media formats. Your local Pearson Canada sales representative can provide you with more details about this service program.

Pearson Custom Library

For enrollments of at least 25 students, you can create your own textbook by choosing the chapters that best suit your own course needs. To begin building your custom text, visit www.pearsoncustomlibrary.com. You may also work with a dedicated Pearson Custom editor to create your ideal text—publishing your own original content or mixing and matching Pearson content. Contact your local Pearson Representative to get started.

ACKNOWLEDGEMENTS

The guidance and recommendations of the following instructors helped us develop our plans for the first Canadian edition and the supplements package. While we could not incorporate every suggestion from every reviewer, we do thank each and every one of you and acknowledge that your feedback was indispensable in developing this text. We greatly appreciate your assistance in making this the best text it could be; you have helped teach a whole new generation of students about the exciting world of economics.

Jim Butko, Niagara College
Michael G. Lanyi, University of Lethbridge
Perry Martens, University of Regina
Vettivelu Nallainayagam, Mount Royal College
Frank Trimnell, Ryerson University
Christopher Willmore, University of Victoria
Rauf Azhar, University of Guelph-Humber
Constantin Colonescu, MacEwan University
Carol Derksen, Red River College
Sigrid Ewender, Kwantlen Polytechnic University
Bruno Fullone, George Brown College
Narine Gregorian, Camosun College
Shahidul Islam, Grant MacEwan University
Nargess Kayhani, Mount Saint Vincent University
Stephen M. Law, Mount Allison University
Joan McEachern, Kwantlen Polytechnic University
Manish Pandey, University of Winnipeg
Fiona T. Rahman, University of Waterloo
Neil Roberts, Kwantlen Polytechnic University
Duane Rockerbie, University of Lethbridge
Rizwan Tahir, Wilfrid Laurier University
Andrew Wong, Grant MacEwan University
Clive Chappel, University of British Columbia
Fred Aswani, McMaster University
Iris Au, University of Toronto, Scarborough
Frank Trimnell, Ryerson University
Christopher Wilmore, University of Victoria
Basil Golovetsky, Simon Fraser University
Hannah M. Holmes, McMaster University
Sandra Wellman, Seneca College
Vladimir Dvoracek, University of the Fraser Valley.
David Gray, University of Ottawa
Brennan Thompson, Ryerson University
Robert Jefferson, Wilfrid Laurier University

A WORD OF THANKS

We greatly appreciate the efforts of the Pearson team. Managing Editor Claudine O'Donnell's energy and direction made this first Canadian edition possible. Developmental Editor Mary Wat and Project Manager Rachel Thompson worked tirelessly to ensure that this text was as good as it could be. We are grateful for the energy and creativity of Marketing Manager Leigh-Anne Graham. Karen Townsend and Imee Salumbides ably managed the extensive MyLab and supplement package that accompanies the book. Anthony Leung and Jerilyn Bockorick turned our manuscript pages into a beautiful published book. We received excellent research assistance from Mike Sherar. We thank Claudia Forgas and Audrey Dorsch for their careful copyediting and proofreading.

Macroeconomics

Canadian Edition

Economics: Foundations and Models

© oah1611/Fotolia

Chapter Outline and Learning Objectives

1.1 Three Key Economic Ideas, page 4
Explain these three key economic ideas:

People are rational.
People respond to incentives.
Optimal decisions are made at the margin.

1.2 The Economic Problems All Societies Must Solve, page 7
Discuss how a society answers these three key economic questions:

What goods and services will be produced?
How will the goods and services be produced?
Who will receive the goods and services produced?

1.3 Economic Models, page 10
Understand what economic models are and aren't, and why they are a good idea.

1.4 The Microeconomics/Macroeconomics Division, page 13
Distinguish between microeconomics and macroeconomics.

1.5 The Language of Economics, page 13
Define important economic terms. (It's not *all* Greek.)

Appendix A: Using Graphs and Formulas, page 22
Review the use of graphs and formulas.

You versus Caffeine

As you study economics, you will start to see the complexity and interconnectedness of the world around you. Something as simple as your morning cup of coffee is actually the result of hundreds of individual choices made by people you have never met.

If you are like 65 percent of Canadians, you had a cup of coffee this morning—you might even be drinking one now. In Colombia, over 3500 kilometres away, someone decided to plant coffee, somebody else picked it, and another group of people brought it to a port. A different group of people loaded it onto a ship, and other people sailed the ship to North America. The coffee beans were then unloaded, transported to a roaster, roasted and ground, and packaged, all by more different people. Finally, the coffee arrived at your local coffee shop, where

yet another group of people brew the coffee for you. This amazing sequence of events happens without any one person or group of people planning it. Yet you get the benefit of all this work by all these different people for less than $5. It's amazing to consider all that's involved in something so simple.

This interconnectedness of people's choices can have major implications for you. In 2011, heavy rains in Colombia reduced the amount of coffee grown there. This change in the weather, so far from Canada, changed what all Canadians had to pay for their morning cup.

AN INSIDE LOOK on **page 16** discusses some of the factors that can change the price of coffee and which types of companies are most likely to change their prices.

Economics in Your Life

How Much Will You Pay for a Cup of Coffee?

The price of coffee is likely to go up in the next year or two. There was a time not long ago when a cup of coffee cost less than a dollar. Suppose you are waiting in line to buy the cup of coffee you count on to keep you awake during class. Is the price likely to be higher than it was last week? We all complain when the price of something we buy regularly goes up, but what determines that price? Consider what might change if the price of coffee doubled over the next six months. As you read this chapter, see if you can answer this question. You can check your answer against the one we provide on page 15 at the end of this chapter.

I n this book, we use economics to answer a wide variety of questions. Just a few examples:

- How are the prices of things you buy every day determined?
- How does government spending and taxation affect the economy?
- Why do governments control the prices of some goods?
- Why are some countries wealthier than others?

Economists don't always agree on the answers to these questions and a lot of others. In fact, there are a number of lively debates on a lot of different issues. In addition, new problems and issues are constantly arising. So, economists are always at work developing new methods to analyze economic questions.

Scarcity A situation in which unlimited wants exceed the limited resources available to fulfill those wants.

All the issues we discuss in this text illustrate a basic fact of life: People have to make choices. We all have to make choices because of **scarcity**. Scarcity means that we don't have enough resources to do everything we want to. Our needs and wants are infinite, but our planet and time are finite. You likely had to choose between spending money on tuition or taking a trip to Europe. Even the richest people in the world have to deal with scarcity of time. Bill Gates, one of the wealthiest people in the world, has to choose between working with his charitable foundation or spending time with his children. Every hour he spends on charity work is an hour he can't spend with his family. **Economics** is the study of the choices consumers, business managers, and government officials (in short, *people*) make in their efforts to make the best use of scarce resources in achieving their goals.

Economics The study of the choices people make to attain their goals, given their scarce resources.

We begin this chapter by discussing three important economic ideas that will come up throughout this book. *People are rational, people respond to incentives*, and *optimal decisions are made at the margin*. We then introduce you to the three basic economic decisions that all societies have had to find answers to since society began: *What* goods and services will be produced? *How* will the goods and services be produced? and *Who* will receive the goods and services produced? Next, we introduce you to the idea of economic models and their role in analyzing economic issues. **Economic models** are simplifications of reality used to analyze real-world issues. We will explain why economists use models and how they construct them. Finally, we will discuss the difference between microeconomics and macroeconomics and introduce you to some of the other important terms that are part of economists' language.

Economic model A simplified version of reality used to analyze real-world economic situations.

1.1 LEARNING OBJECTIVE

Explain these three key economic ideas: People are rational, people respond to incentives, and optimal decisions are made at the margin.

Market A group of buyers and sellers of a good or service and the institutions or arrangements by which they come together to trade.

Three Key Economic Ideas

As you go through your day-to-day life, you interact with many people directly and thousands more indirectly. Whether you are looking for a part-time job, downloading the latest app, or getting a quick cup of coffee, you are interacting with other people through markets. A **market** is a group of buyers and sellers and the institutions (rules) or arrangements by which they come together to trade. Most of economics involves analyzing what happens in markets. Throughout this book, as we study how people make choices and interact in markets, we will return to three important ideas:

1. People are rational.
2. People respond to incentives.
3. Optimal decisions are made at the margin.

People are Rational

Economists generally assume that people are rational. This does not mean that economists think that people are computers with no emotions. It means that people make decisions and take the actions that they *believe* will make them happy. Economists tend to think people consider the costs and benefits of something and only do the things with more benefit than cost. When you buy a cup of coffee, an economist assumes that you thought the benefit was worth at least as much as the time, effort, and money you had to spend getting it. You might be wrong, it could be the worst cup of coffee you have ever had, but when you paid $2, you believed it was worth it. Put simply, economists don't think people deliberately do things to make themselves worse off.

People Respond to Incentives

Many factors go into determining the benefit of something. You might see benefits in terms of religious fulfillment, jealousy, compassion, or even greed. Economists emphasize that consumers and firms consistently respond to *economic* incentives. This fact may seem obvious, but it is often overlooked. For a great example of this, take a look at your local bank and then think of banks shown in American movies. Banks in American movies often have bullet resistant shields and security guards to deter bank robbers. Bullet-resistant plastic shields and armed security guards are unheard of at Canadian bank branches. Why? The shields are expensive, costing up to $20 000. The average loss during a robbery is around just $1200. The economic incentives for banks are clear: It is less costly to put up with robberies and tell staff not to resist robbers than to take additional security measures. Some people are surprised by the lack of security in Canadian banks, but economists aren't.

In each chapter, the *Making the Connection* feature discusses a news story or another application related to the chapter material. Read the following *Making the Connection* for a discussion of whether people respond to incentives even when deciding to have children.

<table>
<tr><td>Making
the
Connection</td><td>**Will Women in Quebec Have More Babies if the Government Pays Them to?**</td></tr>
</table>

The population of Canada is aging as birthrates decline and people live longer. An aging population makes social and pension programs harder to afford as there are fewer young workers paying into the programs and more people drawing benefits. The result will require either reducing payments to seniors or increasing taxes on young workers.

For the population of a country to be relatively stable (without immigration), women must have, on average, 2.1 children each. Canadian women have about 1.6 children on average. This figure is well below what is needed to keep the population stable. To deal with this shortage of people, governments can encourage people from other countries to move to Canada or they can try to encourage Canadian women to have more children.

While some provinces have focused on immigration, Quebec has opted to encourage women to have more children. The provincial government pays parents $500 for their first child, $1000 for their second, and $6000 for their third. While $6000 may not seem like a lot of money for having a child, women in Quebec have more children than the Canadian average (1.72 compared with 1.58). It could be that some women who had just barely decided not to have a third child were convinced by the extra incentive offered by the government.

Sources: Based on Daniel Parent and Ling Wang, "Tax Incentives and Fertility in Canada: Quantum vs Tempo Effects," *Canadian Journal of Economics* 40, no. 2(2007): 371–400; and Statistics Canada, "Crude Birth Rate, Age-Specific and Total Fertility Rates (Live Births), Canada, Provinces and Territories," CANSIM Table 102-4505, http://www5.statcan.gc.ca/cansim/a05?lang=eng&id=1024505.

Your Turn: Test your understanding by doing related problems 1.3 and 1.4 on page 19 at the end of this chapter.

MyEconLab

Optimal Decisions are Made at the Margin

Economics is sometimes referred to as the *marginal science* because of how economists tend to think about decisions. Some decisions are "all or nothing." When you finish your undergraduate degree, you can choose to either get a job or go to graduate school. However, most decisions are not the all-or-nothing type and involve doing a little more or a little less. For example, when you have a job, your choices are not whether to spend everything you earn or to save it all, but how much to save.

Economists use the term *marginal* to mean "extra" or "additional." Should you spend your next hour playing an online game or spend it studying? The *marginal benefit (MB)* of playing another hour is the enjoyment you receive. The *marginal cost (MC)* is the lower grade you receive because you studied less. You aren't the only one who has to make decisions at the margin. McCain Foods has to decide how many kilograms of frozen french-fries to produce per year. Should the company make another million kilos? The marginal benefit of this would be the extra revenue it gets from selling the extra french-fries, and the marginal cost would be the extra wages, materials, and equipment needed to make them. If your goal is to make the *net benefit* (benefit minus cost) as big as possible, then you have a really simple decision rule—*do more of any activity with a marginal benefit greater than the marginal cost.* As long as MB > MC, do more. If you've gotten as much net benefit as possible, you'll find that MB is pretty close to MC. In fact, MB = MC is an easy way of deciding when to do no more of something. When it comes to a firm's profit (revenue – cost), if producing the next unit increases revenue (MB) more than costs (marginal cost), making that unit will increase your profits. If producing the next unit increases costs more than revenue, making that unit will actually reduce profits. If producing the next unit increases revenue by the same amount as it increases costs, stop! You've now maximized profits and net benefits.

People often apply this rule without really thinking about it. Usually you will know whether the extra enjoyment of another hour of gaming is worth the additional cost of spending one hour less studying for your economics midterm without a mathematical formula. However, business people often have to make careful calculations using spreadsheets and such to determine whether the extra revenue of increased production is greater than or less than the additional costs. Economists refer to this sort of analysis as **marginal analysis**.

Marginal analysis Analysis that involves comparing marginal benefits and marginal costs.

In each chapter of this book, you will see the special feature *Solved Problem*. This feature will enhance your understanding of the material by leading you through the steps of solving an applied economic problem. After reading the problem, you can test your understanding by working out the related problems at the end of the chapter and in the study guide. You can also find more *Solved Problems* and tutorials at MyEconLab.

Solved Problem **1.1**

McCain Foods Makes a Decision at the Margin

Suppose McCain Foods is currently selling 10 million kilograms of frozen french-fries per year. Managers at McCain Foods are thinking about increasing production to 11 million kilograms per year. One manager argues, "Increasing production from 10 million to 11 million is good because we will make a total profit of $500 million if we make 11 million kilograms." Do you agree with her reasoning? What, if any, additional information do you need to have to decide whether McCain Foods should produce the extra 1 million kilograms of french-fries? When would making the extra french-fries be a good idea? When would it be a bad idea?

Solving the Problem

Step 1: Review the chapter material. This problem is about making decisions, so you may want to review the section "Optimal Decisions Are Made at the Margin," which begins on this page. Remember to "think marginal" whenever you see the words *additional* or *extra* in economics.

Step 2: Explain whether you agree with the manager. We have seen that any activity should be continued up to the point where marginal benefit is equal to marginal cost. In this case, that means making french-fries up to the point where the additional revenue McCain Foods gets from selling more french-fries is equal to the extra cost of making them. The McCain Foods' manager has not done a marginal analysis, so you should not agree with the manager's reasoning, *yet*. Her statement about total profit doesn't help you decide whether to make the extra french-fries. The manager could be right that making the extra french-fries is a good idea, but she hasn't provided proof—you need more information to know for sure.

Step 3: Explain what additional information you need. You need more information to make the correct decision. You need to know the additional revenue that would be generated by selling the extra french-fries. You also need to know how much the extra potatoes, oil, labour, etc. will cost. In short, you need to know the marginal cost (extra costs) and the marginal benefit (extra revenue).

Step 4: Compare marginal cost and marginal benefit. Once you know the marginal cost and marginal benefit of making the extra million kilograms of french-fries, compare the two. If the marginal cost is greater than the marginal benefit, then making the extra fries is a bad idea. If the marginal cost is less than the marginal benefit, then making the extra french-fries is a good idea.

Your Turn: For more practice, do related problem 1.5 on page 19 at the end of this chapter.

MyEconLab

The Economic Problems all Societies must Solve

1.2 LEARNING OBJECTIVE
Discuss how a society answers these three key economic questions: What goods and services will be produced? How will the goods and services be produced? Who will receive the goods and services produced?

Living in a world of scarcity means that we face **trade-offs**: Doing more of one thing means that we have to do less of something else. The best way to measure the cost of something is the value of what we give up to get it. The value of what we give up to engage in an activity is called the **opportunity cost**. To be accurate, the opportunity cost of something (such as a good or service) is the value of the next best alternative. What is the opportunity cost of spending an extra hour studying? It depends on what you would have chosen to do if you weren't studying. If you would have spent the hour watching TV, then that is the opportunity cost, never mind that you could have spent the same time studying. The easiest way to demonstrate what opportunity cost is all about is with an example. Let's say that a federal government employee, who is currently earning $80 000 a year, is thinking about leaving his or her job to start a consulting company. The opportunity cost of starting the consulting company is the $80 000 salary that is no longer received from the government, even if the person doesn't pay him or herself a salary in the new business.

Since all societies face trade-offs, they must make choices when answering the following three fundamental economic questions:

1. *What* goods and services will be produced?
2. *How* will the goods and services be produced?
3. *Who* will receive the goods and services produced?

Throughout this book, we'll return to these questions. For now, we briefly introduce each one.

Trade-off The idea that because of scarcity, producing more of one good or service means producing less of another good or service.

Opportunity cost The highest-valued alternative that must be given up to engage in an activity.

What Goods and Services will be Produced?

How will a society decide whether to make more economics textbooks or more video games? More daycare spaces or more sports arenas? Of course, "society" doesn't make decisions, individual people do. The answer to the question of what to produce is determined by the choices that consumers, firms, and governments make. Due to the structure of the Canadian economy, every day you help decide what goods and services firms in Canada and around the world make. When you choose to spend your money at the movies instead of at the bookstore, you encourage firms to make more movies and fewer books. Similarly, Bombardier must decide whether it will devote resources to producing new planes or trains. The federal government must also make decisions about what to produce. Will it devote resources to the military or increase payments to parents with children? In each case, consumers, firms, and governments deal with scarcity by trading off one good or service for another. Each choice made comes with an opportunity cost, measured by the value of the best alternative given up.

How will the Goods and Services be Produced?

After figuring out what to make, societies must figure out how to make it. In the Canadian context, we generally think of firms or government making this decision. Producers of goods and services face a trade-off between using more workers and using more machines. For example, movie studios have to choose whether to produce animated films using highly skilled animators to draw each frame by hand or to use fewer animators and powerful computers and software. Firms also have to decide whether to produce in Canada using few workers and many machines or produce in developing countries using many workers with few machines.

Who will Receive the Goods and Services Produced?

In Canada, who receives what is produced depends largely on how income is distributed. Individuals with the highest incomes have the ability to buy the most goods and services. Governments levy taxes and use part of the money to provide income to some people. Governments also use the money collected in taxes to supply goods and services that are not being provided in other ways. The debate over how much taxation and government spending is appropriate will continue as long as societies must address the three fundamental questions.

Centrally Planned Economies versus Market Economies

Societies answer the three questions— what, how, and for whom?—in different ways. We'll talk briefly about the two extremes, but remember that all countries use a combination of both.

Centrally planned economy An economy in which the government decides how economic resources will be allocated.

One extreme is the **centrally planned economy**, in which an individual or group of people (generally the government) directly answers all three questions. From 1917 to 1991, the most important centrally planned economy was the Soviet Union's. In the Soviet Union, government agencies decided what to produce, what production techniques to use, and who would get the goods once they were made. People managing factories and stores reported to the government. These managers had to follow the instructions of government even when what they were producing wasn't what consumers (people) wanted. Centrally planned economies like the Soviet Union's have not been successful in producing low-cost (plentiful), high-quality goods and services. As a result, the material standard of living of the average person in a centrally planned economy tends to be low. All centrally planned economies have also been dictatorships. Dissatisfaction with low living standards and political repression finally led to the collapse of the Soviet Union in 1991. Today only a few small countries, such as Cuba and North Korea, still have largely centrally planned economies. Recently Cuba, under Raúl Castro, has begun to move away from central planning.

Market economy An economy in which the decisions of households and firms interacting in markets allocate economic resources.

At the other end of the spectrum is the **market economy**. Market economies rely on privately owned firms to produce goods and services and to decide how to produce them. A *market* is all potential buyers and sellers of a good or service as well as the rules that determine how buyers and sellers interact. Markets, rather than a government employee, determine who receives the goods and services produced. In this type of economy, firms must produce goods and services that people want to buy or they go out of business. In that sense, it is ultimately consumers who decide what will be produced and how. In a market economy, all trades must be agreed to by all the people involved.

In a market economy, people's income is mostly determined by what they have to sell. For example, if you're a civil engineer and firms are willing to pay you $85 000 a year, that's what you will have to spend on goods and services. If you own a house that you rent out to your friends or own shares in a company, your income will be even higher. Market economies have two distinguishing features: (1) markets directly reward people's hard work, and (2) decision making is shared by everyone in the market. Overall, in a market economy the answers to the three basic questions are provided by everyone.

Market economies do have drawbacks. Luck, both good and bad, plays a role in determining a person's income, and sometimes markets don't work the way we would like them to. In particular, markets are not good at providing important goods and services such as roads, national defence, or health care.

The Modern Mixed Economy

We've seen that there are flaws in how both centrally planned economies and market economies answer the three basic questions. As a result, all modern economies are "**mixed economies**" that use elements of both centrally planned and market economies. In Canada, most of the things you buy in stores—electronics, coffee, food, etc.—are produced by privately owned firms in response to the demands of consumers: The availability of these goods results from a market system answering the three basic questions. At the same time, other goods and services are provided by the government, such as roads, national defence, health care, etc. Even the United States and China are mixed economies that rely on a combination of both the market and central planning to provide people with a variety of goods and services.

Most debates about central planning and markets are about the extent each plays in answering the three questions. Very few people actually still advocate for a total market economy or a completely centrally planned economy. Keep this in mind when listening to the debates of leaders of political parties.

Mixed economy An economy in which most economic decisions result from the interaction of buyers and sellers in markets, but in which the government plays a significant role in the allocation of resources.

Efficiency and Equity

Market economies tend to be more efficient than centrally planned economies. Before we can understand why this is, we must explore two types of efficiency: *productive efficiency* and *allocative efficiency*. **Productive efficiency** occurs when a good or service is produced at the lowest possible cost. **Allocative efficiency** occurs when a country's resources are used to produce the mix of goods and services that consumers want. Markets tend to be efficient because they rely on **voluntary exchange**. When an exchange is voluntary, both the buyer and the seller are made better off by the transaction, or they wouldn't have agreed to it. The voluntary nature of exchange promotes competition that encourages producers to find cheaper methods of producing the goods and services they want to sell, as consumers always wish to pay less. This leads to productive efficiency, as firms that can't match others' low costs go out of business. Competition also promotes allocative efficiency. A firm that uses scarce resources to produce goods and services that consumers don't want to buy goes out of business.

Markets and competition promote efficiency, but they don't guarantee it. Inefficiency can arise from a variety of sources. It often takes time to achieve an efficient outcome. When Blu-ray players were first introduced, firms didn't instantly achieve productive efficiency, as they had to experiment to find the lowest cost method of producing them. Some production processes cause environmental damage. In this case, government intervention can actually increase efficiency; without government action, firms will ignore the cost of damaging the environment, leading to the production of more goods than is in society's best interest.

An economically efficient outcome is not necessarily a desirable one. Many people prefer economic outcomes that they consider fair or equitable, even if those outcomes are less efficient. **Equity** is harder to define than *efficiency*, but it usually involves a fair distribution of economic benefits. For some people, equity involves a more equal distribution of economic benefits than would result from an emphasis on efficiency alone.

Productive efficiency A situation in which a good or service is produced at the lowest possible cost.

Allocative efficiency A state of the economy in which production is in accordance with consumer preferences; in particular, every good or service is produced up to the point where the last unit provides a marginal benefit to society equal to the marginal cost of producing it.

Voluntary exchange A situation that occurs in markets when both the buyer and seller of a product are made better off by the transaction.

Equity The fair distribution of economic benefits.

For example, some people support raising taxes on people with higher incomes to provide funds for programs that aid the poor. Although governments may increase equity by reducing the incomes of high-income people and increasing the incomes of the poor, efficiency may be reduced. People have less incentive to open new businesses, to supply labour, and to save if the government takes a significant amount of the income they earn from working or saving. The result is that fewer goods and services are produced, and less saving takes place. As this example illustrates, *there is often a trade-off between efficiency and equity.* Government policymakers often confront this trade-off.

1.3 LEARNING OBJECTIVE

Understand what economic models are and aren't, and why they're a good idea.

Economic Models

Economists rely on economic theories, or models (we use the words *model* and *theory* interchangeably in this text), to analyze real-world issues from coffee prices to immigration. As mentioned earlier, economic models are simplifications of reality. Economists are not the only ones using models: An engineer may use a computer model of a bridge to test its resistance to earthquakes; a biologist may make a physical model of a nucleic acid to better understand its properties. The main point of a model is to allow people to focus on the interactions between two or more things. Thus a model makes ideas sufficiently explicit and concrete so that individuals, firms, or the government can use them to make decisions. For example, we will see in Chapter 3 that the model of demand and supply is a simplified version of how the prices of products are determined by interactions among buyers and sellers in markets.

Economists use models to answer questions. For example, consider the question from the chapter opener: "How much will you be paying for a cup of coffee?" While this seems like a fairly simple question, it is actually quite complicated. To answer such complex questions like this one, economists use several models to look at different aspects of the issue. For example, they may use a model of how wages are determined to analyze the flexibility different firms have in their cost structures. They may use another model to consider how often people will change their purchasing patterns. Yet another model might be used to explore how growers will react to a change in the price of raw coffee. Sometimes economists can use existing models to analyze an issue, but in other cases, they must develop a new model. To develop a new model, economists generally follow these steps:

1. Decide on the assumptions to use in developing the model.
2. Formulate a testable hypothesis.
3. Use economic data to test the hypothesis.
4. Revise the model if it fails to explain the economic data well.
5. Retain the revised model to help answer similar economic questions in the future.

The Role of Assumptions in Economic Models

Any model, in any discipline, is based on assumptions because models have to be simple to be useful. We cannot analyze an economic issue unless we reduce its complexity at least a little. For example, economic models make *behavioural assumptions* about the motives of consumers and firms. Economists assume that consumers will buy the goods and services that will maximize their well-being or their satisfaction. Similarly, economists assume that firms act to maximize their profits. These assumptions are simplifications because we know they don't describe the motives of every firm or every consumer exactly. How can we know if the assumptions in a model are too simple or too limiting? We discover this when we form hypotheses based on these assumptions and test the hypotheses using real-world information.

Forming and Testing Hypotheses in Economic Models

Economic variable Something measurable that can have different values, such as the price of coffee.

An **economic variable** is something measurable, such as the wages paid to Tim Hortons employees. A *hypothesis* in an economic model is a statement about an economic variable that may be either correct or incorrect. Most hypotheses take the form of predictions. An example of a hypothesis in an economic model is the statement that extreme weather in Colombia will increase the price of coffee in Canada. An economic hypothesis is usually about a *causal relationship*; in this case, the hypothesis states that weather patterns in Colombia *cause* higher prices for coffee in Canada.

All hypotheses need to be tested before they are accepted. To test a hypothesis, we analyze statistics on the relevant economic variables. In our coffee example, we would gather data on coffee prices and other variables that we think might have an impact on the people buying or selling coffee. Testing a hypothesis can be tricky. For example, showing that coffee prices rose following a spate of bad weather in Colombia is not enough to demonstrate that Colombian weather *caused* the price increase. Just because two things are *correlated*—that is, they happen together—does not mean that one caused the other. In this example, perhaps the price increase was caused by an increase in the wages paid to coffee shop employees. Many different economic variables change over any given period of time, which makes testing hypotheses a challenge.

Note that hypotheses must be statements that could, in fact, turn out to be incorrect. Statements such as "high coffee prices are bad" or "high wages for baristas are good" are value judgments rather than hypotheses because there is no way to disprove them.

Economists accept and use an economic model if it leads to hypotheses that are confirmed by statistical analysis. In many cases, the acceptance is tentative pending the gathering and analysis of new data. In fact, economists often refer to a hypothesis having been "not rejected," rather than "accepted." But what if statistical analysis rejects a hypothesis? For example, what if a model generates the hypothesis that bad weather in Colombia leads to higher coffee prices in Canada, but analysis of the data rejects the hypothesis? In this case, the model must be reconsidered. It may be that an assumption used in the model was too simplistic or limiting. What if the model used to determine the effect of weather on Canadian coffee prices didn't take into account Canadian weather patterns—people drink more hot beverages when it's cold outside. If the bad weather in Colombia occurred during the Canadian summer, we might not see an impact on coffee prices.

The process of developing models, testing hypotheses, and revising models occurs not just in economics but in disciplines like physics, chemistry, and biology. This process is often referred to as the *scientific method*. Economics is called a *social science* because it applies the scientific method to the study of interactions among people.

Normative and Positive Analysis

Throughout this book, as we build economic models and use them to answer questions, we need to keep the distinction between *positive analysis* and *normative analysis* in mind. **Positive analysis** concerns facts or logic. Positive statements are concerned with what is and can potentially be disproven. **Normative analysis** is about value judgments, or what *ought* to be. Economics is about positive analysis, which measures the costs and benefits of different courses of action.

Positive analysis Analysis concerned with what is.

Normative analysis Analysis concerned with what ought to be.

We can use a provincial government's minimum wage laws to compare positive and normative analysis. In 2013 Nova Scotia had the highest minimum wage of any province in Canada (Nunavut had an even higher minimum wage). In Nova Scotia, it is illegal to pay a worker less than $10.30 an hour. Without the minimum wage law, some firms and some workers would voluntarily agree to a lower wage. Because of the minimum wage law, some workers have a hard time finding work, and some firms end up paying more for workers. A positive analysis of the minimum wage law uses an economic model to estimate how many workers lose their jobs (or are unable to find one) when the minimum wage increases, the impact of an increase on firms' costs and profits, and the gains to those workers who find jobs at a higher rate of pay. After economists complete this positive analysis, the decision as to whether an increase in the minimum wage was a good idea or a bad idea is a normative one and depends on how people view the trade-offs involved. Supporters of minimum wage laws feel that the losses to employers and to newly unemployed workers are more than offset by the gains to workers who see their pay increase. Opponents of minimum wage laws think the losses are greater than the gains. The assessment depends, in part, on a person's values and political views. The positive analysis an economist provides would play a role in the decision but can't by itself decide the issue one way or another.

In each chapter, you will see a *Don't Let This Happen to You* box like the one below. This box alerts you to common pitfalls in thinking about economic ideas. After reading this box, test your understanding by working out the related problem at the end of the chapter.

Don't Let This Happen to You

Don't Confuse Positive Analysis with Normative Analysis

"Economic analysis has shown that an increase in the minimum wage is a bad idea because it causes unemployment." Is this statement accurate? In 2012, legislation in British Columbia prevented anyone from paying a worker less than $10.25 per hour. This wage is higher than some employers are willing to pay some workers. If the minimum wage were lower, some people who currently can't find a job would be able to find work at a lower wage. Therefore, positive economic analysis indicates that an increase in the minimum wage causes unemployment (although there is a lot of disagreement on how much). *But,* those people who find jobs benefit from the increased minimum wage because they get

paid more. In other words, increasing the minimum wage creates both losers (those who end up unemployed because of the minimum wage legislation and the firms that have to pay workers more) and winners (people who get paid more than they would have before the minimum wage increase).

Should we value the gains to the winners more than the losses to the losers? The answer to this question involves normative analysis. Positive economic analysis can only show you what the consequences of a policy are, not whether a policy is "good" or "bad." The statement at the beginning of this box is incorrect.

MyEconLab
Your Turn: Test your understanding by doing related problem 3.5 on page 20 at the end of this chapter.

Economics as a Social Science

Since economics studies the actions of people, it is a social science. Economics is similar to other social science disciplines like psychology, political science, and sociology. As a social science, economics is all about human behaviour—particularly decision making—in every context, not just the context of business. Economists study issues such as how families decide how many children to have, why some people have a hard time losing weight, and why people often ignore important information when making decisions. Economics also has much to contribute to questions of government policy. As we'll see throughout this book, economists have played an important role in formulating government policies in areas such as the environment, health care, and poverty.

Making
the
Connection

Should the Government of Ontario Increase its Minimum Wage?

The current minimum wage in Ontario is $10.25 per hour, despite the fact that Toronto is one of the most expensive places to live in Canada. Should Ontario increase the minimum wage? Like most questions about economic policy, the answer is, it depends. There are costs and benefits to increasing the minimum wage.

An increase in the minimum wage tends to reduce the number of entry-level jobs. When firms have to pay workers more, they hire fewer people. Entry-level jobs, which tend to be filled by young people, can be the first step in developing a successful career. Youth unemployment is a growing problem in a number of countries, such as Spain and France, that have restrictive labour laws. Moreover, a person's early employment history has a huge impact on lifelong earnings.

Higher labour costs are also difficult for some firms to deal with. Having to pay more for labour means that firms that are able to substitute machinery for workers will have an advantage over those that can't. Increasing the minimum wage tends to give larger firms an advantage over smaller ones, because they can afford the complex machinery to replace people. (Do you think a small retail store could afford the self-scan checkout you see at major retailers?)

Increasing the minimum wage also offers important benefits. Those who can find or keep their jobs get bigger pay cheques. An increase in income can go a long way toward improving the lives of people who depend on minimum wage work for their livelihoods. People with lower incomes may spend more of what they earn than those with higher incomes, so increasing the minimum wage may create more economic opportunities for other people as well.

Whether Ontario should increase its minimum wage rate is a normative question. The answer to that question will be based on how the people of Ontario feel the costs and benefits compare.

Your Turn: Test your understanding by doing related problem 3.3 on page 20 at the end of this chapter.

Should Ontario raise its minimum wage?

© Jim West / Alamy

MyEconLab

Microeconomics and Macroeconomics

Distinguish between microeconomics and macroeconomics.

Economic models can be used to analyze decision making in many areas. We group some of these areas together as *microeconomics* and others as *macroeconomics*. **Microeconomics** is the study of how individual economic agents make choices, how these choices come together to determine what happens in a single market, and the impact of government interventions on market outcomes. When you're talking about microeconomics, you're generally talking about *one* person, *one* firm, or *one* market. Microeconomic issues include explaining how consumers react to changes in prices and how firms decide what prices they should charge. Microeconomics is also used to analyze other issues, such as how individual women decide whether to have children, who is most likely to take illegal drugs, and how to reduce pollution in the most efficient way.

Microeconomics The study of how households and firms make choices, how they interact in markets, and how the government attempts to influence their choices.

Macroeconomics is the study of the economy as a whole. When you're talking about macroeconomics, you're generally talking about a country, province, or region. Macroeconomics focuses on topics such as inflation, unemployment, and economic growth. Some of the big questions in macroeconomics are why economies experience a cycle of booms and busts, why some economies grow much faster than others, and why prices rise faster in some places than in others. Macroeconomics also involves a lot of different policy issues, such as whether and how the government can intervene to prevent recessions.

Macroeconomics The study of the economy as a whole, including topics such as inflation, unemployment, and economic growth.

The division between microeconomics and macroeconomics is not always clear-cut. Many situations have *both* a microeconomic and a macroeconomic aspect. For example, the level of total investment by firms in new machinery and equipment helps determine how quickly an economy grows, which is a macroeconomic issue, but understanding the decisions made by each firm about what to invest in and when to do it is a microeconomic issue.

The Language of Economics

Define important economic terms. (It's not *all* Greek.)

In the following chapters, you'll encounter a number of important economic terms again and again. Becoming familiar with these terms is a necessary step in learning economics—you have to learn to speak the language. Here we provide a brief introduction to a few of these terms. We will discuss them all in greater detail later in the book.

- **Production.** *Production* is the process of making goods and services, often undertaken by entrepreneurs.

- **Entrepreneur.** An *entrepreneur* is someone who operates a business. In a market system, entrepreneurs decide what goods and services to produce and how to produce them. An entrepreneur starting a new business often puts his or her own money at risk. If an entrepreneur is wrong about what consumers want or about the best way to produce goods or services, the money he or she puts up to start the business can be lost. This is not an unusual occurrence: About half of all new businesses close within a few years. Without entrepreneurs willing to take on the risk of starting and running businesses, economic progress would be impossible.

- **Innovation.** There is a difference between *invention* and *innovation*. An invention is the development of a new good or a new process for making a good. An innovation is the practical application of an invention. (Innovation may also be used to refer to any significant improvement in a good or way of making a good.) A lot of time can pass between the appearance of a new idea and its development for widespread use. The first digital electronic computer, the ENIAC—which was the size of a small house (167 m²)—was developed in 1945. ENIAC can be thought of as an invention. However, the first personal computer (an innovation) wasn't introduced until 1981, and it has only been since the 1990s that computers (which experience continual innovations) have become common in workplaces and homes.

- **Technology.** A firm's *technology* is the processes it uses to turn inputs into outputs (i.e., goods and services). In an economic sense, a firm's technology depends on many factors, such as the skill of its managers, the education of its workers, and the quality of its equipment.

- **Firm, company, or business.** A *firm* is an organization that produces a good or service. Most firms produce goods or services in order to earn profit, but there are also non-profit firms, such as universities. Economists tend to use the terms *firm, company,* and *business* interchangeably.

- **Goods.** *Goods* are tangible items that people want, such as books, computers, clothing, etc.

- **Services.** *Services* are activities done for others, such as cutting hair, cleaning houses, or conducting banking transactions.

- **Revenue.** A firm's *revenue* is all the money it receives when it sells goods or services. It is calculated by multiplying the price per unit by the number of units sold.

- **Profit.** A firm's *profit* is the difference between its revenue and its costs. Economists distinguish between *accounting profit* and *economic profit*. In calculating accounting profit, the costs of some economic resources the firm doesn't explicitly pay for are left out—accounting profit only worries about *explicit costs*. Economic profit includes all the costs associated with operating a firm, including *implicit costs* (particularly opportunity costs). When we use the term *profit* in this book, we're referring to *economic profit*. It is very important that you don't confuse profit with revenue.

- **Household.** A *household* consists of all the people occupying a home that make decisions together. Households are the suppliers of all the factors of production (particularly labour) used by firms to make goods and services. Households are also the consumers of all the goods and services produced in an economy.

- **Factors of production or economic resources.** Firms use *factors of production* to produce goods and services. The main factors of production are labour, capital, natural resources—including land—and entrepreneurial ability. Households earn income by supplying firms with these factors of production.

- **Capital.** The word *capital* can refer to *financial capital* or to *physical capital*. Financial capital includes stocks and bonds issued by firms, bank accounts, and holdings of money. However, in economics, *capital* refers to physical capital, which is any manufactured good that is used to make other goods. Examples of physical capital are computers, factory buildings, tools, and trucks. The total amount of physical capital available in a country is referred to as the country's *capital stock*.

- **Human capital.** *Human capital* is the accumulated training, skills, and knowledge that a person has. For example, university-educated workers generally have more skills and are more productive than workers with only high school education. Therefore, people with a university degree are said to have more human capital than people with only a high school diploma.

Economics in Your Life

How Much Will You Pay for a Cup of Coffee?

At the start of the chapter, we asked you "How much will you be paying for a cup of coffee?" Some information that will help you think about the answer to this question appears in *Making the Connection* on page 12. The price of a good is determined by how much someone, like you, is willing to pay for it and how much someone else is willing to sell it for. The costs of producing a cup of coffee, including the opportunity costs, play a very important role in how much you have to lay out for that all important first cup of the day. As the minimum wage increases, coffee-growing lands become increasingly scarce, and more people want to have a cup, the price of coffee will increase. As the price goes up, people will also change their behaviour, and some people might stop drinking coffee all together.

Conclusion

The best way to think of economics is as a group of useful ideas about how individuals make choices. Economists have put these ideas into practice by developing economic models. Consumers, business managers, and government policymakers use these models every day to help make choices. In this book, we explore many key economic models and give examples of how to apply them in the real world. Most students taking an introductory economics course do not major in economics or become professional economists. Whatever your major or career path, the economic principles you'll learn in this book will improve your ability to make choices in many aspects of your life. These principles will also improve your understanding of how decisions are made in business and government.

Reading newspapers and websites is an important part of understanding the current political, economic, and business climates and learning how to apply economic concepts to a variety of real-world issues. At the end of each chapter, you will see a two-page feature titled *An Inside Look*. This feature consists of an excerpt that relates to the company or economic issue introduced at the start of the chapter and also the concepts discussed throughout the chapter. A summary and an analysis, as well as other material, highlight the key economic point of the article. Read *An Inside Look* on the next page to explore some of the key factors that determine the price of a cup of coffee. Test your understanding by answering the *Thinking Critically* questions.

Coffee Prices Set to Soar

HAMILTON SPECTATOR

Canadians will be paying more for store bought coffee in the New Year, as a shrinking global supply and increasing demand continues to push up the price.

A recent spate of extreme weather in Colombia paired with a growing taste for higher quality beans and a diminished global stockpile could result in a 30 to 50 per cent spike in prices, according to one U.S. analyst.

On Wednesday Kraft Canada confirmed that the company's Maxwell House and Nabob Roast & Ground coffees will go up in price on January 30, 2011, the price of roast and ground coffees will go up 7 to 10 per cent. Distributors were informed of the boost a few weeks ago, the company said.

Kraft Canada said the increase "stems from the significant increase in world prices for green coffee." The company boosted prices twice on popular coffee brand products in 2010, the last increasing roast and ground coffee by as much as 12 percent and instant coffee by 16 percent.

South of the border Kraft Foods Inc. cited the same cause was behind Wednesday's boost for Maxwell House and Yuban coffees, with roast and ground coffee prices up 12 per cent and instant coffee prices up about 4 per cent.

Shawn Hackett, president of Hackett Financial Advisors, Inc., a brokerage firm specializing in agricultural commodities in Boynton Florida, predicts "actual coffee prices" or the cost of beans and cups of coffee could rise anywhere from 30 to 50 per cent by 2012.

Coffee closed on the U.S. futures market for (U.S.) $2.175 a pound [Note: like most global markets, the market for coffee uses U.S. Dollars and U.S. units.], about double the cost reported the same time last year. That price is well below historic highs of (U.S.) $3.35 per pound reported in 1977.

Hackett said based on current price increases a conservative estimate would be (U.S.) $4 per pound by the end of 2011.

Caffeine addicts should try to relax. Tim Hortons has no immediate plans to charge more.

"Typically, Tim Hortons books its coffee contracts for at least six months at a time, which protects its restaurant owners and customers from jumps in worldwide future markets," said a spokesperson in an email.

Starbucks said no one was available to comment.

The shortage is being caused by several factors, but poor weather in Colombia is key, he said.

Torrential rainstorms have resulted in loss of life and heavy damage to the current crop. Last year production was down 35 per cent and it was hoped they would recoup those losses in 2010, said Hackett.

Colombia is the largest producer of high-quality, mild washed Arabica. "That is your Starbucks kind of coffee," said Hackett. "The shortest supply is in that kind of coffee which is in the highest demand."

In previous years stockpiles of coffee in Brazil were released to relieve pressure when the market became too tight, but those supplies were depleted this year, said Hackett.

He said because of the massive profits large companies like Starbucks make selling coffee most can afford to eat cost increases until prices stabilize.

Ken Hardy, a professor emeritus of marketing for the Richard Ivey School of Business, said the smaller increase like the one from Kraft are unlikely to impact consumer habits.

Hardy, a board member for Williams Coffee Pub, noted that coffee is a central part of our social habits and a slight price hike won't deter us from buying.

He said if the price for over the counter coffee was going to rise in Canada, the cycle would start with Tim Hortons.

"I think they are the dominant buyer and dominant retail chain . . . they would be the price setter for most coffees."

If prices do rise above $4 and a hefty price hike is passed down to consumers people may start rethinking how much they drink and from where, he said.

Some companies, like Starbucks, don't have a great deal of room to manoeuvre, he said.

"They are already near the ceiling of price tolerance."

Source: Reprinted with permission - Torstar Syndication Services.

Key Points in the Article

This article discusses the impact that weather and tastes in different parts of the world have on the prices Canadians have to pay for a cup of coffee. Bad weather in Colombia means less coffee is available for the entire world. As the global population grows and becomes wealthier, more and more people want to start their day with a cup of coffee. These factors combine to increase the price of coffee.

Analyzing the News

(a) Coffee beans are bought and sold in a global market; companies from all over the world come together to buy and sell coffee beans. It is this global market that determines the price of the basic ingredient of your morning brew. Price changes in this market change the price of coffee not only for Canadians but also for people all over the world.

If suddenly coffee became very unpopular in a country like the United States, Canadians would likely have to pay less for a cup as there would be less competition for the coffee that was grown.

(b) The weather in another part of the world can have a large impact on your life. Bad weather in Colombia can make your morning cup of coffee more expensive, an earthquake in Japan can make electronics harder to get, and brush fires in Russia can make bread cost more here.

(c) Some companies are so important to their markets that other companies follow their lead. In the Canadian coffee shop market, Tim Hortons is the leader. Many smaller firms like Starbucks or Second Cup are hesitant to increase their prices if Tim Hortons does not. This competition among sellers can limit the impact of raw material price changes on consumers, at least for a while.

When the price of something goes up, people often respond by changing their behaviour. For example, if the price of coffee were to double and stay high, you might switch to drinking tea, hot chocolate, or another less-expensive beverage before class starts to save some money. Some people might start bringing their own coffee to work or school in travel mugs. Other people might give up something else, such as going to the movies, so that they can still have their morning coffee at the local coffee shop. People can change their behaviour in response to a change in prices in a number of ways.

Thinking Critically

1. According to the article, heavier-than-normal rains in Colombia reduced the amount of coffee grown there, which led to an increase in the world price of coffee. What do you think would happen if the weather in Colombia was particularly good for growing coffee this year? What do you think will happen to the price of coffee if weather patterns all over the world become more extreme?

2. How do you think you would react if the price of a cup of coffee doubled? How do you think most people would react? What do you think that would mean for the owner of your local coffee shop?

Chapter Summary and Problems

Key Terms

Allocative efficiency, p. 9

Centrally planned economy, p. 8

Economic model, p. 4

Economic variable, p. 10

Economics, p. 4

Equity, p. 9

Macroeconomics, p. 13

Marginal analysis, p. 6

Market, p. 4

Market economy, p. 8

Microeconomics, p. 13

Mixed economy, p. 9

Normative analysis, p. 11

Opportunity cost, p. 7

Positive analysis, p. 11

Productive efficiency, p. 9

Scarcity, p. 4

Trade-off, p. 7

Voluntary exchange, p. 9

Summary

*LO 1.1 Economics is the study of the choices consumers, business managers, and government officials make to attain their goals, given their scarce resources. We must make choices because of **scarcity**, which means that although our wants are unlimited, the resources available to fulfill those wants are limited. Economists assume that people are rational in the sense that consumers and firms use all available information as they take actions intended to achieve their goals. Rational individuals weigh the benefits and costs of each action and choose an action only if the benefits outweigh the costs. Although people act from a variety of motives, ample evidence indicates that they respond to economic incentives. Economists use the word **marginal** to mean extra or additional. The optimal decision is to continue any activity up to the point where the marginal benefit equals the marginal cost.

LO 1.2 Society faces **trade-offs**: Producing more of one good or service means producing less of another good or service. The **opportunity cost** of any activity—such as producing a good or service—is the highest-valued alternative that must be given up to engage in that activity. The choices of consumers, firms, and governments determine what goods and services will be produced. Firms choose how to produce the goods and services they sell. In Canada, who receives the goods and services produced depends largely on how income is distributed in the marketplace. In a **centrally planned economy**, most economic decisions are made by the government. In a **market economy**, most economic decisions are made by consumers and firms. Most economies, including Canada's, are **mixed economies** in which most economic decisions are made by consumers and firms but in which the government also plays a significant role. There are two types of efficiency: productive efficiency and allocative efficiency. **Productive efficiency** occurs when a good or service is produced at the lowest possible cost. **Allocative efficiency** occurs when production is in accordance with consumer preferences. **Voluntary exchange** is a situation that occurs in markets when both the buyer and seller of a product are made better off by the transaction. **Equity** is more difficult to define than efficiency, but it usually involves a fair distribution of economic benefits. Government policymakers often face a trade-off between equity and efficiency.

LO 1.3 An **economic variable** is something measurable that can have different values, such as the wages of software programmers. Economists rely on economic models when they apply economic ideas to real-world problems. **Economic models** are simplified versions of reality used to analyze real-world economic situations. Economists accept and use an economic model if it leads to hypotheses that are confirmed by statistical analysis. In many cases, the acceptance is tentative, however, pending the gathering of new data or further statistical analysis. Economics is a social science because it applies the scientific method to the study of the interactions among individuals. Economics is concerned with positive analysis rather than normative analysis. **Positive analysis** is concerned with what is. **Normative analysis** is concerned with what ought to be. Because economics is based on studying the actions of individuals, it is a social science. As a social science, economics considers human behaviour in every context of decision making, not just in business.

LO 1.4 Microeconomics is the study of how households and firms make choices, how they interact in markets, and how the government attempts to influence their choices. **Macroeconomics** is the study of the economy as a whole, including topics such as inflation, unemployment, and economic growth.

LO 1.5 Becoming familiar with important terms is a necessary step in learning economics. These important economic terms include *capital, entrepreneur, factors of production, firm, goods, household, human capital, innovation, production, profit, revenue, services,* and *technology.*

MyEconLab   Log in to MyEconLab to complete these exercises and get instant feedback.

---

*'Learning Objective' is abbreviated to 'LO' in the end of chapter material.

Review Questions

LO 1.1

1.1 Briefly discuss each of the following economic ideas: People are rational, people respond to incentives, and optimal decisions are made at the margin.

1.2 What is scarcity? Why is scarcity central to the study of economics?

LO 1.2

2.1 Why does scarcity imply that every society and every individual face trade-offs?

2.2 What are the three economic questions that every society must answer? Briefly discuss the differences in how centrally planned, market, and mixed economies answer these questions.

LO 1.3

3.1 Why do economists use models? How are economic data used to test models?

3.2 Describe the five steps by which economists arrive at a useful economic model.

3.3 What is the difference between normative analysis and positive analysis? Is economics concerned mainly with normative analysis or with positive analysis? Briefly explain.

LO 1.4

4.1 Briefly discuss the difference between microeconomics and macroeconomics.

Problems and Applications

LO 1.1

1.1 Bank robberies are on the rise in New Jersey, and according to the FBI, this increase has little to do with the economic downturn. The FBI claims that banks have allowed themselves to become easy targets by refusing to install clear acrylic partitions, called "bandit barriers," which separate bank tellers from the public. Of the 193 banks robbed in New Jersey in 2008, only 23 had these barriers, and of the 40 banks robbed in the first 10 weeks of 2009, only 1 had a bandit barrier. According to a special agent with the FBI, "Bandit barriers are a great deterrent. We've talked to guys who rob banks, and as soon as they see a bandit barrier, they go find another bank." Despite this finding, many banks have been reluctant to install these barriers. Wouldn't banks have a strong incentive to install bandit barriers to deter robberies? Why, then, do so many banks not do so?

Richard Cowen, "FBI: Banks Are to Blame for Rise in Robberies," NorthJersey.com, March 10, 2009.

1.2 The grading system is a powerful resource for teachers. In their book *Effective Grading: A Tool for Learning and Assessment*, Barbara Walvoord and Virginia Anderson state that "teachers must manage the power and complexity of the grading system" and that "teachers must consider grading in their first deliberations about a course."

a. How could the grading system a teacher uses affect the incentives of students to learn the course material?

b. If teachers put too little weight in the grading scale on a certain part of the course, such as readings outside the textbook, how might students respond?

c. Teachers often wish that students came to class prepared, having read the upcoming material. How could a teacher design the grading system to motivate students to come to class prepared?

Barbara E. Walvoord and Virginia Johnson Anderson, Effective Grading: A Tool for Learning and Assessment, Jossey-Bass: San Francisco, 1998, pp. xvii–xviii.

1.3 **[Related to** Making the Connection **on page 5]** Most provincial governments and the federal government in Canada offer programs and payments to encourage Canadians to have more children. The federal government currently pays all parents with children under six years old $100 per month (this is the Universal Child Care Benefit). Why would the Government of Canada make a cash payment to people with small children? How do you think most people respond to this program?

1.4 **[Related to** Making the Connection **on page 5]** Daniel Parent and Ling Wang have found that changes in government subsidies to people who have children don't have an impact on the number of children people have, only on when people have children. They found that more generous subsidies lead people to have children earlier in life than they would have without the subsidies, but that the total number of children people have doesn't change.

a. Why might a government program affect when people have children?

b. Why might a government subsidy not change the number of children people have?

Based on Parent, D. and Wang, L. (2007), Tax incentives and fertility in Canada: quantum vs tempo effects. Canadian Journal of Economics/Revue canadienne d'économique, 40: 371–400. doi: 10.1111/j.1365-2966.2007.00413.x

1.5 **[Related to** Solved Problem 1.1 **on page 6]** Two students are discussing *Solved Problem 1.1*:

Joe: "I think the key additional information you need to know in deciding whether McCain Foods should make 11 million rather than 10 million kilograms of french-fries is the amount of profit they currently make while selling 10 million kilograms. Then we can compare the profit earned from making 11 million to the profit earned from making 10 million. This information is more important than the additional revenue and additional cost of making 1 million more kilograms."

Jill: "Actually, Joe, knowing how much profit changes when McCain Foods makes 1 million more kilograms is exactly the same as knowing the additional revenue and the additional cost."

Briefly evaluate their arguments.

Based on Lauren A. E. Schuker, "Can 3-D Save Hollywood?" Wall Street Journal, March 20, 2009; and "3D Films Struggle," The Economist, July 23–29, 2011.

1.6 [**Related to** Solved Problem 1.1 **on page 6**] Late in the semester, a friend tells you, "I was going to drop my psychology course so I could concentrate on my other courses, but I had already put so much time into the course that I decided not to drop it." What do you think of your friend's reasoning? Would it make a difference to your answer if your friend has to pass the psychology course at some point to graduate? Briefly explain.

Based on Lauren A. E. Schuker, "Can 3-D Save Hollywood?" Wall Street Journal, March 20, 2009; and "3D Films Struggle," The Economist, July 23–29, 2011.

LO 1.2

2.1 Why does Bill Gates, one of the richest people in the world, face scarcity? Does everyone face scarcity? Are there any exceptions?

2.2 Centrally planned economies have been less efficient than market economies.
   a. Has this difference in efficiency happened by chance, or is there some underlying reason?
   b. If market economies are more economically efficient than centrally planned economies, would there ever be a reason to prefer having a centrally planned economy rather than a market economy?

2.3 In a recent paper, economists Patricia M. Flynn and Michael A. Quinn state the following:

> We find evidence that Economics is a good choice of major for those aspiring to become a CEO [chief executive officer]. When adjusting for size of the pool of graduates, those with undergraduate degrees in Economics are shown to have had a greater likelihood of becoming an S&P 500 CEO than any other major.

A list of famous economics majors published by McMaster University includes business leaders Steve Ballmer (CEO of Microsoft), Warren Buffet, Sam Walton (Founder of Walmart), and Scott McNealy (CEO of SUN Microsystems). The list also includes politicians Ronald Reagan (former US president), Stephen Harper (Prime Minister of Canada), Manmohan Singh (Prime Minister of India), and Kofi Annan (former Secretary-General of the United Nations). Why might studying economics be particularly good preparation for being the top manager of a corporation or a leader in government?

Based on Patricia M. Flynn and Michael A. Quinn, " Economics: A Good choice of Major for Future CEOs," Social Science Research Network, November 28, 2006; and Famous Economics Majors, McMaster University; http://www.economics.mcmaster.ca/documents/Famous_Econ.pdf, accessed Feb. 12, 2012.

2.4 Suppose that a local radio station has decided to give away 100 tickets to an Arcade Fire performance it's promoting. It announces that tickets will be given away at 7:00 a.m. on Monday at the radio station's studio.
   a. What groups of people will be most likely to try to get the tickets? Think of specific examples and then generalize.
   b. What is the opportunity cost of distributing tickets in this way?

   c. Productive efficiency occurs when a good or service, such as the distribution of tickets, is produced at the lowest possible cost. Is this an efficient way to distribute the tickets? If possible, think of a more efficient method of distributing the tickets.
   d. Is this an equitable way to distribute the tickets? Explain.

LO 1.3

3.1 Do you agree with the following assertion: "The problem with economics is that it assumes that consumers and firms always make the correct decision. But we know everyone's human, and we all make mistakes."

3.2 Dr. Strangelove's theory is that the price of mushrooms is determined by the activity of subatomic particles that exist in another universe parallel to ours. When the subatomic particles are emitted in profusion, the price of mushrooms is high. When subatomic particle emissions are low, the price of mushrooms is also low. How would you go about testing Dr. Strangelove's theory? Discuss whether this theory is useful.

3.3 [**Related to** Making the Connection **on page 12**] *Making the Connection* explains that there are both positive and normative elements to the debate over raising the minimum wage. What economic statistics would be most useful in evaluating the positive elements of the debate? Assuming that these statistics are available or could be gathered, are they likely to resolve the normative issues in this debate?

3.4 [**Related to the Chapter Opener on page 3**] Recently, Tim Hortons decided to change the sizes of coffee it sold. It essentially increased the size of each cup, so that what was a large is now a medium.
   a. Many other food items, like crackers, are now being sold in smaller quantities than was traditionally the case. Why is takeout coffee different from other goods?
   b. How have the economic incentives for selling coffee changed over the last few years?

3.5 [**Related to** Don't Let This Happen to You **on page 12**] Explain which of the following statements represent positive analysis and which represent normative analysis:
   a. A 50-cent-per-pack tax on cigarettes will lead to a 12 percent reduction in smoking by teenagers.
   b. The federal government should spend more on AIDS research.
   c. Rising paper prices will increase textbook prices.
   d. The price of coffee at Starbucks is too high.

LO 1.4

4.1 Briefly explain whether each of the following is primarily a microeconomic issue or a macroeconomic issue:
   a. The effect of higher cigarette taxes on the quantity of cigarettes sold
   b. The effect of higher income taxes on the total amount of consumer spending
   c. The reasons for the economies of East Asian countries growing faster than the economies of sub-Saharan African countries
   d. The reasons for low rates of profit in the airline industry

4.2 Briefly explain whether you agree with the following assertion: "Microeconomics is concerned with things that happen in one particular place, such as the unemployment rate in one city. In contrast, macroeconomics is concerned with things that affect the country as a whole, such as how the rate of teenage smoking in the United States would be affected by an increase in the tax on cigarettes."

MyEconLab   MyEconLab is an online tool designed to help you master the concepts covered in your course. It will create an adaptive, highly personalized study plan to stimulate and measure your learning. Log in to take advantage of this powerful study aid, and to access quizzes and other valuable course-related material.

Appendix A

LO

Review the use of graphs and formulas.

Using Graphs and Formulas

Graphs are used to illustrate key economic ideas. Graphs appear not just in economics textbooks but also on websites and in newspaper and magazine articles that discuss events in business and economics. Why the heavy use of graphs? Because they serve two useful purposes: (1) They simplify economic ideas, and (2) they make the ideas more concrete so they can be applied to real-world problems. Economic and business issues can be complicated, but a graph can help cut through complications and highlight the key relationships needed to understand the issue. In that sense, a graph can be like a street map.

For example, suppose you take a bus to Toronto to see the CN Tower. After arriving at the downtown bus station, you will probably use a map similar to the one shown below to find your way to the CN Tower.

Maps are very familiar to just about everyone, so we don't usually think of them as being simplified versions of reality, but they are. This map does not show much more than the streets in this part of Toronto and some of the most important places. The names, addresses, and telephone numbers of the people who live and work in the area aren't given. Almost none of the stores and buildings those people work and live in are shown either. The map doesn't indicate which streets allow curbside parking and which don't. In fact, the map shows almost nothing about the messy reality of life in this section of Toronto, except how the streets are laid out, which is the essential information you need to get from the bus station to the CN Tower.

Think about someone who says, "I know how to get around in the city, but I just can't figure out how to read a map." It certainly is possible to find your destination in a

© Valentino Visentini / Alamy

city without a map, but it's a lot easier with one. The same is true of using graphs in economics. It is possible to arrive at a solution to a real-world problem in economics and business without using graphs, but it is usually a lot easier if you do use them.

Often, the difficulty students have with graphs and formulas is a lack of familiarity. With practice, all the graphs and formulas in this text will become familiar to you. Once you are familiar with them, you will be able to use them to analyze problems that would otherwise seem very difficult. What follows is a brief review of how graphs and formulas are used.

Graphs of One Variable

Figure 1A.1 displays values for market shares in the Canadian automobile market, using two common types of graphs. Market shares show the percentage of industry sales accounted for by different firms. In this case, the information is for groups of firms: the "Big Three"—Ford, General Motors, and Chrysler—as well as Japanese firms, European firms, and Korean firms.

Information on economic variables is also often displayed in time-series graphs. Time-series graphs are displayed on a coordinate grid. In a coordinate grid, we can measure the value of one variable along the vertical axis (or *y*-axis) and the value of another variable along the horizontal axis (or *x*-axis). The point where the vertical axis intersects the horizontal axis is called the *origin*. At the origin, the value of both variables is zero. The points on a coordinate grid represent values of the two variables. In Figure 1A.2, we measure the number of automobiles and trucks sold worldwide by Ford Motor Company on the vertical axis, and we measure time on the horizontal axis. In time-series graphs, the height of the line at each date shows the value of the variable measured on the vertical axis. Both panels of Figure 1A.2 show Ford's worldwide sales during each year from 2001 to 2010. The difference between panel (a) and panel (b) illustrates the importance of the scale used in a time-series graph. In panel (a), the scale on the vertical axis is truncated, which means it does not start with zero. The slashes (//) near

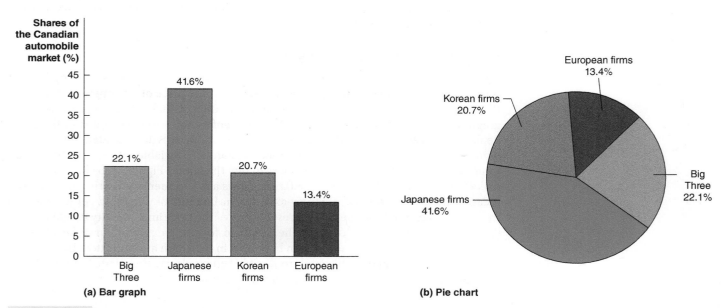

(a) Bar graph   (b) Pie chart

Figure 1A.1 Bar Graphs and Pie Charts

Values for an economic variable are often displayed as a bar graph or as a pie chart. In this case, panel (a) shows market share data for the Canadian automobile industry as a *bar graph*, where the market share of each group of firms is represented by the height of its bar. Panel (b) displays the same information as a *pie chart*, with the market share of each group of firms represented by the size of its slice of the pie.

Source: Data from Global Economic Research, Global Auto Report, Oct. 4, 2012. http://www.gbm.scotiabank.com/English/bns_econ/bns_auto.pdf

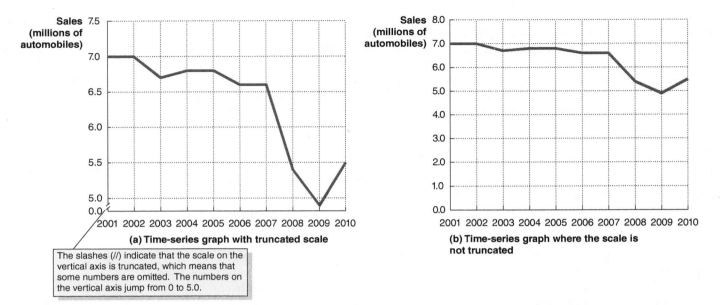

The slashes (//) indicate that the scale on the vertical axis is truncated, which means that some numbers are omitted. The numbers on the vertical axis jump from 0 to 5.0.

Figure 1A.2 **Time-Series Graphs**

Both panels present time-series graphs of Ford Motor Company's worldwide sales during each year from 2001 to 2010. Panel (a) has a truncated scale on the vertical axis, and panel (b) does not. As a result, the fluctuations in Ford's sales appear smaller in panel (b) than in panel (a).

Source: Data from Ford Motor Company, Annual Report, various years.

the bottom of the axis indicate that the scale is truncated. In panel (b), the scale is not truncated. In panel (b), the decline in Ford's sales during 2008 and 2009 appears smaller than in panel (a). (Technically, the horizontal axis is also truncated because we start with the year 2001, not the year 0.)

Graphs of Two Variables

We often use graphs to show the relationship between two variables. For example, suppose you are interested in the relationship between the price of a pepperoni pizza and the quantity of pizzas sold per week in the small town of Sackville, New Brunswick. A graph showing the relationship between the price of a good and the quantity of the good demanded at each price is called a *demand curve*. (As we will discuss later, in drawing a demand curve for a good, we have to hold constant any variables other than price that might affect the willingness of consumers to buy the good.) Figure 1A.3 shows the data collected on price and quantity. The figure shows a two-dimensional grid on which we measure the price of pizza along the *y*-axis and the quantity of pizza sold per week along the *x*-axis. Each point on the grid represents one of the price and quantity combinations listed in the table. We can connect the points to form the demand curve for pizza in Sackville, NB. Notice that the scales on both axes in the graph are truncated. In this case, truncating the axes allows the graph to illustrate more clearly the relationship between price and quantity by excluding low prices and quantities.

Slopes of Lines

Once you have plotted the data in Figure 1A.3, you may be interested in how much the quantity of pizza sold increases as the price decreases. The slope of a line tells us how much the variable we are measuring on the *y*-axis changes as the variable we are measuring on the *x*-axis changes. We can use the Greek letter delta (Δ) to stand for the change in a variable. The slope is sometimes referred to as the *rise* over the *run*. So, we have several ways of expressing slope:

Price (dollars per pizza)	Quantity (pizzas per week)	Points
$15	50	A
14	55	B
13	60	C
12	65	D
11	70	E

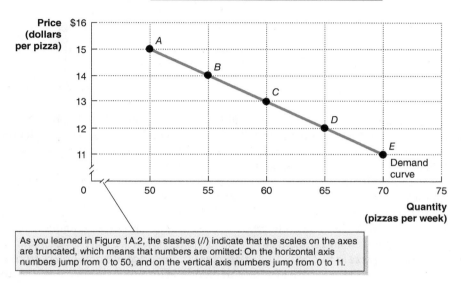

Figure 1A.3

Plotting Price and Quantity Points in a Graph

The figure shows a two-dimensional grid on which we measure the price of pizza along the vertical axis (or *y*-axis) and the quantity of pizza sold per week along the horizontal axis (or *x*-axis). Each point on the grid represents one of the price and quantity combinations listed in the table. By connecting the points with a line, we can better illustrate the relationship between the two variables.

As you learned in Figure 1A.2, the slashes (///) indicate that the scales on the axes are truncated, which means that numbers are omitted: On the horizontal axis numbers jump from 0 to 50, and on the vertical axis numbers jump from 0 to 11.

$$\text{Slope} = \frac{\text{Change in value on the vertical axis}}{\text{Change in value on the horizontal axis}} = \frac{\Delta y}{\Delta x} = \frac{\text{Rise}}{\text{Run}}.$$

Figure 1A.4 reproduces the graph from Figure 1A.3. Because the slope of a straight line is the same at any point, we can use any two points in the figure to calculate the slope of the line. For example, when the price of pizza decreases from $14 to $12, the quantity of pizza sold increases from 55 per week to 65 per week. Therefore, the slope is:

$$\text{Slope} = \frac{\Delta \text{Price of pizza}}{\Delta \text{Quantity of pizza}} = \frac{(\$12 - \$14)}{(65 - 55)} = \frac{-2}{10} = -0.2.$$

The slope of this line gives us some insight into how responsive consumers in Sackville are to changes in the price of pizza. The larger the value of the slope (ignoring the negative sign), the steeper the line will be, which indicates that not many additional pizzas are sold when the price falls. The smaller the value of the slope, the flatter the line will be, which indicates a greater increase in pizzas sold when the price falls.

Taking into Account More Than Two Variables on a Graph

The demand curve graph in Figure 1A.4 shows the relationship between the price of pizza and the quantity of pizza demanded, but we know that the quantity of any good demanded depends on more than just the price of the good. For example, the quantity of pizza demanded in a given week in Sackville can be affected by other variables, such as the price of hamburgers, whether an advertising campaign by local pizza parlours has begun that week, and so on. Allowing the values of any other variables to change will cause the position of the demand curve in the graph to change.

Suppose, for example, that the demand curve in Figure 1A.4 were drawn holding the price of hamburgers constant, at $1.50. If the price of hamburgers rises to $2.00, some consumers will switch from buying hamburgers to buying pizza, and more pizzas will be demanded at every price. The result on the graph will be to shift the line

Figure 1A.4

Calculating the Slope of a Line

We can calculate the slope of a line as the change in the value of the variable on the *y*-axis divided by the change in the value of the variable on the *x*-axis. Because the slope of a straight line is constant, we can use any two points in the figure to calculate the slope of the line. For example, when the price of pizza decreases from $14 to $12, the quantity of pizza demanded increases from 55 per week to 65 per week. So, the slope of this line equals −2 divided by 10, or −0.2.

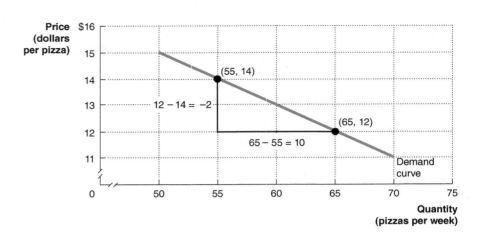

representing the demand curve to the right. Similarly, if the price of hamburgers falls from $1.50 to $1.00, some consumers will switch from buying pizza to buying hamburgers, and fewer pizzas will be demanded at every price. The result on the graph will be to shift the line representing the demand curve to the left.

The table in Figure 1A.5 shows the effect of a change in the price of hamburgers on the quantity of pizza demanded. For example, suppose that at first we are on the line labelled *Demand curve₁*. If the price of pizza is $14 (point *A*), an increase in the price of hamburgers from $1.50 to $2.00 increases the quantity of pizzas demanded from 55 to 60 per week (point *B*) and shifts us to *Demand curve₂*. Or, if we start on *Demand curve₁* and the price of pizza is $12 (point *C*), a decrease in the price of hamburgers from $1.50 to $1.00 decreases the quantity of pizzas demanded from 65 to 60 per week (point *D*) and shifts us to *Demand curve₃*. By shifting the demand curve, we have taken into account the effect of changes in the value of a third variable—the price of hamburgers. We will use this technique of shifting curves to allow for the effects of additional variables many times in this book.

Positive and Negative Relationships

We can use graphs to show the relationships between any two variables. Sometimes the relationship between the variables is negative, meaning that as one variable increases in value, the other variable decreases in value. This was the case with the price of pizza and the quantity of pizzas demanded. The relationship between two variables can also be positive, meaning that the values of both variables increase or decrease together. For example, when the level of total income—or personal disposable income—received by households in Canada increases, the level of total consumption spending, which is spending by households on goods and services, also increases. The table in Figure 1A.6 shows the values (in millions of dollars) for income and consumption spending for the years 2008–2011. The graph plots the data from the table, with personal disposable income measured along the horizontal axis and consumption spending measured along the vertical axis. Notice that the four points do not all fall exactly on the line. This is often the case with real-world data. To examine the relationship between two variables, economists often use the straight line that best fits the data.

Determining Cause and Effect

When we graph the relationship between two variables, we often want to draw conclusions about whether changes in one variable are causing changes in the other variable. Doing so, however, can lead to incorrect conclusions. For example, suppose you graph the number of homes in a neighbourhood that have a fire burning in the fireplace and the number of leaves on trees in the neighbourhood. You would get a relationship like that shown in panel (a) of Figure 1A.7: The more fires burning in the neighbourhood, the fewer leaves the trees have. Can we draw the conclusion from this graph that using a fireplace causes trees to lose their leaves? We know, of course, that such a conclusion

Price (dollars per pizza)	Quantity (pizzas per week)		
	When the Price of Hamburgers = $1.00	When the Price of Hamburgers = $1.50	When the Price of Hamburgers = $2.00
$15	45	50	55
14	50	55	60
13	55	60	65
12	60	65	70
11	65	70	75

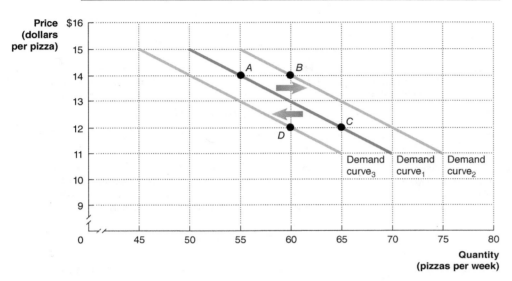

Figure 1A.5

Showing Three Variables on a Graph

The demand curve for pizza shows the relationship between the price of pizzas and the quantity of pizzas demanded, holding constant other factors that might affect the willingness of consumers to buy pizza. If the price of pizza is $14 (point *A*), an increase in the price of hamburgers from $1.50 to $2.00 increases the quantity of pizzas demanded from 55 to 60 per week (point *B*) and shifts us to *Demand curve₂*. Or, if we start on *Demand curve₁* and the price of pizza is $12 (point *C*), a decrease in the price of hamburgers from $1.50 to $1.00 decreases the quantity of pizza demanded from 65 to 60 per week (point *D*) and shifts us to *Demand curve₃*.

would be incorrect. In spring and summer, there are relatively few fireplaces being used, and the trees are full of leaves. In the fall, as trees begin to lose their leaves, fireplaces are used more frequently. And in winter, many fireplaces are being used and many trees have lost all their leaves. The reason that the graph in Figure 1A.7 is misleading about cause and effect is that there is obviously an omitted variable in the analysis—the season

Year	Personal Disposable Income (millions of dollars)	Consumption Spending (millions of dollars)
2008	$953 568	$890 601
2009	966 269	898 215
2010	1 013 778	940 620
2011	1 046 827	980 629

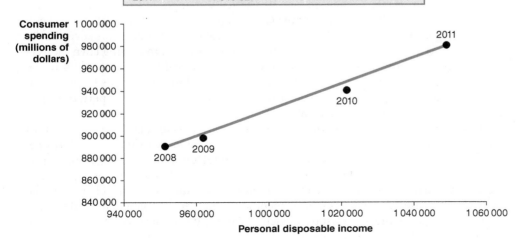

Figure 1A.6

Graphing the Positive Relationship between Income and Consumption

In a positive relationship between two economic variables, as one variable increases, the other variable also increases. This figure shows the positive relationship between personal disposable income and consumption spending. As personal disposable income in Canada has increased, so has consumption spending.

Source: Data from Statistics Canada.

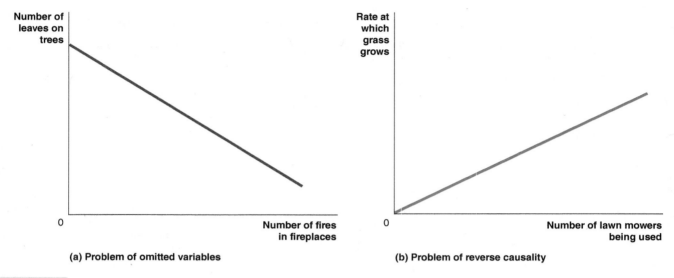

(a) Problem of omitted variables

(b) Problem of reverse causality

Figure 1A.7 **Determining Cause and Effect**

Using graphs to draw conclusions about cause and effect can be hazardous. In panel (a), we see that there are fewer leaves on the trees in a neighbourhood when many homes have fires burning in their fireplaces. We cannot draw the conclusion that the fires cause the leaves to fall because we have an *omitted variable*—the season of the year. In panel (b), we see that more lawn mowers are used in a neighbourhood during times when the grass grows rapidly and fewer lawn mowers are used when the grass grows slowly. Concluding that using lawn mowers causes the grass to grow faster would be making the error of *reverse causality*.

of the year. An omitted variable is one that affects other variables, and its omission can lead to false conclusions about cause and effect.

Although in our example the omitted variable is obvious, there are many debates about cause and effect where the existence of an omitted variable has not been clear. For instance, it has been known for many years that people who smoke cigarettes suffer from higher rates of lung cancer than do nonsmokers. For some time, tobacco companies and some scientists argued that there was an omitted variable—perhaps a failure to exercise or a poor diet—that made some people more likely to smoke and more likely to develop lung cancer. If this omitted variable existed, then the finding that smokers were more likely to develop lung cancer would not have been evidence that smoking caused lung cancer. In this case, however, nearly all scientists eventually concluded that the omitted variable did not exist and that, in fact, smoking does cause lung cancer.

A related problem in determining cause and effect is known as *reverse causality*. The error of reverse causality occurs when we conclude that changes in variable X cause changes in variable Y when, in fact, it is actually changes in variable Y that cause changes in variable X. For example, panel (b) of Figure 1A.7 plots the number of lawn mowers being used in a neighbourhood against the rate at which grass on lawns in the neighbourhood is growing. We could conclude from this graph that using lawn mowers causes the grass to grow faster. We know, however, that in reality, the causality is in the other direction: Rapidly growing grass during the spring and summer causes the increased use of lawn mowers. Slowly growing grass in the fall or winter or during periods of low rainfall causes decreased use of lawn mowers.

Once again, in our example, the potential error of reverse causality is obvious. In many economic debates, however, cause and effect can be more difficult to determine. For example, changes in the money supply, or the total amount of money in the economy, tend to occur at the same time as changes in the total amount of income people in the economy earn. A famous debate in economics was about whether the changes in the money supply caused the changes in total income or whether the changes in total income caused the changes in the money supply. Each side in the debate accused the other side of committing the error of reverse causality.

Are Graphs of Economic Relationships Always Straight Lines?

The graphs of relationships between two economic variables that we have drawn so far have been straight lines. The relationship between two variables is linear when it can be represented by a straight line. Few economic relationships are actually linear. For example, if we carefully plot data on the price of a product and the quantity demanded at each price, holding constant other variables that affect the quantity demanded, we will usually find a curved—or nonlinear—relationship rather than a linear relationship. In practice, however, it is often useful to approximate a nonlinear relationship with a linear relationship. If the relationship is reasonably close to being linear, the analysis is not significantly affected. In addition, it is easier to calculate the slope of a straight line, and it also is easier to calculate the area under a straight line. So, in this book, we often assume that the relationship between two economic variables is linear, even when we know that this assumption is not precisely correct.

Slopes of Nonlinear Curves

In some situations, we need to take into account the nonlinear nature of an economic relationship. For example, panel (a) of Figure 1A.8 shows the hypothetical relationship between Apple's total cost of producing iPhones and the quantity of iPhones produced.

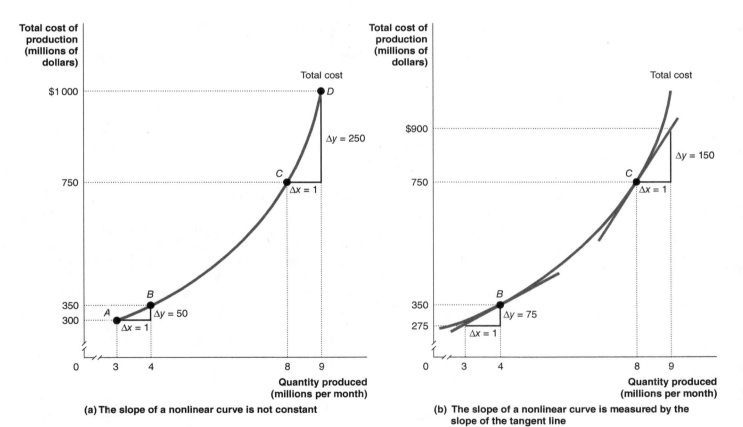

(a) The slope of a nonlinear curve is not constant

(b) The slope of a nonlinear curve is measured by the slope of the tangent line

Figure 1A.8 **The Slope of a Nonlinear Curve**

The relationship between the quantity of iPhones produced and the total cost of production is curved rather than linear. In panel (a), in moving from point A to point B, the quantity produced increases by 1 million iPhones, while the total cost of production increases by $50 million. Farther up the curve, as we move from point C to point D, the change in quantity is the same—1 million iPhones—but the change in the total cost of production is now much larger: $250 million.

Because the change in the y variable has increased, while the change in the x variable has remained the same, we know that the slope has increased. In panel (b), we measure the slope of the curve at a particular point by the slope of the tangent line. The slope of the tangent line at point B is 75, and the slope of the tangent line at point C is 150.

The relationship is curved rather than linear. In this case, the cost of production is increasing at an increasing rate, which often happens in manufacturing. Put a different way, as we move up the curve, its slope becomes larger. (Remember that with a straight line, the slope is always constant.) To see this effect, first remember that we calculate the slope of a curve by dividing the change in the variable on the y-axis by the change in the variable on the x-axis. As we move from point A to point B, the quantity produced increases by 1 million iPhones, while the total cost of production increases by $50 million. Farther up the curve, as we move from point C to point D, the change in quantity is the same—1 million iPhones—but the change in the total cost of production is now much larger: $250 million. Because the change in the y variable has increased, while the change in the x variable has remained the same, we know that the slope has increased.

To measure the slope of a nonlinear curve at a particular point, we must measure the slope of the *tangent line* to the curve at that point. A tangent line will touch the curve only at that point. We can measure the slope of the tangent line just as we would the slope of any other straight line. In panel (b), the tangent line at point B has a slope equal to:

$$\frac{\Delta \text{Cost}}{\Delta \text{Quantity}} = \frac{75}{1} = 75.$$

The tangent line at point C has a slope equal to:

$$\frac{\Delta \text{Cost}}{\Delta \text{Quantity}} = \frac{150}{1} = 150.$$

Once again, we see that the slope of the curve is larger at point C than at point B.

Formulas

We have just seen that graphs are an important economic tool. In this section, we will review several useful formulas and show how to use them to summarize data and to calculate important relationships.

Formula for a Percentage Change

One important formula is the percentage change. The percentage change is the change in some economic variable, usually from one period to the next, expressed as a percentage. An important macroeconomic measure is the real gross domestic product (GDP). GDP is the value of all the final goods and services produced in a country during a year. "Real" GDP is corrected for the effects of inflation. When economists say that the Canadian economy grew 3.0 percent during 2011, they mean that real GDP was 3.0 percent higher in 2011 than it was in 2010. The formula for making this calculation is:

$$\frac{\text{GDP}_{2011} - \text{GDP}_{2010}}{\text{GDP}_{2010}} \times 100$$

or, more generally, for any two periods:

$$\text{Percentage change} = \frac{\text{Value in the second period} - \text{Value in the first period}}{\text{Value in the first period}} \times 100.$$

In this case, real GDP was $1 279 586 million in 2010 and $1 316 622 million in 2011. So, the growth rate of the Canadian economy during 2011 was:

$$\left(\frac{\$1\ 316\ 622 - \$1\ 279\ 586}{\$1\ 279\ 586}\right) \times 100 = 2.89\%.$$

Notice that it doesn't matter that in using the formula, we ignored the fact that GDP is measured in millions of dollars. In fact, when calculating percentage changes, *the*

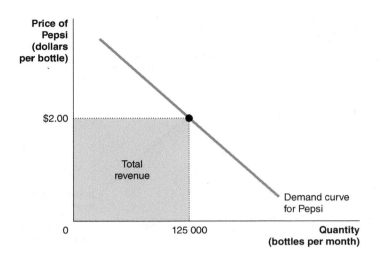

Figure 1A.9

Showing a Firm's Total Revenue on a Graph

The area of a rectangle is equal to its base multiplied by its height. Total revenue is equal to quantity multiplied by price. Here, total revenue is equal to the quantity of 125 000 bottles times the price of $2.00 per bottle, or $250 000. The area of the green-shaded rectangle shows the firm's total revenue.

units don't matter. The percentage increase from $1 279 586 million to $1 316 622 million is exactly the same as the percentage increase from $1 279 586 to $1 316 622.

Formulas for the Areas of a Rectangle and a Triangle

Areas that form rectangles and triangles on graphs can have important economic meaning. For example, Figure 1A.9 shows the demand curve for Pepsi. Suppose that the price is currently $2.00 and that 125 000 bottles of Pepsi are sold at that price. A firm's total revenue is equal to the amount it receives from selling its product, or the quantity sold multiplied by the price. In this case, total revenue will equal 125 000 bottles times $2.00 per bottle, or $250 000.

The formula for the area of a rectangle is:

$$\text{Area of a rectangle} = \text{Base} \times \text{Height}.$$

In Figure 1A.9, the green-shaded rectangle also represents the firm's total revenue because its area is given by the base of 125 000 bottles multiplied by the price of $2.00 per bottle.

We will see in later chapters that areas that are triangles can also have economic significance. The formula for the area of a triangle is:

$$\text{Area of a triangle} = \frac{1}{2} \times \text{Base} \times \text{Height}.$$

The blue-shaded area in Figure 1A.10 is a triangle. The base equals 150 000 – 125 000, or 25 000. Its height equals $2.00 – $1.50, or $0.50. Therefore, its area equals 1/2 × 25 000 × $0.50, or $6250. Notice that the blue area is a triangle only if the demand curve is a straight line, or linear. Not all demand curves are linear. However, the formula for the area of a triangle will usually still give a good approximation, even if the demand curve is not linear.

Summary of Using Formulas

You will encounter several other formulas in this book. Whenever you must use a formula, you should follow these steps:

1. Make sure you understand the economic concept the formula represents.

2. Make sure you are using the correct formula for the problem you are solving.

3. Make sure the number you calculate using the formula is economically reasonable. For example, if you are using a formula to calculate a firm's revenue and your answer is a negative number, you know you made a mistake somewhere.

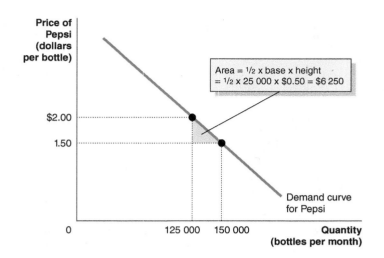

Figure 1A.10

The Area of a Triangle

The area of a triangle is equal to 1/2 multiplied by its base multiplied by its height. The area of the blue-shaded triangle has a base equal to 150 000 – 125 000, or 25 000, and a height equal to $2.00 – $1.50, or $0.50. Therefore, its area equals 1/2 × 25 000 × $0.50, or $6 250.

MyEconLab   Log in to MyEconLab to complete these exercises and get instant feedback.

Problems and Applications

LO Review the use of graphs and formulas.

1A.1 The following table shows the relationship between the price of custard pies and the number of pies Jacob buys per week:

Price	Quantity of Pies	Week
$3.00	6	July 2
2.00	7	July 9
5.00	4	July 16
6.00	3	July 23
1.00	8	July 30
4.00	5	August 6

    a. Is the relationship between the price of pies and the number of pies Jacob buys a positive relationship or a negative relationship?

    b. Plot the data from the table on a graph similar to Figure 1A.3 on page 25. Draw a straight line that best fits the points.

    c. Calculate the slope of the line.

1A.2 The following table gives information on the quantity of glasses of lemonade demanded on sunny and overcast days:

Price (dollars per glass)	Quantity (glasses of lemonade per day)	Weather
$0.80	30	Sunny
0.80	10	Overcast
0.70	40	Sunny
0.70	20	Overcast
0.60	50	Sunny
0.60	30	Overcast
0.50	60	Sunny
0.50	40	Overcast

Plot the data from the table on a graph similar to Figure 1A.5 on page 27. Draw two straight lines representing the two demand curves—one for sunny days and one for overcast days.

1A.3 Using the information in Figure 1A.2 on page 24, calculate the percentage change in auto sales from one year to the next. Between which years did sales fall at the fastest rate?

1A.4 Real GDP in 2008 was $13 162 billion. Real GDP in 2009 was $12 703 billion. What was the percentage change in real GDP from 2008 to 2009? What do economists call the percentage change in real GDP from one year to the next?

1A.5 Assume that the demand curve for Pepsi passes through the following two points:

Price per Bottle of Pepsi	Number of Bottles Demanded
$2.50	100 000
1.25	200 000

a. Draw a graph with a linear demand curve that passes through these two points.

b. Show on the graph the areas representing total revenue at each price. Give the value for total revenue at each price.

1A.6 What is the area of the blue triangle shown in the following figure?

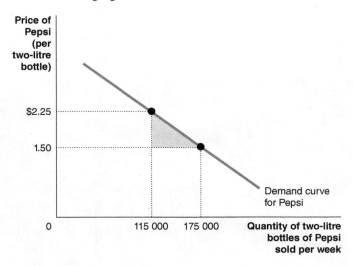

1A.7 Calculate the slope of the total cost curve at point *A* and at point *B* in the following figure.

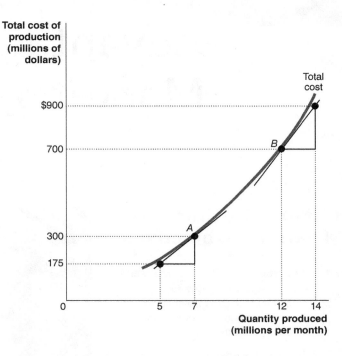

CHAPTER

2

Trade-offs, Comparative Advantage, and the Market System

Chapter Outline and Learning Objectives

2.1 Production Possibilities Frontiers and Opportunity Costs, page 36
Use a production possibilities frontier to analyze opportunity costs and trade-offs.

2.2 Comparative Advantage and Trade, page 42
Understand comparative advantage and explain how it is the basis for trade.

2.3 The Market System, page 48
Explain the basic idea of how a market system works.

OMEO GACAD/AFP/Getty Images

Managers Make Choices at Toyota

When you think of major automakers, Toyota is likely one of the first companies on your list. Founded in Japan in 1937, Toyota is the largest automaker in the world, selling 9.2 million vehicles in 2012. To compete in the automotive market, the managers of Toyota must make many decisions, such as whether to introduce new car models. Toyota doesn't just sell gasoline-powered cars, it also sells diesel-powered cars, hybrids, and is developing all-electric vehicles.

Toyota's managers must also decide whether to concentrate production in Japanese facilities or build new ones in overseas markets. Keeping production in Japan makes it easier for Toyota's managers to supervise production and to employ Japanese workers, who generally have high skill levels and few labour disputes. By building plants in the countries in which it sells its vehicles, Toyota can benefit from paying lower wages, lower transportation costs, and the reduced political friction that results from investing in local economies. Toyota has assembly plants in Cambridge and Woodstock, Ontario, in which it builds the Toyota Corolla, Matrix, and RAV4, and the Lexus RX 350.

Managers also face smaller-scale business decisions. For instance, they must decide how many Toyota Corolla sedans and Lexus RX 350 SUVs to build in the company's Cambridge plant each month. Like other decisions people make, this one involves a trade-off: Producing more Corolla sedans means making fewer RX 350 SUVs.

AN INSIDE LOOK on **page 54** discusses how managers decide between producing hybrid cars and diesel cars, and improving existing gasoline-powered models.

Sources: "GM Loses Global Sales Crown to Toyota," *Globe and Mail*, January 14, 2013, http://www.theglobeandmail.com/globe-investor/gm-loses-global-sales-crown-to-toyota/article7319056/; and Toyota.ca.

Economics in Your Life

The Trade-offs When You Buy a Car

When you buy a car, you probably consider features such as safety, fuel efficiency, and, of course, cost. Most newer cars are more fuel-efficient than older cars. Fuel-efficiency standards have been improving almost continuously over the last 40 years. Of course, newer cars are more expensive than older ones. Very old, inefficient cars can sometimes be bought for very little. Under what circumstances would you be better off buying an older, less fuel-efficient car than a new highly efficient one? Who do you think is most likely to want a car with high fuel efficiency? As you read this chapter, see if you can answer these questions. You can check your answers against those we provide on page 52 at the end of this chapter.

Scarcity A situation in which unlimited wants exceed the limited resources available to fulfill those wants.

Factors of production The inputs used to make goods and services.

A ll economics starts with the recognition of **scarcity**. Scarcity exists because we have unlimited wants but only limited resources available to fulfill those wants. *Scarcity requires trade-offs.* When resources are scarce, having more of one thing means having less of something else. The economic resources, or **factors of production**—the inputs used to make goods and services, such as workers, capital, natural resources, and entrepreneurial ability—are scarce. This means goods and services are scarce. Your time is scarce, which means that you face trade-offs: If you spend an hour studying for an economics exam, you have one less hour to spend playing video games. If your university decides to use some of its scarce budget to buy new computers for the computer labs, those funds will not be available to expand parking lots. In a market system, managers at all firms must make decisions like those made by Toyota's managers. If Toyota decides to devote some of the scarce workers and machinery in its Cambridge plant to producing more RX 350 SUVs, those resources will not be available to produce more Corolla sedans.

Canadian households and firms make many of their decision in markets. Trade is a key activity that takes place in markets. Trade involves the decisions of millions of households and firms spread all over the world. By engaging in trade, people can raise their standard of living. In this chapter, we provide an overview of how the market system coordinates the independent decisions of millions of people. We begin our analysis of the economic consequences of scarcity, the benefits of trade, and the workings of the market system by introducing an important economic model: the *production possibilities frontier.*

2.1 LEARNING OBJECTIVE

Use a production possibilities frontier to analyze opportunity costs and trade-offs.

Production possibilities frontier (PPF) A curve showing the maximum attainable combinations of two products that may be produced with available resources and current technology.

Production Possibilities Frontiers and Opportunity Costs

As we saw in the chapter opener, Toyota operates plants in Cambridge and Woodstock, Ontario, where it assembles Toyota sedans and Lexus RX 350 SUVs. Because the firm's resources—workers, machinery, materials, and entrepreneurial skills—are limited, Toyota faces a trade-off: For example, resources devoted to building sedans can't be used to build RX 350 SUVs, and vice versa. Chapter 1 explained that economic models can be useful to analyze a number of questions. We can use a simple model called the *production possibilities frontier* to analyze the trade-offs Toyota faces in its Cambridge plant. A **production possibilities frontier (PPF)** is a curve showing the maximum attainable combinations of two products that may be produced with available resources and technology. For our purposes, let's assume that Toyota produces only Corolla sedans and RX 350 SUVs at its Cambridge plant, using workers, robots, materials, and other machinery.

Graphing the Production Possibilities Frontier

Figure 2.1 uses a production possibilities frontier to illustrate the trade-offs that Toyota faces. The numbers on the table are plotted on the graph. The line in the graph is Toyota's production possibilities frontier. If Toyota uses all its resources to produce Corolla sedans, it can make 800 per day—point *A* at one end of the production possibilities frontier. If Toyota uses all its resources to produce RX 350 SUVs, it can produce 800 per day—point *E* at the other end of the production possibilities frontier. If Toyota devotes resources to producing both types of vehicles, it could be at a point like *B* where it produces 600 Corolla sedans and 200 RX 350 SUVs.

All the combinations on the frontier (such as *A*, *B*, *C*, *D*, and *E*) or inside it (such as point *F*) are *attainable* with the resources and technology Toyota currently has. Combinations on the frontier are (productively) *efficient* because all available resources are being fully used, and the fewest possible resources are being used to produce a given amount of output. Toyota is getting the most it can. Combinations inside the frontier, such as point *F*, are inefficient because maximum output is not being obtained from the available resources. We can tell *F* is inefficient because Toyota could make 500 SUVs at this factory and still

Toyota's Production Possibilities at Its Cambridge Plant		
Choice	Quantity of Corolla Sedans Produced	Quantity of RX 350 SUVs Produced
A	800	0
B	600	200
C	400	400
D	200	600
E	0	800
F	300	100
G	600	500

Figure 2.1

Toyota's Production Possibilities Frontier

Toyota faces a trade-off: To build one more sedan, it must build one less SUV. The production possibilities frontier illustrates the trade-off Toyota faces. Combinations on the production possibilities frontier—such as points *A, B, C, D,* and *E*—are *technically efficient* because the maximum output is being obtained from the available resources. Combinations inside the frontier—such as point *F*—are *inefficient* because some resources are not being used. Combinations outside the frontier—such as point *G*—are *unattainable* with current resources.

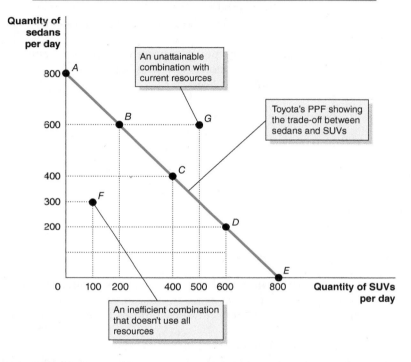

make 300 sedans, instead of only making 100 SUVs and 300 sedans. This would happen if the managers decided to hire a number of workers, but didn't give them anything to do.

Toyota, like most firms, would like to be beyond the frontier—at a point like *G*, where it would be producing 600 sedans and 500 SUVs—but points outside the production possibilities frontier are unattainable with the workers, equipment, materials, and technology currently in use. To be able to produce 600 sedans and 500 SUVs, Toyota would have to hire more workers and buy more equipment.

Notice that if Toyota is producing efficiently and is on the production possibilities frontier, the only way to produce more of one type of vehicle is to produce fewer of another type. Recall from Chapter 1 that the **opportunity cost** of any activity is the highest-valued alternative that must be given up to engage in that activity. For Toyota, the opportunity cost of producing one more SUV is the number of sedans it will not be able to produce because it has shifted those resources to making SUVs. For example, in moving from point *B* to point *C*, the opportunity cost of producing 200 more SUVs per day is the 200 fewer sedans that can be made.

Being on the production possibilities frontier is a good idea, but what point on the production possibilities frontier is best? Choosing the best point on the production possibilities frontier is called **allocative efficiency**. Allocative efficiency occurs when a society is making the combination of goods and services that are most valued by consumers. For example, if consumers want SUVs more than they do sedans (as they did in the 1990s and 2000s), then the allocatively efficient point is likely a point like *E*. If consumers want sedans more than they do SUVs (as they tend to when the price of gas is high) the allocatively efficient point is more likely a point like point *A*.

Opportunity cost The highest-valued alternative that must be given up to engage in an activity.

Allocative efficiency A state of the economy in which production is in accordance with consumer preferences; in particular, every good or service is produced up to the point where the last unit provides a marginal benefit to society equal to the marginal cost of producing it.

Solved Problem **2.1**

Drawing a Production Possibilities Frontier for Pat's Pizza Pit

Pat's Pizza Pit makes both root beer and pizza. Pat has 5 hours a day to spend on making either pizzas or root beer. In 1 hour, Pat can make 2 pizzas or 1 litre of root beer.

a. Use the information given to complete the table below.

	Hours Spent Making		Quantity Made	
Choice	Root Beer	Pizza	Root Beer (litres)	Pizza
A	5	0		
B	4	1		
C	3	2		
D	2	3		
E	1	4		
F	0	5		

b. Use the data from the table you just completed to draw a production possibilities frontier graph illustrating Pat's trade-offs between making pizza and making root beer. Label the vertical axis "Quantity of pizzas made" and the horizontal axis "Quantity of root beer made." Make sure to label the values where Pat's PPF intersects the vertical and horizontal axes.

c. Label the points representing choice *B* and choice *C*. If Pat is at choice *B*, what is her opportunity cost of making more root beer?

Solving the Problem

Step 1: Review the chapter material. This problem is about using production possibilities frontiers to analyze trade-offs, so you may want to review the section "Graphing the Production Possibilities Frontier," which begins on page 36.

Step 2: Answer part (a) by filling in the table. If Pat can produce 1 litre of root beer in one hour, then with choice *A*, she will make 5 litres of root beer and no pizza. Because she can produce 2 pizzas in 1 hour, with choice *B*, she will make 4 litres of root beer and 2 pizzas. Using similar reasoning, you can fill in the remaining cells of the table as follows:

	Hours Spent Making		Quantity Made	
Choice	Root Beer	Pizza	Root Beer (litres)	Pizza
A	5	0	5	0
B	4	1	4	2
C	3	2	3	4
D	2	3	2	6
E	1	4	1	8
F	0	5	0	10

Step 3: Answer part (b) by drawing the production possibilities frontier graph. Using the data in the table shown in Step 2, you should have a graph that looks something like this:

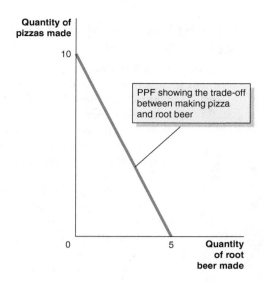

If Pat devotes all 5 hours to making pizza, she will have 10 pizzas. There-fore, her production possibilities frontier will intersect the vertical axis at 10. If she spends all her time making root beer, she will have 5 litres. There-fore, her production possibilities frontier will intersect the horizontal axis at 5.

Step 4: **Answer part (c) by showing choices B and C on your graph.** The points for choices *B* and *C* can be plotted using the information in the table, which gives you the following:

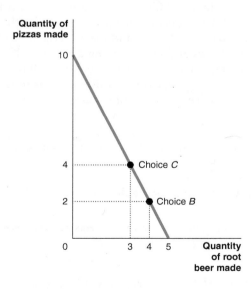

Moving from choice *B* to choice *C* increases Pat's production of pizza from 2 to 4, but lowers her production of root beer by 1 litre (from 4 to 3).

Your Turn: For more practice, do related problem 1.4 on page 57 at the end of this chapter.   MyEconLab

Facing the Trade-offs of Health Care Spending

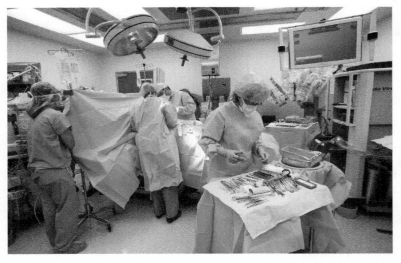

Spending more on health care means spending less on other goods and services.

Governments have to deal with scarcity. If your provincial government spends more on health care, say by paying doctors or nurses more, it has less to spend on other areas such as education. Health care expenditures are the single biggest item in the budgets of all provincial governments, accounting for about 40 percent of spending. The federal government also supports health care spending through the Canada Health Transfer, which is the single biggest transfer of funds from the federal government to provincial governments. In 2011–2012, the federal government transferred about $27 billion dollars to provincial governments to pay for health care.

Canada's population is aging; the number of people who are over 65 is greater than ever before and that number is growing. As the population ages, two things will happen. First, older people need more health care than younger adults, which means governments will be asked to provide more money for health care spending. Second, there will be fewer people of working age to pay the taxes that support health care spending. Moreover, the money to pay for all government spending will become even scarcer than it is now.

Spending more on health care would mean that less funding is available for all the other government programs, such as education, housing, infrastructure, and so on. If governments increase taxes to fund higher health care costs (instead of cutting spending in other areas), people will have less money for the purchases they want to make. Very soon governments will have to make real and meaningful choices about the areas that will receive funding. If doctors and nurses are paid more or more doctors and nurses are hired, who are we going to pay less or what services will receive less funding? Will there be fewer teachers? Fewer police officers? More roads in disrepair? Will we have less money to spend on ourselves? Scarcity of resources means that these sorts of trade-offs have to be made.

Sources: "Canada's demographic time bomb," Financial Post via CBCnews website, April 2, 2011: http://www.cbc.ca/fp/story/2011/04/02/4544389.html#ixzz1RzxLnJHa; Geddes, John, "The health care time bomb," McLean's Magazine, April 12, 2010.

MyEconLab **Your Turn:** Test your understanding by doing related problems 1.5 and 1.6 on page 57 at the end of this chapter.

Increasing Marginal Opportunity Costs

We can use the production possibilities frontier to explore issues concerning the economy as a whole. For example, suppose we divide all the goods and services produced in the economy into just two types: government-provided goods and privately provided goods. In Figure 2.2, we let operations represent government-provided goods and cars represent privately provided goods. If all the country's resources are devoted to producing government-provided goods, 400 operations could be performed in one year. If all the country's resources are devoted to producing privately provided goods, 500 cars could be produced in one year. Devoting resources to producing both types of goods results in the economy being at other points along the production possibilities frontier.

Notice that this production possibilities frontier looks different from the one in Figure 2.1. This PPF is bowed outward rather than a straight line. The fact that the PPF

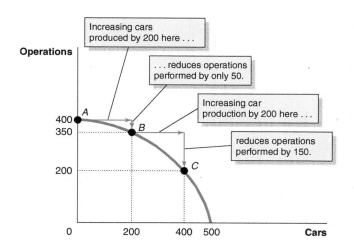

Figure 2.2

Increasing Marginal Opportunity Costs

As the economy moves down the production possibilities frontier, it experiences *increasing marginal opportunity costs* because increasing car production by a given quantity requires larger and larger decreases in the number of operations performed. For example, to increase car production from 0 to 200—moving from point *A* to point *B*—the economy has to give up only 50 operations. But to increase production of cars by another 200 vehicles—moving from point *B* to point *C*—the economy has to give up 150 operations.

is bowed outward tells us that the opportunity cost of producing more cars depends on where the economy currently is on the production possibilities frontier. For example, to increase the production of cars from 0 to 200—moving from point *A* to point *B*—the economy has to give up only 50 operations. To increase the number of cars by another 200 (for a total of 400)—moving from point *B* to point *C*—the economy has to give up another 150 operations.

As the economy moves down the production possibilities frontier, it experiences *increasing marginal opportunity costs*. Marginal opportunity costs increase because some workers, machines, and other resources are better suited to some uses than others. At point *A*, some resources that are best suited to making cars are used to perform operations. To move from point *A* to point *B*, the resources best suited to producing cars (and worst suited to performing operations) are shifted to car production. The result is a large gain in cars made while giving up few operations. As more cars are produced, resources that are better suited to performing operations are switched into car production. As a result, an increasing number of operations must be given up to get the same increase in the production of cars. Economists generally think that production possibilities frontiers are bowed outward (as in this example) rather than linear (as in the Toyota example earlier in the chapter).

The idea of increasing marginal opportunity costs illustrates an important economic concept: *The more resources already devoted to an activity, the smaller the payoff to devoting additional resources to that activity.* For example, the more hours you have already spent studying economics, the smaller the increase in your test grade from each additional hour you spend studying—and the greater the opportunity cost of using the hour in that way. The more funds a firm devotes to research and development during a given year, the smaller the amount of useful knowledge it receives from each additional dollar—and the greater the opportunity cost of using funds in that way. The more money the federal government spends cleaning up the environment during a given year, the smaller the reduction in pollution from each additional dollar—and, once again, the greater the opportunity cost of using the money in that way.

Economic Growth

At any given time, the total resources available to an economy are fixed. Therefore, if Canada produces more cars, it must produce less of something else, operations in our example. Over time the resources available to an economy may increase. For example, both the labour force and the capital stock—the amount of physical capital available to a country—may increase. The increase in the available labour force and the capital stock shifts the production possibilities frontier outward for the Canadian economy and makes it possible to produce more of *both* operations and cars. Panel (a) of Figure 2.3 shows that when an economy gets more resources, it can move from point *A* to point *B*, producing more cars *and* performing more operations.

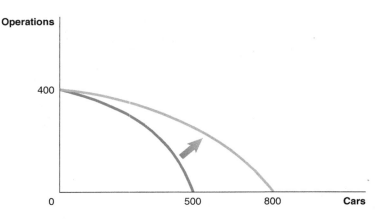

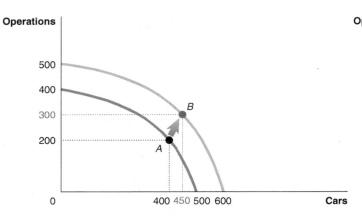

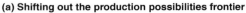

(a) Shifting out the production possibilities frontier

(b) Technological change in the automotive industry

Figure 2.3 **Economic Growth**

Panel (a) shows that as more economic resources become available and technological change occurs, the economy can move from point A to point B, performing more operations and producing more cars. Panel (b) shows the results of technological change in the automobile industry that increases the quantity of cars workers can produce per year while leaving unchanged the maximum quantity of operations that can be performed. Shifts in the production possibilities frontier represent *economic growth*.

Similarly, technological change makes it possible to produce more goods with the same number of workers and the same amount of machinery, which also shifts the production possibilities frontier outward. Technological progress doesn't necessarily affect all sectors of the economy. Panel (b) of Figure 2.3 shows the results of technological progress in the automotive industry—for example, the invention of a better welding robot—that increases the number of cars produced per year but leaves the number of operations performed per year unchanged.

Economic growth The ability of an economy to produce increasing quantities of goods and services.

Shifts in the production possibilities frontier represent **economic growth** because they allow the economy to increase the production of goods and services, which ultimately raises the standard of living. In Canada, and other higher income countries, the market system has aided the process of economic growth, which over the past 200 years has greatly increased the well-being of the average person.

2.2 LEARNING OBJECTIVE

Understand comparative advantage and explain how it is the basis for trade.

Trade The act of buying and selling.

Comparative Advantage and Trade

In Chapter 1 we talked about all the steps and people involved in getting you a cup of coffee. All of these steps and people rely on *trade*. We can use the ideas of production possibilities frontiers and opportunity costs to understand the basic economic activity of **trade**, which is the act of buying and selling. Markets are fundamentally about trade. Sometimes we trade directly, as when children trade one hockey card for another, or you help your friend with her economics homework in exchange for help with your chemistry homework. We often trade indirectly: We sell our labour services as, say, an economist, salesperson, or nurse for money, and then we use the money to buy goods and services. Although in these cases, trade takes place indirectly, ultimately the economist, salesperson, and nurse are trading their services for food, clothing, or video games. One of the great benefits of trade is that it makes it possible for people to become better off by increasing both their production and consumption.

Specialization and Gains from Trade

Consider the following situation: You and your neighbour both have fruit trees on your property. Initially, suppose you have only apple trees and your neighbour only has cherry trees. In this situation, if you both like apples and cherries, there is an obvious opportunity for you both to gain from trade: You give your neighbour some apples and she gives you some cherries, making you both better off.

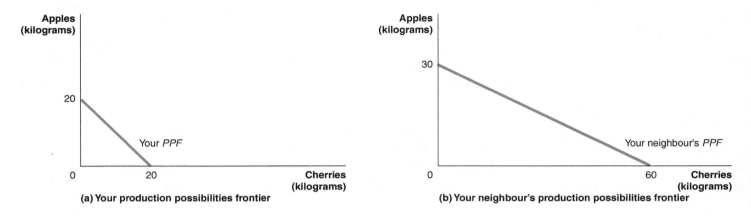

	You		Your Neighbour	
	Apples (kg)	Cherries (kg)	Apples (kg)	Cherries (kg)
Pick nothing but apples	20	0	30	0
Pick nothing but cherries	0	20	0	60

Figure 2.4 **Production Possibilities for You and Your Neighbour, without Trade**

The table in this figure shows how many kilograms of apples and how many kilograms of cherries you and your neighbour can each pick in one week. The graphs in the figure use the data from the table to construct production possibilities frontiers (PPFs) for you and your neighbour. Panel (a) shows your PPF. If you devote all your time to picking apples and none of your time to picking cherries,

you can pick 20 kilograms. If you devote all your time to picking cherries, you can pick 20 kilograms. Panel (b) shows that if your neighbour devotes all her time to picking apples, she can pick 30 kilograms. If she devotes all her time to picking cherries, she can pick 60 kilograms.

What if you both had apple and cherry trees in your yards? In that case, there could still be gains from trade. For example, if your neighbour was really good at picking cherries and you were really good at picking apples, it would make sense for each of you to focus on picking just one kind of fruit and trading after you were done. Things get a little more complicated if your neighbour is better at picking both apples and cherries than you are, but as we will see there are still gains from trade.

We can use production possibilities frontiers to show how you and your neighbour can benefit from trading with you *even if she is better at picking both apples and cherries*. (For simplicity, and because it doesn't change the conclusions, we assume that the PPFs are straight lines.) The table in Figure 2.4 shows how many apples and how many cherries you and your neighbour can pick in one week. The graph in the figure uses the same data to draw PPFs. Panel (a) shows your PPF and Panel (b) shows your neighbour's PPF. If you spend all week picking apples you'll end up with 20 kilograms of apples and no cherries. If you spend all week picking cherries you'll get 20 kilograms of cherries and no apples. If your neighbour spends all week picking apples she will have 30 kilograms of apples and no cherries, while if she spends the week picking nothing but cherries she will have 60 kilograms of cherries and no apples.

The PPFs in Figure 2.4 show how many apples and cherries you and your neighbour can *consume*, if you do not trade. Suppose that when you don't trade with your neighbour you decide to pick and eat 8 kilograms of apples and 12 kilograms of cherries a week (point *A* in panel (a) of Figure 2.5). This combination of apples and cherries is represented by point *A* in panel (a) of Figure 2.5. When your neighbour doesn't trade with you, she picks and consumes 9 kilograms of apples and 42 kilograms of cherries. This combination of apples and cherries is point *C* in panel (b) of Figure 2.5.

After years of ignoring each other—picking and eating apples and cherries independently—suppose your neighbour comes to you with the following proposal: She offers to trade you 15 kilograms of her cherries for 10 kilograms of your apples next week. Should

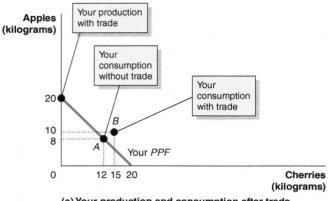

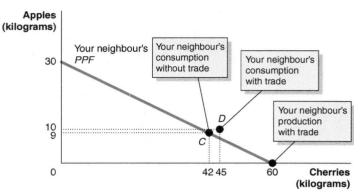

Figure 2.5 **Gains from Trade**

When you don't trade with your neighbour, you pick and consume 8 kilograms of apples and 12 kilograms of cherries per week—point *A* in panel (a). When you neighbour doesn't trade with you, she picks and consumes 9 kilograms of apples and 42 kilograms of cherries per week—point *C* in panel (b). If you specialize in picking apples, you can pick 20 kilograms. If your neighbour specializes in picking

cherries, she can pick 60 kilograms. If you trade 10 kilograms of apples for 15 kilograms of your neighbour's cherries, you will be able to consume 10 kilograms of apples and 15 kilograms of cherries—point *B* in panel (a). You neighbour can now consume 10 kilograms of apples and 45 kilograms of cherries—point *D* in panel (b). You and your neighbour are both better off as a result of the trade.

you accept this offer? Yes! You should accept because you will end up with more apples and more cherries to consume. To take advantage of her proposal, you should specialize in picking only apples rather than splitting your time between picking apples and cherries. This would allow you to pick 20 kilograms of apples. You can then trade 10 kilograms of your apples for 15 kilograms of cherries. As a result of this trading, you end up with 10 kilograms of apples and 15 kilograms of cherries (point *B* in panel (a) of Figure 2.5), 2 kilograms of apples, and 3 kilograms of cherries more than you had last week. You now get to consume a combination of apples and cherries that was unattainable (outside your PPF) to you before!

It might seem like you've got the better of your neighbour, but she is better off too. By specializing in picking cherries, she can pick 60 kilograms. She trades 15 kilograms of cherries to you for 10 kilograms of apples. She ends up with 10 kilograms of apples and 45 kilograms of cherries (point *D* in panel (b) of Figure 2.5), which is 1 kilogram more apples and 3 kilograms more cherries than she had before trading with you. She too can now consume a combination of apples and cherries that was unattainable last week. Table 2.1 summarizes the changes in production and consumption that results from trading with your neighbour. (In this example, we chose one specific rate of trading cherries for apples—15 kilograms of cherries for 10 kilograms of apples. There are, however, many other rates of trading cherries for apples that would also make you and your neighbour both better off.)

Absolute Advantage versus Comparative Advantage

One of the most remarkable aspects of the previous example is that both you and your neighbour benefit from trading, even though your neighbour is better than you at

Table 2.1

A Summary of the Gains from Trade

	You		Your Neighbour	
	Apples (kg)	Cherries (kg)	Apples (kg)	Cherries (kg)
Production and consumption *without* trade	8	12	9	42
Production *with* trade	20	0	0	60
Consumption *with* trade	10	15	10	45
Increased consumption (gains from trade)	2	3	1	3

picking both apples and cherries. **Absolute advantage** is the ability of an individual, a firm, or a country to produce more of a good or service than potential trading partners, using the same amount of resources. Your neighbour has an absolute advantage over you in producing both apples and cherries because she can pick more of each fruit than you can with the same amount of time. Although it seems like you have nothing to offer and she should pick her own apples and cherries, we have already seen that she is (and you are too) better off specializing in cherry picking and leaving the apple picking to you.

We can consider why both you and your neighbour benefit from specializing in picking only one fruit in more detail. First, think about the opportunity cost to each of you of picking each type fruit. We saw from the PPF in Figure 2.4 that if you devoted all your time to picking apples, you would be able to pick 20 kilograms of apples per week. As you move down your PPF and shift time away from picking apples to picking cherries, you have to give up 1 kilogram of apples for each kilogram of cherries you pick (the slope of your PPF is -1). (For a refresher on calculating slopes, see Appendix A, which follows Chapter 1.) Therefore, your opportunity cost of picking 1 kilogram of cherries is 1 kilogram of apples. Put slightly differently, for every kilogram of cherries you pick, you have to give up 1 kilogram of apples. If you were to start off picking nothing but cherries and were thinking about picking some apples, every kilogram of apples you picked would cost you 1 kilogram of cherries. Your opportunity cost of picking apples is 1 kilogram of cherries per kilogram of apples.

Your neighbour's PPF has a different slope, so she faces a different trade-off: As she shifts time from picking apples to picking cherries, she has to give up 0.5 kilogram of apples for every kilogram of cherries she picks (the slope of your neighbour's PPF is -0.5). Her opportunity cost of picking cherries is 0.5 kilogram of apples per kilogram of cherries. If she were going the other way, shifting time from picking cherries to picking apples, she would have to give up 2 kilograms of cherries in order to pick 1 kilogram of apples. Your neighbour's opportunity cost of picking apples is 2 kilograms of cherries per kilogram of apples.

Table 2.2 summarizes the opportunity costs for you and your neighbour of picking apples and cherries. Note that even though your neighbour can pick more of both apples and cherries than you can, the *opportunity cost* of picking apples is higher for her than it is for you, meaning that it costs you less to pick apples than it costs her. Even though she has an absolute advantage in picking both apples and cherries, you have a *comparative advantage* in picking apples. **Comparative advantage** is the ability of an individual, a firm, or a country to produce a good or service at a lower opportunity cost than potential trading partners. In our example, your neighbour has an absolute advantage in picking apples, while you have the comparative advantage in apple picking. At the same time, your neighbour has both the absolute and comparative advantage in picking cherries. As we demonstrated, you are better off specializing in picking apples, and your neighbour is better off specializing in picking cherries. Determining whether a specific trade will lead to gains requires that we know the *exchange ratio*—in this case, the number of kilograms of cherries you would get for each kilogram of apples (or, more often, a price in terms of dollars).

Comparative Advantage and the Gains from Trade

We have just derived an important economic principle: *The basis for trade is comparative advantage, not absolute advantage.* The fastest apple pickers do not necessarily do much apple picking. If the fastest apple pickers have a comparative advantage in something

Absolute advantage The ability of an individual, a firm, or a country to produce more of a good or service than potential trading partners, using the same amount of resources.

Comparative advantage The ability of an individual, a firm, or a country to produce a good or service at a lower opportunity cost than potential trading partners.

Table 2.2

Opportunity Costs of Picking Apples and Cherries

	Opportunity Cost of Apples	Opportunity Cost of Cherries
You	1 kg of cherries	1 kg of apples
Your neighbour	2 kg of cherries	0.5 kg of apples

Don't Let This Happen to You

Don't Confuse Absolute Advantage and Comparative Advantage

First, make sure you know the definitions:

- **Absolute advantage.** The ability of an individual, a firm, or a country to produce more of a good or service than potential trading partners using the same amount of resources. In our example, your neighbour has an absolute advantage over you in both picking apples and picking cherries.
- **Comparative advantage.** The ability of an individual, a firm, or a country to produce a good or service at a lower opportunity cost than potential trading partners. In our example, your neighbour has a comparative advantage in picking cherries, while you have the comparative advantage in picking apples.

Keep these two key points in mind:

1. It is possible to have an absolute advantage in producing something without having a comparative advantage. This is the case with your neighbour and picking apples.
2. It is possible to have a comparative advantage without having an absolute advantage. In our example, you have the comparative advantage in picking apples, even though your neighbour can pick more than you.

MyEconLab

Your Turn: Test your understanding by doing related problem 2.2 on page 57 at the end of this chapter.

else—for example, picking cherries, playing hockey, or being economists—they are better off specializing in that other activity *and so is everyone else*. Individuals, firms, and countries are better off if they specialize in producing goods and services in which they have a comparative advantage and trade to get the other goods and services they aren't producing.

Solved Problem **2.2**

Comparative Advantage and the Gains from Trade

Suppose that Canada and the United States both produce video games and nacho chips. These are the combination of the two goods that each country can produce in one day:

Canada		United States	
Video Games (titles)	Nacho Chips (tonnes)	Video Games (titles)	Nacho Chips (tonnes)
0	60	0	200
10	45	10	160
20	30	20	120
30	15	30	80
40	0	40	40
		50	0

a. Who has the comparative advantage in producing nacho chips? Who has the comparative advantage in producing video games?
b. Suppose that Canada is currently producing (and consuming) 30 video games and 15 tonnes of nacho chips, while the United States is currently producing (and consuming) 10 video games and 160 tonnes of nachos. Demonstrate that Canada and the United States can both be better off if they specialize in producing only one good and engage in trade.
c. Illustrate your answer to question (b) by drawing a PPF for Canada and a PPF for the United States. Show on your PPFs the combinations of video games and nachos produced and consumed in each country before and after trade.

Solving the Problem

Step 1: Review the chapter material. This problem is about comparative advantage, so you may want to review the section "Absolute Advantage versus Comparative Advantage," which begins on page 44.

Step 2: **Answer part (a) by calculating the opportunity costs of each activity for each country and comparing your results to see who has the comparative advantage.** Remember that a country has a comparative advantage when they can produce something at a lower opportunity cost. When Canada produces 1 more video game title, it produces 1.5 tonnes fewer nacho chips. When the United States produces 1 more video game title, it produces 4 tonnes fewer nacho chips. Therefore, Canada's opportunity cost of producing video game titles—1.5 tonnes of nacho chips per video game title—is lower than that of the United States—4 tonnes of nacho chips per video game title. When Canada produces 1 more tonne of nacho chips, it produces 0.67 fewer video game titles. When the United States produces 1 more tonne of nacho chips, it produces 0.25 fewer video game titles. Therefore, the United States' opportunity cost of producing nacho chips—0.25 video game titles per tonne of nacho chips—is lower than Canada's—0.67 video game titles per tonne of nacho chips. We can conclude that Canada has the comparative advantage in producing video game titles and the United States has the comparative advantage in producing nacho chips.

Step 3: **Answer part (b) by showing that specialization makes both Canada and the United States better off.** We know that Canada should specialize where it has a comparative advantage, and so should the United States. This means that Canada should produce video games and the United States should produce nacho chips. If both countries specialize completely, Canada will produce 40 video game titles and 0 tonnes of nacho chips, while the United States will produce 0 video game titles and 200 tonnes of nacho chips. After both countries specialize, Canada could then trade 10 video game titles to the United States in exchange for 20 tonnes of nacho chips. (You should be aware that a lot of other mutually beneficial trades are possible as well.) We can summarize the results in a table:

	Before Trade		After Trade	
	Video Games (titles)	Nacho Chips (tonnes)	Video Games (titles)	Nacho Chips (tonnes)
Canada	30	15	30	20
United States	10	160	10	180

Canadians are better off after trade because they can consume the same number of video games and 5 *more* tonnes of nachos than they could before trade. Americans are better off after trade because they can consume the same amount of nacho chips and 10 *more* video games than before trade.

Step 4: **Answer part (c) by drawing the PPFs.**

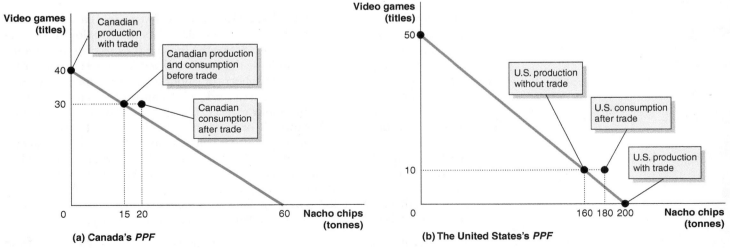

(a) Canada's *PPF*

(b) The United States's *PPF*

Your Turn: For more practice, do related problem 2.3 on page 57 at the end of this chapter.   MyEconLab

Explain the basic idea of how a market system works.

Market A group of buyers and sellers of a good or service and the institutions or arrangements by which they come together to trade.

Product market A market for goods—such as computers—or services—such as haircuts.

Factor market A market for the factors of production, such as labour, capital, natural resources, and entrepreneurial ability.

Entrepreneur Someone who operates a business, bringing together factors of production—labour, capital, and natural resources—to produce goods and services.

The Market System

We have seen that households, firms, and the government face trade-offs and incur opportunity costs because resources are scarce. We have also seen that trade allows people to specialize according to their comparative advantage. By engaging in trade, people can raise their material standard of living—the amount of goods, and services that they get to consume. Of course, trade in the modern world is a lot more complicated than it was in the examples we have considered so far. Trade today involves the decisions of billions of people around the world. But how does an economy make trade possible, and how are the decisions of these billions of people coordinated? In Canada and most other countries, trade is carried out in markets. It is also through markets that these billions of people determine the answers to the three fundamental questions discussed in Chapter 1: What goods and services will be produced? How will the goods and services be produced? Who will receive the goods and services produced?

Recall that the definition of **market** is a group of buyers and sellers of a good or service and the institutions or arrangements by which they come together to trade. Markets take many forms: They can be physical places, such as a farmers' market, a grocery store, or even the Toronto Stock Exchange, or virtual places such as eBay. In a market, the buyers are the people that demand goods or services (demanders), and the sellers are the people willing to supply them (suppliers). Households and firms interact in two types of markets: *product markets* and *factor markets*. **Product markets** are markets for goods—such as computers—or services—such as haircuts. In product markets, households demand the goods and services supplied by firms. **Factor markets** are markets for the *factors of production*. As mentioned earlier, *factors of production* are the inputs used to make goods and services; they are divided into four broad categories:

- *Labour* includes all types of work, from the part-time labour of teens working at McDonald's to the work of CEOs of large corporations.

- *Capital* refers to physical capital, such as computers, machines, and buildings that are used to make other goods.

- *Natural resources* include land, water, oil, iron ore, and other raw materials (or "gifts of nature") that are used in producing goods.

- An **entrepreneur** is someone who operates a business. *Entrepreneurial ability* is the ability to bring the other factors of production together to successfully produce and sell goods and services.

The Circular Flow of Income

Two key groups of people participate in markets:

- A *household* consists of all the individuals in a home. Households are the owners and suppliers of factors of production—particularly labour—employed by firms to make goods and services. Households use the income they receive from selling their factors of production to purchase the goods and services produced by firms. We are familiar with households as suppliers of labour because the majority of people earn most of their money by going to work, which means they are selling their labour services to firms in the labour market. Households also own all the other factors of production, either directly or indirectly, by owning the firms that have these resources. All firms are owned by households. Small firms, like a local coffee shop, might be owned by one person. Large firms, like Toyota, are owned by millions of households that own shares of stock in them. When firms pay profits to the people who own them, the firms are paying for using the capital and natural resources that are supplied to them by those owners. So, we can generalize by saying in factor markets, households are suppliers and firms are demanders.

- *Firms* are suppliers of goods and services. Firms use the funds they receive from selling goods and services to buy the factors of production needed to make the goods and services they sell.

We can use a simple economic model called the **circular-flow diagram** to see how participants in markets are linked. Figure 2.6 shows that in factor markets, households supply labour and other factors of production in exchange for wages and other payments from firms. In product markets, households use the payments they earn in factor markets to purchase the goods and services supplied by firms. Firms produce these goods and services using the factors of production supplied by households. In the figure, the blue arrows show the flow of factors of production from households through factor markets to firms. The red arrows show the flow of goods and services from firms through product markets to households. The green arrows show the flow of funds from firms through factor markets to households and the flow of spending from households through product markets to firms.

Like all models, the circular-flow diagram is a simplified version of reality. For example, Figure 2.6 leaves out the important role of government in buying goods from firms and in making payments, such as employment insurance, to households. The figure also leaves out the roles played by banks, the stock and bond markets, and other parts of the financial system in aiding the flow of funds from lenders to borrowers. Finally, the figure does not show that some goods and services purchased by Canadian households are produced in other countries and some goods and services produced by Canadian firms are sold to households in foreign countries. (The government, financial systems, and international sector are explored in later chapters.) Despite these simplifications, the circular-flow diagram in Figure 2.6 is useful for seeing how product markets, factor markets, and their participants are linked together. One of the great wonders of the market system is that it manages to successfully coordinate the independent activities of so many households and firms.

Circular-flow diagram A model that illustrates how participants in markets are linked.

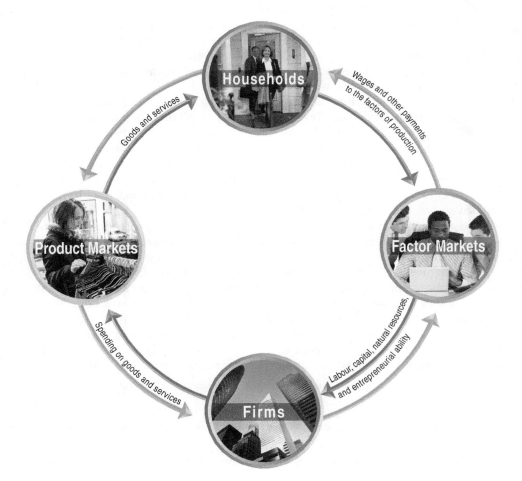

Figure 2.6

A Simple Circular-Flow Diagram

Households and firms are linked together in a circular flow of production, income, and spending. The blue arrows show the flow of the factors of production. In factor markets, households supply labour, entrepreneurial ability, and other factors of production to firms. Firms use these factors of production to make goods and services that they supply to households in product markets. The red arrows show the flow of goods and services from firms to households. The green arrows show the flow of funds. In factor markets, households receive wages and other payments from firms in exchange for supplying the factors of production. Households use these wages and other payments to purchase goods and services from firms in product markets. Firms sell goods and services to households in product markets, and they use the funds to purchase the factors of production from households in factor markets.

The Gains from Free Markets

Free market A market with few government restrictions on how goods or services can be produced or sold, on who can buy or sell goods or services, or on how factors of production can be employed.

A **free market** exists when the government places few restrictions on how goods or services can be produced or sold, on who can buy or sell goods or services, or on how factors of production can be employed. Governments in all modern economies intervene in markets, so no market in the world is completely free. In that sense, we can think of the free market as being a theoretical benchmark against which we can judge actual markets. There are relatively few government restrictions on economic activity in Canada, the United States, Western Europe, Japan, and many other countries. So these countries come fairly close to the free market benchmark. In countries such as Cuba and North Korea, the free market system has been rejected in favour of centrally planned economies with extensive government control of product and factor markets. Countries that come closest to the free market benchmark have much higher standards of living than those with centrally planned economies.

Scottish philosopher Adam Smith is considered the father of modern economics because his book *An Inquiry into the Nature and Causes of the Wealth of Nations*, published in 1776, was an early and very influential argument for the free market system. Smith was writing at a time when extensive government restrictions on markets were

Making the Connection

A Story of the Market System in Action: How Do you Make a PlayBook?

Chris Ratcliffe/Bloomberg via Getty Images

The market coordinates the activities of the many people spread around the world who contribute to the making of such products as a BlackBerry PlayBook.

BlackBerry makes smartphones and used to make the PlayBook. Given that BlackBerry's headquarters are in Waterloo, Ontario, you might think that PlayBooks were made in Ontario. In fact, BlackBerry didn't produce any of the physical parts of the PlayBook, nor did it assemble them to make the finished product. Far from being produced entirely by one company in one place, the PlayBook required the coordinated activities of thousands of workers and many firms from all over the world.

The PlayBook used a CPU made by Texas Instruments, based in Dallas, Texas. But Texas Instruments didn't make the memory components for the PlayBook. Those were produced by SanDisk, which has its headquarters in Milpitas, California, but has manufacturing facilities throughout Asia. These and other PlayBook components—such as screens, speakers, accelerometers, and batteries—were brought together by Quanta Computer in Taiwan for assembly. Once assembled, the PlayBook was shipped all over the world by yet other companies.

All told, a PlayBook contained hundreds of different parts that were designed and manufactured by firms all over the world. Many of these firms were not even aware of which other firms were also producing parts for the PlayBook. Few of the managers of these firms were likely to have met managers of the other firms or have shared knowledge or production schedules with them. In fact, no one person—including Thorsten Heins, the CEO of BlackBerry, and any of the developers of the PlayBook's operating system—knew how to manufacture all the components that went into a PlayBook. Instead, the invisible hand of the market has led the firms involved in producing the PlayBook to contribute their knowledge and resources to the process that ultimately resulted in a PlayBook being available for purchase to people all over the world.

Source: Based on UBM TechInsights, "RIM BlackBerry Playbook Teardown Analysis," http://www.ubmtechinsights.com/teardowns/blackberry-playbook-teardown/.

MyEconLab

Your Turn: Test your understanding by doing related problem 3.2 on page 58 at the end of this chapter.

very common. In many parts of Europe, the *guild system* still prevailed. Under this system, governments would give guilds (organizations of producers) the authority to control the production of a good. For example, the shoemakers' guild controlled who was allowed to produce shoes, how many shoes they could produce, and what price they could charge. In France, the cloth makers' guild even dictated the number of threads in cloth.

Smith argued that such restrictions reduced the income, or wealth, of a country and its people by restricting the quantity of goods produced. Some people at the time supported the restrictions of the guild system because it was in their financial interest to do so. If you were a member of a guild, the restrictions served to reduce the competition you faced. But other people sincerely believed that the alternative to the guild system was economic chaos. Smith argued that these people were wrong and that a country could enjoy a smoothly functioning economic system if firms were freed from guild restrictions.

The Legal Basis of a Successful Market System

As noted earlier, in a free market, government imposes few restrictions. However, the market system cannot work without government, as you can see if you look at some of the failed states around the world. Government must take active steps to provide a *legal environment* that will allow the market system to succeed.

Protection of Private Property For the market system to work well, individuals must be willing to take risks. Someone with $250 000 can be cautious and keep it safely in a bank—or even as cash. But the market system won't work unless a lot of people are willing to risk their savings by investing them in businesses. Investing in businesses is risky in any country. Many businesses fail every year in Canada and other high-income countries. But in high-income countries, someone who starts a new business or invests in an existing business doesn't have to worry that the government, the military, or a criminal gang might decide to seize the business or demand payments for not destroying the business. Unfortunately, in many poor countries, owners of businesses are not well protected from having their businesses seized by government or from having their profits taken by criminals. Where these problems exist, opening a business can be extremely risky. Cash can be concealed easily, but a business is a lot harder to hide and difficult to move.

Property rights are the rights individuals or firms have to the exclusive use of their property, including the right to buy or sell it. Property can be tangible, physical property such as a house, store, or factory. Property can also be intangible, such as the rights to an idea, image, or process.

Property rights in Canada are based on the system of common law that was in effect when Canada was a British colony (with the exception of Quebec, where matters of provincial jurisdiction are based on the civil code system). Both the federal and provincial governments play a role in property rights. The federal government is responsible for intellectual property rights, while provincial governments are responsible for personal and real property. Provincial property rights legislation that concerns goods and services other than land generally has the same name in each province—the Sale of Goods Act. Specifically, this set of acts outlines the obligations of people entering into contracts to buy and sell goods and services. The sale and purchase of land is governed by each province's real estate law, as well as common law (or the civil code, in the case of Quebec). Although seldom used, the federal government has the power to require people to sell their land, which is called *expropriation*. Expropriation law requires that the government "fairly" compensate those from whom it takes land. Unfortunately, many developing countries do not provide the same protection of land property rights.

Enforcement of Contracts and Property Rights Business activity often involves someone agreeing to carry out some action in the future. For example, you borrow

Property rights The rights individuals or firms have to the exclusive use of their property, including the right to buy or sell it.

$20 000 to buy a car and promise the bank—by signing a loan contract—that you will pay back the money (with interest) over the next five years. BlackBerry might also sign a contract with Texas Instruments agreeing to buy 10 000 CPUs for smartphones at a specific price. Usually these agreements take the form of legal contracts. For the market system to work, businesses and individuals have to rely on these contracts being honoured. If one party to a legal contract does not fulfill its obligations—perhaps Texas Instruments doesn't deliver the CPUs on time—the other party to the contract can take Texas Instruments to court to have the deal enforced. Similarly, if one company believes that another has violated a patent or copyright, a lawsuit is likely to follow.

Going to court to enforce a contract or private property rights will be successful only if the court system is independent and judges are able to make impartial decisions on the basis of the law. In Canada and other high-income countries, the court systems have enough independence from other parts of the government and enough protection from threats from outside forces—such as criminals—that they are able to make the decision based on the law. In many developing countries, the court systems lack this independence and will not provide a remedy if the government violates private property rights or if a person with powerful political allies decides to violate a business contract.

If property rights are not well enforced, fewer goods and services will be produced. This reduces economic efficiency, leaving the economy inside its production possibilities frontier and people worse off.

Economics in Your Life

The Trade-offs When You Buy a Car

At the beginning of the chapter, we asked you to think about two questions: Under what circumstances would you be better off buying an older, less fuel-efficient car than a new highly efficient one? Who do you think is most likely to want a car with high fuel efficiency? To answer the first question, you have to think about the trade-off between fuel efficiency and current price. If you buy an older car, you will have to pay less now, but you will have to pay more (in gas) when you drive somewhere. The trade-off is between paying now or paying later. This trade-off would look a lot like the relationship in Figure 2.1 on page 37. What you decide will likely depend on how far or often you plan to drive. If you don't think you will drive much, a cheaper car is probably better for you. That is, you might find you are willing to give up fuel efficiency (future savings) for a lower price (savings now). To have a cheaper and more fuel-efficient car, automakers would have to discover new technologies for making cars. This would shift the PPF out, as in panel (a) of Figure 2.3 on page 42.

To answer the second question, think about the trade-off between purchase price and fuel efficiency. The people most likely to want a fuel-efficient car are people who drive a lot. For them, the savings in gasoline expenses would be more important than the initial purchase price.

Conclusion

We have seen that by trading in markets, people are able to specialize and pursue their comparative advantage. Trading on the basis of comparative advantage makes all participants in trade better off. The key role of markets is to facilitate trade. In fact, the market system is a very effective way of coordinating the decisions of billions of consumers, workers, and firms. At the centre of the market system is the consumer. To be successful, firms must respond to the desires of consumers. These desires are communicated to firms through prices. To explore how markets work, we must study the behaviour of consumers and firms. We continue this exploration of markets in Chapter 3, where we develop the model of demand and supply. Before moving on to Chapter 3, read *An Inside Look* on the next page to learn how managers decide between producing hybrid cars or improving the fuel efficiency of other types of engines.

Toyota Faces a Trade-off

NATIONAL POST

Diesels vs. Hybrids: Who Wins?

Go to any new vehicle launch and invariably one wag will ask whether the car du jour will ever be available with a diesel engine. Ask that question at a Toyota launch and you might need to book off the rest of the morning for the answer.

Toyota, which does supply diesel offerings in markets outside North America, is very adamant about why it thinks diesel is the last thing North America needs.

"We believe in investing in technology that you can use elsewhere rather than in antiquated technology that barely meets the regulatory requirements," says engineer John-Paul Farag, with Toyota Canada's advanced powertrain department.

Antiquated technology? That's fightin' words in some camps. But Farag points to the hiatus diesel vehicles had to take in 2008 when emissions standards changed and the then-current range of diesel vehicles no longer quali-fied. It took new technology, such as selective catalytic conversion and a system to spray urea in catalytic converters, to bring them back to being legal. But the standards are likely to become more restrictive soon, he claims, "and they're right on the edge."

Farag says the technology to clean up diesel fuel emissions runs counter to fuel efficiency, particularly the need to run the engine with a rich fuel mixture at times to generate enough heat to activate the catalytic conversion process.

"I wouldn't be surprised if diesel's on the outside looking in in the near future."

Farag says Toyota is investing heavily in hybrid vehicles because it believes it has greater applications, is more adaptable to future technology and can work with whatever fuel supply is in play. If gasoline gives way to biofuel or hydrogen, the basic concept of hybrid technology applies. Hybrid technology also provides a solid foundation to work toward vehicles that are all-electric, he says.

Porsche has been driving some of its technology toward hybrids, in particular a Panamera hybrid and a Cayenne hybrid, but it hasn't ruled out diesels.

Laurance Yap, public relations manager for Porsche Cars Canada, says the company's interest in hybrids is driven by customer demand, particularly for high-revving, high-performance engines. But it also sells a diesel Cayenne elsewhere in the world and "we're probably going to bring that to Canada as well," he says.

"Diesel will always be complicated to keep within regulations," Yap says, agreeing that diesel is an easier case to make in Europe where the fuel is cleaner than the diesel sold here. "In Europe, cars are taxed on the amount of CO_2 they release, and diesels do release less CO_2 than gasoline models, but they're higher in the stuff that's not taxed—the nitrous oxides and other emissions."

Source: Taylor, Kelly, "Diesels v. hybrids: Who wins?" National Post, June 3, 2011. Material reprinted with the express permission of: National Post, a division of Postmedia Network, Inc.

Key Points in the Article

This article discusses the trade-offs managers at Toyota, Porsche, and other automakers face in attempting to increase fuel efficiency and meet pollution standards. In Canada, emissions standards have become more stringent, requiring that automakers design cars that produce lower emissions. To meet these standards, automakers have had to make a variety of choices. Given that resources are limited, they have faced a trade-off between investing in research and development on hybrids and research and development on cars that burn diesel fuel. In recent years, automakers have focused on research and development on hybrids that use electric batteries or batteries combined with gasoline engines, and have given up on improving diesel engines.

Analyzing the News

ⓐ While Toyota produces diesel-powered cars for other markets, it doesn't offer them to North American consumers. Toyota doesn't offer these cars because emission standards are expensive to meet. In 2008, when the emission standards changed, many manufacturers had to take diesel engines off the market because they generated too much pollution. Toyota's engineer expects that emissions standards will become even tougher in the future, making diesel-powered cars even more expensive.

ⓑ To have diesel-powered cars meet emissions standards, automakers would have to redesign these cars in a way that would increase the amount of fuel they currently use. The increase in fuel use creates an important trade-off for automakers and car buyers. If there is another technology, such as the hybrid engine, that allows cars to be fuel efficient and pollute less, it makes sense for automakers to invest in that technology.

ⓒ Companies face trade-offs in the type of research and development they pursue. Toyota has chosen to invest in hybrid rather than diesel technology. This choice will change the PPF over time, causing it to pivot, as in panel (b) of Figure 2.3 on page 42. When companies successfully invest in research and development, they are able to produce more of their goods or services with the same amount of labour and capital. If Toyota had chosen to invest in both diesel and hybrid engines, its PPF would be represented like the PPF in panel (a) of Figure 2.3.

Thinking Critically

1. Continuing to produce diesel-powered cars will mean that Toyota can produce fewer hybrids than it could if it were to switch all its production to hybrids. Given the generally agreed upon bright future for hybrids, why would Toyota continue to produce diesel-powered cars?

2. Assume that the graph below accurately represents Toyota's production possibilities frontiers at its Canadian plants for 2013 and 2015. Also assume that in 2015 it has customer orders for 500 hybrids per week and 400 diesel-powered cars per week. Explain whether Toyota can fill all of these orders from its Canadian plants.

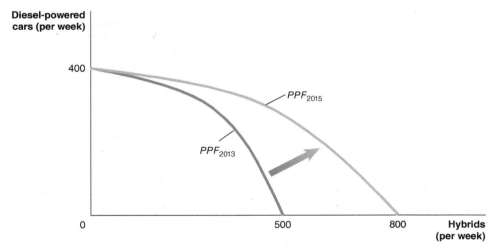

Chapter Summary and Problems

Key Terms

Absolute advantage, p. 45

Allocative efficiency, p. 37

Circular-flow diagram, p. 49

Comparative advantage, p. 45

Economic growth, p. 42

Entrepreneur, p. 48

Factor market, p. 48

Factors of production, p. 36

Free market, p. 50

Market, p. 48

Opportunity cost, p. 37

Product market, p. 48

Production possibilities frontier (PPF), p. 36

Property rights, p. 51

Scarcity, p. 36

Trade, p. 42

Summary

*LO 2.1 The *production possibilities frontier (PPF)* is a curve that shows the maximum attainable combinations of two products that may be produced with available resources. The PPF is used to illustrate the trade-offs that arise from scarcity. Points on the frontier are technically efficient. Points inside the frontier are inefficient, and points outside the frontier are unattainable. The *opportunity cost* of any activity is the highest-valued alternative that must be given up to engage in that activity. Because of increasing marginal opportunity costs, production possibilities frontiers are usually bowed out rather than straight lines. This illustrates the important economic concept that the more resources that are already devoted to any activity, the smaller the payoff from devoting additional resources to that activity is likely to be. *Economic growth* is illustrated by shifting a production possibilities frontier outward.

LO 2.2 Fundamentally, markets are about *trade*, which is the act of buying or selling. People trade on the basis of *comparative advantage*. An individual, a firm, or a country has a comparative advantage in producing a good or service if it can produce the good or service at the lowest opportunity cost. People are usually better off specializing in the activity for which they have a comparative advantage and trading for the other goods and services they need. It is important not to confuse comparative advantage with absolute advantage. An individual, a firm, or a country has an *absolute advantage* in producing a good or service if it can produce more of

that good or service using the same amount of resources. It is possible to have an absolute advantage in producing a good or service without having a comparative advantage.

LO 2.3 A *market* is a group of buyers and sellers of a good or service and the institutions or arrangements by which they come together to trade. *Product markets* are markets for goods and services, such as computers and haircuts. *Factor markets* are markets for the *factors of production*, such as labour, capital, natural resources, and entrepreneurial ability. A *circular-flow diagram* shows how participants in product markets and factor markets are linked. Adam Smith argued in his 1776 book *The Wealth of Nations* that in a *free market*, where the government does not control the production of goods and services, changes in prices lead firms to produce the goods and services most desired by consumers. If consumers demand more of a good, its price will rise. Firms respond to rising prices by increasing production. If consumers demand less of a good, its price will fall. Firms respond to falling prices by producing less of a good. An *entrepreneur* is someone who operates a business. In the market system, entrepreneurs are responsible for organizing the production of goods and services. The market system will work well only if there is protection for *property rights*, which are the rights of individuals and firms to use their property.

MyEconLab   Log in to MyEconLab to complete these exercises and get instant feedback.

Review Questions

LO 2.1

1.1 What is a production possibilities frontier? How can we show economic efficiency on a production possibilities frontier? How can we show inefficiency? What causes a production possibilities frontier to shift outward?

1.2 What does *increasing marginal opportunity costs* mean? What are the implications of this idea for the shape of the production possibilities frontier?

LO 2.2

2.1 What is absolute advantage? What is comparative advantage? Is it possible for a country to have a comparative advantage in producing a good without also having an absolute advantage? Briefly explain.

2.2 What is the basis for trade: absolute advantage or comparative advantage? How can an individual or a country gain from specialization and trade?

LO 2.3

3.1 What is a circular-flow diagram, and what does it demonstrate?

3.2 What is a free market? In what ways does a free market economy differ from a centrally planned economy?

3.3 What are private property rights? What role do they play in the working of a market system? Why are independent courts important for a well-functioning economy?

Problems and Applications

LO 2.1

1.1 Draw a production possibilities frontier that shows the trade-off between the production of cotton and the production of soybeans.

  a. Show the effect that a prolonged drought would have on the initial production possibilities frontier.

  b. Suppose genetic modification makes soybeans resistant to insects, allowing yields to double. Show the effect of this technological change on the initial production possibilities frontier.

1.2 [**Related to the** Chapter Opener **on page 35**] One of the trade-offs Toyota faces is between safety and gas mileage. For example, adding steel to a car makes it safer but also heavier, which results in lower gas mileage. Draw a hypothetical production possibilities frontier that Toyota engineers face that shows this trade-off.

1.3 Suppose you win free tickets to a movie plus all you can eat at the snack bar for free. Would there be a cost to you to attend this movie? Explain.

1.4 [**Related to** Solved Problem 2.1 **on page 38**] You have exams in economics and chemistry coming up, and you have five hours available for studying. The following table shows the trade-offs you face in allocating the time you will spend in studying each subject:

Choice	Hours Spent Studying		Midterm Score	
	Economics	Chemistry	Economics	Chemistry
A	5	0	95	70
B	4	1	93	78
C	3	2	90	84
D	2	3	86	88
E	1	4	81	90
F	0	5	75	91

  a. Use the data in the table to draw a production possibilities frontier graph. Label the vertical axis "Score on economics exam," and label the horizontal axis "Score on chemistry exam." Make sure to label the values where your production possibilities frontier intersects the vertical and horizontal axes.

  b. Label the points representing choice C and choice D. If you are at choice C, what is your opportunity cost of increasing your chemistry score?

  c. Under what circumstances would choice A be a sensible choice?

1.5 [**Related to** Making the Connection **on page 40**] Suppose the minister responsible for Health Canada is trying to decide whether the federal government should spend more on research to find a cure for heart disease. She asks you,

one of her economic advisers, to prepare a report discussing the relevant factors she should consider. Use the concepts of opportunity cost and trade-offs to discuss some of the main issues you would deal with in your report.

1.6 [**Related to** Making the Connection **on page 40**] Suppose your provincial government is deciding which of two sports programs it will pay for (assuming that only one program will be funded). The choices are Sport A, which will allow 24 students to play for 8 months and costs $37 500 per year, and Sport B, which will allow 20 students to play for 8 months and costs $15 000 per year. What factors should the provincial government take into account in making this decision?

LO 2.2

2.1 Look again at the information in Figure 2.4 on page 43. Choose a rate of trading cherries for apples different from the rate used in the text (15 kilograms of cherries for 10 kilograms of apples) that will allow you and your neighbor to benefit from trading apples and cherries. Prepare a table like Table 2.1 on page 44 to illustrate your answer.

2.2 [**Related to** Don't Let This Happen to You **on page 46**] In the 1950s, economist Bela Balassa compared 28 manufacturing industries in the United States and Britain. In every one of the 28 industries, Balassa found that the United States had an absolute advantage. In these circumstances, would there have been any gain to the United States from importing any of these products from Britain? Explain.

2.3 [**Related to** Solved Problem 2.2 **on page 46**] Suppose that France and Germany both produce schnitzel and wine. The following table shows combinations of the goods that each country can produce in a day:

France		Germany	
Wine (bottles)	Schnitzel (kilograms)	Wine (bottles)	Schnitzel (kilograms)
0	8	0	15
1	6	1	12
2	4	2	9
3	2	3	6
4	0	4	3
		5	0

  a. Who has a comparative advantage in producing wine? Who has a comparative advantage in producing schnitzel?

  b. Suppose that France is currently producing 1 bottle of wine and 6 kilograms of schnitzel, and Germany is currently producing 3 bottles of wine and 6 kilograms of schnitzel. Demonstrate that France and Germany can both be better off if they specialize in producing only one good and then engage in trade.

2.4 Can an individual or a country produce beyond its production possibilities frontier? Can an individual or a country consume beyond its production possibilities frontier? Explain.

2.5 Is specialization and trade between individuals and countries more about having a job or about obtaining a higher standard of living? Individually, if you go from a situation of not trading with others (you produce everything yourself) to a situation of trading with others, do you still have a job? Does your standard of living increase? Likewise, if a country goes from not trading with other countries to trading with other countries, does it still have jobs? Does its standard of living increase?

2.6 Some people argue that Canada should import only products that could not be produced here. Do you believe that this would be a good policy? Explain.

LO 2.3

3.1 Identify whether each of the following transactions will take place in the factor market or in the product market and whether households or firms are supplying the good or service or demanding the good or service:

   a. George buys a Toyota Camry hybrid.

   b. Toyota increases employment at its Cambridge plant.

   c. George works 20 hours per week at McDonald's.

   d. George sells land he owns to McDonald's so it can build a new restaurant.

3.2 [**Related to** Making the Connection **on page 50**] In *The Wealth of Nations*, Adam Smith wrote the following (Book I, Chapter II): "It is not from the benevolence of the butcher, the brewer, or the baker, that we expect our dinner, but from their regard to their own interest." Briefly discuss what he meant by this.

3.3 Evaluate the following argument: "Adam Smith's analysis is based on a fundamental flaw: He assumes that people are motivated by self-interest. But this isn't true. I'm not selfish, and most people I know aren't selfish."

3.4 Some economists have been puzzled that although entrepreneurs take on the risk of losing time and money by starting new businesses, on average their incomes are lower than those of people with similar characteristics who go to work at large firms. Economist William Baumol believes part of the explanation for this puzzle may be that entrepreneurs are like people who buy lottery tickets. On average, people who don't buy lottery tickets are left with more money than people who buy tickets because lotteries take in more money than they give out. Baumol argues that "the masses of purchasers who grab up the [lottery] tickets are not irrational if they receive an adequate payment in another currency: psychic rewards."

William J. Baumol, The Microtheory of Innovative Entrepreneurship, (Princeton, NJ: Princeton University Press, 2010).

a. What are "psychic rewards"?

b. What psychic rewards might an entrepreneur receive?

c. Do you agree with Baumol that an entrepreneur is like someone buying a lottery ticket? Briefly explain.

William J. Baumol, *The Microtheory of Innovative Entrepreneurship*, (Princeton, NJ: Princeton University Press, 2010).

3.5 The 2009 International Property Rights Index study states:

Data shows that countries that protect the physical and intellectual property of their people enjoy nearly nine times higher [income per person] . . . than countries ranking lowest in property rights protections. The study . . . compared the protections of physical and intellectual property to economic stability in 115 countries. . . .

How would the creation of property rights be likely to affect the economic opportunities available to citizens of those countries ranking lowest in property rights protections?

Kelsey Zahourek, "Report: Property Rights Linked to Economic Security," International Property Rights Index 2009 Report.

MyEconLab   MyEconLab is an online tool designed to help you master the concepts covered in your course. It will create an adaptive, highly personalized study plan to stimulate and measure your learning. Log in to take advantage of this powerful study aid, and to access quizzes and other valuable course-related material.

Where Prices Come From: The Interaction of Supply and Demand

Chapter Outline and Learning Objectives

3.1 The Demand Side of the Market, page 62
Discuss the variables that influence demand.

3.2 The Supply Side of the Market, page 69
Discuss the variables that influence supply.

3.3 Market Equilibrium: Putting Buyers and Sellers Together, page 73
Use a graph to illustrate market equilibrium.

3.4 The Effect of Demand and Supply Shifts on Equilibrium, page 77
Use demand and supply graphs to predict changes in prices and quantities.

Appendix B: Quantitative Demand and Supply Analysis, page 90
Use quantitative demand and supply analysis.

PhotoXpress/ZUMAPRESS/Newscom

Red Bull and the Market for Energy Drinks

Markets for some products suddenly explode. This was the case in the market for energy drinks. Red Bull was developed in Austria by Dietrich Mateschitz, who based it on a drink he discovered being sold in pharmacies in Thailand. Before Red Bull entered the market, few soft drinks included caffeine. Red Bull didn't enter the Canadian market until 2004, likely due to soft drink regulations. In Canada, caffeine may not be added to a traditional soft drink other than a cola. For example, Mountain Dew sold in the United States has a relatively high amount of caffeine, but the version sold in Canada contains none. Red Bull and other energy drinks are sold in Canada as natural health products, and are therefore subject to different regulations. Despite not being available in Canada before 2004, the Canadian sports and energy drink sector saw $876 million in retail sales in 2012. The market for energy drinks has found a particularly valuable niche with students wanting an extra boost of energy for sports, gaming, or studying. Some people have speculated that energy drinks might replace coffee as the morning drink for the current generation.

The success of Red Bull, Monster Energy, and Rockstar Energy Drink has attracted the attention of huge multinational beverage corporations as well as entrepreneurs looking to introduce new products into a hot market. Coca-Cola signed an agreement to distribute Monster Energy in Canada, 20 US states, and 6 Western European countries, and Pepsi struck a similar deal with Rockstar Energy Drink. A Canadian company that has recently entered the market, DD Beverage Company, produces Beaver Buzz Energy and other energy and sports beverages. Well over 200 energy drinks are now available in the North American marketplace.

The intense competition among firms selling energy drinks is a striking example of how the market responds to changes in consumer tastes. Although intense competition is not always good news for firms trying to sell products, it is great news to consumers. Competition among firms increases the variety of products available and reduces the price consumers pay for those products.

AN INSIDE LOOK on **page 84** discusses Kickstart, PepsiCo's latest high-energy breakfast drink, which the company hopes will attract young consumers who enjoy energy drinks but are looking for an alternative with the promise of health benefits.

Sources: http://www4.agr.gc.ca/AAFC-AAC/display-afficher.do?id=1288818173139&lang=eng, The Calgary Herald, February 3, 2005; "The Buzz Surrounding Energy Drinks", National Geographic, "Why We Love Caffeine", January, 2005.

Economics in Your Life

Red Bull or Beaver Buzz Energy: What's Your Beverage?

Suppose you are about to buy an energy drink and you are choosing between a Red Bull and a Beaver Buzz Energy. As the more established, well-known brand, Red Bull has many advantages over a recent entrant like Beaver Buzz Energy. One strategy DD Beverage Company can use to overcome Red Bull's advantages is to have Beaver Buzz Energy compete based on price and value. Would you choose to buy a can of Beaver Buzz Energy if it had a lower price than a can of Red Bull? Would you be less likely to drink Beaver Buzz Energy if your income dropped? As you read this chapter, see if you can answer these questions. You can check your answers against those we provide on page 82 at the end of this chapter.

I n Chapter 1, we explored how economists use models to predict human behaviour. In Chapter 2, we used the production possibilities frontier model to analyze scarcity and trade-offs. In this chapter, we explore the model of demand and supply, which is the most powerful tool in economics, and use it to explain how prices are determined.

Recall from Chapter 1 that because economic models rely on assumptions, they are simplifications of reality. In some cases, the assumptions of the model may not seem to match the economic situation being analyzed. For example, the model of demand and supply assumes that we are analyzing a *perfectly competitive market*. In a **perfectly competitive market**, there are many buyers and sellers, all the products sold are identical to consumers, and there are no barriers to new firms entering the market. These assumptions are very restrictive and only really describe a very small number of real world markets, such as the global market for wheat or a few other agricultural products. Experience has shown, however, that the model of demand and supply can be very useful in analyzing markets where competition among sellers is intense, even if there are relatively few sellers and the products being sold are not identical. In fact, in recent studies, the model of demand and supply has been successful analyzing markets with as few as four buyers and four sellers. In the end, the usefulness of a model depends on how well it can predict outcomes in a market. As we will see in this chapter, the model of demand and supply is often very useful in predicting changes in quantities and prices in many markets.

We begin exploring the model of demand and supply by discussing consumers and the demand side of the market, before turning to firms and the supply side. As you will see, we will apply this model throughout this book to understand business, the economy, and economic policy.

Perfectly competitive market A market that meets the conditions of (1) many buyers and sellers, (2) all firms selling identical products, and (3) no barriers to new firms entering the market.

Discuss the variables that influence demand.

The Demand Side of the Market

Chapter 2 explained that in a market system, consumers ultimately determine which goods and services will be produced. The most successful businesses are those that respond best to consumer demand. But what determines consumer demand for a product? Many, many things influence the willingness of consumers to buy a particular product. For example, consumers who are considering buying an energy drink, such as Red Bull or Beaver Buzz Energy, will make their decisions based on, among other factors, the amount of money they can spend (income) and the effectiveness of advertising campaigns. The main factor in consumer decisions, however, will be the price. So, it makes sense to begin with price when analyzing the decision of consumers to buy a product. It is important to note that when we discuss demand, we are considering not what a consumer *wants* to buy but what the consumer is both willing and *able* to buy.

Demand Schedules and Demand Curves

Tables that show the relationship between the price of a product and the quantity of the product demanded are called **demand schedules**. The table in Figure 3.1 shows the number of cans of energy drinks consumers would be willing to buy over the course of a month at five different prices. The amount of a good or service that a consumer is willing and able to purchase at a given price is the **quantity demanded**. The graph in Figure 3.1 plots the numbers from the table as a **demand curve**, a curve that shows the relationship between the price of a product and the quantity of the product demanded. (Note that for convenience, we made the demand curve in Figure 3.1 a straight line, or linear. There is no reason to believe that all demand curves are straight lines.) The demand curve in Figure 3.1 shows the **market demand**, or the demand by all the consumers of a given good or service. The market for a product, such as restaurant meals, that is purchased locally would include all the consumers in a city or a relatively small area. The market for a product that is sold internationally, such as energy drinks, would include all the consumers in the world.

Demand schedule A table that shows the relationship between the price of a product and the quantity of the product demanded.

Quantity demanded The amount of a good or service that a consumer is willing and able to purchase at a given price.

Demand curve A curve that shows the relationship between the price of a product and the quantity of the product demanded.

Market demand The demand by all the consumers of a given good or service.

Demand Schedule	
Price (dollars per can)	Quantity (millions of cans per month)
$3.00	60
2.50	70
2.00	80
1.50	90
1.00	100

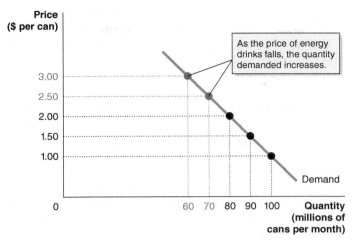

As the price of energy drinks falls, the quantity demanded increases.

Figure 3.1

A Demand Schedule and Demand Curve

As the price changes, consumers change the quantity of energy drinks they are willing to buy. We can show this as a *demand schedule* in a table or as a *demand curve* on a graph. The table and graph both show that as the price of energy drinks falls, the quantity demanded increases. When the price of an energy drink is $3.00, consumers buy 60 million cans per month. When the price drops to $2.50, consumers buy 70 million cans per month. Therefore, the demand curve for energy drinks is downward sloping.

The demand curve in Figure 3.1 slopes downward because consumers will buy more cans over the same time period when the price falls. When the price is $3.00 per can, consumers buy 60 million cans per month. If the price is $2.50 per can, consumers buy 70 million cans per month. Buyers demand a larger quantity of a product as the price falls because the product becomes less expensive relative to other products and because they can afford to buy more at a lower price.

The Law of Demand

The inverse relationship between the price of a product and the quantity of the product demanded is known as the **law of demand**: Holding *everything else* constant, when the price of a product falls, the quantity demanded of the product will increase, and when the price of a product rises, the quantity demanded of the product will decrease. The law of demand holds for any market demand curve. Economists have found only a very few exceptions (after more than 100 years of research).

Law of demand The rule that, holding everything else constant, when the price of a product falls, the quantity demanded of the product will increase, and when the price of a product rises, the quantity demanded of the product will decrease.

What Explains the Law of Demand?

It makes sense that consumers will buy more of a good when the price falls and less of a good when the price rises, but let's take a closer look at why this is true. When the price of energy drinks falls, consumers buy a larger quantity because of two effects, the *substitution effect* and the *income effect*.

The Substitution Effect The **substitution effect** refers to the change in the quantity demanded of a good that results from a change in the relative price of that good. The *relative price* of a good is how much it costs compared with a good that could be purchased instead, a *substitute* good. When the price of energy drinks falls and becomes less expensive relative to coffee (a substitute good), consumers will buy *more* energy drinks and *less* coffee.

Substitution effect The change in the quantity demanded of a good that results from a change in price making the good more or less expensive relative to other goods, holding constant the effect of the price change on consumer purchasing power.

The Income Effect The **income effect** of a price change refers to the change in the quantity demanded of a good that results from the effect of a change in the good's price on consumers' purchasing power. *Purchasing power* is the quantity of goods (and services) a consumer can buy with a fixed amount of income. When the price of a good falls, a consumer can buy more of everything with the same amount of money, including the product whose price fell in the first place. For example, if the price of energy drinks falls, the increased purchasing power of consumers' incomes means that they can buy more energy drinks and other goods with the same amount of money. When the price of a good rises, the decreased purchasing power of consumers' incomes will usually lead them to purchase fewer goods, including the good whose price became higher.

Income effect The change in the quantity demanded of a good that results from the effect of a change in the good's price on consumers' purchasing power.

Note that although we can analyze them separately, the substitution effect and the income effect happen simultaneously whenever a price changes. Thus, a fall in the price of energy drinks leads consumers to buy more energy drinks, both because the cans are now less expensive relative to substitute products (such as coffee) and because the purchasing power of their incomes has increased.

That Magic Latin Phrase *Ceteris Paribus*

You likely noticed that the definition of the law of demand contains the phrase *holding everything else constant*. In constructing the market demand curve for energy drinks, we focused only on the effect that changes in the price of energy drinks would have on how many cans consumers would be willing and able to buy. We were holding constant all other variables that might affect the willingness of consumers to buy energy drinks. Economists refer to the necessity of holding all other variables constant in constructing a demand curve (or any other model) as the **ceteris paribus condition**: *ceteris paribus* is Latin for "all else equal."

What would happen if we allowed a change in a variable—other than price—that might affect the willingness of consumers to buy energy drinks? Consumers would then change the quantity they demanded at each price. We can illustrate this effect by shifting the market demand curve. A shift of a demand curve is *an increase or a decrease in demand*. A movement along a demand curve is *an increase or a decrease in the quantity demanded*. As Figure 3.2 shows, we shift the demand curve to the right if consumers decide to buy more of the good even when the price doesn't change, and we shift the demand curve to the left when consumers decide to buy less of a good even if the price doesn't change.

Variables That Shift Market Demand

Many variables other than price can influence how much of a product consumers are willing and able to buy. These five are the most important:

- Income
- Prices of related goods
- Tastes
- Population and demographics
- Expectations

Ceteris paribus ("all else equal") **condition** The requirement that when analyzing the relationship between two variables—such as price and quantity demanded—other variables must be held constant.

Figure 3.2

Shifting the Demand Curve

When consumers increase the quantity of a product they want to buy at a given price, the market demand curve shifts to the right, from D_1 to D_2. When consumers decrease the quantity of a production they want to buy at a given price, the demand curve shifts to the left from D_1 to D_3.

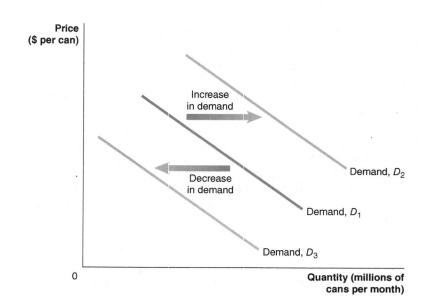

We next discuss how changes in each of these variables affect the market demand curve.

Income The income that consumers have available to spend affects their willingness and ability to buy a good. Suppose the market demand curve in Figure 3.1 on page 63 represents the willingness of consumers to buy energy drinks when average household income is $60 000. If household income rises to $65 000, the demand for energy drinks will increase, which we show by shifting the demand curve to the right. A good is a **normal good** when demand increases following a rise in income and decreases following a fall in income. Most goods are normal goods, but the demand for some goods falls when income rises and rises when income falls. For instance, when your income rises, you might buy fewer hot dogs and more steak. A good is an **inferior good** when demand decreases following a rise in income and increases following a fall in income. So, for you, hot dogs would be an example of an inferior good. Remember, when economists say a good is inferior, they aren't saying anything about the quality of the good, just that the amount people buy falls when income rises.

Normal good A good for which the demand increases as income rises and decreases as income falls.

Inferior good A good for which the demand increases as income falls and decreases as income rises.

Prices of Related Goods The price of other goods can also affect consumers' demand for a product. Goods and services that can be used for the same purpose—such as energy drinks and coffee—are **substitutes**. Two goods are substitutes if, when you

Substitutes Goods and services that can be used for the same purpose.

Making the Connection

Is Beer an Inferior Good?

For most Canadians, a beverage on a hot summer afternoon is part of the culture. In 2012, Canadians drank 8.1 litres of alcohol in various forms per person, including 80.3 litres of beer. This is a profitable industry with the LCBO (Liquor Control Board of Ontario) paying a dividend to the Government of Ontario of $1.63 billion.

How does income affect the choices Canadians make at the liquor store? As Canadians have gotten wealthier, they have changed their drinking habits. There is an underlying trend: Instead of buying beer at the lowest possible price, more and more Canadians are opting for local micro-brewery beer or local wine. In 2009, New Brunswick's alcohol retailer (Alcool NB Liquor) launched its own brand of beer, which provided New Brunswickers with a low-cost alternative, but in July 2011, that brand was discontinued due to lack of sales. During the 2011 fiscal year, the LCBO noticed that the sales of its premium products recovered from the slump that started around the same time as the financial crisis; in Ontario, the volume of sales of alcoholic beverages changed little.

Alcool NB Liquor discontinued its low cost brand of beer as the economy recovered from recession.

What we're seeing from beer sales in particular is that Canadians have begun to treat mainstream beer as an inferior good. As the average income of Canadians rises, they switch from low-cost beverages to more expensive ones. Recall that when economists describe a product as inferior, they aren't necessarily saying it is of poor quality, they're just saying that consumers buy less of it when their incomes rise.

Sources: Statistics Canada – CANSIM Table 183-0019 Series v28463248; David Pett and Jared Lindzon, Financial Post, Jun. 3, 2011; Cigdem Iltan on Thursday, July 7, 2011, MacLean's Magazine.

Your Turn: Test your understanding by doing related problem 1.4 on page 87 at the end of this chapter.

MyEconLab

buy more of one, you buy less of the other. A decrease in the price of a substitute causes the demand curve for a good to shift to the left. An increase in the price of a substitute causes the demand curve for a good to shift to the right.

Suppose that the market demand curve in Figure 3.1 represents the willingness and ability of consumers to buy energy drinks during a week when the average price of coffee is $2.00. If the average price of coffee falls to $1.50, how will the market for energy drinks change? Consumers will demand fewer cans of energy drinks at every price. We show this impact by shifting the demand curve for energy drinks to the left.

Goods and services that are used together—like hamburgers and buns—are **complements**. When two goods are complements, the more consumers buy of one, the more they will buy of the other. A decrease in the price of a complement causes the demand curve for a good to shift to the right. An increase in the price of a complement causes the demand curve to shift to the left.

Many people drink Red Bull, Monster Energy, or Beaver Buzz Energy when working out. So, for these people, energy drinks and gym memberships are complements. Suppose that the market demand curve in Figure 3.1 represents the willingness of consumers to buy energy drinks when the average price of a gym membership is $40 per month. If the price of gym memberships drops to $30 per month, consumers will buy more gym memberships *and* more energy drinks, making the demand curve for energy drinks shift to the right.

Complements Goods and services that are used together.

Tastes Consumers can be influenced by an advertising campaign for a product. If the firms making Red Bull, Monster Energy, Beaver Buzz Energy, or other energy drinks begin to advertise heavily online, consumers are more likely to buy cans at every price, and the demand curve will shift to the right. An economist would say that the advertising campaign has affected consumers' *taste* for energy drinks. Taste is a catchall category that refers to the many subjective elements that can enter into a consumer's decision to buy a product. A consumer's taste for a product can change for many reasons. Sometimes trends play a substantial role. For example, the popularity of low-carbohydrate diets caused a decline in demand for some goods, such as bread and donuts, and an increase in the demand for meat. In general, when consumers' taste for a product increases, the demand curve will shift to the right, and when consumers' taste for a product decreases, the demand curve for the product will shift to the left.

Population and Demographics Population and demographic factors can affect the demand for a product. As the population of Canada increases, so will the number of consumers, and the demand for most products will increase. The **demographics** of a population refers to its characteristics, with respect to age, race, and gender. As the demographics of a country or region change, the demand for particular goods will increase or decrease because different people have different tastes or preferences for those goods. For example, the population of Indo-Canadians (people whose ancestors originate from India) has increased over the last 20 years. Currently there are around 1 million Indo-Canadians, and this number is expected to rise. The increase in the Indo-Canadian population will expand the demand for Indian-made "Bollywood"

Demographics The characteristics of a population with respect to age, race, and gender.

Making the Connection

The Aging Baby Boomers

The average age of Canadians is increasing. After World War II ended in 1945, Canada experienced a "baby boom" as birthrates rose and remained high through the early 1960s. Falling birthrates after 1965 mean that the baby boom generation is larger than the generation before it or those after it. The figure below uses data from Statistics Canada to show how people over the age of 65 have become a significant portion of the population.

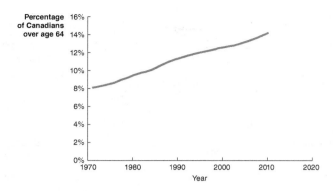

Source: Statistics Canada. Table 051-0001 - Estimates of population, by age group and sex for July 1, Canada, provinces and territories, annual (persons unless otherwise noted) (table), CANSIM (database), Using E-STAT (distributor). Reproduced and distributed on an "as is" basis with the permission of Statistics Canada.

What effects will the aging of the baby boom generation have on the economy? Older people need more medical care than younger adults, which means that there will be greater demand for doctors, nurses, and hospital facilities in the future. In Canada, a growing number of foreign-trained nurses and doctors are being recruited to help meet the growing demand for health care services.

Aging baby boomers will also have an impact on the housing market. Older folks often "downsize" their housing by moving from large, single-family homes with high maintenance costs to smaller homes, condominiums, or apartments. Hence, in coming years, demand for smaller homes may increase, while demand for large homes falls.

Source: Kaleigh Rogers, "Foreign physician Recruits Helping Meet City's Growing Need for Doctors," *CBC.ca*, March 21, 2013, http://www.cbc.ca/hamilton/news/story/2013/03/20/hamilton-foreign-doctors.html.

Your Turn: Test your understanding by doing related problem 1.5 on page 87 at the end of this chapter.

MyEconLab

films and Indo-Canadian cable television channels, as well as other cultural goods and services.

Expectations Consumers choose not only which products to buy but also when to buy them. For instance, if enough consumers become convinced that houses will be selling for lower prices in three months, the demand for houses will decrease now, as some consumers delay their purchases to wait for prices to fall. Alternatively, if enough consumers become convinced that house prices will rise over the next three months, the demand for houses will rise now as some people try to avoid the expected increase in prices.

Expected future prices aren't the only important expectations that affect consumer demand. Consumers also change their purchasing habits when their expected income changes. Most of you are probably consuming more now than your income would suggest. This is because you expect that your income will be higher in the future, meaning that you believe you can afford to consume more now. When the economy slows down and people expect their incomes to be lower in the future, they often put off major purchases or buy different things. How an expected income change affects the demand for a product depends on whether the product is a normal or an inferior good. When incomes are generally falling (e.g., when the economy is doing poorly), people tend to buy more inferior goods, even if their incomes haven't actually changed.

Table 3.1 summarizes the most important variables that cause market demand curves to shift. Note that the table shows the shift in the demand curve that results from an *increase* in each of the variables. A *decrease* in these variables would cause the demand curve to shift in the opposite direction.

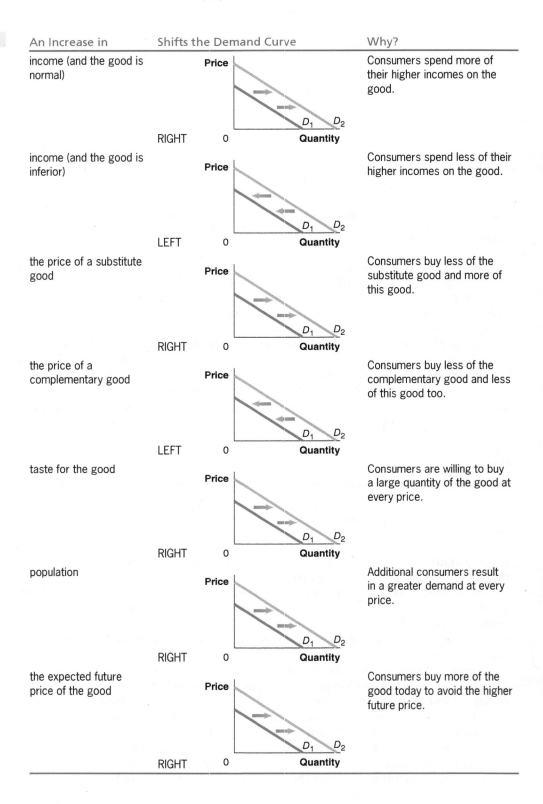

Table 3.1	An Increase in	Shifts the Demand Curve	Why?
Variables That Shift Market Demand Curves	income (and the good is normal)	RIGHT	Consumers spend more of their higher incomes on the good.
	income (and the good is inferior)	LEFT	Consumers spend less of their higher incomes on the good.
	the price of a substitute good	RIGHT	Consumers buy less of the substitute good and more of this good.
	the price of a complementary good	LEFT	Consumers buy less of the complementary good and less of this good too.
	taste for the good	RIGHT	Consumers are willing to buy a large quantity of the good at every price.
	population	RIGHT	Additional consumers result in a greater demand at every price.
	the expected future price of the good	RIGHT	Consumers buy more of the good today to avoid the higher future price.

A Change in Demand versus a Change in Quantity Demanded

It is important to understand the difference between a *change in demand* and a *change in quantity demanded*. A change in demand refers to a shift of the demand curve. A shift occurs if there is a change in one of the variables, *other than the price of the product,* that

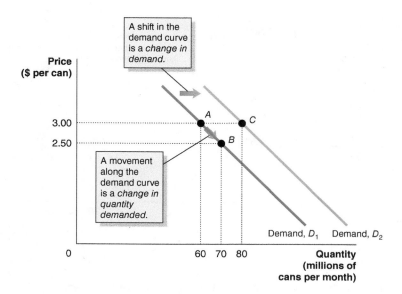

Figure 3.3

A Change in Demand versus a Change in Quantity Demanded

If the price of energy drinks falls from $3.00 to $2.50, the result will be a movement along the demand curve from point A to point B—an increase in quantity demanded from 60 million cans to 70 million cans. If consumers' incomes increase, or if another factor changes that makes consumers want more energy drinks at every price, the demand curve will shift to the right—an increase in demand. In this case, the increase in demand from D_1 to D_2 causes the quantity of energy drinks demanded at a price of $3.00 to increase from 60 million cans at point A to 80 million cans at point C.

affects the willingness of consumers to buy the product. A change in quantity demanded refers to a movement along the demand curve as a result of a change in the product's price. Figure 3.3 illustrates this important distinction. If the price of energy drinks falls from $3.00 to $2.50 per can, the result will be a movement along the demand curve from point A to point B—an increase in quantity demanded from 60 million to 70 million. If consumers' incomes increase, or if another factor changes that makes consumers want more energy drinks *even if the price doesn't change*, the demand curve will shift to the right—an increase in demand. In this case, the increase in demand from curve D_1 to D_2 causes the quantity of energy drinks demanded at a price of $3.00 to increase from 60 million at point A to 80 million at point C.

The Supply Side of the Market

3.2 LEARNING OBJECTIVE

Discuss the variables that influence supply.

Just as many variables influence the willingness and ability of consumers to buy a good or service, many variables also influence the willingness and ability of firms to sell a good or service. The most important of these variables is price. The amount of a good or service that a firm is willing and able to supply at a given price is the **quantity supplied**. Holding all other variables constant (recall the Latin phrase *ceteris paribus*), when the price of a good rises, producing (and selling) that good is more profitable, and the quantity supplied will increase. When the price of a good falls, the good is less profitable to produce, and the quantity supplied will decrease. In addition, as we saw in Chapter 2, devoting more and more resources to the production of a specific good results in increasing marginal costs. If, for example, Red Bull, Monster Energy, and DD Beverage Company increase production of their energy drinks during a given time period, they are likely to find that the cost of producing additional cans increases as they run existing factories for longer hours and pay higher prices for ingredients and higher wages for workers. As the marginal costs of making a product rises as output increases, a firm will supply more of that product only if the price is higher.

Quantity supplied The amount of a good or service that a firm is willing and able to supply at a given price.

Supply Schedules and Supply Curves

A **supply schedule** is a table that shows the relationship between the price of a product and the quantity of the product supplied. The table in Figure 3.4 is a supply schedule showing the quantity of energy drinks that firms would be willing to supply per month at different prices. The graph in Figure 3.4 plots the numbers from the supply schedule as a *supply curve*. A **supply curve** shows the relationship between the price of a product

Supply schedule A table that shows the relationship between the price of a product and the quantity of the product supplied.

Supply curve A curve that shows the relationship between the price of a product and the quantity of the product supplied.

Figure 3.4

A Supply Schedule and Supply Curve

As the price changes, Red Bull, Monster Energy, DD Beverage Company, and other firms producing energy drinks change the quantity they are willing to supply. We can show this as a *supply schedule* in a table or a *supply curve* on a graph. The supply schedule and supply curve both show that as the price of energy drinks rises, firms will increase the quantity they supply. At a price of $2.50 per can, firms will supply 90 million cans. At a price of $3.00 per can, firms will supply 100 million cans.

Supply Schedule	
Price (dollars per can)	Quantity (millions of cans per month)
$3.00	100
2.50	90
2.00	80
1.50	70
1.00	60

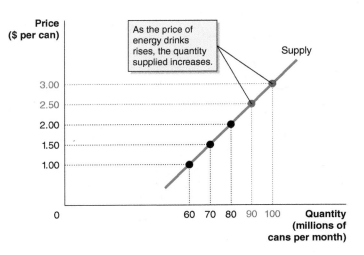

and the quantity of the product supplied. The supply schedule and the supply curve both show that as the price of energy drinks rises, firms will increase the quantity they supply. At a price of $2.50 per can, firms will supply 90 million cans per month. At the higher price of $3.00, firms will supply 100 million. (Once again, we are assuming that the relationship is linear—even though most supply curves are not actually straight lines.)

The Law of Supply

Law of supply The rule that, holding everything else constant, increases in price cause increases in the quantity supplied, and decreases in price cause decreases in the quantity supplied.

The *market supply curve* in Figure 3.4 is upward sloping. We expect most supply curves to be upward sloping based on the **law of supply**, which states that, holding everything else constant, increases in price cause increases in the quantity supplied, and decreases in price result in decreases in the quantity supplied. Notice that the definition of the law of supply—just like the definition of the law of demand—contains the phrase *holding everything else constant*. If only the price of the product changes, there is a movement along the supply curve, which is *an increase or a decrease in the quantity supplied*. As Figure 3.5 shows, if any other variable that affects the willingness of firms to supply a good changes, the supply curve will shift, which is *an increase or a decrease in the quantity supplied*. When firms increase the quantity of a product they would like to sell at a given price, the supply curve shifts to the right. The shift from S_1 to S_3 represents *an*

Figure 3.5

Shifting the Supply Curve

When firms increase the quantity of a product they want to sell at a given price, the supply curve shifts to the right. The shift from S_1 to S_3 represents *an increase in supply*. When firms decrease the quantity of a product they want to sell at a given price, the supply curve shifts to the left. The shift from S_1 to S_2 represents *a decrease in supply*.

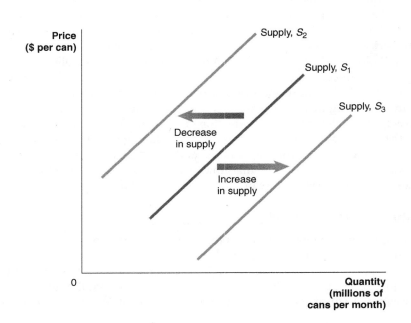

increase in supply. When firms decrease the quantity of a product they would like to sell at a given price, the supply curve shifts to the left. The shift from S_1 to S_2 represents *a decrease in supply.*

Variables That Shift Market Supply

The following are the most important variables that shift the market supply curve:

- Price of inputs
- Technological change
- Prices of substitutes in production
- Number of firms in the market
- Expected future prices

We next discuss how each of these variables affects the market supply curve.

Prices of Inputs   The factor most likely to cause the supply curve for a product to shift is a change in the price of an *input*. An input is anything used in the making of a good or service. For instance, if the price of guarana (a stimulant in many energy drinks) rises, the cost of producing energy drinks will increase, and energy drinks will be less profitable at every price. The supply of energy drinks will decline, and the market supply curve for energy drinks will shift to the left. Similarly, if the price of an input falls, the supply of energy drinks will increase, and the market supply curve for energy drinks will shift to the right. Any time something like wages or interest rates (the price of labour and capital) change, the market supply curve will shift.

Technological Change   A second factor that causes a change in supply is *technological change*. **Technological change** is a positive or negative change in the ability of a firm to produce a given level of output from a given quantity of inputs. Positive technological change occurs when a firm is able to produce *more* output with the same amount of inputs. This change will happen when the *productivity* of workers or machines increases. If a firm can produce more output with the same amount of inputs, its costs will be lower, and the good will be more profitable to produce at any given price. As a result, when positive technological change occurs, a firm will want to sell more of its product at every given price, making the market supply curve shift to the right. Normally, we expect technological change to have a positive impact on a firm's willingness to supply a product.

Negative technological change is rare, although it might be caused by a natural disaster or a war that reduces a firm's ability to supply as much output with a given amount of inputs. Negative technological change will raise a firm's costs, and the good will be less profitable to produce. Therefore, negative technological change causes the market supply curve to shift to the left.

> **Technological change** A change in the quantity of output a firm can produce using a given quantity of inputs.

Prices of Substitutes in Production   Firms often have to choose which goods they will produce at a particular time. Alternative products that a firm could produce with the same inputs are called *substitutes in production*. A number of companies produce both energy drinks and traditional soft drinks. For instance, the Coca-Cola Company produces Full Throttle in addition to the many varieties of Coke it sells. PepsiCo produces Amp in addition to Pepsi, Mountain Dew, and other drinks. If the price of colas falls, producing Pepsi and Coke will be less profitable, and Coca-Cola, PepsiCo, and other soft drink manufacturers will shift some of their productive capacity out of cola production and into making energy drinks. As a result, each company will offer more energy drinks for sale, even if the price doesn't change, so the market supply curve for energy drinks will shift to the right.

Number of Firms in the Market   A change in the number of firms in the market will change supply. When new firms *enter* a market, the supply curve shifts to the right,

Table 3.2

Variables That Shift Market Supply Curves

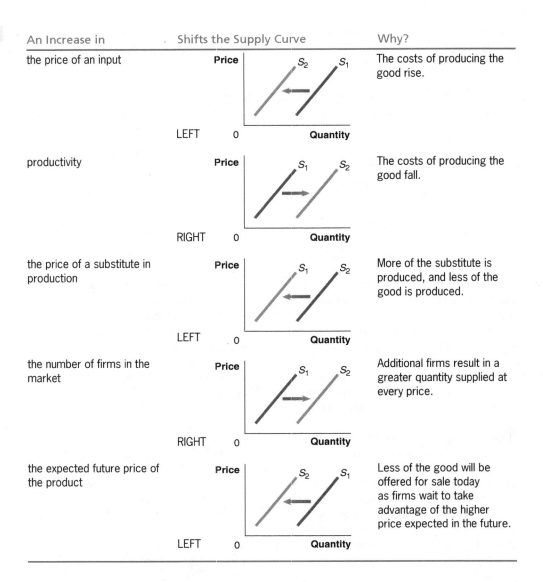

An Increase in	Shifts the Supply Curve	Why?
the price of an input	LEFT	The costs of producing the good rise.
productivity	RIGHT	The costs of producing the good fall.
the price of a substitute in production	LEFT	More of the substitute is produced, and less of the good is produced.
the number of firms in the market	RIGHT	Additional firms result in a greater quantity supplied at every price.
the expected future price of the product	LEFT	Less of the good will be offered for sale today as firms wait to take advantage of the higher price expected in the future.

and when existing firms leave, or *exit*, a market, the supply curve shifts to the left. For example, when Beaver Buzz Energy was introduced, the market supply curve for energy drinks shifted to the right.

Expected Future Prices If a firm expects that the price of its product will be higher in the future than it is today, it has an incentive to decrease supply now and increase supply in the future. For example, if Red Bull believes that prices for energy drinks are temporarily low—perhaps due to low incomes of consumers—it may store some of its production today to sell later on, when it expects prices to be higher.

Table 3.2 summarizes the most important variables that cause market supply curves to shift. Note that the table shows the shift in the supply curve that results from an *increase* in each of the variables. A *decrease* in these variables would cause the supply curve to shift in the opposite direction.

A Change in Supply versus a Change in Quantity Supplied

We noted earlier the important difference between a change in demand and a change in quantity demanded. There is a similar difference between a *change in supply* and a *change in quantity supplied*. A change in supply refers to a shift in the supply curve. The supply curve will shift when there is a change in one of the variables, *other than the price*

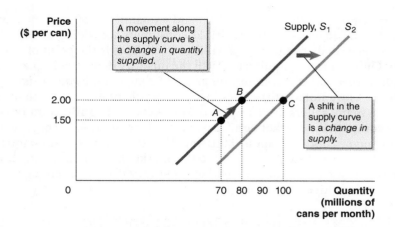

Figure 3.6

A Change in Supply versus a Change in Quantity Supplied

If the price of energy drinks rises from $1.50 to $2.00 per can, the result will be a movement up the supply curve from point *A* to point *B*—an increase in quantity supplied of Red Bull, Monster Energy, Beaver Buzz Energy, and other energy drinks from 70 million to 80 million cans. If the price of an input decreases or another factor changes that causes sellers to supply more of the product at every price, the supply curve will shift to the right—an increase in supply. In this case, the increase in supply from S_1 to S_2 causes the quantity of energy drinks supplied at a price of $2.00 to increase from 80 million cans to 100 million cans.

of the product, that affects the willingness of firms to sell the product. A change in quantity supplied refers to a movement along the supply curve as a result of a change in the product's price. Figure 3.6 illustrates this important distinction. If the price of energy drinks rises from $1.50 to $2.00 per can, the result will be a movement up the supply curve from point *A* to point *B*—an increase in quantity supplied from 70 million cans per month to 80 million cans per month. If the price of an input decreases (or another factor makes sellers supply more of the product at every price), the supply curve will shift to the right—an increase in supply. In this case, the increase in supply from S_1 to S_2 causes the quantity of energy drinks supply to increase from 80 million to 100 million per month even if the price remains at $2.00 per can (note the move from point *B* to point *C* in the figure).

Market Equilibrium: Putting Buyers and Sellers Together

3.3 LEARNING OBJECTIVE

Use a graph to illustrate market equilibrium.

The purpose of markets is to bring buyers and sellers together. As we saw in Chapter 2, instead of being chaotic and disorderly, the interaction of buyers and sellers in markets ultimately results in firms being led to produce the goods and services that consumers want. To understand how this happens, we first need to see how markets work to reconcile the plans of buyers and sellers.

In Figure 3.7, we bring the market demand curve and the market supply curve together. Notice that the demand curve crosses the supply curve at only one point.

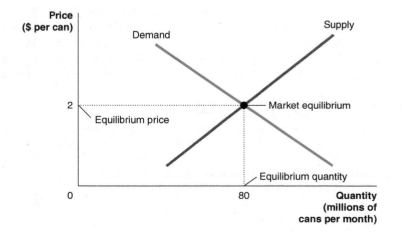

Figure 3.7

Market Equilibrium

Where the demand curve crosses the supply curve determines market equilibrium. In this case, the demand curve for energy drinks crosses the supply curve at a price of $2.00 and a quantity of 80 million cans. Only at this point is the quantity of energy drinks consumers want to buy equal to the quantity of energy drink suppliers are willing to sell: The quantity demanded is equal to the quantity supplied.

Market equilibrium A situation in which quantity demanded equals quantity supplied.

Competitive market equilibrium A market equilibrium with many buyers and many sellers.

Surplus A situation in which the quantity supplied is greater than the quantity demanded.

Shortage A situation in which the quantity demanded is greater than the quantity supplied.

This point represents the price of $2.00 and a quantity of 80 million cans. Only at this point is the quantity of energy drinks consumers are willing to buy equal to the quantity of energy drinks firms are willing to sell. This is the point of **market equilibrium**. Only at market equilibrium will the quantity demanded equal the quantity supplied. In this case, the *equilibrium price* is $2.00 and the *equilibrium quantity* is 80 million. As we noted at the beginning of the chapter, markets that have many buyers and many sellers are competitive markets, and equilibrium in these markets is a **competitive market equilibrium**. In the market for energy drinks, there are many buyers but only about 80 firms. Whether 80 firms are enough for our model of demand and supply to apply to this market is a matter of judgment. In this chapter, we are assuming that the market for energy drinks has enough sellers to be treated as competitive.

How Markets Eliminate Surpluses and Shortages: Getting to Equilibrium

A market that is not in equilibrium moves toward equilibrium. Once a market is in equilibrium, it remains in equilibrium. To see why, consider what happens if the market is not in equilibrium. For instance, suppose that the price in the market for energy drinks is $3.00, rather than the equilibrium price of $2.00. As Figure 3.8 shows, at a price of $3.00 the quantity of energy drinks demanded would be 60 million cans per month, while the quantity supplied would be 100 million cans per month. The quantity supplied is 40 million more than the quantity demanded (100 million − 60 million). When the quantity supplied is greater than the quantity demanded, there is a **surplus** in the market. A surplus means that firms will be unable to sell all the goods they would like and the goods they're producing start piling up. Fortunately, firms have a handy method of getting rid of unwanted inventory, they put it on sale. Remember a sale is just a reduction in price. Cutting the price will simultaneously increase the quantity demanded and decrease the quantity supplied. This adjustment will reduce the surplus, but as long as the price remains above the equilibrium of $2.00, there will be unsold energy drinks and downward pressure on the price. Only when the price has fallen to $2.00 will firms have a reason to stop reducing the price.

What if the price was below market equilibrium, say $0.50? If this were the case the quantity demanded would be 110 million and the quantity supplied would be only 50 million, as shown in Figure 3.8. When the quantity demanded is greater than the quantity supplied, there is a **shortage** in the market. In this case, the shortage is 60 million cans (110 million − 50 million). When a shortage occurs, some consumers will be unable to buy energy drinks at the current price. When this happens, firms will realize they can raise the price without losing sales. A higher price means a decrease in the quantity demanded and an increase in the quantity supplied. The increase in price will reduce the size of the shortage, but as long as the price remains below the equilibrium price of $2.00 there will be a shortage and firms will have an incentive to increase the prices they charge. Only when the price has risen to $2.00 will the market be in equilibrium.

At a competitive equilibrium, all consumers willing to pay the market price will be able to buy as much of the product as they want, and all firms willing to accept the market price will be able to sell as much as they want. As a result, neither consumers nor suppliers will have a reason to do anything differently. This means that the price of energy drinks will stay at $2.00, unless the demand curve, the supply curve, or both shift.

Demand and Supply Both Count

Keep in mind that the interaction of demand and supply determines the equilibrium price. Neither consumers nor firms can dictate what the equilibrium price will be. No firm can sell anything, at any price, unless it can find a willing buyer, and no consumer can buy anything, at any price, without finding a willing seller.

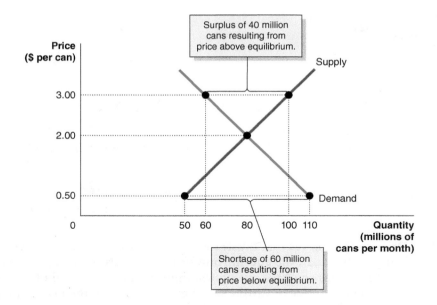

Figure 3.8

The Effect of Surpluses and Shortages on the Market

When the market price is above equilibrium, there will be a *surplus*. In the figure, a price of $3.00 per energy drink results in 100 million cans being supplied but only 60 million cans being demanded, or a surplus of 40 million cans. As the firms that produce Red Bull, Monster Energy, Beaver Buzz Energy, and other drinks cut the price to dispose of the surplus, the price will fall to the equilibrium of $2.00. When the market price is below equilibrium, there will be a *shortage*. A price of $0.50 results in 110 million cans being demanded, but only 50 million cans being supplied, or a shortage of 60 million cans. As firms find that consumers who are unable to find energy drinks for sale are willing to pay more for them, the price will rise to the equilibrium of $2.00.

Solved Problem **3.1**

Demand and Supply Both Count: A Tale of Two Cards

Which hockey card do you think is worth more: Sidney Crosby's rookie card or one of Jacques Plante's distributed free in a box of Quaker Oats? Sidney Crosby is one of the most popular hockey players in recent memory; his jersey sells exceptionally well even though he has missed many games due to concussions and other injuries. Jacques Plante was a goaltender from 1946 to 1975 and played for a number of NHL teams, including the Montreal Canadiens and the Edmonton Oilers. The demand for Sidney Crosby's rookie card is much higher than the demand for Jacques

Plante's cereal-box card. However, at auction, a Sidney Crosby rookie card can be expected to sell for about $5000, while a Jacques Plante cereal-box card can be expected to fetch about $12 000. Use a demand and supply graph to explain how it is that a card of a player from 50 years ago that was distributed free in a box of cereal has a higher price than a card of one of the most popular modern players that was sold in a sealed foil pack, even though the demand for Sidney Crosby's card is certain to be greater than the demand for Jacques Plante's card.

Solving the Problem

Step 1: **Review the chapter material.** This problem is about prices being determined at market equilibrium, so you may want to review the section "Market Equilibrium: Putting Buyers and Sellers Together."

Step 2: **Draw demand curves that illustrate the greater demand for Sidney Crosby's card.** Begin by drawing two demand curves. Label one "Demand for Crosby's card" and the other "Demand for Plante's card." Make sure that the Crosby demand curve is much farther to the right than the Plante demand curve. Make sure you label your axes.

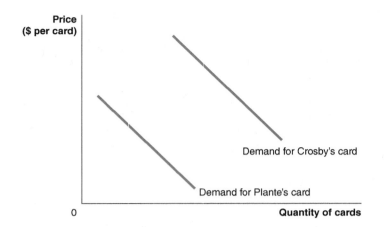

Step 3: **Draw supply curves that illustrate the equilibrium price of Plante's card being higher than the equilibrium price of Crosby's card.** Based on the demand curves you have just drawn, think about how it might be possible for the market price of Crosby's card to be lower than the market price of Plante's card. The only way this can be true is if the supply of Crosby's card is much greater than the supply of Plante's card. (Plante's card was distributed in a cereal box and were therefore easily damaged). In your graph, draw a supply curve for Crosby's card and a supply curve for Plante's card that will result in an equilibrium price of Plante's card of $12 000 and an equilibrium price of Crosby's card of $5000. You have now solved the problem.

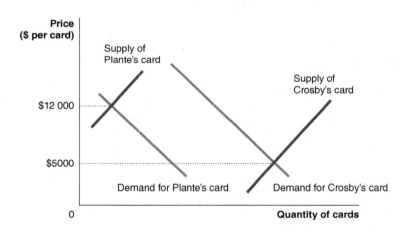

Extra credit: The explanation for this puzzle is that both demand and supply count when determining market price. The demand for Crosby's card is much greater than the demand for Plante's card, but the supply of Crosby's card is also much greater. (Note that the supply curves for the cards of Plante and Crosby are upward sloping, even though only a fixed number of each of these types of cards is available and no more can be produced. The supply curves slope upwards because a higher price will induce more cards to be offered for sale by their current owners.) Try and come up with your own examples of goods with very low demand but very high prices and goods with high demand and very low prices.

Source: http://bleacherreport.com/articles/812055-nhl-the-15-most-valuable-hockey-cards-of-all-time/page/8 and http://bleacherreport.com/articles/812055-nhl-the-15-most-valuable-hockey-cards-of-all-time/page/5

MyEconLab   **Your Turn:** For more practice, do related problem 3.2 on page 88 at the end of this chapter.

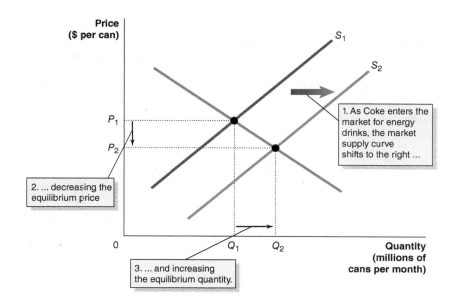

Figure 3.9

The Effect of an Increase in Supply on Equilibrium

If a firm enters a market, as Coca-Cola Company did when it introduced Full Throttle, the equilibrium price will fall, and the equilibrium quantity will rise:

1. As Coke enters the market for energy drinks, a larger quantity of energy drinks will be supplied at every price, so the market supply curve shifts to the right, from S_1 to S_2, which causes a surplus of energy drinks at the original price, P_1.

2. The equilibrium price falls from P_1 to P_2.

3. The equilibrium quantity rises from Q_1 to Q_2.

The Effect of Demand and Supply Shifts on Equilibrium

3.4 LEARNING OBJECTIVE

Use demand and supply graphs to predict changes in prices and quantities.

We have seen that the interaction of demand and supply in markets determines the quantity of a good that is produced and the price at which it sells. We have also seen that several variables cause demand curves to shift, and other variables cause supply curves to shift. As a result, demand and supply curves in most markets are constantly moving around, and the prices and quantities that represent equilibrium are constantly changing. In this section, we look at how shifts in demand and supply curves affect equilibrium price and quantity.

The Effect of Shifts in Supply on Equilibrium

When Coke started selling the energy drink Full Throttle, the market supply curve for energy drinks shifted to the right. Figure 3.9 shows the supply curve shifting from S_1 to S_2. When the supply curve shifts to the right, there will be a surplus at the original equilibrium price, P_1. The surplus is eliminated as the equilibrium price falls to P_2, and the equilibrium quantity rises from Q_1 to Q_2. If existing firms exit the market, the supply curve will shift to the left, causing the equilibrium price to rise and the equilibrium quantity to fall.

Making the Connection | **The Falling Price of LCD TVs**

Research on flat-screen televisions using liquid crystal displays (LCDs) began way back in the 1960s. However, it was surprisingly difficult to produce a television with a price low enough for many consumers to purchase. One researcher noted, "In the 1960s, we used to say 'In 10 years, we're going to have the TV on the wall.' ... We said the same thing in the "70s and then in the "80s." A key technical problem in manufacturing LCD TVs was making glass large, thin, and clean enough to be used as LCD screens. Finally in 1999, Corning Inc., developed a manufacturing process that produced glass that was less than 1 millimetre thick and very clean because it didn't come into contact with machinery.

Corning's breakthrough led to what the *Wall Street Journal* described as a "race to build new, better factories." For years, the leading firms were Korea's Samsung Electronics and LG Phillips LCD, Taiwan's AU Optronics, and Japan's Sharp Corporation. But in recent years, new firms, such as Vizio, and existing firms, such as Matsushita (the makers of Panasonic), have entered the market or expanded their offerings. Matsushita's Japanese factory can produce as many as 15 million LCD screens a year. The figure below shows how the entry of new firms and the expansion of existing firms has driven down the price of LCD TVs.

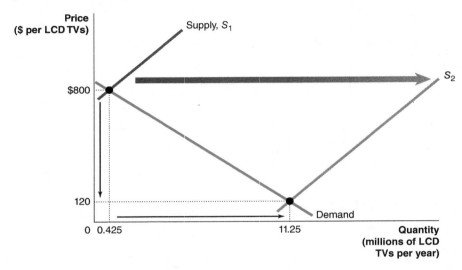

Sources: Daisuke Wakabayashi and Christopher Lawton, "TV Makers Confront a Stakeout," *Wall Street Journal*, January 20, 2009; David Richards, "Sony and Panasonic Flat Screen Kings," Smarthouse.com, February 13, 2007; and Evan Ramstad, "Big Display: Once a Footnote, Flat Screens Grow into Huge Industry," Wall Street Journal, August 30, 2004.

 MyEconLab

Your Turn: Test your understanding by doing related problem 4.7 on page 89 at the end of this chapter.

The Effect of Shifts in Demand on Equilibrium

Because energy drinks are generally a normal good, when incomes increase, the market demand for energy drinks shifts to the right. Figure 3.10 shows the effect of a demand curve shifting to the right, from D_1 to D_2. This shift causes a shortage at the original

Figure 3.10

The Effect of an Increase in Demand on Equilibrium

Increases in income will cause equilibrium price and quantity to rise:

1. Because energy drinks are a normal good, as income grows, the quantity demanded increases at every price, and the market demand curve shifts to the right, from D_1 to D_2, which causes a shortage of energy drinks at the original price, P_1.

2. The equilibrium price rises from P_1 to P_2.

3. The equilibrium quantity rises from Q_1 to Q_2.

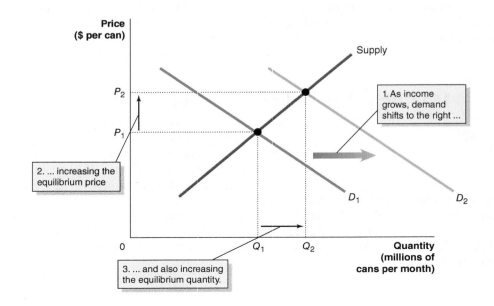

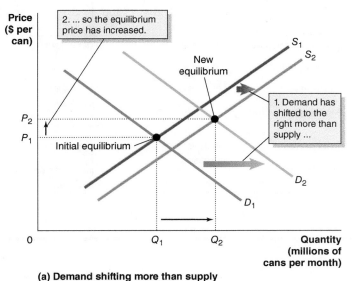

(a) Demand shifting more than supply

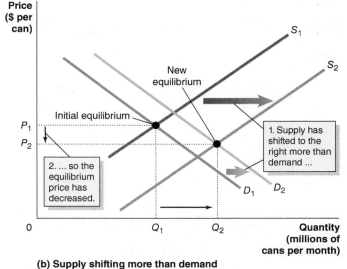

(b) Supply shifting more than demand

Figure 3.11 **Shifts in Demand and Supply**

Whether the price of a product rises or falls over time depends on whether demand shifts to the right more than supply. In panel (a), demand shifts to the right more than supply, and the equilibrium price rises:

1. Demand shifts to the right more than supply.
2. The equilibrium price rises from P_1 to P_2.

In panel (b), supply shifts to the right more than demand, and the equilibrium price falls:

1. Supply shifts to the right more than demand.
2. The equilibrium price falls from P_1 to P_2.

equilibrium price, P_1. To eliminate this new shortage, equilibrium price rises to P_2, and the equilibrium quantity rises from Q_1 to Q_2. In contrast, if the price of a substitute good, such as coffee, were to fall, the demand for energy drinks would decrease, shifting the demand curve for energy drinks to the left. When the demand curve shifts to the left, the equilibrium price and quantity both decrease.

The Effect of Shifts in Demand and Supply over Time

Whenever only demand or only supply shifts, we can easily predict the effect on equilibrium price and quantity. Things are more complicated when *both* supply and demand shift at the same time. For instance, in many markets, the demand curve shifts to the right over time as populations and incomes grow. The supply often shifts to the right over time too, as new firms enter the market or technology improves. Whether the equilibrium price rises or falls over time depends on which shift is bigger. If the shift in the demand curve is bigger than the shift in the supply curve, the price will rise. If the shift in the supply curve is bigger than the shift in the demand curve, the price will fall. Panel (a) of Figure 3.11 shows that when demand shifts to the right more than supply, the equilibrium price rises. But as panel (b) shows, when supply shifts to the right more than demand, the equilibrium price falls.

Table 3.3 summarizes all possible combinations of shifts in demand and supply over time and the effects of the shifts on equilibrium price (*P*) and quantity (*Q*). For example, the entry in red in the table shows that if the demand curve shifts to the right and the supply curve also shifts to the right, the equilibrium quantity will increase, while the equilibrium price may increase, decrease, or remain unchanged. To be sure you understand each entry in the table, draw demand and supply graphs to check whether you can reproduce the predicted changes in equilibrium price and quantity. If the entry in the table says the predicted change in equilibrium price or quantity can be either an increase or a decrease, draw two graphs similar to panels (a) and (b) of Figure 3.11—one showing the equilibrium price or quantity increasing and the other showing it decreasing. Note also that in the ambiguous cases where either price or quantity might increase or decrease, it is also possible that price or quantity might remain unchanged. Be sure you understand why.

Table 3.3

How Shifts in Demand and Supply Affect Equilibrium Price (*P*) and Quantity (*Q*)

	Supply Curve Unchanged	Supply Curve Shifts Right	Supply Curve Shifts to the Left
Demand curve unchanged	Q unchanged P unchanged	Q increases P decreases	Q decreases P increases
Demand curve shifts right	Q increases P increases	Q increases P increases or decreases	Q increases or decreases P increases
Demand curve shifts left	Q decreases P decreases	Q increases or decreases P decreases	Q decreases P increases or decreases

Solved Problem **3.2**

High Demand and Low Prices in the Lobster Market

For many communities in the Maritimes, the lobster fishery is an essential part of the local economy. Lobster is fished only in season, and different communities are allowed to fish at different times of the year. For example, the fishing season for the area of Yarmouth, Nova Scotia, is from late November to the end of May. It isn't uncommon for the price of lobster to fluctuate during the season. In some cases, it can change from below $5 per pound to $8 or $9 per pound. A patch of really bad weather can drive up the price quickly, but so does Christmas (lobster tends to be a popular part of winter festivities in Canada, Europe, and other parts of the world).

What would happen if the weather just before Christmas was particularly good, allowing fishers to spend more time on the water and catch more lobster?

Solving the Problem

Step 1: **Review the chapter material.** This problem is about how shifts in demand and supply curves affect the equilibrium price, so you may want to review the section "The Effect of Shifts in Demand and Supply over Time."

Step 2: **Draw the demand and supply graph.** Draw a demand and supply graph, showing the market equilibrium before the Christmas rush and with normal weather. Label the equilibrium price $6.00. Label both the demand and supply curves "Typical."

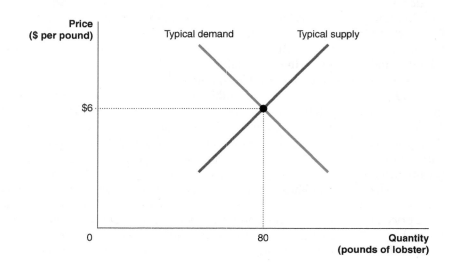

Step 3: **Add a demand and supply curve.** Add a demand curve to account for the increase in the demand for lobster from Europe. Add a supply curve to account for the nicer-than-usual weather.

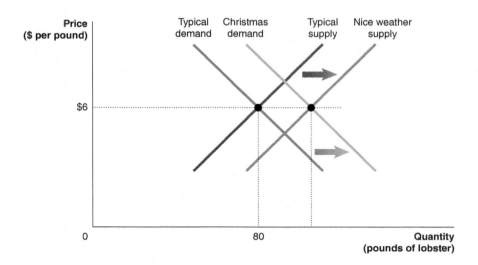

Step 4: **Explain the graph.** After studying the graph, you should see how the two events of increased demand from Europe and the nicer-than-usual weather combine to move the equilibrium price. The increase in supply due to the nicer-than-usual weather is offset by some of the increase in demand from Europeans. We can't say for sure which way the price will go. The price of lobster will rise if the shift in demand is greater than the shift in supply. If the shift in supply is greater than the shift in demand, prices will actually fall. All that we can say for certain is that the quantity of lobster sold (and eaten) will go up.

Source: Province of Nova Scotia, "Lobster Fishing Seasons in Atlantic Canada," *Nova Scotia Fisheries and Aquaculture*, May 17, 2012, http://www.gov.ns.ca/fish/marine/map/lobarea.shtml.

Your Turn: For more practice, do related problems 4.3 and 4.4 on page 88 at the end of this chapter.   MyEconLab

Don't Let This Happen to You

Remember: A Change in a Good's Price Does *Not* Cause the Demand or Supply Curve to Shift

Suppose a student is asked to draw a demand and supply graph to illustrate how an increase in the price of oranges would affect the market for apples, other variables being constant. He draws the graph on the left below and explains it as follows: "Because apples and oranges are substitutes, an increase in the price of oranges will cause an initial shift to the right in the demand curve for apples, from D_1 to D_2. However, because this initial shift in the demand curve for

apples results in a higher price for apples, P_2, consumers will find apples less desirable, and the demand curve will shift to the left, from D_2 to D_3, resulting in a final equilibrium price of P_3." Do you agree or disagree with the student's analysis?

You should disagree. The student has correctly understood that an increase in the price of oranges will cause the demand curve for apples to shift to the right. But the second demand curve shift the student describes, from D_2 to D_3, will not take place. Changes in the price of a product do not result in shifts in the product's demand curve. Changes in the price of a product result only in movements along a demand curve.

The graph on the right below shows the correct analysis. The increase in the price of oranges causes the demand curve for apples to increase from D_1 to D_2. At the original price, P_1, the increase in demand initially results in a shortage of apples equal to $Q_3 - Q_1$. But, as we have seen, a shortage causes the price to increase until the shortage is eliminated. In this case, the price will rise to P_2, where the quantity demanded and the quantity supplied are both equal to Q_2. Notice that the increase in price causes a decrease in the *quantity demanded*, from Q_3 to Q_2, but does not cause a decrease in demand.

MyEconLab
Your Turn: Test your understanding by doing related problems 4.6 and 4.7 on page 89 at the end of this chapter.

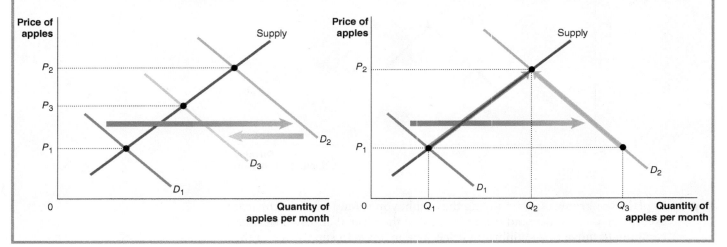

Shifts in a Curve versus Movements along a Curve

When analyzing markets using demand and supply curves, it is important to remember that *when a shift in a demand or supply curve causes a change in equilibrium price, the change in price does not cause a further shift in demand or supply.* For instance, suppose an increase in supply causes the price of a good to fall, while everything else that affects the willingness of consumers to buy the good is constant. The result will be an increase in the quantity demanded, but not an increase in demand. For demand to increase, the whole curve must shift. The point is the same for supply: If the price of the good falls but everything else that affects the willingness of sellers to supply the good is constant, the quantity supplied decreases, but the supply does not. For supply to decrease, the whole curve must shift.

Economics in Your Life

Red Bull or Beaver Buzz Energy: What's Your Beverage?

At the beginning of the chapter, we asked you to consider two questions: Would you choose to buy a can of Beaver Buzz Energy if it had a lower price than a can of Red Bull? Would you be less likely to drink Beaver Buzz Energy if your income dropped? To determine the answer to the first question, you have to recognize that Beaver Buzz Energy and Red Bull are substitutes. If you consider the two drinks to be very close substitutes, then you are likely to buy the one with the lower price. In the market, if consumers generally believe that Beaver Buzz Energy and Red Bull are close substitutes, a fall in the price of Beaver Buzz Energy will increase the quantity of Beaver Buzz Energy demanded and decrease the demand for Red Bull. Suppose that you are currently leaning toward buying Red Bull because you believe that it is better tasting than Beaver Buzz Energy. If a decrease in your income made you more likely to buy Beaver Buzz Energy, then you consider Beaver Buzz Energy as an inferior good.

Conclusion

The interaction of demand and supply determines market equilibrium. The model of demand and supply is a powerful tool for predicting how changes in the actions of consumers and firms will cause changes in equilibrium prices and quantities. As we have seen in this chapter, we can use the model to analyze markets that do not meet all of the requirements for being perfectly competitive. As long as there is intense competition among sellers, the model of demand and supply can often successfully predict changes in prices and quantities.

Before moving on to Chapter 4, read *An Inside Look* on the next page for a discussion of PepsiCo's Kickstart, a high-energy breakfast drink that the company hopes will help it capture part of the market for energy drinks.

PepsiCo Tries to Create a New Category of Drinks That Promises Energy and Health Benefits

MAIL ONLINE

Mountain Dew for Breakfast? Soda Giant's New Morning Beverage Is Packed with Caffeine and Vitamins (Just Don't Call It an Energy Drink)

If you don't like coffee or tea, Mountain Dew has a new breakfast drink that might perk you up.

PepsiCo Inc. is rolling out a new drink called Kickstart this month that has Mountain Dew flavour but is made with 5% juice and Vitamins B and C, along with an extra jolt of caffeine.

The company, based in Purchase, N.Y., is hoping to boost sales by reaching Mountain Dew fans at a new time of day: morning.

PepsiCo said it doesn't consider Kickstart to be an energy drink, noting that it still has far less caffeine than drinks such as Monster and Red Bull and none of the mysterious ingredients that have raised concerns among lawmakers and consumer advocates.

But Kickstart, which comes in flavours such as "energizing orange citrus" and "energizing fruit punch," could nevertheless give the company a side-door into the fast-growing energy drink market without getting tangled in any of its controversies.

It also comes in the same 16-ounce cans as popular energy drinks made by Monster Beverage Corp., which also offers options with juice content.

Simon Lowden, chief marketing officer for PepsiCo's Americas beverages, says the idea for Kickstart came about after the company learned through consumer research that Mountain Dew fans were looking for an alternative to traditional morning drinks such as coffee, tea and juice.

Kickstart was developed independently from a Taco Bell breakfast drink last year.

"They didn't really see anything that fit their needs," he said.

Lowden said Kickstart was developed independently from a Taco Bell breakfast drink introduced last year that combines Mountain Dew and orange juice.

With the growth of energy drinks such as Monster and Red Bull expected to slow, Kickstart could also signal the emergence of a new category that plays off the promise of energy and other health benefits, said John Sicher, publisher of the trade journal *Beverage Digest*.

In a nod to the growing concerns about sugary drinks, for example, Kickstart also uses artificial sweeteners to reduce its caloric content to about half that of regular soda; a can has 80 calories.

"It's a very interesting experiment capturing a number of attributes," Sicher said, likening it to Starbucks' Refreshers drinks, which promise "natural energy" from green coffee extract.

PepsiCo and the Coca-Cola Co. have largely watched the growth of energy drinks from the sidelines.

The promise of "energy" has been a big seller in the beverage industry in recent years, with the energy drink market increasing 17% in 2011 even as broader soft drink consumption has continued to decline, according to *Beverage Digest*. PepsiCo and the Coca-Cola Co. have largely watched that growth from the sidelines, however, with players such as Monster Beverage and Red Bull dominating the market.

But the surging popularity of energy drinks has also led to sharper scrutiny. This summer, New York's attorney general launched an investigation into the marketing prices of energy drink makers including Monster and PepsiCo, which also makes Amp. Lawmakers and consumer advocacy groups have also called on the Food and Drug Administration to investigate the safety of the high levels of caffeine in energy drinks for younger people.

Although Kickstart may look like an energy drink, it has far less caffeine, at 92 milligrams for a 16-ounce can. A comparable amount of regular Mountain Dew would have 72 milligrams of caffeine while a can of PepsiCo's Amp energy drink has 142 milligrams, according to the Center for Science in the Public Interest.

By comparison, a 16-ounce cup of Starbucks coffee has 330 milligrams of caffeine.

Source: Associated Press, "Mountain Dew for Breakfast? Soda Giant's New Morning Beverage Is Packed with Caffeine and Vitamins (Just Don't Call It an Energy Drink)," *Mail Online*, February 11, 2013, http://www.dailymail.co.uk/femail/article-2277065/Mountain-Dew-breakfast-Soda-giants-new-morning-beverage-packed-caffeine-vitamins-just-dont-energy-drink.html.

Key Points in the Article

PepsiCo has introduced a new product intended to fill the space between traditional coffee/tea and the more caffeinated energy drinks. Soft drink giants Coca Cola and PepsiCo hadn't entered the caffeinated drink market with the same intensity they have other drinks markets, but PepsiCo is now focusing on increasing its sales in this market. Kickstart is based on a mix of orange juice and Mountain Dew, which was developed by Taco Bell (that's owned by Yum! Brands Inc., which was part of PepsiCo).

Analyzing the News

(a) In addition to the growth in the demand for energy drinks, demand for healthier drinks has expanded as well. PepsiCo is hoping to capture parts of both markets by offering a product that fits into both categories. The new product also addresses some of the concerns about the large amount of caffeine in energy drinks by offering much less in Kickstart.

(b) The energy drink market has been dominated by Red Bull and Monster Energy, two firms that are not part of either major soft drink maker (Coca Cola and PepsiCo). Kickstart also offers less sugar than many other soft drinks by using artificial sweeteners, thereby reducing the calories in the new product. By trying to meet the concerns of different consumers, PepsiCo is entering not only the energy drink market, but also the market for vitamin-fortified drinks at the same time.

(c) As energy drinks have become more popular, many people have become concerned about the impact of large doses of caffeine on health, particularly in younger consumers. Kickstart has much less caffeine than an energy drink or even a medium-sized coffee at some of the most popular coffee shops in Canada.

Thinking Critically

1. How would you show the impact of the launch of Kickstart on the market for energy drinks in a graph?
2. If health researchers find strong evidence that high-caffeine beverages damage the health of younger consumers, what would be the impact on the market for energy drinks?

Chapter Summary and Problems

Key Terms

Ceteris paribus ("all else equal") condition, p. 64

Competitive market equilibrium, p. 74

Complements, p. 66

Demand curve, p. 62

Demand schedule, p. 62

Demographics, p. 66

Income effect, p. 63

Inferior good, p. 65

Law of demand, p. 63

Law of supply, p. 70

Market demand, p. 62

Market equilibrium, p. 74

Normal good, p. 65

Perfectly competitive market, p. 62

Quantity demanded, p. 62

Quantity supplied, p. 69

Shortage, p. 74

Substitutes, p. 65

Substitution effect, p. 63

Supply curve, p. 69

Supply schedule, p. 69

Surplus, p. 74

Technological change, p. 71

Summary

*LO 3.1 The model of demand and supply is the most powerful tool in economics. The model applies exactly only to *perfectly competitive markets*, where there are many buyers and sellers, all the products sold are identical, and there are no barriers to new sellers entering the market. But the model can also be useful in analyzing markets that don't meet all these requirements. The *quantity demanded* is the amount of a good or service that a consumer is willing and able to purchase at a given price. A *demand schedule* is a table that shows the relationship between the price of a product and the quantity of the product demanded. A *demand curve* is a graph that shows the relationship between the price of a good and the quantity of the good demanded. *Market demand* is the demand by all consumers of a given good or service. The *law of demand* states that *ceteris paribus*—holding everything else constant—the quantity of a product demanded increases when the price falls and decreases when the price rises. Demand curves slope downward because of the *substitution effect*, which is the change in quantity demanded that results from a price change that makes one good more or less expensive relative to another good, and the income effect, which is the change in quantity demanded of a good that results from the effect of a change in the good's price on consumer purchasing power. Changes in income, the prices of related goods, tastes, population and demographics, and expectations all cause the demand curve to shift. *Substitutes* are goods that can be used for the same purpose. *Complements* are goods that are used together. A *normal good* is a good for which demand increases as income increases. An *inferior good* is a good for which demand decreases as income increases. *Demographics* refers to the characteristics of a population with respect to age, race, and gender. A change in demand refers to a shift of the demand curve. A change in quantity demanded refers to a movement along the demand curve as a result of a change in the product's price.

LO 3.2 The *quantity supplied* is the amount of a good that a firm is willing and able to supply at a given price. A *supply* schedule is a table that shows the relationship between the price of a product and the quantity of the product supplied. A *supply curve* shows on a graph the relationship between the price of a product and the quantity of the product supplied. When the price of a product rises, producing the product is more profitable, and a greater amount will be supplied. The *law of supply* states that, holding everything else constant, the quantity of a product supplied increases when the price rises and decreases when the price falls. Changes in the prices of inputs, technology, the prices of substitutes in production, expected future prices, and the number of firms in a market all cause the supply curve to shift. *Technological change* is a positive or negative change in the ability of a firm to produce a given level of output with a given quantity of inputs. A change in supply refers to a shift of the supply curve. A change in quantity supplied refers to a movement along the supply curve as a result of a change in the product's price.

LO 3.3 *Market equilibrium* occurs where the demand curve intersects the supply curve. A *competitive market equilibrium* has a market equilibrium with many buyers and many sellers. Only at this point is the quantity demanded equal to the quantity supplied. Prices above equilibrium result in *surpluses*, with the quantity supplied being greater than the quantity demanded. Surpluses cause the market price to fall. Prices below equilibrium result in *shortages*, with the quantity demanded being greater than the quantity supplied. Shortages cause the market price to rise.

LO 3.4 In most markets, demand and supply curves shift frequently, causing changes in equilibrium prices and quantities. Over time, if demand increases more than supply, equilibrium price will rise. If supply increases more than demand, equilibrium price will fall.

MyEconLab   Log in to MyEconLab to complete these exercises and get instant feedback.

---

*'Learning Objective' is abbreviated to 'LO' in the end of chapter material.

Review Questions

LO 3.1

1.1 What is a demand schedule? What is a demand curve?

1.2 What is the difference between a change in demand and a change in the quantity demanded?

1.3 What are the main variables that will cause the demand curve to shift? Give an example of each.

LO 3.2

2.1 What is a supply schedule? What is a supply curve?

2.2 What is the difference between a change in supply and a change in the quantity supplied?

2.3 What is the law of supply? What are the main variables that will cause a supply curve to shift? Give an example of each.

LO 3.3

3.1 What do economists mean by *market equilibrium*?

3.2 What do economists mean by a *shortage*? By a *surplus*?

3.3 What happens in a market if the current price is above the equilibrium price? What happens if the current price is below the equilibrium price?

LO 3.4

4.1 Draw a demand and supply graph to show the effect on the equilibrium price in a market in the following two situations:

a. The demand curve shifts to the right.

b. The supply curve shifts to the left.

4.2 If, over time, the demand curve for a product shifts to the right more than the supply curve does, what will happen to the equilibrium price? What will happen to the equilibrium price if the supply curve shifts to the right more than the demand curve? For each case, draw a demand and supply graph to illustrate your answer.

Problems and Applications

LO 3.1

1.1 For each of the following pairs of products, state which are complements, which are substitutes, and which are unrelated.

a. Gasoline and electric car batteries

b. Houses and household appliances

c. UGG boots and Kindle e-readers

d. iPads and Kindle e-readers

1.2 [**Related to the** Chapter Opener **on page 61**] Many people are concerned about the health effects of consuming large quantities of energy drinks. In fact, Health Canada began a review of its regulation of the energy drink industry in 2012. One proposal, not made by Health Canada but by others, is that energy drinks only be sold in pharmacies or liquor stores. What impact do you think this proposal would have on the market for energy drinks? What do you think will happen to the price of these products?

1.3 Imagine that the table below shows the quantity demanded of UGG boots at five different prices in 2012 and in 2013:

	Quantity Demanded	
Price	2012	2013
$160	5000	4000
170	4500	3500
180	4000	3000
190	3500	2500
200	3000	2000

Name two different variables that could cause the quantity demanded of UGG boots to change as indicated from 2012 to 2013.

1.4 [**Related to** Making the Connection **on page 65**] A student makes the following argument:

The chapter says that Canadian consumers, as a group, have begun to treat mainstream beer as an inferior good and wine as a normal good. But I like the taste of mainstream beer better than I like the taste of wine, so for me wine is an inferior good and beer is a normal good.

Do you agree with the student's reasoning? Briefly explain.

1.5 [**Related to the** Making the Connection **on page 67**] Name three products whose demand is likely to increase rapidly if the following demographic groups increase at a faster rate than the population as a whole:

a. Teenagers

b. Children under age five

c. Recent immigrants

1.6 Suppose the following table shows the price of a base model Toyota Prius hybrid and the quantity of Priuses sold for three years. Do these data indicate that the demand curve for Priuses is upward sloping? Explain.

Year	Price	Quantity
2010	$24 880	35 265
2011	24 550	33 250
2012	25 250	36 466

1.7 Richard Posner is a US federal court judge who also writes on economic topics. A newspaper reporter summarized Posner's view on the effect of online bookstores and e-books on the demand for books:

Posner's [argument] is that the disappearance of bookstores is to be celebrated and not mourned, partly because e-books and online stores will reduce the cost of books and thus drive up demand for them.

Do you agree with Posner's statements as given by the reporter? Briefly explain.

Christopher Shea, "Judge Posner Hails the Demise of Bookstores," Wall Street Journal, January 13, 2011.

LO 3.2

2.1 Briefly explain whether each of the following statements describes a change in supply or a change in the quantity supplied:

    a. To take advantage of high prices for snow shovels during a snowy winter, Alexander Shovels, Inc., decides to increase output.

    b. The success of the Apple iPad leads more firms to begin producing tablet computers.

    c. In the six months following the Japanese earthquake and tsunami in 2011, production of automobiles in Japan declined by 20 percent.

2.2 Suppose that the following table shows the quantity supplied of UGG boots at five different prices in 2012 and in 2013:

	Quantity Supplied	
Price	2012	2013
$160	300 000	200 000
170	350 000	250 000
180	400 000	300 000
190	450 000	350 000
200	500 000	400 000

    Name two different variables that would cause the quantity supplied of UGG boots to change as indicated in the table from 2012 to 2013.

2.3 Will each firm in the tablet computer industry always supply the same quantity as every other firm at each price? What factors might cause the quantity of tablet computers supplied by different firms to be different at a particular price?

2.4 If the price of a good increases, is the increase in the quantity of the good supplied likely to be smaller or larger, the longer the time period being considered? Briefly explain.

LO 3.3

3.1 Briefly explain whether you agree with the following statement: "When there is a shortage of a good, consumers eventually give up trying to buy it, so the demand for the good declines, and the price falls until the market is finally in equilibrium."

3.2 [**Related to** Solved Problem 3.1 **on page 75**] In *The Wealth of Nations*, Adam Smith discussed what has come to be known as the "diamond and water paradox":

    Nothing is more useful than water: but it will purchase scarce anything; scarce anything can be had in exchange for it. A diamond, on the contrary, has scarce any value in use; but a very great quantity of other goods may frequently be had in exchange for it.

    Graph the market for diamonds and the market for water. Show how it is possible for the price of water to be much lower than the price of diamonds, even though the demand for water is much greater than the demand for diamonds.

Adam Smith, An Inquiry into the Nature and Causes of the Wealth of Nations, Vol. I, (Oxford, UK: Oxford University Press, 1976 original edition, 1776).

3.3 If a market is in equilibrium, is it necessarily true that all buyers and all sellers are satisfied with the market price? Briefly explain.

LO 3.4

4.1 As oil prices rose during 2006, the demand for alternative fuels increased. Ethanol, one alternative fuel, is made from corn. According to an article in the *Wall Street Journal*, the price of tortillas, which are made from corn, also rose during 2006: "The price spike [in tortillas] is part of a ripple effect from the ethanol boom."

    a. Draw a demand and supply graph for the corn market and use it to show the effect on this market of an increase in the demand for ethanol. Be sure to indicate the equilibrium price and quantity before and after the increase in the demand for ethanol.

    b. Draw a demand and supply graph for the tortilla market and use it to show the effect on this market of an increase in the price of corn. Once again, be sure to indicate the equilibrium price and quantity before and after the increase in the demand for ethanol.

    c. During 2009, the demand for gasoline had fallen, lowering its price. The demand for ethanol had declined as well. In response, ethanol producers asked regulators to raise the allowable amount of ethanol in gasoline blends from 10 percent to 15 percent. If regulators were to agree to this proposal, what would be the likely effect on tortilla prices?

Based on Stephen Power, "Industry Seeks to Raise Ethanol Levels in Fuel," Wall Street Journal, March 7, 2009; and Mark Gongloff, "Tortilla Soup," Wall Street Journal, January 25, 2007.

4.2 [**Related to** Making the Connection **on page 77**] During 2013, the demand for LCD TVs appeared to be falling. At the same time, some industry observers expected that several smaller TV manufacturers might exit the market. Use a demand and supply graph to analyze the effects of these factors on the equilibrium price and quantity of LCD TVs. Clearly show on your graph the old equilibrium price and quantity and the new equilibrium price and quantity. Can you tell for certain whether the new equilibrium price will be higher or lower than the old equilibrium price? Briefly explain.

4.3 [**Related to** Solved Problem 3.2 **on page 80**] The demand for watermelons is highest during summer and lowest during winter. Yet watermelon prices are normally lower in summer than in winter. Use a demand and supply graph to demonstrate how this is possible. Be sure to carefully label the curves in your graph and to clearly indicate the equilibrium summer price and the equilibrium winter price.

4.4 [**Related to** Solved Problem 3.2 **on page 80**] Tourism is an important part of the economies of the Maritime provinces. The tourist season is generally the summer months; with June, July, and August being the most popular months. Shediac, New Brunswick, and Prince Edward Island as a whole are particularly popular with tourists. The lobster fishing season in Shediac doesn't begin until mid-August and ends in mid-October. Use a demand and supply graph to explain whether lobster prices would be higher or lower if the lobster fishing season were to begin in June and end in August.

4.5 An article in the *Wall Street Journal* noted that the demand for Internet advertising was declining at the same time that the number of websites accepting advertising was increasing. After reading the article, a student argues: "From this information, we know that the price of Internet ads should fall, but we don't know whether the total quantity of Internet ads will increase or decrease." Is the student's analysis correct? Illustrate your answer with a demand and supply graph.

Based on Martin Peers, "Future Shock for Internet Ads?" Wall Street Journal, February 17, 2009.

4.6 [**Related to** Don't Let This Happen to You **on page 81**] A student writes the following: "Increased production leads to a lower price, which in turn increases demand." Do you agree with the student's reasoning? Briefly explain.

4.7 [**Related to** Don't Let This Happen to You **on page 81**] A student was asked to draw a demand and supply graph to illustrate the effect on the tablet computers market of a fall in the price of displays used in tablet computers, holding everything else constant. She drew the graph below and explained it as follows:

> Displays are an input to tablet computers, so a fall in the price of displays will cause the supply curve for tablets to shift to the right (from S_1 to S_2). Because this shift in the supply curve results in a lower price (P_2), consumers will want to buy more tablets, and the demand curve will shift to the right (from D_1 to D_2). We know that more tablets will be sold, but we can't be sure whether the price of tablets will rise or fall. That depends on whether the supply curve or the demand curve has shifted farther to the right. I assume that the effect on supply is greater than the effect on demand, so I show the final equilibrium price (P_3) as being lower than the initial equilibrium price (P_1).

Explain whether you agree or disagree with the student's analysis. Be careful to explain exactly what—if anything—you find wrong with her analysis.

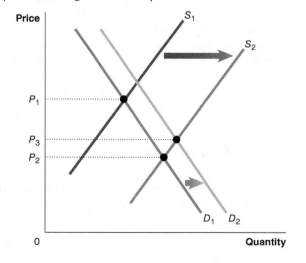

4.8 Proposals have been made to increase government regulation of firms providing child-care services by, for instance, setting education requirements for child-care workers. Suppose that these regulations increase the quality of child-care and cause the demand for child-care services to increase. At the same time, assume that complying with the new government regulations increases the costs of firms providing child-care services. Draw a demand and supply graph to illustrate the effects of these changes in the market for child-care services. Briefly explain whether the total quantity of child-care services purchased will increase or decrease as a result of regulation.

4.9 The following graphs show the supply and demand curves for two markets. One of the markets is for BMW automobiles, and the other is for a cancer-fighting drug, without which lung cancer patients will die. Briefly explain which graph most likely represents which market.

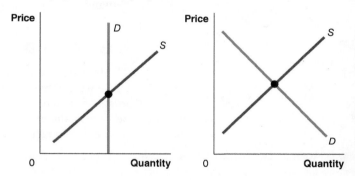

Appendix B

LO
Use quantitative demand and supply analysis.

Quantitative Demand and Supply Analysis

Graphs help us understand economic change *quantitatively*. For instance, a demand and supply graph can tell us that if household incomes rise, the demand curve for a normal good will shift to the right, and its price will rise. Often, though, economists, business managers, and policymakers want to know more than the qualitative direction of change; they want a *quantitative estimate* of the size of the change.

In this chapter, we carried out qualitative analysis of market equilibriums. We saw that an increase in demand would increase the market price and an increase in supply would decrease the market price. To better understand how different shifts in the market impact price and quantity, we need to know how large the effects are. A quantitative analysis of market equilibrium will tell us how much prices and quantities change after a demand or supply curve shifts.

Demand and Supply Equations

The first step in a quantitative analysis is to supplement our use of demand and supply curve with demand and supply *equations*. We noted briefly in this chapter that economists often statistically estimate equations for demand curves. Supply curves can also be statistically estimated. For example, suppose that economists have estimated that the demand for apartments in Toronto is:

$$Q^D = 3\,000\,000 - 1000P$$

and the supply of apartments is:

$$Q^S = -450\,000 + 1300P.$$

We have used Q^D for the quantity of apartments demanded per month, Q^S for the quantity of apartments supplied per month, and P for the apartment rent, in dollars per month. In reality, both the quantity of apartments demanded and quantity of apartments supplied will depend on more than just the rental price of apartments in Toronto. For instance, the demand for apartments in Toronto will also depend on the average incomes of families in the Toronto area and on the rents of apartments in surrounding cities. For simplicity, we will ignore these other factors.

The competitive market equilibrium occurs when the quantity demanded equals the quantity supplied, or:

$$Q^D = Q^S.$$

We can use this equation, which is called an *equilibrium condition*, to solve for the equilibrium monthly apartment rent by setting the quantity demanded from the demand equation equal to the quantity demanded from the supply equation:

$$3\,000\,000 - 1000P = -450\,000 + 1300P$$

$$3\,450\,000 = 2300P$$

$$P = \frac{3\,450\,000}{2300} = \$1500.$$

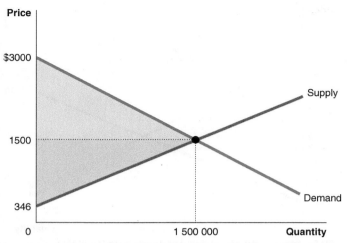

Figure 3B.1a

Graphing Supply and Demand Equations

After statistically estimating supply and demand equations, we can use the equations to draw supply and demand curves. In this case, as panel (a) shows, the equilibrium rent for apartments is $1500 per month, and the equilibrium quantity of apartments rented is 1 500 000. The supply equation tells us that at a rent of $346, the quantity of apartments supplied will be zero. The demand equation tells us that at a rent of $3000, the quantity of apartments demanded will be zero. Panel (b), below, shows the shift in the equilibrium price from $1500 to $1283 when the demand for apartments decreases.

(a) Determining the equilibrium apartment price (monthly rent) in Toronto

We can then substitute this price back into either the demand equation or the supply equation to find the equilibrium quantity of apartments rented:

$$Q^D = 3\,000\,000 - 1000P = 3\,000\,000 - 1000(1500) = 1\,500\,000$$

$$Q^S = -450\,000 + 1300P = -450\,000 + 1300(1500) = 1\,500\,000.$$

Panel (a) of Figure 3B.1 shows in a graph *the same information as we just found using algebra.*

If the economy of Toronto is not performing as well as it has in the past, fewer people are likely to want to live in Toronto, all else being equal. We can represent this idea by reducing the number of apartments that would be rented at every price. This makes the new demand equation:

$$Q^D = 2\,500\,000 - 1000P$$

and the supply equation remains unchanged:

$$Q^S = -450\,000 + 1300P.$$

The new equilibrium price is:

$$2\,500\,000 - 1000P = -450\,000 + 1300P$$

$$2\,950\,000 = 2300P$$

$$P = \frac{2\,950\,000}{2300} = \$1283.$$

The new quantity of apartments rented can be found by substituting this price into either the demand equation or the supply equation:

$$Q^D = 2\,500\,000 - 1000P = 2\,500\,000 - 1000(1283) = 1\,217\,000$$

$$Q^S = -450\,000 + 1300P = -450\,000 + 1300(1283) = 1\,217\,000.$$

When the demand for apartments decreases, the equilibrium price falls from $1500 to $1283, and the equilibrium number of apartments rented falls from 1 500 000 to 1 217 000. Panel (b) of Figure 3B.1 illustrates the result of this shift. Notice that the qualitative results (a decrease in price and quantity) match the quantitative results we just found.

Figure 3B.1b

Graphing Supply and Demand Equations

The process of finding the new equilibrium remains the same no matter whether the demand curve, the supply curve, or both shifts. You set the quantity demanded equal to the quantity supplied and solve for price. Then you substitute the price you found into either the demand equation or the supply equation.

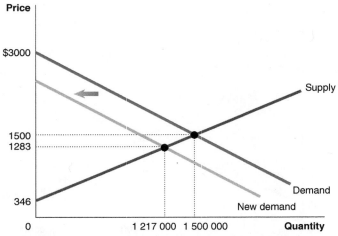

(b) Determining the equilibrium apartment price (monthly rent) in Toronto: when demand decreases

MyEconLab   Log in to MyEconLab to complete these exercises and get instant feedback.

LO Use quantitative demand and supply analysis.

Review Questions

3B.1 In a linear demand equation, what economic information is conveyed by the intercept on the price axis? Similarly, what information is conveyed by the intercept on the price axis in a linear supply equation.

Problems and Applications

3B.1 Suppose that you have been hired to analyze wages in a simple market. The demand for labour and supply of labour can be represented by the following equations:

$$\text{Demand:} \quad L^D = 100 - 4W$$

$$\text{Supply:} \quad L^S = 6W$$

a. Calculate the equilibrium wage (price) and quantity of labour employed in this market.

b. A new employer enters the market causing labour demand to become:

$$\text{New Demand: } L^D = 120 - 4W$$

Calculate the new equilibrium wage (price) and quantity of workers employed in this market.

3B.2 Suppose the demand and supply of leather shoes can be represented by the following equations:

$$Q^D = 200 - 2P$$

$$Q^S = 2P$$

a. Calculate the equilibrium price and quantity in this market.

b. Assume that an increase in the cost of leather causes the supply of shoes to change to:

$$Q^S = -50 + 2P$$

Calculate the new equilibrium price and quantity in this market.

c. Assume that in addition to the increase in the price of leather, the demand for leather shoes falls due to a change in fashion and is now as follows:

$$150 - 2P$$

Calculate the equilibrium price and quantity in this market. Remember to use the same supply curve as in part (b).

CHAPTER 4

GDP: Measuring Total Production and Income

Chapter Outline and Learning Objectives

4.1 Gross Domestic Product Measures Total Production, page 96
Explain how total production is measured.

4.2 Does GDP Measure What We Want It to Measure? page 104
Discuss whether GDP is a good measure of well-being.

4.3 Real GDP versus Nominal GDP, page 107
Discuss the difference between real GDP and nominal GDP.

4.4 Other Measures of Total Production and Total Income, page 110
Become familiar with other measures of total production and total income.

AP Photo/Canadian Press, Jason Kryk

The Health of the Canadian Economy

Many different factors impact the health of the Canadian economy. One of those factors is exports. It was not a surprise to most people when the Canadian economy slowed down in the second quarter of 2011. The global economy, particularly the economy of the United States, was not growing. When the economies of other countries aren't doing well, they tend to buy fewer of our exports.

Canadian exporters were feeling the effects of the *business cycle,* which refers to the alternating periods of economic expansion and recession that occur in all economies. Production and employment increase during expansions and fall during recessions. Whether the general level of economic activity is increasing is important to all kinds of firms, and it is also important to workers wondering whether they will be able to keep their jobs and to college and university students wondering whether they will be able to find jobs when they gradu-

ate. One US study found that college students who graduate during a recession have to search longer to find a job and end up accepting jobs that, on average, pay 10 percent less than the jobs accepted by students who graduate during expansions. What is more, students who graduate during a recession will continue to earn less for as long as 15 years after they graduate. A similar Canadian study showed that those graduating from university during a recession had lower earnings for 10 years or more. The overall state of the economy is clearly important to you!

AN INSIDE LOOK on **page 114** discusses the effects of falling exports on the Canadian economy.

Sources: Lisa B. Kahn, "The Long-Term Labour Market Consequences of Graduating from College in a Bad Economy," Labour Economics, Vol. 17, No. 2, April 2010, pp.303-316; Oreopoulos, P., von Wachter, T., & Heisz, A. (2012). The short- and long-term career effects of graduating in a recession. American Economic Journal: 4(1), 1-29.

Economics in Your Life

What's the Best Country for You to Work In?

Suppose that an airline offers you a job after graduation in 2014. The firm has offices in the United Kingdom and China, and because you are fluent in both English and Mandarin, you get to choose the country in which you will work and live. Gross domestic product (GDP) is a measure of an economy's total production of goods and services, so one factor in your decision is likely to be the growth rate of GDP in each country. Based on the International Monetary Fund's forecasts for 2014, GDP will grow by 1.5 percent in the United Kingdom and 8.2 percent in China. What effects do these very different growth rates have on your decision to work and live in one country or the other? If China's much larger growth rate does not necessarily lead you to decide to live and work in China, why not? As you read this chapter, see if you can answer these questions. You can check your answers against those we provide on page 112 at the end of this chapter.

Microeconomics The study of how households and firms make choices, how they interact in markets, and how the government attempts to influence their choices.

Macroeconomics The study of the economy as a whole, including topics such as inflation, unemployment, and economic growth.

Business cycle Alternating periods of economic expansion and economic recession.

Expansion The period of a business cycle during which total production and total employment are increasing.

Recession The period of a business cycle during which total production and total employment are decreasing.

Economic growth The ability of an economy to produce increasing quantities of goods and services.

Inflation rate The percentage increase in the price level from one year to the next.

As we saw in Chapter 1, we can divide economics into the subfields of microeconomics and macroeconomics. **Microeconomics** is the study of how households and firms make choices, how they interact in markets, and how the government attempts to influence their choices. **Macroeconomics** is the study of the economy as a whole, including topics such as inflation, unemployment, and economic growth. In microeconomic analysis, economists generally study individual markets, such as the market for tablet computers. In macroeconomic analysis, economists study factors that affect many markets at the same time. As we saw in the chapter opener, one important macroeconomic issue is the business cycle. The **business cycle** refers to the alternating periods of expansion and recession that the Canadian economy has experienced since Canada became a country. A business cycle **expansion** is a period during which total production and total employment are increasing. A business cycle **recession** is a period during which total production and total employment are decreasing. In the following chapters, we will discuss the factors that influence the business cycle and policies the government may use to reduce its effects.

Another important macroeconomic topic is **economic growth**, which refers to the ability of an economy to produce increasing quantities of goods and services. Economic growth is important because an economy that grows very slowly fails to raise living standards. In some countries in Africa, very little economic growth occurred from the 1950s to 2000, and as a result many people remain in severe poverty. Macroeconomics analyzes both what determines a country's rate of economic growth and the reasons growth rates differ so much among countries.

Macroeconomics also analyzes what determines the total level of employment in an economy. As we will see, in the short run, the level of employment is significantly affected by the business cycle, but in the long run, the effects of the business cycle disappear, and other factors determine the level of employment. A related issue is why some economies are more successful than others in maintaining high levels of employment over time. Yet another important macroeconomic issue is what determines the **inflation rate**, or the percentage increase in the average level of prices from one year to the next. As with employment, inflation is affected both by the business cycle and by other long-run factors. Finally, macroeconomics is concerned with the linkages among economies: international trade and international finance.

Macroeconomic analysis provides information that consumers and firms need in order to understand current economic conditions and to help predict future conditions. A family may be reluctant to buy a house if employment is declining, as declining employment makes it more likely that someone in that family will lose their job. Similarly, firms may be reluctant to invest in building new factories or to hire new workers if they expect that future sales may be weak.

In this chapter and in Chapter 5, we begin our study of macroeconomics by considering how best to measure key macroeconomic variables. As we will see, there are important issues to think about when deciding how to measure macroeconomic variables. We start by considering the most common measure of total production and total income in an economy.

4.1 LEARNING OBJECTIVE

Explain how total production is measured.

Gross Domestic Product Measures Total Production

There are few days in which *gross domestic product (GDP)* is *not* in the news. In this section, we explore what GDP is and how it is measured. We also explore why knowledge of GDP is important to consumers, firms, and government policymakers.

Measuring Total Production: Gross Domestic Product

Gross domestic product (GDP) The market value of all final goods and services produced in a geographic area (country) during a period of time, typically one year.

Economists measure total production by **gross domestic product (GDP)**. GDP is the market *value* of all *final* goods and services produced in a geographic area (a country, typically) during a *period of time*. In Canada, Statistics Canada produces estimates of

GDP data which are released every three months. GDP is a central concept in macroeconomics, so we need to consider its definition carefully.

GDP Is Measured Using Market Values, Not Quantities The word *value* is important in the definition of GDP. In microeconomics, we tend to think about production in terms of quantity: the number of cups of coffee sold per day, the number of barrels of oil pumped, the number of cars made by automakers, and so on. When we measure total production in an economy, we can't just add together the quantities of every good and service because the result would be a meaningless mess. Barrels of oil would be added to cans of energy drinks, the number of cars, and so on. This really would be like adding apples to oranges, so to speak. Instead of making a list of all the different goods and services produced (or trying to add apples and oranges), we measure production by taking the *value*, in dollar terms, of all the goods and services produced.

GDP Includes Only the Market Value of Final Goods and Services In measuring GDP, we include only the value of *final goods and services*. A **final good or service** is one that is purchased by its final user and is not included in the production of any other good or service. Examples of final goods are things like a hamburger you buy to eat for lunch and a computer purchased by a business. Some goods and services, though, become part of other goods and services. Let's consider the car seats made by Magna International in London, Ontario, for Toyota cars. These car seats are considered **intermediate goods**, while the Toyota cars they're installed in are considered final goods. In calculating GDP, we include the value of the car, but not that of the car seats. If we included the value of the car seats, we would be *double counting*: The value of a car seat would be counted once when it was sold to Toyota and a second time when Toyota sold the car, with the seat installed, to a consumer.

Final good or service A good or service purchased by a final user.

Intermediate good or service A good or service that is an input into another good or service, such as car seats.

GDP Includes Only Current Production GDP includes only production that takes place during the indicated time period. For example, GDP in 2014 includes only the goods and services made during that year. In particular, GDP does *not* include the value of used goods. If you buy a new copy of this text for your winter class, the purchase is included in GDP; if you then sell your copy to a friend who is taking the class in the fall, that transaction is not included in GDP.

Solved Problem **4.1**

Calculating GDP

Suppose that a very simple economy produces only four goods and services: energy drinks, pizzas, textbooks, and paper. Assume that all paper in this economy is used to make either textbooks or pizza boxes. Use the information in the following table to compute GDP for 2014.

Production and Price Statistics for 2014

Product	Quantity	Price per Unit
Energy drinks (24 cans)	100	$ 50.00
Pizzas	80	10.00
Textbooks	20	100.00
Paper	2000	0.10

Solving the Problem

Step 1: **Review the chapter material.** This problem is about gross domestic product, so you may want to review the section "Measuring Total Production: Gross Domestic Product" on page 96.

Step 2: **Determine which goods and services listed in the table should be included in the calculation of GDP.** GDP is the value of all final goods and services. Therefore, we need to calculate the value of all the final goods and services listed in the table. Energy drinks, pizzas, and textbooks are final goods. Paper would be a final good if a consumer bought it to use in a printer. Here we assumed that all paper is purchased by publishers and pizza producers as an intermediate good. The value of intermediate goods (paper, in this case) is not included in GDP.

Step 3: **Calculate the value of the three final goods and services listed in the table.** Value is equal to the quantity produced multiplied by the price per unit, so we multiply the numbers in the quantity column by the numbers in the price-per-unit column.

Product	Quantity	Price per Unit	Value
Energy drinks	100	$ 50	$5000
Pizzas	80	10	800
Textbooks	20	100	2000

Step 4: **Add the value for each of the three final goods and services to find GDP.** GDP = Value of energy drinks produced + Value of pizzas produced + Value of textbooks produced = $5000 + $800 + $2000 = $7800.

MyEconLab   **Your Turn:** For more practice, do related problem 1.5 on page 117 at the end of this chapter.

Production, Income, and the Circular-Flow Diagram

When we measure the value of total production in the economy by calculating GDP, we are simultaneously measuring the value of total income. To see why the value of total production is equal to the value of total income, consider what happens to the money you spend on a single product. Suppose you buy an iPad for $450 at Future Shop. *All* of that $450 must end up as someone's income. Apple and Future Shop will receive some of the $450 as profits, workers at Apple will receive some as wages, the salesperson who sold you the iPad will receive some as salary, the firms that sell parts to Apple will receive some as profits, the workers of those firms will receive some as wages, and so on. Every penny must end up as someone's income. (Note, however, that any sales tax—such as the GST or HST— on the iPad will be collected by the store and sent to the government, without ending up as anyone's income until the government spends it.) Therefore, if we add up the value of every good and service sold in the economy (expenditures), we must get a total that is equal to the value of all the income in the economy.

The circular-flow diagram in Figure 4.1 was introduced in Chapter 2 to illustrate the interaction of firms and households in markets. We use it here to illustrate the flow of spending and money in the economy. Firms sell goods and services to three groups: domestic households, foreign firms and households, and the government. Expenditures by foreign firms and households (shown as "Rest of the World" in the diagram) on domestically produced goods and services are called *exports*. For example, Air Canada sells many tickets to passengers in Europe and Asia. As we note at the bottom of Figure 4.1, we can measure GDP by adding up the total expenditures of these three groups on goods and services.

Firms use the *factors of production*—labour, capital, natural resources, and entrepreneurship—to produce goods and services. Households supply the factors of production to firms in exchange for income. We divide income into four categories: wages, interest, rent, and profit. Firms pay wages to households in exchange for the services of labour, interest for the use of capital, and rent for natural resources such as land. Profit is the income that remains after a firm has paid wages, interest, and rent. Profit is the return to entrepreneurs for organizing the other factors of production and for taking on the risk of producing and selling goods and services.

As Figure 4.1 shows, federal, provincial, and local governments make payments of wages and interest to households in exchange for hiring workers and for other factors of production. Governments also make *transfer payments* to households.

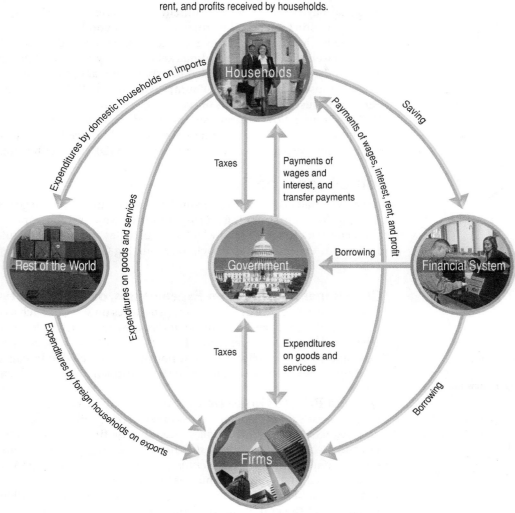

GDP can be measured by total wages, interest, rent, and profits received by households.

GDP can be measured by total expenditures on goods and services by households, firms, government, and the rest of the world.

Figure 4.1 The Circular Flow and the Measurement of GDP

The circular-flow diagram illustrates the flow of spending and money in the economy. Firms sell goods and services to three groups: domestic households, foreign firms and households, and the government. To produce goods and services, firms use factors of production: labour, capital, natural resources, and entrepreneurship. Households supply the factors of production to firms in exchange for income in the form of wages, interest, profit, and rent. Firms make payments of wages and interest to households in exchange for hiring workers and other factors of production. The sum of wages, interest, rent, and profit is total income in the economy. We can measure GDP as the total income received by

households. The diagram also shows that households use their income to purchase goods and services, pay taxes, and save. Firms and the government borrow the funds that flow from households into the financial system. We can measure GDP either by calculating the total value of expenditures on final goods and services or by calculating the value of total income.

Photo credits : (top) JupiterImages; (left) Bill Aron/PhotoEdit; (bottom) Mikael Damkier/Alamy; (right) Eric Gevaert/Shutterstock; (centre) Yoshio Tomii/SuperStock

Transfer payments include social program payments (e.g., Old Age Security and Guaranteed Income Supplement) and unemployment insurance payments. These payments are not included in GDP because they are not received in exchange for producing a new good or service. The sum of wages, interest, rent, and profit is the total income in the economy. As we note at the top of Figure 4.1, we can measure GDP as the total income received by households.

The diagram also allows us to trace the ways that households use their income. Households spend some of their income on goods and services. Some of this spending is on domestically produced goods and services and some is on foreign-produced goods and services. Spending on foreign-produced goods and services is known as *imports*.

Transfer payments Payments by the government to households for which the government does not receive a new good or service in return.

Households also use some of their income to pay taxes to the government. (Note that firms also pay taxes to the government.) Even after paying taxes to the government, households don't spend all of their income on goods and services; some income is deposited in chequing or savings accounts in banks or used to buy stocks and/or bonds. Banks, as well as stock and bond markets, make up the *financial system*, which allows firms to borrow the money needed to expand and adopt new technologies. In fact, as we will discuss in Chapter 6, no country without a well-developed financial system has been able to sustain high levels of economic growth.

The circular-flow diagram shows that we can measure GDP either by calculating the total value of expenditures on final goods and services or by calculating the value of total income. We get the same dollar amount of GDP using either approach.

Components of GDP

Statistics Canada divides the data on GDP into four major categories of expenditures: consumption, investment, government purchases, and net exports. Economists use these categories to understand why GDP fluctuates and to forecast future GDP. Here, we focus on the expenditure approach to calculating GDP, as this will be the focus of much of the rest of the text.

(C) Personal Consumption Expenditures, or "Consumption" Expenditures made by households are divided into expenditures on *services*, such as financial planning, massages, education, and haircuts; *non-durable goods*, such as food; *semi-durable goods*, such as clothing and footwear; and *durable goods*, such as cars, appliances, and furniture. The spending by households on new houses is not included in **consumption**. Instead, spending on new houses is included in the investment category, which we discuss next.

Consumption Spending by households on goods and services, not including spending on new houses.

(I) Gross Private Domestic Investment, or "Investment" Spending on *gross private domestic investment*, or simply **investment**, is divided into three categories. *Business gross fixed capital formation* is spending by firms on new factories, office buildings, and machinery. *Residential structures* is spending by households and firms on new houses. Finally, *business investment in inventories* are included in investment. Inventories are goods that have been purchased but not yet sold. If Toyota has $20 000 000 worth of unsold cars at the beginning of the year and $35 000 000 million worth of unsold cars at the end of the year, then the firm has spent $15 000 000 on inventory investment during the year.

Investment Spending by firms on new factories, office buildings, machinery, and additions to inventories, plus spending by households and firms on new houses.

(G) Government Consumption and Gross Investment, or "Government Purchases" **Government purchases** are spending by federal, provincial, and local

Government purchases Spending by federal, provincial, and local governments on goods and services.

Don't Let This Happen to You

Remember What Economists Mean by *Investment*

Notice that the definition of *investment* in this chapter is narrower than in everyday use. For example, people often say they are investing in the stock market or in rare coins. As we have seen, economists reserve the word *investment* for purchases of machinery, factories, and houses. Economists don't include purchases of stocks or rare coins or deposits in savings accounts in the definition of investment because these activities don't result in the production of new goods. For example, a share of Microsoft stock rep-

resents part ownership of that company. When you buy a share of Microsoft stock, nothing new is produced; there is just a transfer of that small piece of ownership of Microsoft. Similarly, buying a rare coin or putting $1000 into a savings account does not result in an increase in production. GDP is not affected by any of these activities, so they are not included in the economic definition of investment.

MyEconLab
Your Turn: Test your understanding by doing related problem 1.6 on page 117 at the end of this chapter.

governments on goods and services, such as teachers' salaries, highways, and hospitals. Again, government spending, when referring to GDP, does not include transfers to individuals because such payments do not represent the production of a new good or service.

(NX) Net Exports of Goods and Services, or "Net Exports"

Net exports are equal to *exports* minus *imports*. **Exports** are goods and services produced in Canada and purchased by foreign firms, households, and governments. We add exports to our other categories of expenditures because otherwise we would not be including all spending on new goods and services produced in Canada. For example, if a farmer in Saskatchewan sells wheat to China, the value of the wheat is included in GDP because it represents production in Canada. **Imports** are goods and services produced in foreign countries and purchased by Canadian firms, households and governments. We subtract imports from total expenditures because otherwise we would be including spending that does not represent production of new goods and services in Canada. For example, if Canadian consumers buy $50 million worth of IKEA furniture manufactured in Sweden, that spending is included in Canadian consumption expenditures, even though it doesn't represent Canadian production. Therefore to avoid including the foreign production, $50 million of the IKEA imports is subtracted because it was included under the measurement of C, Consumption.

Net exports The value of a country's total exports minus the value of a country's total imports.

Exports Goods and services produced domestically but sold to foreign households or firms.

Imports Goods and services bought domestically but produced in other countries.

An Equation for GDP and Some Actual Values

A simple equation sums up the components of GDP:

$$Y = C + I + G + NX$$

The equation tells us that GDP (represented by the letter Y in this equation) equals consumption (C) plus investment (I) plus government purchases (G) plus net exports (NX). Figure 4.2 shows the value of the components of GDP for the year 2012. The graph in the figure highlights that consumption is by far the largest component of GDP. The table provides a more detailed breakdown and shows several interesting points.

Components of GDP (millions of dollars)		
Consumption		$986 268
Durable goods	$119 260	
Semi-durable goods	70 978	
Non-durable goods	250 666	
Services	545 364	
Investment		360 167
Business fixed investment	196 170	
Residential structures	126 008	
Business inventories	7 903	
Government Purchases		469 373
Government spending on goods and services	394 667	
Government investment	74 706	
Net Exports		−36 444
Exports	545 827	
Imports	582 271	
Total GDP		$1 817 604

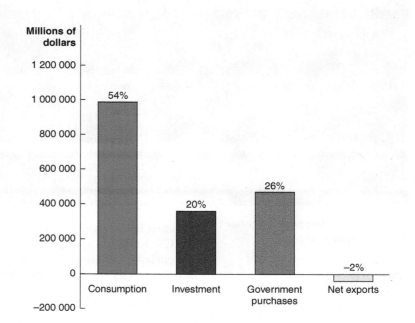

Figure 4.2 Components of GDP in 2012

Consumption accounts for 54 percent of GDP, far more than any of the other components. In recent years, net exports typically have been negative, which reduces GDP. Note that the subtotals may not sum to the totals for each category because of rounding.

Source: CANSIM Table 380-0002. Series v498918, v498919, v498924, v498925, v498926, v498927, v498932, v498935, v498938. Reproduced and distributed on an "as is" basis with the permission of Statistics Canada.

Note: Adjusting entries ignored for simplicity.

- Consumer spending on services is greater than the sum of all other types of consumer spending. This greater spending on services reflects the continuing trend in Canada and other high-income countries away from the production of goods and toward the production of services. As the populations of these countries have become, in general, both older and wealthier, their demand for services such as financial advice has increased faster than their demand for goods.

- Business fixed investment is the largest component of investment. As we will see in later chapters, spending by firms on new factories, computers, and machinery can fluctuate.

- Purchases made by government accounts for just over one-quarter of every dollar spent in Canada. The majority of government spending is classified as spending on goods and services rather than investment.

- In 2012, imports were larger than exports, so net exports were negative. We discuss in Chapter 14 why imports are larger than exports in Canada.

Making
the
Connection

Do Canadians Spend Too Much?

We saw in Figure 4.2 that in 2012, consumption was 54 percent of GDP in Canada. In comparison, as the figure below shows, American consumption accounts for a much greater share of GDP—over 70 percent! The role that consumption plays in the American economy is larger than that of any other country in the Organisation for Economic Cooperation and Development (OECD). Comparing the role of consumption in the American economy to its role in other developed economies can be somewhat misleading. The United States is the only developed economy in which citizens have to pay for most of their health care directly. This means that some of the spending that is categorized as "consumption" in the United States is categorized as "government spending" in countries such as Canada. A comparison of Canadian consumption spending to UK consumption

Consumer spending plays a key role in the Canadian economy.

spending is somewhat more telling, as both have socialized health care systems.

Consumption spending in the United Kingdom accounts for almost two-thirds (66 percent) of GDP even though that country's health care system is similar to Canada's. In fact, as you can see in the graph below, the role that consumption plays in the Canadian economy, while below average (63 percent), is far from the highest or lowest in the group.

Does this mean that Canadians should not be concerned about the role consumption spending plays in the economy? Not necessarily. Demographics are going to play a role in the sustainability of the Canadian economy. For this level of consumption spending to be sustainable, older Canadians have to have sufficient savings to see them through their retirement years. This isn't generally the case. As a result, it seems likely that Canadians will have to spend less in the future, causing consumer spending to account for less of Canadian GDP. The same applies to virtually all developed countries, particularly the United States.

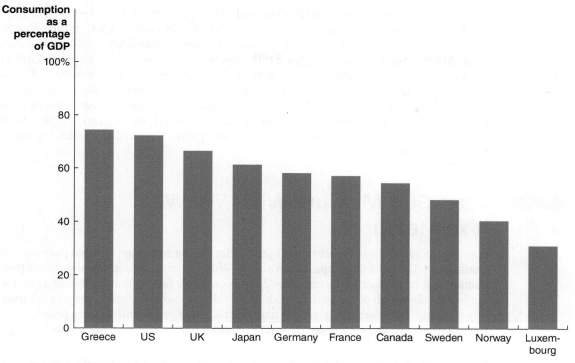

Source: Data from OECD National Accounts at a Glance, http://stats.oecd.org/Index.aspx?DataSetCode=NAAG_2011

Your Turn: Test your understanding by doing related problem 1.7 on page 117 at the end of this chapter.   MyEconLab

Measuring GDP Using the Value-Added Method

We have seen that GDP can be calculated by adding together all expenditures on final goods and services. An alternative way of calculating GDP is the *value-added method.* **Value added** refers to the additional market value a firm gives a product and is equal to the difference between the price the firm paid for intermediate goods and the price for which it sells the finished product. Table 4.1 gives a hypothetical example of the value added by each firm involved in the production of a diamond ring—from the diamond's extraction from a diamond mine in the Northwest Territories to the ring's sale at a local jewellery store.

Suppose Diavik Diamond Mine sells a diamond it has just extracted to a gem cutter for $500. If, for simplicity, we ignore any inputs the mining company purchased from other firms—such as drilling equipment, trucks, and so on—then the mining company's value added is $500. The gem cutter then cuts the diamond into the familiar diamond shape and sells the stone to a jewellery designer for $700; the gem cutter has added $200 in value to the stone. The jewellery designer then designs and makes

Value added The market value a firm adds to a product.

Firm	Value of Product	Value Added	
Diavik Diamond Mine	Value of raw diamond = $500	Value added by diamond miner	= $500
Gem cutter	Value of cut diamond = $700	Value added by diamond cutter = ($700 − $500)	= $200
Jewellery designer	Value of set diamond = $1000	Value added by jewellery designer = ($1000 − $700)	= $300
Jewellery store	Value of diamond ring = $1500	Value added by jewellery store = ($1500 − $1000)	= $500
	Total Value Added		= $1500

Table 4.1

Calculating Value Added

a ring for the diamond and sets the diamond in the ring. This ring is then sold to your local jewellery store for $1000. The jewellery designer has added $300 in the value to the ring. The jewellery store cleans and displays the ring and helps you pick it out. In selling you the diamond ring for $1500, the jewellery store added another $500 to the value of the ring. Notice that *the price of the diamond ring at the jewellery store is exactly equal to the sum of the value added by each firm involved in the production of the ring.* Similarly, we can calculate GDP by adding up the market value of every final good and service produced during a particular period. Or, we can arrive at the same value for GDP by adding the value added of every firm involved in producing those final goods and services.

4.2 LEARNING OBJECTIVE

Discuss whether GDP is a good measure of well-being.

Does GDP Measure What We Want It to Measure?

Economists use GDP to measure total production in the economy. For that purpose, we would like GDP to be as comprehensive as possible, not overlooking any significant production that takes place in the economy. Most economists believe that GDP does a good—but not flawless—job of measuring production. GDP is also sometimes used as a measure of well-being. Although it is generally true that the more goods and services people have, the better off they are, we will see that GDP provides only a rough measure of well-being.

Shortcomings of GDP as a Measure of Total Production

When Statistics Canada calculates GDP, it does not include two types of production: production in the home and production in the underground economy.

Household production Goods and services people produce for themselves.

Household Production With very few exceptions, Statistics Canada does not attempt to estimate the value of goods and services that are not bought and sold in markets. If a carpenter makes and sells bookcases, the value of those bookcases will be counted in GDP. If you make the bookcases yourself, this is **household production**. *Household production* refers to goods and services people produce for themselves. The most important type of household production is the services a homemaker provides to the family. If a person has been looking after children, cleaning, and preparing family meals, the value of these services is not included in GDP. If the person decides to work outside the home, enrols the children in daycare, hires a cleaning service, and chooses to have the family eat all their meals at restaurants, the value of all these services will be included in GDP, even though the production of these services has not really changed.

Underground economy Buying and selling of goods and services that is concealed from the government to avoid taxes or regulations or because the goods and services are illegal.

The Underground Economy Individuals and firms sometimes conceal the buying and selling of goods and services, in which case their production isn't counted in GDP. Individuals and firms hide these transactions for three basic reasons: They are dealing in illegal goods and services—such as drugs or prostitution; they want to avoid paying taxes on the income they earn; or they want to avoid government regulation. These concealed transactions are referred to as the **underground economy**. Estimates of the size of the underground economy are very difficult to make because the people involved want to avoid detection. An estimate by Statistics Canada puts the size of the underground economy at $36 billion dollars, or about 2.2 percent of GDP. This is relatively small compared to other countries. Estimates of the American underground economy vary a great deal, but it is likely no more than 10 percent of GDP ($1.4 trillion). The underground economy in some low-income countries, such as Zimbabwe or Peru, may be as much as half of measured GDP.[1]

---

[1]Grant, Tavia. "Canada's underground economy tops $30-billion," The Globe and Mail, June 28, 2011.

Is not counting household production or production in the underground economy a serious shortcoming of GDP? Most economists would say "no" because the most important use of GDP is to measure changes in how the economy is performing over short periods of time, such as from one year to the next. For this purpose, omitting household production or production in the underground economy won't have much effect, as these forms of production are unlikely to change quickly.

We also use GDP statistics to measure how production of goods and services grows over fairly long periods of a decade or more. For this purpose, omitting household production and production in the underground economy may be more important. For example, in the 1960s, the proportion of women working outside the home was much smaller, so the production of most women was not included in GDP. Since the 1960s the proportion of women working outside the home has increased dramatically and the products of their labour is now included in GDP.

Shortcomings of GDP as a Measure of Well-Being

The main purpose of GDP is to measure a country's total production. GDP is also used by some people as a measure of well-being. For example, news articles often include tables that show the levels of *real* GDP per person in different countries. Real GDP per capita is calculated by dividing the value of real GDP in a country by that country's population. (We'll discuss how real GDP is calculated in the next section.) These articles imply that people in countries with higher levels of real GDP per capita are better off. Although increases in GDP often do lead to increases in the well-being of the population, it is important to be aware that GDP is not a perfect measure of well-being for several reasons.

The Value of Leisure Is Not Included in GDP If an economics professor decides to retire, GDP will decline even though the professor may value increased leisure more than the income earned teaching undergrad economics courses. The professor's well-being has increased, but GDP has decreased. In the 1800s it was not uncommon for someone to work 60 hours a week. Today, most Canadians work less than 40 hours per week. If Canadians still worked 60 hours per week, GDP would be much higher, but it isn't hard to imagine that well-being would be much lower as we would have less time for leisure activities.

GDP Does Not Consider the State of the Environment When you get your clothes cleaned at a dry cleaner, the value of that service is included in GDP. If the chemicals used to clean your shirt pollute the air or water, GDP is not adjusted to compensate for the costs of the pollution. Similarly, the value of cigarettes produced is included in GDP, but the cost of lung cancer that some smokers develop is not included in GDP.

We should note, however, that increasing GDP often leads countries to devote more resources to protecting the environment. Canada, the United States, and European countries have tougher emissions standards than many developing countries. Environmental regulation is expensive to enforce, and developing countries may be reluctant to spend scarce resources on pollution reduction rather than health care or education. China is an excellent example of this; levels of pollution in China are much higher than in Western countries. According to the World Health Organization, 7 of the 10 most polluted cities in the world are in China, but as Chinese GDP continues to rise, the Chinese government is likely to devote more resources to protecting and cleaning up the environment.

GDP Is Not Adjusted for Changes in Crime and Other Social Problems An increase in crime reduces well-being but may actually increase GDP if it leads to greater spending on police, security guards, and alarm systems. GDP is also not adjusted for changes in divorce rates, drug addiction, or other factors that may affect people's well-being.

GDP Measures the Size of the Pie but Not How the Pie Is Divided When a country's GDP increases, the country has more goods and services, but those goods and services may be very unequally distributed. Therefore, GDP per person may not provide a good description of what the typical person consumes.

To summarize, we can say that a person's well-being depends on many factors that are not considered when calculating GDP. We have to remember that GDP is designed to measure the size of the economy (total production), and it should not be a surprise that GDP is an imperfect measure of well-being.

Making the Connection | GDP and Happiness

As we have seen, GDP has limitations as a measure of the well-being of the people who live in a country. Although GDP was not designed to measure the well-being of a country's people, it isn't uncommon for people to compare countries based on GDP and conclude that people in one country are better off than those in another because their GDP is higher. It turns out that this approach isn't entirely unreasonable.

The OECD (an international organization that conducts research on a variety of issues related to economic performance, education, well-being, and other issues) has developed a way of measuring well-being that does not simply compare GDP per person. The OECD Better Life Index takes into consideration the categories of housing, income, jobs, community, education, environment, governance, health, life satisfaction, safety, and work-life balance.

When you give equal weight to all of the different categories (you can explore the index and change the weights given to each category by going to **www.oecdbetterlifeindex.org**), a very clear relationship emerges between GDP per person and well-being. Countries with relatively low GDP per person such as Mexico and Chile also have low Better Life Index scores. Countries such as Canada, Australia, and the United States have high Better Life Index scores. You can see this relationship in the graph below.

Well-being and wealth
OECD Better Life Index (10 = best) and GDP per person, 2009*

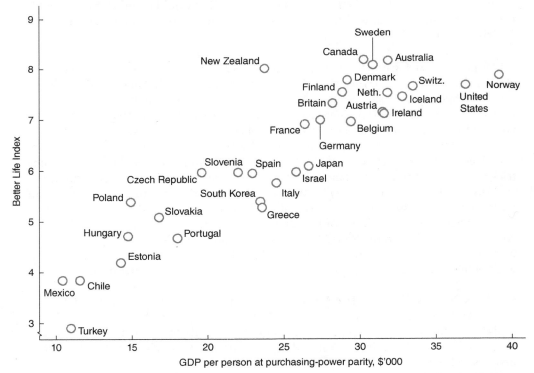

*or latest available year

Source: Data from, Well-being and wealth: OECD Better Life index (10=best) and GDP per person, 2009, The Organisation for Economic Cooperation and Development.

Why might a country like New Zealand score so much higher on the Better Life Index than its GDP would suggest? A lot of factors can influence how content people are. One of these factors is climate. New Zealand has a comfortable climate (compared with Canada, Sweden, and Australia), great scenery, and, unlike other countries in the region, not much of the wildlife is likely to kill you. New Zealanders may also have more trust in one another and their government.

So while GDP per person isn't a perfect measure of well-being, it actually performs pretty well.

Source: Economist, "The Pursuit of Happiness," May 24, 2011, http://www.economist.com/blogs/dailychart/2011/05/well-being_and_wealth.

Your Turn: Test your understanding by doing related problem 2.3 on page 117 at the end of this chapter.

MyEconLab

Real GDP versus Nominal GDP

GDP is measured in value terms, so we have to be careful about interpreting changes over time. To see why, consider interpreting an increase in the total value of pickup truck production from $40 billion in 2013 to $44 billion in 2014. Can we be sure that because $44 billion is 10 percent more than $40 billion, the number of trucks produced in 2014 is also 10 percent more than in 2013? We can draw this conclusion only if the average price of a truck hasn't changed between 2013 and 2014. In fact, when GDP increases from one year to the next, the increase is due in part to increases in production of goods and services and partly due to increases in prices. Given that we're mainly interested in GDP as a measure of production, we need a way of separating the price changes from the quantity changes.

Calculating Real GDP

We can separate the price changes from the quantity changes by calculating a measure of production called *real GDP*. **Nominal GDP** is calculated by summing the *current* values of final goods and services. **Real GDP** is calculated by designating a particular year as the *base year* and then using the prices of goods and services in the base year to calculate the value of goods and services in all other years. For instance, if the base year is 2007, real GDP for 2013 would be calculated by using the price of goods and services from 2007. By always using the same prices, we know that changes in real GDP represent changes in the quantity of goods and not changes in prices.

Nominal GDP The value of final goods and services evaluated at current-year prices.

Real GDP The value of final goods and services evaluated at base-year prices.

One drawback of calculating real GDP using base-year prices is that, over time, prices may change relative to each other. For example the price of cellphones has fallen dramatically over the last 10 years relative to the price of pizzas. Because this change is not reflected in base-year prices, real GDP is somewhat distorted. The further away from the base year we are, the bigger this problem becomes. To address this problem, Statistics Canada began to use *chain-weighted prices*, and it now publishes real GDP statistics in both 2007 base-year prices and as "chained (2007) dollars."

The details of calculating real GDP using chain-weighted prices are more complicated than we need to discuss here, but the basic idea is straightforward. Starting with the base year, take the average of prices in that year and prices in the following year. Then use this average to calculate real GDP in the year after the base year (2008 if the base year is 2007). For the next year—two years after the base year (2009)—calculate real GDP by taking an average of prices in that year and the previous year. In this way, prices in each year are "chained" to prices from the previous year, and the distortion from changes in relative prices is minimized. Essentially, chain-weighting involves using an average price for goods rather than just the base year price.

Holding prices constant means that the *purchasing power* of a dollar remains the same from one year to the next. Ordinarily, the purchasing power of a dollar falls over the years, as price increases reduce the amount of goods and services that a dollar can buy.

Solved Problem **4.2**

Calculating Real GDP

Suppose that a very simple economy only produces the following three final goods and services: energy drinks, pizzas, and textbooks. Use the information in the table below to compute real GDP for the year 2014. Assume that the base year is 2007.

Product	2007 Quantity	2007 Price	2014 Quantity	2014 Price
Energy drinks	80	$ 40	100	$ 50
Pizza	90	11	80	10
Textbooks	15	90	20	100

Solving the Problem

Step 1: Review the chapter material. This problem is about calculating real GDP, so you may want to review the section "Calculating Real GDP."

Step 2: Calculate the value of the three goods and services listed in the table, using the quantities for 2014 and the prices for 2007. The definition above tells us that real GDP is the value of all final goods and services, evaluated at base-year prices. In this case, the base year is 2007, and we are given information on the price of each product in that year:

Product	2014 Quantity	2007 Price	Value
Energy drinks	100	$40	$4000
Pizzas	80	11	880
Textbooks	20	90	1800

Step 3: Add up the values for the three products to find real GDP. Real GDP for 2014 equals the sum of:

Quantity of energy drinks in 2014 × Price of energy drinks in 2007 = $4000 +
Quantity of pizzas in 2014 × Price of pizzas in 2007 = $880 +
Quantity of textbooks in 2014 × Price of textbooks in 2007 = $1800
For a real GDP of $6680.

Extra credit: Notice that the quantities of each good produced in 2007 were irrelevant for calculating real GDP in 2014. Notice also that the value of $6680 for real GDP in 2014 is lower than the value of nominal GDP, $7800, which we calculated in *Solved Problem 4.1* on page 97.

MyEconLab **Your Turn:** For more practice, do related problem 3.1 on page 118 at the end of this chapter.

Comparing Real GDP and Nominal GDP

Real GDP holds prices constant, which makes it a better measure than nominal GDP of changes in the production of goods and services from one year to the next. In fact, growth in the economy is almost always measured as growth in real GDP. If a headline in the *Globe and Mail* states "Canadian Economy Grew at 2.4% Last Year," the article will report that real GDP grew at 2.4 percent during the previous year.

We describe real GDP as being measured in "base-year dollars." For example, with a base year of 2007, nominal GDP in 2012 was $1817.6 billion and real GDP for 2012 was $1658.2 billion in 2007 dollars. Real GDP is smaller than nominal GDP in years after the base year because prices tend to rise over time. In the base year, nominal GDP and real GDP are the same because both are calculated using the same set of prices. In

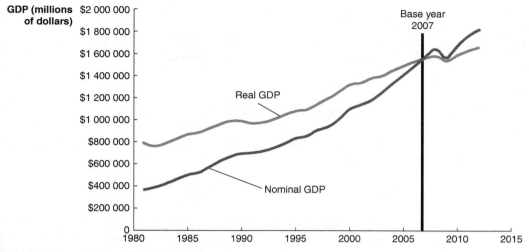

Figure 4.3 Nominal GDP and Real GDP, 1981–2012

Currently, the base year for calculating GDP is 2007. In the years before 2007, prices were, on average, lower than in 2007, so nominal GDP was lower than real GDP. In 2007, nominal and real GDP were equal. Since 2007, prices have been, on average, higher than in 2007, so nominal GDP is higher than real GDP.

Source: CANSIM Table 380-0002, Series v498918 and v41707125. Reproduced and distributed on an "as is" basis with the permission of Statistics Canada.

years before the base year, real GDP will be larger than nominal GDP because prices in years prior to the base year are lower. Figure 4.3 shows movements in real and nominal GDP over time using 2007 as the base year. As you can see, before 2007, nominal GDP is lower than real GDP. In 2007 they are the same, and after 2007 nominal GDP is larger than real GDP.

The GDP Deflator

Economists and policymakers are not just interested in the level of total production, as measured by real GDP, but also in the *price level*. The **price level** measures the average prices of goods and services in the economy. One of the goals of economic policy is a stable price level. We can use values for nominal GDP and real GDP to compute a measure of the price level called the *GDP deflator*. We calculate the **GDP deflator** by using this formula:

$$\text{GDP Deflator} = \frac{\text{Nominal GDP}}{\text{Real GDP}} \times 100.$$

> **Price level** A measure of the average prices of goods and services in the economy.
>
> **GDP deflator** A measure of the price level, calculated by dividing nominal GDP by real GDP and multiplying by 100.

To see why the GDP deflator is a measure of the price level, think about what would happen if prices of goods and services rose while production remained the same. In that case, nominal GDP would increase, but real GDP would remain constant, so the GDP deflator would increase. In reality, both prices and production increase in most years, but the more prices increase relative to the increase in production, the more nominal GDP increases relative to real GDP, and the higher the value for the GDP deflator. Increases in the GDP deflator allow economists and policymakers to track increases in the price level over time.

Remember that in the base year (currently 2007), nominal GDP and real GDP are the same number. This also means that the GDP deflator will always be 100 in the base year. The following table gives the values of nominal and real GDP in 2011 and 2012.

	2011	2012
Nominal GDP	$1762.4 billion	$1817.6 billion
Real GDP	$1628.3 billion	$1658.2 billion

We can use this information to calculate the value for the GDP deflator for 2011 and 2012.

For 2011, we get:

$$\text{GDP Deflator} = \frac{\text{Nominal GDP}}{\text{Real GDP}} \times 100 = \frac{\$1762.4}{\$1628.3} \times 100 = 108.2.$$

For 2012, we get:

$$\text{GDP Deflator} = \frac{\text{Nominal GDP}}{\text{Real GDP}} \times 100 = \frac{\$1817.6}{\$1658.2} \times 100 = 109.6.$$

From these values for the GDP deflator, we can calculate that the price level rose by 1.29 percent between 2011 and 2012:

$$\frac{109.6 - 108.2}{108.2} \times 100 = 1.29\%.$$

In Chapter 5, we will see that economists and policymakers also rely on another measure of the price level, known as the *consumer price index*. In addition, we will discuss the strengths and weaknesses of different measures of the price level.

4.4 LEARNING OBJECTIVE

Become familiar with other measures of total production and total income.

Other Measures of Total Production and Total Income

National income accounting refers to the methods government agencies use to track total production and total income in the economy. In Canada, the statistical tables containing this information are called the National Economic Accounts. Every quarter, Statistics Canada releases the National Economic Accounts containing data on several measures of total production and total income. We have already discussed the most commonly used measure of total production and total income: gross domestic product (GDP). In addition to GDP, Statistics Canada also calculates the following four measures of production and income: gross national product, national income, household income, and personal household income.

Gross National Product (GNP)

We have seen that GDP is the value of final goods and services produced within Canada's borders. *Gross national product (GNP)* is the value of final goods and services produced by the labour and resources of Canadians, even if the production takes place outside of Canada. Canadian firms have facilities in other countries, and foreign firms have facilities in Canada. Many Canadian mining companies operate mines in South America, Africa, and elsewhere. Foreign companies also operate mines in Canada. GDP excludes foreign production by Canadian firms, but includes Canadian production by foreign firms. For Canada, GNP is very similar to GDP. For example, in 2012 GDP at market prices was $1817.6 billion and GNP at market prices was $1784.8 billion, a difference of only 1.8 percent.

For many years, GNP was the main measure of total production used by different countries and economists around the world. However, in many countries, a significant share of domestic production takes place in foreign-owned facilities. For those countries, GDP is much larger than GNP and is a more accurate measure of the level of production taking place within the country's borders. As a result, many countries and international agencies now prefer using GDP to using GNP.

National Income

In producing goods and services, some machinery, equipment, and buildings wear out and have to be replaced. The value of this worn-out machinery, equipment, and buildings is *depreciation*. In the National Economic Account tables, depreciation is often referred to as the *consumption of fixed capital*. If we subtract this value from GDP we are left with *national income*.

Measure	Billions of dollars
GDP	$1818
GNP	1785
National income (net)	1489
Household income	1177
Household disposable income	1028

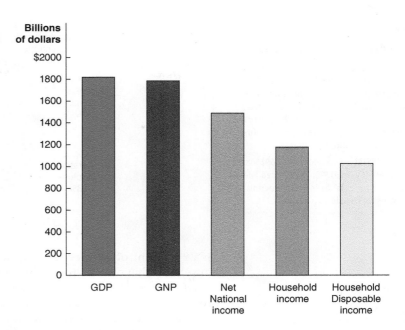

Figure 4.4 **Measures of Total Production and Total Income, 2013**

The most important measure of total production and total income is gross domestic product (GDP). As we will see in later chapters, for some purposes, the other measures of total production and total income shown in the figure turn out to be more useful than GDP.

Sources: CANSIM Table 380-0015 (Series v1992225, v499722, v499724) and Cansim Table 384-0012 (Series v691566 and v691567). Reproduced and distributed on an "as is" basis with the permission of Statistics Canada.

Previously in this chapter, we stressed that the value of total production is equal to the value of total income. This point is not strictly true if by "value of total production" we mean GDP and by "value of total income" we mean national income because national income will always be smaller than GDP by an amount equal to depreciation. In practice, though, the difference between the value of GDP and national income doesn't change the predictions made in macroeconomic models.

Household Income

Household income is income received by households. To calculate household income, we subtract the earnings that corporations retain rather than pay to shareholders in the form of dividends. We also add in the payments received by households from the government in the form of *transfer payments* or interest on government bonds.

Household Disposable Income

Household disposable income is equal to household income minus personal tax payments, such as federal income tax. It is the best measure of the income households actually have to spend.

Figure 4.4 shows the values of these measures for 2012 in a table and a graph.

The Division of Income

Figure 4.1 illustrates the important fact that we can measure GDP in terms of total expenditure or as the total income received by households. GDP calculated as the sum of income payments to households is sometimes referred to as *gross domestic income.* Figure 4.5 shows the division of total income among labour income, corporate operating surplus, small business income, and taxes on production and imports (but not income taxes). Labour income is the payments that households receive from supplying labour to firms (that they don't own) and government. This accounts for 50 percent of all income received in Canada. Corporate operating surplus accounts

Figure 4.5

The Division of Income, 2012

We can measure GDP in terms of total expenditure or as the total income received by households. The largest component of income received by households is labour income, which is more than the profits received by sole proprietors and the profits received by corporations combined.

Source: CANSIM Series v691567, v691568, v691570, v691571, v691572. Reproduced and distributed on an "as is" basis with the permission of Statistics Canada.

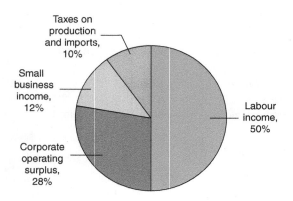

for 28 percent of all income in Canada, and includes the profits that get paid to households that own shares in these corporations. Small business income, also called *mixed income*, makes up 12 percent of income. This category covers the wages and profits earned by owners of unincorporated businesses. Finally, taxes on production and imports account for 10 percent of GDP. These taxes are included in the calculation because they are included in the market price of the goods and services that Canadians buy.

Economics in Your Life

What's the Best Country for You to Work In?

At the beginning of the chapter we posed two questions: What effects should the United Kingdom's and China's two very different GDP growth rates have on your decision to live and work in one country or the other? And if China's much higher growth rate does not necessarily lead you to decide to live and work in China, why not? This chapter has shown that although it is generally true that the more goods and services people have, the better off they are, GDP provides only a rough measure of well-being. GDP does not include the value of leisure; nor is it adjusted for pollution and other negative effects of production, crime, or any other social problems. So, in deciding where to live and work, you would need to balance China's much higher growth rate of GDP against these other considerations. You would also need to take into account that although China's *growth rate* is higher than the United Kingdom's, the United Kingdom's current *level* of real GDP per person is much higher than China's.

Source: OECD Factbook.

Conclusion

In this chapter, we have begun the study of macroeconomics by examining an important concept: how a nation's total production and income can be measured. Understanding GDP is important for understanding the business cycle and the process of long-run economic growth. In Chapter 5, we discuss the issues involved in measuring two other key economic variables: the unemployment rate and the inflation rate.

Read *An Inside Look* on the next page for a discussion of the effects of falling exports on the Canadian economy.

A Slowdown in the Export of Goods and Services Shrinks the Canadian Economy in 2011

TORONTO STAR

Canada's Economy Shrinks for First Time in Two Years

The Canadian economy shifted into reverse gear in the second quarter, as falling exports dragged down consumer, business, and government spending.

The negative growth in the April to June period is the first time the economy has shrunk in two years. Combined with recent stock market turmoil, stalling economic growth in the U.S., and continuing debt worries in Europe, it raises the spectre of the country sliding back into recession.

But federal Finance Minister Jim Flaherty, along with economists, say unless consumer spending or the housing market drop off sharply in coming months, a return to recession is unlikely.

Flaherty said that he expects modest growth in the second half of this year.

A recession is typically defined as two consecutive quarters of economic decline.

"The good news in (the) data release is that our domestic economy remains strong, with consumption, and particularly business investment, continuing to expand," Flaherty said Wednesday.

He made the comments while touring a 14,000-square-foot expansion of the Ryerson University School of Image Arts, paid for by the federal and provincial governments.

Canada's gross domestic product, or GDP, contracted at an annualized rate of 0.4 per cent for the three months ended June 30, according to Statistics Canada.

"It wasn't a huge surprise. We were expecting that the Canadian economy did stall in the second quarter with a high risk of a contraction," said Diana Petramala, an economist with TD Economics.

While the higher Canadian dollar has contributed to slower exports, the second quarter's decline was mostly a result of temporary factors, economists say.

Exports of goods and services fell 2.1 per cent, the first decline since the third quarter of 2010. Within that category, energy exports fell 6.7 per cent due to wildfires in Alberta and maintenance shutdowns at oil refineries. Auto production was also down as a result of continuing supply problems resulting from the March earthquake and tsunami in Japan.

"If you take away those factors, growth was probably marginally positive," Petramala said.

Still domestic demand was higher. Business investment in machinery and equipment grew by 7 percent in the second quarter. Investment in computers and other office equipment registered double-digit growth, up 13 percent in the period, StatsCan said.

Consumer spending on goods and services was up 0.4 per cent for the quarter.

Government spending was also up 0.4 per cent.

TD does not expect the economy to shrink again in the third quarter. "That being said, we're not expecting a robust rebound. U.S. economic growth is chugging along at a modest pace and global growth has slowed substantially, and that will weigh on Canadian exports," Petramala said.

In June, the GDP rose 0.2 per cent, slightly above expectations.

The "firmer monthly figure provides a better starting point" for the third quarter, Sherry Cooper, chief economist for BMO Financial Group, wrote in a research note.

"As many of the factors holding back Q2 have dissipated, we should see a return to growth in the second half of the year. Even so, we're only expecting a mediocre 2 per cent annualized pace, which should keep the Bank of Canada pinned to the sidelines into 2012."

StatsCan also lowered its take on the first quarter to an annual growth rate of 3.6 per cent, down from the 3.9 per cent initially reported.

The small revisions didn't bother economists, who point out that Canada's growth rate for the period was still twice that of the U.S.

"We still think that going into next quarter consumer spending and business investment will keep up the momentum. Residential construction may come down a little bit, but it will be a soft landing, rather than anything dramatic," said Leslie Levesque, senior economist with IHS Global Insight.

Key Points in the Article

Exports make up a key component of Canadian GDP even though net exports are a relatively small share of GDP. Canadians sell a great deal of goods and services to other countries, but they also buy many goods and services from other countries. When demand for Canadian-produced products falls in other parts of the world, firms tend to cut back their production. When the production of goods and services for export falls, GDP falls too. The drop in exports may cause the total amount of goods and services produced in Canada to shrink.

Analyzing the News

(a) Statistics Canada (StatsCan) releases GDP data in three-month blocks, called *quarters*. Although it isn't an official definition, many economists consider a *recession* to be two consecutive quarters (six months) in which GDP falls. Economists and government analysts track this data carefully, and many even forecast how GDP will change. This drop in Canada's total production was not unexpected by most analysts.

(b) The value of the Canadian dollar, relative to the US dollar, has an important effect on Canadian exports. When the Canadian dollar increases in value, it makes the goods and services produced in Canada more expensive to foreigners. As we saw in Chapter 3, when something costs more, people tend to buy less of it.

Canadian exports also depend on what is happening in other economies, particularly the US economy. The American economy did not have a particularly good second quarter of 2011. Natural disasters in other parts of the world can also have a dramatic impact on the Canadian economy. Many of the automotive plants in Canada buy parts from Japanese manufacturers as well as Canadian producers. The 2011 earthquake and tsunami in Japan meant that many of these parts makers were shut down and not able to provide Canadian assembly plants with key parts. As a result, many of these plants reduced production, causing GDP to fall.

(c) Even though exports play a key role in the Canadian economy, they are not the only important element in determining total production. Investment in capital (new machines, buildings, and other equipment) is also very important. In the second quarter of 2011, the purchasing of new capital by firms grew by 7 percent. This investment helps offset the fall in exports.

Consumption and government spending are important as well. While exports were falling, consumer spending and government spending both rose. Consumption spending and government spending don't always follow the same pattern as exports.

A change in Canada's total production depends on all the different categories of spending discussed in this chapter. We must be aware of what is happening to consumer spending, investment by firms, government spending, *and* net exports to understand what is happening to GDP and to predict how GDP might change in the future.

Thinking Critically

1. Canadian exports depend a lot on what is happening in the United States, but the article points out that the Canadian economy is doing much better than the US economy. Why do you think this might be the case?

2. Over the past 20 years, the prices of many of the goods Canada exports (wheat, oil, potash, etc.) have risen. Over the same period, the prices of many of the goods Canada imports (clothing, consumer electronics, etc.) have stayed the same or fallen. What impact do you think this change in relative prices has likely had on real GDP?

Chapter Summary and Problems

Key Terms

Business cycle, p. 96

Consumption, p. 100

Economic growth, p. 96

Expansion, p. 96

Exports, p. 101

Final good or service, p. 97

GDP deflator, p. 109

Government purchases, p. 101

Gross domestic product (GDP), p. 96

Household production, p. 104

Imports, p. 101

Inflation rate, p. 96

Intermediate good or service, p. 97

Investment, p. 100

Macroeconomics, p. 96

Microeconomics, p. 96

Net exports, p. 101

Nominal GDP, p. 107

Price level, p. 109

Real GDP, p. 107

Recession, p. 96

Transfer payments, p. 99

Underground economy, p. 104

Value added, p. 103

Summary

*LO 4.1 Economics is divided into the subfields of *microeconomics*—which studies how households and firms make choices—and *macroeconomics*—which studies the economy as a whole. An important macroeconomic issue is the *business cycle*, which refers to alternating periods of economic expansion and economic recession. An *expansion* is a period during which production and employment are increasing. A *recession* is a period during which production and employment are decreasing. Another important macroeconomic topic is *economic growth*, which refers to the ability of the economy to produce increasing quantities of goods and services. Macroeconomics also studies the *inflation rate*, or the percentage increase in the price level from one year to the next. Economists measure total production by *gross domestic product (GDP)*, which is the value of all final goods and services produced in an economy during a period of time. A *final good or service* is purchased by a final user. An *intermediate good or service* is an input into another good or service and is not included in GDP. When we measure the value of total production in the economy by calculating GDP, we are simultaneously measuring the value of total income. GDP is divided into four major categories of expenditures: consumption, investment, government purchases, and net exports. Government transfer payments are not included in GDP because they are payments to individuals for which the government does not receive a good or service in return. We can also calculate GDP by adding up the value added of every firm involved in producing final goods and services.

LO 4.2 GDP does not include household production, which refers to goods and services people produce for themselves, nor does it include production in the *underground economy*, which consists of concealed buying and selling. The underground economy in some developing countries may be more than half of measured GDP. GDP is not a perfect measure of well-being because it does not include the value of leisure, it is not adjusted for pollution or other negative effects of production, and it is not adjusted for changes in crime and other social problems.

LO 4.3 *Nominal GDP* is the value of final goods and services evaluated at current-year prices. *Real GDP* is the value of final goods and services evaluated at *base-year* prices. By keeping prices constant, we know that changes in real GDP represent changes in the quantity of goods and services produced in the economy. When the *price level*, the average prices of goods and services in the economy, is increasing, real GDP is greater than nominal GDP in years before the base year and less than nominal GDP for years after the base year. The *GDP deflator* is a measure of the price level and is calculated by dividing nominal GDP by real GDP and multiplying by 100.

LO 4.4 The most important measure of total production and total income is gross domestic product (GDP). As we will see in later chapters, for some purposes, the other measures of total production and total income shown in Figure 4.4 are actually more useful than GDP. These measures are gross national product (GNP), national income, household income, and household disposable income.

MyEconLab   Log in to MyEconLab to complete these exercises and get instant feedback.

---

*'Learning Objective' is abbreviated to 'LO' in the end of chapter material.

Review Questions

LO 4.1

1.1 Why in microeconomics do we measure production in terms of quantity, but in macroeconomics we measure production in terms of market value?

1.2 If Statistics Canada added up the values of every good and service sold during the year, would the total be larger or smaller than GDP?

1.3 In the circular flow of income, why must the value of total production in an economy equal the value of total income?

1.4 Describe the four major categories of expenditures in GDP and write the equation used to represent the relationship between GDP and the four expenditure categories.

LO 4.2

2.1 Why does the size of a country's GDP matter? How does it affect the quality of life of the country's people?

2.2 Why is GDP an imperfect measure of economic well-being? What types of production does GDP not measure? Even if GDP included these types of production, why would it still be an imperfect measure of economic well-being?

LO 4.3

3.1 Why does inflation make nominal GDP a poor measure of the increase in total production from one year to the next? How does Statistics Canada deal with the problem inflation causes with nominal GDP?

3.2 What is the GDP deflator, and how is it calculated?

LO 4.4

4.1 What is the difference between GDP and GNP? Briefly explain whether the difference is important for Canada.

4.2 What are the differences between national income, household income, and household disposable income?

Problems and Applications

LO 4.1

1.1 A student remarks: "It doesn't make sense that intermediate goods are not counted in GDP. A computer chip is an intermediate good, and without it a PC won't work. So why don't we count the computer chip in GDP?" Provide an answer for the student's question.

1.2 Briefly explain whether each of the following transactions represents the purchase of a final good.
   a. The purchase of wheat from a wheat farmer by a bakery
   b. The purchase of a frigate by the federal government
   c. The purchase of a French wine by a Canadian consumer
   d. The purchase of a new airliner by WestJet

1.3 [**Related to the** Chapter Opener **on page 95**] Which component of GDP will be affected by each of the following transactions involving Ford Motor Company? If you believe that none of the components of GDP will be affected by the transactions, briefly explain why.
   a. You purchase a new Ford Edge (built in Oakville, Ontario) from a Ford dealer.
   b. You purchase a 2010 Ford Edge from a friend.
   c. Ford purchases seats for the Ford Edge from Magna International, located in Aurora, Ontario.
   d. Ford purchases new machine tools to use in its Oakville plant.

1.4 Is the value of a house built in 2000 and resold in 2013 included in the GDP of 2013? Briefly explain. Would the services of the real estate agent who helped sell (or buy) the house in 2013 be counted in GDP for 2013? Briefly explain.

1.5 [**Related to** Solved Problem 4.1 **on page 98**] Suppose that a simple economy produces only four goods: textbooks, hamburgers, shirts, and cotton. Assume that all the cotton is used in the production of shirts. Use the information in the following table to calculate nominal GDP for 2014:

Production and Price Statistics for 2014		
Product	Quantity	Price
Textbooks	100	$60.00
Hamburgers	100	2.00
Shirts	50	25.00
Cotton	80	0.60

1.6 [**Related to** Don't Let This Happen to You **on page 100**] Briefly explain whether you agree with the following statement: "In years when people buy many shares of stock, investment will be high and, therefore, so will GDP."

1.7 [**Related to** Making the Connection **on page 102**] In 2012, Mark Carney, then governor of the Bank of Canada, expressed serious concern about the household debt of Canadians. In fact, in a *Financial Post* article he identified increasing household debt as the biggest domestic risk to the Canadian economy. The fear is that Canadians will have to cut debt and build up savings in the near future. Why does cutting debt and increasing personal savings affect consumer spending? What would happen to GDP and incomes if the majority of consumers decided to reduce their spending and pay down their debts at the same time?

Sources: Household debt still biggest risk: BoC, by Gordon Isfeld, Postmedia News Mar 8, 2012, accessed on March 14, 2012 at http://business.financialpost.com/2012/03/08/bank-of-canada-holds-rates-2/; Karina Frayter, "Economists: Consumers Won't Save the Economy," USAToday.com, October 2, 2011.

1.8 For the total value of expenditures on final goods and services to equal the total value of income generated from producing those final goods and services, all the money that a business receives from the sale of its product must be paid out as income to the owners of the factors of production. How can a business make a profit if it pays out as income all the money it receives?

LO 4.2

2.1 Which of the following are likely to increase measured GDP, and which are likely to reduce it?
   a. The fraction of women working outside the home increases.
   b. There is a sharp increase in the crime rate.
   c. Higher tax rates cause some people to hide more of the income they earn.

2.2 Does the fact that the typical Canadian works less than 40 hours per week today and worked 60 hours per week in 1890 indicate whether the economic well-being of Canadians today versus 1890 is higher or lower? Or, can we use the difference between real GDP per capita today and in 1890 alone to measure differences in economic well-being? Briefly explain.

2.3 [**Related to** Making the Connection **on page 106**] Each year, the United Nations publishes the Human Development Report, which provides information on the standard of living in nearly every country in the world. The report includes data on real GDP per person and also contains a broader measure of the standard of living called the Human Development Index (HDI). The HDI combines data on gross national income (GNI) per person with data on life expectancy at birth, average years of schooling, and expected years of schooling. (GNI is a measure of the total income per person in a country.) The following table shows values for GNI per person and the HDIs for several

countries. Prepare one list that ranks countries from highest GNI per person to lowest and another list that ranks countries from highest HDI to lowest. Briefly discuss possible reasons for any differences in the rankings of countries in your two lists. (All values in the table are for the year 2012.)

Country	Real GNI per Person (2005 Dollars)	HDI
Australia	$34 340	0.938
Greece	20 511	0.860
China	7 945	0.699
Iran	10 695	0.742
Norway	48 688	0.955
Canada	35 369	0.911
Singapore	52 613	0.895
South Korea	28 231	0.909
United Arab Emirates	42 716	0.818
United States	43 480	0.937
Zimbabwe	424	0.397

Data from United Nations Development Programme, "The Human Development Index," (http:/hdr.undp.org/en/statistics/hdi/). Retrieved March 14, 2012.

LO 4.3

3.1 [**Related to** Solved Problem 4.2 **on page 108**] Suppose the information in the table on the next page is for a simple economy that produces only four goods and services: textbooks, hamburgers, shirts, and cotton. Assume that all the cotton is used in the production of shirts.

Product	2007 Quantity	2007 Price	2012 Quantity	2012 Price	2013 Quantity	2013 Price
Textbooks	90	$50.00	100	$60.00	100	$65.00
Hamburgers	75	2.00	100	2.00	120	2.25
Shirts	50	30.00	50	25.00	65	25.00
Cotton	100	0.80	800	0.60	120	0.70

   a. Use the information in the table to calculate real GDP for 2012 and 2013, assuming that the base year is 2007.

   b. What is the growth rate of real GDP from 2012?

3.2 The movie *Avatar* overtook *Titanic* as the highest-grossing movie of all time. An article on Forbes.com notes that "the average ticket price in 2008 (*Avatar* was released in 2009) was $7.18, up 56% from prices in 1997 when *Titanic* was in theaters." The article states that "a look at domestic grosses (box-office receipts) adjusted for inflation shows a more realistic view of *Avatar*'s performance."

   a. Why would adjusting for inflation show a more realistic view of *Avatar*'s performance at the box office?

   b. Which would be a more accurate measure of how well a movie has performed at the box office: the dollar value of tickets sold or the number of tickets sold? Why don't newspapers report the number of tickets sold rather than the dollar value of tickets sold? Would comparing the total number of tickets sold by all movies in 1939 with the total number of tickets sold by all movies in 2011 be a good way to measure how the relative importance of movies in the economy has changed over time? Briefly explain.

Dorthy Pomerantz, "Is Avator Really King of the Box Office?" Forbes.com, January 27, 2010.

LO 4.4

4.1 Suppose a country has many of its citizens temporarily working in other countries, and many of its firms have facilities in other countries. Furthermore, relatively few citizens of foreign countries are working in this country, and relatively few foreign firms have facilities in this country. In these circumstances, which would you expect to be larger for this country, GDP or GNP? Briefly explain.

4.2 Suppose the amount the federal government collects in personal income taxes increases, while the level of GDP remains the same. What will happen to the values of national income, household income, and household disposable income?

4.3 If you were attempting to forecast the level of consumption spending by households, which measure of total production or total income might be most helpful to you in making your forecast? Briefly explain.

Unemployment and Inflation

Vladimir Melnik/Shutterstock

Chapter Outline and Learning Objectives

5.1 Measuring the Unemployment Rate and the Labour Force Participation Rate, page 122
> Define the unemployment rate and the labour force participation rate and understand how they are computed.

5.2 Types of Unemployment, page 126
> Identify the four types of unemployment.

5.3 Explaining Unemployment, page 129
> Explain what factors determine the unemployment rate.

5.4 Measuring Inflation, page 131
> Define price level and inflation rate, and understand how they are computed.

5.5 Using Price Indexes to Adjust for the Effects of Inflation, page 135
> Use price indexes to adjust data for the effects of inflation.

5.6 Real versus Nominal Interest Rates, page 136
> Distinguish between the nominal interest rate and the real interest rate.

5.7 Does Inflation Impose Costs on the Economy? page 137
> Discuss the problems inflation can cause.

Canadian Manufacturers Grow While Others Shrink

When we study macroeconomics, we are looking at the big picture: total production, total employment, and the price level. Of course, the big picture is made up of millions of consumers, workers, and firms. The actions of all these individuals come together to determine how many people will find jobs and how many will lose them.

One sector of the economy that receives a great deal of media and political attention is the manufacturing sector. Manufacturing firms make goods (rather than provide services), and their hiring decisions can have a major impact on the entire economy. As such, economists, policymakers, and other firms would all like to know when manufacturing firms are planning to expand or contract as early as possible to understand how employment and the economy overall will be affected.

One way to assess the coming employment picture is the Purchasing Managers' Index (PMI). Produced in 28 countries, the PMI is a monthly survey of firms' plans to purchase goods and services as well as their assessment of how they feel the economy will do over the next few months (i.e., "better than before," "worse than before," or "the same"). Think about the PMI index as a continuum: If all firms surveyed report that they are going to lay off workers and shut down operations, the PMI would be 0; if most firms surveyed report that they are likely to cut back operations (indicating a negative economic out-

look), the PMI would be below 50; if all firms surveyed report that they are going to keep production the same as in previous months, the PMI would be 50; if most firms surveyed report that they expect to expand operations (indicating a positive economic outlook), the PMI would be above 50; and if all firms surveyed report that they expect to hire more employees and expect the economy to improve, the PMI would be 100.

In April 2013, the PMI for Canada's manufacturing sector was 50.1, indicating that Canadian manufacturers were unlikely to change the number of workers they employ or to increase production. Canada's outlook was very different from that of many other countries at the time. For example, the April 2013 PMI for the eurozone was 46.9, which predicted job losses for that region. Forecasting the number of jobs that will be created or lost in an economy is exceptionally difficult, but the PMI gives us a starting point.

In this chapter, we will focus on measuring changes in unemployment as well as changes in the price level, or inflation. Both unemployment and inflation are major economic and political problems, so it is important to understand how they are measured.

AN INSIDE LOOK on **page 140** further discusses the PMI and employment in the Canadian manufacturing sector.

Sources: Based on Kim Covert, Manufacturing growth and unemployment. Postmedia News, National Post Sept. 2, 2011.

Economics in Your Life

Should You Change Your Career Plans If You Graduate during a Recession?

Suppose you are in your second year of your degree, majoring in economics and finance. You plan to find a job in the banking industry after graduation. The banking industry has seen much less growth in the aftermath of the global financial crisis. Due to the recession caused by the financial crisis, unemployment in the entire economy is still quite high. After meeting with some older students, you learn that many of them already have jobs in the energy industry. Should you switch your major to natural resource/energy economics? As you read this chapter, see if you can answer these questions. You can check your answers against those we provide on page 139 at the end of this chapter.

U nemployment and inflation are the macroeconomic problems most discussed in the media and during political campaigns. For many people, the state of the economy can be described by just two measures: the unemployment rate and the inflation rate. In the 1960s, Arthur Okun, an American economist, coined the term *misery index*, which adds the inflation rate and the unemployment rate together to give a rough measure of the state of the economy. As we will see in later chapters, although inflation and unemployment are important problems, the long-run success of an economy is generally judged by its ability to generate high levels of real GDP per person. We devote this chapter to discussing how unemployment and inflation rates are measured. In particular, we'll look closely at the measures produced by Statistics Canada on a monthly basis.

5.1 LEARNING OBJECTIVE

Define the unemployment rate and the labour force participation rate, and understand how they are computed.

Unemployment rate The percentage of the labour force that is unemployed.

Measuring the Unemployment Rate and the Labour Force Participation Rate

On the first Friday of every month at 7:00 a.m., Statistics Canada (also called StatsCan) reports its estimate of the previous month's **unemployment rate**. The estimates are widely reported in newspapers, radio, TV, and on blogs. If the unemployment rate is higher or lower than expected, investors and firms are likely to change their views on the health of the economy. The unemployment rate can also have a major impact on the outcome of elections. In many provincial and federal elections the party in power does well if the unemployment has been steady or falling. If the unemployment rate is rising, a change in government is much more likely.

The unemployment rate is one of the key macroeconomic statistics, but how does Statistics Canada prepare its estimates, and how accurate are these estimates? We explore the answers to these questions in this section.

The Labour Force Survey

Each month, Statistics Canada conducts the Labour Force Survey (LFS) to collect the data needed to compute the unemployment rate. The LFS involves interviewing about 56 000 households to gain information on people's labour market activities as well as the demographic makeup of the people living in the household. The LFS focuses only on the **working age population**, people 15 years of age and older who are legally entitled to work in Canada.

Working age population People 15 years of age and older who are legally entitled to work in Canada.

Participants in the survey are put into one of three categories: *employed, unemployed*, or *not in the labour force*.

- **Employed:** Anyone who did paid work, unpaid work for a family business, or worked for themselves is considered "employed." Also considered employed is anyone who would normally have worked but did not due to illness, disability, family crisis, vacation, or labour dispute (strike or lockout). Essentially, anyone with a job is classified as employed.

- **Unemployed:** People who don't have a job but are willing and able to work and have looked for work in the last four weeks are considered "unemployed." This category includes people who have been temporarily laid off, or will be starting a new job within four weeks. The most important part of the definition of *unemployed* is the requirement that an individual must have looked for work in the last four weeks. If someone doesn't have a job and hasn't looked for one in the last four weeks, that person is placed in the category that is described next.

- **Not in the labour force:** People who were unable or unwilling to do paid work are considered to be outside the labour force. This category includes people who would like to have a job, but have given up looking for one.

We need one more definition before we can show you how to calculate the unemployment rate and the participation rate. We need to define *labour force* clearly. The **labour force** is all the people who are working or actively looking for work. Essentially, the labour force is all the people who could be working on very short notice. Statistics Canada calculates the size of the labour force by adding up all the people who were classified as employed and all the people who were classified as unemployed. Figure 5.1 shows how the population is broken down into the different categories we discussed. The numbers in the figure are taken from the April 2013 estimates.

Labour force The sum of employed and unemployed workers in the economy.

The unemployment rate is calculated as follows:

$$\text{Unemployment rate} = \frac{\text{Number of unemployed}}{\text{Labour force}} \times 100.$$

Using the numbers from Figure 5.1, we can see that the unemployment rate for April 2013 was:

$$\text{Unemployment Rate} = \frac{1\ 403\ 700}{18\ 893\ 800} \times 100 = 7.4\%.$$

The **labour force participation rate**, or simply the *participation rate*, is calculated as follows:

Labour force participation rate The percentage of the working age population in the labour force.

$$\text{Participation rate} = \frac{\text{Labour force}}{\text{Working age population}} \times 100.$$

For April 2013 the participation rate was:

$$\text{Participation rate} = \frac{18\ 893\ 800}{28\ 588\ 700} \times 100 = 66\%.$$

Another measure of the state of the economy is the **employment–population ratio**. The employment–population ratio measures the portion of the population engaged in paid work. It is calculated as follows:

Employment–population ratio A measure of the portion of the population engaged in paid work.

$$\text{Employment–population ratio} = \frac{\text{Number of employed}}{\text{Working age population}} \times 100$$

For April 2013, the employment–population ratio was:

$$\text{Employment–population ratio} = \frac{17\ 490\ 100}{28\ 588\ 700} \times 100 = 61\%.$$

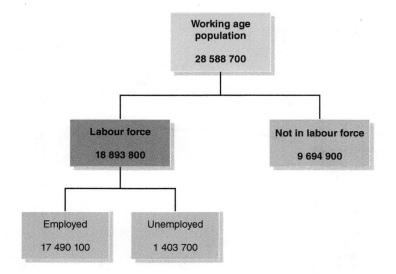

Figure 5.1

The Employment Status of the Working Age Population, April 2013

In April 2013, the working age population of Canada was 28 million. The working age population is divided into those in the labour force (19 million) and those not in the labour force (9 million). The labour force is divided into the employed (17.7 million) and the unemployed (1.3 million). Those not in the labour force are further divided into different groups. The most important of these groups from an economic standpoint are the discouraged workers (18 900). These are people who would like to have a job but who have given up looking for work.

Source: Data from CANSIM Table 282-0001 series v2091030, v2091051, v2091072, v2091135, and CANISM Table 282-0085 series v2440390.

Problems with Measuring the Unemployment Rate

Although Statistics Canada reports the unemployment rate measured to a tenth of a percentage point, it is not a perfect measure of the current state of joblessness in the economy. One problem that Statistics Canada faces is distinguishing between people who are not in the labour force. During a recession, some unemployed people who are having a hard time finding a job will stop looking for work. Remember that only people who have actively looked for work in the last four weeks are counted as "unemployed" by Statistics Canada. So, even though these **discouraged workers** are willing and able to work, they are counted as "not in the labour force."

Another problem with the unemployment rate is that everyone with a job is considered "employed," even if they are only working a few hours a week. The "employed" category includes everyone with a full-time or a part-time job. Some part-time workers would like to have a full-time job, but they can only find part-time work. The unemployment rate doesn't tell us how many people are in this situation. Both of these issues mean that the unemployment rate *understates* problems in the labour market.

There are other measurement problems, however, that cause the measured unemployment rate to *overstate* the extent of joblessness. These problems arise because the LFS doesn't verify the responses of people included in the survey. Some people who claim to be unemployed and actively looking for work may not be looking. A person might claim to be actively looking for a job to remain eligible for Employment Insurance. In this case, a person who is actually not in the labour force is counted as unemployed. Other people might be employed but not in a legal activity—such as selling drugs—or might want to conceal a legitimate job to avoid paying taxes. In these cases, individuals who are actually working are counted as unemployed. These inaccurate responses to the LFS bias the unemployment rate upward. We can conclude that, although the unemployment rate provides useful information about the employment situation in the country, it is far from an exact measure of joblessness.

Discouraged workers People who are available for work but have not looked for a job during the previous four weeks because they believe no jobs are available for them.

Trends in Labour Force Participation

The labour force participation rate is important because it determines the amount of labour that will be available to the economy from a given population. The higher the labour force participation rate, the more labour is available and the higher a country's levels of GDP and GDP per person. Figure 5.2 highlights two important trends in labour force participation rates of adults over 15 years old since 1976—the rising participation of women and the falling participation of men.

Figure 5.2

Trends in the Labour Force Participation Rate of Men and Women, 1976 to 2013

The labour force participation rate of men has declined gradually since 1976, but the participation rate of women has increased significantly over the same period of time, making the overall labour force participation rate higher today than it was in 1976.

Source: CANSIM Table 282-0001 Series v2091408 v2091618. Reproduced and distributed on an "as is" basis with the permission of Statistics Canada.

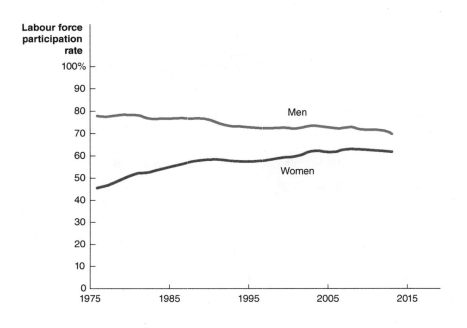

Length of Time Unemployed	2007	2009
Less than 4 weeks	39.9%	33.6%
5 to 13 weeks	25.9	28.7
14 to 25 weeks	13.3	16.8
26 weeks or more	14.0	19.5

Note: Numbers may not sum to 100 due to rounding.

Table 5.1

Length of Unemployment Before and During Recession
When the economy is shrinking, as in a recession, it is much harder for people to find new jobs. This makes the length of time people are unemployed a good indicator of the state of joblessness in the economy.

Source: CANSIM Table 282-0048 Series v2349181, v2349182, v2349183, v2349184, v2349185. Reproduced and distributed on an "as is" basis with the permission of Statistics Canada.

The labour force participation rate of males over 15 years old has fallen from 78.4 percent in 1981 to 70 percent in 2013. Some of this decline is due to older men retiring earlier and younger men staying in school longer. There has also been a decline in the participation of males who are not in school but are too young to retire.

The decline in labour force participation by men has been offset by the increase in participation by women. The labour force participation rate for women in Canada rose from 45.7 per cent in 1976 to 62.4 per cent in 2010. As a result, the overall labour force participation increased from 61.5 to a high of 62.7 in 2008. The increase in the labour force participation rate for women has several explanations, including changing social attitudes, federal and provincial legislation, increasing wages, and families in general having fewer children.

How Long Are People Typically Unemployed?

The longer a person is unemployed, the greater the hardship. During the Great Depression, some people were unemployed for years at a time. In the modern Canadian economy, the typical person remains unemployed for a relatively short period of time. Table 5.1 shows the breakdown of unemployment spells (a "spell" of unemployment is the length of time someone is unemployed) for 2009—the middle of the recent recession. It also shows the same data from 2007—just before the US financial crisis.

In an economic boom, the length of time a person is unemployed tends to be quite short. In an economic boom, many new firms are started and existing firms expand, increasing the opportunities for people to find work. In a recession, on the other hand, few firms are started and many reduce the number of workers they employ, making it exceptionally difficult for people to find new jobs.

Job Creation and Job Destruction over Time

One important fact about employment is little known: Thousands of jobs are created and lost in the Canadian economy every year. In April 2013, 162 500 more people had jobs than the year before. This means there were at least 162 500 more jobs than just a year earlier. In fact, the number of jobs created over that period of time was much larger as some firms cut workers and went out of business altogether. The really good news was that there was an increase in the number of full-time jobs (183 900) and a decline in part-time work (–21 500). Some provinces gained jobs and others lost them. British Columbia, for example, lost 6600 employees from April 2012 to April 2013. Ontario, on the other hand, saw employment rise by 70 700. Saskatchewan saw the fastest growth in employment at 3.1 percent, while New Brunswick and Newfoundland struggled the most seeing employment drop by 1.2 percent each.

Different industries saw changes as well. The manufacturing industry saw employment fall over the previous year by 52 000 people. Over the same time period, employment in public administration rose by 25 000 from a year earlier. Transportation and warehousing actually saw little change in the number of employees from the previous year.[1]

---

[1]*Source:* Data from Statistics Canada – The Daily for September 9, 2011.

Changes in the overall unemployment rate don't show you the whole picture of what is happening in the economy. Even when the unemployment rate is rising, some firms are hiring new employees and creating jobs. By the same token, even when the unemployment rate is falling, some firms are laying off workers or are going out of business entirely.

5.2 LEARNING OBJECTIVE

Identify the four types of unemployment.

Types of Unemployment

As Figure 5.3 illustrates, the unemployment rate follows the business cycle, rising during recessions and falling during expansions. Notice, though, that the unemployment rate never falls to zero. To understand why this is true, we need to discuss the four types of unemployment.

- Frictional unemployment
- Structural unemployment
- Cyclical unemployment
- Seasonal unemployment

Frictional Unemployment and Job Search

Workers have different skills, interests, and abilities. Jobs have different skill requirements, working conditions, and pay levels. As a result, a new worker entering the labour force or a worker who has lost a job probably will not find an acceptable job right away. Most workers spend at least some time engaging in *job search*, just as most firms spend time searching for a new person to fill a job opening. **Frictional unemployment** is short-term unemployment that arises from the process of matching workers with jobs. Some frictional unemployment is unavoidable. As we have seen, the Canadian economy creates and destroys jobs all the time. The process of job search takes time, so there will always be some workers who are frictionally unemployed because they are between jobs and in the process of finding new ones.

Would eliminating all frictional unemployment be good for the economy? No, because some frictional unemployment actually increases economic efficiency. Frictional unemployment occurs because workers and firms take the time necessary to

Frictional unemployment Short-term unemployment that arises from the process of matching workers with jobs.

Figure 5.3

The Unemployment Rate in Canada, January 1976 to April 2013

The unemployment rate rises during recessions and falls during expansions. It's not hard to tell when the Canadian economy was performing poorly by looking at the unemployment rate. There were recessions in the early 1980s, early 1990s, and again as of 2008.

Source: Table 282-0087 Series v2064894. Reproduced and distributed on an "as is" basis with the permission of Statistics Canada.

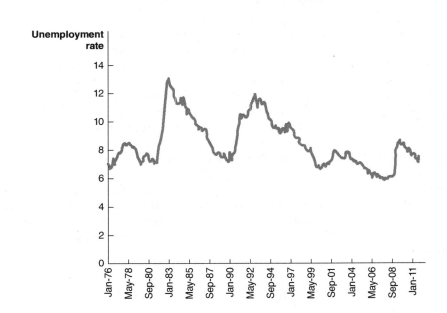

ensure a good match between the attributes of workers and the characteristics of jobs. By devoting time to job search, workers end up with jobs they find more satisfying and in which they can be more productive. Of course, having more productive and better-satisfied workers is also in the best interest of firms.

Structural Unemployment

By 2009, computer-generated three-dimensional animation, which was used in movies like *Shrek*, *Cars*, and *Up*, had become much more popular than traditional hand-drawn two-dimensional animation (which was used in *Snow White*). Many people who were highly skilled in hand-drawn animation lost their jobs at Walt Disney Pictures, Dreamworks, and other animation houses. To become employed again, these animators either had to become skilled in computer-generated animation or find new occupations. In the meantime, they were unemployed. Economists consider these animators *structurally unemployed.* **Structural unemployment** arises from a persistent mismatch between the job skills or attributes of workers and the requirements of jobs. While frictional unemployment is short term, structural unemployment can last for longer periods because workers need time to learn new skills. Caterpillar, makers of heavy equipment, closed an engine plant in London, Ontario, in 2012. The plant's closure meant that many people who worked as mechanics became unemployed. Some of the people previously employed at the plant found jobs in other industries. However, those with highly specialized skills had a difficult time finding new jobs without retraining.

Structural unemployment
Unemployment that arises from a persistent mismatch between the skills and attributes of workers and the requirements of jobs.

Structural unemployment can also arise due to a mismatch between the location of workers and the location of new jobs. Those who have lost jobs in the fisheries of Newfoundland and Labrador have often had to relocate to the Prairies to find jobs as labourers. Before these people decided to move to find new jobs, they were structurally unemployed.

Workers that lack even basic skills, such as literacy, or have addictions to alcohol or other drugs find it particularly difficult to train for new jobs. These workers may remain structurally unemployed for years.

Cyclical Unemployment

When the economy moves into recession, many firms find their sales falling and cut back on production. As production falls, firms start laying off workers. Workers who lose their jobs because of a recession are experiencing **cyclical unemployment**. For example, in February of 2009, Chrysler announced that it would temporarily close its assembly plant in Brampton, Ontario, due to low sales. Chrysler and other automakers have low sales when the economy is in a recession. The laid-off Chrysler employees experienced cyclical unemployment.

Cyclical unemployment
Unemployment caused by a business cycle recession.

Seasonal Unemployment

Some unemployment is due to seasonal factors, such as weather or the fluctuation in demand for some products during different times of the year. For example, ski resorts typically reduce their hiring during the summer months. Department stores increase their hiring in November and December and reduce their hiring after New Year's Day. In the fisheries, employment increases when the season opens and is much lower for the rest of the year. Construction workers often experience **seasonal unemployment** during the winter. Seasonal unemployment can make unemployment rates seem artificially high during some months and artificially low in others. As a result, Statistics Canada publishes two sets of unemployment figures each month: one that is *seasonally adjusted* and another that is not seasonally adjusted. The seasonally adjusted data eliminate the effects of seasonal unemployment. Economists and policymakers use the seasonally adjusted unemployment statistics as a more accurate reflection of the state of the labour market. From this point forward, when we talk about the unemployment rate, you can assume that we are discussing the seasonally adjusted unemployment rate.

Seasonal unemployment
Unemployment that is due to seasonal factors, such as weather or the fluctuation in demand for some products during different times of the year.

Full Employment

As the economy moves through the expansion phase of the business cycle, cyclical unemployment eventually drops to zero. The unemployment rate will not be zero, however, because of frictional and structural unemployment. As Figure 5.3 shows, the unemployment rate in Canada hasn't been below 6 percent in the last 35 years. When the only remaining unemployment is structural and frictional unemployment, the economy is said to be at *full employment.*

Natural rate of unemployment The normal rate of unemployment, consisting of frictional unemployment plus structural unemployment.

Economists consider frictional and structural unemployment as the normal underlying level of unemployment in the economy. The sum of frictional and structural unemployment is referred to as the **natural rate of unemployment**. The fluctuations around the natural rate of unemployment, which we see in Figure 5.3, are mainly due to changes in cyclical unemployment. Unfortunately, economists disagree on the exact value of the natural rate of unemployment, and there is good reason to believe it varies over time. Many estimate that the natural rate of unemployment for Canada is between 6.5 percent and 7.5 percent. The natural rate of unemployment is also sometimes called the *full-employment rate of unemployment.*

You will notice that the official rate of unemployment as reported by Statistics Canada is different from the natural rate of employment most of the time. The natural rate is a theoretical concept that represents the portion of the labour force that would be unemployed if everything in the economy was going well and only structural and frictional unemployment occur. The official rate of unemployment reported by Statistics Canada is a measure of what is actually happening in the economy, and includes cyclical unemployment in addition to structural and frictional unemployment. The official rate of unemployment is equal to the natural rate of unemployment only when cyclical unemployment is zero.

Making the Connection | ## How Should We Categorize the Unemployment of Laid-off Canada Post Employees?

In July 2011, Canada Post cut 200 call-centre positions in Manitoba, Ontario, New Brunswick, and Nova Scotia, and outsourced the call centre services. These job losses were a consequence of falling mail volumes. Due to greater use of the internet and email, and as a result of the recent recession, the demand for Canada Post's services has dropped.

We can categorize the unemployment caused by Canada Post's decision in three ways: cyclical unemployment, frictional unemployment, or structural unemployment. To know which type of unemployment applies in this case, we have to consider the situation more carefully.

Workers that lose their jobs due to the state of the economy are classified as *cyclically unemployed.* Canada Post also delivers a lot of advertising and promotional material for businesses. The demand for this service is sensitive to the business cycle. If Canada Post's layoffs were in response to businesses cutting back on advertising during a recession, the laid-off workers would be classified as *cyclically unemployed.*

The people who lost their jobs at Canada Post fit into more than one category of unemployment.

Frictional unemployment occurs when new entrants to the labour force or displaced workers search for a new job. In New Brunswick and Nova Scotia, several companies supply call-centre services to a wide variety of firms across North America. If the laid-off workers are able to find work at one of these other call-centre companies fairly quickly, they would be classified as *frictionally unemployed.*

Structural unemployment occurs when a new technology or production process leads to a mismatch between the skills of workers and the requirements of jobs. In this case, Canada Post's services have been replaced in large part by the Internet and email. Moreover the existence of technology that allows call-centre services to be provided from virtually anywhere means that the organization doesn't have to provide call-centre services in-house. If the laid-off workers are unable to find work at another call centre and must learn new skills to find other work, they would be classified as *structurally unemployed*.

Source: Harleen Kaur, "Canada Post to Layoff Large Number of Employees," *CanadaUpdates*, April 24, 2011, http://www.canadaupdates.com/content/canada-post-layoff-large-number-employees-16379.html.

Your Turn: Test your understanding by doing related problem 2.3 on page 143 at the end of this chapter.

MyEconLab

Explaining Unemployment

We have seen that some unemployment is a result of the business cycle. In later chapters, we will explore the causes of the business cycle, which will help us understand the causes of cyclical unemployment. In this section, we will look at the factors that determine the levels of frictional and structural unemployment.

Government Policies and the Unemployment Rate

Workers generally search for jobs by sending out resumés, registering with Internet job sites such as Monster.ca, and getting referrals from friends and relatives. Firms fill job openings by advertising in newspapers, listing openings online, participating in job fairs, and recruiting on university campuses. Government policy can aid these private efforts. Governments can help reduce the level of frictional unemployment by pursuing policies that speed up the process of matching employees with employers. Governments can reduce structural unemployment by implementing policies that aid worker retraining.

Some government policies, however, can add to the level of frictional and structural unemployment. These government policies increase the unemployment rate either by increasing the time workers devote to searching for jobs, by providing disincentives for firms to hire workers, or by keeping wages above the market clearing wage (or *equilibrium wage*).

Employment Insurance Suppose that you have been in the labour force for a few years, but have just lost your job. You could probably find a low-wage job immediately if you needed to—perhaps at Walmart or McDonald's. Instead, you decide to search for a better, higher-paying job by sending out resumés and responding to want ads and online job postings. Remember from Chapter 1 that the *opportunity cost* of any activity is the highest-valued alternative that you must give up to engage in that activity. In this case, the opportunity cost of continuing to search for a job is the salary you are giving up at the job you didn't take (say, at McDonald's). The longer you search, the greater your chances of finding a better, higher-paying job, but the longer you search, the more salary you have given up by not working, so the greater the total cost of searching.

In Canada and most other industrial countries, people are eligible for payments from the government if they become unemployed. The Canadian program for supporting unemployed workers is called *Employment Insurance (EI)*. While conditions and payments vary by region, EI will replace 55 percent of your earnings up to a maximum of $501 per week (in 2013). The unemployed receiving EI payments spend more time searching for jobs because the opportunity cost of job search is lower. The additional time people spend searching for a job raises the unemployment rate (recall the definition of *unemployed* that appears on page 122). Does this mean that EI is a bad idea? Most economists would say no. If not for the EI program, unemployed workers would suffer very large declines in their income, which would lead them to greatly reduce spending, which would make any recession worse. EI helps the unemployed maintain their incomes and spending, which also reduces the personal hardship of being unemployed. Finally, EI helps both workers and firms make "good matches." Allowing unemployed people to spend more time searching for an appropriate job means more people find jobs that are appropriate to their skills and tastes. The better the match between employer and employee, the more productive the economy will be.

Minimum Wage Laws   Each province and territory in Canada sets the lowest legal wage that firms can pay workers. Currently, the highest minimum wage is $11.00 an hour in Nunavut, and the lowest is $9.75 an hour in Alberta. If the minimum wage is set above the market clearing wage (determined by the demand and supply of labour), the quantity of labour supplied will be greater than the quantity of labour demanded. Some workers will be unemployed who would have been employed if there were no minimum wage. As a result, the unemployment rate will be higher than it would be without a minimum wage. Economists agree that the current minimum wage is above the market clearing wage for some workers, but they disagree on the amount of unemployment that minimum wages cause. Teenagers, with relatively few job-related skills, are one of the groups most likely to receive the minimum wage. Some studies have estimated that a 10 percent increase in the minimum wage reduces teenage employment by about 2 percent. Despite this impact on teenagers, most economists agree that current minimum wages have only a small impact on the overall unemployment rate.

Labour Unions

Labour unions are organizations of workers that bargain with employers for higher wages and better working conditions for their members. In unionized industries, the wage is usually above the market clearing wage. This higher wage results in employers in unionized industries hiring fewer workers. Does this reduction in hiring by unionized firms significantly increase the unemployment rate? Most economists would say the answer is no. Overall, about 31.5 percent of Canadian workers belong to a union. The vast majority of government employees, 75 percent, are members of a union. In the private sector, only 17.5 percent of workers are unionized.[2] This means that most of the workers not able to find jobs in unionized industries are able to find jobs in other areas.

Efficiency Wages

Many firms pay wages that are higher than the market clearing wage, not because the government requires them to or because a union has negotiated a contract, but because they believe doing so will increase their profits. This may seem strange at first: Wages are the largest cost for many employers, so paying higher wages seems like a good way for firms to reduce profits rather than increase them. The key to understanding why firms might want to pay higher wages is that the level of wages can influence worker productivity. Many studies have shown that workers are motivated to work harder by higher wages. An **efficiency wage** is a higher-than-market wage that a firm pays to motivate workers to be more productive. Can't firms ensure that workers work hard by supervising them? In some cases, they can. For example, when you phone a call centre, you often hear this message: "This call may be monitored for quality assurance and training purposes." In many situations, however, it is much harder to monitor workers. Many firms must rely on workers being motivated enough to work hard. By paying a

Efficiency wage A higher-than-market wage that a firm pays to increase worker productivity.

---

[2]*Source:* Statistics Canada. Table 282-0001 - Labour force survey estimates (LFS), by sex and detailed age group, unadjusted for seasonality, computed annual average (persons unless otherwise noted) (table), CANSIM (database), Using E-STAT (distributor). Reproduced and distributed on an "as is" basis with the permission of Statistics Canada.

wage above the market clearing wage, a firm raises the cost to workers of losing their jobs because many other available jobs pay less. The increase in productivity that results from paying a higher wage can more than offset the extra cost of the wage, meaning that the firm's costs of production actually falls.

When firms pay efficiency wages, the quantity of labour supplied will exceed the quantity of labour demanded. As with minimum wage laws or unions, a supply of labour larger than the demand for labour leads to unemployment. Efficiency wages are another reason we don't see an unemployment rate of zero, even in an economic boom.

Making the Connection | Why Does Costco Pay Its Workers More than Walmart?

The concept of efficiency wages raises the possibility that firms might find it more profitable to pay higher wages even when they don't have to. We might expect that a firm would maximize profits by paying the lowest wages at which it was possible to hire all the workers the firm needs. But if low wages significantly reduce worker productivity, then paying higher wages can actually reduce costs and increase profits. Walmart and Costco are international competitors in the discount department store industry, but the two have taken different approaches to compensating their employees.

Walmart employs about 85 000 people in Canada and about 2.1 million employees worldwide. Costco employs thousands of people in Canada and almost 150 000 employees around the world. While Walmart generally pays new employees the minimum wage, Costco pays new employees well above the minimum wage—$2 or $3 above, in some cases.

Why does Costco pay so much more to its employees than Walmart does? Costco's chief executive officer, Jim Sinegal, argues that paying high wages reduces employee turnover, and raises morale and productivity: "Paying good wages and keeping your people working for you is very good business . . . Imagine that you have 120,000 loyal ambassadors out there who are constantly saying good things about Costco. It has to be a significant advantage for you." However, it is likely that the higher wages Costco pays are not entirely due to an efficiency wage strategy. Unlike Walmart, Costco charges a fee of at least $50 per year to shop in its stores. The typical Costco store stocks only about 4000 items, as opposed to the 100 000 items carried by the average Walmart store. Costco stores also sells more big-ticket items, such as higher-priced jewellery and consumer electronics. As a result, the average income of Costco customers is a lot higher than the average income of Walmart customers. One observer concludes that Costco pays higher wages than Walmart "because it requires higher-skilled workers to sell higher-end products to its more affluent customers." So, even if Costco were not pursuing a strategy of paying efficiency wages, it is likely that it would still have to pay higher wages than Walmart.

Sources: Alan B. Goldberg and Bill Ritter. "Costco CEO Finds Pro-Worker Means Profitability," ABCNews.com, August 2, 2006; Lori Montgomery, "Maverick CEO Joins Push to Raise Minimum Wage," Washington Post, January 30, 2007; and John Tierney, "The Good Goliath," New York Times, November 29, 2005.

Your Turn: Test your understanding by doing related problem 2.4 on page 143 at the end of this chapter.

MyEconLab

Measuring Inflation

One of the facts of economic life is that the prices of most goods and services rise over time, a process known as **inflation**. As a result, the cost of living continually rises. In 1914, in the United States, Henry Ford famously began paying his workers $5 a day, more than twice what Ford's competitors were paying. While it would be illegal for anyone in Canada to work for as little as $5 an *hour* today, at the time, Ford's $5 workday meant his employees could enjoy a comfortable middle-class lifestyle. In 1914, you could buy a number of goods with just a nickel or even a penny. Today, even dollar stores charge more than a dollar for most things.

5.4 LEARNING OBJECTIVE
Define price level and inflation rate, and understand how they are computed.

Inflation A general increase in the prices of goods and services over time.

Price level A measure of the average prices of goods and services in the economy.

Inflation rate The percentage increase in the price level from one year to the next.

Knowing how employment and unemployment statistics are compiled is important in understanding what they mean. The same is true of the statistics on the cost of living. As we saw in Chapter 4, the **price level** measures the average prices of goods and services in the economy. The **inflation rate** is the percentage increase in the price level from one year to the next. In Chapter 4, we introduced the *GDP deflator* as a measure of the price level. The GDP deflator is the broadest measure we have of the price level because it includes the price of every final good and service produced in the country. Recall that the GDP deflator is calculated as the ratio of Nominal GDP to Real GDP times 100.

The GDP deflator isn't the best measure of price level in every circumstance, as it includes goods and services that households don't consume (like large scale electric generators) and does not include many of the goods and services that households consume. In particular, the GDP deflator excludes the price of imports and includes the price of goods made for export. In this chapter we introduce you to another measure of price level that better reflects the cost of living, called the *consumer price index*. We also briefly discuss a third measure of the price level, called the *producer price index*.

The Consumer Price Index

The idea behind the *consumer price index (CPI)* is to measure changes in the prices faced by the average household. To figure out what goods and services the average household buys, Statistics Canada conducts the Survey of Household Spending each year. The survey asks 16 758 Canadian households about their purchasing habits, including what they buy, how much they buy, and where they buy it. Based on the results of the survey, Statistics Canada constructs a shopping list, or basket of goods and services, that the average household buys. The types of goods and services that are included in the basket are updated every few years to reflect changing purchasing habits. The most recent basket of goods and services is based on what consumers bought in 2011. The prices of the goods and services in the basket are researched in stores in various cities across the country each month to ensure they are up to date.

The weight of each good and service in the basket (somewhat like the amount of each item put into a shopping basket) is based on the results of the Survey of Household Spending. Figure 5.4 shows the goods and services included in the basket, grouped into eight broad categories.

The **consumer price index (CPI)** is an average of the prices of the goods and services in the basket. One year is chosen as the base year, and the value of the CPI is set

Consumer price index (CPI) An average of the prices of the goods and services purchased by a typical household.

Figure 5.4

The CPI Basket, 2011

Statistics Canada surveys 16 758 Canadian households on their spending habits. The results are used to construct a basket of goods and services purchased by a typical household. The chart shows these goods and services, grouped into eight broad categories. The percentages represent the expenditure shares of the categories within the basket. The categories of shelter, transportation, and food account for about two-thirds of the basket.

Source: Data from http://www.statcan.gc.ca/imdb-bmdi/document/2301_D48_T9_V1-eng.htm

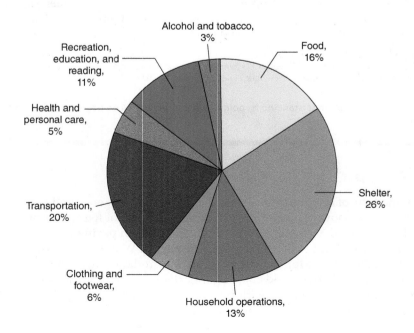

equal to 100 for that year. In any year other than the base year, the CPI is equal to the ratio of the dollar amount necessary to buy the basket of goods and services in that year to the dollar amount required to purchase the same basket of goods and services in the base year, multiplied by 100. Because the CPI measures the price of the goods and services that the average household buys, it is a fairly good indicator of the cost of living.

A simple example can clarify how the CPI is constructed. For the purposes of this example, we assume that the basket has only three products in it: root beer, pizzas, and movies:

	Base Year (2002)			2014		2015	
Product	Quantity	Price	Expenditures	Price	Expenditures (on base-year quantities)	Price	Expenditures (on base-year quantities)
Root beer	1	$50.00	$50.00	$100.00	$100.00	$85.00	$85.00
Pizzas	20	10.00	200.00	15.00	300.00	14.00	280.00
Movies	20	25.00	500.00	25.00	500.00	27.50	550.00
TOTAL			$750.00		$900.00		$915.00

Suppose that during the base year of 2002, a survey determines that each month the typical family purchases 1 case of root beer, 20 pizzas, and 20 movies. At 2002 prices, the typical family must spend $750.00 to purchase this basket of goods and services. The CPI for every year after the base year is determined by dividing the amount necessary to purchase the basket in that year by the amount required in the base year, multiplied by 100. Notice that the quantities of the products purchased in 2014 and 2015 are irrelevant in calculating the CPI because *we are assuming that households buy exactly the same basket of goods every month*. Using the numbers in the table, we can calculate the CPI for 2014 and 2015:

Formula	Applied to 2014	Applied to 2015
$CPI = \dfrac{\text{Expenditures now}}{\text{Expenditures in base year}} \times 100$	$\dfrac{\$900}{\$750} \times 100 = 120$	$\dfrac{\$915}{\$750} \times 100 = 122$

How do we interpret values such as 120 or 122? The first thing to recognize is that they are *index numbers*, which means that they are not measured in dollars or any other units. *The CPI is intended to measure changes in the price level over time.* We can't use the CPI to tell us in an absolute sense how high the price level is—only how much it has changed over time. We measure the inflation rate as the percentage increase in the CPI from one year to the next. For our simple example, the inflation rate in 2015 would be the percentage change in the CPI from 2014 to 2015:

$$\frac{122 - 120}{120} \times 100 = 1.7\%$$

Because the CPI is a measure of the changes in the cost of living, we can also say that the cost of living increased by 1.7 percent between 2014 and 2015.

Is the CPI Accurate?

The CPI is the most widely reported measure of inflation. Policymakers use the CPI to track the state of the economy. Businesses use it to help set the prices they charge and the wages they pay their employees. Each year, the federal government increases payments to seniors based on the CPI over the previous year.

It is important that the CPI be as accurate as possible, but there are four biases that cause changes in the CPI to overstate the true rate of inflation experienced by households:

- **Substitution bias.** In constructing the CPI, Statistics Canada assumes that each month, households purchase exactly the same amount of each product in the basket. In fact, households are likely to buy less of a product when its price increases relative to other goods. For example, if apple prices rise rapidly while orange prices fall, households will reduce their apple purchases and increase their orange purchases. Therefore, the prices of the basket households actually buy will rise less than the prices of the basket Statistics Canada uses to compute the CPI.

- **Increase in quality bias.** Over time, most products included in the CPI improve in quality: Cars become safer and more fuel efficient, computers become faster and have more memory, and so on. Increases in the prices of these products partly reflect their improved quality and partly are pure inflation.

- **New product bias.** The CPI shopping list isn't updated every time a new product comes out (or an existing product becomes unpopular). This means that new products introduced between updates are not included in the basket. For example, iPads weren't available when the basket was last updated, so any change in the price of iPads won't be captured by the CPI (if iPads largely replace other, more expensive devices such as desktop computers, that wouldn't be captured either). This bias applies to all new products that become popular quickly.

- **Outlet bias.** During the 1990s, consumers began to increase their purchases from discount stores such as Walmart and Costco. Over the past decade, the Internet has also become a significant retail source for Canadians. If the CPI basket is not updated to reflect changes in where people buy things, the CPI will overstate inflation.

Most economists believe these biases cause changes in the CPI to overstate the true rate of inflation from 0.5 percentage point to 1 percentage point. That is, if the CPI indicates that the inflation rate was 3 percent, the true inflation rate is probably between 2 and 2.5 percent.

Don't Let This Happen to You

Don't Miscalculate the Inflation Rate

Suppose you are given the data in the following table and are asked to calculate the inflation rate for 2015:

Year	CPI
2014	216
2015	219

It is tempting to avoid calculations and simply to report that the inflation rate in 2015 was 119 percent because 219 is a 119 percent increase from 100. But 119 would be the wrong inflation rate. A value for the CPI of 219 in 2015 tells us that the price level in 2015 was 119 percent higher than in the base year, but the inflation rate is the percentage increase from the previous year, not from the base year. The correct calculation of the inflation rate for 2015 is:

$$\left(\frac{219 - 216}{216}\right) \times 100 = 1.4\%$$

MyEconLab

Your Turn: Test your understanding by doing related problem 4.1 on page 144 at the end of this chapter.

The Producer Price Index

Producer price index (PPI) An average of the prices received by producers of goods and services at all stages of production.

In addition to the GDP deflator and the CPI, Statistics Canada also computes the **producer price index (PPI)**. Like the CPI, the PPI tracks the prices of a basket of goods and services. However, unlike the CPI, the PPI tracks the prices that firms receive for goods and services at all stages of production. The PPI includes the prices of intermediate goods (such as flour, cotton, yarn, steel, and lumber) and raw materials (such as coal and crude oil). If the prices of these goods rise, the cost to firms of producing final goods and services will rise, which may lead firms to increase the prices of the goods and services they sell to consumers. Changes in the PPI can give an early warning of future movements in the CPI.

Using Price Indexes to Adjust for the Effects of Inflation

5.5 LEARNING OBJECTIVE

Use price indexes to adjust data for the effects of inflation.

You are likely to receive a much higher salary after graduation than your parents or professor did when they started looking for their first job, say 25 years ago. On the other hand, prices were much lower 25 years ago than they are today. Put another way, the purchasing power of a dollar was much higher 25 years ago because the prices of most goods and services were much lower. Price indexes such as the CPI give us a way of adjusting for the effects of inflation so that we can compare dollar values from different years. For example, suppose your mother received a salary of $20 000 in 1986. By using the CPI, we can calculate what $20 000 in 1986 would be equivalent to in 2013. The CPI was 64.4 in January 1986 and 121.9 in January 2013. As 121.9/64.4 = 1.9, we know that on average prices were 1.9 times as high in January 2013 as they were in January 1986. We can use this result to inflate a salary of $20 000 received in 1986 to its value in terms of 2013 purchasing power:

$$\text{Value in 2013 dollars} = \text{Value in 1986 dollars} \times \frac{\text{CPI in 2013}}{\text{CPI in 1986}}$$

$$= \$20\ 000 \times \frac{121.9}{64.4} = \$38\ 000.$$

Our calculation shows that if you were paid a salary of $38 000 in 2013, you would be able to purchase roughly the same amount of goods and services that your mother could have purchased with a salary of $20 000 in 1986. Economic variables that are calculated in current-year prices are referred as *nominal variables*. The calculation we have just made used a price index to adjust a nominal variable—your mother's starting salary—for the effects of inflation.

For some purposes, we are interested in tracking changes in an economic variable over time rather than seeing what its value would be in today's dollars. In that case, to correct for the effects of inflation, we can divide the nominal variable by a price index and multiply by 100 to obtain a *real variable*. The real variable will be measured in dollars of the base year for the price index. Currently the base year for the CPI is 2002.

Solved Problem **5.1**

Calculating Real Hourly Wages

Suppose your economics professor is complaining about how lucky students have it today compared with when your professor was an undergraduate student. In those days, while working through an undergraduate degree, your professor had to take a part-time job that paid the minimum wage of $5 an hour, way back in 1992. Your professor moans that the minimum wage where you live is $10 an hour. You can make twice as much today! Is your professor right in complaining about "how easy young folks have it today"?

Solving the Problem

Step 1: Review the chapter material. This problem is about using price indexes to correct for inflation, so you may want to review the section "Using Price Indexes to Adjust for the Effects of Inflation" above on this page.

Step 2: Calculate the real hourly wage for each year. To calculate the real hourly wage for each year, divide the nominal hourly wage by the CPI and multiply by 100. In this case:

Real 1992 Wage	Real 2013 Wage
$\dfrac{\$5}{84} \times 100 = \$5.95$	$\dfrac{\$10}{121.9} \times 100 = \$8.20$

We can conclude that someone earning minimum wage today is in fact earning more than your professor did as an undergraduate student.

Source: Statistics Canada. Table 326-0020 - Consumer Price Index (CPI), 2009 basket, monthly (2002=100 unless otherwise noted) (table), CANSIM (database), Using E-STAT (distributor). Reproduced and distributed on an "as is" basis with the permission of Statistics Canada.

MyEconLab **Your Turn:** For more practice, do related problems 5.1 and 5.2 on page 144 at the end of this chapter.

5.6 LEARNING OBJECTIVE

Distinguish between the nominal interest rate and the real interest rate.

Nominal interest rate The stated interest rate on a loan.

Real interest rate The nominal interest rate minus the inflation rate.

Real versus Nominal Interest Rates

The difference between real and nominal values is important when borrowing and lending money. The *interest rate* is the cost of borrowing money expressed as a percentage of the amount borrowed. If a firm borrowed $1000 from you for a year and charge an interest rate of 6 percent, the firm will have to pay back $1060, or 6 percent more than you lent them. But is $1060 received a year from now really 6 percent more than $1000 today? If prices rise during the year, you will not be able to buy as much with the $1060 you receive at the end of the year than you would have if you had $1060 at the beginning of the year. Your true return from lending the $1000 is equal to the percentage change in your purchasing power after taking into account the effects of inflation.

The stated interest rate on a loan is the **nominal interest rate**. The **real interest rate** corrects the nominal interest rate for the effect of inflation on the purchasing power of money. Essentially, the real interest rate is the amount of extra buying power you pay back (or get, if you're the lender) when a loan is repaid. As a simple example, suppose that the only good you purchase is coffee, and at the beginning of the year a cup of coffee costs $2.00. With $1000, you can buy 500 cups of coffee. If you lend the $1000 out for one year at an interest rate of 6 percent, you will receive $1060 at the end of the year. Suppose the inflation rate during the year is 2.5 percent, so the price of coffee has risen to $2.05 by the end of the year. How has your purchasing power increased as a result of making the loan? At the beginning of the year, your $1000 could have bought 500 cups of coffee. At the end of the year, your $1060 can buy $1060/$2.05 = 517 cups of coffee. In other words, you can purchase 3.4 percent more coffee than you could at the beginning of the year. In this case, the real interest rate you received from lending was 3.4 percent. For low rates of inflation, a convenient approximation of the real interest rate is:

$$\text{Real interest rate} = \text{Nominal interest rate} - \text{Inflation rate.}$$

In our example, we can calculate the real interest rate by using this formula as 6 percent − 2.5 percent = 3.5 percent, which is close to the 3.4 percent we calculated above (this result would be even closer if we included the 0.0731707 of a cup of coffee you could have bought with the $1060 you had at the end of the year that we left out due to rounding). Holding the nominal interest rate constant, the higher the inflation rate, the lower the real interest rate. Notice that if the inflation rate turns out to be higher than expected, borrowers pay and lenders receive a lower real interest rate than either of them expected. For example, if the actual inflation rate is 5 percent instead of the 2.5 both you and the borrower expected, the real interest rate will be 1 percent instead of the 3.5 percent you thought you were going to get. This is bad news for you, but good news for your borrower.

You have likely heard people talk about a number of different interest rates. The *prime rate* is the rate at which the most credit-worthy businesses can borrow. The *conventional mortgage rate* is the rate at which the most credit-worthy individuals can borrow to purchase a house. The *overnight rate* is the rate at which banks can borrow from other banks for a period of 24 hours. The *bank rate* is the rate at which the Bank of Canada (our central bank) will lend to commercial banks. In general, all of the interest rates tend to move up when the bank rate increases and down when the bank rate falls. Figure 5.5 shows the key nominal interest rate in the Canadian economy and an estimate of the real interest rate. In periods when inflation is high, as was the case in the early 1980s, the

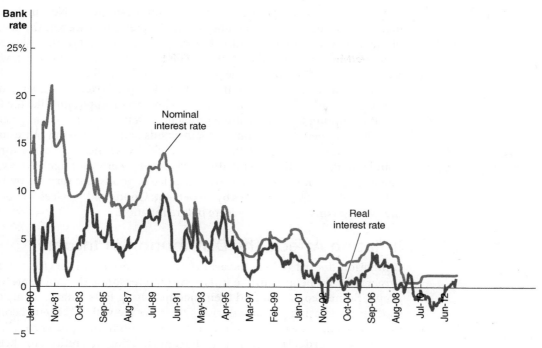

Figure 5.5   Nominal and Real Interest Rates, January 1980 to April 2013

The real interest rate is equal to the nominal interest rate minus the inflation rate. The real interest rate provides a better measure of the true cost of borrowing and the true return to lending than does the nominal interest rate. The nominal interest rate in the figure is the bank rate. The inflation rate is measured by the percentage change in the CPI from the same month one year earlier.

Sources: Data from CANSIM Table 326-0020 (series v41690973) and CANSIM series v122530, and author's calculations.

nominal interest rate is high and the gap between the nominal interest rate and the real interest rate is large. When inflation is low, as was the case in the recession of 2008 to 2009, the nominal interest rate is low and the gap between the nominal interest rate and the real interest rate is quite small.

It is difficult to know whether a particular nominal interest rate involves a high cost of borrowing or a low cost of borrowing. In August 1980, the nominal interest rate was 10.45 percent, which seems fairly high, but once we account for inflation, the real interest rate was actually *negative* 0.5 percent. A negative real interest rate means that the total amount you pay back from your loan can buy *less* than the amount you borrowed in the first place. By the same token, a low nominal interest rate doesn't always mean that borrowing is cheap. In June 1994, the nominal interest rate was almost 7 percent, but inflation was effectively zero at that time. This means that the real interest rate was actually 7 percent.

Does Inflation Impose Costs on the Economy?

5.7 LEARNING OBJECTIVE

Discuss the problems inflation can cause.

Imagine waking up tomorrow and finding that the price of everything has doubled. The prices of food, gas, computers, movies, pizzas, and beer have all doubled. But suppose that all wages and salaries have also doubled. Will this doubling of prices and wages matter? Think about walking into Best Buy, expecting to spend $250 on a new iPod. Instead, you find that iPods now cost $500. Will you leave without one? Probably not, because you're now getting paid $50 000 per year instead of the $25 000 per year you were making yesterday. Even though prices have doubled, your purchasing power has stayed exactly the same.

This hypothetical situation makes an important point: Nominal incomes generally increase with inflation. Remember from Chapter 4 that we can think of the $250 price of the iPod as representing either the value of the product or the value of all the income generated in producing the product. The two amounts are the same, whether the iPod sells for $250 or $500. When the price of the iPod rises from $250 to $500, that extra $250 ends up as income that goes to the workers at Apple, Foxcomm (the manufacturers of the iPod), sales staff at Best Buy, and the stockholders of Apple, just like the first $250 did.

It's tempting to think that the problem with inflation is that, as prices rise, consumers can no longer afford to buy as many goods and services, but our example shows that this isn't always the case. Rising prices don't always mean we can afford less (ask your grandparents what they could afford when they were your age). An expected inflation rate of 10 percent will raise the average price of goods and services by 10 percent, but it will also raise average incomes by 10 percent. Goods and services will be as affordable to the average consumer as they were before inflation.

Inflation Affects the Distribution of Income

If inflation doesn't reduce the affordability of goods and services to the average consumer, why do people dislike inflation? One reason is that there are very few *average people*. Some people will find their incomes rising faster than the rate of inflation, and so their purchasing power will rise. Other people will find their incomes rising more slowly than the rate of inflation, causing their purchasing power to fall. People on fixed incomes are particularly likely to be hurt by inflation. If a retired worker receives a fixed pension of $2000 per month, over time, inflation will reduce the purchasing power of that payment. In this way, inflation can change the distribution of income in a way that strikes many as being unfair.

The extent to which inflation redistributes income depends in part on whether the inflation is *anticipated*—in which case consumers, workers, and firms can see it coming and can prepare for it—or *unanticipated*—in which case they do not see it coming and do not prepare for it.

The Problem with Anticipated Inflation

Like many of life's problems, inflation is easier to deal with if you see it coming. Suppose that everyone knows that the inflation rate for the next 10 years will be 10 percent per year. Workers know that unless their wages go up by at least 10 percent per year, the real purchasing power of their wages will fall. Businesses will be willing to increase workers' wages enough to compensate for inflation because they know that the prices they can charge for their products will also increase. Lenders will realize that the loans they make will be paid back with dollars that are worth less than they were a year before, so they charge higher interest rates to compensate for this fact. Borrowers are willing to pay the higher interest rates because they also know the dollars they pay back will buy less than the ones they borrowed. So far, there do not seem to be any costs to anticipated inflation.

Even when inflation is perfectly anticipated, some individuals will experience a cost. Inevitably, there will be a redistribution of income, as some people's incomes do not grow at the same rate as anticipated inflation. In addition, firms and consumers have to hold some paper money to facilitate their buying and selling. Anyone holding paper money will find its purchasing power decreasing every year by the rate of inflation. To avoid this cost, firms and workers will try to hold as little paper money as possible, but they will have to hold some. In addition, to keep up with inflation, firms will have to change the price stickers on products and on shelves, which means paying someone to do it. Restaurants will have to reprint their menus more often to make sure their prices keep up with inflation. The costs to firms of changing the prices they charge for their products are called **menu costs**. At moderate levels of anticipated inflation, menu costs are relatively small, but when anticipated inflation is high, menu costs and the costs of holding paper money can be substantial. Finally, even anticipated inflation acts to raise the taxes paid by investors and raises the cost of capital for business investment. These effects arise because investors are taxed on the nominal interest payments they receive rather than on the real interest payments.

Menu costs The costs to firms of changing prices.

The Problem with Unanticipated Inflation

In any advanced economy—such as Canada's—households, workers, and firms routinely enter into contracts that commit them to make or receive payments for years in the future. For example, your university will have negotiated a contract with your professors, which commits the university to pay them a specific wage or salary for the duration of the contract (usually three to four years). When people buy houses, they usually borrow most of the amount they need from a bank. These loans, called *mortgages*, commit a borrower to make fixed monthly payments for the length of the loan. Most mortgage loans are for periods of 25 years but must be renewed several times over the length of the loan.

To make these long-term commitments, households and firms must forecast the rate of inflation. If a firm believes the inflation rate over the next three years will be 6 percent per year, signing a three-year contract with a union that calls for wage increases of 8 percent per year may seem reasonable because the firm may be able to raise its prices by at least the rate of inflation each year. If the firm believes that inflation will only be 2 percent per year, paying wages that increase by 8 percent per year may significantly reduce profits or even force the firm out of business.

When people borrow or lend money, they must forecast the rate of inflation so they can calculate the real rate of interest. In the 1980s, it was not uncommon for banks to charge interest rates of 18 percent or more on a mortgage. This seems really high by today's standards, seeing that the interest rates on mortgages are generally 4 or 5 percent. However, inflation rates in the 1980s were 10 percent or so compared with the 2 to 3 percent we see today.

When the actual inflation rate turns out to be very different from the expected inflation rate, some people gain and some people lose. This outcome seems unfair to most people because they are either winning or losing only because something they did not expect has happened. This apparently unfair redistribution is a key reason why people dislike unanticipated inflation.

Economics in Your Life

Should You Change Your Career Plans If You Graduate during a Recession?

At the beginning of the chapter, we asked whether layoffs in the banking industry should cause you to change your major and give up your plans to pursue a career as a banker and switch your major to natural resource/energy economics instead. We have learned in this chapter that unemployment rates are higher and layoffs more common in a recession than in an economic expansion. Because you're only in your second year of your degree, you have a few years before you graduate, by then the recession is likely to have ended and the unemployment rate will have fallen. You might also want to investigate whether the layoffs in the banking industry represent a permanent contraction in the size of the industry or a temporary decline due to the recession. If the reduction of banking sector jobs is more likely to be permanent, then you might consider a career in the energy industry. If the layoffs appear to be related mostly to the current recession, then you probably don't need to change your career path.

Conclusion

Inflation and unemployment are key macroeconomic problems. Elections are often won and lost on the basis of which candidate and party is able to convince the public that they can best deal with these problems. Many economists, however, would argue that, in the long run, maintaining high rates of growth of real GDP per person is the most important macroeconomic concern. Only when real GDP per person is increasing will a country's standard of living increase. In Chapter 6, we discuss the important issue of economic growth.

Read *An Inside Look* on the next page for a discussion of the application of the Purchasing Manager's Index in predicting the expansion or contraction of the Canadian manufacturing sector.

The Link between the Demand for Manufactured Products and Employment

POSTMEDIA NEWS

Manufacturing Grows

Canada is bucking an international trend of manufacturing contraction, according to a report released Thursday by the Royal Bank.

On a day when reports showed the purchasing managers indexes of several major economies dropping below 50, the line which indicates a contraction, RBC's new monthly Canadian manufacturing purchasing managers index rose to 54.9, up from 53.1 in July—a broad-based advance that included all four of Canada's major regions.

The Canadian manufacturing sector saw increases in both output and new orders in August, the report said.

"Panellists attributed growth of new work to greater demand and new client wins," it said. "Subsequently, firms employed additional staff to cope with the increase in workloads."

The international story is different, however, with the eurozone PMI dropping to 49 in August, "with every major economy coming in below expectation," notes Scotiabank chief currency strategist Camilla Sutton. Germany, which dropped to 50.9, was the only major economy in the zone to have a reading above 50.

"The global economy is already fairly fragile, and weaker-than-expected growth is a significant risk to the major European economies as it complicates austerity measures and threatens the viability of current estimates," Ms. Sutton added.

China's PMI is also at 50.9, which suggests that while there is growth, strong demand from earlier in the year has fallen off, she said.

Also on Thursday, the Institute for Supply Management in the U.S. reported its index of national factory activity slowed to 50.6 from 50.9 in July - a decline, but above the line that signals a contraction and a much better result than the 48.5 analysts had expected.

On Wednesday, Statistics Canada reported the country's economy shrank in the second quarter, which was largely blamed on a number of external factors, including the earthquake and tsunami in Japan in March, which disrupted automotive supply chains, and wildfires in Alberta, which led to lower production levels in the oilsands.

"Today's report supports the view that the supply-chain problems in manufacturing, which arose from the natural disasters that hit Japan in March, have started to reverse," said Paul Ferley, assistant chief economist at RBC. "This augurs well for a rebound in manufacturing activity for the second half of the year."

Along with the headline PMI, the RBC survey tracks changes in output, new orders, employment, inventories, prices and supplier delivery times.

The volume of new orders rose at the fastest rate since April, RBC reported, with increasing orders from abroad, especially the U.S.—good news in a week that saw Canada's trade deficit widen due to a slowdown in exports and an increase in imports.

Firms depleted inventories to fill orders for the second month in a row, and also stepped up production to meet the new demand, in turn adding more jobs to meet production goals, RBC said.

"Employment in the manufacturing sector increased during August," the report said. "Notably, the rate of growth was the fastest in three months. Almost 22% of surveyed firms hired additional staff, while 9% reported job losses. Job creation was generally linked to greater production requirements."

Quebec was the only province to post manufacturing job losses last month.

Source: Covert, Kim, "Canada's Manufacturing Sector Sees Gain in August: RBC," Postmedia News, Sept. 2, 2011. Material reprinted by the express permission of: National Post, a division of Postmedia Network, Inc.

Key Points in the Article

This article discusses some the effects of growing demand for manufactured products has on the economy. When orders for manufactured products increase, more workers are hired to produce the goods ordered. In an effort to predict which way unemployment will move over the upcoming months, the Royal Bank of Canada (RBC) asks purchasing managers about the plans their firms have for the upcoming months. The responses are combined to create the Purchasing Managers' Index (PMI). Values over 50 indicate that firms plan to expand their operations and values below 50 are good indicators that firms will reduce their operations and lay off workers.

Analyzing the News

Canadian manufacturers had a particularly difficult recession. Employment in the sector fell, and some firms went out of business. In August 2011, the PMI indicated that manufacturers all over Canada were expecting to expand rather than contract over the coming months. Analysts believe the positive outlook for Canadian manufacturers is due to increasing demand in many parts of the world, primarily developing countries, and Canadian manufacturers competing successfully against firms in other countries.

Other developed countries aren't doing as well as Canada. Eurozone (countries that use the euro as their currency) manufacturers indicated that they expected their businesses to shrink, except for those in Germany. These firms are not seeing the same increase in demand for their products and are expecting less support for their businesses from the government over the foreseeable future.

China and the United States both showed signs of weak expansion in the PMI. The 50.9 value of the index in both countries suggests that, on average, purchasing managers did not expect their firms to grow much if at all over the next few months.

The manufacturing sector still plays an important role in the Canadian economy, accounting for about 12.5 percent of real GDP in 2013. Employment in the manufacturing sector plays a large role in determining the unemployment rate for the entire economy. As manufacturers get more orders for their products, they increase production and hire more labour. This generally makes the unemployment rate fall.

Thinking Critically

1. The article points out the link between the manufacturing sector and the overall unemployment rate. If the PMI in your region of the country is 48.5, what could you expect to happen to the unemployment rate in the near future? What type of unemployment would you expect to see change and why?

2. The PMI is not always an accurate predictor of future economic activity. Sometimes the PMI for the manufacturing sector will predict economic growth, but the economy actually ends up shrinking. Why isn't the PMI always accurate? Why might this occur?

Chapter Summary and Problems

Key Terms

Consumer price index (CPI), p. 132

Cyclical unemployment, p. 127

Discouraged workers, p. 124

Efficiency wage, p. 130

Employment–population ratio, p. 123

Frictional unemployment, p. 126

Inflation, p. 131

Inflation rate, p. 132

Labour force, p. 123

Labour force participation rate, p. 123

Menu costs, p. 138

Natural rate of unemployment, p. 128

Nominal interest rate, p. 136

Price level, p. 132

Producer price index (PPI), p. 134

Real interest rate, p. 136

Seasonal unemployment, p. 127

Structural unemployment, p. 127

Unemployment rate, p. 122

Working age population, p. 122

Summary

*LO 5.1 Statistics Canada uses the results of the Labour Force Survey to calculate the *unemployment rate*, the *labour force participation rate*, and the *employment ratio*. The *labour force* is the total number of people who have jobs plus the number of people who do not have jobs but are actively looking for them. The *unemployment rate* is the percentage of the labour force that is unemployed. *Discouraged workers* are people who are available for work but who are not actively looking for a job because they believe no jobs are available for them. Discouraged workers are not counted as unemployed. The *labour force participation rate* is the percentage of the working age population in the labour force. Since the 1970s, the participation rate of women has been rising, while the labour force participation of men has been falling. The employment–population ratio measures the portion of the working age population that is employed. Except for severe recessions, the typical unemployed person finds a new job or returns to his or her previous job within a few months. Each year, thousands of jobs are created in Canada, and thousands of jobs are destroyed.

LO 5.2 There are four types of unemployment: frictional, structural, cyclical, and seasonal. *Frictional unemployment* is short-term unemployment that arises from the process of matching workers with jobs. *Structural unemployment* arises from a persistent mismatch between the job skills or attributes of workers and the requirements of jobs. *Cyclical unemployment* is caused by a business cycle recession. *Seasonal unemployment* is due to factors such as weather, variations in tourism, legislation that restricts activities to certain times of year, and other calendar-related events. The *natural rate of unemployment* is the normal rate of unemployment, consisting of frictional unemployment plus structural unemployment. The natural rate of unemployment is also sometimes called the *full-employment rate of unemployment*.

LO 5.3 Government policies can reduce the level of frictional and structural unemployment by aiding in the search for jobs and the retraining of workers. Some government policies, however, can add to the level of frictional, structural, and seasonal unemployment. Employment Insurance payments can raise the unemployment rate by extending the time that unemployed workers search for jobs and can reduce the incentive for seasonal workers to look for off-season work. Government policies in Canada (and most high-income countries) have led to unemployment rates that are historically higher than in the United States. Wages above market levels can also increase unemployment. Wages may be above market levels because of minimum wage laws, labour unions, and efficiency wages. An *efficiency wage* is a higher-than-market wage that a firm pays to increase worker productivity.

LO 5.4 The *price level* measures the average prices of goods and services in the economy. The *inflation rate* is equal to the percentage change in the price level from one year to the next. Statistics Canada compiles data on three different measures of the price level: the consumer price index (CPI), the GDP deflator, and the producer price index (PPI). The *consumer price index (CPI)* is an average of the prices of goods and services purchased by a typical household. Changes in the CPI are the best measure of changes in the cost of living as experienced by the typical household. Biases in the construction of the CPI cause changes in it to overstate the true inflation rate from 0.5 percentage point to 1 percentage point. The *producer price index (PPI)* is an average of prices received by producers of goods and services at all stages of production.

LO 5.5 Price indexes are designed to measure changes in the price level over time, not the absolute level of prices. To correct for the effects of inflation, we can divide a *nominal variable* by a price index and multiply by 100 to obtain a *real variable*. The real variable will be measured in dollars of the base year for the price index.

LO 5.6 The stated interest rate on a loan is the *nominal interest rate*. The *real interest rate* is the nominal interest rate minus the inflation rate. Because it is corrected for the effects of inflation, the real interest rate provides a better measure of the true cost of borrowing and the true return from lending than does the nominal interest rate.

LO 5.7 Inflation does not reduce the affordability of goods and services to the average consumer, but it does impose costs on the economy. When inflation is anticipated, its main costs are that paper money loses some of its value and firms incur *menu costs*. *Menu costs* include the costs of changing prices on products and printing new catalogues. When inflation is unanticipated, the actual inflation rate can turn out to be different from the expected inflation rate. As a result, income is redistributed as some people gain and some people lose.

MyEconLab   Log in to MyEconLab to complete these exercises and get instant feedback.

*'Learning Objective' is abbreviated to 'LO' in the end of chapter material.

Review Questions

LO 5.1

1.1 How is the unemployment rate measured? What are the three conditions someone needs to meet to be counted as unemployed?

1.2 What are the problems in measuring the unemployment rate? In what ways does the official Statistics Canada measure of the unemployment rate *overstate* the true degree of unemployment? In what ways does the official Statistics Canada measure of the unemployment rate *understate* the true degree of unemployment?

LO 5.2

2.1 What are the four types of unemployment?

2.2 What is the natural rate of unemployment? What is the relationship between the natural rate of unemployment and full employment? Would it be better for economists to define full employment as being an unemployment rate equal to zero?

LO 5.3

3.1 What effect does the payment of Employment Insurance have on the unemployment rate? On the severity of recessions?

3.2 Discuss the effect of each of the following on the unemployment rate.
a. Provincial minimum wage laws
b. Labour unions
c. Efficiency wages

LO 5.4

4.1 Briefly describe the three major measures of the price level.

4.2 What potential biases exist in calculating the consumer price index?

LO 5.5

5.1 What is the difference between a nominal variable and a real variable?

5.2 Briefly explain how you can use data on nominal wages for 2004 to 2012 and data on the consumer price index for the same years to calculate the real wage for these years.

LO 5.6

6.1 What is the difference between the nominal interest rate and the real interest rate?

6.2 The chapter explains that it is impossible to know whether a particular nominal interest rate is "high" or "low." Briefly explain why.

LO 5.7

7.1 Why do nominal incomes generally increase with inflation? If nominal incomes increase with inflation, does inflation reduce the purchasing power of the average consumer? Briefly explain.

7.2 How can inflation affect the distribution of income?

Problems and Applications

LO 5.1

1.1 Fill in the missing values in the following table of data collected in the Labour Force Survey in February 2012:

Working Age Population	
Employment	16 877 000
Unemployment	
Unemployment rate	7.7%
Labour force	
Labour force participation rate	65.6%
Employment–population ratio	

CANSIM Table 282-0001 Series v2091030, v2091051, v2091072, v2091135, v2091177, v2091198, v2091219. Reproduced and distributed on an "as is" basis with the permission of Statistics Canada.

1.2 Is it possible for the total number of people who are unemployed to increase while the unemployment rate decreases? Briefly explain.

1.3 In February 2012, the unemployment rate fell to 7.7 percent, despite the fact that Statistics Canada reported that 2800 jobs were lost. How could the unemployment rate fall when the number of jobs in the economy is also decreasing? Further, the same report identifies that 9100 full-time jobs were created during the month. How is it possible to have the same report saying that the economy lost 2800 jobs at the same time 9100 new full-time jobs were created?

LO 5.2

2.1 Macroeconomic conditions affect the decisions firms and families make. Why, for example, might a student graduating from college enter the job market during an economic expansion but apply for graduate school during a recession?

2.2 A politician makes the following argument: "The economy would operate more efficiently if frictional unemployment were eliminated. Therefore, a goal of government policy should be to reduce the frictional rate of unemployment to the lowest possible level." Briefly explain whether you agree with this argument.

2.3 [**Related to** Making the Connection **on page 129**] What advice for finding a job would you give someone who is frictionally unemployed? What advice would you give someone who is structurally unemployed? What advice would you give someone who is cyclically unemployed?

2.4 [**Related to** Making the Connection **on page 131**] Describe the advantages and disadvantages of efficiency wages.

LO 5.3

3.1 If Parliament eliminated the Employment Insurance system, what would be the effect on the level of frictional unemployment? What would be the effect on the level of real GDP? Would well-being in the economy be increased? Briefly explain.

3.2 Why do you think the minimum wage in Newfoundland and Labrador was set at only $0.50 per hour in 1965? Wouldn't this wage have been well below the equilibrium wage?

3.3 Costco typically pays its workers higher wages than does Walmart. One analyst argues that Costco pays higher wages "because it requires higher-skilled workers to sell higher-cost products to more affluent customers." If this analyst is correct, can we conclude that Costco is paying efficiency wages and Walmart is not? Briefly explain.

Based on Lori Montgomery, "Maverick Costco CEO Joins Push to Raise Minimum Wage," *Washington Post*, January 30, 2007.

LO 5.4

4.1 [**Related to** Don't Let This Happen to You **on page 134**] Briefly explain whether you agree or disagree with the following statement: "I don't believe the government price statistics. The CPI for 2010 was 218, but I know that the inflation rate couldn't have been as high as 118 percent in 2010."

4.2 In calculating the consumer price index for the year, why does Statistics Canada use the quantities in the basket of goods and services rather than the quantities purchased during the current year?

4.3 The new house price index issued by Statistics Canada is an indicator of housing price trends in Canada. The base year for the index is June 2007. The following table lists index numbers for January 2011 and January 2012 for six cities.

City	January 2011	January 2012
Halifax	111.6	112.6
Montreal	112.8	115.0
Toronto	107.8	114.2
Regina	142.1	149.7
Calgary	95.9	95.8
Vancouver	98.4	98.4

a. Calculate the percentage change in housing prices from January 2011 to January 2012 for each of these six cities. In which city did housing prices change the most? The least?

b. Can you determine on the basis of these numbers which city had the most expensive homes in January 2012? Briefly explain.

Data from CANSIM Table 327-0046 Series: v53600443, v53600458, v53600467, v53600500, v53600509, v53600518.

LO 5.5

5.1 [**Related to** Solved Problem 5.1 **on page 135**] Use the information in the following table to determine the percentage changes in the US and French *real* minimum wages between 1957 and 2010. Does it matter for your answer that you have not been told the base year for the US CPI or the French CPI? Was the percentage increase in the price level greater in the United States or in France during these years?

	United States		France	
Year	Minimum Wage (dollars per hour)	CPI	Minimum Wage (euros per hour)	CPI
1957	$1.00	27	€0.19	10
2010	7.25	215	8.86	128

Based on John M. Abowd, Francis Kramarz, Thomas Lemieux, and David N. Margolis, "Minimum Wages and Youth Employment in France and the United States," in D. Blanchflower and R. Freeman, eds., Youth Employment and Joblessness in Advanced Countries, (Chicago: University of Chicago Press, 1999), pp. 427–472 (the value for the minimum wage is given in francs; it was converted to euros at a conversion rate of 1 euro = 6.55957 francs); Insee online data bank, www.insee.fr; U.S. Department of Labor; and U.S. Bureau of Labor Statistics.

5.2 [**Related to** Solved Problem 5.1 **on page 135**] The recession that began in 2008 was one of the most important economic events for the G7 countries of the last 70 years. Canada's performance during the recession was one of the best in the developed world. Use the data in the table below to calculate the percentage decline in real GDP between 2007 and 2009.

CANSIM Series v3260022 and v464937. Reproduced and distributed on an "as is" basis with the permission of Statistics Canada.

Year	Nominal GDP (billions of dollars)	Consumer Price Index (2002 = 100)
2007	$1529.6	111.45
2009	1529.0	114.45

Data from Statistics Canada, CANSIM Tables 380-0064 and 176-0043.

LO 5.6

6.1 Suppose you were borrowing money to buy a car. Which of these situations would you prefer: The interest rate on your car loan is 20 percent and the inflation rate is 19 percent OR the interest rate on your car loan is 5 percent and the inflation rate is 2 percent? Briefly explain.

6.2 Suppose that the only good you purchase is hamburgers and that at the beginning of the year, the price of a hamburger is $2.00. Suppose you lend $1000 for one year at an interest rate of 5 percent. At the end of the year, a hamburger costs $2.08. What is the real rate of interest you earned on your loan?

6.3 During the 1990s, Japan experienced periods of deflation (negative inflation) and low nominal interest rates that approached zero percent. Why would lenders of funds agree to a nominal interest rate of almost zero percent? (Hint: Were real interest rates in Japan also low during this period?)

LO 5.7

7.1 What are menu costs? What effect has the internet had on the size of menu costs?

7.2 Suppose that the inflation rate turns out to be much higher than most people expected. In that case, would you rather have been a borrower or a lender? Briefly explain.

MyEconLab   MyEconLab is an online tool designed to help you master the concepts covered in your course. It will create an adaptive, highly personalized study plan to stimulate and measure your learning. Log in to take advantage of this powerful study aid, and to access quizzes and other valuable course-related material.

Economic Growth, the Financial System, and Business Cycles

Chapter Outline and Learning Objectives

6.1 Long-Run Economic Growth, page 148
Discuss the importance of long-run economic growth.

6.2 Saving, Investment, and the Financial System, page 155
Discuss the role of the financial system in facilitating long-run economic growth.

6.3 The Business Cycle, page 162
Explain what happens during the business cycle.

Doug Steakley/Getty Images

Economic Growth and the Business Cycle at Bombardier

In 1937, Joseph-Armand Bombardier invented a snowmobile to help people navigate snowy roads in Quebec. In 1942, he founded L'Auto-Neige Bombardier Limitée and began manufacturing 12-passenger snowmobiles. Bombardier also developed a personal snowmobile, the Ski-Doo, in 1959. Short-run changes in the state of the economy can dramatically change the opportunities facing firms. When the oil crisis of 1973 hit, the demand for Ski-Doos fell by half and Bombardier had to look for new markets and new products, eventually finding a new niche, making train cars for subways and mass-transit systems.

Long-run economic growth provides firms with new opportunities as people's incomes grow. In 1986, Bombardier added another product line to its manufacturing business: the Canadair Regional Jet (CRJ), a 50-seat short-haul passenger aircraft. Today, the CRJ line of regional jets is the world's most successful regional aircraft program.

Bombardier now employs more than 30 300 people worldwide and produces aerospace and transportation products.

Despite having the most successful regional aircraft program in the world, Bombardier is still subject to the business cycle. When global demand falls, demand for Bombardier's products falls as well. On September 21, 2011, Bombardier announced that it would slow production of regional jets due to a decrease in new orders.

In this chapter, we provide an overview of long-run growth and the business cycle and their importance for firms, consumers, and the economy as a whole.

AN INSIDE LOOK on **page 168** discusses how the business cycle affected Bombardier's production plans as the global economy recovered from a recession.

Sources: http://www.financialpost.com/news/Bombardier+regional+production/5433138/story.html and http://www.bombardier.com/en/corporate.

Economics in Your Life

Do You Help the Economy More If You Spend or If You Save?

Suppose that you have received an income tax refund cheque from the federal government. You are not sure what to do with the money, so you ask your two roommates for advice. One roommate tells you that if you want to help the economy, you should save all the money because a country's economic growth depends on the amount of saving by households. The other roommate disagrees and advises you to spend all the money because consumer spending is a major component of gross domestic product (GDP), and your spending would help increase production and create more jobs. Which of your two roommates is right? As you read this chapter, see if you can answer this question. You can check your answer against the one we provide on page 166 at the end of this chapter.

A successful economy is capable of increasing production of goods and services faster than the growth in population. Increasing production faster than population growth is the only way that the standard of living of the average person in a country can increase. Unfortunately, some economies around the world are not growing at all or growing slowly compared with their rate of population growth. In some countries of sub-Saharan Africa, living standards are barely higher than, or in a few cases lower than, they were 50 years ago. Most people in these low-growth countries live in the same poverty their ancestors did. In Canada and most developed countries, however, living standards are much higher than they were 50 years ago. An important topic in macroeconomics is why some countries grow much faster than others.

As we will see, one determinant of economic growth is the ability of firms to expand their operations, buy additional equipment, train workers, and adopt new technologies. To carry out these activities, firms must acquire funds from households, either directly through financial markets—such as the stock and bond markets—or indirectly through financial intermediaries—such as banks. Financial markets and financial intermediaries together make up the *financial system*. In this chapter, we will present an overview of the financial system and see how funds flow from households to firms through the *market for loanable funds*.

Expansion The period of a business cycle during which total production and total employment are increasing.

Recession The period of a business cycle during which total production and total employment are decreasing.

Business cycle Alternating periods of economic expansion and economic recession.

Dating back to at least the early nineteenth century, the Canadian economy has experienced periods of expanding production and employment followed by periods of recession, during which production and employment fall. As we noted in Chapter 4, these alternating periods of **expansion** and **recession** are called the **business cycle**. The business cycle is not uniform: Each period of expansion is not the same length, nor is each period of recession, but every period of expansion in Canadian history has been followed by a period of recession, and every recession has been followed by a period of expansion.

In this chapter, we begin to explore two key aspects of macroeconomics: the long-run growth that has steadily raised living standards in Canada and the short-run fluctuations of the business cycle.

6.1 LEARNING OBJECTIVE

Discuss the importance of long-run economic growth.

Long-Run Economic Growth

Most people in Canada, the United States, Western Europe, Japan, and other advanced countries expect that over time their standard of living will improve. They expect that year after year, firms will introduce new and improved products, new prescription drugs and better medical techniques will allow them to be healthier and live longer, and their ability to afford the goods and services they desire will increase. For most people, these are reasonable expectations.

Figure 6.1 illustrates two important points about GDP per capita. First, GDP per capita has been rising over the last 50-plus years; this is what we mean when we talk about "economic growth." Second, GDP per capita fluctuates from year to year; economic growth hasn't been smooth. In fact, since 1961, GDP per capita in Canada has fallen during three periods. These drops and rises over the short-run are due to the business cycle.

Long-run economic growth The process by which rising productivity increases the average standard of living.

The process of **long-run economic growth** brought the typical Canadian from the standard of living of 1961 to the standard of living we see today. The best measure of standard of living is real GDP per person, which is usually referred to as *real GDP per capita*. So we measure long-run economic growth by increases in real GDP per capita over long periods of time, generally decades or more. We use real GDP rather than nominal GDP to adjust for changes in the price level over time. Figure 6.1 shows the real GDP per capita for Canada from 1961 to 2012.

In 1961, Canada enjoyed one of the highest living standards in the world with real GDP per capita of about $16 000 (in 2007 dollars). Even though Canada was one of the wealthiest countries in the world, most households had one television with only a few channels, household air conditioning was unheard of, and long-distance calls

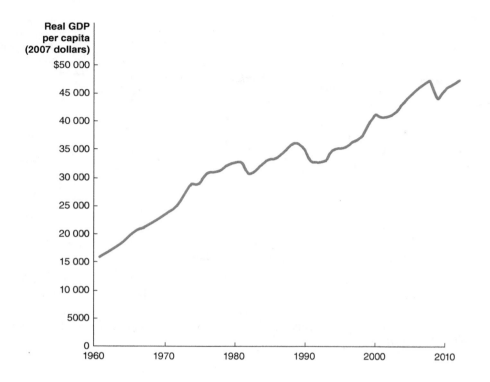

Figure 6.1

Real GDP per Capita, 1961–2012

Measured in 2007 dollars, real GDP per capita in Canada grew from about $16 000 per person in 1961 to about $47 000 per person in 2012. The average Canadian in 2012 could buy 2.9 times as many goods and services in 2012 as the average Canadian in 1961.

Sources: Data on nominal GDP and the GDP deflator since 1961 are from Statistics Canada CANSIM II, series V3862688 and V3860248. Values from 1870 to 1960 are from Urquhart (1988). Since 1971 the population series is from Statistics Canada CANSIM II, series V466668. From 1921 to 1970 it is from Statistics Canada CANSIM I, series D892580. From 1870 to 1920 it is from Urquhart (1988).

were very expensive. In 2012, real GDP per capita was about $47 000 (again in 2007 dollars). The purchasing power of the average Canadian today is almost three times as much as the average Canadian in 1961. As big as this increase in real GDP per capita is, it actually understates the true increase in the standard of living that Canadians enjoy today. Many of the products we now take for granted, such as personal computers and cellphones, didn't exist in 1961. If you were attending university in 1961, you wouldn't have been able to purchase a reasonably sized computer, no matter your income.

Of course, the quantity of goods and services you can purchase is not a perfect indicator of how happy or content you might be. The level of crime, spiritual well-being, pollution, and many other factors ignored in calculating GDP contribute to a person's happiness. Nevertheless, economists rely heavily on comparisons of real GDP per capita because it is the best means of comparing the performance of one economy over time or the performance of different economies at any one particular time.

Making
the
Connection

Economic Prosperity and Health

We can see the direct impact of economic growth on living standards by looking at health in high-income countries over the past 50 years. The research of Robert Fogel, winner of the Nobel Prize in Economics, highlights the close connection between economic growth, improvements in technology, and improvements in human physiology. One important measure of health is life expectancy at birth. As the graph below shows, life expectancy since 1960 has increased. Men born in 1960 could expect to live 68.2 years, while women born in the same year could expect to live 74.2 years. A man born in 2010 could expect to live to the age of 79.2, and a woman with the same birth year can expect to reach 83.6 years old.

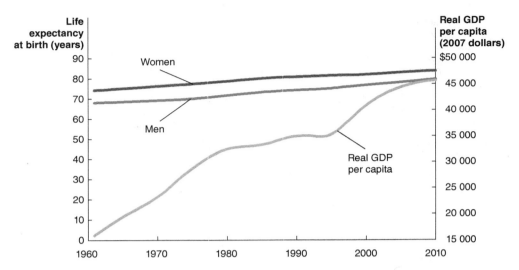

There is a similar relationship between life expectancy at birth and real GDP per capita when we compare different countries. Countries with high real GDP per capita, such as Canada, Sweden, and Switzerland also have high life expectancies. Countries with very low real GDP per capita, such as Chad, Zimbabwe, and Togo, also have very low life expectancies.

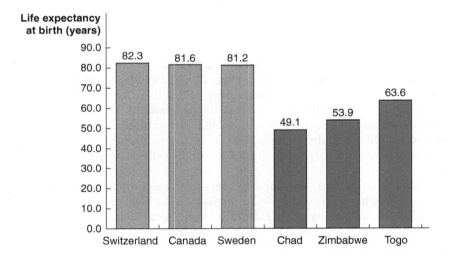

When countries produce more goods and services, more of those goods and services can be devoted to providing health care to people. Higher real GDP per capita is also linked to access to more and better-quality food.

Sources: http://www.osfi-bsif.gc.ca/app/DocRepository/1/eng/oca/studies/cppmrt_e.pdf [[new report expected in 2012?]], and The Economist Pocket World in Figures, 2011 edition.

MyEconLab   **Your Turn:** Test your understanding by doing related problem 1.2 on page 171 at the end of this chapter.

Calculating Growth Rates and the Rule of 70

The growth rate of real GDP or real GDP per capita during a particular year is equal to the percentage change from the previous year. For example, measured in prices of the year 2007, real GDP was $1 598 760 in 2011 and rose to $1 644 639 million in 2012. We calculate the growth of real GDP in 2012 as follows:

$$\frac{\$1\ 644\ 639\ \text{million} - \$1\ 598\ 760\ \text{million}}{\$1\ 598\ 760\ \text{million}} \times 100 = 2.9\%$$

For longer periods of time, we can use the *average annual growth rate*. For example, the real GDP in Canada was $966 112 million in 1990 and $1 553 488 million in 2010. To find the average annual growth rate during this 20-year period, we compute the annual growth rate that would result in $966 112 million increasing to $1 553 488 million over 20 years. In this case, the growth rate is 2.4 percent. That is, if $966 112 million grows at an average rate of 2.4 percent per year, after 20 years, it will have grown to $1 553 488 million.

For shorter periods of time, we get approximately the same answer by averaging the growth rate for each year. For example, real GDP in Canada shrank by 0.2 percent in 2008 (which is the same as growing at −0.2 percent per year), shrank again by 2 percent in 2009, and grew by 2.9 percent in 2010. So the average annual growth rate for the period 2008 to 2010 was 0.23 percent, which is the average of the three annual growth rates:

$$\frac{-0.2\% - 2\% + 2.9\%}{3} = 0.23\%.$$

Note that when discussing long-run economic growth, we usually shorten "average annual growth rate" to "growth rate."

We can judge how rapidly an economic variable is growing by calculating the number of years it would take to double. For example, if real GDP per capita in a country doubles, say, every 20 years, most people in the country will experience significant increases in their standard of living over the course of their lives. If real GDP per capita doubles only every 100 years, increases in the standard of living will occur too slowly to notice. One easy way to calculate approximately how many years it will take real GDP per capita to double is to use the *rule of 70*. The formula for the rule of 70 is as follows:

$$\text{Number of years to double} = \frac{70}{\text{Growth rate}}$$

For example, if real GDP per capita is growing at a rate of 5 percent per year, it will take 70/5 = 14 years to double. If real GDP per capita is growing at a rate of 2 percent per year, it will double in 70/2 = 35 years to double. These examples illustrate an important point that we will discuss further in Chapter 7: Small differences in growth rates can have large effects on how rapidly the standard of living in a country increases. Finally, notice that the rule of 70 applies not only to growth in real GDP per capita but also to growth in any variable. For example, if you invest $1000 in the stock market and your investment grows at an average annual rate of 7 percent, your investment will double to $2000 in 10 years.

What Determines the Rate of Long-Run Growth?

In Chapter 7, we explore the sources of economic growth in more detail and discuss why growth in Canada and other high-income countries has been so much faster than in poorer countries (until fairly recently). For now, we will focus on the basic point that *increases in real GDP per capita depend on increases in labour productivity*. **Labour productivity** is the quantity of goods and services that can be produced by one worker or by one hour of work. In analyzing long-run growth, economists usually measure labour productivity as output per hour of work to avoid the effects of fluctuations in the length of the workday or in the fraction of the population employed. If the quantity of goods and services consumed by the average person is to increase, the quantity of goods and services produced per hour of work must also increase. Why in 2012 was the average Canadian able to consume almost three times as much as the average Canadian in 1961? The simple answer is because the average Canadian worker was three times more productive in 2012 than the average Canadian worker in 1961.

If increases in labour productivity are the key to long-run economic growth, what causes labour productivity to increase? Economists believe two key factors determine

Labour productivity The quantity of goods and services that can be produced by one worker or by one hour of work.

labour productivity: the quantity of capital per hour worked and the level of technology. Therefore, economic growth occurs if the quantity of capital per hour worked increases and if technological change occurs.

Increases in Capital per Hour Worked Workers today in high-income countries, such as Canada, have more physical capital available than workers in low-income countries. Canadian workers today have much more capital than Canadian workers in 1961. **Capital** refers to manufactured goods that are used to produce other goods and services. Examples of capital are computers, factories, buildings, machines and tools, warehouses, and trucks. The total amount of physical capital available in a country is known as the country's *capital stock*.

Capital Manufactured goods that are used to produce other goods and services.

As the capital stock per hour worked increases, worker productivity increases. A secretary with a personal computer can produce more documents per day than a secretary with a manual typewriter. A worker with a backhoe can dig a bigger hole in a day than a worker equipped with just a shovel.

Human capital refers to the accumulated knowledge and skills workers acquire from education, training, or from life experience. For example, workers with a university education generally have more skills and are more productive than workers who have only a high school degree. Increases in human capital are particularly important in stimulating economic growth.

Technological Change Economic growth depends more on technological change than on increases in capital per hour worked. *Technology* refers to the processes a firm uses to turn inputs into outputs of goods and services. Technological change is an increase in the quantity of output firms can produce using a given quantity of inputs. Technological change can come from many sources. For example, a firm's managers may rearrange a factory floor or the layout of a retail store to increase production and sales. Most technological change, however, is embodied in new machinery, equipment, or software.

A very important point is that just accumulating more inputs—such as labour, capital, or natural resources—will not ensure that an economy experiences economic growth unless technological change also occurs. For example, the Soviet Union failed to maintain a high rate of economic growth, even though it continued to increase the quantity of capital available per hour worked. The Soviet system experienced little technological change.

In implementing technological change, *entrepreneurs* are critical. Recall from Chapter 2 that an entrepreneur is someone who operates a business, bringing together the factors of production—labour, capital, and natural resources—to produce goods and services. In a market economy, entrepreneurs make crucial decisions about whether to introduce new technology to produce better or lower-cost products. Entrepreneurs also decide whether to allocate the firm's resources to research and development that can result in new technologies. One of the difficulties centrally planned economies have in sustaining economic growth is that managers employed by the government are typically much slower to develop and adopt new technologies than entrepreneurs in a market system.

Solved Problem 6.1

The Role of Technological Change in Economic Growth

Between 1960 and 1995, real GDP per capita in Singapore grew at an average annual rate of 6.2 percent. This very rapid growth rate means that the level of real GDP per capita was doubling about every 11.3 years. In 1995, Alwyn Young published an article in which he argued that Singapore's growth depended more on increases in capital per hour worked, increases in the labour force participation rate, and the transfer of workers from agricultural to non-agricultural jobs than on technological change. If Young's analysis was correct, predict what was likely to happen to Singapore's growth rate in the years after 1995.

Solving the Problem

Step 1: **Review the chapter material.** This problem is about what determines the rate of long-run growth, so you may want to review the section "What Determines the Rate of Long-Run Growth?" on page 151.

Step 2: **Predict what happened to the growth rate in Singapore after 1995.** As countries begin to develop, they often experience an increase in the labour force participation rate, as workers who were not part of the paid labour force respond to rising wages. Many workers also leave the agricultural sector— where output per hour worked is often low—for the non-agricultural sector. These changes increase real GDP per capita, but they are "one-shot" changes that eventually come to an end (you cannot have a participation rate greater than 100 percent, for example). Similarly, as we already noted, increases in capital per hour worked cannot sustain high rates of economic growth unless they are accompanied by technological change.

We can conclude that Singapore was unlikely to sustain its high growth rates in the years after 1995. In fact, from 1996 to 2012, the growth of real GDP per capita slowed to an average rate of 3.2 percent per year. Although this growth rate is similar to high income countries (like Canada), it leads to a doubling of real GDP per capita only every 22 years, rather than every 11.3 years.

Sources: Alwyn Young, "The Tyranny of Numbers: Confronting the Statistical Realities of the East Asian Growth Experience," Quarterly Journal of Economics, Vol 11, NO. 3, August 1995, pp.641-680; and International Monetary Fund, World Economic Outlook Database, April 2009.

Your Turn: For more practice, do related problem 1.6 on page 171 at the end of this chapter.

MyEconLab

Finally, an additional requirement for economic growth is that the government must provide secure rights to private property. As we saw in Chapter 2, a market system cannot function unless rights to private property are secure. In addition, the government can help the market system work and aid economic growth by establishing an independent court system that enforces contracts between private individuals. Many economists would also say that the government has a role in facilitating the development of an efficient financial system, as well as systems of education, transportation, and communication.

Making
the
Connection

Rapid Economic Growth in Botswana

Economic growth in much of sub-Saharan Africa has been very slow. As desperately poor as most of these countries were in 1960, some are even poorer today. However, the growth rate in one country in this region stands out as being exceptionally rapid. The graph below shows the average annual growth rate in real GDP per capita between 1960 and 2009 for Botswana and the six most populous sub-Saharan countries. Botswana's average annual growth rate over this 49-year period was more than three times as great as Tanzania's, which was the second-fastest growing country in the group. Botswana may seem an unlikely country to experience rapid growth because it has been hit hard by the HIV epidemic. Despite the disruptive effects of the epidemic, growth in real per capita GDP continued to be rapid through 2007 (although the global recession did reduce growth in 2008 and 2009).

What explains Botswana's rapid growth rate? Several factors have been important. Botswana avoided the civil wars that plagued other African countries during these years. The country also benefited from earnings from exporting diamonds. But many economists believe the pro-growth policies of its government are the most important reason for the country's success.

The government of Botswana has protected private property, avoided political instability, limited corruption, and allowed freedom of the press and democracy. While these things may seem a straightforward recipe for providing an environment in which economic growth can occur, as we will see in Chapter 8, such policies can be very difficult to implement in practice.

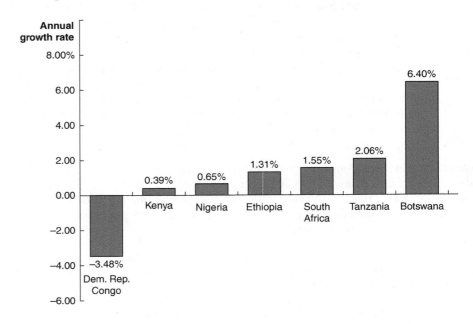

Source: Author's calculations on data from Alan Heston, Robert Summers and Bettina Aten, Penn World Table Version 7.0, Center for International Comparisons of Production, Income and Prices at the University of Pennsylvania, May 2011.

MyEconLab

Your Turn: Test your understanding by doing related problem 1.7 on page 171 at the end of this chapter.

Potential GDP

Potential GDP The level of real GDP attained when all firms are producing at capacity.

In thinking about long-run economic growth, the concept of *potential GDP* is useful. **Potential GDP** is the level of real GDP attained when all firms are producing at capacity. The capacity of a firm is *not* the maximum output the firm is capable of producing. A Bombardier assembly plant could operate 24 hours per day for 365 days per year and would be at its maximum production level. The plant's capacity, however, is measured by its production when operating on normal hours, using a normal workforce. If all firms in the economy were operating at capacity, the level of total production of final goods and services would equal potential GDP. Potential GDP will increase over time as the labour force grows, new factories are built, new machinery and equipment are installed, and technological change takes place.

In Canada, the Bank of Canada estimates and reports the "output gap," which is the percentage difference between *actual* GDP and *potential* GDP. Sometimes the output gap is negative, and at other times it is positive. When the output gap is negative, actual real GDP is below potential real GDP and the economy is not making full use of its resources. When the output gap is positive, real GDP is above potential GDP and the economy is using its resources in an unsustainable way or, more accurately, the economy is using resources in a way that will lead to inflation. Figure 6.2 shows the output gap for the Canadian economy since 1981. You can see that actual GDP was below potential GDP quite a few times in the last 30 years. The major deviations of actual GDP from potential GDP correspond to recessions. The Canadian economy experienced recessions in the early 1980s, early 1990s, and a third in the late 2000s.

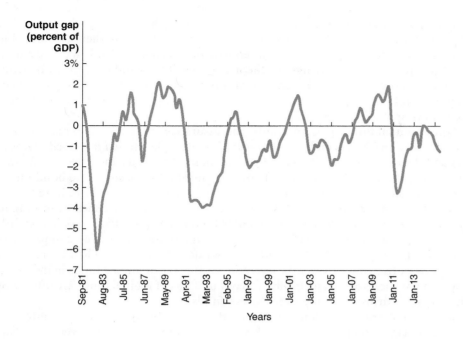

Figure 6.2

The Output Gap

The Bank of Canada measures the output gap as the difference between actual GDP and potential GDP as a percentage of potential GDP. When the output gap is positive, actual GDP is larger than potential GDP; when the output gap is negative, actual GDP is smaller than potential GDP. A negative output gap is associated with a recession.

Data from Bank of Canada. http://www.bankofcanada.ca/rates/indicators/capacity-and-inflation-pressures/product-market-definitions/product-market-historical-data/

Saving, Investment, and the Financial System

6.2 LEARNING OBJECTIVE

Discuss the role of the financial system in facilitating long-run economic growth.

The process of economic growth depends on the ability of firms to expand their operations, buy additional equipment, train workers, and adopt new technologies. Firms can pay for some of these activities from *retained earnings*, which are profits that are reinvested in the firm rather than paid to the firm's owners. For many firms, retained earnings are not sufficient to finance the rapid expansion required in economies with high rates of economic growth. Firms can also get funds from households, either directly through financial markets—such as stock and bond markets—or indirectly through financial intermediaries—such as banks. Financial markets and financial intermediaries together make up the **financial system**. Without a well-functioning financial system, economic growth is almost impossible because firms will be unable to expand and adopt new technologies. As we noted earlier, no country without a well-developed financial system has been able to sustain high levels of economic growth.

Financial system The system of financial markets and financial intermediaries through which firms acquire funds from households.

An Overview of the Financial System

The financial system channels funds from savers to borrowers and channels the returns on borrowed funds back to savers. Through **financial markets**, such as the stock market or the bond market, firms raise funds by selling financial securities directly to savers. A *financial security* is a document—sometimes an electronic one—that states the terms under which funds pass from the buyer of the security (the lender) to the seller (the borrower). *Stocks* are financial securities that represent partial ownership of a firm. If you buy one share of Bell Canada, you will own relatively close to a billionth of the company (specifically, you will own one share out of 752.3 million shares). *Bonds* are financial securities that represent promises to repay a fixed amount in the future. When Bell Canada sells a bond, the firm promises to pay the purchaser of the bond an interest payment each year for the term of the bond, as well as a final payment that includes the original amount borrowed.

Financial markets Markets where financial securities, such as stocks and bonds, are bought and sold.

    Financial intermediaries, such as banks, mutual funds, pension funds, and insurance companies, act as go-betweens for borrowers and lenders. In effect, financial intermediaries borrow funds from savers and lend them to borrowers. When you deposit funds in your checking account, you are lending that money to the bank. The bank may then lend your funds (along with money from other savers) to an entrepreneur who wants to start a business. Suppose Lena wants to open a laundry. Rather than Lena

Financial intermediaries Firms, such as banks, mutual funds, pension funds, and insurance companies, that borrow funds from savers and lend them to borrowers.

having to ask 100 people to each lend her $100, the bank acts as a go-between. The bank pools the funds from 100 people, each who deposited $100 in their accounts, and makes a single loan of $10 000 to Lena. Intermediaries, such as the bank in this example, pay interest to savers in exchange for the use of their funds and earn profit by lending money to borrowers and charging borrowers a higher rate of interest on loans. For example, a bank might pay 2 percent interest on a savings account, but charge you 6 percent on your student loan.

Banks, mutual funds, pension funds, and insurance companies also make investments in stocks and bonds on behalf of savers. For example, *mutual funds* sell shares to savers and then use the funds to buy a portfolio of stocks, bonds, mortgages, and other financial securities. Banks, for example, offer many alternative stock and bond funds. Some funds hold a wide range of stocks or bonds, while others specialize in securities issued by firms in a particular industry or sector of the economy, such as mining or manufacturing. Other funds invest as an index fund in a fixed market basket of securities, such as shares of the S&P/TSX 60, which includes the stocks of 60 companies in 10 sectors of the economy ("S&P" stands for "Standard & Poor's," and "TSX" stands for "Toronto Stock Exchange"). Over the last 30 years, the role of mutual funds in the financial system has increased dramatically. Today, hundreds of mutual funds are offered by banks and other firms and compete for savers' funds.

In addition to matching households wanting to save with firms that want to borrow, the financial system provides three key services for savers and borrowers: risk sharing, liquidity, and information. *Risk* is the chance that the value of a financial asset will change relative to what you expect. For example, you may buy that share of Bell Canada at a price of $38, only to have the price fall to $20. Most individual savers are not gamblers and seek a steady return on their savings, rather than erratic swings between high and low (negative) earnings. The financial system provides risk sharing by allowing savers to spread their money among many financial assets. For example, you can divide your money among a bank certificate of deposit, individual bonds, and a mutual fund.

Liquidity is the ease with which one asset can be converted into a different asset. Generally, when talking about liquidity, we think in terms of exchanging a financial asset for money. The financial system provides the service of liquidity by providing savers with markets in which they can sell their financial assets. For example, you can easily sell your share of Bell Canada stock at the Toronto Stock Exchange. You don't have to ask everyone you meet if they want to buy a small piece of the company.

A third service that the financial system provides savers is the collection and communication of *information*, or facts about borrowers and expectations about returns on financial securities. For example, Lena's Laundry may want to borrow $10 000 from you. Finding out what Lena intends to do with the funds and how likely she is to pay you back is likely costly and time-consuming. By depositing $100 in the bank, you are, in effect, allowing the bank to gather this information for you. Because banks specialize in gathering information on borrowers, they are often able to do it faster and at a lower cost than individual savers. The financial system plays an important role in communicating information. If you read a news story announcing that an automaker has invented a car with an engine that runs on water, how would you determine the effect of that discovery on the firm's profits? Financial markets do some of the job for you by incorporating information into the prices of stocks, bonds, and other financial securities. In this example, the expectation of higher future profits for that automaker would boost the prices of their stocks and bonds.

The Macroeconomics of Saving and Investment

We've seen that the funds available to firms through the financial system come from saving. When firms use funds to purchase machinery or build new factories, they are engaging in investment. In this section, we explore the macroeconomics of saving and investment. A key point we will develop is that the *total value of saving in the economy must equal the total value of investment*. We saw in Chapter 4 that *national income accounting* refers to the methods government agencies use to track total production and total income in the economy. We can use some relationships from national income accounting to understand why total saving must equal total investment.

We begin with the relationship between GDP (Y) and its components, consumption (C), investment (I), government purchases (G), and net exports (NX):

$$Y = C + I + G + NX$$

Remember that GDP is a measure of both total production in the economy and total income.

In an *open economy*, there is interaction with other economies in terms of trading goods and services as well as borrowing and lending. Virtually all economies today are open economies, although a lot of variation exists in the degree of openness. In a *closed economy*, there is no trading, borrowing, or lending with other economies. For simplicity, we will develop the relationship between saving and investment in a closed economy. This allows us to focus on the most important points in a simpler framework. We will consider the case for an open economy in Chapter 14.

In a closed economy, net exports are zero, so we can rewrite the relationship between GDP and its components as follows:

$$Y = C + I + G$$

If we rearrange this relationship, we have an expression for investment in terms of the other variables:

$$I = Y - C - G$$

This expression tells us that in a closed economy, investment spending is equal to total income minus consumption spending and minus government purchases.

We can also derive an expression for total saving. *Private saving* is equal to what households retain from their income after purchasing goods and services (C) and paying taxes (T). Households receive income in two ways; by supplying the factors of production to firms (Y) and as transfers from government (TR). Recall that transfer payments include social program payments and employment insurance payments. We can write the resulting relationship between private savings ($S_{Private}$) as follows:

$$S_{Private} = Y + TR - C - T$$

The government also engages in saving. *Public saving* (S_{Public}) equals the amount of tax revenue the government retains after paying for government purchases and making transfer payment to households:

$$S_{Public} = T - G - TR$$

So, total savings in the economy (S) is equal to the sum of private saving and public saving:

$$S = S_{Private} + S_{Private}$$

or:

$$S = (Y + TR - C - T) + (T - G - TR)$$

or:

$$S = Y - C - G$$

The right side of this expression is identical to the expression we derived earlier for investment spending. So, we conclude that total saving must equal total investment:

$$S = I$$

When the government spends the same amount as it collects in taxes, there is a *balanced budget*. When the government spends more than it collects in taxes, there is a *budget deficit*. When there is a budget deficit, T is less than $G + TR$, which means that public savings is negative. Negative savings is sometimes referred to as *dissaving*. How can public saving be negative? When the federal government runs a budget deficit, the government must sell bonds to borrow the money needed to fund the spending not paid for with taxes. In this case, rather than adding to the total amount of saving in the economy, the federal government subtracts from it. Put slightly differently, the government is using up some of the savings that would have otherwise been used to finance investment. We can conclude that, holding all other factors constant (*ceteris paribus*), there is a lower level of investment spending in the economy when there is a budget deficit than when the government has a balanced budget.

When the government spends less than it collects in taxes, there is a *budget surplus*. A budget surplus increases public saving and thus increases the total level of saving in the economy. A higher level of saving results in a higher level of investment spending. Therefore, holding everything else constant (*ceteris paribus*, again), investment spending is higher when the government runs a surplus than when the government has a balanced budget.

The Market for Loanable Funds

Market for loanable funds The interaction of borrowers and lenders that determines the market interest rate and the quantity of loanable funds exchanged.

We have seen that the value of total saving must equal the value of total investment, but we have not yet discussed how this equality is actually brought about in the financial system. We can think of the financial system as being composed of many markets through which funds flow from lenders to borrowers: the market for certificates of deposit at banks, the market for stocks, the market for bonds, the market for mutual fund shares, and so on. For simplicity, we can think of all these different markets as making up the market for *loanable funds*. In the model of the **market for loanable funds**, the interaction between borrowers and lenders determines the market interest rate and the quantity of loanable funds exchanged. As we will discuss in Chapter 14, firms can also borrow from savers in other countries. For the remainder of this chapter, we will assume that there are no interactions between households and firms in Canada and those in other countries.

Demand and Supply in the Loanable Funds Market The demand for loanable funds is determined by the willingness of firms to borrow money to engage in new investment projects, such as building new factories or buying new equipment. In determining whether to borrow funds, firms compare the return they expect to make on an investment with the interest rate they must pay to borrow the needed funds. For example, if Rona is considering opening several new stores and expects to earn a return of 15 percent on its investment, the investment will only be profitable if Rona can borrow at an interest rate of less than 15 percent. If Rona could only borrow at an interest rate of 20 percent, it would pay more for its investment than it would get, so opening the new stores would not be a good idea. If Rona could borrow at an interest rate of 10 percent, it would get more from its investment than it would pay, so opening the new stores would be a good idea.

In Figure 6.3, the demand for loanable funds is downward sloping because the lower the interest rate, the more investment projects firms can profitably undertake, and the greater the quantity of loanable funds they will demand.

The supply of loanable funds is determined by the willingness of households to save and by the extent of government saving or dissaving. When households save, they reduce the amount of goods and services they can consume and enjoy right now. The willingness of households to save rather than consume their incomes today will be determined in part by the interest rate they receive when they lend their savings. The higher the interest rate, the greater the reward for saving and the larger the amount of funds households will save. Therefore, the supply curve for loanable funds in Figure 6.3 is upward sloping: The greater the interest rate, the bigger the reward for saving, and households will save (lend) more of their income.

In Chapter 5, we discussed the distinction between the *nominal interest rate* and the *real interest rate*. The nominal interest rate is the stated interest rate on a loan. The real interest rate corrects the nominal interest rate for the impact of inflation and is equal to

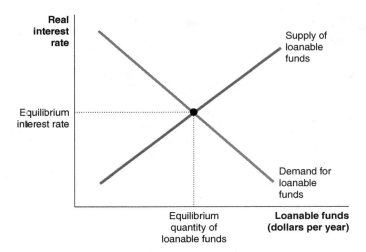

Figure 6.3

The Market for Loanable Funds

The demand for loanable funds is determined by the willingness of firms to borrow money to engage in new investment projects. The supply of loanable funds is determined by the willingness of households to save and by the extent of government saving or dissaving. Equilibrium in the market for loanable funds determines the real interest rates and the quantity of loanable funds exchanged.

the nominal interest rate minus the inflation rate. Because both borrowers and lenders are concerned with the real interest rate they receive or pay, equilibrium in the market for loanable funds determines the real interest rate rather than the nominal interest rate.

Explaining Movements in Saving, Investment, and Interest Rates Equilibrium in the market for loanable funds determines the quantity of loanable funds that will flow from lenders to borrowers each period. It also determines the real interest rate that lenders will receive and that borrowers must pay. We draw the demand curve for loanable funds the same way we draw any demand curve, by holding everything but the real interest rate (i.e., the price of loanable funds) constant. A number of factors can influence how much firms want to borrow, and a change in any of those factors will cause the demand curve to shift.

If the profitability of new investments increases dues to technological change, for example, firms will increase their demand for loanable funds at all real interest rates. Figure 6.4 shows the impact of an increase in demand in the market for loanable funds. As with the markets we discussed in Chapter 3, an increase in demand in the market for loanable funds shifts the demand curve to the right. In the new equilibrium, the interest rate increases from r_1 to r_2, and the equilibrium quantity of funds loaned increases from L_1 to L_2. Notice that an increase in the quantity of funds loaned means that both the quantity of saving by households and the quantity of investment by firms

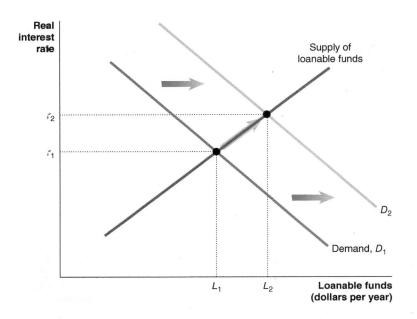

Figure 6.4

An Increase in the Demand for Loanable Funds

An increase in the demand for loanable funds increases the equilibrium interest rate from r_1 to r_2, and it increases the equilibrium quantity of loanable funds from L_1 to L_2. As a result, saving and investment both increase.

Figure 6.5

Figure 6.5

An Increase in the Supply of Loanable Funds

An increase in the supply of loanable funds decreases the interest rate from r_1 to r_2, and it increases the equilibrium quantity of loanable funds from L_1 to L_2. As a result, both saving and investment increase.

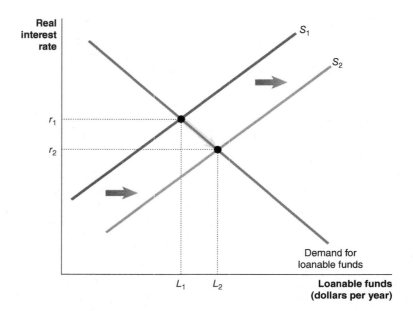

have increased. Increasing investment increases the capital stock and helps increase economic growth.

We also assume that everything other than the real interest rate that might have an impact on the supply of loanable funds is held constant when we draw the supply curve in Figure 6.3. If something other than the real interest rate changes how much people want to save, the supply of loanable funds will shift. If households change their beliefs so that saving is more important to them, they will save more at every real interest rate, causing the supply of loanable funds to shift to the right. You can see this change in Figure 6.5.

We can also use the market for loanable funds to examine the impact of a government budget deficit. Putting aside the effects of foreign saving—which we will consider in Chapter 14— recall that if the government begins running a budget deficit, it reduces the total amount of saving in the economy. Suppose the government increases spending, which results in a budget deficit. We illustrate the effects of the budget deficit in Figure 6.6 by shifting the supply of loanable funds to the left. In the new equilibrium, the interest rate is higher, and the equilibrium quantity of loanable funds is lower. Running a deficit has reduced the level of total saving in the economy and, by increasing the interest rate, has also reduced the level of investment spending by firms. By borrowing to finance

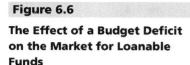

Figure 6.6

The Effect of a Budget Deficit on the Market for Loanable Funds

When the government begins running a budget deficit, the supply of loanable funds shifts to the left. The equilibrium interest rate increases from r_1 to r_2, and the equilibrium quantity of loanable funds falls from L_1 to L_2. As a result, saving and investment both decline.

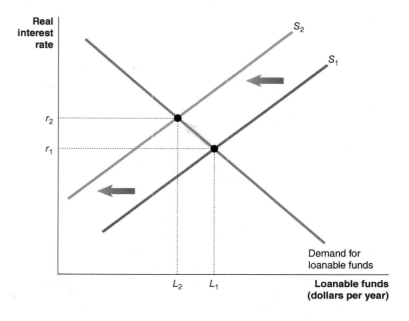

its budget deficit, the government will have *crowded out* some firms that would have otherwise borrowed to finance investment. **Crowding out** refers to a decline in investment spending as a result of an increase in government purchases. In Figure 6.6, the decline in investment spending due to crowding out is shown by the movement from L_1 to L_2 on the demand for loanable funds curve. Lower investment spending means that capital stock and the quantity of capital per worker will not be as high as it would have been without the government budget deficit.

Crowding out A decline in private investment expenditures as a result of an increase in government purchases.

A government budget surplus has the opposite effect of a deficit. A budget surplus increases the total amount of saving in the economy, shifting the supply of loanable funds to the right. In the new equilibrium, the interest rate will be lower, and the quantity of loanable funds will be higher. We can conclude that a budget surplus increases the level of saving and investment.

In practice, however, the impact of government budget deficits and surpluses on the equilibrium interest rate is relatively small. (This finding reflects in part the importance of global saving in determining the interest rate.) Small does not mean non-existent, of course. Further, paying off government debt in the future may require higher taxes, which can depress economic growth. In 2013 (at the time of writing), many economists and policymakers around the world were concerned that the large deficits projected for most developed countries might become an obstacle to economic growth.

Solved Problem **6.2**

How Does a Consumption Tax Affect Saving, Investment, the Interest Rate, and Economic Growth?

Some economists and policymakers have suggested that governments should rely less on income taxes and rely more on consumption taxes (such as the GST and HST) to generate revenue. Under an income tax, households pay taxes on all income earned. Under a consumption tax, households pay taxes only on the income they spend.

Households would pay taxes on saved income only if they spent the money later on. Use the market for loanable funds model to analyze the effect on saving, investment, the interest rate, and economic growth of switching from an income tax to a consumption tax as the primary source of government revenue.

Solving the Problem

Step 1: Review the chapter material. This problem is about applying the market for loanable funds model, so you may want to review the section "Explaining Movements in Saving, Investment, and Interest Rates" on page 159.

Step 2: Explain the effect of switching from an income tax to a consumption tax. Households are interested in the return they receive from saving after they have paid their taxes. For example, consider someone who puts savings in a certificate of deposit at an interest rate of 4 percent and whose tax rate is 25 percent. Under an income tax, this person's after-tax return to saving is 3 percent [$4 \times (1 - 0.25)$]. Under a consumption tax, income that is saved is not taxed, so the return rises to 4 percent. We can conclude that moving from an income tax to a consumption tax would increase the return to saving, causing the supply of loanable funds to increase.

Step 3: Draw a graph of the market for loanable funds to illustrate your answer. The supply curve for loanable funds will shift to the right as the after-tax return to saving increases under the consumption tax. The equilibrium interest rate will fall, and the levels of saving and investment will both increase. As a result of the increase in investment, the capital stock and the capital per worker will rise, which means that the rate of economic growth should increase. Note that the size of the fall in the interest rate and the size of the increase in loanable funds shown in the graph are both larger than the effects that most economists would expect from the replacement of the income tax with a consumption tax.

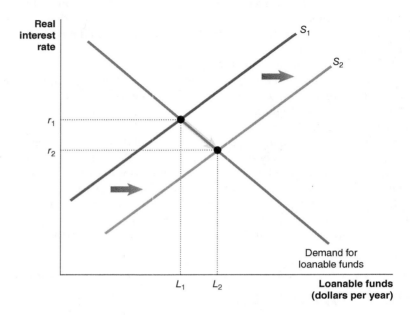

Your Turn: For more practice, do related problem 2.10 on page 172 at the end of this chapter.

MyEconLab

The Business Cycle

Figure 6.1 illustrates the massive increase in the standard of living Canadians have enjoyed over the last 50-plus years. But close inspection of the figure reveals that real GDP per capita did not increase every year during the last 50 years. For example, GDP per capita actually fell in the early 1980s, the early 1990s, and again in 2008. What accounts for these deviations from the long-run upward trend?

Some Basic Business Cycle Definitions

The fluctuations in real GDP per capita shown in Figure 6.1 reflect the underlying fluctuations in real GDP. Dating back as long as Canada has been a country, the economy has experienced a business cycle that consists of alternating periods of expanding and contracting economic activity. Given that real GDP is our best measure of economic activity, the business cycle is usually illustrated using movements in real GDP.

During the *expansion phase* of the business cycle, production, employment, and income are increasing. The period of expansion ends with a *business cycle peak*. Following the business cycle peak, production, employment, and income decline as the economy enters the *recession phase* of the business cycle. The recession comes to an end with a *business cycle trough*, after which another period of expansion begins. Figure 6.7 illustrates the phases of the business cycle. Panel (a) shows an idealized business cycle, with real GDP increasing smoothly in an expansion to a business cycle peak and then decreasing smoothly in a recession to a business cycle trough, which is followed by another expansion. Panel (b) shows the somewhat messier reality of an actual business cycle by plotting fluctuations in real GDP from 2001 to 2010. The figure shows that the expansion that began in the 1990s (not shown on the graph) continued through the early 2000s until the business cycle peak in 2008. The economy then entered a recession from 2008 to 2009, when the trough of the business cycle was reached, and the next

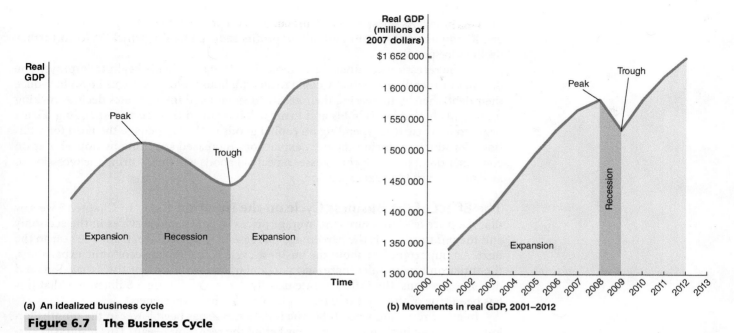

(a) An idealized business cycle

(b) Movements in real GDP, 2001–2012

Figure 6.7   The Business Cycle

Panel (a) shows an idealized business cycle with real GDP increasing smoothly in an expansion to a business cycle peak and then decreasing smoothly in a recession to a business cycle trough, which is followed by another expansion. The periods of expansion are shown in green, and the period of recession is shown in red. Panel (b) shows the actual movements in real GDP from 2001 to 2012. The recession that began in 2008 was a particularly deep recession.

(b) CANSIM Table 380-0002 series v41707150. Reproduced and distributed on an "as is" basis with the permission of Statistics Canada.

period of expansion began in 2009. Using yearly data disguises some of the movement in real GDP around the actual business cycle. GDP is typically reported in quarters, and it is not uncommon to have real GDP slow down for a single quarter and then continue rising, even though the period in question is generally thought of as an expansion. This inconsistency in real GDP movements can make the exact beginning of a recession (or peaks and troughs for that matter) difficult to identify.

How Do We Know When the Economy Is in a Recession?

Statistics Canada produces many statistics that make it possible to monitor the economy. Statistics Canada does not officially decide when a recession begins or when it ends. In Canada, there is no official beginning or end to a recession. However, elaborating on our earlier definition, there is general agreement that a recession is defined as two consecutive quarters of negative real GDP growth. That is six months of falling real GDP.

What Happens during the Business Cycle

Each business cycle is different. The lengths of the expansion and recession phases and which sectors of the economy are most affected are rarely the same in any two cycles. Most business cycles share certain characteristics. As the economy nears the end of an expansion, interest rates are usually rising, and the wages of workers are usually rising faster than prices. As a result of rising interest rates and wages, the profits of firms will be falling. Typically, toward the end of an expansion, both households and firms will have substantially increased their debts. These debts are the result of the borrowing firms and households undertake to help finance their spending during the expansion.

A recession will often begin with a decline in spending by firms on capital goods, such as machinery, equipment, new factories, and new office buildings, or by households on new houses and consumer durables, such as furniture and automobiles. As spending declines, firms selling capital goods and consumer durables will find their sales declining. As sales decline, firms cut back on production and begin to lay off workers. Rising unemployment and falling profits reduce income, which leads to further declines in spending.

As the recession continues, economic conditions gradually begin to improve. The declines in spending eventually come to an end; households and firms begin to reduce their debt, thereby increasing their ability to spend; and interest rates decline, making it more likely that households and firms will borrow to finance new spending. Firms begin to increase their spending on capital goods as they anticipate the need for additional production during the next expansion. Increased spending by households on consumer durables and by businesses on capital goods will finally bring the recession to an end and start the next expansion.

The Effect of the Business Cycle on the Inflation Rate   In Chapter 5 we saw that the *price level* measures the average prices of goods and services in the economy and the *inflation rate* is the percentage increase in the price level from one year to the next. An important fact about the business cycle is that during economic expansions, the inflation rate usually increases, particularly near the end of the expansion, and during recessions, the inflation rate usually decreases. Figure 6.8 illustrates that this has been true of the last three recessions Canada has experienced.

In every recession since 1980, the inflation rate has been lower in the months following a recession than in the months before the recession began. This result isn't surprising. During a business cycle expansion, spending by businesses and households is strong, and producers of goods and services find it easy to raise prices. As spending declines during a recession, firms have a harder time selling their goods and services and are less likely to increase prices.

Figure 6.8

The Effect of Recessions on the Inflation Rate

Toward the end of a typical expansion, the inflation rate begins to rise; these times are marked with blue shading. Recessions, marked by red shading, cause the inflation rate to fall. By the end of a recession, the inflation rate is below what it had been at the beginning of the recession.

CANSIM Table 326-0020 series v41690973. Reproduced and distributed on an "as is" basis with the permission of Statistics Canada.

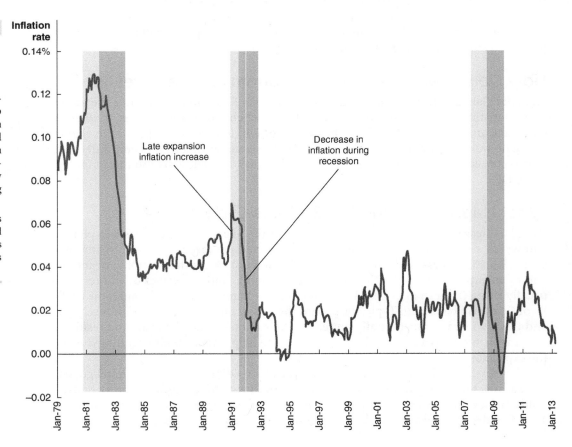

Don't Let This Happen to You

Don't Confuse the Price Level with the Inflation Rate

Do you agree with the following statement: "The consumer price index is a widely used measure of the inflation rate"? This statement sounds like it might be correct, but it's wrong. As we saw in Chapter 5, the consumer price index is a measure of the *price level*, not of the inflation rate. We can measure the inflation rate as the *percentage change* in the consumer price index from one year to the next. In macroeconomics, it is important not to confuse the level of a variable with the change in the variable. To give another example, real GDP does not measure economic growth. Economic growth is measured by the percentage change in real GDP from one year to the next.

MyEconLab

Your Turn: Test your understanding by doing related problem 3.4 on page 172 at the end of this chapter.

The Effect of the Business Cycle on the Unemployment Rate Recessions cause the inflation rate to fall, but they cause the unemployment rate to increase. As firms see their sales decline, they begin to reduce production and lay off workers. Figure 6.9 shows that this has been true of the recessions since 1980. Notice in the figure that large increases in the unemployment rate correspond to recessions and decreases in the inflation rate.

You should also notice that the unemployment rate continues to rise even after most economists believe that a particular recession has ended. This is typical, and is caused by two factors. First, even though employment begins to increase as a recession ends, it may increase more slowly than the growth in the labour force that results from population growth. If employment grows more slowly than the labour force, the unemployment rate will rise. Further, some workers who became discouraged during the recession and stopped looking for work (and therefore aren't classified as *unemployed*) re-enter the labour force once the economy begins to recover. These returning workers increase the number of people in the labour force. Second, not all firms expand at the same rate after a recession. Some firms who laid off workers during a recession may be particularly slow to call workers back even after a recession is over.

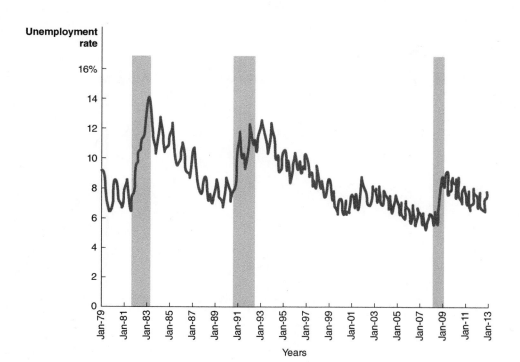

Figure 6.9

How Recessions Affect the Unemployment Rate

Unemployment rises during recessions and falls during expansions. The reluctance of firms to hire new employees as well as the re-entry of discouraged workers into the labour force during the early stages of a recovery mean that the unemployment rate usually continues to rise even after the recession has ended.

CANSIM Table 282-0001 Series v2091177. Reproduced and distributed on an "as is" basis with the permission of Statistics Canada.

Economics in Your Life

Do You Help the Economy More If You Spend or If You Save?

At the beginning of the chapter we posed a question: Which of your two roommates is right: The one who argues that you would help the economy more by saving your income tax refund cheque, or the one who argues that you should spend it? In this chapter, we have seen that consumption spending promotes the production of more consumption goods and services—such as coffee and donuts—and fewer investment goods and services—such as physical capital and education. Saving—not consuming—is necessary to fund investment expenditure. So, saving your refund cheque will help the economy grow over the long run. But if the economy is in a recession, spending your refund cheque will spur more production of consumption goods. In a sense, then, both of your roommates are correct: Spending your cheque will help stimulate the economy during a recession, while saving it will help the economy grow over time.

Conclusion

The Canadian economy remains a remarkable engine for improving the well-being of Canadians. The standard of living we enjoy today is much higher than it was 100 years ago or even 50 years ago. But households and firms still have to deal with the ups and downs of the business cycle. In the following chapters, we will continue our analysis of this basic fact of macroeconomics: Ever-increasing long-run prosperity is achieved in the context of short-run stability.

Read *An Inside Look* for a discussion of the effects of the worldwide recession on the Canadian manufacturing of airplanes.

Bombardier and the Global Recession

Bombardier Cuts Regional Jet Production

a Bombardier Inc. said Tuesday it would be cutting production rates for its regional jets next year after several key sales campaigns for the aircraft failed to materialize.

But the Montreal manufacturer said it would reduce any job losses resulting from the production cuts by moving employees to other aircraft programs, including its business jets and its new CSeries aircraft.

b "Although several sales campaigns for our CRJ aircraft are making progress and the long-term prospects for the CRJ program remain positive, the reduced pace of orders has made a review of our production plans necessary," said Guy Hachey, Bombardier Aerospace president, in a statement. "For these reasons and after careful consideration, a CRJ aircraft production decrease is warranted in the short term."

The production cuts were widely expected with the Montreal manufacturer recording only three regional jet orders so far this year, and management warning on its past two quarterly calls that a decision on whether to cut production rates for the CRJ would be imminent if no new orders were placed.

Bombardier's regional jet orders have hit a lull as airlines around the globe keep a careful eye on their balance sheets and push off new aircraft orders due to current economic turmoil.

The result is that Bombardier's backlog has dwindled to nine months' worth of work on its Q400 program, and 15 months for its CRJs, said Cameron Doerksen, National Bank Financial analyst. The company typically targets between 18 to 21 months' worth of work for both, he noted.

Bombardier has already announced it would slow production of its Q400s, and the move to do the same with the CRJ planes will begin in January 2012.

"There remain several campaigns for new CRJ orders underway, but even if Bombardier is successful in one or more, it will likely not be enough to sustain the current production rate," Mr. Doerksen said in a note to clients. "[Tuesday's] announcement is not a surprise and we believe already priced into the stock."

Bombardier did not reveal how much it would reduce its regional jet production rates. But Mr. Doerksen said he expected the rates would fall to 2.5 aircraft per month, or a little more than 30 aircraft a year, down from 3.5 a month, or 40 to 45 a year.

As a result, he lowered his delivery forecast for Bombardier's regional jets to 28 next year, from 41 previously. But he said he expects reduced deliveries will only trim Bombardier's earnings per share in fiscal 2012 to 54¢ a share, down from 56¢ a piece previously. He kept his $6.50-a-share price target on the stock, and his outperform rating.

"We believe that the CRJ is among Bombardier's lowest margin aircraft," he said. "As a result, a reduced production rate should not have a significant impact on profitability."

Source: Deveau, Scott, "Bombardier and the Global Recession," Financial Post, Sept. 21, 2011. Material reprinted with the express permission of: National Post, a division of Postmedia Network, Inc.

Key Points in the Article

Bombardier has had difficulty in selling its regional passenger jets during the last recession. Many airlines around the world postponed buying new jets until the financial markets (the market for loanable funds essentially) and the other markets are more stable. The cut in production of regional jets was likely to have an impact on the number of employees Bombardier's air plane manufacturing business needs. As a result, analysts thought some lay-offs were likely.

Analyzing the News

(a) When companies increase output, they generally hire more workers. Similarly, if companies need to reduce output, they need fewer workers. In some cases, firms can move workers from one part of the company that will produce less output to other parts of the company that are expanding. Instead of job losses, the result is fewer new people hired than would have otherwise been the case. Moving workers from one part of a company to another isn't always an option in bad economic times. When firms can't move workers, not only fewer new workers are hired, but also many older workers lose their jobs.

(b) Bombardier is having to reduce its production of regional aircraft in part because of the global recession and the ongoing economic uncertainty in many countries. The regional airlines that would otherwise buy Bombardier's jets are waiting to see whether the demand for air travel remains strong before replacing older planes or expanding their travel options. The outcome is fewer orders and, as a result, fewer workers.

Thinking Critically

1. Suppose the Canadian government regulated airline ticket prices. How might such a policy affect the profitability of Canadian airlines during a weak economy? How do you think this policy might influence Bombardier's production of regional aircraft?

2. Suppose the Canadian government decides to provide Canadian airlines with low-interest loans, regardless of their creditworthiness, in an attempt to help airlines purchase CRJ aircraft. Would such a policy be likely to succeed? Briefly explain.

Chapter Summary and Problems

Key Terms

Business cycle, p. 148

Capital, p. 152

Crowding out, p. 161

Expansion, p. 148

Financial intermediaries, p. 155

Financial markets, p. 155

Financial system, p. 155

Labour productivity, p. 151

Long-run economic growth,
p. 148

Market for loanable funds,
p. 158

Potential GDP, p. 154

Recession, p. 148

Summary

*LO **6.1** The Canadian economy has experienced both *long-run economic growth* and the *business cycle*. The *business cycle* refers to alternating periods of economic expansion and economic recession. *Long-run economic growth* is the process by which rising productivity increases the standard of living of the typical person. Because of economic growth, the typical Canadian today can buy almost three times as much as the typical Canadian in 1961. Long-run growth is measured by increases in real GDP per capita. Increases in real GDP per capita depend on increases in labour productivity. *Labour productivity* is the quantity of goods and services that can be produced by one worker or by one hour of work. Economists believe that two key factors determine labour productivity: the quantity of capital per hour worked and the level of technology. *Capital* refers to manufactured goods that are used to produce other goods and services. *Human capital* is the accumulated knowledge and skills workers acquire from education, training, or their life experiences. Economic growth occurs if the quantity of capital per hour worked increases and if technological change occurs. Economists often discuss economic growth in terms of growth in *potential GDP*, which is the level of GDP attained when all firms are producing at capacity.

LO **6.2** Financial markets and financial intermediaries together comprise the *financial system*. A well-functioning financial system is an important determinant of economic growth. Firms acquire funds from households, either directly through

financial markets—such as the stock and bond markets—or indirectly through *financial intermediaries*—such as banks. The funds available to firms come from saving. There are two categories of saving in the economy: private saving by households and public saving by the government. The value of total saving in the economy is always equal to the value of total investment spending. In the model of the *market for loanable funds*, the interaction of borrowers and lenders determines the market interest rate and the quantity of loanable funds exchanged.

LO **6.3** During the *expansion* phase of the business cycle, production, employment, and income are increasing. The period of expansion ends with a business cycle peak. Following the business cycle peak, production, employment, and income decline during the *recession* phase of the cycle. The recession comes to an end with a business cycle trough, after which another period of expansion begins. The inflation rate usually rises near the end of a business cycle expansion and then falls during a recession. The unemployment rate declines during the later part of an expansion and increases during a recession. The unemployment rate often continues to increase even after an expansion has begun. Economists have not found a method to predict when recessions will begin and end. Recessions are difficult to predict because they are due to more than one cause. Until the recession of 2008, the Canadian economy had not experienced a recession since the early 1990s.

MyEconLab   Log in to MyEconLab to complete these exercises and get instant feedback.

Review Questions

LO **6.1**

1.1 By how much did real GDP per capita in Canada increase between 1961 and 2012? Discuss whether the increase in real GDP per capita is likely to be greater or less than the true increase in living standards.

1.2 What is the rule of 70? If real GDP per capita grows at a rate of 7 percent per year, how many years will it take to double?

1.3 What is the most important factor in explaining increases in real GDP per capita in the long run?

1.4 What is potential real GDP? Does potential real GDP remain constant over time?

LO **6.2**

2.1 Why is the financial system of a country important for long-run economic growth? Why is it essential for economic growth that firms have access to adequate sources of funds?

2.2 Briefly explain why the total value of saving in the economy must equal the total value of investment.

2.3 What are loanable funds? Why do businesses demand loanable funds? Why do households supply loanable funds?

---

*'Learning Objective' is abbreviated to 'LO' in the end of chapter material.

LO 6.3

3.1 What are the names of the following events that occur during a business cycle?
   a. The high point of economic activity
   b. The low point of economic activity
   c. The period between the high point of economic activity and the following low point
   d. The period between the low point of economic activity and the following high point

---

Problems and Applications

LO 6.1

1.1 Briefly discuss whether you would rather live in Canada in 1900 with an income of $1 000 000 or Canada in 2014 with an income of $50 000. Assume that the incomes for both years are in 2014 dollars.

1.2 [**Related to** Making the Connection **on page 149**] Think about the relationship between economic prosperity and life expectancy. What implications does this relationship have for the size of the health care sector of the economy? In particular, is this sector likely to expand or contract in coming years?

1.3 A question from Chapter 5 asked about the relationship between real GDP and the standard of living in a country. Based on what you read about economic growth in this chapter, elaborate on the importance of growth in GDP, particularly real GDP per capita, to the quality of life of a country's citizens.

1.4 Use the table to answer the following questions.

Year	Real GDP (billions of 2005 dollars)
1990	$8034
1991	8015
1992	8287
1993	8523
1994	8871

   a. Calculate the growth rate of real GDP for each year from 1991 to 1994.
   b. Calculate the average annual growth rate of real GDP for the period from 1991 to 1994.

1.5 Real GDP per capita in Canada, as mentioned in the chapter, grew from about $16 000 per person in 1961 to about $47 000 per person in 2012, which represents an annual growth rate of 2.4 percent. If Canada continues to grow at this rate, how many years will it take for real GDP per capita to double? If government attempts to balance the budget and reduce the annual growth rate to 1.8 percent, how many years will it take for real GDP per capita to double?

1.6 [**Related to** Solved Problem 6.1 **on page 152**] An article in the *Economist* magazine compares Panama to Singapore. It quotes Panama's president as saying: "We copy a lot from Singapore and we need to copy more." The article observes that "Panama is not even one-fifth as rich as its Asian model on a per-person basis. But Singapore would envy its growth: from 2005 to 2010 its economy expanded by more than 8% a year, the fastest rate in the Americas." Judging from the experience of Singapore, if Panama is to maintain these high growth rates, what needs to be true about the sources of Panama's growth?

Based on "A Singapore for Central America?" *Economist*, July 14, 2011.

1.7 [**Related to** Making the Connection **on page 153**] If the keys to Botswana's rapid economic growth seem obvious, why have other countries in the region had difficulty following them?

LO 6.2

2.1 Suppose that you can receive an interest rate of 3 percent on a certificate of deposit at a bank that is charging borrowers 7 percent on new car loans. Why might you be unwilling to loan money directly to someone who wants to borrow from you to buy a new car, even if that person offers to pay you an interest rate higher than 3 percent?

2.2 Consider the following data for a closed economy:
   $Y = \$11$ trillion
   $C = \$8$ trillion
   $I = \$2$ trillion
   $TR = \$1$ trillion
   $T = \$3$ trillion
   Use these data to calculate the following:
   a. Private saving
   b. Public saving
   c. Government purchases
   d. The government budget deficit or budget surplus

2.3 Consider the following data for a closed economy:
   $Y = \$12$ trillion
   $C = \$8$ trillion
   $G = \$2$ trillion
   $S_{Public} = -\$0.5$ trillion
   $T = \$2$ trillion
   Use these data to calculate the following:
   a. Private saving
   b. Investment spending
   c. Transfer payments
   d. The government budget deficit or budget surplus

2.4 In problem 2.3, suppose that government purchases increase from $2 trillion to $2.5 trillion. If the values for Y and C are unchanged, what must happen to the values of S and I? Briefly explain.

2.5 Use the graph below to answer the following questions:
   a. Does the shift from S_1 to S_2 represent an increase or a decrease in the supply of loanable funds?
   b. With the shift in supply, what happens to the equilibrium quantity of loanable funds?
   c. With the change in the equilibrium quantity of loanable funds, what happens to the quantity of saving? What happens to the quantity of investment?

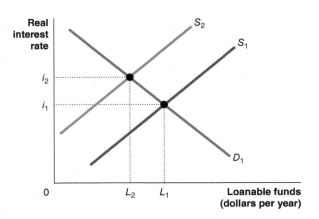

2.6 Use this graph to answer the questions that follow:

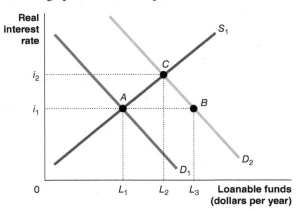

a. With the shift in the demand for loanable funds, what happens to the equilibrium real interest rate and the equilibrium quantity of loanable funds?

b. How can the equilibrium quantity of loanable funds increase when the real interest rate increases? Doesn't the quantity of loanable funds demanded decrease when the interest rate increases?

2.7 Suppose the economy is currently in a recession and that economic forecasts indicate that the economy will soon enter an expansion. What is the likely effect of the expansion on the expected profitability of new investment in plant and equipment? In the market for loanable funds, graph and explain the effect of the forecast of an economic expansion, assuming that borrowers and lenders believe the forecast is accurate. What happens to the equilibrium real interest rate and the quantity of loanable funds? What happens to the quantity of saving and investment?

2.8 Firms care about their after-tax rate of return on investment projects. In the market for loanable funds, graph and explain the effect of an increase in taxes on business profits. (For simplicity, assume no change in the federal budget deficit or budget surplus.) What happens to the equilibrium real interest rate and the quantity of loanable funds? What will be the effect on the quantity of investment by firms and the economy's capital stock in the future?

2.9 The federal government has been cutting spending to reduce budget deficits.

a. Use a market for loanable funds graph to illustrate the effect of shrinking federal budget deficits. What happens to the equilibrium real interest rate and the quantity of loanable funds? What happens to the quantity of saving and investment?

b. Now suppose that households believe that the return to balanced budgets will lead to lower taxes in the near future, and households decrease their saving in anticipation of paying those lower taxes. Briefly explain how your analysis in part (a) will be affected.

2.10 [**Related to** Solved Problem 6.2 **on page 162**] Savers are taxed on the nominal interest payments they receive rather than the real interest payments. Suppose the government shifted from taxing nominal interest payments to taxing only real interest payments. (That is, savers could subtract the inflation rate from the nominal interest rate they received and only pay taxes on the resulting real interest rate.) Use a market for loanable funds graph to analyze the effects of this change in tax policy. What happens to the equilibrium real interest rate and the equilibrium quantity of loanable funds? What happens to the quantity of saving and investment?

LO 6.3

3.1 [**Related to the** Chapter Opener **on page 147**] Briefly explain whether production of each of the following goods is likely to fluctuate more or less than real GDP does during the business cycle:
   a. Ford F-150 pickup trucks
   b. McDonald's Big Macs
   c. Kenmore refrigerators
   d. Huggies diapers
   e. Bombardier passenger aircraft

3.2 No agency in Canada is responsible for declaring when recessions begin and end. Can you think of reasons why Statistics Canada, which is a federal government agency, might not want to take on this responsibility?

3.3 Some firms actually prosper by expanding during recessions. What risks do firms take when they pursue this strategy? Are there circumstances in particular industries under which a more cautious approach might be advisable? Briefly explain.

3.4 [**Related to** Don't Let This Happen to You **on page 165**] "Real GDP in 2012 was $1.6 trillion. This value is a large number. Therefore, economic growth must have been high during 2012." Briefly explain whether you agree with this statement.

MyEconLab   MyEconLab is an online tool designed to help you master the concepts covered in your course. It will create an adaptive, highly personalized study plan to stimulate and measure your learning. Log in to take advantage of this powerful study aid, and to access quizzes and other valuable course-related material.

Long-Run Economic Growth: Sources and Policies

Newscom

Chapter Outline and Learning Objectives

7.1 Economic Growth over Time and around the World, page 176
> Define economic growth, calculate economic growth rates, and describe global trends in economic growth.

7.2 What Determines How Fast Economies Grow? page 181
> Use the economic growth model to explain why growth rates differ across countries.

7.3 Economic Growth in Canada, page 189
> Discuss fluctuations in productivity growth in Canada.

7.4 Why Isn't the Whole World Rich? page 191
> Explain economic catch-up and discuss why many poor countries have not experienced rapid economic growth.

7.5 Growth Policies, page 200
> Discuss government policies that foster economic growth.

Google's Dilemma in China

Google was founded in 1998 by Larry Page and Sergey Brin. By 2011, Google employed more than 28 000 people and had annual revenues exceeding US$29 billion. But Google encountered problems when expanding into China in 2006. The Chinese government insisted on regulating how people in that country access the Internet. In setting up Google.cn, Google had to agree to block searches of sensitive topics, such as the 1989 pro-democracy demonstrations in Tiananmen Square.

In late 2009, hackers stole some of Google's most important intellectual property by breaking into its computer system. Company executives suspected that Chinese government officials were involved in the theft. In January 2010, Google decided it would no longer cooperate with the Chinese government to censor Internet searchers and moved its Chinese search service from the mainland to Hong Kong.

Google's problems highlight one of the paradoxes of China in recent years: very rapid economic growth occurring in the context of government regulations that can stifle that growth. From the time the Communist Party seized control of China in 1949 until the late 1970s, the government controlled production, and the country experienced very little economic growth. China moved away from a *centrally planned economy* in 1978, and real GDP per capita grew at a rate of 6.5 percent per year between 1979 and 1995; it grew at the white-hot rate of more than 9 percent per year between 1996 and 2010. These rapid growth rates have transformed the Chinese economy: Real GDP per capita today is 10 times higher than it was 50 years ago.

But, as the experience of Google has shown, China is not a democracy, and the Chinese government has failed to fully establish the rule of law, particularly with respect to the consistent enforcement of property rights. This is a problem for the long-term prospects of the Chinese economy because without the rule of law, entrepreneurs cannot fulfill their role in the market system of bringing together the factors of production—labour, capital, and natural resources—to produce goods and services.

AN INSIDE LOOK on **page 204** discusses China's long-term plan to decrease its reliance on investment spending as a means of achieving sustainable economic growth.

Sources: Based on Steven Levy, "Inside Google's China Misfortune," Fortune, April 15, 2011; and Kathrin Hille, "China Renews Google's Website License," Financial Times, September 7, 2011.

Economics in Your Life

Would You Be Better Off without China?

Suppose that you could choose to live and work in a world with the Chinese economy growing very rapidly or in a world with the Chinese economy as it was before 1978—very poor and growing slowly. Which world would you choose to live in? How does the current high-growth, high-export Chinese economy affect you as a consumer? How does it affect you as someone about to start a career? As you read the chapter, see if you can answer these questions. You can check your answers against those we provide on page 203 at the end of this chapter.

Economic growth is not inevitable. For most of human history, no sustained increases in output per capita occurred, and, in the words of the philosopher Thomas Hobbes, the lives of most people were "poor, nasty, brutish, and short." Sustained economic growth first began with the Industrial Revolution in England in the late eighteenth century. From there, economic growth spread to the United States, Canada, and the countries of Western Europe. Following World War II, rapid economic growth also began in Japan and, eventually, in several other Asian countries, but the economies of many other countries stagnated, leaving their people mired in poverty.

Real GDP per capita is the best measure of a country's standard of living because it represents the ability of the average person to buy goods and services. Economic growth occurs when real GDP per capita increases. Why have countries such as Canada, the United States, and the United Kingdom, which had high standards of living at the beginning of the twentieth century, continued to grow rapidly? Why have countries such as Argentina, which at one time had relatively high standards of living, failed to keep pace? Why was the Soviet Union unable to sustain the rapid growth rates of its early years? Why are some countries that were very poor at the beginning of the twentieth century still very poor today? And why have some countries, such as South Korea and Japan, that once were very poor now become much richer? What explains China's very rapid recent growth rates? In this chapter, we will develop a *model of economic growth* that helps us answer these important questions.

Define economic growth, calculate economic growth rates, and describe global trends in economic growth.

Economic Growth over Time and around the World

You live in a world that is very different from the world when your grandparents were young. You can listen to music on an iPod that fits in your pocket; your grandparents played vinyl records on large stereo systems. You can pick up a cellphone or send a text message to someone in another city, province, or country; your grandparents mailed letters that took days or weeks to arrive. More important, you have access to health care and medicines that have prolonged life and improved its quality. In many poorer countries, however, people endure grinding poverty and have only the bare necessities of life, just as their great-grandparents did.

The difference between you and people in poor countries is that you live in a country that has experienced substantial economic growth. With economic growth, an economy produces both increasing quantities of goods and services and better goods and services. It is only through economic growth that living standards can increase, but through most of human history, no economic growth took place. Even today, billions of people are living in countries where economic growth is extremely slow.

Economic Growth from 1 000 000 BCE to the Present

In 1 000 000 BCE (Before the Christian Era), our ancestors survived by hunting animals and gathering edible plants. Farming was many years in the future, and production was limited to food, clothing, shelter, and simple tools. Bradford DeLong, an economist at the University of California, Berkeley, estimates that in those primitive circumstances, GDP per capita was about $140 per year in 2010 dollars, which was the minimum amount necessary to sustain life. DeLong estimates that real GDP per capita worldwide was still $140 in the year 1300 CE. In other words, no sustained economic growth occurred between 1 000 000 BCE and 1300 CE (Christian Era).

A peasant toiling on a farm in France in the year 1300 was no better off than his ancestors thousands of years before. In fact, for most of human existence, the typical person had only the bare minimum of food, clothing, and shelter necessary to sustain life. Few people survived beyond age 40, and most people suffered from debilitating illnesses.

Significant economic growth did not begin until the **Industrial Revolution**, which started in England around the year 1750. The production of cotton cloth in factories using machinery powered by steam engines marked the beginning of the Industrial Revolution. Before that time, production of goods had relied almost exclusively on human or animal power. The use of mechanical power spread to the production of many other goods, greatly increasing the quantity of goods each worker could produce. First England and then other countries, such as Canada, the United States, France, and Germany, experienced *long-run economic growth*, with sustained increases in real GDP per capita that eventually raised living standards in those countries to the high levels of today.

Industrial Revolution The application of mechanical power to the production of goods, beginning in England around 1750.

Making the Connection | Why Did the Industrial Revolution Begin in England?

The Industrial Revolution was a key turning point in human history. Before the Industrial Revolution, economic growth was slow and halting. After the Industrial Revolution, economic growth became rapid and sustained in a number of countries. Although historians and economists agree on the importance of the Industrial Revolution, they have not reached a consensus on why it happened in the time and place that it did. Why the eighteenth century and not the sixteenth century or the twenty-first century? Why England and not China or India or Africa or Japan?

There is always a temptation to read history backward. We know when and where the Industrial Revolution occurred; therefore, it had to happen where it did and when it did. But what was so special about England in the eighteenth century? Nobel Laureate Douglass North, of Washington University in St. Louis, has argued that institutions in England differed significantly from those in other countries in ways that greatly aided economic growth. North believes that the Glorious Revolution of 1688 was a key turning point. After that date, the British Parliament, rather than the king, controlled the government. The British court system also became independent of the king. As a result, the British government was credible when it committed to upholding private property rights, protecting wealth, and eliminating arbitrary increases in taxes. These institutional changes gave entrepreneurs the incentive to make the investments necessary to use the important technological developments of the second half of the eighteenth century—particularly the spinning jenny and the water frame, which were used in the production of cotton textiles, and the steam engine, which was used in mining and in the manufacture of textiles and other products. Without the institutional changes, entrepreneurs would have been reluctant to risk their property or their wealth by starting new businesses.

Although not all economists agree with North's specific argument about the origins of the Industrial Revolution, we will see that most economists accept the idea that economic growth is not likely to occur unless a country's government provides the type of institutional framework North describes.

The British government's guarantee of property rights set the stage for the Industrial Revolution.

Sources: Based on Douglass C. North, *Understanding the Process of Economic Change* (Princeton, NJ: Princeton University Press, 2005); and Douglass C. North and Barry R. Weingast, "Constitutions and Commitment: The Evolution of Institutions Governing Public Choice in Seventeenth-Century England," *Journal of Economic History* Vol. 49, No. 4, December 1989.

Your Turn: Test your understanding by doing related problem 1.1 on page 207 at the end of this chapter.

MyEconLab

Figure 7.1

Average Annual Growth Rates for the World Economy

World economic growth was essentially zero in the years before 1300, and it was very slow—an average of only 0.2 percent per year—before 1800. The Industrial Revolution made possible the sustained increases in real GDP per capita that have allowed some countries to attain high standards of living.

Source: Data from J. Bradford DeLong, "Estimating World GDP, One Million B.C.– Present," working paper, University of California, Berkeley.

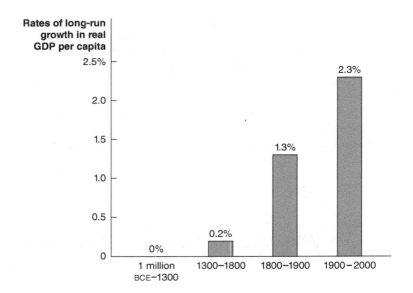

Figure 7.1 shows how growth rates of real GDP per capita for the entire world have changed over long periods. Prior to 1300, there were no sustained increases in real GDP per capita. Over the next 500 years, to 1800, there was very slow growth. Significant growth began in the nineteenth century, as a result of the Industrial Revolution. A further acceleration in growth occurred during the twentieth century, as the average growth rate increased from 1.3 percent per year to 2.3 percent per year.

Small Differences in Growth Rates Are Important

The difference between 1.3 percent and 2.3 percent may seem trivial, but over long periods, small differences in growth rates can have a large effect. For example, suppose you have $100 in a savings account earning an interest rate of 1.3 percent, which means you will receive an interest payment of $1.30 this year. If the interest rate on the account is 2.3 percent, you will earn $2.30. The difference of an extra $1.00 interest payment seems insignificant. But if you leave the interest as well as the original $100 in your account for another year, the difference becomes greater because now the higher interest rate is applied to a larger amount—$102.30—and the lower interest rate is applied to a smaller amount—$101.30. This process, known as *compounding*, magnifies even small differences in interest rates over long periods of time. Over a period of 50 years, your $100 would grow to $312 at an interest rate of 2.3 percent but to only $191 at an interest rate of 1.3 percent.

The principle of compounding applies to economic growth rates as well as to interest rates. For example, in 1950, real GDP per capita in Argentina was $5474 (measured in 2005 dollars), which was larger than Italy's real GDP per capita of $5361. Over the next 60 years, the economic growth rate in Italy averaged 2.8 percent per year, while in Argentina, the growth rate was only 1.4 percent per year. Although this difference in growth rates of only 1.4 percentage points may seem small, in 2010, real GDP per capita in Italy had risen to $27 930, while real GDP per capita in Argentina was only $12 931. In other words, because of a relatively small difference in the growth rates of the two economies, the standard of living of the typical person in Italy went from being below that of the typical person in Argentina to being much higher. The important point to keep in mind is this: *In the long run, small differences in economic growth rates result in big differences in living standards.*

Why Do Growth Rates Matter?

Why should anyone care about growth rates? Growth rates matter because an economy that grows too slowly fails to raise living standards. In some countries in Africa and

Asia, very little economic growth has occurred in the past 50 years, so many people remain in severe poverty. In high-income countries, only 4 out of every 1000 babies die before they are one year old. In the poorest countries, more than 100 out of every 1000 babies die before they are one year old, and millions of children die annually from diseases that could be avoided by having access to clean water or that could be cured by using medicines that cost only a few dollars.

Although their problems are less dramatic, countries that experience slow growth have also missed opportunities to improve the lives of their citizens. For example, the failure of Argentina to grow as rapidly as the other countries that had similar levels of GDP per capita in 1950 has left many of its people in poverty. Life expectancy in Argentina is lower than in Canada and other high-income countries, and nearly twice as many babies in Argentina die before age one.

Don't Let This Happen to You

Don't Confuse the Average Annual Percentage Change with the Total Percentage Change

When economists talk about growth rates over a period of more than one year, the numbers are always *average annual percentage changes* and *not* total percentage changes. For example, in Canada, real GDP per capita was $11 596 in 1950 and $39 370 in 2011. The percentage change in real GDP per capita between these two years is:

$$\left(\frac{\$39\ 370 - \$11\ 596}{\$11\ 596}\right) \times 100 = 240\%.$$

However, this is *not* the growth rate between the two years. The growth rate between these two years is the rate at which $11 596 in 1950 would have to grow on average *each year* to end up as $39 370 in 2011, which is 2.0 percent.

In general, the average annual growth rate between year 0 (in this case, 1950) and year *t* (in this case, 2011) can be calculated as follows:

$$\text{Average annual growth rate} = \left[\frac{y_t}{y_0}\right]^{1/t} - 1.$$

MyEconLab
Your Turn: Test your understanding by doing related problem 1.4 on page 208 at the end of this chapter.

"The Rich Get Richer and…"

We can divide the world's economies into two groups: the *high-income countries*, sometimes also referred to as the *industrial countries*, and the poorer countries, or *developing countries*. The high-income countries include the countries of Western Europe, Australia, Canada, Japan, New Zealand, and the United States. The developing countries include most of the countries of Africa, Asia, and Latin America. In the 1980s and 1990s, a small group of countries, mostly East Asian countries such as Singapore, South Korea, and Taiwan, experienced high rates of growth and are sometimes referred to as the *newly industrializing countries*. Figure 7.2 shows the levels of GDP per capita around the world in 2010. GDP is measured in US dollars, corrected for differences across countries in the cost of living. In 2010, GDP per capita ranged from a high of $82 600 in Luxembourg to a low of $300 in the African countries of Burundi and Democratic Republic of the Congo. To understand why the gap between rich and poor countries exists, we need to look at what causes economies to grow.

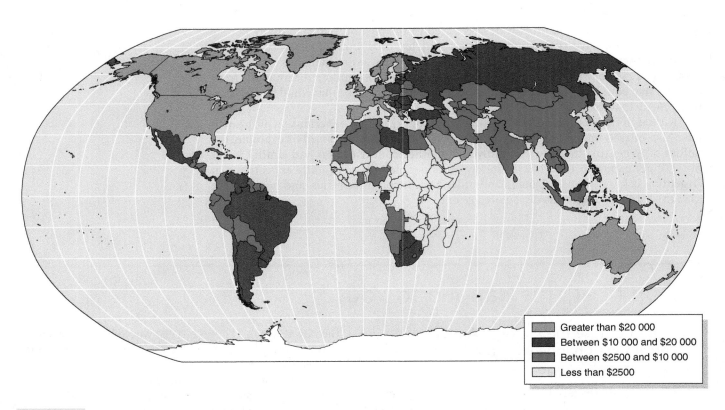

Figure 7.2 **GDP per Capita, 2010**

GDP per capita is measured in US dollars, corrected for differences across countries in the cost of living.

Legend:
Greater than $20 000
Between $10 000 and $20 000
Between $2500 and $10 000
Less than $2500

Making the Connection

Is Income All That Matters?

The more income you have, the more goods and services you can buy. When people are surviving on very low incomes of $2 per day or less, their ability to buy even minimal amounts of food, clothing, and housing is limited. So, most economists argue that unless the incomes of the very poor increase significantly, they will be unable to attain a higher standard of living. In some countries—primarily those coloured in yellow in Figure 7.2—the growth in average income has been very slow, or even negative, over a period of decades. Many economists and policymakers have concluded that the standard of living in these countries has been largely unchanged for many years.

Recently, however, some economists have argued that if we look beyond income to other measures of the standard of living, we can see that even the poorest countries have made significant progress in recent decades. For example, Charles Kenny, an economist with the World Bank, argues that "those countries with the lowest quality of life are making the fastest progress in improving it—across a range of measures including health, education, and civil and political liberties." For example, between 1960 and 2010, deaths among children declined, often by more than 50 percent, in nearly all countries, including most of those with the lowest incomes. Even in sub-Saharan Africa, where growth in incomes has been very slow, the percentage of children dying before age five has decreased by more than 30 percent over the past 50 years. Similarly, the percentage of people able to read and write has more than doubled in sub-Saharan Africa since 1970. Many more people now live in democracies where basic civil rights are respected than at any other time in world history. Although some countries, such as Somalia, Democratic Republic of the Congo, and Afghanistan, have suffered from civil wars, political instability has also decreased in many countries in recent years, which has reduced the likelihood of dying from violence.

What explains these improvements in health, education, democracy, and political stability? William Easterly, an economist at New York University, has found that although at any given time, countries that have a higher income also have a higher standard of living, over time increases in income *within a particular country* typically have very little effect on the country's standard of living in terms of health, education, individual rights, political stability, and similar factors. Kenny's argument and Easterly's finding are connected: Some increases in living standards do not require significant increases in income. The key factors in raising living standards in low-income countries have been increases

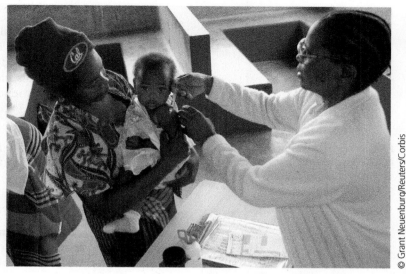

In sub-Saharan Africa and other parts of the world, increases in technology and knowledge are leading to improvements in health care and the standard of living.

in technology and knowledge—such as the development of inexpensive vaccines that reduce epidemics or the use of mosquito-resistant netting that reduces the prevalence of malaria—that are inexpensive enough to be widely available. Changes in attitudes, such as placing a greater value on education, particularly for girls, or increasing support for political freedoms, have also played a role in improving conditions in low-income countries.

There are limits, of course, to how much living standards can increase if incomes stagnate. Ultimately, much higher rates of economic growth will be necessary for low-income countries to significantly close the gap in living standards with high-income countries.

Sources: Based on Charles Kenny, Getting Better (New York: Basic Books, 2011); Ursula Casabonne and Charles Kenny, "The Best Things in Life Are (Nearly) Free: Technology, Knowledge, and Global Health," Center for Global Development Working Paper No. 252, May 31, 2011; and William Easterly, "Life during Growth," Journal of Economic Growth, Vol. 4, No. 3, September 1999, pp. 239-276.

Your Turn: Test your understanding by doing related problems 1.5 and 1.6 on page 208 at the end of this chapter.

MyEconLab

What Determines How Fast Economies Grow?

To explain changes in economic growth rates over time within countries and differences in growth rates among countries, we need to develop an *economic growth model*. An **economic growth model** explains growth rates in real GDP per capita over the long run. The average person can buy more goods and services only if the average worker produces more goods and services. Recall that **labour productivity** is the quantity of goods and services that can be produced by one worker or by one hour of work. Because of the importance of labour productivity in explaining economic growth, the economic growth model focuses on the causes of long-run increases in labour productivity.

How can a country's workers become more productive? Economists believe two key factors determine labour productivity: the quantity of capital per hour worked and the level of technology. Therefore, the economic growth model focuses on technological change and changes over time in the quantity of capital available to workers in explaining changes in real GDP per capita. Recall that **technological change** is a change in the quantity of output firms can produce using a given quantity of inputs.

7.2 LEARNING OBJECTIVE

Use the economic growth model to explain why growth rates differ across countries.

Economic growth model A model that explains growth rates in real GDP per capita over the long run.

Labour productivity The quantity of goods and services that can be produced by one worker or by one hour of work.

Technological change A change in the quantity of output a firm can produce using a given quantity of inputs.

There are three main sources of technological change:

- **Better machinery and equipment.** Beginning with the steam engine during the Industrial Revolution, the invention of new machinery has been an important source of rising labour productivity. Today, continuing improvements in computers, factory machine tools, electric generators, and many other machines contribute to increases in labour productivity.

- **Increases in human capital.** Capital refers to *physical capital*, including computers, factory buildings, machine tools, warehouses, and trucks. The more physical capital workers have available, the more output they can produce. **Human capital** is the accumulated knowledge and skills that workers acquire from education and training or from their life experiences. As workers increase their human capital through education or on-the-job training, their productivity also increases. The more educated workers are, the greater is their human capital.

- **Better means of organizing and managing production.** Labour productivity increases if managers can do a better job of organizing production. For example, the *just-in-time system*, first developed by Toyota Motor Corporation, involves assembling goods from parts that arrive at the factory at exactly the time they are needed. With this system, Toyota needs fewer workers to store and keep track of parts in the factory, so the quantity of goods produced per hour worked increases.

Note that technological change is *not* the same thing as more physical capital. New capital can embody technological change, as when a faster computer chip is embodied in a new computer. But simply adding more capital that is the same as existing capital is not technological change. To summarize, we can say that a country's standard of living will be higher the more capital workers have available on their jobs, the better the capital, the more human capital workers have, and the better the job business managers do in organizing production.

The Per-Worker Production Function

The economic growth model explains increases in real GDP per capita over time as resulting from increases in just two factors: the quantity of physical capital available to workers and technological change. Often when analyzing economic growth, we look at increases in real GDP *per hour worked* and increases in capital *per hour worked*. We use measures of GDP per hour and capital per hour rather than per person so that we can analyze changes in the underlying ability of an economy to produce more goods with a given amount of labour without having to worry about changes in the fraction of the population working or in the length of the workday. We can illustrate the economic growth model using the **per-worker production function**, which is the relationship between real GDP per hour worked and capital per hour worked, *holding the level of technology constant*. Figure 7.3 shows the per-worker production function as a graph. In the figure, we measure capital per hour worked along the horizontal axis and real GDP per hour worked along the vertical axis. Letting K stand for capital, L stand for labour, and Y stand for real GDP, real GDP per hour worked is Y/L, and capital per hour worked is K/L. The curve represents the production function. Notice that we do not explicitly show technological change in the figure. We assume that as we move along the production function, the level of technology remains constant. As we will see, we can illustrate technological change using this graph by *shifting up* the curve representing the production function.

The figure shows that increases in the quantity of capital per hour worked result in movements up the per-worker production function, increasing the quantity of output each worker produces. When *holding technology constant*, however, equal increases in the amount of capital per hour worked lead to *diminishing* increases in output per hour worked. For example, increasing capital per hour worked from $20 000 to $30 000 increases real GDP per hour worked from $200 to $350, an increase of $150. Another $10 000 increase in capital per hour worked, from $30 000 to $40 000, increases real

Human capital The accumulated knowledge and skills that workers acquire from education and training or from their life experiences.

Per-worker production function The relationship between real GDP per hour worked and capital per hour worked, holding the level of technology constant.

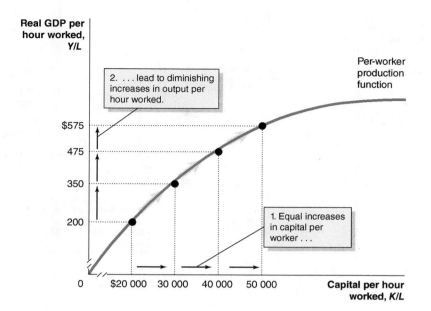

Figure 7.3

The Per-Worker Production Function

The per-worker production function shows the relationship between capital per hour worked and real GDP per hour worked, holding technology constant. Increases in capital per hour worked increase output per hour worked, but at a diminishing rate. For example, an increase in capital per hour worked from $20 000 to $30 000 increases real GDP per hour worked from $200 to $350. An increase in capital per hour worked from $30 000 to $40 000 increases real GDP per hour worked only from $350 to $475. Each additional $10 000 increase in capital per hour worked results in a progressively smaller increase in output per hour worked.

GDP per hour worked from $350 to $475, an increase of only $125. Each additional $10 000 increase in capital per hour worked results in progressively smaller increases in real GDP per hour worked. In fact, at very high levels of capital per hour worked, further increases in capital per hour worked will not result in any increase in real GDP per hour worked. This effect results from the *law of diminishing returns*, which states that as we add more of one input—in this case, capital—to a fixed quantity of another input—in this case, labour—output increases by smaller additional amounts.

Why are there diminishing returns to capital? Consider a simple example in which you own a copy store. At first you have 10 employees but only 1 copy machine, so each of your workers is able to produce relatively few copies per day. When you buy a second copy machine, your employees will be able to produce more copies. Adding additional copy machines will continue to increase your output—but by increasingly smaller amounts. For example, adding a twentieth copy machine to the 19 you already have will not increase the copies each worker is able to make by nearly as much as adding a second copy machine did. Eventually, adding additional copying machines will not increase your output at all.

Which Is More Important for Economic Growth: More Capital or Technological Change?

Technological change helps economies avoid diminishing returns to capital. Let's consider two simple examples of the effects of technological change. First, suppose that you have 10 copy machines in your copy store. Each copy machine can produce 10 copies per minute. You don't believe that adding an eleventh machine identical to the 10 you already have will significantly increase the number of copies your employees can produce in a day. Then you find out that a new copy machine has become available that produces 20 copies per minute. If you replace your existing machines with the new machines, the productivity of your workers will increase. The replacement of existing capital with more productive capital is an example of technological change.

Or suppose that you realize that the layout of your store could be improved. Maybe the paper for the machines is on shelves at the back of the store, which requires your workers to spend time walking back and forth whenever the machines run out of paper. By placing the paper closer to the copy machines, you can improve the productivity of your workers. Reorganizing how production takes place so as to increase output is also an example of technological change.

Figure 7.4

Technological Change Increases Output per Hour Worked

Technological change shifts up the production function and allows more output per hour worked with the same amount of capital per hour worked. For example, along Production function₁ with $50 000 in capital per hour worked, the economy can produce $575 in real GDP per hour worked. However, an increase in technology that shifts the economy to Production function₂ makes it possible to produce $675 in real GDP per hour worked with the same level of capital per hour worked.

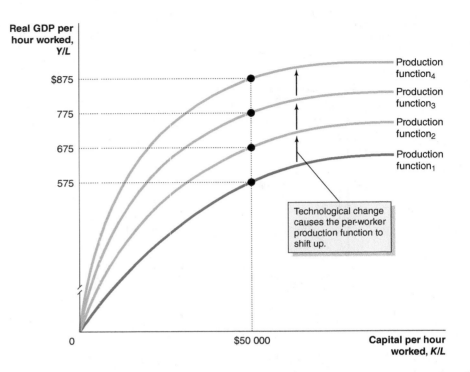

Technological Change: The Key to Sustaining Economic Growth

Figure 7.4 shows the effect of technological change on the per-worker production function. Technological change shifts up the per-worker production function and allows an economy to produce more real GDP per hour worked with the same quantity of capital per hour worked. For example, if the current level of technology puts the economy on Production function₁, then when capital per hour worked is $50 000, real GDP per hour worked is $575. Technological change that shifts the economy to Production function₂ makes it possible to produce $675 in goods and services per hour worked with the same level of capital per hour worked. Further increases in technology that shift the economy to higher production functions result in further increases in real GDP per hour worked. Because of diminishing returns to capital, continuing increases in real GDP per hour worked can be sustained only if there is technological change. Remember that a country will experience increases in its standard of living only if it experiences increases in real GDP per hour worked. Therefore, we can draw the following important conclusion: *In the long run, a country will experience an increasing standard of living only if it experiences continuing technological change.*

Making
the
Connection | ## What Explains the Economic Failure of the Soviet Union?

The economic growth model can help explain one of the most striking events of the twentieth century: the economic collapse of the Soviet Union. The Soviet Union was formed from the old Russian Empire following the Communist revolution of 1917. Under Communism, the Soviet Union was a centrally planned economy where the government owned nearly every business and made all production and pricing decisions. In 1960, Nikita Khrushchev, the leader of the Soviet Union, addressed the United Nations in New York City. He declared to Canada and the other democracies, "We will bury you. Your grandchildren will live under Communism."

Many people at the time took Khrushchev's boast seriously. Capital per hour worked grew rapidly in the Soviet Union from 1950 through the 1980s. At first, these increases in capital per hour worked also produced rapid increases in real GDP per hour worked. Rapid increases in real GDP per hour worked during the 1950s caused some economists in Canada to predict incorrectly that the Soviet Union would someday surpass Canada economically. In fact, diminishing returns to capital meant that the additional factories the Soviet Union was building resulted in smaller and smaller increases in real GDP per hour worked.

The Soviet Union did experience some technological change—but at a rate much slower than in Canada and other high-income countries. Why did the Soviet Union fail the crucial requirement for growth: implementing new technologies? The key reason is that in a centrally planned economy, the people managing most businesses are government employees and not entrepreneurs or independent business people, as is the case in market economies. Soviet managers had little incentive to adopt new ways of doing things. Their pay depended on producing the quantity of output specified in the government's economic plan, not on discovering new, better, and lower-cost ways to produce goods. In addition, these managers did not have to worry about competition from either domestic or foreign firms.

Entrepreneurs and managers of firms in Canada, by contrast, are under intense competitive pressure from other firms. They must constantly search for better ways of producing the goods and services they sell. Developing and using new technologies is an important way to gain a competitive edge and higher profits. The drive for profit provides an incentive for technological change that centrally planned economies are unable to duplicate. In market economies, decisions about which investments to make and which technologies to adopt are made by entrepreneurs and managers who have their own money on the line. Nothing concentrates the mind like having your own funds at risk.

In hindsight, it is clear that a centrally planned economy, such as the Soviet Union's, could not, over the long run, grow faster than a market economy. The Soviet Union collapsed in 1991, and contemporary Russia now has a more market-oriented system, although the government continues to play a much larger role in the economy than does the government in Canada.

Your Turn: Test your understanding by doing related problem 2.6 on page 209 at the end of this chapter.

The fall of the Berlin Wall in 1989 symbolized the failure of Communism.

MyEconLab

Solved Problem **7.1**

Using the Economic Growth Model to Analyze the Failure of the Soviet Economy

Use the economic growth model and the information in *Making the Connection* on page 180 to analyze the economic problems the Soviet Union encountered.

Solving the Problem

Step 1: Review the chapter material. This problem is about using the economic growth model to explain the failure of the Soviet economy, so you may want to review *Making the Connection* on page 184.

Step 2: Draw a graph like Figure 7.3 (on page 183) to illustrate the economic problems of the Soviet Union. For simplicity, assume that the Soviet Union experienced no technological change.

The Soviet Union experienced rapid increases in capital per hour worked from 1950 through the 1980s, but its failure to implement new technology meant that output per hour worked grew at a slower and slower rate.

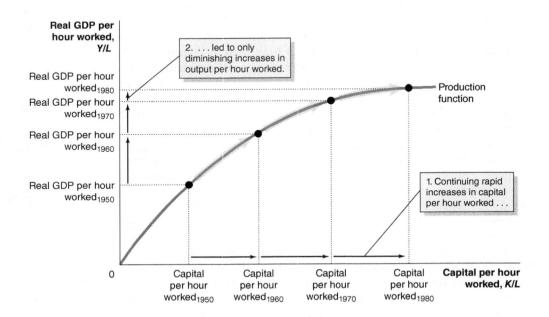

Extra credit: The Soviet Union hoped to raise the standard of living of its citizens above that enjoyed in Canada, the United States, and other high-income countries. Its strategy was to make continuous increases in the quantity of capital available to its workers. The economic growth model helps us understand the flaws in this policy for achieving economic growth.

MyEconLab **Your Turn:** For more practice, do related problems 2.3 and 2.4 on pages 208–209 at the end of this chapter.

New Growth Theory

The economic growth model we have been using was first developed in the 1950s by Nobel Laureate Robert Solow of MIT. According to this model, productivity growth is the key factor in explaining long-run growth in real GDP per capita. In recent years, some economists have become dissatisfied with this model because it does not explain the factors that determine productivity growth. What has become known as the **new growth theory** was developed by Paul Romer, an economist at Stanford University, to provide a better explanation of the sources of productivity change. Romer argues that the rate of technological change is influenced by how individuals and firms respond to economic incentives. Earlier accounts of economic growth did not explain technological change or attributed it to factors such as chance scientific discoveries.

Romer argues that the accumulation of *knowledge capital* is a key determinant of economic growth. Firms add to an economy's stock of knowledge capital when they engage in research and development or otherwise contribute to technological change. We have seen that accumulation of physical capital is subject to diminishing returns: Increases in capital per hour worked lead to increases in real GDP per hour worked but

New growth theory A model of long-run economic growth that emphasizes that technological change is influenced by economic incentives and so is determined by the working of the market system.

at a decreasing rate. Romer argues that the same is true of knowledge capital *at the firm level*. As firms add to their stock of knowledge capital, they increase their output but at a decreasing rate. At the level of the entire economy rather than just individual firms, however, Romer argues that knowledge capital is subject to *increasing returns*. Increasing returns can exist because knowledge, once discovered, becomes available to everyone. The use of physical capital, such as a computer or machine tool, is *rival* because if one firm uses it, other firms cannot, and it is *excludable* because the firm that owns the capital can keep other firms from using it. The use of knowledge capital, such as the chemical formula for a drug that cures cancer, is nonrival, however, because one firm's using that knowledge does not prevent another firm from using it. Knowledge capital is also nonexcludable because once something like a chemical formula becomes known, it becomes widely available for other firms to use (unless, as we discuss shortly, the government gives the firm that invents a new product the legal right to its exclusive use).

Because knowledge capital is nonrival and nonexcludable, firms can *free ride* on the research and development of other firms. Firms free ride when they benefit from the results of research and development they did not pay for. For example, transistor technology was first developed at Western Electric's Bell Laboratories in the 1950s and served as the basic technology of the information revolution. Bell Laboratories, however, received only a tiny fraction of the immense profits that were eventually made by all the firms that used this technology. Romer points out that firms are unlikely to invest in research and development up to the point where the marginal cost of the research equals the marginal return from the knowledge gained because *other* firms gain much of the marginal return. Therefore, there is likely to be an inefficiently small amount of research and development, slowing the accumulation of knowledge capital and economic growth.

Government policy can help increase the accumulation of knowledge capital in three ways:

- **Protecting intellectual property with patents and copyrights.** Governments can increase the incentive to engage in research and development by giving firms the exclusive rights to their discoveries for a period of years. The Canadian government grants patents to companies that develop new products or new ways of making existing products. A **patent** gives a firm the exclusive legal right to a new product for a period of 20 years from the date a patent on the product is applied for. For example, a pharmaceutical firm that develops a drug that cures cancer can secure a patent on the drug, keeping other firms from manufacturing the drug without permission. The profits earned during the period the patent is in force provide firms with an incentive for undertaking the research and development. The patent system has drawbacks, however. In filing for a patent, a firm must disclose information about the product or process. This information enters the public record and may help competing firms develop products or processes that are similar but that do not infringe on the patent. To avoid this problem, a firm may try to keep the results of its research a *trade secret*, without patenting it. (A famous example of a trade secret is the formula for Coca-Cola.) Tension also arises between the government's objectives of providing patent protection that gives firms the incentive to engage in research and development and making sure that the knowledge gained through the research is widely available, which increases the positive effect of the knowledge on the economy. Economists debate the features of an ideal patent system.

    Patent The exclusive right to produce a product for a period of 20 years from the date the patent is applied for.

    Just as a new product or a new method of making a product receives patent protection, books, films, and other artistic works receive *copyright* protection. Under Canadian copyright law, the creator of a book, a film, or other artistic work has the exclusive right to use, produce, reproduce, and alter that work. Copyright lasts the creator's lifetime plus 50 years, after which the work becomes part of the public domain.

- **Subsidizing research and development.** The government can use subsidies to increase the quantity of research and development that takes place. In Canada, the federal government conducts some research directly. The government also subsidizes research by providing grants to researchers in universities through a number of agencies. Finally, the government provides tax benefits to firms that invest in research and development.

- **Subsidizing education.** People with technical training carry out research and development. If firms are unable to capture all the profits from research and development, they will pay lower wages and salaries to technical workers. These lower wages and salaries reduce the incentive to workers to receive this training. If the government subsidizes education, it can increase the number of workers who have technical training. In Canada, the government subsidizes education by directly providing free education from grades kindergarten through 12 and by providing support for public colleges and universities. The government also provides student loans at reduced interest rates.

These government policies can bring the accumulation of knowledge capital closer to the optimal level.

Joseph Schumpeter and Creative Destruction

The new growth theory has revived interest in the ideas of Joseph Schumpeter. Born in Austria in 1883, Schumpeter served briefly as that country's finance minister. In 1932, he became an economics professor at Harvard. Schumpeter developed a model of growth that emphasized his view that new products unleash a "gale of creative destruction" that drives older products—and, often, the firms that produced them—out of the market. According to Schumpeter, the key to rising living standards is not small changes to existing products but, rather, new products that meet consumer wants in qualitatively better ways. For example, in the early twentieth century, the automobile displaced the horse-drawn carriage by meeting consumer demand for personal transportation in a way that was qualitatively better. In the early twenty-first century, the DVD and the DVD player displaced the VHS tape and the VCR by better meeting consumer demand for watching films at home. Downloading or streaming movies from the Internet may be in the process of displacing the DVD just as the DVD displaced the VHS tape.

To Schumpeter, the entrepreneur is central to economic growth: "The function of entrepreneurs is to reform or revolutionize the pattern of production by exploiting an invention or, more generally, an untried technological possibility for producing new commodities or producing an old one in a new way."

The profits an entrepreneur hopes to earn provide the incentive for bringing together the factors of production—labour, capital, and natural resources—to start new firms and introduce new goods and services. Successful entrepreneurs can use their profits to finance the development of new products and are better able to attract funds from investors.

Thomas Malthus and Endogenous Population Growth

So far, we have assumed that the population growth rate is constant and *exogenous* (i.e., a factor arising from outside the model). By contrast, English economist Thomas Malthus, who wrote *An Essay on the Principle of Population* in 1798, considered the population growth rate to be *endogenous* (i.e., a factor determined by the model). He argued that an increase in real income per person will have a positive effect on the population growth rate. He believed that a higher standard of living leads to better nutrition, sanitation, and medical care, and thus to population growth. He also believed that an increase in the standard of living encourages greater fertility and inevitably leads to further population growth.

Although Malthus did not construct a formal economic model, if we formalize his idea that an increase in real income per person will have a positive effect on the population growth rate, then we find that although improvements in technology lead to an increase in real income per person, they also lead to an increase in population and, thus, no improvement in the long-run standard of living. In fact, the Malthusian model of economic growth predicts that government population control policies are the only means for improvement in the long-run standard of living.

The Malthusian model is consistent with ideas on economic growth before the Industrial Revolution. During that period, population grew over time as did aggregate production (which was mainly agricultural), but there were no significant improvements in real income per person. In fact, the standard of living was very similar over time and across countries, which was consistent with the Malthusian model.

However, the predictions of Thomas Malthus regarding the positive effect of real income per person on population growth and the inability of economies to produce long-run improvements in the standard of living were ultimately wrong. Recent cross-country data show that higher real GDP per person matches up with a lower (not higher) population growth rate. Moreover, Malthus did not predict the Industrial Revolution and the sustained growth in the standard of living that took place in the nineteenth and twentieth centuries in economies around the world, even in the absence of any significant government population control policies.

Economic Growth in Canada

7.3 LEARNING OBJECTIVE

Discuss fluctuations in productivity growth in Canada.

The economic growth model can help us understand the record of growth in Canada. Figure 7.5 shows average annual growth rates in real GDP per person since 1870. As Canada experienced the Industrial Revolution during the nineteenth century, Canadian firms increased the quantities of capital per worker. New technologies such as the steam engine, the railroad, and the telegraph also became available. Together, these factors resulted in an average annual growth rate of real GDP per person of 1.7 percent from 1870 to 1900.

By the twentieth century, technological change had been institutionalized. Many large corporations began to set up research and development facilities to improve the quality of their products and the efficiency with which they produced them. Universities also began to conduct research that had business applications. The accelerating rate of technological change led to more rapid growth rates.

Economic Growth in Canada since 1950

Continuing technological change allowed the Canadian economy to avoid the diminishing returns to capital that stifled growth in other economies, such as the Soviet economy.

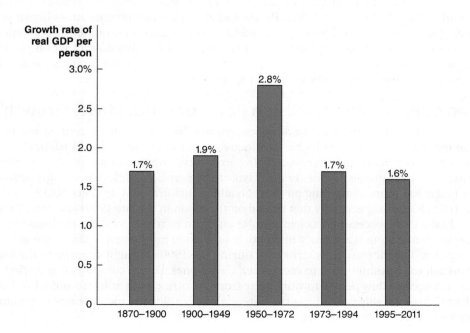

Figure 7.5

Average Annual Growth Rates in Real GDP per Person in Canada

The growth rate in Canada increased from 1870 through the mid-1970s. Then growth slowed considerably.

Sources: Data on nominal GDP and the GDP deflator since 1961 are from Statistics Canada, CANSIM Table II, series V3862688 and V3860248; values from 1870 to 1960 are from M. C. Urquhart, "Canadian Economic Growth 1870–1985" (Discussion paper no. 734, Institute for Economic Research, Queens University, Kingston, ON, 1988); since 1971, the population series is from Statistics Canada, CANSIM Table II, series V466668; from 1921 to 1970, the population series is from Statistics Canada, CANSIM Table I, series D892580; and from 1870 to 1920, the population series is from Urquhart (1988).

In fact, until the 1970s, the growth rate of the Canadian economy increased over time. As Figure 7.5 shows, growth in the first half of the twentieth century was faster than growth during the nineteenth century, and growth in the immediate post–World War II period from 1950 to 1972 was faster yet. Then the unexpected happened: For more than 20 years, from 1973 to 1994, the growth rate of real GDP per person decreased. The growth rate during these years was more than 1 percentage point per year lower than during the 1950 to 1972 period. Beginning in the mid-1990s, the growth rate declined again, although it remained at roughly the same rate as for the 1973 to 1994 period.

What Caused the Productivity Slowdown from 1973 to 1994?

Several explanations have been offered for the productivity slowdown of the mid-1970s to mid-1990s, but none is completely satisfying. Some economists argue that productivity really didn't slow down; it only *appears* to have slowed down because of problems in measuring productivity accurately. After 1970, services—such as haircuts and financial advice—became a larger fraction of GDP, and goods—such as automobiles and hamburgers—became a smaller fraction. It is more difficult to measure increases in the output of services than to measure increases in the output of goods. For example, before banks began using automated teller machines (ATMs) in the 1980s, you could withdraw money only by going to a bank before closing time—which was usually 3:00 p.m. Once ATMs became available, you could withdraw money at any time of the day or night at a variety of locations. This increased convenience from ATMs does not show up in GDP. If it did, measured output per person would have grown more rapidly.

There may also be a measurement problem in accounting for improvements in the environment and in health and safety. During these years, new laws required firms to spend billions of dollars reducing pollution, improving workplace safety, and redesigning products to improve their safety. This spending did not result in additional output that would be included in GDP—although it may have increased overall well-being. If these increases in well-being had been included in GDP, measured output per person would have grown more rapidly. In the early 1980s, many economists thought the rapid oil price increases that occurred between 1974 and 1979 explained the productivity slowdown, but the productivity slowdown continued after Canadian firms had fully adjusted to high oil prices. In fact, it continued into the late 1980s and early 1990s, when oil prices declined.

Canada was not alone in experiencing the slowdown in productivity. All the high-income countries, including the United States, experienced a growth slowdown between the mid-1970s and the mid-1990s. Because all the high-income economies began producing more services and fewer goods and enacted stricter environmental regulations at about the same time, explanations of the productivity slowdown that emphasize measurement problems become more plausible. In the end, though, economists are still debating why the productivity slowdown took place.

Can Canada Maintain High Rates of Productivity Growth?

Some economists argue that the development of a "new economy" based on information technology can lead to higher productivity growth in the future. In particular, the spread of ever-faster and increasingly less expensive computers has made communication and data processing easier and faster than ever before. Today, a single desktop computer has more computing power than all the mainframe computers NASA used to control the *Apollo* spacecrafts that landed on the moon in the late 1960s and early 1970s.

Faster data processing has had a major effect on nearly every firm. Business record keeping, once done laboriously by hand, is now done more quickly and accurately by computer. The increase in Internet use during the 1990s brought changes to the ways firms sell to consumers and to each other. Cellphones, laptop computers, and wireless Internet access allow people to work away from the office, both at home and while travelling. These developments have the potential to significantly increase labour productivity and the standard of living.

Why Isn't the Whole World Rich?

The economic growth model tells us that economies grow when the quantity of capital per hour worked increases and when technological change takes place. This model seems to provide a good blueprint for developing countries to become rich: (1) Increase the quantity of capital per hour worked, and (2) use the best available technology. There are economic incentives for both of these things to happen in poor countries. The profitability of using additional capital or better technology is generally greater in a developing country than in a high-income country. For example, replacing an existing computer with a new, faster computer will generally have a relatively small payoff for a firm in Canada. In contrast, installing a new computer in a Zambian firm where records have been kept by hand is likely to have an enormous payoff.

This observation leads to an important conclusion: *The economic growth model predicts that poor countries will grow faster than rich countries.* If this prediction is correct, we should observe poor countries catching up to rich countries in levels of GDP per capita (or income per capita). Has this **catch-up**—or *convergence*—actually occurred? Here we come to a paradox: If we look only at the countries that currently have high incomes, we see that the lower-income countries have been catching up to the higher-income countries, but the developing countries as a group have not been catching up to the high-income countries as a group.

Catch-up: Sometimes but Not Always

We can construct a graph that makes it easier to see whether catch-up is happening. In Figure 7.6, the horizontal axis shows the initial level of real GDP per capita, and the vertical axis shows the rate at which real GDP per capita is growing. We can then plot points on the graph for rich and poor countries. Each point represents the combination of a country's initial level of real GDP per capita and its growth rate over the following years. Low-income countries should be in the upper-left part of the graph because they would have low initial levels of real GDP per capita but fast growth rates. High-income countries should be in the lower-right part of the graph because they would have high initial levels of real GDP per capita but slow growth rates.

7.4 LEARNING OBJECTIVE

Explain economic catch-up and discuss why many poor countries have not experienced rapid economic growth.

Catch-up The prediction that the level of GDP per capita (or income per capita) in poor countries will grow faster than in rich countries.

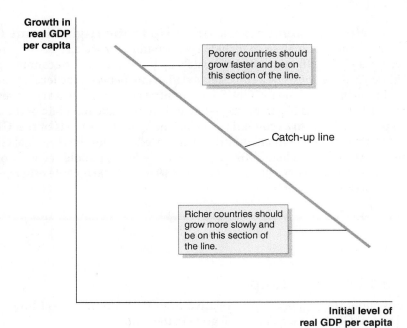

Figure 7.6

The Catch-up Predicted by the Economic Growth Model

According to the economic growth model, countries that start with lower levels of real GDP per capita should grow faster (points near the top of the line) than countries that start with higher levels of real GDP per capita (points near the bottom of the line).

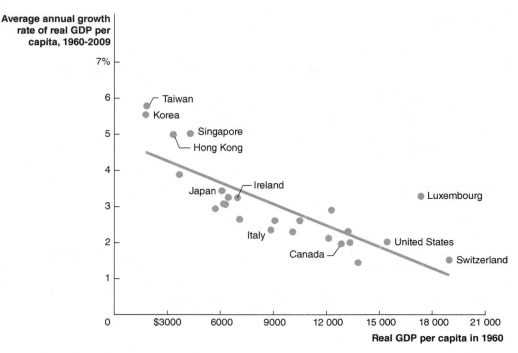

Figure 7.7   There Has Been Catch-up among High-Income Countries

If we look only at countries that currently have high incomes, we see that countries such as Taiwan, Korea, and Singapore that had the lowest incomes in 1960 grew the fastest between 1960 and 2009. Countries such as Switzerland and the United States that had the highest incomes in 1960 grew the slowest.

Note: Data are real GDP per capita in 2005 US dollars. Each point in the figure represents one high-income country.

Source: Authors' calculations from data in Alan Heston, Robert Summers, and Bettina Aten, Penn World Table Version 7.0, Center for International Comparisons of Production, Income and Prices at the University of Pennsylvania, June 3, 2011.

Catch-up among the High-Income Countries If we look at only the countries that currently have high incomes, we can see the catch-up predicted by the economic growth model. Figure 7.7 shows that the high-income countries that had the lowest incomes in 1960, such as Taiwan, Korea, and Singapore, grew the fastest between 1960 and 2009. Countries that had the highest incomes in 1960, such as Switzerland and the United States, grew the slowest.

Are the Developing Countries Catching Up to the High-Income Countries? If we expand our analysis to include every country for which statistics are available, it becomes more difficult to find the catch-up predicted by the economic growth model. Figure 7.8 does not show a consistent relationship between the level of real GDP in 1960 and growth from 1960 to 2009. Some countries that had low levels of real GDP per capita in 1960, such as Niger, Madagascar, and Democratic Republic of the Congo, actually experienced *negative* economic growth: They had *lower* levels of real GDP per capita in 2009 than in 1960. Other countries that started with low levels of real GDP per capita, such as Malaysia and South Korea, grew rapidly. Some middle-income countries in 1960, such as Venezuela, hardly grew between 1960 and 2009, while others, such as Israel, experienced significant growth.

Solved Problem **7.2**

The Economic Growth Model's Prediction of Catch-up

The economic growth model makes predictions about the relationship between an economy's initial level of real GDP

per capita relative to other economies and how fast the economy will grow in the future.

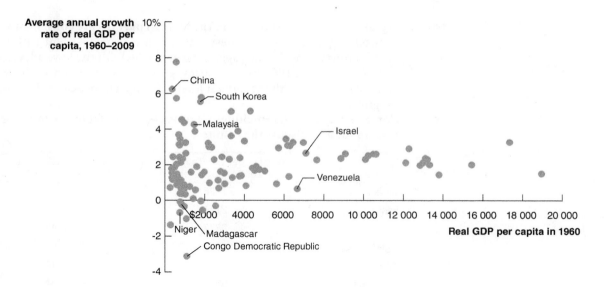

Figure 7.8   Most of the World Hasn't Been Catching Up

If we look at all countries for which statistics are available, we do not see the catch-up predicted by the economic growth model. Some countries that had low levels of real GDP per capita in 1960, such as Niger, Madagascar, and Democratic Republic of the Congo, actually experienced *negative* economic growth. Other countries that started with low levels of real GDP per capita, such as Malaysia and South Korea, grew rapidly. Some middle-income countries in 1960, such as Venezuela, hardly grew between 1960 and 2009, while others, such as Israel, experienced significant growth.

Note: Data are real GDP per capita in 2005 US dollars. Each point in the figure represents one country.

Sources: Authors' calculations from data in Alan Heston, Robert Summers, and Bettina Aten, Penn World Table Version 7.0, Center for International Comparisons of Production, Income and Prices at the University of Pennsylvania, June 3, 2011.

---

a. Consider the statistics in the following table:

Country	Real GDP per Capita in 1960 (2005 US dollars)	Annual Growth in Real GDP per Capita, 1960–2009
Taiwan	$1826	5.78%
Panama	2171	3.21
Brazil	2877	2.43
Algeria	4077	0.81
Venezuela	6662	0.64

Are these statistics consistent with the economic growth model? Briefly explain.

b. Now consider the statistics in the following table:

Country	Real GDP per Capita in 1960 (2005 US dollars)	Annual Growth in Real GDP per Capita, 1960–2009
Japan	$6094	3.44%
Belgium	10 241	2.52
United Kingdom	12 842	1.97
New Zealand	13 803	1.44

Are these statistics consistent with the economic growth model? Briefly explain.

c. Construct a new table that lists all nine countries, from lowest real GDP per capita in 1960 to highest, along with their growth rates. Are the statistics in your new table consistent with the economic growth model?

Solving the Problem

Step 1: Review the chapter material. This problem is about catch-up in the economic growth model, so you may want to review the section "Why Isn't the Whole World Rich?" which begins on page 191.

Step 2: Explain whether the statistics in the table in part (a) are consistent with the economic growth model. These statistics are consistent with the economic growth model. The countries with the lowest levels of real GDP per capita in 1960 had the fastest growth rates between 1960 and 2009, and the countries with the highest levels of real GDP per capita had the slowest growth rates.

Step 3: Explain whether the statistics in the table in part (b) are consistent with the economic growth model. These statistics are also consistent with the economic growth model. Once again, the countries with the lowest levels of real GDP per capita in 1960 had the fastest growth rates between 1960 and 2009, and the countries with the highest levels of real GDP per capita had the slowest growth rates.

Step 4: Construct a table that includes all nine countries from the tables in parts (a) and (b) and discuss the results.

Country	Real GDP per Capita in 1960 (2005 US dollars)	Annual Growth in Real GDP per Capita, 1960–2009
Taiwan	$ 1826	5.78%
Panama	2171	3.21
Brazil	2877	2.43
Algeria	4077	0.81
Japan	6094	3.44
Venezuela	6662	0.64
Belgium	10 241	2.52
United Kingdom	12 842	1.97
New Zealand	13 803	1.44

The statistics in the new table are not consistent with the predictions of the economic growth model. For example, New Zealand and the United Kingdom had higher levels of real GDP per capita in 1960 than did Algeria and Venezuela. The economic growth model predicts that New Zealand and the United Kingdom should, therefore, have grown more slowly than Algeria and Venezuela. The data in the table show, however, that New Zealand and the United Kingdom grew faster. Similarly, Belgium grew faster than Brazil, even though its real GDP per capita was already much higher than Brazil's in 1960.

Extra credit: The statistics in these tables confirm what we saw in Figures 7.7 and 7.8 on pages 192–193: There has been catch-up among the high-income countries, but there has not been catch-up if we include in the analysis all the countries of the world.

MyEconLab **Your Turn:** For more practice, do problems 4.1 and 4.2 on page 209 at the end of this chapter.

Why Haven't Most Western European Countries, Canada, and Japan Caught Up to the United States?

Figure 7.7 indicates that there has been catch-up among the high-income countries over the past 50 years. If we look at the catch-up of other high-income countries to the United States, we discover a surprising fact: Over the past 20 years, other high-income countries have actually fallen further behind the United States rather than catching up to it. Figure 7.9 shows real GDP per capita in Canada, Japan, and the five largest economies in Western Europe relative to real GDP per capita in the United States. The blue bars show real GDP per capita in 1990 relative to the United States, and the red bars show real GDP per capita in 2010 relative to the United States. In each case, relative levels of real GDP per capita were lower in 2010 than they were in 1990. Each of these countries experienced significant catch-up to the United States between 1960 and 1990, but they have experienced no catch-up since 1990.

Why have other high-income countries had trouble completely closing the gap in real GDP per capita with the United States? Many economists believe there are two main explanations: the greater flexibility of US labour markets and the greater efficiency of the US financial system. US labour markets are more flexible than labour markets in

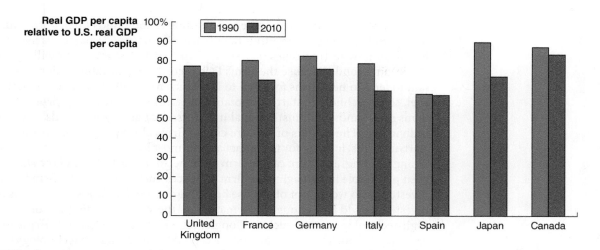

Figure 7.9 Other High-Income Countries Have Stopped Catching Up to the United States

The blue bars show real GDP per capita in 1990 relative to the United States, and the red bars show real GDP per capita in 2010 relative to the United States. In each case, relative levels of real GDP per capita are lower in 2010 than they were in 1990, which means that these countries have ceased catching up to the United States.

Sources: Authors' calculations from data in Alan Heston, Robert Summers, and Bettina Aten, Penn World Table Version 7.0, Center for International Comparisons of Production, Income and Prices at the University of Pennsylvania, June 3, 2011; U.S. Central Intelligence Agency, The World Factbook, online version, www.cia.gov/library/publications/the-world-factbook.

other countries for several reasons. In many European countries, government regulations make it difficult for firms to fire workers and thereby make firms reluctant to hire workers in the first place. As a result, many younger workers have difficulty finding jobs, and once a job is found, a worker tends to remain in it even if his or her skills and preferences are not a good match for the characteristics of the job. In the United States, by contrast, government regulations are less restrictive, workers have an easier time finding jobs, and workers change jobs fairly frequently. This high rate of job mobility ensures a better match between workers' skills and preferences and the characteristics of jobs, which increases labour productivity. Many European countries also have restrictive work rules that limit the flexibility of firms to implement new technologies. These rules restrict the tasks firms can ask workers to perform and the number of hours they work. So, the rules reduce the ability of firms to use new technologies that may require workers to learn new skills, perform new tasks, or work during the night or early mornings.

Workers in the United States tend to enter the labour force earlier, retire later, and experience fewer long spells of unemployment than do workers in Europe. As we noted in Chapter 5, unemployed workers in the United States typically receive smaller government payments for a shorter period of time than do unemployed workers in Canada and most of the countries of Western Europe. Because the opportunity cost of being unemployed is lower in those countries, the unemployment rate tends to be higher, and the fraction of the labour force that is unemployed for more than one year also tends to be higher. Studies have shown that workers who are employed for longer periods tend to have greater skills, greater productivity, and higher wages. Many economists believe that the design of the US unemployment insurance program has contributed to the greater flexibility of US labour markets and to higher rates of growth in labour productivity and real GDP per capita.

As we have seen, technological change is essential for rapid productivity growth. To obtain the funds needed to implement new technologies, firms turn to the financial system. It is important that funds for investment be not only available but also allocated efficiently. Large corporations can raise funds by selling stocks and bonds in financial markets. US corporations benefit from the efficiency of US financial markets. The level of legal protection of investors is relatively high in US financial markets, which encourages both US and foreign investors to buy stocks and bonds issued by US firms. The volume of trading in US financial markets also ensures that investors will be able to quickly sell the stocks and bonds they buy. This *liquidity* serves to attract investors to US markets.

Smaller firms that are unable to issue stocks and bonds often obtain funding from banks. Entrepreneurs founding new firms—"start-ups"—particularly firms that are based on new technologies, generally find that investors are unwilling to buy their stocks and bonds because the firms lack records of profitability. Banks are also reluctant to lend to new firms founded to introduce new and unfamiliar technologies. However, some technology start-ups obtain funds from *venture capital firms*. Venture capital firms raise funds from institutional investors, such as pension funds, and from wealthy individuals. The owners of venture capital firms closely examine the business plans of start-up firms, looking for those that appear most likely to succeed. In exchange for providing funding, a venture capital firm often becomes part owner of the start-up and may even play a role in managing the firm. A successful venture capital firm is able to attract investors who would not otherwise be willing to provide funds to start-ups because the investors would lack enough information on the start-up. A number of well-known US high-technology firms, such as Google, relied on venture capitals firms to fund their early expansion. The ability of venture capital firms to finance technology-driven start-up firms may be giving the United States an advantage in bringing new products and new processes to market.

Why Don't More Low-Income Countries Experience Rapid Growth?

The economic growth model predicts that the countries that were very poor in 1960 should have grown rapidly over the next 50 years. As we have just seen, a few did, but most did not. Why are many low-income countries growing so slowly? There is no single answer, but most economists point to four key factors:

- Failure to enforce the rule of law

- Wars and revolutions

- Poor public education and health

- Low rates of saving and investment

Property rights The rights individuals or firms have to the exclusive use of their property, including the right to buy or sell it.

Rule of law The ability of a government to enforce the laws of the country, particularly with respect to protecting private property and enforcing contracts.

Failure to Enforce the Rule of Law In the years since 1960, increasing numbers of developing countries, including China, have abandoned centrally planned economies in favour of more market-oriented economies. For entrepreneurs in a market economy to succeed, however, the government must guarantee private **property rights** and enforce contracts. Unless entrepreneurs feel secure in their property, they will not risk starting a business. It is also difficult for businesses to operate successfully in a market economy unless they can use an independent court system to enforce contracts. The **rule of law** refers to the ability of a government to enforce the laws of the country, particularly with respect to protecting private property and enforcing contracts. The failure of many developing countries to guarantee private property rights and to enforce contracts has hindered their economic growth.

Consider, for example, the production of shoes in a developing country. Suppose the owner of a shoe factory signs a contract with a leather tannery to deliver a specific quantity of leather on a particular date for a particular price. On the basis of this contract, the owner of the shoe factory signs a contract to deliver a specific quantity of shoes to a shoe wholesaler. This contract specifies the quantity of shoes to be delivered, the quality of the shoes, the delivery date, and the price. The owner of the leather tannery uses the contract with the shoe factory to enter into a contract with cattle ranchers for the delivery of hides. The shoe wholesaler enters into contracts to deliver shoes to retail stores, where they are sold to consumers. For the flow of goods from cattle ranchers to shoe customers to operate efficiently, each business must carry out the terms of the contract it has signed. In developed countries, such as Canada, businesses know that if they fail to carry out a contract, they may be sued in court and forced to compensate the other party for any economic damages.

Many developing countries do not have functioning, independent court systems. Even if a court system does exist, a case may not be heard for many years. In some countries, bribery of judges and political favouritism in court rulings are common. If firms cannot enforce contracts through the court system, they will insist on carrying out only face-to-face cash transactions. For example, the shoe manufacturer will wait until the leather producer brings the hides to the factory and will then buy them for cash. The wholesaler will wait until the shoes have been produced before making plans for sales to retail stores. Production still takes place, but it is carried out more slowly and inefficiently. With slow and inefficient production, firms have difficulty finding investors willing to provide them with the funds they need to expand.

<table>
<tr><td>Making
the
Connection</td><td>## What Do Parking Tickets in New York City Tell Us about Poverty in the Developing World?</td></tr>
</table>

In many developing countries, government officials insist on receiving bribes to process most transactions. For example, someone may need to pay an official before being allowed to open a shoe store or to purchase farm land. This corruption represents a breakdown in the rule of law. Generally, the more corrupt a country's government, the lower the country's growth rate. Economists at the World Bank have developed an index that ranks the countries of the world from most corrupt to least corrupt. The figure below compares GDP per capita in the 20 most corrupt and the 20 least corrupt countries. GDP per capita is more than 10 times higher in the least corrupt countries than in the most corrupt countries.

But does corruption cause countries to be poor, or does a country's being poor lead to its being corrupt? Some economists have made the controversial argument that corruption may be the result of culture. If a culture of corruption exists in a country, then the country may have great difficulty establishing an honest government that is willing to enforce the rule of law. Economists Raymond Fisman of the Columbia Business School and Edward Miguel of the University of California, Berkeley, came up with an ingenious method of testing whether a culture of corruption exists in some countries. Every country in the world sends delegates to the United Nations in New York City. Under international law, these delegates cannot be prosecuted for violating US laws, including parking regulations. So, a delegate to the United Nations can double park or park next to a fire hydrant and ignore any parking ticket he or she would receive.

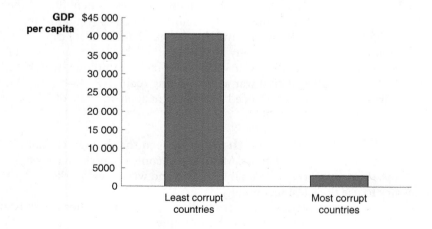

Fisman and Miguel argue that if a culture of corruption exists in some countries, the delegates from these countries will be more likely to ignore parking tickets than will the delegates from countries without a culture of corruption. Fisman and Miguel gathered statistics on the number of parking violations per delegate and compared the statistics to the World Bank's index of corruption. They found that as the level of corruption in a country increases, so does the number of parking violations by the country's United Nations delegates. For example, the figure below shows that the 15 percent of countries that are most corrupt had more than 10 times as many parking violations as the 15 percent of countries that are least corrupt.

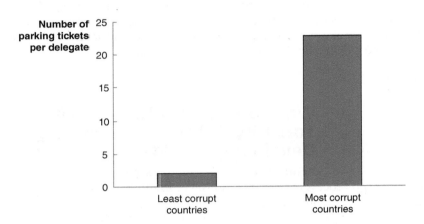

Of course, ignoring parking regulations is a relatively minor form of corruption. But if Fisman and Miguel are correct, and a culture of corruption has taken hold in some developing countries, then it may be a difficult task to reform their governments enough to establish the rule of law.

Sources: Based on Raymond Fisman and Edward Miguel, Economic Gangsters, (Princeton, NJ: Princeton University Press, 2008), Chapter 4; Daniel Kaufmann, Aart Kraay, and Massimo Mastruzzi, Governance Matters V: Aggregate Governance Indicators, 1996-2007, World Bank working paper; International Monetary Fund, World Economic Outlook Database, April 2009.

MyEconLab **Your Turn:** Test your understanding by doing related problem 4.4 on page 210 at the end of this chapter.

Wars and Revolutions Many of the countries that were very poor in 1960 have experienced extended periods of war or violent changes of government during the years since. These wars have made it impossible for countries such as Afghanistan, Angola, Ethiopia, the Central African Republic, and the Congo to accumulate capital or adopt new technologies. In fact, conducting any kind of business has been very difficult. The positive effect on growth of ending war was shown in Mozambique, which suffered through almost two decades of civil war and declining real GDP per capita. With the end of civil war, Mozambique experienced a strong annual growth rate of 3.7 percent in real GDP per capita from 1990 to 2009.

Poor Public Education and Health We have seen that human capital is one of the determinants of labour productivity. Many low-income countries have weak public school systems, so many workers are unable to read and write. Few workers acquire the skills necessary to use the latest technology.

Many low-income countries suffer from diseases that are either nonexistent or treated readily in high-income countries. For example, few people in developed countries suffer from malaria, but more than 1 million Africans die from it each year.

Treatments for AIDS have greatly reduced deaths from this disease in Canada, the United States, and Europe. But millions of people in low-income countries continue to die from AIDS. These countries often lack the resources, and their governments are often too ineffective, to provide even routine medical care, such as childhood vaccinations.

People who are sick work less and are less productive when they do work. Poor nutrition or exposure to certain diseases in childhood can leave people permanently weakened and can affect their intelligence as adults. Poor health has a significant negative effect on the human capital of workers in developing countries.

Low Rates of Saving and Investment To invest in factories, machinery, and computers, firms need funds. Some of the funds can come from the owners of the firm and from their friends and families; firms in high-income countries raise most of their funds from bank loans and selling stocks and bonds in financial markets. In most developing countries, stock and bond markets do not exist, and often the banking system is very weak. In high-income countries, the funds that banks lend to businesses come from the savings of households. In high-income countries, many households are able to save a significant fraction of their income. In developing countries, many households barely survive on their incomes and, therefore, have little or no savings.

The low savings rates in developing countries can contribute to a vicious cycle of poverty. Because households have low incomes, they save very little. Because households save very little, few funds are available for firms to borrow. Lacking funds, firms do not invest in the new factories, machinery, and equipment needed for economic growth. Because the economy does not grow, household incomes remain low, as do their savings, and so on.

The Benefits of Globalization

One way for a developing country to break out of the vicious cycle of low saving and investment and low growth is through foreign investment. **Foreign direct investment (FDI)** occurs when corporations build or purchase facilities in foreign countries. **Foreign portfolio investment** occurs when an individual or a firm buys stocks or bonds issued in another country. Foreign direct investment and foreign portfolio investment can give a low-income country access to funds and technology that otherwise would not be available. Until recently, many developing countries were reluctant to take advantage of this opportunity.

Foreign direct investment (FDI) The purchase or building by a corporation of a facility in a foreign country.

Foreign portfolio investment The purchase by an individual or a firm of stocks or bonds issued in another country.

From the 1940s through the 1970s, many developing countries closed themselves off from the global economy. They did this for several reasons. During the 1930s and early 1940s, the global trading and financial system collapsed as a result of the Great Depression and World War II. Developing countries that relied on exporting to the high-income countries were hurt economically. Also, many countries in Africa and Asia achieved independence from the colonial powers of Europe during the 1950s and 1960s and were afraid of being dominated by them economically. As a result, many developing countries imposed high tariffs on foreign imports and strongly discouraged or even prohibited foreign investment. This made it difficult to break out of the vicious cycle of poverty.

The policies of high tariff barriers and avoiding foreign investment failed to produce much growth, so by the 1980s, many developing countries began to change policies. The result was **globalization**, which refers to the process of countries becoming more open to foreign trade and investment.

Globalization The process of countries becoming more open to foreign trade and investment.

If we measure globalization by the fraction of a country's GDP accounted for by exports, we see that globalization and growth are strongly positively associated. Figure 7.10 shows that developing countries that were more globalized grew faster during the 1990s than developing countries that were less globalized. Globalization has benefited developing countries by making it easier for them to get investment funds and technology.

Figure 7.10

Globalization and Growth

Developing countries that were more open to foreign trade and investment grew much faster during the 1990s than developing countries that were less open.

Source: Data from David Dollar, "Globalization, Inequality, and Poverty since 1980," World Bank Research Observer, Vol. 20, No. 2, Fall 2005, pp. 145-175.

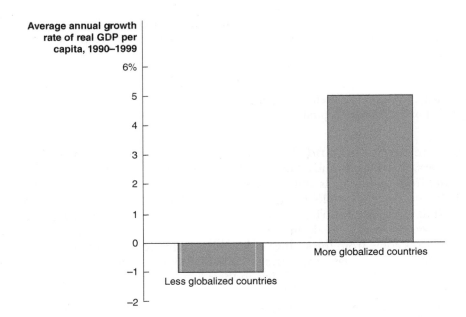

Growth Policies

What can governments do to promote long-run economic growth? We have seen that even small differences in growth rates compounded over the years can lead to major differences in standards of living. Therefore, there is potentially a very high payoff to government policies that increase growth rates. We have already discussed some of these policies in this chapter. In this section, we explore additional policies.

Enhancing Property Rights and the Rule of Law

A market system cannot work well unless property rights are enforced. Entrepreneurs are unlikely to risk their own funds, and investors are unlikely to lend their funds to entrepreneurs, unless property is safe from being arbitrarily seized. We have seen that in many developing countries, the rule of law and property rights are undermined by government *corruption*. In some developing countries, it is impossible for an entrepreneur to obtain a permit to start a business without paying bribes, often to several different government officials. Is it possible for a country to reform a corrupt government bureaucracy?

Property rights are unlikely to be secure in countries that are afflicted by wars and civil strife. For a number of countries, increased political stability is a necessary prerequisite to economic growth.

7.5 LEARNING OBJECTIVE

Discuss government policies that foster economic growth.

Making the Connection | **Will China's Standard of Living Ever Exceed That of Canada?**

In 2010, GDP per capita in Canada was more than six times higher than GDP per capita in China. However, the growth rate of real GDP per capita in Canada has averaged only 1.9 percent per year since 1980, compared with China's average rate of 8.9 percent per year over the same time period. If these growth rates were to continue, then China's standard of living would exceed the Canadian standard of living in the year 2038. However, for China to maintain its high rates of growth in real GDP per capita, it would have to maintain high rates of productivity growth, which is unlikely for several reasons. First, Canada invests more in activities, such as research and development, that result in new technologies and increases in productivity. Second, much of China's growth is likely due to the transition from a centrally planned economy to a market economy, so China's growth rate is likely to decrease as the transition is completed.

Another looming problem is demographic. Because of China's low birthrate, the country will soon experience a decline in its labour force. Over the next two decades, the population of men and women between 15 and 29 years will fall by roughly 100 million, or about 30 percent. China will also experience a large increase in older workers, a group that will likely be less educated and less healthy than younger workers. Given current trends, the US Census Bureau projects fewer people under age 50 in China in 2030 than today, including fewer people in their twenties and early thirties, and many more people in their sixties and older. China still has potential sources for enhancing productivity, including the migration of rural workers to more productive urban jobs and the wider application of technical know-how. These factors can fuel future growth, but at some point, China's demographic problems could slow growth.

Some economists argue that China may have overinvested in physical capital, such as bullet trains.

Perhaps most troubling for China is the fact that, as we saw in the chapter opener, the country remains autocratic, with the Communist Party refusing to allow meaningful elections and continuing to limit freedom of expression. Secure property rights and the rule of law have never been fully established in China. Some observers believe that the lack of political freedom in China may ultimately lead to civil unrest, which could slow growth rates. Whether or not civil unrest eventually develops, the lack of democracy in China may already be resulting in problems that could slow growth in the near future. Nouriel Roubini, an economist at New York University, argues that China's Communist Party may be repeating some of the mistakes committed by the Soviet Communist Party decades ago. He argues that by employing policies that have resulted in investment being 50 percent of GDP, the government may have boosted short-term growth at the expense of the health of the economy in the long term. He notes the following:

> China is rife with overinvestment in physical capital, infrastructure, and property. To a visitor, this is evident in sleek but empty airports and bullet trains…highways to nowhere, thousands of colossal new central and provincial government buildings, ghost towns, and brand-new aluminum smelters kept closed to prevent global prices from plunging.

China has been engaged in an economic experiment: Can a country maintain high rates of economic growth in the long run while denying its citizens basic political rights?

Sources: Based on Nicholas Eberstadt, "The Demographic Future," *Foreign Affairs*, Vol. 89, No. 6, November/December 2010, pp. 54-64; Nouriel Roubini, "Beijing's Empty Bullet Trains," *Slate*, April 14, 2011.

Your Turn: Test your understanding by doing related problem 5.2 on page 210 at the end of this chapter.

MyEconLab

Improving Health and Education

Recently, many economists have become convinced that poor health is a major impediment to growth in some countries. The research of Nobel Laureate Robert Fogel emphasizes the important interaction between health and economic growth. As people's health improves and they become stronger and less susceptible to disease, they also become more productive. Recent initiatives in developing countries to increase vaccinations against infectious diseases, to improve access to treated water, and to improve sanitation have begun to reduce rates of illness and death.

We discussed earlier in this chapter Paul Romer's argument that there are increasing returns to knowledge capital. Nobel Laureate Robert Lucas of the University of Chicago similarly argues that there are increasing returns to *human* capital. Lucas argues that productivity increases as the total stock of human capital increases but that these productivity increases are not completely captured by individuals as they decide how much education to purchase. Therefore, the market may produce an inefficiently low level of education and training unless education is supported by the government. Some researchers have been unable to find evidence of increasing returns to human capital, but many economists believe that government subsidies for education have played an important role in promoting economic growth.

The rising incomes that result from economic growth can help developing countries deal with the brain drain. The *brain drain* refers to highly educated and successful individuals leaving developing countries for high-income countries. This migration occurs when successful individuals believe that economic opportunities are very limited in the domestic economy. Rapid economic growth in India and China in recent years has resulted in more entrepreneurs, engineers, and scientists deciding to remain in those countries rather than leave for Canada, the United States, or other high-income countries.

Policies That Promote Technological Change

One of the lessons from the economic growth model is that technological change is more important than increases in capital in explaining long-run growth. Government policies that facilitate access to technology are crucial for low-income countries. The easiest way for developing countries to gain access to technology is through foreign direct investment, where foreign firms are allowed to build new facilities or to buy domestic firms. Recent economic growth in India has been greatly aided by the Indian government's relaxation of regulations on foreign investment. Relaxing these regulations made it possible for India to gain access to the technology of BlackBerry, Dell, Microsoft, and other multinational corporations.

In high-income countries, government policies can aid the growth of technology by subsidizing research and development. As we noted previously, in Canada, the federal government conducts some research and development on its own and also provides grants to researchers in universities. Tax breaks to firms undertaking research and development also facilitate technological change.

Policies That Promote Saving and Investment

We noted in Chapter 6 that firms turn to the loanable funds market to finance expansion and research and development. Policies that increase the incentives to save and invest will increase the equilibrium level of loanable funds and may increase the level of real GDP per capita. As we also discussed in Chapter 6, tax incentives can lead to increased savings. In Canada, many workers are able to save for retirement by placing funds in Registered Retirement Savings Plans (RRSPs). Income placed in these plans is not taxed until it is withdrawn during retirement. Because the funds are allowed to accumulate tax-free, the return is increased, which raises the incentive to save.

Governments also increase incentives for firms to engage in investment in physical capital by using *investment tax credits*. Investment tax credits allow firms to deduct from their taxes some fraction of the funds they have spent on investment. Reductions in the taxes firms pay on their profits also increase the after-tax return on investments.

Is Economic Growth Good or Bad?

Although we didn't state so explicitly, in this chapter we have assumed that economic growth is desirable and that governments should undertake policies that will increase growth rates. It seems undeniable that increasing the growth rates of very low-income countries would help relieve the daily suffering that many people in those countries endure. But some people are unconvinced that, at least in the high-income countries, further economic growth is desirable.

The arguments against further economic growth tend to be motivated either by concern about the effects of growth on the environment or by concern about the effects of the globalization process that has accompanied economic growth in recent years. In 1973, the Club of Rome published a controversial book titled *The Limits to Growth*, which predicted that economic growth would likely grind to a halt in Canada and other high-income countries because of increasing pollution and the depletion of natural resources, such as oil. Although these dire predictions have not yet come to pass, many people remain concerned that economic growth may be contributing to global warming, deforestation, and other environmental problems.

Some people believe that globalization has undermined the distinctive cultures of many countries, as imports of food, clothing, movies, and other goods have displaced domestically produced goods. We have seen that allowing foreign direct investment is an important way in which low-income countries can gain access to the latest technology. Some people, however, see multinational firms that locate in low-income countries as unethical because they claim the firms are paying very low wages and are failing to follow the same safety and environmental regulations they are required to follow in high-income countries.

As with many other normative questions, economic analysis can contribute to the ongoing political debate over the consequences of economic growth, but it cannot settle the issue.

Economics in Your Life

Would You Be Better Off without China?

At the beginning of the chapter, we asked you to imagine that you could choose to live and work in a world with the Chinese economy growing very rapidly or in a world with the Chinese economy as it was before 1978—very poor and growing slowly. Which world would you choose to live in? How does the current high-growth, high-export Chinese economy affect you as a consumer? How does it affect you as someone about to start a career?

It's impossible to walk into stores in Canada without seeing products imported from China. Many of these products were at one time made in Canada. Imports from China replace domestically produced goods when the imports are either less expensive or of higher quality than the domestic goods they replace. Therefore, the rapid economic growth that has enabled Chinese firms to be competitive with firms in Canada has benefited you as a consumer: You have lower-priced goods and better goods available for purchase than you would if China had remained very poor. As you begin your career, there are some Canadian industries that, because of competition from Chinese firms, will have fewer jobs to offer. Expanding trade changes the types of products each country makes, and, therefore, the types of jobs available, but it does not affect the total number of jobs. So, the economic rise of China will affect the mix of jobs available to you in Canada but will not make finding a job any more difficult.

Conclusion

For much of human history, most people have had to struggle to survive. Even today, two-thirds of the world's population lives in extreme poverty. The differences in living standards among countries today are a result of many decades of sharply different rates of economic growth. According to the economic growth model, increases in the quantity of capital per hour worked and increases in technology determine how rapidly increases will occur in real GDP per hour worked and a country's standard of living. The keys to higher living standards seem straightforward: Establish the rule of law, provide basic education and health care for the population, increase the amount of capital per hour worked, adopt the best technology, and participate in the global economy. However, for many countries, these policies have proved very difficult to implement.

Having discussed what determines the growth rate of economies, we will turn in the following chapters to the question of why economies experience short-run fluctuations in output, employment, and inflation. First, read *An Inside Look* on page 204 for a discussion of the Chinese government's attempts to become less dependent on investment spending for economic growth.

Despite a Plan for Change, Investment Still Spurs China's Growth

REUTERS

Analysis: China Unlikely to Cool Investment as Its Growth Engine

China's long-term plan to cut reliance on investment as a growth engine is clashing with its short-term need for protection against a worsening global outlook.

Beijing has made it clear that consumption, not investment, must eventually do more of the work to drive the world's No. 2 economy.

But with debt troubles in Canada and Europe casting doubt on world-wide demand, it's likely China will keep investing by the billions for now, even if that takes Beijing further from its ultimate goal.

Chinese consumers are a long way from becoming big spenders, so massive investment is still the fastest and easiest way for China to prop up its economy if push comes to shove....

Without doubt, having heavy investment carries a price. Analysts say it generates waste and excess capacity, fuels inflation and produces diminishing economic returns. State investment is like an unsustainable life-support system that China needs to wean itself off.

In 2009—the last year for which figures are available—investment made up 65 percent of China's gross domestic product, a far higher share than in other major or Asian economies. Household consumption, however, accounted for just 35 percent, compared with 70 percent in Canada.

Unstable, Unbalanced, Uncoordinated

In the words of China Premier Wen Jiabao, the Chinese growth model is on all counts unstable, unbalanced, uncoordinated and ultimately unsustainable.

Some of the more bearish economists argue that wasteful investment is inflating a property price bubble and saddling banks with bad loans, sowing the seeds of a future crisis.

An example of healthier investment, economists say, would be companies stepping up capital expenditures on improving China's manufacturing technologies....

Rebalancing, Some Day

On the surface, China seems serious about following through on promises to invest less to rebalance its economy, and it has good reasons to be wary of repeating its 2008 spending spree.

Some of the 4 trillion yuan ($626 billion) stimulus package announced in 2008 was squandered on ill-advised projects and economists now worry that a sizable fraction of loans to local governments won't be repaid.

Banks may be wary of extending more large loans, making it difficult for local governments to invest their way to growth in the future....

Homes Priced Out of Reach

Soaring property prices have put homes out of reach for many ordinary Chinese, and that has become a source of public ire. Keenly aware of that, Beijing wants to build more public homes to keep them affordable.

And with the real estate market accounting for a quarter of total investment in the first half of this year, China could get decent bang for its buck if it ramps up spending in the sector....

To be sure, Beijing says it wants to cure China of its penchant for investment-driven growth. Under its broad five-year economic plan starting from 2011, it envisions a fairer Chinese economy where consumption climbs on rising incomes....

Few Big Spenders

Many analysts have said that Chinese consumers cannot pull their weight as big spenders because the bulk of national income goes to the state instead of workers. A flimsy social safety net encourages high saving rates.

For younger workers, consumption tends to be higher, but between expensive housing and strong cultural pressure to support aging parents and grandparents, they too face limits on how much they can spend.

In a paper published last month, the International Monetary Fund outlined key reforms China should implement to empower its consumers.

It called for a liberalization of financial markets; a reduction in personal income taxes; better healthcare services, increasing the cost of land, energy and pollution; raising dividend payouts from state firms, and improving labor mobility.

However, it would be years before these reforms take effect....

Key Points in the Article

The Chinese economy has been growing at a rapid pace over the past decade, due in large part to high levels of investment. However, the Chinese government has stated that its recent growth will be unsustainable without a shift away from investment spending. The government has established a five-year economic plan that calls for greater reliance on consumption as a means to sustain economic growth. Many analysts believe that achieving this goal will not happen anytime soon because (1) a majority of national income goes to the government instead of workers, and (2) other reforms are needed before Chinese consumers have the willingness and the financial ability to significantly increase consumption.

Analyzing the News

a As you read in the chapter, the quantity of capital available to workers is a source of long-run economic growth. From 1996 to 2010, China experienced an annual growth rate of real GDP per capita of more than 9 percent. Much of this growth came from investment in capital goods. In 2009, investment spending accounted for 65 percent of Chinese GDP, a far higher percentage than in other major economies, and consumption was only 35 percent. In contrast, consumption spending is 70 percent of GDP in Canada and the United States. Relying on investment as a means of economic growth is not a long-run solution, though, as eventually an economy encounters diminishing returns to capital. Because of diminishing returns to capital, further increases in the quantity of capital would result in even smaller increases in real GDP per worker. The production function in the figure below illustrates this point: An increase in capital per hour worked from $(K/L)_{2014}$ to $(K/L)_{2015}$ leads to an increase in output per hour worked from $(Y/L)_{2014}$ to $(Y/L)_{2015}$. This increase in output per hour is much smaller than the increase resulting from the same size increase in capital per hour worked from $(K/L)_{2001}$ to $(K/L)_{2002}$, when the level of capital per hour worked was much smaller.

b Chinese Premier Wen Jiabao understands that the country's current economic growth model is unsustainable in the long run, yet China has continued on the path of high rates of investment. A main reason for this strategy has been a decrease in worldwide demand caused by the global economic downturn. While this investment strategy is not sustainable in the long run, some economists have suggested that increasing government expenditures on research and development in an effort to improve China's manufacturing technologies would be a good option for the Chinese economy.

c A primary reason that China has yet to succeed in increasing consumption is because Chinese consumers have low incomes and high savings rates. A large portion of Chinese national income currently goes to the government rather than to workers, although China has announced its desire to increase income levels to encourage more consumption. Increasing consumption may take time, though, as the following reforms may be needed to encourage consumers to increase spending: reduced personal income taxes, liberalized financial markets, and improved labour mobility.

Thinking Critically

1. What policies can the Chinese government pursue to raise the country's long-run economic growth without further increases in investment spending? How would these policies affect China's per-worker production function?

2. According to the article, consumption in China has not grown significantly because a "flimsy social safety net encourages high saving rates." Explain what the article means by "flimsy social safety net." Why would a flimsy social safety net lead to high saving rates and low rates of consumption? Briefly explain.

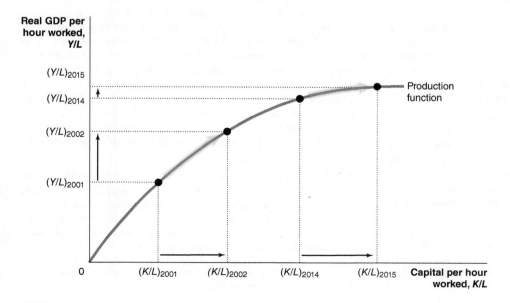

Continuous increases in capital per hour worked lead to smaller and smaller increases in output per hour worked.

Chapter Summary and Problems

Key Terms

Catch-up, p. 191

Economic growth model, p. 181

Foreign direct investment (FDI), p. 199

Foreign portfolio investment, p. 199

Globalization, p. 199

Human capital, p. 182

Industrial Revolution, p. 177

Labour productivity, p. 181

New growth theory, p. 186

Patent, p. 187

Per-worker production function, p. 182

Property rights, p. 196

Rule of law, p. 196

Technological change, p. 181

Summary

*LO 7.1 Until around 1300, most people survived with barely enough food. Living standards began to rise significantly only after the *Industrial Revolution* began in England in the 1700s, with the application of mechanical power to the production of goods. The best measure of a country's standard of living is its level of real GDP per capita. Economic growth occurs when real GDP per capita increases, thereby increasing the country's standard of living.

LO 7.2 An *economic growth model* explains changes in real GDP per capita in the long run. *Labour productivity* is the quantity of goods and services that can be produced by one worker or by one hour of work. Economic growth depends on increases in labor productivity. Labour productivity will increase if there is an increase in the amount of *capital* available to each worker or if there is an improvement in *technology. Technological change* is a change in the ability of a firm to produce a given level of output with a given quantity of inputs. There are three main sources of technological change: better machinery and equipment, increases in human capital, and better means of organizing and managing production. *Human capital* is the accumulated knowledge and skills that workers acquire from education and training or from their life experiences. We can say that an economy will have a higher standard of living the more capital it has per hour worked, the more human capital its workers have, the better its capital, and the better the job its business managers do in organizing production.

The *per-worker production function* shows the relationship between capital per hour worked and output per hour worked, holding technology constant. *Diminishing returns to capital* means that increases in the quantity of capital per hour worked will result in diminishing increases in output per hour worked. Technological change shifts up the per-worker production function, resulting in more output per hour worked at every level of capital per hour worked. The economic growth model stresses the importance of changes in capital per hour worked and technological change in explaining growth in output per hour worked. *New growth theory* is a model of long-run economic growth that emphasizes that technological change is influenced by how individuals and firms respond to economic incentives.

One way governments can promote technological change is by granting *patents*, which are exclusive rights to a product for a period of 20 years from the date the patent is applied for. To Joseph Schumpeter, the entrepreneur is central to the "creative destruction" by which the standard of living increases as qualitatively better products replace existing products.

LO 7.3 Productivity in Canada grew rapidly from the end of World War II until the mid-1970s. Growth then slowed down. Economists continue to debate the reasons for the growth slowdown. Leading explanations for the productivity slowdown are measurement problems, high oil prices, and a decline in labour quality. Because the United States, Western Europe, and Japan experienced a productivity slowdown at the same time as Canada, explanations that focus on factors affecting only Canada are unlikely to be correct.

LO 7.4 The economic growth model predicts that poor countries will grow faster than rich countries, resulting in *catch-up*. In recent decades, some poor countries have grown faster than rich countries, but many have not. Some poor countries do not experience rapid growth for four main reasons: wars and revolutions, poor public education and health, failure to enforce the rule of law, and low rates of saving and investment. The *rule of law* refers to the ability of a government to enforce the laws of the country, particularly with respect to protecting private property and enforcing contracts. *Globalization* has aided countries that have opened their economies to foreign trade and investment. *Foreign direct investment (FDI)* is the purchase or building by a corporation of a facility in a foreign country. *Foreign portfolio investment* is the purchase by an individual or firm of stocks or bonds issued in another country.

LO 7.5 Governments can attempt to increase economic growth through policies that enhance property rights and the rule of law, improve health and education, subsidize research and development, and provide incentives for savings and investment. Whether continued economic growth is desirable is a normative question that cannot be settled by economic analysis.

MyEconLab   Log in to MyEconLab to complete these exercises and get instant feedback.

---

*'Learning Objective' is abbreviated to 'LO' in the end of chapter material.

Review Questions

LO 7.1

1.1 Why does a country's rate of economic growth matter?

1.2 Explain the difference between the total percentage increase in real GDP between 2002 and 2012 and the average annual growth rate in real GDP between the same years.

LO 7.2

2.1 What are the consequences for growth of diminishing returns to capital? How are some economies able to maintain high growth rates despite diminishing returns to capital?

2.2 Why are firms likely to underinvest in research and development, which slows the accumulation of knowledge capital, slowing economic growth? Briefly discuss three ways in which government policy can increase the accumulation of knowledge capital.

2.3 What is the *new growth theory*? How does the new growth theory differ from the growth theory developed by Robert Solow?

LO 7.3

3.1 Describe the record of productivity growth in Canada from 1870 to the present. What explains the slowdown in productivity growth from the mid-1970s?

LO 7.4

4.1 Why does the economic growth model predict that poor countries should catch up to rich countries in income per capita? Have poor countries been catching up to rich countries?

4.2 In what ways do Canada and the United States have greater flexibility in their labour markets and greater efficiency in their financial system compared with other higher income countries, such as those in Europe? How might this greater flexibility in labour markets and greater efficiency in financial markets lead to higher growth rates in real GDP per capita?

4.3 What are the main reasons many poor countries have experienced slow growth?

4.4 What does *globalization* mean? How have developing countries benefited from globalization?

LO 7.5

5.1 Briefly describe three government policies that can increase economic growth.

5.2 Can economics arrive at the conclusion that economic growth will always improve economic well-being? Briefly explain.

Problems and Applications

LO 7.1

1.1 [**Related to** Making the Connection **on page 177**] Economists Carol Shiue and Wolfgang Keller of the University of Texas at Austin published a study of "market efficiency" in the eighteenth century in England, other European countries, and China. If the markets in a country are efficient, a product should have the same price wherever in the country it is sold, allowing for the effect of transportation costs. If prices are not the same in two areas within a country, it is possible to make profits by buying the product where its price is low and reselling it where its price is high. This trading will drive prices to equality. Trade is most likely to occur, however, if entrepreneurs feel confident that their gains will not be seized by the government and that contracts to buy and sell can be enforced in the courts. Therefore, in the eighteenth century, the more efficient a country's markets, the more its institutions favoured long-run growth. Shiue and Keller found that in 1770, the efficiency of markets in England was significantly greater than the efficiency of markets elsewhere in Europe and in China. How does this finding relate to Douglass North's argument concerning why the Industrial Revolution occurred in England?

Based on Carol H. Shiue and Wolfgang Keller, "Markets in China and Europe on the Eve of the Industrial Revolution," American Economic Review, Vol. 97, No. 4, September 2007, pp. 1189–1216.

1.2 Use the data on real GDP in this table to answer the questions that follow.

Country	2007	2008	2009	2010
Brazil	1295.7	1362.6	1353.8	1455.2
Mexico	8806.7	8911.4	8362.4	8815.3
Thailand	4259.5	4368.4	4265.1	4597.0

Note: All values are in billions of units of domestic currency at constant prices.

Data from International Monetary Fund.

a. Which country experienced the highest rate of economic growth during 2008 (that is, for which country did real GDP increase the most from 2007 to 2008)?

b. Which country experienced the worst economic recession during 2009? Briefly explain.

c. Which country experienced the highest average annual growth rate between 2008 and 2010?

d. Does it matter for your answer that each country's real GDP is measured in a different currency? Briefly explain.

1.3 Andover Bank and Lowell Bank each sell one-year certificates of deposit (CDs). The interest rates on these CDs are given in the following table for a three-year period:

Bank	2011	2012	2013
Andover Bank	5%	5%	5%
Lowell Bank	2	6	7

Suppose that you deposit $1000 in a CD in each bank at the beginning of 2011. At the end of 2011, you take your $1000 and any interest earned and invest it in a CD for the following year. You do this again at the end of 2012. At the end of 2013, will you have earned more on your Andover Bank CDs or on your Lowell Bank CDs? Briefly explain.

1.4 **[Related to** Don't Let This Happen to You **on page 179]** Use the data for Canada in this table to answer the following questions:

Year	Real GDP per Capita (2005 prices)
2006	$43 332
2007	43 726
2008	43 178
2009	41 313
2010	42 205

a. What was the percentage change in real GDP per capita between 2006 and 2010?

b. What was the average annual growth rate in real GDP per capita between 2006 and 2010? (*Hint:* Remember that the average annual growth rate for relatively short periods can be approximated by averaging the growth rates for each year during the period.)

1.5 **[Related to** Making the Connection **on page 181]** In his book *The White Man's Burden*, William Easterly reports the following:

> A vaccination campaign in southern Africa virtually eliminated measles as a killer of children. Routine childhood immunization combined with measles vaccination in seven southern Africa nations starting in 1996 virtually eliminated measles in those countries by 2000. A national campaign in Egypt to make parents aware of the use of oral rehydration therapy from 1982 to 1989 cut childhood deaths from diarrhea by 82 percent over that period.

a. Is it likely that real GDP per capita increased significantly in southern Africa and Egypt as a result of the near elimination of measles and the large decrease in childhood deaths from diarrhea? If these events did not increase real GDP per capita, is it still possible that they increased the standard of living in southern Africa and Egypt? Briefly explain.

b. Which seems more achievable for a developing country: the elimination of measles and childhood deaths from diarrhea or sustained increases in real GDP per capita? Briefly explain.

William Easterly, The White Man's Burden: Why the West's Efforts to Aid the Rest Have Done So Much Ill and So Little Good, (New York: The Penguin Press, 2006), p. 241.

1.6 **[Related to** Making the Connection **on page 181]** Economist Charles Kenny of the World Bank has argued the following:

> The process technologies—institutions like laws and inventory management systems— that appear central to raising incomes per capita flow less like water and more like bricks. But ideas and inventions—the importance of

ABCs and vaccines for DPT—really might flow more easily across borders and over distances.

If Kenny is correct, what are the implications of these facts for the ability of low-income countries to rapidly increase their rates of growth of real GDP per capita in the decades ahead? What are the implications for the ability of these countries to increase their standards of living? Briefly explain.

From Charles Kenny, Getting Better, (New York: Basic Books, 2011), p. 117.

LO 7.2

2.1 According to a study by an economist at the Bank of Canada Bank of Minneapolis, during the mid-1980s, managers at iron mines in Canada and Canada increased output per hour worked by 100 percent through changes in work rules that increased workers' effort per hour worked and increased the efficiency of workers' effort. Briefly explain whether this increase in output per hour worked is an example of an improvement in technology.

Based on James A. Schmitz, Jr., "What Determines Labor Productivity? Lessons from the Dramatic Recovery of the U.S. and Canadian Iron-Ore Industries Following Their Early 1980s Crisis," Federal Reserve Bank of Minneapolis Research Department Staff Report 286, February 2005.

2.2 Which of the following will result in a movement along China's per-worker production function, and which will result in a shift of China's per-worker production function? Briefly explain.

a. Capital per hour worked increases from 5 million yuan per hour worked to 6 million yuan per hour worked.

b. The Chinese government doubles its spending on support for university research.

c. A reform of the Chinese school system results in more highly trained Chinese workers.

2.3 **[Related to** Solved Problem 7.1 **on page 185]** Use the graph at the top of the next column to answer the following questions:

a. True or false: The movement from point *A* to point *B* shows the effects of technological change.

b. True or false: The economy can move from point *B* to point *C* only if there are no diminishing returns to capital.

c. True or false: To move from point *A* to point *C*, the economy must increase the amount of capital per hour worked and experience technological change.

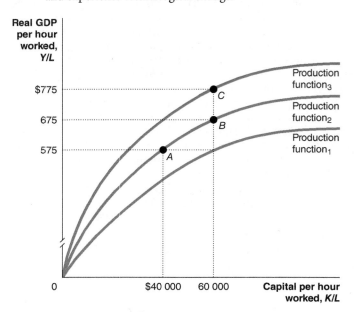

2.4 [**Related to** Solved Problem 7.1 **on page 185**] Shortly before the fall of the Soviet Union, economist Gur Ofer of Hebrew University of Jerusalem wrote this: "The most outstanding characteristic of Soviet growth strategy is its consistent policy of very high rates of investment, leading to a rapid growth rate of [the] capital stock." Explain why this turned out to be a very poor growth strategy.

Gur Ofer, "Soviet Economic Growth, 1928–1985," Journal of Economic Literature, Vol. 25, No. 4, December 1987, p. 1,784.

2.5 Why is the role of the entrepreneur much more important in the new growth theory than in the traditional economic growth model?

2.6 [**Related to** Making the Connection **on page 185**] *Making the Connection* argues that a key difference between market economies and centrally planned economies, such as that of the former Soviet Union, is as follows:

> In market economies, decisions about which investments to make and which technologies to adopt are made by entrepreneurs and managers with their own money on the line. In the Soviet system, these decisions were usually made by salaried bureaucrats trying to fulfill a plan formulated in Moscow.

But in large corporations, investment decisions are often made by salaried managers who do not have their own money on the line. These managers are spending the money of the firm's shareholders rather than their own money. Why, then, do the investment decisions of salaried managers in Canada tend to be better for the long-term growth of the economy than were the decisions of salaried bureaucrats in the Soviet Union?

LO 7.3

3.1 Figure 7.5 shows average annual growth rates in real GDP per person in Canada for various periods from 1870 onward. How might the growth rates in the figure be different if they were calculated for real GDP *per hour worked* instead of per person? (*Hint:* How do you think the number of hours worked per person has changed in Canada since 1870?)

3.2 An article in the *Wall Street Journal* observes for the United States: "For 2008, productivity grew an astounding 2.8% from 2007 even as the economy suffered through its worst recession in decades." How is it possible for labour productivity in the United States (output per hour worked) to increase if output (real GDP) is falling?

From Brian Blackstone, "Productivity Proves Resilient," Wall Street Journal, April 29, 2009.

3.3 Economist Robert Gordon of Northwestern University has argued the following:

> My interpretation of the [information] revolution is that it is increasingly burdened by diminishing returns. The push to ever smaller devices runs up against the fixed size of the human finger that must enter information on the device. Most of the innovations since 2000 have been directed to consumer enjoyment rather than business productivity, including video games, DVD players, and iPods. iPhones are nice, but the ability to reschedule business meetings and look up corporate documents while on the road already existed by 2003.

If Gordon's observations about the information revolution are correct, what are the implications for future labour productivity growth rates?

From Robert J. Gordon, "Revisiting U.S. Productivity Growth over the Past Century with a View of the Future," National Bureau of Economic Research Working Paper 15834, March 2010.

LO 7.4

4.1 [**Related to** Solved Problem 7.2 **on page 193**] Briefly explain whether the statistics in the following table are consistent with the economic growth model's predictions of catch-up.

Country	Real GDP per Capita in 1960	Growth in Real GDP per Capita, 1960–2009
China	$ 363	6.23%
Uganda	655	1.16
Madagascar	1268	–0.23
Ireland	6971	3.25
United States	15 438	2.02

Authors' calculations from data in Alan Heston, Robert Summers, and Bettina Aten, *Penn World Table Version 7.0*, Center for International Comparisons of Production, Income and Prices at the University of Pennsylvania, June 3, 2011.

4.2 [**Related to** Solved Problem 7.2 **on page 193**] In the following figure, each dot represents a country, with its initial real GDP per capita and its growth rate of real GDP per capita.

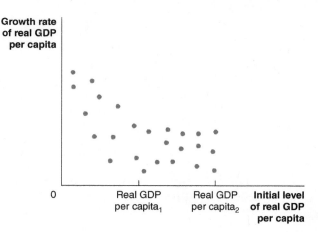

a. For the range of initial GDP per capita from 0 to Real GDP per capita$_2$, does the figure support the economic growth model's prediction of catch-up? Briefly explain.

b. For the range of initial GDP per capita from 0 to Real GDP per capita$_1$, does the figure support the catch-up prediction? Briefly explain.

c. For the range from initial Real GDP per capita$_1$ to Real GDP per capita$_2$, does the figure support the catch-up prediction? Briefly explain.

4.3 An opinion column in the *Economist* argued, "Globalisation, far from being the greatest cause of poverty, is its only feasible cure." What does globalization have to do with reducing poverty?

From Clive Crook, "Globalisation and Its Critics," Economist, September 27, 2001.

4.4 [**Related to** Making the Connection **on page 197**] The relationship that Raymond Fisman and Edward Miguel found between the extent of corruption in a country and the number of parking violations committed by the country's United Nations delegates in New York isn't perfect. For example, "Ecuador and Colombia both have perfectly clean parking slates, despite the experts' view of them as fairly corrupt places." Does this observation invalidate Fisman and Miguel's conclusions about whether the parking violations data provide evidence in favour of there being a culture of corruption in some countries? Briefly explain.

Based on Raymond Fisman and Edward Miguel, Economic Gangsters (Princeton, NJ: Princeton University Press, 2009), p. 89.

4.5 The Roman Empire lasted from 27 BCE to 476 CE. The empire was wealthy enough to build such monuments as the Roman Colosseum. Roman engineering skill was at a level high enough that aqueducts built during the empire to carry water long distances remained in use for hundreds of years. Yet the empire's growth rate of real GDP per capita was very low, perhaps zero. Why didn't the Roman Empire experience sustained economic growth? What would the world be like today if it had? (*Note:* There are no definite answers to this question; it is intended to get you to think about the preconditions for economic growth.)

LO 7.5

5.1 [**Related to the** Chapter Opener **on page 175**] In discussing the future of China, the *Economist* magazine observed:

> And there are…clear limits to the march of freedom in China; although personal and economic freedoms have multiplied, political freedoms have been disappointingly constrained since Hu Jintao became president in 2003.

Briefly discuss whether the limits on political freedom in China are likely to eventually become an obstacle to its continued rapid economic growth.

From "China's Dash for Freedom," Economist, July 31, 2008.

5.2 [**Related to** Making the Connection **on page 200**] In China, why may a lower birthrate lead to slower growth in real GDP per capita? Why might high levels of spending on investment in China lead to high rates of growth in the short run, but not in the long run?

5.3 Is it likely to be easier for the typical developing country to improve the state of public health or to improve the average level of education? Briefly explain.

5.4 Briefly explain which of the following policies are likely to increase the rate of economic growth in Canada.

  a. The government passes an investment tax credit, which reduces a firm's taxes if it installs new machinery and equipment.

  b. The government passes a law that allows taxpayers to reduce their income taxes by the amount of provincial sales taxes they pay.

  c. The government provides more funds for low-interest loans to college students.

5.5 Economist George Ayittey, in an interview on PBS about economic development in Africa, stated that of the 54 African countries, only 8 had a free press. For Africa's economic development, Ayittey argued strongly for the establishment of a free press. Why would a free press be vital for the enhancement of property rights and the rule of law? How could a free press help reduce corruption?

Based on George Ayittey, Border Jumpers, Anchor Interview Transcript, WideAngle, PBS.org, July 24, 2005.

5.6 More people in high-income countries than in low-income countries tend to believe that rapid rates of economic growth are not desirable. Recall the concept of a "normal good" from Chapter 3. Does this concept provide insight into why some people in high-income countries might be more concerned with certain consequences of rapid economic growth than are people in low-income countries?

Aggregate Expenditure and Output in the Short Run

Chapter Outline and Learning Objectives

8.1 The Aggregate Expenditure Model, page 214
> Understand how macroeconomic equilibrium is determined in the aggregate expenditure model.

8.2 Determining the Level of Aggregate Expenditure in the Economy, page 217
> Discuss the determinants of the four components of aggregate expenditure and define marginal propensity to consume and marginal propensity to save.

8.3 Graphing Macroeconomic Equilibrium, page 230
> Use a 45°-line diagram to illustrate macroeconomic equilibrium.

8.4 The Multiplier Effect, page 235
> Describe the multiplier effect and use the multiplier formula to calculate changes in equilibrium GDP.

8.5 The Aggregate Demand Curve, page 241
> Understand the relationship between the aggregate demand curve and aggregate expenditure.

Appendix C: The Algebra of Macroeconomic Equilibrium, page 250
> Apply the algebra of macroeconomic equilibrium.

AP Photo/Mary Altaffer

Fluctuating Demand at Tim Hortons

Tim Hortons coffee is part of Canadian culture. There is a Tim Hortons outlet in just about every small town in the country, and it's hard to go to a rink or a mall and not see someone taking a sip from that famous brown paper cup. Many people seem to need that cup of coffee from "Timmy's" to get through their morning.

Just like most other businesses, Tim Hortons outlets have to worry about the wider economy. When people lose their jobs or are worried about their financial future, they tend to cut back on spending. That morning cup of coffee at the local coffee shop can be one of those things that people decide to do without when times are tight.

Tim Hortons has seen its sales fall in many of the small Canadian towns where the area's main employer has shut down or scaled back operations. The employers in many of these small towns have faced challenges due to the sluggish Canadian and American economies. When firms have a hard time making sales, they reduce output and sometimes lay off workers. These workers then stop making some purchases. If people buy fewer cups of coffee, in turn, Tim Hortons may find it necessary to reduce the hours of work of its employees or even to lay off a few of its employees.

This is just one example of how some firms that cut production can reduce the total spending, or *aggregate expenditure*, of an economy. In this chapter, we will explore how changes in aggregate expenditure affect the level of total production in the economy.

AN INSIDE LOOK on **page 244** discusses how a slow economy can hurt Tim Hortons sales.

Source: Based on Hollie Shaw "Tim Hortons earnings fall short of forecasts," Financial Post, May 9, 2012.

Economics in Your Life

When Consumer Confidence Falls, Is Your Job at Risk?

Suppose that while taking your degree, you work part-time at a local Tim Hortons. One morning you read a local newspaper's story that consumer confidence in the economy has fallen and, as a result, many households expect their future income to be much less than their current income. Should you be concerned about losing your job? What factors should you consider in deciding how likely your boss is to lay you off? As you read the chapter, see if you can answer these questions (pay particular attention to *Making the Connection*, "Do Changes in Consumer Confidence Affect Consumption Spending?" on page 219). You can check your answers against those we provide on page 243 at the end of this chapter.

Aggregate expenditure (AE) Total spending in the economy: the sum of consumption, planned investment, government purchases, and net exports.

I n Chapter 7, we analyzed the determinants of long-run economic growth. In the short-run, as we saw in Chapter 6, the economy experiences a business cycle around the long-run upward trend in real GDP. In this chapter, we begin by exploring the causes of the business cycle by examining the effect of changes in total spending on real GDP.

During some years, total spending in the economy, or **aggregate expenditure (AE)**, and total production of goods and services increase by the same amount. If this happens, most firms will sell what they expected to sell. These firms are not likely to increase or decrease their production. This means there won't be large changes in the total number of workers employed. During other years, total spending in the economy increases more than total production. In these years, firms will increase their production and hire more workers in order to meet the demands of consumers. Sometimes, however, the increase in total spending in the economy is less than total production. As a result, firms reduce their production and potentially lay off a few workers, which can trigger a slowdown in more sectors of the economy—potentially leading to a recession. In this chapter, we will explore why changes in total spending play such an important role in the economy.

Understand how macroeconomic equilibrium is determined in the aggregate expenditure model.

Aggregate expenditure model A macroeconomic model that focuses on the short-run relationship between total spending and real GDP, assuming that the price level is constant.

The Aggregate Expenditure Model

The business cycle involves the interaction of many different economic variables. A simple model called the *aggregate expenditure model* can help us understand the relationships among some of these variables. Recall from Chapter 6 that nominal GDP is the current market value of all final goods and services produced in a country in a year. Real GDP corrects nominal GDP for the effects of inflation. The **aggregate expenditure model** focuses on the short-run relationship between total spending and real GDP. A central assumption of this model is that the price level doesn't change. This means we don't have to worry about a difference between real GDP and nominal GDP. In Chapter 9, we will develop a more complete model of the business cycle that relaxes the assumption of constant prices.

The key idea of the aggregate expenditure model is that *in any particular year, the level of real GDP is determined mainly by the level of aggregate expenditure*. To understand the relationship between aggregate expenditure and real GDP, we need to look more closely at the components of aggregate expenditure.

Aggregate Expenditure

Economists first began to study the relationship between changes in aggregate expenditure and changes in GDP during the Great Depression of the 1930s. Canada, the United States, the United Kingdom, and other industrial countries suffered declines in real GDP of 25 percent or more during the early part of the 1930s. In 1936, British economist John Maynard Keynes published one of the most important books in economics, *The General Theory of Employment, Interest, and Money*, that systematically analyzed the relationship between changes in aggregate expenditure and changes in GDP. Keynes identified four components of aggregate expenditure (which we discussed in Chapter 4), that together equal GDP: consumption, investment, government purchases, and net exports. The four components that make up planned aggregate expenditure (*AE*) are very similar:

- **Consumption (C):** This is spending by households on goods and services; it includes everything from food to haircuts to snowmobiles.

- **Planned Investment (I_p):** This is the planned spending by firms on capital goods, such as factories, office buildings, and machines, and by households on new homes.

- **Government Purchases (G):** This is spending by local, provincial, and federal governments on goods and services, such as the armed forces, bridges and roads, and the salaries of RCMP officers.

- **Net Exports (*NX*):** This is spending by foreign firms and households on goods and services produced in Canada minus the spending by Canadian firms and households on goods and services produced in other countries.

In this chapter, we use the term *planned aggregate expenditure* for the most part because we are focusing on the desired (rather than the actual) spending of an economy in a given period, which is represented by the following equation:

Planned aggregate expenditure = Consumption + Planned investment
+ Government purchases + Net exports

or:

$$AE = C + I_p + G + NX.$$

Governments around the world gather statistics on aggregate expenditure based on these four components. Economists and business analysts usually explain changes in GDP in terms of changes in these four components of spending.

The Difference between Planned Investment and Actual Investment

As you likely know, not everything goes as planned. This is true for businesses as well as university students. You likely noticed that we included "planned investment" rather than "investment" in the equation above. How is it that the amount businesses plan to spend on investment can be different from the amount they actually end up spending?

Understanding how the difference can arise begins with thinking about how firms go about selling goods. In many cases, firms don't wait for a customer to purchase something before they produce it. Instead they produce it, and hold it in *inventory*, while waiting for a customer to make a purchase. **Inventories** are simply products that have been produced but not yet sold to the consumer. Changes in inventories are included as part of investment spending, along with spending on machinery, equipment, office buildings, and factories.

Inventories Goods that have been produced but not yet sold.

In the case of Tim Hortons, actual investment would include its bakeries and stores as well as any doughnuts or cans of coffee it hadn't sold yet. For a retailer, all of the products in the store are part of inventory. Businesses need some inventory in order to sell to consumers. A difference between planned and actual investment arises when firms don't sell the amount of a product they were planning to.

For example, Chapters may want to have 5 copies of *SuperFreakonomics* on its shelves at all times. Assume that it already has 5 copies. If it expects to sell 95 more copies, it would then order 95 copies of the book. If it sells 95 copies, its inventory remains unchanged at 5 copies of the book. If it only sells 90 copies of the book, it has an unplanned increase in inventory of 5 books, leaving it with a total of 10. In short, changes in inventories often depend on sales of goods, which firms can't always predict with perfect accuracy.

For the economy as a whole, we can say that actual investment spending will be greater than planned investment spending when there is an unplanned increase in inventories. Actual investment spending will be less than planned investment spending when there is an unplanned decrease in inventories. *Therefore, actual investment will equal planned investment only when there is no unplanned change in inventories.* In this chapter, we use I_p to represent planned investment. We will also assume that the government data on investment spending (not including inventories) compiled by Statistics Canada represent planned spending. This is a simplification because some of the spending on inventories would be planned by firms.

Macroeconomic Equilibrium

Macroeconomic equilibrium is similar to microeconomic equilibrium. In a microeconomic equilibrium, such as in the market for apples, neither buyers nor sellers have any incentive to change their plans. Equilibrium in the market for apples occurs when the quantity of apples demanded is equal to the quantity of apples supplied, thus neither producers nor consumers have an incentive to change their behaviour. This means apples producers are selling the amount they planned to. When equilibrium in the apple market is achieved, the quantity of apples produced and sold will not change unless the demand for apples or the supply of apples changes. For the economy as a whole, macroeconomic equilibrium occurs where total spending, or planned aggregate expenditure, equals total production, or GDP[1]:

Planned aggregate expenditure = GDP.

As we saw in Chapter 7, in the long run, real GDP in Canada grows, and the standard of living rises over time. In this chapter, we are interested in understanding why GDP fluctuates in the short run. To simplify the analysis of macroeconomic equilibrium, we assume that the economy is not growing. In Chapter 9, we discuss the more realistic case of macroeconomic equilibrium in a growing (or shrinking) economy. If we assume that the economy is not growing, equilibrium GDP will not change unless planned aggregate expenditure changes.

Getting to Macroeconomic Equilibrium

In Chapter 3, where we discussed equilibrium in the market for a single good, we assumed that price would adjust so that the quantity demanded would equal the quantity supplied. In the macroeconomic equilibrium model, we assume that the price level is constant, so price adjustments can't cause the market to move to equilibrium. Instead, firms' responses to unplanned inventory investment will lead to equilibrium.

The easiest way to show that the economy will move toward an output level that is equal to planned aggregate expenditure is to consider what would happen if the two were not equal. As an example, let's look at how a manager at Chapters might respond to different levels of sales of *SuperFreakonomics*.

If planned aggregate expenditure is greater than GDP, firms have sold more than they expected to sell. For our Chapters example, the store may have planned to sell 95 copies of *SuperFreakonomics*, but actually sold 100. It has seen a reduction in its inventories of 5 books. As a result, Chapters has an unplanned investment in inventories of −5 (meaning that inventories have fallen by 5—the minus sign tells you that inventories have decreased). How would the manager respond to such a change in inventories? The manager would likely order more copies of *SuperFreakonomics* this time, say 100 copies. If stores and producers in the economy are experiencing similar unplanned drops in inventories, everyone will increase their orders and the output of the economy (GDP) will increase. To increase production, firms have to hire more workers, and employment rises. In summary, *when planned aggregate expenditure is greater than GDP, inventories will decline, and (as a result of firms' reactions to the drop in inventories) GDP and total employment will increase.*

If planned aggregate expenditure is less than GDP, firms have not sold as much as they expected to sell. For our Chapters example, the store may have planned to sell 95 copies of *SuperFreakonomics*, but instead only sold 90. It has seen an unplanned increase in its inventories of 5 books (it now has 10 in stock when it wanted only 5). How would the manager respond to such an unplanned increase in inventories? The manager would likely order fewer copies of *SuperFreakonomics*, say 85 copies, in hopes of selling all of the copies ordered this time. If many other stores and producers throughout the economy have experienced similar unplanned increases in inventories, they too will decrease their orders. In response to the decrease in orders, firms will cut back production and GDP will decrease. To decrease production, firms generally have to lay off workers, leading to lower employment. Managers of small-town Tim Hortons may have to take such actions when major employers in the area close. In summary, *when planned aggregate expenditure is less than GDP, inventories will increase, and (as a result of firms' reactions to the increase in inventories) GDP and total employment will decrease.*

---

[1]Another way to think of this idea is to make planned aggregate expenditure equal to actual aggregate expenditure. Macroeconomic equilibrium occurs when the plans of producers such as Tim Hortons are realized, or most firms get production "right."

If ...	then ...	and ...
planned aggregate expenditure equals GDP	inventories don't change	the economy is in macroeconomic equilibrium.
planned aggregate expenditure is less than GDP	inventories rise	GDP and employment decrease.
planned aggregate expenditure is greater than GDP	inventories fall	GDP and employment increase.

Table 8.1

The Relationship between Planned Aggregate Expenditure and GDP

Only when planned aggregate expenditure is equal to GDP will firms sell what they expected to sell. In that case, their unplanned inventory investments are 0, and they won't have an incentive to increase or decrease their production. The economy will be in macroeconomic equilibrium. Table 8.1 summarizes the relationship between planned aggregate expenditure and GDP.

This process of increasing and decreasing planned aggregate expenditure causes the year-to-year changes we see in GDP. Economists devote a lot of time and energy to forecasting what will happen to each component of planned aggregate expenditure. Those who are really good at it can make a lot of money working for business or government. When economists forecast that planned aggregate expenditure will decline in the future, that is equivalent to forecasting that GDP will decline and that the economy will enter a recession. Individuals and firms closely watch these forecasts because changes in GDP can have dramatic consequences. When GDP increases, wages, profits, and job opportunities also tend to increase. When GDP declines, it can be bad news for a lot of workers, firms, and job seekers.

When economists forecast that planned aggregate expenditure is likely to decline and the economy is headed for a recession, the federal and provincial governments may implement *macroeconomic policies* in an attempt to head off the decrease in expenditure and keep the economy from falling into recession. We discuss macroeconomic policies in Chapters 11 and 12.

Determining the Level of Aggregate Expenditure in the Economy

To better understand how macroeconomic equilibrium is determined in the aggregate expenditure model, we look more closely at the components of planned aggregate expenditure. Table 8.2 lists the four components of aggregate expenditure for 2012. Each component is measured in *real* terms, meaning that it is corrected for inflation by being measured in billions of 2007 dollars. Consumption is clearly the largest component of aggregate expenditure. Government purchases, including some items considered government investment, is the second-largest component, followed closely by planned investment (not including inventories). Net exports are negative because in 2012, unlike most years before the mid-2000s, Canada imported more goods and services than it exported. Next we consider the variables that determine each of the four components of aggregate expenditure.

8.2 LEARNING OBJECTIVE

Discuss the determinants of the four components of aggregate expenditure and define marginal propensity to consume and marginal propensity to save.

Expenditure Category	Real Expenditure (billions of 2007 dollars)
Consumption	$924.18
Planned investment	327.80
Government purchases	415.23
Net exports	−45.06

Table 8.2

Components of Aggregate Expenditure, 2012

Source: CANSIM Table 380-0002, series v41707126, v41707134, v41707131, v41707142, v41707145. Reproduced and distributed on an "as is" basis with the permission of Statistics Canada.

Figure 8.1

Real Consumption

Consumption follows a smooth, upward trend, interrupted only infrequently by brief recessions.

Source: CANSIM Table 380-0002 series v41975012. Reproduced and distributed on an "as is" basis with the permission of Statistics Canada.

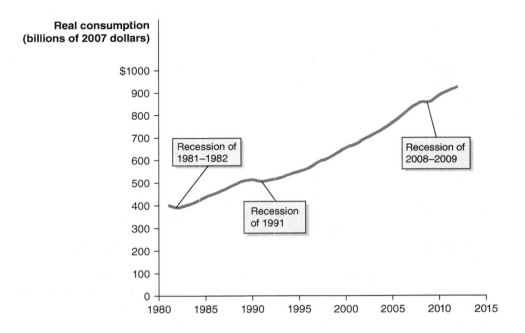

Consumption

Figure 8.1 shows real consumption from 1981 to 2012. Notice that consumption generally follows a smooth, upward trend. Only during periods of recession does consumption decline. You can see this as drops in consumption between 1981 and 1982, as well as between 1991 and 1992 and is flat between 2008 and 2009 then shrinks between 2009 and 2010. The Canadian economy was in or recovering from a recession during these periods.

The following are the five most important variables that determine the level of consumption:

- Current disposable income

- Household wealth

- Expected future income

- The price level

- The interest rate

We will discuss how changes in each of these variables affect consumption in turn.

Current Disposable Income The most important determinant of consumption is the current disposable income of households. Recall from Chapter 4 that disposable income is the income remaining to households after they have paid the personal income tax and received government *transfer payments,* such as social security payments. For most households, the higher their disposable income the more they spend, and the lower their disposable income the less they spend. Macroeconomic consumption is the total of all consumption by Canadian households. So, we would expect consumption to increase when the current disposable income of households increases and to decrease when current disposable income decreases. As was discussed in Chapter 4, total income in Canada increases in most years. Only during recessions, which have not occurred that often in the last 30 years, does total income decline. The main reason why consumption in Figure 8.1 shows such a strong upward trend is that incomes have been rising over the same period of time.

Asset Anything of value owned by a person or a firm.

Household Wealth Consumption depends in part on the wealth of households. A household's *wealth* is the value of its *assets* minus the value of its *liabilities*. An **asset** is anything of value owned by a person or a firm, and a **liability** is any debt or obligation owed by a person or firm. A household's assets include its home, stock and bond holdings, bank accounts, and cars. A household's liabilities include any loans that must be paid back, such as student loans, mortgages, and car loans. A household with $10 million in wealth is likely to spend more than a household with $10 000 in wealth, even if both have the same disposable income. Therefore, when the wealth of households increases, consumption is likely to increase, and when the wealth of households decreases, consumption is likely to decrease.

Liability Anything owed by a person or a firm.

The value of stocks held by households is an important indicator of household wealth. When stock prices increase, household wealth increases, and so should consumption. For example, a family whose stock holdings have increased in value from $50 000 to $100 000 may be willing to spend a larger portion of their disposable income because that household will be less concerned with saving for the future. A decline in stock prices is likely to lead to a decline in consumption. Economists who have studied the determinants of consumption have concluded that permanent increases in wealth have a larger impact than temporary increases. A recent estimate of the effect of changes in wealth on consumption spending indicates for a permanent $1 increase in household wealth, consumption spending increases by 4 to 5 cents per year.

Expected Future Income   Consumption depends in part on expected future income. Most people prefer to keep their consumption fairly stable from year to year, even if their income changes a lot. Some salespeople, for example, earn most of their income from commissions (fixed percentages of the price) on the products they sell. A salesperson might have high income in some years and much lower incomes in other years. Most people in this situation keep their consumption steady and do not increase it much in good years and do not reduce it much in bad years.

The same can be said of most students in Canada. Canadian students generally spend much more of their income than people who are not students with the same income. In fact many students even borrow to improve their consumption possibilities. This may be because students believe their future incomes will be much higher than their current incomes.

If we looked only at the current income of people in the early stages of their lives, we might have difficulty estimating people's current consumption. Instead, we need to take people's expected future income into account.

Making the Connection | Do Changes in Consumer Confidence Affect Consumption Spending?

Since 1980, the Conference Board of Canada has conducted surveys of consumers and calculated the *Consumer Confidence Index*. This index is intended to capture the expectations of consumers about the future. The survey is based on the following four questions:

1. Considering everything, would you say that your family is better or worse off financially than six months ago?
2. Again, considering everything, do you think that your family will be better off, the same, or worse off financially six months from now?
3. How do you feel the job situation and overall employment will be in this community six months from now?
4. Do you think that right now is a good or bad time for the average person to make a major outlay for items such as a home, car or other major item?

The percentages of positive and negative responses for each question are calculated. The index value for each question is:

$$\text{Value} = \frac{\text{Percentage of positive responses}}{\text{Percentage of positive responses } + \text{ Percentage of negative responses}}$$

The index is the average of the values for the four questions, adjusted so that the index is 100 in 2002 (see the graph below).

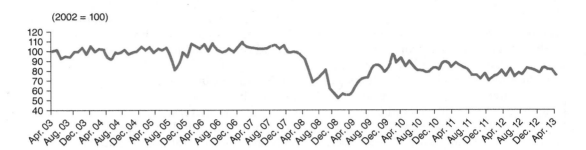

It is fairly clear that consumers have not been feeling very confident about the Canadian economy since 2007. Consumer confidence also fell in the late 1980s, preceding the recession of the early 1990s. The downturn in 2012–2013 may indicate a coming recession.

Andy Kwan of Chinese University Hong Kong and John Cotsomitis of Concordia University have studied the relationship between the Consumer Confidence Index and the Canadian economy. It turns out that the Consumer Confidence Index is a good predictor of household spending in Canada. The link between spending and expected future income is supported by their study. They find spending increases when consumers are more confident about the future and falls when they are less confident. Consumer confidence data are also widely reported in the press and on the evening news. You too can use the Consumer Confidence Index to predict what will happen to consumer spending in the near future.

Source: Do Changes in Consumer Confidence Affect Consumption Spending? The Conference Board of Canada: http://www.conferenceboard.ca/topics/economics/Consumer_confidence.aspx. Reused by permission.

MyEconLab

Your Turn: Test your understanding by doing related problem 2.4 on page 247 at the end of this chapter.

The Price Level Recall from Chapter 5 that the *price level* is a measure of the average prices of goods and services in the economy. Consumption is affected by changes in the price level. It is tempting to assume that an increase in prices will reduce consumption by making goods and services less affordable. In fact, the effect of an increase in the price of one product on the quantity demanded of that product is different from the effect of an increase in the price level on *total* spending by households on goods and services. Changes in the price level affect consumption through the impact on real household wealth. An increase in price level leads to a reduction in the *real* value of wealth. For example, if you have $2000 in a chequing account, the higher the price level, the fewer goods you can buy with that $2000. If the price level falls, the more you can buy. Therefore, as the price level rises, the *real* value of your wealth falls, and so will your consumption. Conversely, if the price level falls, which almost never happens in Canada, your real wealth and thus your consumption will increase.

Nominal interest rate The stated interest rate on a loan.

Real interest rate The nominal interest rate minus the inflation rate.

The Interest Rate Finally, consumption also depends on the interest rate. When the interest rate is high, the reward for saving is increased, and households are likely to save more and spend less. In Chapter 5, we discussed the difference between the *nominal interest rate* and the *real interest rate*. The **nominal interest rate** is the stated interest rate on a loan or a financial asset such as a bond. The **real interest rate** corrects the nominal interest rate for the impact of inflation and is equal to the nominal interest rate minus the inflation rate.[2] Households are concerned with the payments they will make or receive after the effects of inflation are taken into account. As a result, consumption spending depends on the real interest rate.

Consumption spending is divided into three categories: spending on *services*, such as education and haircuts; spending on *nondurable goods*, such as food and clothing; and spending on *durable goods*, such as cars and furniture. Spending on durable goods is most likely to be affected by changes in the interest rate because a high real interest rate increases the cost of borrowing to purchase durable goods. The monthly payments on a four-year car loan will be higher if the real interest rate is 4 percent than if the real interest rate is 2 percent. *You can check this out for yourself at* **www4.bmo.com/popup/ loans/Calculator.html.**

The Consumption Function Panel (a) in Figure 8.2 shows the relationship between consumption spending and disposable income from the years 1981 to 2012, where both consumption and disposable income are measured in billions of 2007 dollars. Each of the dots represents a combination of consumption spending and disposable income for a given year. The straight line in panel (b) shows the estimated relationship between consumption and disposable income. The fact that most of the points lie almost on the line means we can say *consumption is a function of disposable income.* The relationship between consumption and disposable income is called the **consumption function.**

The slope of the consumption function is particularly important. It is called the **marginal propensity to consume** (*MPC*). It is calculated as the change in consumption

Consumption function The relationship between consumption spending and disposable income.

Marginal propensity to consume (*MPC*) The slope of the consumption function: The amount by which consumption spending changes when disposable income changes.

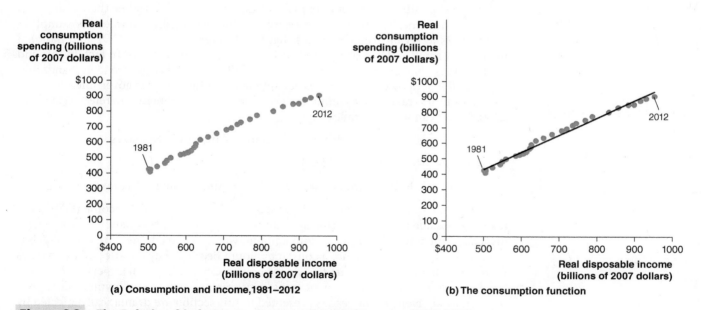

(a) Consumption and income, 1981–2012

(b) The consumption function

Figure 8.2   The Relationship between Consumption and Income, 1981–2012

Panel (a) shows the relationship between consumption and income. The points represent combinations of real consumption spending and real disposable income for the years 1981–2012. In panel (b), we draw a straight line though the points from panel (a). The line, which represents the relationship between consumption and disposable income, is called the *consumption*

function. The slope of the consumption function is the marginal propensity to consume.

Sources: Data Sources: CANSIM Table 380-0004 series v498991 and v498998, and CANSIM Table 236-0021 series v41693271.

---

[2]This relationship is sometimes known as the *Fisher equation*, named for the famous economist Irving Fisher. The relationship is often simplified to $r = i -$ inflation, where r is the real interest rate and i is the nominal interest rate.

divided by the change in disposable income. Using the Greek letter delta, Δ, to represent "change in," C to represent consumption, and YD to represent disposable income, we can write the formula for MPC as follows:

$$MPC = \frac{\text{Change in consumption}}{\text{Change in disposable income}} = \frac{\Delta C}{\Delta YD}$$

For example, between 2011 and 2012, consumption spending increased by $31.4 billion, while disposable income increased by $39.0 billion. The marginal propensity to consume was, therefore:

$$\frac{\Delta C}{\Delta YD} = \frac{\$31.4 \text{ billion}}{\$39.0 \text{ billion}} = 0.80$$

The value for the MPC tells us the part of an extra dollar of disposable income that households spend. Between 2011 and 2012, households spent 80 cents out of every additional dollar of disposable income. As the relationship is very close to a straight line, we can apply the MPC to determine how consumption will change as disposable income changes. For example, if disposable income were to increase by $10 000, consumption spending would increase by $10 000 × 0.80, or $8000. This can be expressed by the formula:

Change in consumption = MPC × Change in disposable income.

The Relationship between Consumption and National Income

We have seen that consumption spending by households depends on disposable income. We now shift our attention slightly to the similar relationship that exists between consumption spending and GDP. We make this shift because we are interested in using the aggregate expenditure model to explain changes in real GDP rather than changes in disposable income. The first step in examining the relationship between consumption and GDP is to recall from Chapter 4 that the differences between GDP and national income are small and can be ignored without affecting our analysis. In fact, in this and the following chapters, we will use the terms *GDP* and *national income* interchangeably. Also recall that disposable income is equal to national income plus government transfer payments minus taxes. Taxes minus government transfer payments are referred to as *net taxes*. So, we can write the following:

Disposable income = National income − Net taxes.

We can rearrange the equation like this:

National income = GDP = Disposable income + Net taxes.

The table in Figure 8.3 shows hypothetical values for national income (GDP), net taxes, disposable income, and consumption spending. Notice that national income and disposable income differ by a constant amount, which is equal to net taxes of $1000 billion. In reality, net taxes are not a constant amount because they are affected by changes in income. As income rises, net taxes rise because some taxes, such as personal income tax, increase and some government transfer payments, such as employment insurance payments, fall. None of the results presented in this section are dramatically affected by this simplifying assumption.

The graph in Figure 8.3 shows a line similar to the consumption function shown in Figure 8.2. We defined the marginal propensity to consume (MPC) as the change in consumption divided by the change in disposable income, which is the slope of the consumption function. In fact, notice that if we calculate the slope of the line in Figure 8.3 between points A and B, we get a result that will not change whether we use the values for national income or the values for disposable income. Using the values for national income:

$$\frac{\Delta C}{\Delta Y} = \frac{\$5250 \text{ billion} - \$3750 \text{ billion}}{\$7000 \text{ billion} - \$5000 \text{ billion}} = 0.75.$$

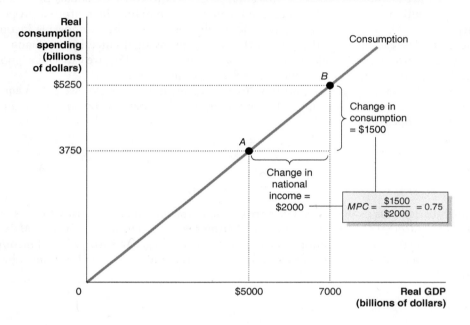

National Income or GDP (billions of dollars)	Net Taxes (billions of dollars)	Disposable Income (billions of dollars)	Consumption (billions of dollars)	Change in National Income (billions of dollars)	Change in Disposable Income (billions of dollars)
$ 1000	$1000	$ 0	$ 750	—	—
3000	1000	2000	2250	$2000	$2000
5000	1000	4000	3750	2000	2000
7000	1000	6000	5250	2000	2000
9000	1000	8000	6750	2000	2000
11 000	1000	10 000	8250	2000	2000
13 000	1000	12 000	9750	2000	2000

Figure 8.3

The Relationship between Consumption and National Income

Because national income differs from disposable income only by net taxes—which, for simplicity, we assume are constant—we can graph the consumption function using national income rather than disposable income. We can also calculate the *MPC*, which is the slope of the consumption function, using either the change in national income or the change in disposable income and always get the same value. The slope of the consumption function between point *A* and point *B* is equal to the change in consumption—$1500 billion—divided by the change in national income—$2000 billion—or 0.75.

Using the corresponding values for disposable income from the table:

$$\frac{\Delta C}{\Delta YD} = \frac{\$5250 \text{ billion} - \$3750 \text{ billion}}{\$6000 \text{ billion} - \$4000 \text{ billion}} = 0.75.$$

It should not be surprising that we get the same result in either case. National income (real GDP) and disposable income differ by a constant amount, so changes in the two numbers always give the same value, as shown in the last columns of the table in Figure 8.3. Therefore we can graph the consumption function using national income rather than using disposable income. We can also calculate the *MPC* using either the change in real GDP or the change in disposable income and always get the same value.

Income, Consumption, and Saving

To complete our discussion of consumption, we can look briefly at the relationships among income, consumption, and saving. Households either spend their income, save it, or use it to pay taxes. For the economy as a whole, we can write the following:

National income = Consumption + Saving + Taxes

When national income increases, there must be some combination of an increase in consumption, an increase in saving, and an increase in taxes:

Change in national income = Change in consumption + Change in saving + Change in taxes.

Using symbols, where Y represents national income (GDP), C represents consumption, S represents saving, and T represents taxes, we can write the following:

$$Y = C + S + T$$

and

$$\Delta Y = \Delta C + \Delta S + \Delta T.$$

To simplify, we can assume that taxes are always a constant amount, in which case $\Delta T = 0$, so the following is also true:

$$\Delta Y = \Delta C + \Delta S.$$

Marginal propensity to save (MPS) The amount by which saving changes when disposable income changes.

We have already seen that the marginal propensity to consume equals the change in consumption divided by the change in income. We can define the **marginal propensity to save (MPS)** as the amount by which saving increases when disposable income increases. We can measure the MPS as the change in saving divided by the change in disposable income. In calculating the MPS, as in calculating MPC, we can safely ignore the difference between national income and disposable income.

If we divide the last equation above by the change in income, ΔY, we get an equation that shows the relationship between the marginal propensity to consume and the marginal propensity to save:

$$\frac{\Delta Y}{\Delta Y} = \frac{\Delta C}{\Delta Y} + \frac{\Delta S}{\Delta Y}$$

or

$$1 = MPC + MPS.$$

This equation tells us that when taxes are constant, the marginal propensity to consume plus the marginal propensity to save must always equal 1. Think of MPC and MPS as what people do with an additional dollar of income. If you get an extra dollar of income, and you spend 75 cents, what did you do with the remaining 25 cents? You must have saved it!

Solved Problem 8.1

Calculating the Marginal Propensity to Consume and the Marginal Propensity to Save

Fill in the blanks in the following table. For simplicity, assume that taxes are zero. Show that MPC plus MPS equals 1.

Real GDP (Y)	Consumption (C)	Saving (S)	Marginal Propensity to Consume (MPC)	Marginal Propensity to Save (MPS)
$900	$300		—	—
1000	800			
1100	900			
1200	900			
1300	1040			

Solving the Problem

Step 1: Review the chapter material. This problem is about the relationship among income, consumption, and saving, so you may want to review the section "Income, Consumption, and Saving" on page 223.

Step 2: **Fill in the table.** We know that $Y = C + S + T$. With taxes equal to zero, this equation becomes $Y = C + S$. We can use this equation to fill in the "Saving" column. We can use the equation for MPC and MPS to fill in the other two columns.

$$MPC = \frac{\Delta C}{\Delta Y}$$

$$MPS = \frac{\Delta S}{\Delta Y}$$

For example, to calculate the value of MPC in the second row of the table, we have:

$$MPC = \frac{\Delta C}{\Delta Y} = \frac{\$860 - \$800}{\$1000 - \$900} = \frac{\$60}{\$100} = 0.6.$$

To calculate the value of MPS in the second row of the table, we have:

$$MPS = \frac{\Delta S}{\Delta Y} = \frac{\$140 - \$100}{\$1000 - \$900} = \frac{\$40}{\$100} = 0.4.$$

Real GDP (Y)	Consumption (C)	Saving (S)	Marginal Propensity to Consume (MPC)	Marginal Propensity to Save (MPS)
$900	$800	$100	—	—
1000	860	140	0.6	0.4
1100	920	180	0.6	0.4
1200	980	220	0.6	0.4
1300	1040	260	0.6	0.4

Step 3: **Show that _MPC_ plus _MPS_ equals 1.** At every level of national income, the MPC is 0.6 and MPS is 0.4. Therefore, the MPC plus MPS is always equal to 1.

Your Turn: For more practice, do related problem 2.5 on page 247 at the end of this chapter.

MyEconLab

Planned Investment

Figure 8.4 shows movements in real investment spending from 1981 to 2012. Notice that while investment generally does have an upward trend, it is not as smooth as

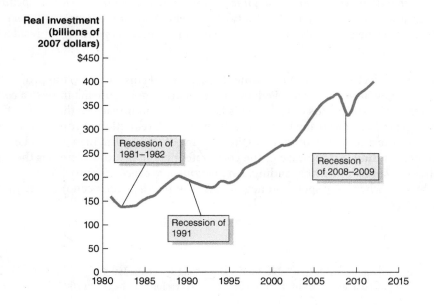

Figure 8.4

Real Investment

Investment is subject to larger changes than is consumption. Investment declined significantly during the recessions of 1981–1982, 1991, and 2008–2009.

Source: CANSIM Table 380-0002 Series v41707134. Reproduced and distributed on an "as is" basis with the permission of Statistics Canada.

consumption. Investment declined significantly in 1982, from 1991 to 1994, and in 2009. As you might have guessed, the Canadian economy was in or recovering from a recession during these periods.

The four most important variables that determine the level of investment are as follows:

- Expectations of future profits
- Interest rate
- Taxes
- Cash flow

Expectations of Future Profits Investment goods, such as factories, office buildings, and machinery, are long lived. A firm is unlikely to build a new factory unless it believes demand for its product will remain strong for at least several years. When the economy moves into a recession, many firms delay buying investment goods, even if the demand for their own product is strong, because they fear the recession may become worse. During an expansion, some firms may become optimistic and begin to increase spending on investment goods even before the demand for their own product has increased. The key point is this: *The optimism or pessimism of firms is an important determinant of investment spending.*

Residential construction (the building of houses) is included in investment spending. Since 1990, residential construction in Canada has averaged about 32.5 percent of total investment spending. The swings in residential construction can be substantial, ranging from a high of 40 percent to a low of 28 percent of total investment spending. The decline in spending on residential construction in 2008 contributed to the recession, and the increase in spending contributed to the recovery.[3]

Interest Rate Some business investment is financed by borrowing, which takes the form of issuing corporate bonds or receiving loans from banks. Households also borrow to finance most of their spending on new homes. The higher the interest rate, the more expensive it is for firms and households to borrow. Firms and households are interested in the cost of borrowing after taking inflation into account, meaning it is the real interest rate that influences investment spending. The higher the real interest rate, the more interest has to be repaid, which means borrowing is more expensive. Therefore, holding everything else that affects investment constant, there is an inverse relationship between investment spending and the real interest rate. *A higher real interest rate results in less investment spending, while a lower real interest rate results in more investment spending.* As we will discuss in Chapter 12 the ability of households to borrow money at very low real interest rates helps explain the rapid increase in American spending on residential construction from 2002 to 2006.[4]

Taxes Taxes affect the level of investment spending. Firms focus on the profits that remain after they have paid taxes. Federal and provincial governments impose a *corporate income tax* on the profits of firms. This tax will have an impact on the benefit firms receive, or get to keep, from any investment they make. A reduction in corporate income tax increases the after-tax profitability (the amount of money the firm gets to keep) of investment spending. An increase in the corporate income tax rate decreases the after-tax profitability of investment spending. An *investment tax incentive* provides firms with a tax reduction when they spend on new investment goods, which can increase investment spending.

---

[3]*Sources:* Statistics Canada, CANSIM Table 380-0002; and author's calculations.
[4]This expansion played a large part in sparking the global recession that began in 2007.

Cash Flow Many firms do not borrow to finance spending on new factories, machinery, and other investments. Instead, they use their own funds. **Cash flow** is the difference between the cash revenues received by a firm and the cash spending by the firm. Neither noncash receipts nor noncash spending is included in cash flow. For example, tax laws allow firms to count depreciation to replace worn out or obsolete machinery as a cost, even when new machinery that has not been purchased would represent noncash spending. The depreciation of existing equipment does not count toward cash flow. The largest contributor to cash flow is profit. The more profitable a firm is, the greater its cash flow and the greater its ability to finance investment. During periods of recession, many firms experience reduced profits, which in turn reduces their ability to finance spending on new factories or machines.

Cash flow The difference between the cash revenues received by a firm and the cash spending by the firm.

Making the Connection | ## The Hills and Valleys of Snowmobile Purchases

Bombardier Recreational Products (BRP), the first company to mass-manufacturer snowmobiles, is facing lower sales of its Ski-Doos in the current economic climate. Snowmobiles are durable goods, and spending on durable goods tends to follow the business cycle. During recessions, households cut back on spending on snowmobiles as they do on other luxury or entertainment items. Firms that use snowmobiles are likely to cut back on new purchases during recessions as well, because they view the machines as an investment, and, as we've seen, investment falls during recessions.

Often households and firms will "make do" with their current machines in a recession rather than buy new ones. As the first graph below shows, snowmobiles sales in Canada tend to follow the state of the economy. Sales fell approximately 17.4 percent from 2009 to 2011, more than 12 percent from 1990 to 1991, and by more than 27 percent between 1981 and 1982. Clearly there are other factors that affect the number of snowmobiles sold—snowfall in a given year, the price of gasoline, the size of the rural population, etc.—but income still plays an important part. The trend has been a decline in snowmobile sales since the mid-1990s. This trend had reversed in 2005, but the industry still had not returned to its higher level of sales in 2008. Certainly, the current economic conditions do not encourage the purchase of snowmobiles.

Changes in real GDP even impact snowmobile sales.

© Fotosearch/AGE Fotostock

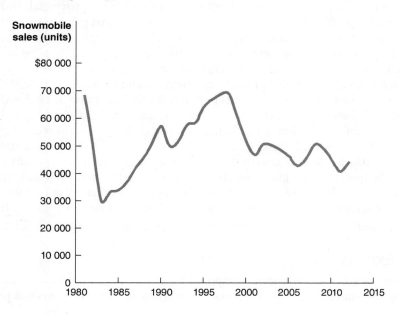

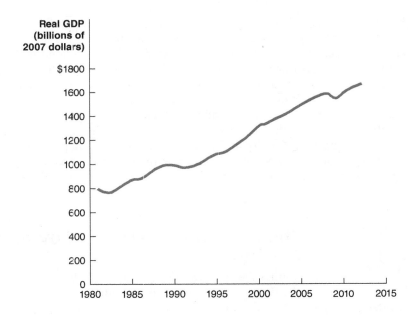

It is interesting to note that BRP has continually expanded its product line into areas other than snowmobiles. In 1968 the Sea-Doo was launched. This small watercraft is in many ways a Ski-Doo for the summer. In 1997 BRP entered the all-terrain vehicle market with a personal "quad," and in 2007 BRP launched its first on-road vehicle called the Spider. BRP is likely expanding its product line for two reasons. First, the general decline in snowmobile sales would encourage it to apply its expertise to other areas. Second, many firms attempt to diversify their product lines to minimize their exposure to the risk of an economic downturn as not all products will see their demand reduced by the same amount when the economy enters a recession.

Sources: Data from International Snowmobile Manufacturers Association.

MyEconLab   **Your Turn:** Test your understanding by doing related problem 2.6 on page 248 at the end of the chapter.

Government Purchases

Total government purchases include all spending by federal, provincial, and local governments for goods and services. Recall from Chapter 4 that government purchases do not include transfer payments, such as social welfare payments by the federal government, or pension payments to retired police officers and firefighters, because the government does not receive a good or service in return.

Figure 8.5 shows levels of real government purchases from 1981 to 2012. Government purchases grew for most of this period, with the exception of 1993 to 1997, when the federal Liberal government of Jean Chrétien undertook a series of spending cuts to reduce Canada's federal budget deficit. As a result of these cuts, the federal government started to take in more in taxes than it spent, and the debt of the country started to fall. More recently, the federal government has engaged in spending programs designed to reduce the impact of the global recession. We see a major increase in government purchases between 2009 and 2010 (during which the federal government focused on its economic stimulus plans), but we see government purchases grow slowly in 2011 and 2012 (during which the federal government focused on reducing the deficit).

Net Exports

Net exports equal exports minus imports. We can calculate net exports by taking the value of spending by foreign firms and households on goods and services produced in

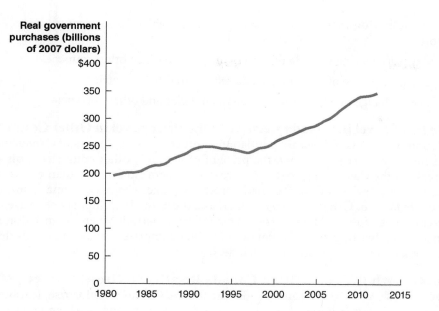

Figure 8.5

Real Government Purchases

Government purchases grew steadily for most of the 1981–2012 period. However, in the mid-1990s, concern about the federal budget deficit caused real government purchases to fall from 1992 to 1997. Real government purchases also grew slowly in 2011 and 2012, a period during which the federal government focused on reducing the deficit.

Source: CANSIM Table 380-0002 series v41707131. Reproduced and distributed on an "as is" basis with the permission of Statistics Canada.

Canada and *subtracting* the value of spending by Canadian firms and households on goods and services produced in other countries. Figure 8.6 illustrates movements in real net exports from 1981 through 2012.

For most of this period net exports were positive. This means foreign firms and households bought more from Canada than Canadian firms households bought from them. For Canada, a fall in net exports is often associated with a recession, *in the United States!* This is because the United States is Canada's biggest trading partner, with approximately 80 percent of our exports going to American firms and households. When the United States enters a recession, the demand for Canadian products and services decreases. This lower demand makes it hard for Canadian firms to sell products in the United States, causing our exports to fall. Canadian imports don't follow the same decreasing pattern as exports when the United States is in recession, so a drop in net exports is the result. We will explore the behaviour of net exports further in Chapter 15.

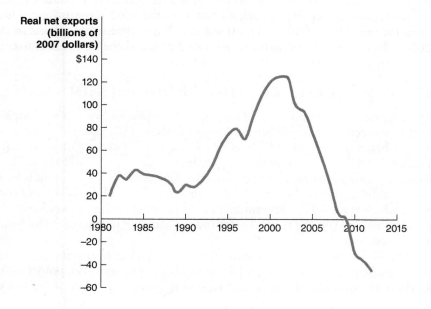

Figure 8.6

Real Net Exports

Net exports were positive for most of the period between 1981 and 2012. Net exports have usually increased when the American economy is booming and decreased when the United States enters a recession.

Source: CANSIM Table 380-0002 Series v41707145 and Series v41707142. Reproduced and distributed on an "as is" basis with the permission of Statistics Canada.

The following are the three most important variables that determine the level of net exports:

- The price level in Canada relative to the price levels in other countries
- The growth rate of GDP in Canada relative to other countries
- The exchange rate between the Canadian dollar and other currencies

The Price Level in Canada Relative to the Price Level in Other Countries If inflation in Canada is lower than inflation in other countries, prices of Canadian products increase more slowly than the price of products in other countries. This slower increase in the Canadian price level increases the demand for Canadian products. The relative rise in prices of foreign-made products makes Canadian demand for foreign products fall. So, Canadian exports increase and Canadian imports decrease, which increases net exports. The reverse happens during periods when the inflation rate in Canada is higher than the inflation rates in other countries: Canadian exports decrease and Canadian imports increase, which decreases net exports.

The Growth Rate of GDP in Canada Relative to Growth Rates in Other Countries As GDP rises in Canada, the incomes of households rise, leading them to increase their purchases of all goods and services, including goods and services produced in other countries. As a result, imports rise. When incomes in other countries rise, their households will increase their purchases of goods and services, including some goods and services made in Canada. As a result, Canadian exports (which are other country's imports) rise. When incomes in Canada rise faster than in other countries, Canadian imports rise more than exports. As a result, Canada's net exports fall.

The Exchange Rate between the Canadian Dollar and Other Currencies As the value of the Canadian dollar rises, the foreign currency price of Canadian products sold in other countries rises, and the dollar price of foreign products sold in Canada falls. For example suppose the exchange rate between the Japanese yen and the Canadian dollar is ¥100 Japanese yen for 1 Canadian dollar, or ¥100 = $1. At this exchange rate, someone in Canada could buy ¥100 for $1, or someone in Japan could buy $1 for ¥100. Leaving aside transportation costs, an item that sells for $10 in Canada will sell for ¥1000 in Japan, and a Japanese product that sells for ¥1000 in Japan will sell for $10 in Canada. If the exchange rate changes to ¥150 = $1, the value of the dollar has risen as it takes more yen to buy $1. Under the new exchange rate, a product that still sells for $10 in Canada will now cost ¥1500, reducing the quantity demanded by Japanese consumers. The Japanese product that sells in Japan for ¥1000, will now sell in Canada for $6.67, increasing the quantity demanded by Canadian consumers. An increase in the value of the dollar will reduce exports and increase imports, so net exports will fall. A decrease in the value of the dollar will increase exports and reduce imports, so net exports will rise. The decline in net exports we've seen since 2004 is due, at least in part, to the increase in the value of the Canadian dollar.

Use a 45°-line diagram to illustrate macroeconomic equilibrium.

Graphing Macroeconomic Equilibrium

Having examined the components of aggregate expenditure, we can now look more closely at macroeconomic equilibrium. We saw earlier in the chapter that macroeconomic equilibrium occurs when GDP is equal to aggregate expenditure. We can use a graph called the *45°-line diagram* to illustrate macroeconomic equilibrium. (The 45°-line diagram is also sometimes referred to as the *Keynesian cross* because it is based on the analysis of John Maynard Keynes.) To become familiar with this diagram, consider Figure 8.7, which is a 45°-line diagram that shows the relationship between the quantity of cups of coffee sold (on the vertical axis) and the quantity of cups of coffee produced (on the horizontal axis).

The line on the diagram forms an angle of 45° with the horizontal axis. The line represents all the points that are equal distances from both axes. So, points such as A and B, where the number of cups of coffee sold equals the number of cups of coffee

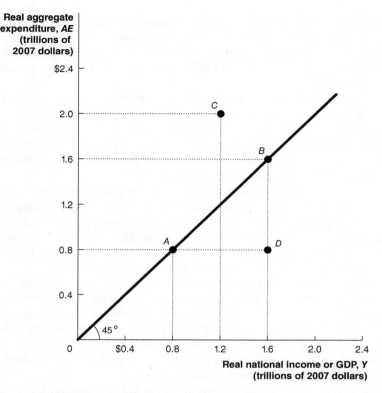

Figure 8.7

An Example of the 45°-Line Diagram

The 45° line shows all the points that are equal distances from both axes. Points such as *A* and *B*, at which the quantity produced equals the quantity sold, are on the 45° line. Points such as *C*, at which the quantity sold is greater than the quantity produced, lie above the line. Points such as *D*, at which the quantity sold is less than the quantity produced, lie below the line.

produced, lie on the 45° line. Points such as *C*, where the quantity sold is greater than the quantity produced, lie above the line. Points such as *D*, where the quantity sold is less than the quantity produced lie below the line.

Figure 8.8 is similar to Figure 8.7, except that it measures real national income, or real GDP[5] (*Y*), on the horizontal axis and planned real aggregate expenditure (*AE*) on

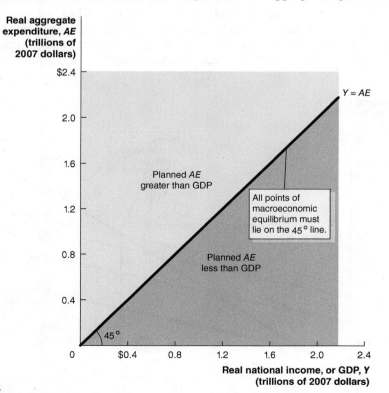

Figure 8.8

The Relationship between Planned Aggregate Expenditure and GDP in a 45°-Line Diagram

Every point of macroeconomic equilibrium is on the 45° line, where planned aggregate expenditure equals GDP. At points above the line, planned aggregate expenditure is greater than GDP. At points below the line, planned aggregate expenditure is less than GDP.

[5]Keep in mind that GDP can be used to represent each of the following: (1) income, (2) actual expenditure, and (3) production.

the vertical axis. Because macroeconomic equilibrium occurs where planned aggregate expenditure equals GDP, *we know that all points of macroeconomic equilibrium must lie along the 45° line.* For all points above the 45° line, planned aggregate expenditure will be greater than GDP. For all points below the 45° line, planned aggregate expenditure will be less than GDP.

The 45° line shows many potential points of macroeconomic equilibrium. During any particular year, only one of these points will represent the actual level of equilibrium real GDP, given the actual level of planned real expenditure. To determine this point, we need to draw a line on the graph to show the *aggregate expenditure function.* The aggregate expenditure function shows us the amount of planned aggregate expenditure that will occur at every level of national income, or GDP.

Changes in GDP have a much greater impact on consumption than on planned investment, government purchases, or net exports. We assume for simplicity that the variables that determine planned investment, government purchases, and net exports all remain constant, as do the variables other than GDP that affect consumption. For example, we assume that a firm's level of planned investment at the beginning of the year will not change during the year, even if the level of GDP changes.

Figure 8.9 shows the aggregate expenditure function on the 45°-line diagram. The lowest upward sloping line (the dark blue one), C, represents the consumption function, as shown in Figure 8.2. The quantities of planned investment, government purchases, and net exports are constant because we assumed the variables they depend on are constant. So, the level of planned aggregate expenditure at any level of GDP is the amount of consumption spending at that level of GDP plus the sum of the constant amounts of planned investment, government purchases, and net exports. In Figure 8.9, we add each component of spending successively to the consumption function line to arrive at the line representing planned aggregate expenditure (AE). The $C + I_p$ line (the red one) is higher than the C line by the constant amount of planned investment. The $C + I_p + G$ line (the light blue one) is higher than the $C + I_p$ line by the constant amount of government purchases. The $C + I_p + G + NX$ line (the pink one) is higher than the $C + I_p + G$ line by the constant amount of net exports. (In some years, such as 2010, NX is negative and the $C + I_p + G + NX$ will be *lower* than the $C + I_p + G$ line.) The $C + I_p + G + NX$ line shows all four components of expenditure and is the aggregate expenditure (AE) function. At the point where the AE line crosses the 45° line, planned aggregate expenditure is equal to GDP, and the economy is in macroeconomic equilibrium.

Figure 8.9

Macroeconomic Equilibrium on the 45°-Line Diagram

Macroeconomic equilibrium occurs where the AE line crosses the 45° line. The lowest upward-sloping line, C, represents the consumption function. The quantities of planned investment, government purchases, and net exports are constant because we assumed that the variables they depend on are constant. So, the total of planned aggregate expenditure at any level of GDP is the amount of consumption at that level of GDP plus the sum of the constant amounts of planned investment, government purchases, and net exports. We successively add each component of spending to the consumption function line to arrive at the line representing aggregate expenditure.

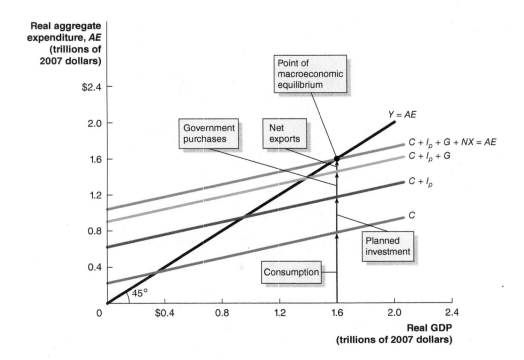

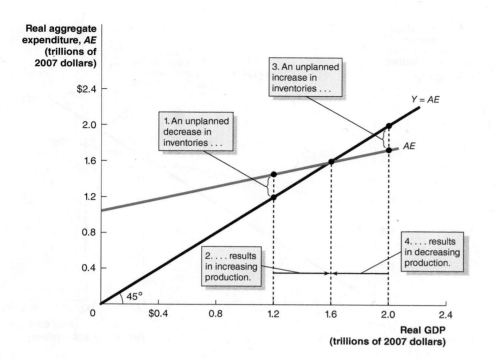

Figure 8.10

Macroeconomic Equilibrium

Macroeconomic equilibrium occurs where the AE line crosses the 45° line. In this case, that occurs at GDP of $1.6 trillion. If GDP is less than $1.6 trillion, the corresponding point on the AE line is above the 45° line, planned aggregate expenditure is greater than total production, firms will experience an unplanned decrease in inventories, and GDP will increase. If GDP is greater than $1.6 trillion, the corresponding point on the AE line is below the 45° line, planned aggregate expenditure is less than total production, firms will experience an unplanned increase in inventories, and GDP will decrease.

Figure 8.10 makes the relationship between planned aggregate expenditure and GDP clearer by showing only the 45° line and the AE line. The figure shows that the AE line intersects the 45° line at a level of GDP of $1.6 trillion. Therefore, $1.6 trillion represents the equilibrium level of real GDP. To see why this is true, consider what would happen if real GDP were only $1.2 trillion. By moving vertically from $1.2 trillion on the horizontal axis up to the AE line, we see that planned aggregate expenditure will be greater than $1.2 trillion at this level of real GDP. Whenever total spending is greater than total production, firms' inventories will fall. The fall in inventories is equal to the vertical distance between the AE line, which shows the level of total spending and the 45° line which shows the $1.2 trillion in total production. Unplanned declines in inventories lead firms to increase their production.[6] As real GDP increases from $1.2 trillion, so will total income and, therefore, consumption. The economy will move up the AE line as consumption increases. The gap between total spending and total production will fall, but so long as the AE line is above the 45° line, inventories will continue to decline, and firms will continue to expand production. When real GDP rises to $1.6 trillion, inventories stop falling, and the economy will be in macroeconomic equilibrium.

As Figure 8.10 shows, if GDP is initially $2 trillion, planned aggregate expenditure will be less than GDP, and firms will experience an unplanned increase in inventories. Rising inventories lead firms to decrease production. As GDP falls from $2 trillion, consumption will also fall, which causes the economy to move down the AE line. The gap between planned aggregate expenditure and GDP will fall, but as long as the AE line is below the 45° line, inventories will continue to rise and firms will continue to cut production. When GDP falls to $1.6 trillion, inventories will stop rising, and the economy will be in macroeconomic equilibrium.

Showing a Recession on the 45°-Line Diagram

Notice that *macroeconomic equilibrium can occur at any point on the 45° line.* Ideally, we would like equilibrium to occur at *potential real GDP.* At potential real GDP, firms

---

[6]This is what happened at the Chapters bookstore we discussed earlier, when the manager had ordered 95 copies of *SuperFreakonomics* and sold 100.

Figure 8.11

Showing a Recession on the 45°-Line Diagram

When the *AE* line intersects the 45° line at a level of GDP below potential GDP, the economy is in recession. The figure shows that potential GDP is $2 trillion, but because planned aggregate expenditure is too low, the equilibrium level of GDP is only $1.6 trillion, where the *AE* line intersects the 45° line. As a result, some firms will be operating below their normal capacity, and unemployment will be above the natural rate of unemployment. We can measure the shortfall in planned aggregate expenditure as the vertical distance between the *AE* line and the 45° line at the level of potential GDP.

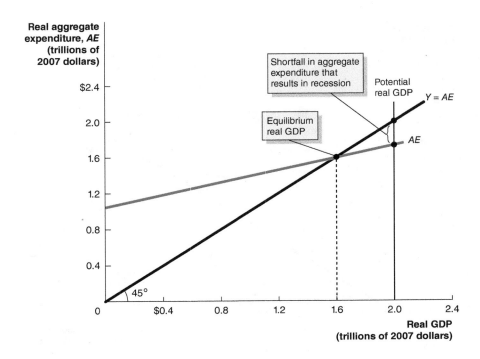

will be operating at the normal level of capacity, and the economy will be at the *natural rate of unemployment*. As we saw in Chapter 5, at the natural rate of unemployment, the economy will be at *full employment*: Everyone in the labour force who wants a job will have a job, except the structurally and frictionally unemployed. However, for equilibrium to occur at the level of potential GDP, planned aggregate expenditure must be high enough. As Figure 8.11 shows, if there is insufficient total spending, equilibrium will occur at a lower level of real GDP. Many firms will be operating below their normal capacity, and the unemployment rate will be above the natural rate of unemployment.

Suppose the level of potential real GDP is $2 trillion. As Figure 8.11 shows, when GDP is $2 trillion, planned aggregate expenditure is below $2 trillion, perhaps because firms have become pessimistic about their future profitability and have reduced their investment spending. For example firms are worried about future revenues the boss might not buy doughnuts for the office staff as often. The shortfall in planned aggregate expenditure that leads to the recession can be measured as the vertical distance between the *AE* line and the 45° line at the level of potential real GDP. This shortfall is equal to the unplanned increase in inventories that would occur if the economy was initially at a level of GDP of $2 trillion. The unplanned increase in inventories measures the amount by which current planned aggregate expenditure is too low for the current level of production to be the equilibrium level. Or, put another way, if any of the four components of aggregate expenditure increased by this amount, the *AE* line would shift upward and intersect the 45° line at a GDP of $2 trillion, and the economy would be in macroeconomic equilibrium at full employment.

Figure 8.11 shows that macroeconomic equilibrium will occur where GDP is $1.6 trillion. This is a full 10 percent below the potential real GDP of $2 trillion. As a result, many firms will be operating below their normal capacity, and the unemployment rate will be well above the natural rate of unemployment. The economy will remain at this level of real GDP until there is an increase in one or more of the components of aggregate expenditure.

The Important Role of Inventories

Whenever planned aggregate expenditure is less than real GDP, some firms will experience unplanned increases in inventories. If firms do not cut back their production

Table 8.3   Macroeconomic Equilibrium

Real GDP (Y)	Consumption (C)	Planned Investment (I_p)	Government Purchases (G)	Net Exports (NX)	Planned Aggregate Expenditure (AE)	Unplanned Inventory Investment	Real GDP Will ...
$800	$740	$125	$125	-$30	$960	-$160	increase
1200	1060	125	125	-30	1280	-80	increase
1600	1380	125	125	-30	1600	0	be in equilibrium
2000	1700	125	125	-30	1920	80	decrease
2400	2020	125	125	-30	2240	160	decrease

Note: The values are in billions of 2007 dollars.

promptly when spending declines, they will accumulate inventories. If firms accumulate excess inventories, then even if spending quickly returns to normal levels, firms will have to sell their excess inventories before they can return to producing at normal levels.

A Numerical Example of Macroeconomic Equilibrium

In forecasting real GDP, economists rely on quantitative models of the economy. We can increase our understanding of the causes of changes in real GDP by considering a simple numerical example of macroeconomic equilibrium. Although simplified, this example captures some of the key features contained in the sort of quantitative models that economic forecasters use. Table 8.3 shows several hypothetical combinations of real GDP and planned aggregate expenditure. The first column lists real GDP. The next four columns list levels of the four components of planned aggregate expenditure that occur at the corresponding level of real GDP. We assume that planned investment, government purchases, and net exports do not change as GDP changes. Because consumption depends on GDP, it increases as GDP increases.

In the first row, GDP of $800 billion (or $0.8 trillion) results in consumption of $740 billion. Adding consumption, planned investment, government purchases, and net exports across the row gives planned aggregate expenditure of $960 billion, which is shown in the sixth column. In this row, planned aggregate expenditure is more than GDP so inventories will fall by $160 billion. This unplanned decline in inventories will lead firms to increase production, and GDP will increase. GDP will continue to increase until it reaches $1600 billion. At that level of GDP planned aggregate expenditure is also $1600 billion, unplanned changes in inventories are zero, and the economy has reached a macroeconomic equilibrium.

In the last row of Table 8.3, GDP of $2400 billion results in consumption of $2020 billion and planned aggregate expenditure of $2240 billion. Now planned aggregate expenditure is less than GDP, so inventories increase by $160 billion. This unplanned increase in inventories will lead firms to decrease production, and GDP will decrease. GDP will continue to decrease until it reaches $1600 billion, unplanned inventory investment is zero, and the economy is in a macroeconomic equilibrium.

Only when real GDP equals $1600 billion will the economy be in macroeconomic equilibrium. At other levels of real GDP, planned aggregate expenditure will be higher or lower than GDP, and the economy will be expanding or contracting.

The Multiplier Effect

To this point, we have seen that aggregate expenditure determines real GDP in the short run and we have seen how the economy adjusts if it is not in equilibrium. We have also seen that whenever aggregate expenditure changes, there will be a new level

8.4 LEARNING OBJECTIVE

Describe the multiplier effect and use the multiplier formula to calculate changes in equilibrium GDP.

Figure 8.12

The Multiplier Effect

The economy begins at point *A*, at which equilibrium real GDP is $1.6 trillion. An $80 billion increase in planned investment shifts up aggregate expenditure from AE_1 to AE_2. The new equilibrium is at point *B*, where real GDP is $2 trillion, which is potential real GDP. Because of the multiplier effect, an $80 billion increase in investment results in a $400 billion increase in equilibrium real GDP.

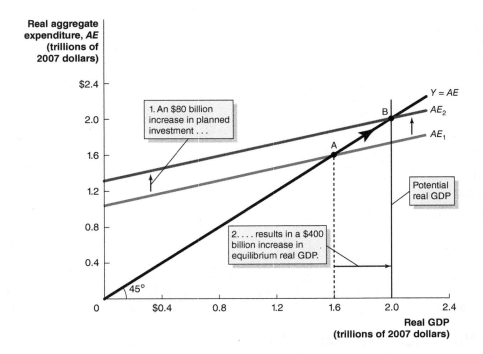

Autonomous expenditure An expenditure that does not depend on the level of GDP.

Multiplier The increase in equilibrium real GDP divided by the increase in autonomous expenditure.

of equilibrium real GDP. In this section, we will look more closely at the effects of changes in aggregate expenditure on equilibrium real GDP. We begin the discussion with Figure 8.12, which illustrates the effects of an increase in planned investment spending. We assume that the economy starts in equilibrium at point *A*, at which real GDP is $1.6 trillion. Remember that there are no unplanned changes in inventories at this level of output under current conditions. Now assume that firms become more optimistic about their future profitability and increase spending on factories, machinery, and equipment by $80 billion. This increase in planned investment shifts the *AE* line up by $80 billion from AE_1 to AE_2. (Notice the vertical distance between the two *AE* curves is $80 billion.) The new equilibrium occurs at point *B*, at which real GDP is $2 trillion, which is also potential real GDP in this story.

Notice that the initial $80 billion increase in planned investment results in a $400 billion increase in equilibrium real GDP. The increase in planned investment has had a *multiplied effect* on equilibrium real GDP. It is not only planned investment that will have this multiplied effect; any increase in *autonomous expenditure* will shift the aggregate expenditure function upward and lead to a multiplied increase in equilibrium GDP. **Autonomous expenditure** does not depend on the level of GDP. In the aggregate expenditure model we have been using, planned investment spending, government purchases, and net exports are all autonomous expenditures. Consumption actually has both an autonomous component, which does not depend on the level of GDP, and a nonautonomous (also known as *induced*) component that does depend on the level of GDP. For example, if households decide to spend more of their incomes, which also means saving less, at every level of income, there will be an autonomous increase in consumption spending. The increase in autonomous consumption spending will cause the aggregate expenditure function to shift up, just like the increase in planned investment did. If, however, it is an increase in real GDP that causes households to increase their spending, as indicated in the consumption function, the economy will move up along the aggregate expenditure function, and the increase in consumption spending will be nonautonomous.

The ratio of the increase in equilibrium real GDP to the increase in autonomous expenditure is called the **multiplier**. The series of induced increases in consumption spending that result from an initial increase in autonomous expenditure is called the

multiplier effect. The multiplier effect occurs because an initial increase in autonomous expenditure sets off a series of increases in real GDP.

We can look more closely at the multiplier effect shown in Figure 8.12. Suppose the whole $80 billion increase in investment spending shown in the figure consists of firms building additional factories and office buildings. Initially, this additional spending will cause the construction of factories and office buildings to increase by $80 billion, so GDP will also increase by $80 billion. Remember that increases in production result in equal increases in national income. So, this increase in real GDP of $80 billion is also an increase in national income of $80 billion. In this example, the income is received as wages and salaries by the employees of the construction firms, as profits by the owners of the firms, and so on. After receiving this additional income, these workers, managers, and owners will increase their consumption of cars, appliances, furniture, and many other products (such as Tim Hortons coffee). If the marginal propensity to consume (*MPC*) is 0.8, we know the increase in consumption spending will be $64 billion. This additional $64 billion in spending will cause the firms making cars, appliances, coffee, and other products to increase production by $64 billion, so GDP will rise by $64 billion. This increase in GDP means national income will increase by another $64 billion. This increase in income will be received by the workers, managers, and owners of the firms producing the cars, appliances, coffee, and other products. These workers, managers, and owners will, in turn, increase their consumption spending, and the process of increasing production, income, and consumption will continue.

Eventually, the total increase in consumption will be $320 billion (the equilibrium change in real GDP is $400 billion and the marginal propensity to consume is 0.8, so consumer spending is $320 billion higher in the new equilibrium). This $320 billion increase in consumption combined with the initial $80 billion increase in investment spending will result in a total change in equilibrium GDP of $400 billion. We can think of the multiplier effect occurring in rounds of spending. In round 1, there is an increase of $80 billion in autonomous expenditure—the $80 billion in planned investment spending in our example—which causes GDP to rise by $80 billion. In round 2, induced expenditure rises by $64 billion (which equals the $80 billion in increase in real GDP in round 1 multiplied by the *MPC*). The $64 billion in induced expenditure in round 2 causes a $64 billion increase in real GDP, which leads to a $51.2 billion increase in induced expenditure in round 3, and so on. The final column sums up the total increases in expenditure, which equal the total increase in GDP. In each round, the additional induced expenditure becomes smaller because the *MPC* is less than 1. By round 10, additional induced expenditure is only $10.74 billion, and the total increase in GDP from the beginning of the process is $357.05 billion. By round 20, the process is almost complete: Additional induced expenditure is only $1.15 billion, and the total increase in GDP is $395.39 billion. Eventually, the process will be finished, although we can't say precisely how many rounds of spending it will take, so we just label the last round "*n*" instead of giving it a specific number.

We can calculate the value of the multiplier in our example by dividing the increase in equilibrium real GDP by the increase in autonomous expenditure:

$$\frac{\Delta Y}{\Delta I} = \frac{\text{Change in real GDP}}{\text{Change in investment spending}} = \frac{\$400 \text{ billion}}{\$80 \text{ billion}} = 5.$$

With a multiplier of 5, each increase in autonomous expenditure of $1 will result in an increase in equilibrium GDP of $5.

A Formula for the Multiplier

Table 8.4 shows that during the multiplier process, each round of increases in consumption is smaller than the previous round, so, eventually, the increases will come to an end, and we will have a new macroeconomic equilibrium. But how do we know that when we

Multiplier effect The process by which an increase in autonomous expenditure leads to a larger increase in real GDP.

Table 8.4

The Multiplier Effect in Action

	Additional Autonomous Expenditure	Additional Induced Expenditure (C)	Total Additional Expenditure = Total Additional GDP
Round 1	$80 billion	$0	$80.00 billion
Round 2	0	64.00 billion	144.00 billion
Round 3	0	51.20 billion	195.20 billion
Round 4	0	40.96 billion	236.16 billion
Round 5	0	32.77 billion	268.93 billion
.	.	.	.
.		.	.
.		.	.
Round 10	0	10.74 billion	357.05 billion
.		.	.
.		.	.
.		.	.
Round 20	.	1.15 billion	395.39 billion
.		.	.
Round n	0	0	400.00 billion

add all the increases in GDP, the total will be $400 billion? We can show this is true by first writing out the total change in equilibrium GDP:

The total change in equilibrium GDP equal the initial increase in planned investment spending = $80 billion

Plus the first induced in consumption = $MPC \times$ $80 billion

Plus the second induced increase in consumption = $MPC \times (MPC \times$ $80 billion)

Plus the third induced increase in consumption = $MPC \times (MPC \times (MPC \times$ $80 billion))

Plus the fourth induced increase in consumption = $MPC \times MPC \times (MPC \times (MPC \times$ $80 billion))

And so on ...
Equivalently:

Total change in GDP = $80 billion + $MPC \times$ $80 billion + $MCP^2 \times$ $80 billion + $MPC^3 \times$ $80 billion + $MPC^4 \times$ $80 billion + ...

Where the ellipses (...) indicate the pattern continues on for an infinite number of similar terms. If we factor out the $80 billion from each term in the expression, we have:

Total change in GDP = $80 billion $\times (1 + MPC + MCP^2 + MPC^3 + MPC^4 + ...)$

Mathematicians have shown an expression like the one in parentheses above sums to:

$$\frac{1}{1 - MPC}.$$

In this case, the MPC is equal to 0.8. So, we can calculate the change in equilibrium GDP = $80 billion $\times [1/(1 - 0.8)]$ = $80 billion $\times$ 5 = $400 billion. We have also arrived at a general formula for the multiplier:

$$Multiplier = \frac{\text{Change in equilibrium real GDP}}{\text{Change in autonomous expenditure}} = \frac{1}{1 - MPC}.$$

In this case, the multiplier is $1/(1 - 0.8)$, or 5, which means that for each additional \$1 of autonomous spending, equilibrium GDP will increase by \$5. An \$80 billion increase in planned investment spending results in a \$400 billion increase in equilibrium GDP. Notice that the value of the multiplier depends on the value of the *MPC*. In particular, the larger the value of the *MPC*, the larger the value of the multiplier will be. For example, if the *MPC* were 0.9 instead of 0.8, the multiplier would increase from 5 to $1/(1 - 0.9) = 10$.

Summarizing the Multiplier Effect

You should note four key points about the multiplier effect:

1. The multiplier effect occurs both when autonomous expenditure increases and when it decreases. For example, with an *MPC* of 0.8, a *decrease* in planned investment of \$80 billion will cause a *decrease* in equilibrium income of \$400 billion.
2. The multiplier effect makes the economy more sensitive to changes in autonomous expenditure than it would be otherwise. The recent declines in exports have set off a series of declines in production, income, and spending. These declines have caused firms that clearly do not export, like barbers, to experience declines in sales. The multiplier effect means a decline in spending in one sector will cause declines in spending and production in other sectors of the economy.
3. The larger the *MPC* (all else equal), the larger the value of the multiplier. With an *MPC* of 0.8, the multiplier is 5, but with an *MPC* of 0.5, the multiplier is only 2. This direct relationship between the value of the *MPC* and the value of the multiplier holds true because the larger the *MPC*, the more additional consumption takes place after each rise (or fall) in the multiplier process.
4. The formula for the multiplier, $1/(1 - MPC)$, is oversimplified because it ignores many real-world complications, such as the effect of increased GDP on imports, inflation, interest rates, and income taxes. These effects combine to cause the simple formula we've presented to overstate the true value of the multiplier. Beginning in Chapter 12, we will start to take these real-world complications into account.

Solved Problem **8.2**

Using the Multiplier Formula

Use the information in the table to answer the questions that follow.

Real GDP (Y)	Consumption (C)	Planned Investment (I_p)	Government Purchases (G)	Net Exports (NX)
\$800	\$690	\$100	\$100	−\$50
900	770	100	100	−50
1000	850	100	100	−50
1100	930	100	100	−50
1200	1010	100	100	−50

Note: The values are in billions of 2007 dollars.

a. What is the equilibrium level of real GDP?
b. What is the *MPC*?
c. Suppose government purchases increase by \$20 billion. What will the new equilibrium level of real GDP be? Use the multiplier formula to determine your answer.

Solving the Problem

Step 1: Review the chapter material. This problem is about the multiplier process so you may want to review the section "The Multiplier Effect," which begins on page 235.

Step 2: Determine equilibrium GDP. Just as in *Solved Problem 8.1*, we can find macroeconomic equilibrium by calculating the level of planned aggregate expenditure for each level of real GDP.

Real GDP (Y)	Consumption (C)	Planned Investment (I_p)	Government Purchases (G)	Net Exports (NX)	Planned Aggregate Expenditure (AE)
$800	$690	$100	$100	–$50	$840
900	770	100	100	–50	920
1000	850	100	100	–50	1000
1100	930	100	100	–50	1080
1200	1010	100	100	–50	1160

Note: The values are in billions of 2007 dollars.

Step 3: **Calculate the *MPC*.**

$$MPC = \frac{\Delta C}{\Delta Y}.$$

In this example:

$$MPC = \frac{\$80 \text{ billion}}{\$100 \text{ billion}} = 0.8.$$

Step 4: **Use the multiplier formula to calculate the new equilibrium level of real GDP.**
We could find the new level of equilibrium real GDP by constructing a new table with government purchases at the new ($120 billion) level. This would take a lot more time than the multiplier method, however.

$$\text{Multiplier} = \frac{1}{1 - MPC} = \frac{1}{1 - 0.8} = 5.$$

So:
Change in equilibrium real GDP = Change in autonomous expenditure × 5.
Or:
Change in equilibrium real GDP = $20 billion × 5 = $100 billion.
Therefore:
New level of equilibrium GDP = $1000 billion + $100 billion
= $1100 billion.

MyEconLab   **Your Turn:** For more practice, do related problem 4.2 on page 249 at the end of this chapter.

Don't Let This Happen to You

Understand Why Protectionism Doesn't Raise the Multiplier

We have seen that there is a link between net exports and real GDP in this chapter. When net exports increase, autonomous expenditure increases, and the result is an increase in real GDP. As you learned, net exports are equal to exports minus imports. Net exports will increase whenever exports rise or imports fall. Increasing exports can be very difficult; this is what various trade missions attempt to do. Another way to make net exports rise is to restrict imports, which can be done with the imposition of tariffs. Tariffs are taxes on imports, which increase the cost

of imports to domestic consumers. The desired result is an increase in net exports and an increase in real GDP.

Tariffs are a tempting option for governments looking to stimulate an economy in a recession. Instead of increasing government spending (which often means more government borrowing), a government could restrict imports, expecting that GDP will increase as citizens substitute domestically produced goods for imported ones. In this situation, the multiplier tells us that GDP will rise by more than imports fell.

The problem with this strategy is that it only works if your country alone uses it. If other countries impose tariffs on the products your country exports, your net exports will fall. When one country imposes tariffs on the exports of another, the situation usually ends with both countries imposing tariffs. This situation is sometimes called a *trade war*. Recently, the United States imposed tariffs on tires made in China. The Chinese government responded by imposing tariffs on US-produced automotive products and chicken meat. While these tariffs aren't likely to hurt either economy that much, other trade restrictions have done a lot of damage to a large number of economies.

For example, the Smoot Hawley Tariff Act, a US tariff law passed in 1930, caused problems for the world economy. The act increased the tariffs on more than 20 000 goods imported into the United States to record levels. Most countries that traded with the United States, including Canada, responded by imposing their own tariffs on US-produced goods. In fact, Canada acted before the bill was passed, adding tariffs to 16 products that made up about 30 percent of US exports to Canada. The increase in tariffs around the world resulted in a reduction in global trade of about 66 percent. Not only did many economies shrink as a result of the tariffs, but consumers around the world faced much higher prices for many products. Tariffs may seem like a good way to improve the domestic economy at first, but usually lead to a decrease in exports and GDP, as well as imports.

MyEconLab

Your Turn: Test your understanding by doing related problem 4.8 on page 249 at the end of this chapter.

The Paradox of Thrift

We saw in Chapters 6 and 7 that an increase in savings can increase the rate of economic growth in the long run by providing funds for investment. In the short run, if households save more of their income and spend less of it, aggregate expenditure and real GDP will decline. In discussing the aggregate expenditure model, John Maynard Keynes argued that if many households decide at the same time to increase their saving and reduce their spending, they may make themselves worse off by causing aggregate expenditure to fall, thereby pushing the economy into a recession. The lower incomes in the recession might mean that total saving does not increase, despite the attempt by many individuals to increase their own saving. Keynes referred to this outcome as the *paradox of thrift* because what appears to be something favourable for the long-run performance of the economy might be counterproductive in the short run.

The paradox is sometimes observed at the beginning of recessions. Households that expect negative economic times reduce their spending in case they lose their jobs, and thus their incomes. As households switch from spending to saving, the aggregate expenditure in the economy falls. Firms respond to the fall in aggregate spending by reducing their production. A reduction in production means laying off workers. In some cases, people trying to protect themselves from a recession end up contributing to one.

The Aggregate Demand Curve

8.5 LEARNING OBJECTIVE
Understand the relationship between the aggregate demand curve and aggregate expenditure.

When demand for a product increases, firms usually respond by increasing production, but they are also likely to increase prices. Similarly, when demand falls, production falls, but often, prices do as well. We would expect, then, that an increase or a decrease in aggregate expenditure to affect not just real GDP but the *price level* as well. Will a change in price level, in turn, affect the components of aggregate expenditure? In fact, as we will see, increases in the price level cause aggregate expenditure to fall, and decreases in the price level cause aggregate expenditure to rise. There are three main reasons for this relationship. We discussed the first two reasons earlier in this chapter, when considering the factors that determine consumption and net exports:

- A rising price level decreases consumption by decreasing the real value of household wealth; a falling price level has the reverse effect.

- If the price level in Canada rises relative to the price levels of other countries, Canadian exports become relatively more expensive, and foreign imports become less

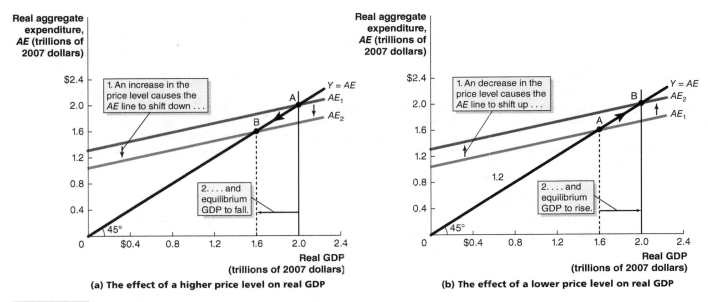

Figure 8.13   The Effect of a Change in the Price Level on Real GDP

In panel (a), an increase in the price level results in declining consumption, planned investment, and net exports and causes the aggregate expenditure line to shift down from AE_1 to AE_2. As a result, equilibrium real GDP declines from $2 trillion to $1.6 trillion. In panel (b), a decrease in the price level results in rising consumption, planned investment, and net exports and causes the aggregate expenditure line to shift up from AE_1 to AE_2. As a result, equilibrium real GDP increases from $1.6 trillion to $2 trillion.

expensive, causing net exports to fall. A falling price level in Canada has the opposite effect.

- When prices rise, firms and households need more money to finance buying and selling. If the central bank (the Bank of Canada) does not increase the money supply, the result will be an increase in the interest rate. In Chapter 11 we will analyze this result in more detail. As we discussed earlier in this chapter, a higher rate of interest means lower investment spending as firms borrow less to finance the building of factories or the purchase of new machines. Even households borrow less to finance the purchase of new homes. A falling price level has the opposite effect: Other things being equal, lower interest rates mean a higher level of investment spending.

We can now incorporate the effect of a change in the price level into the basic aggregate expenditure model, in which equilibrium real GDP is determined by the intersection of the aggregate expenditure (AE) line and the 45°-line. Remember that we measure the price level as an index number with a value of 100 in the base year. If the price level rises from say 100 to 103, consumption, planned investment, and net exports will all fall, causing the AE line to shift down on the 45°-line diagram. The AE line shifts down because with higher prices, less spending will occur in the economy at every level of GDP. Panel (a) of Figure 8.13 shows that the downward shift of the AE line results in a lower level of equilibrium real GDP.

If the price level falls from, say, 100 to 97, then planned investment, consumption, and net exports will all rise. As panel (b) of Figure 8.13 shows, the AE line will shift up, which will cause equilibrium real GDP to increase.

Figure 8.14 summarizes the effect of changes in the price level on real GDP. The table shows the combinations of price level and real GDP from Figure 8.13. The graph plots the numbers from the table. In the graph, the price level is measured on the vertical axis, and real GDP is measured on the horizontal axis. The relationship shown in Figure 8.14 between the price level and the level of planned aggregate expenditure is known as the **aggregate demand (AD) curve**.

Aggregate demand (AD) curve A curve that shows the relationship between the price level and the level of planned aggregate expenditure in the economy, holding constant all other factors that affect aggregate expenditure.

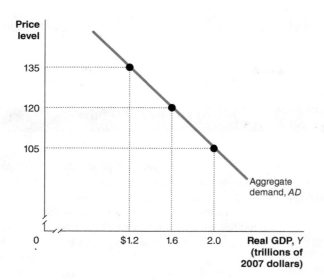

Price level	Equilibrium real GDP
105	$2.0 trillion
120	1.6 trillion
135	1.2 trillion

Figure 8.14

The Aggregate Demand Curve

The aggregate demand (*AD*) curve shows the relationship between the price level and the level of planned aggregate expenditure in the economy. When the price level is 105, real GDP is $2 trillion. An increase in the price level to 120 causes consumption, planned investment, and net exports to fall, which reduces real GDP to $1.6 trillion.

Economics in Your Life

When Consumer Confidence Falls, Is Your Job at Risk?

At the beginning of this chapter, we asked you to suppose that you work part-time at a local Tim Hortons. You have learned that consumer confidence in the economy has fallen and that many households expect their future income to be dramatically lower than their current income. Should you be concerned about losing your job? We have seen that if consumers expect their future incomes to decline (see *Making the Connection*, "Do Changes in Consumer Confidence Affect Consumption Spending?") they will cut their consumption spending. Consumption spending is about 63 percent of total expenditure in the economy. So if the decline in consumer confidence is correct in forecasting the decline in consumption, then aggregate expenditure and real GDP are likely to decline as well. If the economy moves into a recession, spending at Tim Hortons is likely to fall; this could reduce your location's sales and possibly cost you a job. Before you panic, though, keep in mind surveys of consumer confidence are not always accurate predictors of recessions, so you may not end up in your parents' basement after all.

Conclusion

In this chapter, we examined a key macroeconomic idea: In the short run, the level of GDP is determined mainly by the level of aggregate expenditure. When economists forecast changes in GDP, they do so by forecasting changes in the four components of aggregate expenditure. We constructed an aggregate demand curve by asking what would happen to the level of aggregate expenditure when the price level changes.

But our story is incomplete. In the next chapter, we will analyze the aggregate supply curve. Then, we will use the aggregate demand curve *and* the aggregate supply curve to show how equilibrium real GDP and the equilibrium price level are determined at the same time. We will also need to discuss the roles that the financial system and government policy play in determining real GDP in the short run. We will cover these important topics in the next three chapters.

Read *An Inside Look* for a discussion of the effects of declining aggregate expenditure on the demand for coffee and other products at Tim Hortons.

Tim Hortons Depends on the Broader Economy

FINANCIAL POST

Tim Hortons Earnings Fall Short of Forecasts

Some Tim Hortons Inc. customers in Canada have been feeling the pinch of higher gas prices and unemployment, even though overall system-wide transactions rose in the first quarter.

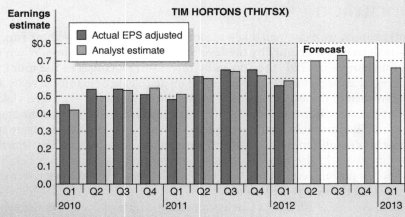

"We think that in some cases they are not coming as often as they'd like to come because of their financial situation," chief executive Paul House told analysts during a conference call Wednesday, citing transaction declines in certain Canadian regions with heavy manufacturing.

Canada's biggest coffee and baked goods chain reported net income rose 10% in the three-month period ended April 1, though earnings slightly missed analyst expectations.

Mr. House said Tim Hortons operated in many towns across the country where one sole manufacturer had accounted for a large percentage of the employment there, but is now no longer operating. "You cannot help but feel that at store level, because of the loss of income."

Increased global competition and industry productivity improvements have put pressure on Canada's manufacturing sector. Factory employment in this country hit a 35-year nadir last year, according to Statistics Canada.

Nevertheless, the company saw gains during the period thanks to strong sales of several new menu items, including a new egg-whites only breakfast sandwich, lattes and smoothies in Canada, and panini sandwiches in the U.S.

Tim Hortons posted profit of $88.8-million, or 56¢ a share, compared with earnings of $80.7-million, (48¢), in the same period a year ago. That fell short of the mean estimate of 59¢ per share from analysts polled by Bloomberg.

Revenue climbed 12.1% to $721.3-million and same-store sales, a key measure of foodservice performance at outlets open for a year or more, rose 5.2% in Canada and 8.5% in the U.S.

"In the U.S. we are seeing traction in our core markets," Mr. House said.

Tim Hortons also announced that Mr. House, who is also the company's executive chairman and president, will stay on as CEO until December 2013 or until a new CEO is appointed, whichever comes first. Mr. House, who first acted as CEO in the middle of the last decade and led the company through a blockbuster period of growth, was put into the role again on an interim basis a year ago after Don Schroeder stepped down.

Tim Hortons said its operating costs were up 7.3% in the period compared with first quarter of last year.

The company also said the Humane Society of the United States has withdrawn its shareholder proposal demanding Tim Hortons address the pig and hen housing systems its suppliers use, originally to be presented at Thursday's annual general meeting. Tim Hortons recently announced several initiatives to improve the living standards of pigs and chickens, including a call for plans to eliminate gestation stalls for sows and a goal of purchasing 10% of its eggs from more humane hen housing systems.

"Overall, although sales were above our expectation, higher-than-expected cost of sales was an offset," Peter Sklar, analyst at BMO Capital Markets, said in a note to clients.

Tim Hortons, which has 4042 restaurants, opened 22 outlets in Canada during the quarter and seven in the U.S.

Source: Shaw, Hollie, "Tim Hortons earnings fall short of forecasts" Financial Post, May 9, 2012. Material reprinted by express permission of: National Post, a division of Postmedia Network, Inc.

TIM HORTONS (THI/TSX)

Earnings estimate

- ■ Actual EPS adjusted
- ■ Analyst estimate

Forecast

$0.8
0.7
0.6
0.5
0.4
0.3
0.2
0.1
0.0

Q1 Q2 Q3 Q4 | Q1 Q2 Q3 Q4 | Q1 Q2 Q3 Q4 | Q1
2010 | 2011 | 2012 | 2013

Sources: Bloomberg News; Andrew Barr/National Post

Key Points in the Article

The article discusses the sales and profits of Tim Hortons. The company did not earn as much profit as people expected in the first three months of 2012. Tim Hortons management offer two explanations. First, the company didn't sell as much as expected in some parts of Canada, possibly because some of their traditional customers have lost jobs and are cutting back on their spending. Second, the company faced an increase in costs.

Analyzing the News

(a) Tim Hortons has stores in many small towns across Canada. Many of these towns have only one major employer. Some of these firms have seen demand for their products fall due to slow growth in the US economy and increased global competition. When these employers face difficulties and have to reduce production, they lay off workers. When these workers have lower incomes, or even just fear they will have lower incomes in the future they reduce their spending, meaning lower demand for other goods and services—such as Tim Hortons coffee. The result is a decrease in demand for Canadian products in other parts of the world which can reduce demand in the entire economy, not just for firms that produce goods for export.

(b) As manufacturing becomes more competitive and productivity increases around the world, demand for Canadian products can fall if producers in Canada don't keep pace. Changes in the costs of production in other parts of the world, either due to changes in exchange rates or labour costs, can also reduce demand for Canadian made products. When Canadian goods become expensive relative to goods produced in other countries, demand for our exports falls, and producers of these goods (many of which are located in smaller towns) reduce their workforce or sometimes go out of business entirely.

(c) Changes in how firms produce goods and services also play an important role in determining a firm's costs. When costs increase, firms generally have less retained profits from which to finance investments. This can reduce demand now, as firms make fewer investments, and in the future as firms end up with less capital to use in the production process. Some changes in the production process are worthwhile and should be pursued, but all come with a cost.

Thinking Critically

1. Suppose the federal government decides to send a $1000 cheque to every consumer that can prove they purchased at least 10 cups of Tim Hortons coffee in the last year. How would this program affect Canadian aggregate expenditure and equilibrium real GDP?

2. Suppose in order to aid the Canadian take-out coffee industry, the federal government enacts a law that makes it illegal to purchase take-out coffee from firms whose headquarters are located in other countries. How would this law affect aggregate expenditure and equilibrium GDP in Canada? In what way does your answer depend on how the governments of other countries react to the new law? Briefly explain your answer.

Chapter Summary and Problems

Key Terms

Asset, p. 218

Aggregate demand (*AD*) curve, p. 242

Aggregate expenditure (*AE*), p. 214

Aggregate expenditure model, p. 214

Autonomous expenditure, p. 236

Cash flow, p. 227

Consumption function, p. 221

Inventories, p. 215

Liability, p. 219

Marginal propensity to consume (*MPC*), p. 221

Marginal propensity to save (*MPS*), p. 224

Multiplier, p. 236

Multiplier effect, p. 237

Nominal interest rate, p. 220

Real interest rate, p. 220

Summary

*LO **8.1** *Aggregate expenditure (AE)* is the total amount of spending in the economy. The *aggregate expenditure model* focuses on the relationship between total spending and real GDP in the short run, assuming that the price level is constant. In any particular year, the level of GDP is determined by the level of total spending, or aggregate expenditure, in the economy. The four components of aggregate expenditure are consumption (*C*), planned investment (I_p), government purchases (*G*), and net exports (*NX*). When aggregate expenditure is greater than GDP, there is an unplanned decrease in *inventories*, which are goods that have been produced but not yet sold, and GDP and total employment will increase. When aggregate expenditure is less than GDP, there is an unplanned increase in inventories, and GDP and total employment will decline. When aggregate expenditure is equal to GDP, firms will sell what they expected to sell, production and employment will be unchanged, and the economy will be in macroeconomic equilibrium.

LO **8.2** The five determinants of consumption are current disposable income, household wealth, expected future income, the price level, and the interest rate. The *consumption function* is the relationship between consumption and disposable income. The *marginal propensity to consume (MPC)* is the change in consumption divided by the change in disposable income. The *marginal propensity to save (MPS)* is the change in saving divided by the change in disposable income. The determinants of planned investment are expectations of future profitability, real interest rate, taxes, and *cash flow*, which is the difference between the cash revenues received by a firm and the cash spending by the firm. Government purchases include spending by the federal government, provincial governments, and local governments for goods and services. Government purchases do not include transfer payments, such as social security payments by the federal government or pension payments by local governments to retired police officers and firefighters. The three determinants of net exports are changes in the price level in Canada relative to changes in the price levels in other countries, the growth rate of GDP in Canada relative to the growth rates of GDP in other countries, and the exchange rate between the Canadian dollar and other currencies.

LO **8.3** The 45°-line diagram shows all the points where aggregate expenditure equals real GDP. On the 45°-line diagram, macroeconomic equilibrium occurs where the line representing the aggregate expenditure function crosses the 45° line. The economy is in recession when the aggregate expenditure line intersects the 45° line at a level of GDP that is below potential GDP. Numerically, macroeconomic equilibrium occurs when:

Consumption + Planned investment + Government purchases + Net Exports = GDP.

LO **8.4** *Autonomous expenditure* is expenditure that does not depend on the level of GDP. An autonomous change is a change in expenditure not caused by a change in income. An induced change is a change in aggregate expenditure caused by a change in income. An autonomous change in expenditure will cause rounds of induced changes in expenditure. Therefore, an autonomous change in expenditure will have a multiplier effect on equilibrium GDP. The *multiplier effect* is the process by which an increase in autonomous expenditure leads to a larger increase in real GDP. The *multiplier* is the ratio of the change in equilibrium GDP to the change in autonomous expenditure. The formula for the multiplier is

$$\frac{1}{1 - MPC}.$$

Because of the paradox of thrift, an attempt by many individuals to increase their saving may lead to a reduction in aggregate expenditure and a recession.

LO **8.5** Increases in the price level cause a reduction in consumption, investment, and net exports. This causes the aggregate expenditure function to shift down on the 45°-line diagram, leading to a lower equilibrium real GDP. A decrease in the price level leads to a higher equilibrium real GDP. The *aggregate demand (AD) curve* shows the relationship between the price level and the level of aggregate expenditure, holding constant all factors other than the price level that affect aggregate expenditure.

MyEconLab   Log in to MyEconLab to complete these exercises and get instant feedback.

---

*'Learning Objective' is abbreviated to 'LO' in the end of chapter material.

Review Questions

LO 8.1

1.1 What is the key idea in the aggregate expenditure macroeconomic model?

1.2 What are inventories? What usually happens to inventories at the beginning of a recession? At the beginning of an expansion?

1.3 Which of the following does the aggregate expenditure model seek to explain: long-run economic growth, the business cycle, inflation, and cyclical unemployment?

LO 8.2

2.1 In the aggregate expenditure model, why is it important to know the factors that determine consumption spending, investment spending, government purchases, and net exports?

2.2 Give an example of each of the four categories of aggregate expenditure.

2.3 What are the four main determinants of investment? How would a change in interest rates affect investment?

2.4 What are the three main determinants of net exports? How would an increase in the growth rate of GDP in the BRIC nations (Brazil, Russia, India, and China) affect Canadian net exports?

LO 8.3

3.1 What is the meaning of the 45° line in the 45°-line diagram?

3.2 Use a 45°-line diagram to illustrate macroeconomic equilibrium. Make sure your diagram shows the aggregate expenditure function and the level of equilibrium real GDP and that your axes are properly labelled.

3.3 What does the slope of the aggregate expenditure line equal? How is the slope of the aggregate expenditure line related to the slope of the consumption function?

3.4 What is the difference between aggregate expenditure and consumption spending?

LO 8.4

4.1 What is the multiplier effect? Use a 45°-line diagram to illustrate the multiplier effect of a decrease in government purchases.

4.2 What is the formula for the multiplier? Explain why this formula is considered to be too simple.

LO 8.5

5.1 Briefly explain the difference between aggregate expenditure and aggregate demand.

5.2 Briefly explain which components of aggregate expenditure are affected by a change in the price level.

Problems and Applications

LO 8.1

1.1 Into which category of aggregate expenditure would each of the following transactions fall?
   a. The Jones family buys a new car.
   b. The Toronto School Board buys 12 new school buses.
   c. The Jones family buys a newly constructed house from the Garcia Construction Co.

1.2 Suppose Apple plans to produce 2.2 million iPhones in Canada this year. The company expects to sell 2.1 million and add 100 000 to the inventories in its stores.
   a. Suppose that at the end of the year, Apple has sold 1.9 million iPhones. What was Apple's planned investment? What was Apple's actual investment?
   b. Now suppose that at the end of the year, Apple has sold 2.3 million iPhones. What was Apple's planned investment? What was Apple's actual investment?

1.3 In the first quarter of 2012, manufacturing inventories increased by $680 196. Can we tell from this information whether aggregate expenditure was higher or lower than GDP during the first quarter of 2012? If not, what other information would you need?

Data from Statistics Canada CANSIM Table 304-0014 Series v802764.

LO 8.2

2.1 [**Related to the** Chapter Opener **on page 213**] Suppose Tim Hortons is forecasting demand for its products during the next year. How will the forecast be affected by each of the following?
   a. A survey shows a sharp rise in consumer confidence that income growth will be increasing.
   b. Real interest rates are expected to increase.
   c. The exchange rate value of the Canadian dollar is expected to increase.

   d. Planned investment spending in the economy is expected to decrease.

2.2 Draw the consumption function and label each axis. Show the effect of an increase in income on consumption spending. Does the change in income cause a movement along the consumption function or a shift of the consumption function? How would an increase in expected future income or an increase in household wealth affect the consumption function? Would these increases cause a movement along the consumption function or a shift of the consumption function?

2.3 Unemployed workers receive Employment Insurance payments from the government. Does the existence of Employment Insurance make it likely that consumption will fluctuate more or fluctuate less over the business cycle than it would in the absence of Employment Insurance? Briefly explain.

2.4 [**Related to** Making the Connection **on page 220**] Why might a small business owner be willing to pay for the detailed consumer confidence data of the Consumer Confidence Index?

2.5 [**Related to** Solved Problem 8.1 **on page 225**] Fill in the blanks in the following table. Assume for simplicity that taxes are zero. Also assume that the values represent billions of 2007 dollars.

Real GDP (Y)	Consumption (C)	Saving (S)	Marginal Propensity to Consume (MPC)	Marginal Propensity to Save (MPS)
$900	$800		—	—
1000	875			
1100	950			
1200	1025			
1300	1100			

2.6 [**Related to** Making the Connection **on page 228**] We saw that sales of snowmobiles are linked to changes in the economy. Based on this linkage, do you think BRP pays attention to the Consumer Confidence Index? Why or why not?

LO 8.3

3.1 At point *A* in the following graph, is planned aggregate expenditure greater than, equal to, or less than GDP? What about at point *B*? At point *C*? For points *A* and *C*, indicate the vertical distance that measures the unintended change in inventories.

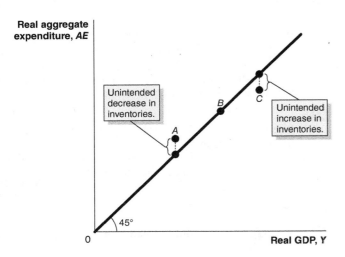

3.2 Suppose we drop the assumption that net exports do not depend on real GDP. Draw a graph with the value of net exports on the vertical axis and the value of real GDP on the horizontal axis. Now, add a line representing the relationship between net exports and real GDP. Does your net exports line have a positive or negative slope? Briefly explain.

3.3 Consider the following table, which shows business investment in inventories for each quarter from the first quarter of 2007 to the first quarter of 2012, measured in millions of 2007 dollars. Provide a macroeconomic explanation for this pattern. (Hint: When did the recession during this period begin and end?)

Year	Quarter	Inventory Investment (Millions of 2007 Dollars)
2007	Q1	$ 3360
	Q2	−2822
	Q3	15 570
	Q4	19 644
2008	Q1	6061
	Q2	9512
	Q3	11 856
	Q4	4699
2009	Q1	−2364
	Q2	−7779
	Q3	−4807
	Q4	−4807
2010	Q1	2663
	Q2	−2508
	Q3	4841
	Q4	−6805
2011	Q1	8965
	Q2	12 153
	Q3	6462
	Q4	2179
2012	Q1	2061
	Q2	7298
	Q3	14 091
	Q4	3875
2013	Q1	6031

Data from Statistics Canada, CANSIM Table 380-0064.

3.4 Fill in the missing values in the following table. Assume that the value of the *MPC* does not change as real GDP changes. Also assume that the values represent billions of 2007 dollars.

Real GDP (Y)	Consumption (C)	Planned Investment (I_p)	Government Purchases (G)	Net Exports (NX)	Planned Aggregate Expenditures (AE)	Unplanned Change in Inventories
$900	$760	$120	$120	−$40		
1000	840	120	120	−40		
1100		120	120	−40		
1200		120	120	−40		
1300		120	120	−40		

a. What is the value of the *MPC*?
b. What is the value of equilibrium real GDP?

LO 8.4

4.1 In Figure 8.12, the economy is initially in equilibrium at point *A*. Aggregate expenditure and real GDP both equal $6 trillion. The increase in investment of $1 trillion increases aggregate expenditure to $7 trillion. If real GDP increases to $7 trillion, will the economy be in equilibrium? Briefly explain. What happens to aggregate expenditure when real GDP increases to $7 trillion?

4.2 [**Related to** Solved Problem 8.2 **on page 239**] Use the information in the following table to answer the following questions. Assume that the values represent billions of 2007 dollars.

Real GDP (Y)	Consumption (C)	Planned Investment (I_p)	Government Purchases (G)	Net Exports (NX)
$800	$730	$100	$100	−$50
900	790	100	100	−50
1000	850	100	100	−50
1100	910	100	100	−50
1200	970	100	100	−50

    a. What is the equilibrium level of real GDP?
    b. What is the *MPC*?
    c. Suppose net exports increase by $40 billion. What will be the new equilibrium level of real GDP? Use the multiplier formula to determine your answer.

4.3 If the marginal propensity to consume is 0.75, by how much will an increase in planned investment spending of $40 billion shift up the aggregate expenditure line? By how much will it increase equilibrium real GDP?

4.4 Explain whether each of the following would cause the value of the multiplier to be larger or smaller.
    a. An increase in real GDP increases imports.
    b. An increase in real GDP increases interest rates.
    c. An increase in in real GDP increases the marginal propensity to consume.
    d. An increase in real GDP causes the average tax rate paid by households to decrease.
    e. An increase in real GDP increases the price level.

4.5 Suppose booming economies in the BRIC nations (Brazil, Russia, India, and China) cause net exports to rise by $75 billion in Canada. If the *MPC* is 0.8, what will be the change in equilibrium GDP?

4.6 Would a larger multiplier lead to longer and more severe recessions or shorter and less severe recessions? Briefly explain.

4.7 Use the following graph to answer the questions.

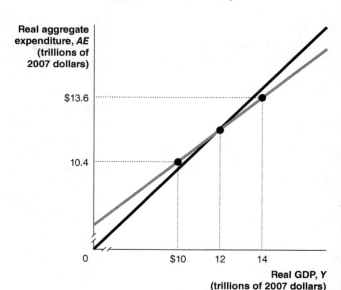

    a. What is the value of equilibrium real GDP?
    b. What is the value of the *MPC*?
    c. What is the value of the multiplier?

4.8 [**Related to** Don't Let This Happen to You **on page 240**] Statistics Canada estimates that the multiplier for nonresidential construction projects in Quebec is 1.52, but only 1.07 for construction projects in Nunavut. Why might this be the case?

Statistics Canada, *Provincial Input-Output Multipliers, 2009*, Catalogue No. 15F0046XDB.

LO 8.5

5.1 Briefly explain why the aggregate expenditure line is upward sloping, while the aggregate demand curve is downward sloping.

5.2 Briefly explain whether you agree with the following statement: "The reason the aggregate demand curve slopes downward is that when the price level is higher, people cannot afford to buy as many goods and services."

Appendix C

The Algebra of Macroeconomic Equilibrium

In this chapter, we relied primarily on graphs and tables to illustrate the aggregate expenditure model of short-run real GDP. Graphs help us understand economic change *qualitatively*. When we write an economic model using equations, we make it easier to make *quantitative estimates*. When economists forecast future movements in GDP, they often rely on *econometric models*. An econometric model is an economic model written in the form of equations, where each equation has been statistically estimated, using methods similar to the methods used in estimating demand curves that we briefly described in Chapter 3. We can use equations to represent the aggregate expenditure model described in this chapter.

The following equations are based on the example shown in Table 8.3 on page 235. Y stands for real GDP, and the numbers (with the exception of the MPC) represent billions of dollars.

1. $C = 100 + 0.8Y$ Consumption function

2. $I_p = 125$ Planned investment function

3. $G = 125$ Government spending function

4. $NX = -30$ Net export function

5. $Y = C + I_p + G + NX$ Equilibrium condition

The first equation is the consumption function. The MPC is 0.8, and 100 is autonomous consumption, which is the level of consumption that does not depend on income. If we think of the consumption function as a line on the 45°-line diagram, 100 would be the intercept, and 0.8 would be the slope. The "functions" for the other three components of planned aggregate expenditure are very simple because we have assumed that these components are not affected by GDP and, therefore, are constant. Economists who use this type of model to forecast GDP would, of course, use more realistic investment, government, and net export functions. The *parameters* of the functions—such as the value of autonomous consumption and the value of the MPC in the consumption function—would be estimated statistically, using data on the values of each variable over a period of years.

In this model, GDP is in equilibrium when it equals planned aggregate expenditure. Equation 5—the equilibrium condition—shows us how to calculate equilibrium in the model: We need to substitute equations 1 through 4 into equation 5. Doing so gives us the following:

$$Y = 100 + 0.8Y + 125 + 125 - 30.$$

We need to solve this expression for Y to find equilibrium GDP. The first step is to subtract $0.8Y$ from both sides of the equation:

$$Y - 0.8Y = 100 + 125 + 125 - 30.$$

Then, we solve for Y:

$$0.2Y = 320.$$

Or:

$$Y = \frac{320}{0.2} = 1600.$$

To make this result more general, we can replace particular values with general values represented by letters:

1. $C = \overline{C} + MPC(Y)$ Consumption function

2. $I_p = \overline{I}_p$ Planned investment function

3. $G = \overline{G}$ Government spending function

4. $NX = \overline{NX}$ Net export function

5. $Y = C + I_p + G + NX$ Equilibrium condition

The letters with bars over them represent fixed, or autonomous, values. So, for example, $\overline{C}$ represents autonomous consumption, which had a value of 100 in our original example. Now, solving for equilibrium, we get

$$Y = \overline{C} + MPC(Y) + \overline{I} + \overline{G} + \overline{NX},$$

or

$$Y - MPC(Y) = \overline{C} + \overline{I} + \overline{G} + \overline{NX},$$

or

$$Y(1 - MPC) = \overline{C} + \overline{I} + \overline{G} + \overline{NX},$$

or

$$Y = \frac{\overline{C} + \overline{I} + \overline{G} + \overline{NX}}{1 - MPC}.$$

Remember that $1/(1 - MPC)$ is the multiplier, and all four variables in the numerator of the equation represent autonomous expenditure. Therefore, an alternative expression for equilibrium GDP is:

Equilibrium GDP = Autonomous expenditure Multiplier.

MyEconLab   Log in to MyEconLab to complete these exercises and get instant feedback.

LO The Algebra of Macroeconomic Equilibrium.

Review Questions

8A.1 Write a general expression for the aggregate expenditure function. If you think of the aggregate expenditure function as a line on the 45°-line diagram, what would be the intercept and what would be the slope, using the general values represented by letters?

8A.2 Find equilibrium GDP using the following macroeconomic model (where the numbers, with the exception of the MPC, represent billions of dollars).

1. $C = 150 + 0.75Y$ Consumption function
2. $I_p = 100$ Planned investment function
3. $G = 100$ Government spending function
4. $NX = 25$ Net export function
5. $Y = C + I_p + G + NX$ Equilibrium condition

8A.3 For the macroeconomic model in problem 8A.2, write the aggregate expenditure function. For GDP of $1600, what is the value of aggregate expenditure, and what is the value of the unintended change in inventories? For GDP of $1200, what is the value of aggregate expenditure, and what is the value of the unintended change in inventories?
[[Answer: When GDP = 1600, AE = 1575, and unplanned inventory investment = 25. When GDP = 1200, AE = 1275, and unplanned inventory investment = −75.]]

8A.4 Suppose that autonomous consumption is 50, government purchases are 100, planned investment spending is 125, net exports are −25, and the MPC is 0.9. What is equilibrium GDP?
[[Answer: Y = 2500.]]

CHAPTER

9

Aggregate Demand and Aggregate Supply Analysis

Chapter Outline and Learning Objectives

9.1 Aggregate Demand, page 254
Identify the determinants of aggregate demand and distinguish between a movement along the aggregate demand curve and a shift of the curve.

9.2 Aggregate Supply, page 262
Identify the determinants of aggregate supply and distinguish between a movement along the short-run aggregate supply curve and a shift of the curve.

9.3 Macroeconomic Equilibrium in the Long Run and the Short Run, page 267
Use the aggregate demand and aggregate supply model to illustrate the difference between short-run and long-run macroeconomic equilibrium.

9.4 A Dynamic Aggregate Demand and Aggregate Supply Model, page 272
Use the dynamic aggregate demand and aggregate supply model to analyze macroeconomic conditions.

Appendix D: Macroeconomic Schools of Thought, page 287
Understand macroeconomic schools of thought.

© David Buzzard / Alamy

Canadian National Railway and the Business Cycle

In terms of land area, Canada is the second-largest country in the world. As you can imagine, businesses involved in moving goods around a country this large are an important part of the economy.

Canadian National Railway (CN) was formed in 1919 by the federal government from the remains of several failed Canadian railway companies. CN was returned to the private sector in 1995. Since it was privatized, CN has expanded to the United States. It is now Canada's largest freight railway—operating in eight provinces and one territory—as well as the only transcontinental rail network in North America. In 2012, CN alone moved more than 300 million tonnes of freight.

Despite its size, CN is subject to the business cycle just like other firms. During recessions, as demand for goods falls, CN handles less cargo on its network. When the economy is expanding, CN handles more cargo and longer trains more often. When the price of oil or labour rises, CN often has to increase its prices, and firms find it more expensive to get their goods to market. Increases in the price of a key good or service, such as transportation, tend to reduce the supply of goods and services in all parts of the economy.

To understand the relationship between the business cycle and firms such as CN, we need to explore how production, employment, and prices interact throughout the business cycle.

AN INSIDE LOOK on **page 280** discusses how CN, like other firms providing freight services, can be an indicator of the state of the economy.

Source: Canadian National Railway, 2012 Annual Report.

Economics in Your Life

Is an Employer Likely to Cut Your Pay during a Recession?

Suppose that you have worked as a barista for a local coffeehouse for two years. From on-the-job training and experience, you have honed your coffee-making skills and mastered the perfect latte. Then the economy moves into a recession, and sales at the coffeehouse decline. Is the owner of the coffeehouse likely to cut the prices of lattes and other drinks? Suppose the owner asks to meet with you to discuss your wages for the next year. Is the owner likely to cut your pay? As you read this chapter, see if you can answer these questions. You can check your answers against those we provide on page 278 at the end of this chapter.

W e saw in Chapter 6 that the Canadian economy has experienced a long-run upward trend in real gross domestic product (GDP). This upward trend has resulted in the standard of living in Canada being much higher today than it was just 50 years ago. In the short run, however, real GDP fluctuates around the long-run upward trend because of the business cycle. Fluctuations in GDP lead to fluctuations in employment. These fluctuations in real GDP and employment are the most visible and dramatic part of the business cycle. During recessions, we are more likely to see factories close, businesses declare bankruptcy, and workers lose their jobs. During expansions, we are more likely to see new businesses open and new jobs created. In addition to these changes in output and employment, the business cycle causes changes in wages and prices. Some firms react to a decline in sales by cutting back on production, but they may also cut the prices they charge and the wages they pay. Other firms respond to a recession by raising prices and workers' wages by less than they would have in an expansion.

In this chapter, we expand our story of the business cycle by developing the aggregate demand and aggregate supply model. This model will help us analyze the effects of recessions and expansions on production, employment, and prices.

9.1 LEARNING OBJECTIVE

Identify the determinants of aggregate demand and distinguish between a movement along the aggregate demand curve and a shift of the curve.

Aggregate demand and aggregate supply model A model that explains short-run fluctuations in real GDP and the price level.

Price level A measure of the average prices of goods and services in the economy.

Aggregate demand (AD) curve A curve that shows the relationship between the price level and the quantity of real GDP demanded by households, firms, and the government.

Short-run aggregate supply (SRAS) curve A curve that shows the relationship in the short run between the price level and the quantity of real GDP supplied by firms.

Aggregate Demand

To understand what happens during the business cycle, we need an explanation of why real GDP, the unemployment rate, and the inflation rate fluctuate. We have already seen that fluctuations in the unemployment rate are caused mainly by fluctuations in real GDP. In this chapter, we use the **aggregate demand and aggregate supply model** to explain fluctuations in real GDP and the **price level**. As Figure 9.1 shows, real GDP and the price level in this model are determined in the short run by the intersection of the *aggregate demand curve* and the *aggregate supply curve*. Fluctuations in real GDP and the price level are caused by shifts in the aggregate demand curve, the aggregate supply curve, or both.

The **aggregate demand (AD) curve** shows the relationship between the price level and the quantity of real GDP demanded by households, firms, and the government. The **short-run aggregate supply (SRAS) curve** shows the relationship between the price level and the quantity of real GDP supplied by firms *in the short run*. The aggregate demand and short-run aggregate supply curves in Figure 9.1 should seem familiar. They are similar to the individual market demand and supply curves we explored in Chapter 3. However, because these curves apply to the whole economy, rather than to a single market, the aggregate demand and aggregate supply model is quite different from the model of demand and supply in individual markets. Because we're dealing with the economy as a whole, we need *macroeconomic* explanations of why the aggregate demand curve is downward sloping, why the short-run aggregate supply curve is upward sloping, and why the curves shift. We begin by explaining why the aggregate demand curve is downward sloping.

Why Is the Aggregate Demand Curve Downward Sloping?

We saw in Chapter 5 that GDP has four components: consumption (C), investment (I), government purchases (G), and net exports (NX). If we let Y stand for real GDP, we can write the following:

$$Y = C + I + G + NX.$$

The aggregate demand curve is downward sloping because a fall in the price level increases the quantity of real GDP demanded. To understand why this is true, we need to look at how changes in the price level affect each of the components of aggregate demand. We begin with the assumption that government purchases are determined by the policy decisions of lawmakers and are not influenced by changes in the price level.

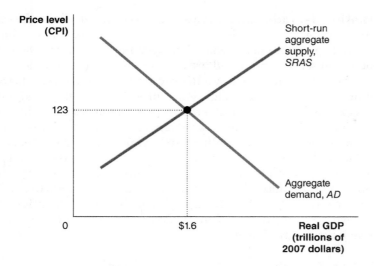

Figure 9.1

**Aggregate Demand and
Aggregate Supply**

In the short run, real GDP and the price
level are determined by the intersection of
the aggregate demand curve and the short-
run aggregate supply curve. In the figure,
real GDP is measured on the horizontal axis,
and the price level is measured on the vertical axis by the CPI. In this example, the
equilibrium real GDP is $1.6 trillion and the
equilibrium price level is 123.

We can then consider the effect of changes in the price level on each of the three remaining components of real GDP: consumption, investment, and net exports.

The Wealth Effect: How a Change in the Price Level Affects Consumption

Current income is the most important variable determining the consumption of
households. As income rises, consumption will rise, and as income falls, consumption will fall. But consumption also depends on household wealth. A household's
wealth is the difference between the value of its assets and the value of its debts.
Consider two households, both with incomes of $80 000 per year. The first house-
hold has wealth of $5 million, while the second has wealth of $50 000. The first
household is likely to spend a lot more of its income than the second household. So,
as total household wealth rises, consumption will rise. Some household wealth is
held in cash or other *nominal assets* that lose value as the price level rises and gain
value as the price level falls. For instance, if you have $10 000 in cash, a 10 percent
increase in the price level will reduce the purchasing power of that cash by 10 percent. When the price level rises, the *real value* of household wealth falls, meaning
higher price levels lead to lower consumption spending by households. When the
price level falls, the real value of household wealth rises, and so consumption goes
up. The impact of the price level on consumption is called the *wealth effect*, and is
one reason the aggregate demand curve is downward sloping.

The Interest-Rate Effect: How a Change in the Price Level Affects

Investment When prices rise, households and firms need more money to finance
buying and selling. Therefore, when the price level rises, households and firms will try
to increase the amount of money they hold by withdrawing funds from banks, borrowing from banks, or selling financial assets, such as stocks or bonds. These actions
tend to drive up the interest rate charged on bank loans and the interest rate on bonds.
(In Chapter 11, we analyze in more detail the relationship between money and interest rates.) A higher interest rate raises the cost of borrowing for firms and households.
As a result, firms will borrow less to build new factories or install new machinery and
equipment, and households will borrow less to buy new houses. To a smaller extent,
consumption will also fall as households borrow less to finance spending on cars, furniture, and other durable goods. So, because a higher price level increases the interest
rate and reduces investment spending, it also reduces the quantity of goods and services
demanded. A lower price level will decrease the interest rate and increase investment
spending, thereby increasing the quantity of goods and services demanded. This impact
of the price level is known as the *interest-rate effect*, and is a second reason the aggregate
demand curve is downward sloping.

The International-Trade Effect: How a Change in the Price Level Affects Net Exports *Net exports* equals spending by foreign households and firms on goods and services produced in Canada minus spending by Canadian households and firms on goods and services produced in other countries. If the price level in Canada increases relative to the price levels in other countries, Canadian exports will become relatively more expensive, and foreign-made products (i.e., imports) will become relatively less expensive. Some consumers in foreign countries will shift from buying Canadian products to buying domestic products, and some Canadian consumers will also shift from buying Canadian products to buying imported products. Canadian exports will fall, and Canadian imports will rise, causing net exports to fall, thereby reducing the quantity of goods and services demanded. A lower price level in Canada relative to other countries has the reverse effect, causing net exports to rise, increasing the quantity of goods and services demanded. This impact of the price level on net exports is known as the *international-trade effect*, and is a third reason the aggregate demand curve is downward sloping.

Shifts of the Aggregate Demand Curve versus Movements along It

An important point to remember is that the aggregate demand curve tells us the relationship between the price level and the quantity of real GDP demanded, *holding everything else constant*. If the price level changes but other variables that affect the willingness of households, firms, and the government to spend are unchanged, the economy will move along a stationary aggregate demand curve. If any variable other than the price level changes, the aggregate demand curve will shift. For example, if government purchases increase and the price level remains the same, the aggregate demand curve will shift to the right at every price level. Or, if firms become pessimistic about the future profitability of investment and cut back spending on factories and equipment, the aggregate demand curve will shift to the left. There is a simple way to tell if a change causes a movement along a curve or a shift of the curve. If the variable that changed is on either the *x*-axis or *y*-axis, you're dealing with a *movement* along the curve. If the variable that changed isn't on either of the axes, you're dealing with a *shift* of the curve.

Variables That Shift the Aggregate Demand Curve

The variables that cause the aggregate demand curve to shift fall into three categories:

* Changes in government policy

Don't Let This Happen to You

Understand Why the Aggregate Demand Curve Is Downward Sloping

The aggregate demand curve and the demand curve for a single product are both downward sloping—but for different reasons. When we draw a demand curve for a single product, such as apples, we know that it will slope downward because as the price of apples rises, apples become more expensive relative to other products—such as oranges—and consumers will buy fewer apples and more of the other products. In other words, consumers substitute other products for apples. When the overall price level rises, the prices of all domestically produced

goods and services are rising, so consumers have no other domestic products to which they can switch. The aggregate demand curve slopes downward for the reasons given on pages 254–256: A lower price level raises the real value of household wealth (which increases consumption), lowers interest rates (which increases investment and consumption), and makes Canadian exports less expensive and foreign imports more expensive (which increases net exports).

MyEconLab
Your Turn: Test your understanding by doing related problem 1.2 on page 283 at the end of this chapter.

- Changes in the expectations of households and firms
- Changes in foreign variables

Changes in Government Policy As we will discuss further in Chapters 11 and 12, the federal government uses monetary and fiscal policy to shift the aggregate demand curve. **Monetary policy** involves actions that the Bank of Canada—the nation's central bank—takes to manage the money supply and interest rates and to ensure the flow of funds from lenders to borrowers. The Bank of Canada takes these actions to achieve its inflation target. For example, by lowering interest rates, the Bank of Canada can lower the cost to firms and households of borrowing. Lower borrowing costs increases consumption and investment spending, which shifts the aggregate demand curve to the right. Higher interest rates shift the aggregate demand curve to the left. **Fiscal policy** involves changes in federal taxes and purchases that are intended to achieve macroeconomic policy objectives. As government purchases are one component of aggregate demand, an increase in government purchases shifts the aggregate demand curve to the right, and a decrease in government purchases shifts the aggregate demand curve to the left. An increase in personal income taxes reduces the amount of disposable income for households. Higher personal income taxes reduce consumption spending and shift the aggregate demand curve to the left. Lower personal income taxes increase consumption spending and shift the aggregate demand curve to the right. Increases in business taxes reduce the profitability of investment and shift the aggregate demand curve to the left. Lower business taxes make investments more appealing to firms and shift the aggregate demand curve to the right.

> **Monetary policy** The actions the Bank of Canada takes to manage the money supply and interest rates to pursue macroeconomic policy goals.

> **Fiscal policy** Changes in federal taxes and purchases that are intended to achieve macroeconomic policy objectives.

Changes in Expectations of Households and Firms If households become more optimistic about their future incomes, they are likely to increase their current consumption. This increased consumption will shift the aggregate demand curve to the right. If households become more pessimistic about their future incomes, the aggregate demand curve will shift to the left. Similarly, if firms become more optimistic about the future profitability of investment spending, the aggregate demand curve will shift to the right. If firms become more pessimistic, the aggregate demand curve will shift to the left.

Changes in Foreign Variables If firms and households in other countries buy fewer Canadian goods or if firms and households in Canada buy more foreign goods, net exports will fall, and the aggregate demand curve will shift to the left. As we saw in Chapter 5, when real GDP increases, so does the income available for consumers to spend. If real GDP in Canada increases faster than real GDP in other countries, Canadian imports will increase faster than Canadian exports, making net exports fall. Net exports will also fall if the *exchange rate* between the Canadian dollar and foreign currencies rises because the price in a foreign currency of Canadian products sold in other countries will rise, and the dollar price of foreign products sold in Canada will fall. For example, if the current exchange rate between the dollar and the euro is $1 = €1, then a $300 BlackBerry exported from Canada to France will cost €300 in France, and a €50 bottle of French wine will cost $50 in Canada. If the exchange rate rises to $1 = €1.50, then the BlackBerry will increase to €450 in France, causing its sales to fall. At the same time, the $1 = €1.50 exchange rate will make the cost of the French wine fall from $50 to $33.33 per bottle in Canada, causing its sales to increase. Canadian exports will fall, Canadian imports will rise, and the aggregate demand curve will shift to the left.

An increase in net exports at every price level will shift the aggregate demand curve to the right. Net exports will increase if real GDP grows more slowly in Canada than in other countries or if the value of the dollar falls against other currencies. A change in net exports that results from a change in the price level in Canada will result in a movement along the aggregate demand curve, *not* a shift of the aggregate demand curve.

Making
the
Connection

The Role of Exports in Aggregate Demand

Exports are a key component of aggregate demand for most modern economies. Some people believe that countries in which exports make up a large portion of aggregate demand are more vulnerable to economic problems that arise in other parts of the world. One country's exports are another country's imports. When a country enters a recession, purchases of all goods and services, including imports, fall. This means that a recession in one country can cause a recession in another country. While trade allows countries to specialize in goods and services in which they have a comparative advantage, it also exposes countries involved in trade to recessions started in other countries.

Germany is one country that exports a lot of what it produces to other countries. Some commentators speculated that countries such as Germany would be permanently damaged by the global recession of 2007–2009. Prior to the financial crisis in 2007, which sparked the global recession, Germany exported almost half of everything it made (see the graph below). For comparison, China and Canada exported 37 percent and 35 percent, respectively. The United States, by contrast, only exported 13 percent of its output. While German exports outside Europe have increased since the end of the global recession, Germany's European trading partners are still not purchasing many German products.

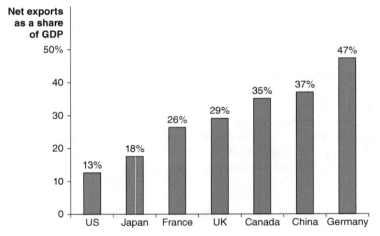

In Germany, the *Mittelstand* are small and medium-sized firms, often family owned and operated. Many *Mittelstand* manufacture machinery, optical equipment, and other scientific and engineering products. These products are generally inputs into the production process and require a highly skilled labour force. Many *Mittelstand* sell the majority of their products outside of Germany. Some larger German firms, particularly in the chemical and automotive industries, also export a good deal of their output. So, the deep global recession of 2007–2009 was particularly bad news for Germany. From the first quarter of 2008 to the first quarter of 2009, German exports declined almost 20 percent. Over the same time, the country's real GDP fell 7 percent, the largest decline in nearly 30 years.

In 2009, German policymakers debated whether a policy response to the global recession was needed. Angela Merkel, the chancellor of Germany, and her advisers believed that Germany still had a comparative advantage in making things that required highly skilled engineers, and thus exports would grow quickly once the global recession was over. In order to protect this comparative advantage, the government instituted payroll subsidies in export industries that allowed firms to retain their skilled workers. However, some argued against this approach, concerned that the demand for Germany's exports would grow much slower than expected after the recession due to an increase in saving rates and a corresponding decrease in the level of consumption in the United States and some European countries. As well, increased competition from developing countries in the production and sale of goods that require strong engineering skills was reducing Germany's comparative advantage. Some believed that an alternative approach would be to encourage greater entrepreneurship, hoping that doing so would help Germany develop comparative advantages in other areas. For example, Germany has few firms in knowledge-based industries, such as software and computing. However, such firms have contributed greatly to the growth of both the United States and India in recent years.

The effects of the global recession of 2007–2009 and the ensuing euro crisis continue to unfold and change the economies of countries around the world. The slow growth in European Union countries continues to mean slow growth in demand for German exports.

Sources: Marcus Walker, "Germany Can Change to Confront the Export Slump – But Will It?" Wall Street Journal, June 29, 2009; Organization for Economic Cooperation and Development.

Your Turn: Test your understanding by doing related problem 1.3 on page 283 at the end of this chapter.

MyEconLab

Solved Problem **9.1**

Movements along the Aggregate Demand Curve versus Shifts of the Aggregate Demand Curve

Suppose the current price level is 123, and the current level of real GDP is $1.6 trillion. Illustrate each of the following situations on a graph.

The price level rises to 127, while everything else remains exactly the same.

Firms become more pessimistic and reduce their investment spending. Assume that the price level remains constant.

Solving the Problem

Step 1: Review the chapter material. This problem is about understanding the difference between movements along an aggregate demand curve and shifts of an aggregate demand curve, so you may want to review the section "Shifts of the Aggregate Demand Curve versus Movements along It," which begins on page 256.

Step 2: To answer part (a), draw a graph that shows a movement along the aggregate demand curve. Because there will be a movement along the aggregate demand curve but no shift of the aggregate demand curve, your graph should look like this:

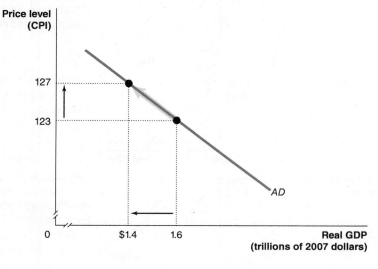

We don't have enough information to be certain what the new level of real GDP demanded will be. We only know that it has to be less than the initial $1.6 trillion; the graph shows this value as $1.4 trillion. **To answer part (b), draw a graph that shows a leftward shift of the aggregate demand curve.** We know that the aggregate demand curve will shift left, but we don't have enough information to determine how far left it will shift. Let's assume that the shift is $200 billion (or $0.2 trillion). In that case, your graph should look like this:

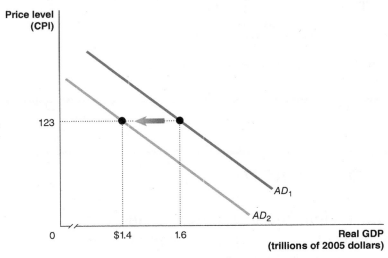

The graph shows a parallel shift in the aggregate demand curve so that at every price level, the quantity of real GDP demanded declines by $200 billion. For example, if the price level remains at 123, the quantity of real GDP demanded will fall from $1.6 trillion to $1.4 trillion.

MyEconLab   **Your Turn:** For more practice, do related problem 1.4 on page 283 at the end of this chapter.

Table 9.1 summarizes the most important variables that cause the aggregate demand curve to shift. The table shows the shift in the aggregate demand curve that results from an *increase* in each of the variables. A *decrease* in these variables would cause the aggregate demand curve to shift in the opposite direction.

Table 9.1

Variables that Shift the Aggregate Demand Curve

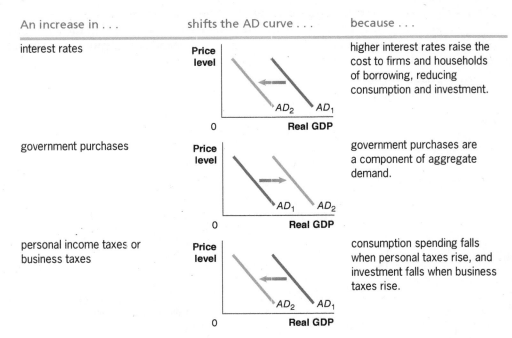

An increase in . . .	shifts the AD curve . . .	because . . .
interest rates		higher interest rates raise the cost to firms and households of borrowing, reducing consumption and investment.
government purchases		government purchases are a component of aggregate demand.
personal income taxes or business taxes		consumption spending falls when personal taxes rise, and investment falls when business taxes rise.

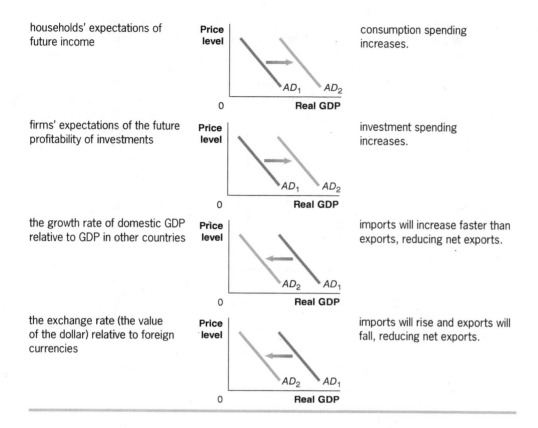

households' expectations of future income → consumption spending increases.

firms' expectations of the future profitability of investments → investment spending increases.

the growth rate of domestic GDP relative to GDP in other countries → imports will increase faster than exports, reducing net exports.

the exchange rate (the value of the dollar) relative to foreign currencies → imports will rise and exports will fall, reducing net exports.

Making the Connection | # Predicting Shifts of the Aggregate Demand Curve

Predicting the state of the economy is a multi-million-dollar business, and people use a variety of methods to forecast where the economy is heading. The MacDonald-Laurier Institute (an independent think-tank based in Ottawa) produces a composite leading index, called the *MLI Leading Economic Indicator*, which combines nine predictors of the future health of the Canadian economy. This indicator includes things like the state of the housing market, the predicted state of the US economy, what is happening in the markets for manufactured goods and financial products, and the number of new claims for Employment Insurance. When the index rises, the economy is expected to grow, and when the index falls, the economy is expected to shrink. The Composite Index of Leading Indicators has a decent track record of predicting the health of the economy.

The MLI Leading Economic Indicator is an imperfect predictor of the future state of the economy. In particular, the index does not include any direct measurements of the mood of consumers and producers.

A variety of other economic indicators exist, ranging from the completely logical to the truly quirky.

On the logical side of the spectrum are the Conference Board of Canada's Index of Consumer Confidence and the Ivey Business School's Ivey Purchasing Managers Index; the former measures the plans of consumers, and the latter measures the activities of producers. The Index of Consumer Confidence is based on the views of households about current and expected economic conditions, including whether now is a good time to make a major purchase (such as a house); the index is issued monthly. The Ivey Purchasing Managers Index measures the change in the value of purchases made by purchasing managers across the country each month. An increase in the Index of Consumer Confidence indicates that consumers are planning to spend more, and an increase in the Purchasing Managers Index indicates that firms are spending more than they did in the previous month. Increases in either index suggest that the economy is growing.

On the quirky side of the spectrum, there is no shortage of economic indicators. For example, in the 1920s, economist George Taylor noted a relationship between stock market prices and the length of women's skirts. According to Taylor's Hemline Index, as the economy improves, skirts get shorter, and as the economy worsens, skirts get longer. This fashion trend is still reported in the media as an economic indicator.

Leonard Lauder, CEO of Estée Lauder, created the Lipstick Index, which proposes that lipstick sales tend to increase as the economy declines. The rise in lipstick sales is likely due to people substituting a relatively cheap luxury for a more expensive one, such as new clothing. Meanwhile, the Skinny Tie Width indicator proposes two points: (1) necktie sales go up during tough economic times because men want to show their bosses that they are serious and working hard, and (2) during economic downturns, neckties get skinnier, while as the economy improves, neckties get wider and more colourful.

All of these indicators have one thing in common; they reflect the state of aggregate demand in the economy. The state of aggregate demand, as we shall see, plays a key role in determining the phase of the business cycle of the economy.

Sources: Statistics Canada, Composite Index of Leading Indicators http://www.statcan.gc.ca/tables-tableaux/sum-som/l01/cst01/cpis03a-eng.htm, Conference Board of Canada, Consumer Confidence Index: http://www2.conferenceboard.ca/weblinx/ica/Default.htm, Richard Ivey School of Business and the Purchasing Management Association of Canada, Ivey Purchasing Manager's Index: http://iveypmi.uwo.ca/English/Welcomeeng.htm, New York Times, The Hemline Index, Updated: http://www.nytimes.com/2008/10/19/business/worldbusiness/19iht-19lewin.17068071.html?_r=1, The Economist, Lip Service: What lipstick sales tell you about the economy: http://www.economist.com/displaystory.cfm?story_id=12998233, Financial Times, The Information: The Tie Index: http://www.ft.com/cms/s/2/15f88980-e695-11dd-8e4f-0000779fd2ac.html.

MyEconLab

Your Turn: Test your understanding by doing related problem 1.5 on page 283 at the end of this chapter.

9.2 LEARNING OBJECTIVE

Identify the determinants of aggregate supply and distinguish between a movement along the short-run aggregate supply curve and a shift of the curve.

Aggregate Supply

The aggregate demand curve is only half of the aggregate demand and aggregate supply model. Now we turn to aggregate supply, which shows the effect of changes in the price level on the quantity of goods and services that firms are willing and able to provide. Because the impact of changes in the price level on aggregate supply is very different in the short run as compared with the long run, we use two aggregate supply curves: one for the long run and one for the short run. We start by discussing the long-run aggregate supply curve.

The Long-Run Aggregate Supply Curve

In the long run, the level of real GDP is determined by the supply of inputs—the labour force and the capital stock—and the available technology. The labour force is the number of workers available to be employed. The capital stock is the amount of physical capital (e.g., factories, office buildings, machinery, and equipment) available. The supply of both factors is determined by the decisions people have made in the past. The current labour force is based on people's decisions to have children or immigrate, made years ago. The current capital stock is based on firm's investment decisions made in previous years. This leads to a level of output the economy can produce when markets clear. The level of real GDP in the long run is referred to as **potential GDP**, or *full-employment GDP*. At potential GDP, firms will operate at their normal level of capacity, and the only unemployment we will observe will be structural and frictional. Because potential GDP is determined by decisions made in the past, it is not influenced by changes in the price level. The **long-run aggregate supply (*LRAS*) curve** shows the relationship between the price level and the quantity of real GDP supplied. As Figure 9.2 shows, whether the price level is 119, 123, or 127, potential GDP remains the same. Therefore, the long-run aggregate supply (*LRAS*) curve is a vertical line at potential GDP.

Potential GDP The level of real GDP attained when all firms are producing at capacity.

Long-run aggregate supply (*LRAS*) curve A curve that shows the relationship in the long run between the price level and the quantity of real GDP supplied.

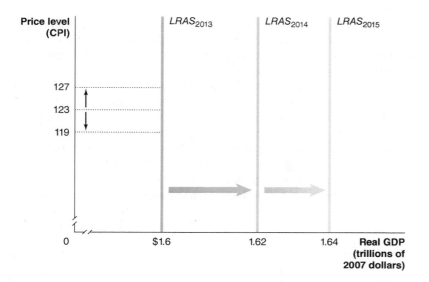

Figure 9.2

The Long-Run Aggregate Supply Curve

Changes in the price level do not affect the level of aggregate supply in the long run. Therefore, the long-run aggregate supply (*LRAS*) curve is a vertical line at potential GDP. For instance, the price level was 123 in 2013, and potential GDP was $1.6 trillion. If the price level had been 127, or if it had been 119, long-run aggregate supply would still have been a constant $1.6 trillion. Each year, the long-run aggregate supply curve shifts to the right, as the number of workers in the economy increases, more machinery and equipment are accumulated, and technological change occurs.

Figure 9.2 also shows that the *LRAS* curve shifts to the right each year. This shift occurs because potential GDP increases almost every year, as we accumulate more machinery, the labour force grows, and technology improves. Figure 9.2 shows potential GDP increasing from $1.6 trillion in 2013 to $1.62 trillion in 2014 to $1.64 trillion in 2015.

The Short-Run Aggregate Supply Curve

While the *LRAS* curve is vertical, the short-run aggregate supply curve (*SRAS*) is upward sloping. The *SRAS* curve is upward sloping because, over the short run, as the price level increases, the quantity of goods and services firms are willing to supply will increase. The main reason firms behave this way is that, *as prices of final goods and services rise, prices of inputs—such as the wages of workers or the price of natural resources—rise more slowly.* Profits increase when the prices of the goods and services firms sell rise faster than the prices they pay for inputs. Therefore, a higher price level leads to higher profits and increases the willingness of firms to supply more goods and services. A secondary reason the *SRAS* curve slopes upward is that, as the price level rises or falls, some firms are slow to adjust their prices. A firm that is slow to raise its prices when the price level is increasing may find its sales increase and, therefore, will increase production. A firm that is slow to reduce its prices when the price level is decreasing may find its sales falling and cut production as a result.

Why do some firms adjust prices more slowly than others, and why might the wages of workers and the prices of other inputs change more slowly than the prices of final goods and services? Most economists believe the explanation is that *some firms and workers fail to accurately predict changes in the price level.* If firms and workers could predict the future price level exactly, the short-run aggregate supply curve would be the same as the long-run aggregate supply curve.

But how does the failure of workers and firms to perfectly predict the price level result in an upward sloping *SRAS* curve? Economists are not in complete agreement on this point, but we can briefly discuss the three most common explanations:

1. Contracts make some wages and prices "sticky."
2. Firms are often slow to adjust wages.
3. Menu costs make some prices sticky.

Contracts Make Some Wages and Prices "Sticky" Prices or wages are said to be "sticky" when they do not respond quickly to changes in demand or supply. Contracts can make wages or prices sticky. For example, suppose Purolator Courier negotiates a three-year contract with Teamsters Canada (the union for truck drivers, package handlers, and other employees) during a time when the economy is in recession and the volume of packages being shipped is falling. Suppose that after the union signs the contract, the economy begins to expand rapidly, and the volume of packages shipped increases, so that Purolator can raise the rates it charges. Purolator will find that shipping more packages will be profitable because the prices it charges are rising while the wages it pays its workers are fixed by contract. Or a steel mill might have signed a multiyear contract to buy coal, which is used to make steel, at a time when the demand for steel was stagnant. If the demand for steel (and thus the price of steel) begins to rise rapidly, producing additional steel will be profitable because the cost of coal to the steel firm will remain fixed by contract. In both of these examples, rising prices lead to higher output. If these examples are representative of enough firms in the economy, a rising price level should lead to a greater quantity of goods and services supplied. In other words, the short-run aggregate supply curve will be upward sloping.

Notice, though, that if the workers at Purolator or the managers of the coal companies had accurately predicted what would happen to prices, this prediction would have been reflected in the contracts, and Purolator and the steel mill would not have earned greater profits when prices rose. In that case, rising prices would not lead to higher output.

Firms Are Often Slow to Adjust Wages We just noted that the wages of union workers remain fixed by contract for several years. Many non-union workers also have their wages or salaries adjusted only once a year. For instance, suppose that you accept a job at a management consulting firm in June at a salary of $65 000 per year. The firm probably will not adjust your salary until the following June, even if the prices it can charge for its services rise after you are first hired. If firms are slow to adjust wages, a rise in the price level will increase the profitability of hiring more workers and producing more output. Similarly, a fall in the price level will decrease the profitability of hiring more workers and producing more output. Once again, we have an explanation for why the short-run aggregate supply curve slopes upward.

It is worth noting that firms are often slower to *cut* wages than to increase them. Cutting wages can have a negative effect on the morale and productivity of workers and can also cause some of a firm's best workers to quit and look for jobs elsewhere.

Menu costs The costs to firms of changing prices.

Menu Costs Make Some Prices Sticky Firms base their prices today partly on what they expect future prices to be. For instance, before printing its menus, a restaurant has to decide the prices it will charge for meals. Some firms still print catalogues that list the prices of their products. If demand for their products is higher or lower than the firms had expected, they may want to charge prices different from those printed in their menus or catalogues. Changing prices would be costly, however, because it would involve printing new menus or catalogues. The costs to firms of changing prices are called **menu costs**. To see why menu costs can lead to an upward-sloping short-run aggregate supply curve, consider the effect of an unexpected increase in the price level. In this case, firms will want to increase the prices they charge. Some firms, however, may not be willing to increase prices because of menu costs. The firms that don't increase their prices will find their sales increasing (because their prices are lower than those of other firms), which will cause them to increase output. Once again, we have an explanation for a higher price level leading to a larger quantity of goods and services supplied.

Shifts of the Short-Run Aggregate Supply Curve versus Movements along It

It is important to remember the difference between a shift in a curve and a movement along it. The short-run aggregate supply curve tells us the short-run relationship between the price level and the quantity of goods and services firms are willing to supply, *holding everything else that can affect the willingness of firms to supply goods and services constant*. If the price level changes, but nothing else does, the economy will move up or down a stationary aggregate supply curve. If any variable other than the price level changes, the aggregate supply curve will shift.

Variables That Shift the Short-Run Aggregate Supply Curve

We now briefly discuss the five most important variables that cause the short-run aggregate supply curve to shift.

Increases in the Labour Force and in the Capital Stock A firm will supply more output at every price if it has more workers and more physical capital. The same is true of the economy as a whole. So, as the labour force and the capital stock grow, firms will supply more output at every price level, and the short-run aggregate supply curve will shift to the right. In Japan, for example, the population is aging and the labour force is shrinking. Holding other things constant, this decrease in the labour force causes the short-run aggregate supply curve in Japan to shift to the left.

Technological Change As positive technological change takes place, the productivity of workers and machinery increases, which means firms can produce more goods and services with the same amount of labour and machinery. This increase in productivity reduces firms' costs of production and, thus, allows them to produce more output at every price level. As a result, the short-run aggregate supply curve shifts to the right.

Expected Changes in the Future Price Level If workers and firms believe that the price level is going to increase by 3 percent during the next year, they will try to adjust their wages and prices accordingly. For instance, if a labour union believes there will be 3 percent inflation next year, it knows that wages must rise by 3 percent to preserve the purchasing power of those wages. Similar adjustments by other workers and firms will result in costs increasing throughout the economy by 3 percent. The result, shown in Figure 9.3, is that the short-run aggregate supply curve shifts to the left, so that any level of real GDP is associated with a price level that is 3 percent higher. In general, *if workers and firms expect the price level to increase by a certain percentage, the SRAS curve will shift by that amount,* holding constant all other variables that can shift the SRAS curve.

Adjustments of Workers and Firms to Errors in Past Expectations about the Price Level Workers and firms sometimes make incorrect predictions about the price level. As time passes, they will attempt to compensate for these errors. Suppose, for example, that Teamsters Canada signs a contract with Purolator Courier that provides for only small wage increases because the company and the union both expect only small increases in the price level. If increases in the price level turn out to be unexpectedly large, the union will take this into account when negotiating the next contract. The higher wages Purolator workers receive under the new contract will increase Purolator's costs and result in Purolator needing to receive higher prices to produce the same level of output. If workers and firms across the economy are adjusting to the price level being higher than expected, the SRAS curve will shift to the left. If they are adjusting to the price level being lower than expected, the SRAS curve will shift to the right.

Unexpected Changes in the Price of an Important Natural Resource An unexpected event that causes the short-run aggregate to shift to the left is called a

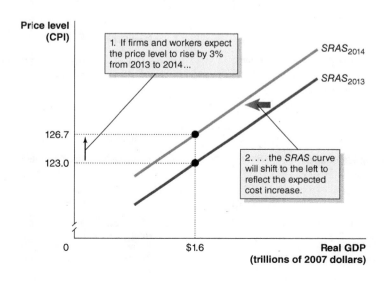

Figure 9.3

How Expectations of the Future Price Level Affect the Short-Run Aggregate Supply Curve

The SRAS curve shifts to reflect worker and firm expectations of future prices.

1. If workers and firms expect that the price level will rise by 3 percent, from 123 to 126.7, they will adjust their wages and prices by that amount.
2. Holding constant all other variables that affect aggregate supply, the short-run aggregate supply curve will shift to the left.

If workers and firms expect that the price level will be lower in the future, the short-run aggregate supply curve will shift to the right.

Supply shock An unexpected event that causes the short-run aggregate supply curve to shift.

supply shock. Supply shocks are often caused by unexpected increases or decreases in the prices of important natural resources. For example, an unexpected increase or decrease in the price of a key natural resource can cause firms' costs to be different from what they had expected. Oil prices can be particularly volatile. Some firms use oil in the production process. Other firms use products, such as plastics, that are made from oil. If oil prices rise unexpectedly, the costs of production will rise for these firms. Some utilities also burn oil to generate electricity, so electricity prices will rise. Rising oil prices lead to rising gasoline prices, which raise transportation costs for firms. Because firms face rising costs, they will supply the same level of output only if they receive higher prices, and the short-run aggregate supply curve will shift to the left.

Because the Canadian economy has experienced at least some inflation in virtually every year since the 1930s, workers and firms always expect next year's price level to be higher than this year's price level. Holding everything else constant, expectations of a higher price level will cause the SRAS curve to shift to the left. But everything else is never constant because the Canadian labour force and the Canadian capital stock are also increasing, and technology is always changing—factors that shift the SRAS curve to the right. The direction in which the SRAS curve shifts in a particular year depends on how large an impact these variables have during that year.

Table 9.2 summarizes the most important variables that cause the SRAS curve to shift. The table shows the shift in the SRAS curve that results from an *increase* in each

Table 9.2

Variables That Shift the Short-Run Aggregate Supply Curve

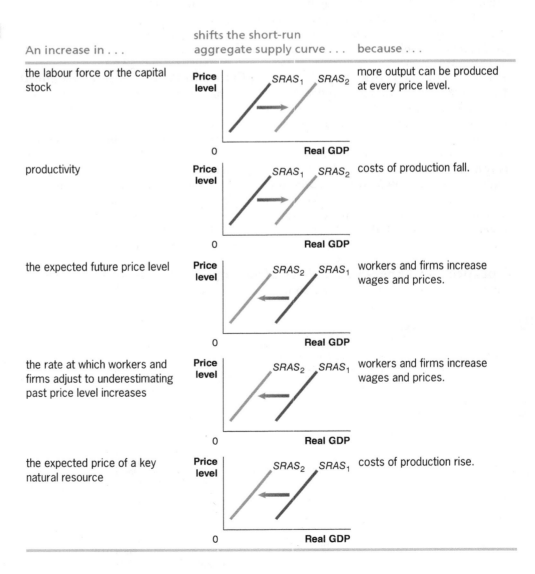

of the variables. A *decrease* in these variables would cause the *SRAS* curve to shift in the opposite direction.

Macroeconomic Equilibrium in the Long Run and the Short Run

9.3 LEARNING OBJECTIVE

Use the aggregate demand and aggregate supply model to illustrate the difference between short-run and long-run macroeconomic equilibrium.

Now that we have discussed the components of the aggregate demand and aggregate supply model, we can use it to analyze changes in real GDP and the price level. In Figure 9.4, we bring the aggregate demand curve, the short-run aggregate supply curve, and the long-run aggregate supply curve together in one graph, to show the *long-run macroeconomic equilibrium* for the economy. In the figure, equilibrium occurs at real GDP of $1.6 trillion and a price level of 123. Notice that in the long-run equilibrium, the short-run aggregate supply curve and the aggregate demand curve intersect at a point on the long-run aggregate supply curve. Because equilibrium occurs at a point on the long-run aggregate supply curve, we know the economy is at potential GDP: Firms will be operating at their normal capacity, and everyone who wants a job will have one—except for the structurally and frictionally unemployed. We know, however, that the economy is often not in long-run macroeconomic equilibrium. In the following section, we discuss the economic forces that can push the economy out of its long-run macroeconomic equilibrium.

Recessions, Expansions, and Supply Shocks

Because the full analysis of the aggregate demand and aggregate supply model can be complex, we begin with a simplified case, using two assumptions:

1. The economy has not been experiencing any inflation. The price level is currently 123, and workers and firms expect the price level to remain at 123.
2. The economy is not experiencing any long-run growth. Potential GDP is $1.6 trillion and will be $1.6 trillion in the future.

These assumptions are simplifications because in reality, the Canadian economy has experienced at least some inflation in virtually every year since the 1930s, and the potential GDP also increases every year. However, these assumptions allow us to focus on the key ideas of the aggregate demand and aggregate supply model. In this section, we examine the short-run and long-run effects of recessions, expansions, and supply shocks.

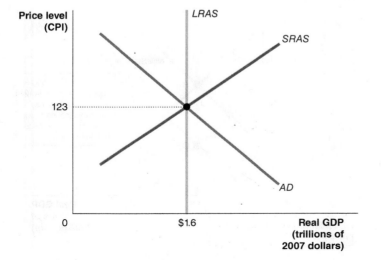

Figure 9.4

Long-Run Macroeconomic Equilibrium

In long-run macroeconomic equilibrium, the *AD* and *SRAS* curves intersect at a point on the *LRAS* curve. In this case, equilibrium occurs at real GDP of $1.6 trillion and a price level of 123.

Recession

The Short-Run Effect of a Decline in Aggregate Demand

Suppose that rising interest rates cause firms to reduce spending on factories and equipment and cause households to reduce spending on new homes. The decline in investment that results will shift the aggregate demand curve to the left, from AD_1 to AD_2, as shown in Figure 9.5. The economy moves from point A to a new *short-run macroeconomic equilibrium*, where the AD_2 curve intersects the SRAS curve at point B. In the new short-run equilibrium, real GDP has declined from $1.6 trillion to $1.56 trillion and is below potential GDP. This lower level of GDP will result in declining profitability for many firms and layoffs for some workers—in short, the economy will be in recession.

Adjustment Back to Potential GDP in the Long Run

We know that the recession will eventually end because there are forces at work that push the economy back to potential GDP in the long run. Figure 9.5 shows how the economy moves from recession back to potential GDP. The shift from AD_1 to AD_2 initially leads to a short-run equilibrium, with the price level having fallen from 123 to 120 (point B). Firms will be willing to accept lower prices due to lower sales. In addition, the unemployment resulting from the recession will make workers more willing to accept lower wages. As a result, the SRAS curve will shift to the right, from $SRAS_1$ to $SRAS_2$. At this point, the economy will be back in long-run equilibrium (point C). The shift from $SRAS_1$ to $SRAS_2$ will not happen instantly. It may take the economy several years to return to potential GDP. The important conclusion is that a decline in aggregate demand causes a recession in the short run, but in the long run it causes only a decline in the price level.

Economists refer to the process of adjustment back to potential GDP just described as an *automatic mechanism* because it occurs without any actions by the government. An alternative to waiting for the automatic mechanism to end a recession is for the government to use monetary or fiscal policy to shift the AD curve to the right and restore potential GDP more quickly. We will discuss monetary and fiscal policy in Chapters 11 and 12. Economists debate whether it is better to wait for the automatic mechanism to end a recession or whether government intervention is a better solution.

Figure 9.5

The Short-Run and Long-Run Effects of a Decrease in Aggregate Demand

In the short run, a decrease in aggregate demand causes a recession. In the long run, it causes only a decrease in the price level.

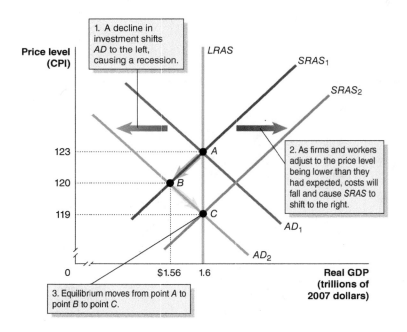

Making the Connection

Does the Canadian Economy Import Recessions?

We've discussed the four components that make up GDP. A decline in any one of these components will cause the aggregate demand (*AD*) curve to shift to the left, causing a recession. Remarkably, Canada has experienced only three recessions in the last 30 years: one in the early 1980s, another in the early 1990s, and the most recent from late 2008 to 2009. Many people believe that a decline in the American economy necessarily means a recession in Canada, as a recession in the United States usually means a fall in Canadian net exports. This link has been considered so important, that the state of the US economy is included in the MLI Leading Economic Indicator, one of the official predictors of the future state of the Canadian economy. Although a drop in our exports to the United States won't make our economy grow faster, it may not be as damaging as many believe.

Lowe's and other American home-improvement retailers sell Canadian lumber and wood products in the US market.

Consider the two US recessions of the last 10 years. The United States entered a recession at the end of 2001, while Canada did not. The recession that began in 2007 with the bursting of the US housing bubble and the subsequent financial crisis caused Canada to enter a recession, but this recession was relatively short-lived and was not as damaging to the Canadian economy as many feared that it would be. One key reason Canada has been able to avoid the worst of the last two US recessions is that it has decoupled from (i.e., become less dependent on) the US economy. The United States is still by far the largest consumer of Canadian exports, but Canadian producers have found additional markets for their products. This is particularly true of raw materials. The Canadian economy didn't follow the United States into recession in 2001. It did follow the United States into recession in 2008. One of the main differences between these events was the price of natural resources. In 2007–2008, the prices of natural resources such as oil, potash, and timber fell dramatically, reducing the value Canadian producers received for these materials. In 2001, however, the prices of these natural resources didn't fall nearly as much, which meant that Canadian producers of these materials were able to continue to earn the same or similar profits and to employ the same number of workers.

Countries in Asia also led the way out of recession in 2010. Like Canada, many developing economies in Asia have begun to become less dependent on the US economy and are focusing more so on trade with China and Japan. The continued recovery and growth of Asian economies may not be as dependent on the state of the American economy as it once was.

Your Turn: Test your understanding by doing related problem 3.3 on page 284 at the end of this chapter.

MyEconLab

Expansion

The Short-Run Effect of an Increase in Aggregate Demand

Suppose that instead of becoming pessimistic, many firms become optimistic about the future profitability of new investment, as happened during the information and telecommunication boom of the late 1990s and the real-estate boom of the 2000s. The resulting increase in investment will shift the *AD* curve to the right, as shown in Figure 9.6. Equilibrium moves from point *A* to point *B*. Real GDP rises from $1.6 trillion to $1.64 trillion, and the price level rises from 123 to 126. The economy will be operating above potential GDP: Firms are operating beyond their normal capacity, and some workers who would ordinarily be structurally or frictionally unemployed or who would normally not be in the labour force are employed.

Figure 9.6

The Short-Run and Long-Run Effects of an Increase in Aggregate Demand

In the short run, an increase in aggregate demand causes an increase in real GDP. In the long run, it causes only an increase in the price level.

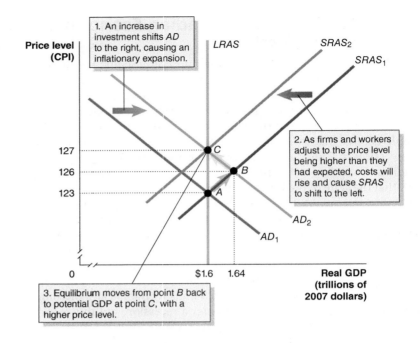

1. An increase in investment shifts AD to the right, causing an inflationary expansion.

2. As firms and workers adjust to the price level being higher than they had expected, costs will rise and cause SRAS to shift to the left.

3. Equilibrium moves from point B back to potential GDP at point C, with a higher price level.

Adjustment Back to Potential GDP in the Long Run Just as an automatic mechanism brings the economy back to potential GDP from a recession, an automatic mechanism brings the economy back from a short-run equilibrium beyond potential GDP. Figure 9.6 illustrates this mechanism. The shift from AD_1 to AD_2 initially leads to a short-run equilibrium, with the price level rising from 123 to 126 (point B). Workers and firms will begin to adjust to the price level being higher than they had expected. Workers will push for higher wages—because each dollar of wages is able to buy fewer goods and services than before—and firms will charge higher prices. In addition, the low level of unemployment resulting from the expansion will make it easier for workers to negotiate for higher wages, and the increase in demand will make it easier for firms to increase their prices. As a result, the SRAS will shift to the left, from $SRAS_1$ to $SRAS_2$. At this point, the economy will be back in long-run equilibrium. Once again, the shift from $SRAS_1$ to $SRAS_2$ will not happen instantly. The process of returning to potential GDP may stretch out for more than a year.

Supply Shock

The Short-Run Effect of a Supply Shock Suppose oil prices increase substantially. This supply shock will increase costs for many firms and cause the SRAS curve to shift to the left, as shown in panel (a) of Figure 9.7. Notice that the price level is higher in the new short-run equilibrium (126 rather than 123), but real GDP is lower ($1.56 trillion rather than $1.6 trillion). This unpleasant combination of inflation and recession is called **stagflation**.

Stagflation A combination of inflation and recession, usually resulting from a supply shock.

Adjustment Back to Potential GDP in the Long Run The recession caused by a supply shock increases unemployment and reduces output. This eventually results in workers being willing to accept lower wages and firms being willing to accept lower prices. In panel (b) of Figure 9.7, the short-run aggregate supply curve shifts from $SRAS_2$ to $SRAS_1$, moving the economy from point B to point A. The economy is back to potential GDP at the original price level. It may take several years for this process to be completed. An alternative would be to use monetary or fiscal policy to shift the aggregate demand curve to the right. Using policy in this way would bring the economy back to potential GDP more quickly but would result in a permanently higher price level.

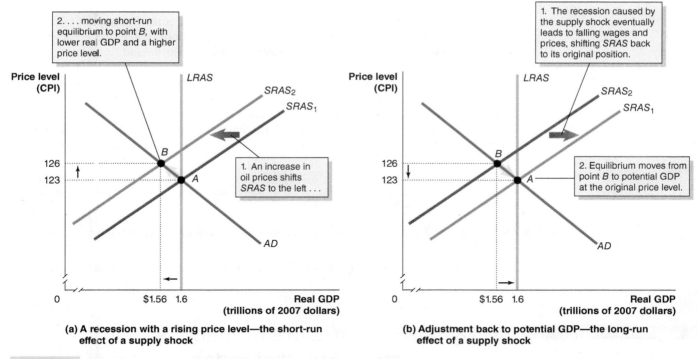

Figure 9.7   The Short-Run and Long-Run Effects of a Supply Shock

Panel (a) shows that a supply shock, such as a large increase in oil prices, will cause a recession and a higher price level in the short run. The recession caused by the supply shock increases unemployment and reduces output. In panel (b), rising unemployment and falling output result in workers being willing to accept lower

wages and firms being willing to accept lower prices. The short-run aggregate supply curve shifts from $SRAS_2$ to $SRAS_1$. Equilibrium moves from point B back to potential GDP and the original price level at point A.

Making the Connection

Does Government Intervention Help Fight a Recession?

As we have seen, economists agree that an automatic mechanism brings the economy back to potential GDP in the long run. But governments and people don't always want to wait for the long run—we don't really know how long the long run is. The length of time it takes for the economy to correct itself plays a role in determining whether federal policymakers should use monetary and fiscal policies to offset the effects of shifts in aggregate demand and aggregate supply.

The global recession led to a Canadian recession in late 2008. As a result of the global recession, Canadian net exports and domestic spending decreased, causing the aggregate demand curve to shift to the left, moving the economy into a recession. The federal government responded to the recession by introducing the politically named, "Economic Action Plan." The Economic Action Plan, introduced in the 2009 federal budget, greatly increased government spending in a wide variety of areas and introduced some income tax breaks as well. The purpose of the increased spending and reduced taxes was to offset the leftward shift in the aggregate demand curve, thus reducing the length and intensity of the recession for Canadians.

In 2009, as the Canadian economy made the transition from recession to growth once more, debate began over the effectiveness of the government's stimulus efforts to limit the impact of the recession. In particular, Niels Veldhuis, president of the Fraser Institute, and Charles Lammam, an associate director at the Fraser Institute, argue that the government's actions did little to spur the recovery of the Canadian economy. They believe that the recovery was driven by

During recessions, governments often increase their spending to stimulate the economy.

increases in private spending and investment instead of the increase in government spending and reduced taxation. While their analysis ignores the impact of the government's stimulus efforts on consumer and investor confidence, the evidence they present against a direct link between government intervention and Canada's economic turnaround is fairly strong.

Both sides of the debate over the effectiveness of government intervention in the economy have their supporters. Why do economists vary in their economic forecasts and policy advice? A key reason is that economists don't always agree on the specific assumptions they should use in building models. One thing economists can agree on is that the aggregate demand and aggregate supply model plays an important role in the development of economic policy.

Source: Based on "The Stimulus Didn't Work: Government stimulus spending had virtually no effect on Canada's economic recovery." Neils Veldhuis and Charles Lammam in Fraser Forum, May 2010, p.17 to 19. http://www.fraserinstitute.org/commerce.web/product_files/fraserforum-may2010.pdf

MyEconLab

Your Turn: Test your understanding by doing related problem 3.7 on page 285 at the end of this chapter.

9.4 LEARNING OBJECTIVE

Use the dynamic aggregate demand and aggregate supply model to analyze macroeconomic conditions.

A Dynamic Aggregate Demand and Aggregate Supply Model

The basic aggregate demand and aggregate supply model used so far in this chapter provides important insights into how short-run macroeconomic equilibrium is determined. Unfortunately, the model also provides some misleading results. For instance, it incorrectly predicts that a recession caused by the aggregate demand curve shifting to the left will cause the price level to fall, which has not happened for an entire year since the 1930s. The difficulty with the basic model arises from the following two assumptions we made: (1) The economy does not experience continuing inflation, and (2) the economy does not experience long-run growth. We can develop a more useful aggregate demand and aggregate supply model by dropping these assumptions. The result will be a model that takes into account that the economy is not *static*, with an unchanging level of potential GDP and no continuing inflation, but *dynamic*, with potential GDP that grows over time and inflation that continues every year. We can create a *dynamic aggregate demand aggregate supply model* by making changes to the basic model that incorporate the following important macroeconomic facts:

- Potential GDP increases continually, shifting the long-run aggregate supply curve to the right.

- During most years, the aggregate demand curve shifts to the right.

- Except during periods when workers and firms expect high rates of inflation, the short-run aggregate supply curve shifts to the right.

Figure 9.8 illustrates how incorporating these macroeconomic facts changes the basic aggregate demand and aggregate supply model. We start in panel (a), in which $SRAS_1$ and AD_1 intersect at point A, at a price level of 123 and real GDP of \$1.6 trillion. Because this intersection occurs at a point on $LRAS_1$, we know the economy is in long-run equilibrium. As panel (b) shows, the long-run aggregate supply curve shifts to the right, from $LRAS_1$ to $LRAS_2$. This shift occurs because during the year, potential GDP increases as the Canadian labour force and the Canadian capital stock increase and technological progress occurs. The short-run aggregate supply curve shifts from $SRAS_1$ to $SRAS_2$. This shift occurs because the same variables that cause the long-run aggregate supply curve to shift to the right will also increase the quantity of goods and

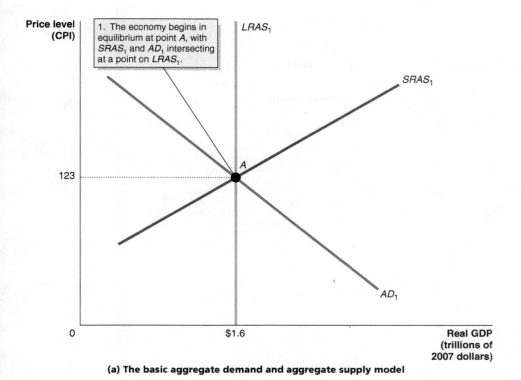

(a) The basic aggregate demand and aggregate supply model

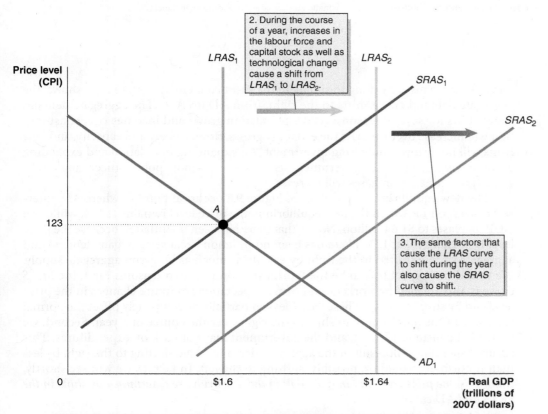

(b) The effect of increases in the labour force and capital stock as well as technological change

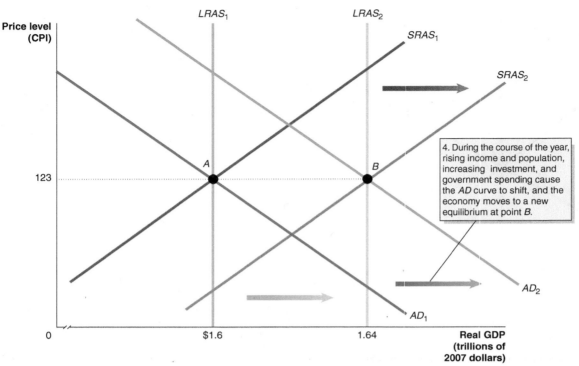

(c) The effect of increased spending by consumers, firms, and the government

Figure 9.8 **A Dynamic Aggregate Demand and Aggregate Supply Model**

We start with the basic aggregate demand and aggregate supply model in panel (a). In the dynamic model, increases in the labour force and capital stock as well as technological change cause the long-run aggregate supply to shift over the course of a year from $LRAS_1$ to $LRAS_2$. Typically, these same factors cause the short-run aggregate supply curve to shift from $SRAS_1$ to $SRAS_2$, as in panel (b). Aggregate demand will shift from AD_1 to AD_2 if, as is usually the case, spending by consumers, firms, and the government increases during the year. The shift in the aggregate demand curve is added to the model in panel (c).

services that firms are willing to supply in the short run. Finally, as panel (c) shows, the aggregate demand curve shifts to the right, from AD_1 to AD_2. The aggregate demand curve shifts for several reasons: As the population grows and incomes rise, consumption will increase over time. As the economy grows, firms will expand capacity, and new firms will be formed, increasing investment. An expanding population and expanding economy require increased government services, such as more police officers and teachers, so government purchases will increase.

The new equilibrium in panel (c) of Figure 9.8 occurs at point B, where AD_2 intersects $SRAS_2$ on $LRAS_2$. In the new equilibrium, the price level remains at 123, while real GDP increases to $1.64 trillion. Notice that there has been no inflation because the price level is unchanged, at 123. There has been no inflation because aggregate demand and aggregate supply shifted to the right by exactly as much as long-run aggregate supply. We would not expect this to be the typical situation for two reasons. First, the $SRAS$ curve is also affected by workers' and firms' expectations of future changes in the price level and by supply shocks. These variables can partially or completely offset the normal tendency of the $SRAS$ curve to shift to the right over the course of a year. Second, we know that consumers, firms, and the government may cut back on expenditures. This reduced spending will result in the aggregate demand curve shifting to the right by less than it normally would or, possibly, shifting to the left. In fact, as we will see shortly, *changes in the price level and in real GDP in the short run are determined by shifts in the SRAS and AD curves.*

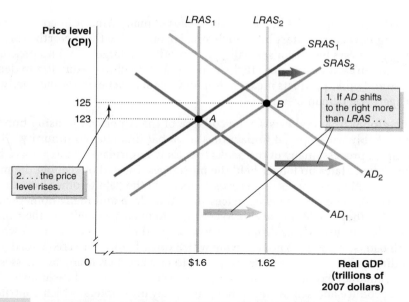

Figure 9.9 **Using Dynamic Aggregate Demand and Aggregate Supply to Understand Inflation**

The most common cause of inflation is total spending increasing faster than total production.

1. The economy begins at point A, with real GDP of $1.6 trillion and a price level of 123. An increase in full-employment real GDP from $1.6 trillion

to $1.62 trillion causes long-run aggregate supply to shift from $LRAS_1$ to $LRAS_2$. Aggregate demand shifts from AD_1 to AD_2.

2. Because AD shifts to the right by more than the $LRAS$ curve, the price level in the equilibrium rises from 123 to 125.

What Is the Usual Cause of Inflation?

The dynamic aggregate demand and aggregate supply model provides a more accurate explanation than the basic model of the source of most inflation. If total spending in the economy grows faster than total production, prices rise. Figure 9.9 illustrates this point by showing that if the AD curve shifts to the right by more than the $LRAS$ curve, inflation results because equilibrium occurs at a higher price level, point B. In the new equilibrium, the $SRAS$ curve has shifted to the right by less than the $LRAS$ curve because the anticipated increase in prices offsets some of the technological change and increases the labour force and capital stock that occur during the year. Although inflation generally results from total spending growing faster than total production, a shift to the left of the short-run aggregate supply curve can also cause an increase in the price level, as we saw earlier, in the discussion of supply shocks.

As we saw in Figure 9.8, if aggregate demand increases by the same amount as short-run and long-run aggregate supply, the price level will not change. In this case, the economy experiences economic growth without inflation.

The Canadian Recession of 2008–2009

We can use the dynamic aggregate demand and aggregate supply model to analyze the recession of 2008–2009. The recession that began in late 2008 was brought on by a combination of several factors:

- **The recession in the United States.** Although we have discussed the decoupling of the Canadian economy from the US economy earlier in the chapter, this process is far from complete. Many of the manufactured goods produced in Canada are ultimately destined for American consumers. The automotive industry provides a particularly striking example. The combination of high oil (and, therefore, gas) prices and the bursting of the housing bubble caused many American consumers to stop buying new cars or start buy much smaller ones. The three North American car manufacturers had been specializing in producing large SUV and pick-up trucks that weren't known for their fuel efficiency. The resulting reduction in demand for these and other products meant a drop in Canadian net exports and a leftward shift in aggregate demand.

- **The global financial crisis.** The collapse of the American housing bubble had a remarkably wide-spread impact on the global financial community. Through a complex process, many of the banks that issued mortgages on expensive homes in the United States no longer held the mortgages. Instead of keeping the mortgages and collecting payments themselves, banks sold the debt to other investors around the world. When US housing prices started to drop and many homeowners realized that they would not be able to continue to make payments on their mortgages, the value of these debts dropped. Banks around the world, unsure of who owned such bad debt and thus not knowing which other banks were creditworthy, stopped lending to businesses, people, and even to one another. Many businesses, including Canadian export companies, rely on credit. If this credit is unavailable, they can't produce and sell. Instead, they have to lay off workers, which contributes to a recession in Canada. The reduction in the availability of credit caused the short-run aggregate supply curve to shift to the left.

- **The rapid drop in commodity prices.** Canada is a major exporter of commodities, including oil. When the prices of these goods drop, the value of Canadian net exports falls. The drop in the value of these products makes producing them less profitable. Firms will often reduce their output and lay off workers when prices fall like this—for example, the Canadian unemployment rate rose from 5.6 in October of 2008 to 9.1 in August of 2009. The result is a leftward shift in Canadian aggregate demand.

Figure 9.10 illustrates the beginning of the Canadian recession, by showing the economy's short-run macroeconomic equilibrium in 2008 and 2009. In the

Figure 9.10

The Beginning of the Canadian Recession of 2008–2009

Between 2008 and 2009, *AD* shifted to the left as Canadian exports fell. Due to the reduction in the availability of credit and the ongoing process of increasing wages and the prices of other important inputs such as electricity, the short-run aggregate supply shifted to the left, from $SRAS_{2008}$ to $SRAS_{2009}$. As a result, the equilibrium for 2009 occurred at real GDP of $1.54 trillion and a price level of 114.4. A large gap opened between short-run equilibrium real GDP and potential GDP. Not surprisingly, unemployment rose from 5.6 percent to 9.1 percent. The price level increased from 114.1 to 114.4, so the inflation rate was a relatively low 0.3 percent.

Sources: CANSIM Tables 380-0064 and 326-0020; and Bank of Canada, *Indicators of Capacity and Inflation Pressures for Canada* (Output Gap).

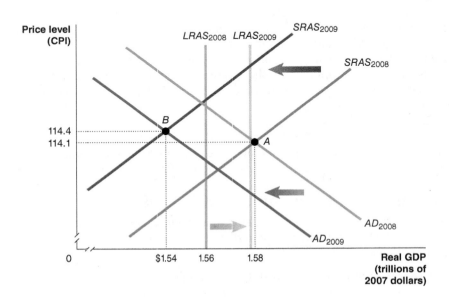

figure, short-run equilibrium for the year ending 2008 occurs where AD_{2008} intersects $SRAS_{2008}$ at real GDP of $1.58 trillion dollars and a price level of 114.1 (point A). At point A, real GDP is greater than the potential GDP of $1.56 trillion as shown by $LRAS_{2008}$. During 2009, aggregate demand shifted to the left from AD_{2008} to AD_{2009}. At the same time, the short-run aggregate supply curve shifted to the left from $SRAS_{2008}$ to $SRAS_{2009}$ due to the continuing increase in wages throughout the economy. The short-run equilibrium for 2009 occurred at real GDP of $1.54 trillion and a price level of 114.4 (point B). A large gap opened between short-run equilibrium real GDP and potential GDP. Not surprisingly, unemployment rose from 5.6 percent to 9.1 percent. The price level increased from 114.1 to 114.4, so the inflation rate was a relatively low 0.3 percent.

Both the federal government and the Bank of Canada responded to the recession very strongly. The federal government expanded spending and cut taxes. The Bank of Canada reduced its key interest rate to historic lows. Both policies were intended to shift the aggregate demand curve to the right to close the gap between short-run equilibrium and potential GDP. We will explore monetary and fiscal policies in Chapters 11 and 12.

Solved Problem 9.2

Showing the Millennium Economic Boom on a Dynamic Aggregate Demand and Aggregate Supply Graph

The booming economy of 2000–2001 clearly shows how a demand shock affects the economy. Throughout 2000 and into 2001, the value of the Canadian dollar was low and falling compared with the American dollar. The low value of the Canadian dollar combined with growing economies in the United States and much of the world meant that demand for Canadian products was high. Based on this information and the statistics in the following table, draw a dynamic aggregate demand and aggregate supply graph showing macroeconomic equilibrium for 2000 and 2001.

Provide a brief explanation of your graph and predict what is likely to happen to the price level in the future.

	Actual Real GDP (Trillions of 2007 Dollars)	Potential GDP (Trillions of 2007 Dollars)	Price Level (CPI)
2000	$1.32	$1.30	95.4
2001	$1.34	$1.35	97.8

Solving the Problem

Step 1: Review the chapter material. This problem is about using the dynamic aggregate demand and aggregate supply model, so you may want to review the section "A Dynamic Aggregate Demand and Aggregate Supply Model," which begins on page 272.

Step 2: Use the information in the table to draw the graph. You need to draw six curves: $SRAS_{2000}$, $SRAS_{2001}$, $LRAS_{2000}$, $LRAS_{2001}$, AD_{2000}, and AD_{2001}. You know the two $LRAS$ curves will be vertical lines at the values given for potential GDP in the table. Because of the large aggregate demand shock, the AD curve has shifted to the right significantly. While the $SRAS$ will have shifted to the left, this shift needs to be relatively small to get the results we see from the data. Your graph should look like this:

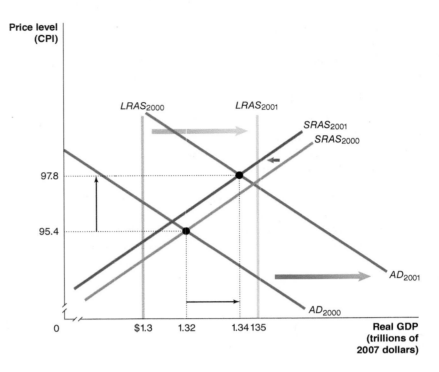

Step 3: **Explain your graph.** *LRAS*$_{2000}$ and *LRAS*$_{2001}$ are at the levels of potential GDP for each year. Macroeconomic equilibrium for 2000 occurs where the *AD*$_{2000}$ curve intersects the *SRAS*$_{2000}$ curve with a real GDP of $1.32 trillion dollars and a price level of 95.4. Macroeconomic equilibrium for 2001 occurs where *AD*$_{2001}$ intersects the *SRAS*$_{2001}$ curve with real GDP equal to $1.34 trillion and a price level of 97.8. The rightward shift of the *AD* curve was much larger than the leftward shift of the *SRAS* curve. The result is an increase in real GDP as well as an increase in the price level.

Sources: CANSIM Tables 380-0064 and 326-0020; and Bank of Canada, *Indicators of Capacity and Inflation Pressures for Canada* (Output Gap).

MyEconLab   **Your Turn:** For more practice, do related problem 4.3 on page 285 at the end of this chapter.

Is an Employer Likely to Cut Your Pay during a Recession?

At the beginning of this chapter, we asked you to consider whether during a recession your employer is likely to reduce your pay and cut the prices of the products he or she sells. In this chapter, we saw that even during a recession, the price level rarely falls. Although some firms reduced prices during the Canadian recession of 2008–2009, most firms did not. So, the owner of the coffeehouse where you work will probably not cut the price of lattes unless sales have declined drastically. We also saw that most firms are more reluctant to cut wages than to increase them because wage cuts can have a negative effect on worker morale and productivity. Some firms did cut wages in response to the recession, but given that you are a highly skilled barista, your employer is unlikely to cut your wages for fear that you might quit and work for a competitor.

Conclusion

Chapter 3 demonstrated the power of the microeconomic model of demand and supply in explaining how the prices and quantities of individual products are determined. This chapter showed that we need a different model to explain the behaviour of the whole economy. We saw that the macroeconomic model of aggregate demand and aggregate supply explains fluctuations in real GDP and the price level. Fluctuations in real GDP, employment, and the price level have led the federal government to implement macroeconomic policies. We will explore these policies in Chapter 12 and Chapter 13, but first, in Chapter 11, we consider the role money plays in the economy.

Read *An Inside Look* on the next page for a discussion of how CN's prospects improved as the economy recovered from the Canadian recession of 2008–2009.

Higher Freight Volumes Signal Good News for the Canadian Economy

THE GAZETTE

CN a Bellwether of the Economy

(a) In many ways, investing in Canadian National Railway is a play on Canada itself.

The railroad mirrors the Canadian economy quite accurately, carrying a mix of natural resources and manufactured goods across the country. Its route structure through the U.S. to the Gulf of Mexico reflects the patterns of North American trade.

So when Montreal-based CN reported a 21-per-cent increase in first-quarter net income this week, it provided another confirmation that the economy is on the mend.

"The economy is gaining traction, and I think we are on a firm path to a gradual recovery," chief executive Claude Mongeau said after yesterday's annual meeting.

That doesn't mean there aren't pockets of concern, particularly in the U.S.

"Some sectors are still having difficulty, there is still a lot of consumer debt," he noted.

For example, shipments of forest products to the U.S. are down, reflecting the lower level of demand for lumber in the weak housing sector and the falling consumption of paper products.

(b) "The U.S. recession was a lot deeper than Canada's," he said, but elsewhere the recovery is kicking in strongly.

"In China and India and some of the new emerging markets, pretty much across the world, there's been a lot of stimulus."

CN is seeing that show up in growing demand for lumber in Asian markets.

(c) The strong Canadian dollar is a challenge, given its impact on exports to the U.S., but Mongeau didn't sound too concerned.

"It means the Canadian economy, the Canadian fiscal situation is in order. As our dollar appreciates, that means as a nation we are more wealthy. This is a good thing."

While conceding that it's forcing exporters to adjust, he added: "The dollar at parity is not a new thing. The dollar was at $1.10 U.S. not too long ago. Most of the manufacturing sectors know they have to focus on productivity."

The higher dollar affects revenue from the U.S., but "helps us with buying fuel, it helps us with paying our interest, which is (U.S.) dollar-denominated."

The bottom-line impact is that "for every cent of appreciation, our reported results lose two cents of earnings per share."

Mongeau took over the CEO's job from the retired Hunter Harrison, whose obsession with "precision railroading" turned CN into a finely-tuned machine with the best ratio of expenses to revenue in the business.

Mongeau says he wants to build on the legacy laid down by Harrison and his predecessor, Paul Tellier, who spearheaded the 1996 privatization of the railway.

Analysts continue to marvel at CN's success in good times and bad. Brian Yarbrough, a U.S. analyst at brokerage firm Edward Jones, says CN has done a "great job of controlling costs."

"If you look at their first quarter, their volumes were up 16 per cent, yet they were able to do that with just 100 additional people on a base of 22,000 employees and with no additional cars.

"They've done a great job of improving productivity, and they continue to improve their metrics. We think they are the best-run railroad in North America."

CN has also done a good job of managing the balance sheet, he added.

"Look at all the companies that cut their dividends, yet they are raising the dividend seven per cent after a tough year."

About 20 per cent of the company's business depends on the U.S. market alone, while another 30 per cent is Canada-U.S. trade. Yarbrough said while the U.S. recovery is lagging, U.S. railroads have begun to report solid increases in volumes.

The question, he said, is whether "this is just inventory restocking or user demand. That's the big wild card."

Investors knocked $1.51, or 2.4 per cent, off the price of CN shares, which closed yesterday at $62.21 on the Toronto Stock Exchange. Some are taking profits after a good run that has seen CN shares climb from the $44-range last July, said Chris Sears, a research analyst at MacDougall, MacDougall and MacTier.

Sears raised his 12-month target to $75.

The company's operating ratio is so strong, he argued, that as the recovery strengthens and top-line revenue grows, there will be plenty of leverage on earnings.

Source: Hadekel, Peter, "Earnings provided another confirmation things are on mend," The Gazette, April 28, 2010. Material reprinted by express permission of: National Post, a division of Postmedia Network, Inc.

Key Points in the Article

The article discusses the performance of CN as the Canadian economy began to recover from the recession of 2008–2009. Companies that carry freight are particularly vulnerable to changes in the state of the economy. When a company receives fewer orders, it needs to ship fewer goods, and those companies that carry freight see demand for their services fall in turn. As the economy recovers, more producers order raw materials and sell finished products, both of which have to be shipped. As a result, companies such as CN will be quick to see an increase in demand for their services when the economy recovers. The improvement in CN's business generally means good news for the Canadian economy.

The article also discusses the importance of exports to the Canadian economy and the role the value of the Canadian dollar, relative to the US dollar, can have on the economy. While a higher value of the domestic currency generally makes business more difficult for exporters, it isn't bad news for everybody.

Analyzing the News

(a) Freight hauling is central to any economy and is an excellent indicator of the conditions firms face in completely different industries. Many economic analysts pay close attention to the profitability of freight hauling and the volume of freight that travels on the country's roads and railways. The Canadian recession of 2008–2009 saw a significant decrease in the volume of goods being shipped in Canada, the United States, and around the world. A change in the volume of goods being shipped is an indication that aggregate demand has shifted to the left. This overall shift can be difficult to see from the output or sales of a single firm in a different industry.

(b) The traditional wisdom is that if the US economy isn't doing well, the Canadian and even the global economy will have difficulty doing well. At the time the article was written, the United States had not yet recovered from the recession brought on by the collapse of the housing bubble and financial crisis. Many of the larger emerging market economies were in an excellent position to stimulate their economies to offset the loss of exports to the United States and did so. As a result, the demand for Canadian products increased, particularly the demand for raw materials, in areas outside of North America.

(c) An increase in the value of the Canadian dollar relative to the US dollar is usually a cause for concern for exporters. As we saw in the chapter, an increase in the value of the Canadian dollar makes Canadian products more expensive for other countries to import and the products produced in other countries less expensive for Canadian consumers. The result is generally a decrease in the value of net exports and a leftward shift of the aggregate demand curve. Mongeau argues that an increase in value of the Canadian dollar wouldn't have much effect on the value of Canadian exports, because that higher value wasn't new. The value of the Canadian dollar has been on an upward trend for the last 5 to 10 years. As a result, Canadian producers of exports have had to improve their productivity to reduce the price at which they can afford to sell their output. Mongeau also points out that many important commodities are priced in American currency, and an increase in the relative value of the Canadian dollar makes these inputs, such as fuel, cheaper. The reduction in the price of inputs shifts the short-run aggregate supply curve to the right.

Thinking Critically

1. Show the effects of a government's economic stimulus spending and a significant reduction in the costs of inputs (such as the wages of workers or the price of natural resources) in an aggregate demand and aggregate supply graph.

2. In the second quarter of 2010, the Canadian unemployment rate began to fall. Where would the *AD* and *SRAS* intersect, relative to the *LRAS* curve in 2010, given the drop in the unemployment rate?

3. Given the link between various goods and the state of the economy, what do you think the increase in the volume of freight being carried by CN will do to the amount of lipstick sold? What about the number of wide and more colourful neckties?

Chapter Summary and Problems

Key Terms

Aggregate demand (*AD*) curve, p. 254

Aggregate demand and aggregate supply model, p. 254

Fiscal policy, p. 257

Long-run aggregate supply (*LRAS*) curve, p. 262

Menu costs, p. 264

Monetary policy, p. 257

Potential GDP, p. 262

Price level, p. 254

Short-run aggregate supply (*SRAS*) curve, p. 254

Stagflation, p. 270

Supply shock, p. 266

Summary

*LO **9.1** The *aggregate demand and aggregate supply model* enables us to explain short-run fluctuations in real GDP and price level. The *aggregate demand curve* shows the relationship between the *price level* and the level of planned aggregate expenditures by households, firms, and the government. The *short-run aggregate supply curve* shows the relationship in the short run between the price level and the quantity of real GDP supplied by firms. *The long-run aggregate supply curve* shows the relationship in the long run between the price level and the quantity of real GDP supplied. The four components of aggregate demand are consumption (*C*), investment (*I*), government purchases (*G*), and net exports (*NX*). The aggregate demand curve is downward sloping because a decline in the price level causes consumption, investment, and net exports to increase. If the price level changes but all else remains constant, the economy will move up or down a stationary aggregate demand curve. If any variable other than the price level changes, the aggregate demand curve will shift. The variables that cause the aggregate demand curve to shift are divided into three categories: changes in government policy, changes in the expectations of households and firms, and changes in foreign variables. For example, *monetary policy* involves the actions the Bank of Canada takes to manage the money supply and interest rates to pursue macroeconomic policy objectives. When the Bank of Canada takes actions to change interest rates, consumption and investment spending will change, shifting the aggregate demand curve. *Fiscal policy* involves changes in taxes and purchases that are intended to achieve macroeconomic policy objectives. Changes in federal taxes and purchases shift the aggregate demand curve.

LO **9.2** The *long-run aggregate supply curve* is a vertical line because in the long run, real GDP is always at its potential level and is unaffected by the price level. The short-run aggregate supply curve slopes upward because workers and firms fail to predict accurately the future price level. The three main explanations of why this failure results in an upward-sloping aggregate supply curve are that (1) contracts make some wages and prices "sticky"; (2) firms are often slow to adjust wages; and (3) menu costs make some prices sticky. *Menu costs* are the costs to firms of changing prices on menus or in catalogues. If the price level changes but all else remains constant, the economy will move up or down a stationary aggregate supply curve. If any variable other than the price level changes, the aggregate supply curve will shift. The aggregate supply curve shifts as a result of increases in the labour force and capital stock, technological change, expected increases or decreases in the future price level, adjustments of workers and firms to errors in past expectations about the price level, and unexpected increases or decreases in the price of an important raw material. A *supply shock* is an unexpected event that causes the short-run aggregate supply curve to shift.

LO **9.3** In long-run macroeconomic equilibrium, the aggregate demand and short-run aggregate supply curves intersect at a point on the long-run aggregate supply curve. In short-run macroeconomic equilibrium, the aggregate demand and short-run aggregate supply curves often intersect at a point off the long-run aggregate supply curve. An automatic mechanism drives the economy to long-run equilibrium. If short-run equilibrium occurs at a point below potential GDP, wages and prices will fall, and the short-run aggregate supply curve will shift to the right until potential GDP is restored. If short-run equilibrium occurs at a point beyond potential GDP, wages and prices will rise, and the short-run aggregate supply curve will shift to the left until potential GDP is restored. Real GDP can be temporarily above or below its potential level, either because of shifts in the aggregate demand curve or because supply shocks lead to shifts in the aggregate supply curve. *Stagflation* is a combination of inflation and recession, usually resulting from a supply shock.

LO **9.4** To make the aggregate demand and aggregate supply model more realistic, we need to make it dynamic by incorporating three facts that were left out of the basic model: (1) Potential GDP increases continually, shifting the long-run aggregate supply curve to the right; (2) during most years, aggregate demand shifts to the right; and (3) except during periods when workers and firms expect high rates of inflation, the aggregate supply curve shifts to the right. The dynamic aggregate demand and aggregate supply model allows us to analyze macroeconomic conditions, including the beginning of the 2008–2009 Canadian recession.

MyEconLab   Log in to MyEconLab to complete these exercises and get instant feedback.

---

*'Learning Objective' is abbreviated to 'LO' in the end of chapter material.

Review Questions

LO 9.1

1.1 Explain the three reasons the aggregate demand curve slopes downward.

1.2 What variables cause the *AD* curve to shift? For each variable, identify whether an increase in that variable will cause the *AD* curve to shift to the right or to the left.

LO 9.2

2.1 Explain why the long-run aggregate supply curve is vertical.

2.2 What variables cause the long-run aggregate supply curve to shift? For each variable, identify whether an increase in that variable will cause the long-run aggregate supply curve to shift to the right or to the left.

2.3 Why does the short-run aggregate supply curve slope upward?

2.4 What variables cause the short-run aggregate supply curve to shift? For each variable, identify whether an increase

in that variable will cause the short-run aggregate supply curve to shift to the right or to the left.

LO 9.3

3.1 What is the relationship among the *AD*, *SRAS*, and *LRAS* curves when the economy is in long-run macroeconomic equilibrium?

3.2 Why are the long-run effects of an increase in aggregate demand on price and output different from the short-run effects?

LO 9.4

4.1 What are the key differences between the basic aggregate demand and aggregate supply model and the dynamic aggregate demand and aggregate supply model?

4.2 In the dynamic aggregate demand and aggregate supply model, what is the result of aggregate demand increasing more quickly than potential GDP? What is the result of aggregate demand increasing more slowly than potential GDP?

Problems and Applications

LO 9.1

1.1 Explain how each of the following events would affect the aggregate demand curve.
   a. An increase in the price level
   b. Higher provincial income taxes
   c. Higher interest rates

1.2 [**Related to** Don't Let This Happen to You **on page 256**] A student was asked to draw an aggregate demand and aggregate supply graph to illustrate the effect of an increase in aggregate supply. The student drew the following graph:

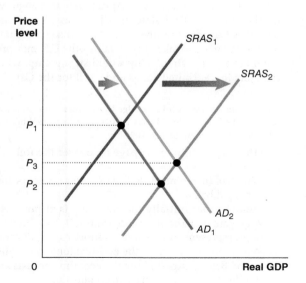

The student explains the graph as follows:

An increase in aggregate supply causes a shift from $SRAS_1$ to $SRAS_2$. Because this shift in

the aggregate supply curve results in a lower price level, there will be an increase in consumption, investment, and net exports. This change causes the aggregate demand curve to shift to the right, from AD_1 to AD_2. We know that real GDP will increase, but we can't be sure whether the price level will rise or fall because that depends on whether the aggregate supply curve or the aggregate demand curve has shifted farther to the right. I assume that aggregate supply shifts out farther than aggregate demand, so I show the final price level, P_3, as being lower than the initial price level, P_1.

Explain whether you agree with the student's analysis. Be careful to explain exactly what—if anything—you find wrong with this analysis.

1.3 [**Related to** Making the Connection **on page 259**] It is common for news stories in Canada to report on recessions and slowdowns in the United States and other parts of the world. American news, even business news, does not provide nearly the same level of reporting on the state of economies outside the United States. Why might this be the case?

1.4 [**Related to** Solved Problem 9.1 **on page 259**] Explain whether the following will cause a shift of the *AD* curve or a movement along the *AD* curve:
   a. Firms become more optimistic about future sales and increase their spending on machinery and equipment.
   b. The Canadian economy experiences 6 percent inflation.

1.5 [**Related to** Making the Connection **on page 261**] (a) What do you think is likely to happen to the economy if you notice a lot of long skirts and skinny neckties? (b) Give an example of something that you think could be a leading indicator of the current state and future health of the Canadian economy.

1.6 In a 2010 article in the *Winnipeg Free Press*, Export Development Canada's chief economist Peter Hall stated:

> The bad news, in a nutshell, was that the global economic recovery is shaky, at best. And the next six to seven months . . . will determine whether the recovery takes hold, or the economy slides back into a recession . . . the global economy will muddle through and shift into full recovery mode in 2011. . . . The sectors that should see the biggest export gains this year are energy—particularly oil and hydro electricity—industrial goods, and forestry, . . . [a]nd the ones that are likely to see modest improvement are motor vehicles, and machinery and equipment. The only sector that's expected to see a drop in exports is agri-food, which will also be hurt by an oversupply of some grains and punitive protectionist measures in key export markets like China and the United States.

Why would some sectors recover more quickly than others? What problems would this variable recovery pose for the Canadian economy? Why would China and the United States be especially punitive given the global economic climate?

Murray McNeill, "Global Economy in 'Critical Zone,'" *Winnipeg Free Press*, May 22, 2010, http://www.winnipegfreepress.com/business/global-economy-in-critical-zone-94563914.html. Reprinted with permission from the Winnipeg Free Press.

LO 9.2

2.1 Explain how each of the following events would affect the long-run aggregate supply curve.
  a. A higher price level
  b. An increase in the quantity of capital goods
  c. Technological change

2.2 An article in the *Economist* noted that "the economy's potential to supply goods and services [is] determined by such things as the labour force and capital stock, as well as inflation expectations." Do you agree with this list of the determinants of potential GDP? Briefly explain.

Based on "Money's Muddled Message," Economist, May 19, 2009.

2.3 Explain how each of the following events would affect the short-run aggregate supply curve.
  a. An increase in the price level
  b. An increase in what the price level is expected to be in the future
  c. An unexpected increase in the price of an important raw material
  d. An increase in the labour force participation rate

2.4 Workers and firms often enter into contracts that fix prices or wages, sometimes for years at a time. If the price level turns out to be higher or lower than was expected when the contract was signed, one party to the contract will lose out. Briefly explain why, despite knowing this, workers and firms still sign long-term contracts.

LO 9.3

3.1 Draw a basic aggregate demand and aggregate supply graph (with *LRAS* constant) that shows the economy in long-run equilibrium.

  a. Assume that there is a large increase in demand for Canadian exports. Show the resulting short-run equilibrium on your graph. In this short-run equilibrium, is the unemployment rate likely to be higher or lower than it was before the increase in exports? Briefly explain. Explain how the economy adjusts back to long-run equilibrium. When the economy has adjusted back to long-run equilibrium, how have the values of each of the following changed relative to what they were before the increase in exports:
    i. Real GDP
    ii. The price level
    iii. The unemployment rate
  b. Assume that there is an unexpected increase in the price of oil. Show the resulting short-run equilibrium on your graph. Explain how the economy adjusts back to long-run equilibrium. In this short-run equilibrium, is the unemployment rate likely to be higher or lower than it was before the increase in exports? Briefly explain. When the economy has adjusted back to long-run equilibrium, how have the values of each of the following changed relative to what they were before the increase in exports:
    i. Real GDP
    ii. The price level
    iii. The unemployment rate

3.2 List four variables that would cause a decrease in real GDP (if large enough, a recession). Indicate whether changes in each variable increase or decrease aggregate demand or short-run aggregate supply. Next, state four variables that would cause an increase in the price level (short-run inflation). Indicate whether changes in the variable increase or decrease aggregate demand or short-run aggregate supply.

3.3 [**Related to** Making the Connection **on page 269**] According to an article in the *Lethbridge Herald* "the Canadian economy got a double-barrelled blast of good news Friday, with both the domestic and U.S. labour markets reporting stunning job creation gains for April [2010] that augur well for the recovery." They state that "[a]s massive and unexpected as Canada's improvement was—to some the number was too good to take fully on faith—the U.S. may prove the most encouraging." Why would strong employment numbers in the United States bode well for the Canadian economy?

The Canadian Press with Lethbridge Herald files, "Job gains signal recovery" Lethbridge Herald, May 7, 2010. http://www.lethbridgeherald.com/content/view/187496/109/

3.4 Use the graph on the next page to answer the following questions:
  a. Which of the points A, B, C, or D can represent a long-run equilibrium?
  b. Suppose that initially the economy is at point A. If aggregate demand increases from AD_1 to AD_2, which point represents the economy's short-run equilibrium? Which point represents the eventual long-run equilibrium? Briefly explain how the economy adjusts from the short-run to the long-run equilibrium.

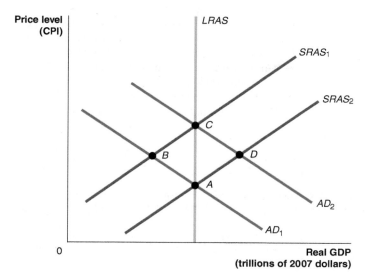

3.5 In the chapter, we saw that goods such as lipstick, neckties, and hemlines could be used as indicators of future developments in the economy. Why do these goods work as economic indicators? What other goods or services can you think of that could also play a similar role in forecasting the economy?

3.6 Consider the data in the following table for the years 2000 and 2001:

Year	Actual Real GDP (Millions of 2007 Dollars)	Potential GDP (millions of 2007 Dollars)	Unemployment Rate (Annual Average)
2000	$1 319 435	$1 304 921	6.8%
2001	$1 341 712	$1 341 712	7.2%

   a. In 2000, actual real GDP was greater than potential GDP. Explain how this is possible.

   b. Even though real GDP in 2001 was greater than that in 2000, the unemployment rate increased between 2000 and 2001. Why did this increase in unemployment occur?

   c. Was the inflation rate in 2001 likely to have been higher or lower than the inflation rate in 2000? Does your answer depend on whether the slowdown was caused by a change in a component of aggregate demand or by a supply shock?

Data from StatsCan tables 282-0002 and 380-0017, Bank of Canada Potential GDP estimates from Office of the Parliamentary Budget Officer, Estimates of Canada's Potential GDP and Output Gap – A Comparative Analysis, April 28, 2010 http://www2.parl.gc.ca/sites/pbo-dpb/documents/Potential_GDP.pdf

LO 9.4

4.1 Draw a dynamic aggregate demand and aggregate supply graph showing the economy moving from potential GDP in 2013 to potential GDP in 2014, with no inflation. Your graph should contain the *AD*, *SRAS*, and *LRAS* curves for both 2013 and 2014 and should indicate the short-run macroeconomic equilibrium for each year and the directions in which the curves have shifted. Identify what must happen to have growth during 2014 without inflation.

4.2 According to the Bank of Canada, the only sustained period of deflation in Canada occurred in the 1930s as a result of the Great Depression. "Deflation can be particularly harmful when caused by a protracted sharp contraction in spending (as in the 1930s), which triggers a persistent fall in the general level of prices." Why is this type of deflation so harmful? (*Hint:* Think about which curve will shift in this case and think about how consumers might react to consistently falling prices.)

Bank of Canada Fact Sheet: Disinflation and Deflation, http://www.bankofcanada.ca/en/backgrounders/bg-i6.html

4.3 [**Related to** Solved Problem 9.2 **on page 277**] Look at the table in *Solved Problem 9.2*. The price level for 2000 is given as 95.4, and the price level for 2001 is given as 97.8. The values for the price level are just below 100. What does this indicate about inflation during these years? Briefly explain.

4.4 In the graph below, suppose that the economy moves from point A in year 1 to point B in year 2. Using the graph, briefly explain your answer to each of the questions.

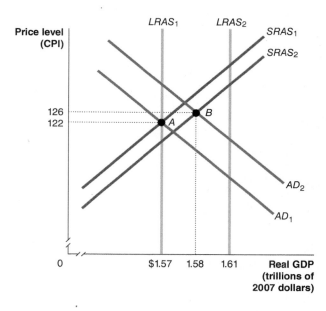

   a. What is the growth rate in potential GDP from year 1 to year 2?

   b. Is the unemployment rate in year 2 higher or lower than in year 1?

   c. What is the inflation rate in year 2?

   d. What is the growth rate of real GDP in year 2?

4.5 In May 2010, the Reed Job Index reported that demand for new workers was growing, but the salary on offer of new jobs was declining. How is this strong evidence that the economy has entered the recovery phase of the business cycle?

Based on Helen Gilbert, "Jobs demand up in May, but salaries for new starters fall" Personnel Today, June 1, 2010. http://www.personnel-today.com/articles/2010/06/01/55762/jobs-demand-up-in-may-but-salaries-for-new-starters-fall.html

4.6 [**Related to** An Inside Look **on page 280**] An article in the *Montreal Gazette* refers to CN as an "economic bellwether."
   a. What is an economic bellwether?
   b. Briefly compare how sensitive CN's sales are likely to be to changes in the business cycle to how sensitive the following firms' sales are likely to be to changes in the business cycle. (In other words, explain whether CN's sales are likely to fluctuate more or less than the sales of each of these other firms as the economy moves from recession to expansion and back to recession.)
   - Tim Hortons (a chain of restaurants specialized in coffee and baked goods)
   - Kent Homes (a home builder)
   - Harlequin Romance Ltd. (a novel publisher)

Appendix D

Macroeconomic Schools of Thought

Macroeconomics became a separate field of economics in 1936, with the publication of John Maynard Keynes's book *The General Theory of Employment, Interest, and Money*. Keynes, an economist at the University of Cambridge in England, was attempting to explain the devastating Great Depression of the 1930s. As we discussed in Chapter 8, real GDP in Canada and other industrial countries fell by more than 25 percent between 1929 and the mid-1930s. In 1930, the unemployment rate in Canada was estimated at 30 percent. The Canadian economy did not truly recover until the start of World War II in 1939. To explain what Canada and other industrial countries were experiencing, Keynes developed a version of the aggregate demand and aggregate supply model. The widespread acceptance during the 1930s and 1940s of Keynes's model became known as the **Keynesian revolution**.

In fact, using the aggregate demand and aggregate supply model remains the most widely accepted approach to analyzing macroeconomic issues. Because the model has been modified significantly from Keynes's day, many economists who use the model today refer to themselves as *new Keynesians*. The new Keynesians emphasize the importance of the stickiness of wages and prices in explaining fluctuations in real GDP. A significant number of economists, however, dispute whether using the aggregate demand and aggregate supply model, as we have discussed it in this chapter, is the best way to analyze macroeconomic issues. These alternative *schools of thought* use models that differ significantly from the standard aggregate demand and aggregate supply model. We can briefly consider each of the three major alternative models:

1. The monetarist model
2. The new classical model
3. The real business cycle model

LO
Understand macroeconomic schools of thought.

Keynesian revolution The name given to the widespread acceptance during the 1930s and 1940s of John Maynard Keynes's macroeconomic model.

The Monetarist Model

The monetarist model—also known as the *neo-Quantity Theory of Money model*—was developed beginning in the 1940s by Milton Friedman, an economist at the University of Chicago who was awarded the Nobel Prize in Economics in 1976. Friedman argued that the Keynesian approach overstates the amount of macroeconomic instability in an economy. In particular, he argued that an economy will ordinarily be at potential real GDP. In the book *A Monetary History of the United States: 1867–1960*, written with Anna Jacobson Schwartz, Friedman argued that most fluctuations in real output were caused by fluctuations in the money supply rather than by fluctuations in consumption spending or investment spending. Friedman and Schwartz argued that the severity of the Great Depression in the United States was caused by the central banks, particularly the American central bank, allowing the quantity of money to fall dramatically.

Central banks are responsible for managing the amount of money circulating in the economy. As we will discuss further in Chapter 11, central banks historically focused more on controlling interest rates than on controlling the money supply. Friedman argued that central banks should change their practices and adopt a **monetary growth rule**, which is a plan for increasing the quantity of money at a fixed rate. Friedman believed that adopting a monetary growth rule would reduce fluctuations in real GDP, employment, and inflation.

Monetary growth rule A plan for increasing the quantity of money at a fixed rate that does not respond to changes in economic conditions.

Monetarism The macroeconomic theories of Milton Friedman and his followers, particularly the idea that the quantity of money should be increased at a constant rate.

Friedman's ideas, which are referred to as **monetarism**, attracted significant support during the 1970s and early 1980s, when developed economies experienced high rates of unemployment and inflation. The support for monetarism declined during the late 1980s and 1990s, when the unemployment and inflation rates in developed economies were relatively low. In Chapter 10, we will discuss the *quantity theory of money*, which underlies the monetarist model.

The New Classical Model

The new classical model was developed in the mid-1970s by a group of economists including Nobel Laureate Robert Lucas of the University of Chicago, Nobel Laureate Thomas Sargent of New York University, and Robert Barro of Harvard University. Some of the views held by the new classical macroeconomists are similar to those held by economists before the Great Depression. Keynes referred to the economists before the Great Depression as "classical economists." Like the classical economists, the new classical macroeconomists believe that the economy normally will be at potential real GDP. They also believe that wages and prices adjust quickly to changes in demand and supply. Put another way, they believe the stickiness in wages and prices emphasized by the new Keynesians is unimportant.

Lucas argues that workers and firms have *rational expectations*, meaning that they form their expectations of the future values of economic variables, such as the inflation rate, by making use of all available information, including information on variables—such as changes in the quantity of money—that might affect aggregate demand. If the actual inflation rate is lower than the expected inflation rate, the actual real wage will be higher than the expected real wage. These higher real wages will lead to a recession because they will cause firms to hire fewer workers and cut back on production. As workers and firms adjust their expectations to the lower inflation rate, the real wage will decline, and employment and production will expand, bringing the economy out of recession. The ideas of Lucas and his followers are referred to as the **new classical macroeconomics**. Supporters of the new classical model agree with supporters of the monetarist model that central banks should adopt a monetary growth rule. They argue that a monetary growth rule will make it easier for workers and firms to accurately forecast the price level, thereby reducing fluctuations in real GDP.

New classical macroeconomics The macroeconomic theories of Robert Lucas and others, particularly the idea that workers and firms have rational expectations.

The Real Business Cycle Model

Beginning in the 1980s, some economists, including Nobel Laureates Finn Kydland of Carnegie Mellon University and Edward Prescott of Arizona State University, began to argue that Lucas was correct in assuming that workers and firms formed their expectations rationally and that wages and prices adjust quickly to supply and demand but was wrong about the source of fluctuations in real GDP. They argue that fluctuations in real GDP are caused by temporary shocks to productivity. These shocks can be negative, such as a decline in the availability of oil or other raw materials, or positive, such as technological change that makes it possible to produce more output with the same quantity of inputs.

Real business cycle model A macroeconomic model that focuses on real, rather than monetary, causes of the business cycle.

According to this school of thought, shifts in the aggregate demand curve have no impact on real GDP because the short-run aggregate supply curve is vertical. Other schools of thought believe that the short-run aggregate supply curve is upward sloping and that only the *long-run* aggregate supply curve is vertical. Fluctuations in real GDP occur when a negative productivity shock causes the short-run aggregate supply curve to shift to the left—reducing real GDP—or a positive productivity shock causes the short-run aggregate supply curve to shift to the right—increasing real GDP. Because this model focuses on "real" factors—productivity shocks—rather than changes in the quantity of money to explain fluctuations in real GDP, it is known as the **real business cycle model**.

Making
the
Connection

Karl Marx: Capitalism's Severest Critic

The schools of macroeconomic thought we have discussed in this appendix are considered part of mainstream economic theory because of their acceptance of the market system as the best means of raising living standards in the long run. One quite influential critic of mainstream economic theory was Karl Marx. Marx was born in Trier, Germany, in 1818. After graduating from the University of Berlin in 1841, he began a career as a political journalist and agitator. His political activities caused him to be expelled first from Germany and then from France and Belgium. In 1849, he moved to London, where he spent the remainder of his life.

In 1867, Marx published the first volume of his greatest work, *Das Kapital*. Marx read closely the most prominent mainstream economists, including Adam Smith, David Ricardo, and John Stuart Mill. But Marx believed that he understood how market systems would evolve in the long run much better than those earlier authors. Marx argued that the market system would eventually be replaced by a Communist economy, in which the workers would control production. He believed in the *labour theory of value*, which attributed all of the value of a good or service to the labour embodied in it. According to Marx, the owners of businesses—capitalists—did not earn profits by contributing anything of value to the production of goods or services. Instead, capitalists earned profits because their "monopoly of the means of production"—their ownership of factories and machinery—allowed them to exploit workers by paying them wages that were much lower than the value of workers' contribution to production.

Marx argued that the wages of workers would be driven to levels that allowed only bare survival. He also argued that small firms would eventually be driven out of business by larger firms, forcing owners of small firms into the working class. Control of production would ultimately be concentrated in the hands of a few firms, which would have difficulty selling the goods they produced to the impoverished masses. A final economic crisis would lead the working classes to rise up, seize control of the economy, and establish Communism. Marx died in 1883, without having provided a detailed explanation of how the Communist economy would operate.

Karl Marx predicted that a final economic crisis would lead to the collapse of the market system.

Marx had relatively little influence on mainstream thinking in the United States, but several political parties in Europe were guided by his ideas. In 1917, the Bolshevik party seized control of Russia and established the Soviet Union, the first Communist state. Although the Soviet Union was a vicious dictatorship under Vladimir Lenin and his successor, Joseph Stalin, its prestige rose when it avoided the macroeconomic difficulties that plagued the market economies during the 1930s. By the late 1940s, Communist parties had also come to power in China and the countries of Eastern Europe. Poor economic performance contributed to the eventual collapse of the Soviet Union and its replacement by a market system, although one in which government intervention is still widespread. The Communist Party remains in power in China, but the economy is evolving toward a market system. Today, only North Korea and Cuba have economies that claim to be based on the ideas of Karl Marx.

Key Terms

Keynesian revolution, p. 287

Monetarism, p. 288

Monetary growth rule, p. 287

New classical macroeconomics, p. 288

Real business cycle model, p. 288

Money, Banks, and the Bank of Canada

Chapter Outline and Learning Objectives

10.1 What Is Money, and Why Do We Need It? page 292
Define money and discuss the four functions of money.

10.2 How Is Money Measured in Canada Today? page 295
Discuss the definitions of the money supply used in Canada today.

10.3 How Do Banks Create Money? page 299
Explain how banks create money.

10.4 The Bank of Canada, page 306
Discuss the policy tools the Bank of Canada uses to manage the money supply.

10.5 The Quantity Theory of Money, page 313
Explain the quantity theory of money, and use it to explain how high rates of inflation occur.

Marco Di Lauro/Getty Images

Coca-Cola Dries Up as Money Floods Zimbabwe

People in Africa buy 36 billion bottles of Coca-Cola a year. In 2008, Zimbabwe, a country in southern Africa, ran out of locally produced Coke for the first time in at least 40 years. Because they could not obtain US dollars, local Coke bottlers were not able to import from the United States the concentrated syrup used to make the soft drink. A meagre amount of Coke was imported from South Africa, but a single bottle sold for around 15 billion Zimbabwean dollars! Zimbabwe was suffering the effects of an inflation rate so high that it is called a *hyperinflation*. Zimbabwe's hyperinflation was of epic proportions, perhaps the worst in world history. When it was first introduced in 1980, 1 Zimbabwean dollar was worth 1.47 US dollars. By the end of 2008, the exchange rate was 1 US dollar to 2 *billion* Zimbabwean dollars, and prices for some large transactions in Zimbabwe were calculated in quadrillions (15 zeros) and quintillions (18 zeros).

In addition to the Coke shortage, Zimbabweans were suffering shortages of fuel, food, and other basic goods. As the value of the Zimbabwean currency fell against other currencies, it was difficult for local businesses such as the Coke bottlers to find anyone willing to exchange US dollars for Zimbabwean dollars. What made Zimbabwe's currency almost worthless? The government of Zimbabwe had decided to pay for all of its expenses by printing more and more money. The faster the government printed money, the faster

© Glenda Powers/Fotolia

prices rose. Eventually, both foreigners and local residents refused to accept the Zimbabwean dollar in exchange for goods and services, and the country's economy plunged into a devastating recession, with real GDP falling more than 12 percent during 2008. In early 2009, the government issued 100 trillion dollar bills, not enough for a bus ticket in Harare, Zimbabwe's capital city. Eventually, in 2009, a new Zimbabwean government took the drastic step of abandoning its own currency and making the US dollar the country's official currency.

AN INSIDE LOOK on **page 318** discusses whether central banks around the world could achieve superior results using different monetary policy strategies.

Sources: Based on Angus Shaw, "Coca Cola Dries Up in Zimbabwe," newzimbabwe.com, December 1, 2008; Patrick McGroarty and Farai Mutsaka, "How to Turn 100 Trillion Dollars into Five and Feel Good About It," Wall Street Journal, May 11, 2011; Marcus Walker and Andrew Higgins, "Zimbabwe Can't Paper Over Its Million-Percent Inflation Anymore," Wall Street Journal, July 2, 2008; and "Wait and See," Economist, February 5, 2009.

Economics in Your Life

What If Money Became Increasingly Valuable?

Most people are used to the fact that as prices rise each year, the purchasing power of money falls. You will be able to buy fewer goods and services with $1000 one year from now than you can buy today, and you will be able to buy even fewer goods and services the year after that. In fact, with an inflation rate of just 3 percent, in 25 years, $1000 will buy only what $475 can buy today. Suppose, though, that you could live in an economy where the purchasing power of money rose each year? What would be the advantages and disadvantages of living in such an economy? As you read the chapter, see if you can answer these questions. You can check your answers against those we provide on page 317 at the end of this chapter.

I n this chapter, we will explore the role of money in the economy. We will see how the banking system creates money and what policy tools the Bank of Canada uses to manage the quantity of money. We will also look at the crisis in the global banking system during the past few years. At the end of the chapter, we will explore the link between changes in the quantity of money and changes in the price level. What you learn in this chapter will serve as an important foundation for understanding monetary policy and fiscal policy, which we study in the next three chapters.

Define money and discuss the four functions of money.

Money Assets that people are generally willing to accept in exchange for goods and services or for payment of debts.

Asset Anything of value owned by a person or a firm.

What Is Money, and Why Do We Need It?

Could an economy function without money? We know the answer to this question is "yes" because there are many historical examples of economies in which people traded goods for other goods rather than using money. For example, Canada's indigenous people historically traded furs for European products without using money. Most economies, though, use money. What is money? The economic definition of **money** is any asset that people are generally willing to accept in exchange for goods and services or for payment of debts. An **asset** is anything of value owned by a person or a firm. There are many possible kinds of money: In West Africa, at one time, cowrie shells served as money. During World War II, prisoners of war used cigarettes as money.

Barter and the Invention of Money

To understand the importance of money, let's consider further the situation in economies that do not use money. These economies, where goods and services are traded directly for other goods and services, are called *barter economies*. Barter economies have a major shortcoming. To illustrate this shortcoming, consider a farmer on the recently settled prairies. Suppose the farmer needed another cow and proposed trading a spare plough to a neighbour for one of the neighbour's cows. If the neighbour did not want the plough, the trade would not happen. For a barter trade to take place between two people, each person must want what the other one has. Economists refer to this requirement as a *double coincidence of wants*. The farmer who wants the cow might eventually be able to obtain one if he first trades with some other neighbour for something the neighbour with the cow wants. However, it may take several trades before the farmer is ultimately able to trade for what the neighbour with the cow wants. Locating several trading partners and making several intermediate trades can take considerable time and energy.

Commodity money A good used as money that also has value independent of its use as money.

The problems with barter give societies an incentive to identify a product that most people will accept in exchange for what they have to trade. For example, in colonial times, animal skins were very useful in making clothing. The European demand for beaver fur meant that beaver pelts often traded as money among settlers and indigenous groups. A good used as money that also has value independent of its use as money is called a **commodity money**. Historically, once a good became widely accepted as money, people who did not have an immediate use for it would be willing to accept it. An early settler or a member of an indigenous group might not really want a beaver pelt, but would take it knowing that it could be traded for something they really did want.

Trading goods and services is much easier when money becomes available. People only need to sell what they have for money and then use the money to buy what they want. If our fictitious farmer could find someone to buy his plough, he could use the money to buy the cow he wanted. The neighbour with the cow would accept the money because she knows she could use it to buy what she wanted. When money is available, people are less likely to produce everything or nearly everything they need themselves and more likely to specialize.

Most people in modern economies are highly specialized. They do only one thing—work as a nurse, an accountant, or an engineer—and use the money they earn to buy everything else they need. As we discussed in Chapter 2, people become much more productive by specializing because they can pursue their *comparative advantage*. The high income levels in modern economies are based on the specialization that money makes possible. We can now answer the question, "Why do we need money?" *By making exchange easier, money allows people to specialize and become more productive.*

The Functions of Money

Anything used as money—whether a beaver pelt, a cowrie seashell, cigarettes, or a dollar bill—should fulfill the following four functions:

- Medium of exchange
- Unit of account
- Store of value
- Standard of deferred payment

Medium of Exchange Money serves as a medium of exchange when sellers are willing to accept it in exchange for goods or services. When the local supermarket accepts your $5 bill in exchange for bread and milk, the $5 bill is serving as a medium of exchange. With a medium of exchange, people can sell goods and services for money and use the money to buy what they want. An economy is more efficient when a single good is recognized as a medium of exchange.

Unit of Account In a barter system, each good has many prices. A cow may be worth two ploughs, 20 bushels of wheat, or six axes. Once a single good is used as money, each good has a single price rather than many prices. This function of money gives buyers and sellers a *unit of account*, a way of measuring value in the economy in terms of money. Because the Canadian economy uses dollars as money, each good has a price in terms of dollars.

Store of Value Money allows value to be stored easily. If you do not use all your dollars to buy goods and services today, you can hold the rest to use in the future. Money is not the only store of value, however. Any asset—shares of Coca-Cola stock, Canada bonds, real estate, or Renoir paintings, for example—represents a store of value. Financial assets, such as stocks and bonds, offer an important benefit relative to holding money because they pay a higher rate of interest or may increase in value in the future. Other assets also have advantages relative to money because they provide services. A house, for example, offers you a place to sleep.

Why, then, do people hold any money? The answer has to do with *liquidity*, or the ease with which an asset can be converted into the medium of exchange. Because money is the medium of exchange, it is the most liquid asset. If you want to buy something and you need to sell an asset to do so, you are likely to incur a cost. For example, if you want to buy a car and need to sell bonds or stocks in order to do so, you will need to pay a commission to your broker. To avoid such costs, people are willing to hold some of their wealth in the form of money, even though other assets offer a greater return as a store of value.

Standard of Deferred Payment Money is useful because it can serve as a standard of deferred payment in borrowing and lending. Money can facilitate exchange at a *given point in time* by providing a medium of exchange and unit of account. Money can facilitate exchange *over time* by providing a store of value and a standard of deferred payment. For example, a computer manufacturer may buy hard drives from another firm in exchange for the promise of making payment in 60 days.

How important is it that money be a reliable store of value and standard of deferred payment? People care about how much food, clothing, and other goods and services their dollars will buy. The value of money depends on its purchasing power, which refers to its ability to buy goods and services. Inflation causes a decline in purchasing power because with rising prices, a given amount of money can purchase fewer goods and services. When inflation reaches the levels seen in Zimbabwe, money is no longer a reliable store of value or standard of deferred payment.

What Can Serve as Money?

Having a medium of exchange helps make transactions easier, allowing the economy to work more efficiently. The next logical question is this: What can serve as money? That is, which assets should be used as the medium of exchange? We saw earlier that an asset must, at a minimum, be generally accepted as payment to serve as money. In practical terms, however, it must be even more.

Five criteria make a good suitable for use as a medium of exchange:

1. The good must be *acceptable* to (i.e., usable by) most people.
2. It should be of *standardized quality* so that any two units are identical.
3. It should be *durable* so that value is not lost by spoilage.
4. It should be *valuable* relative to its weight so that amounts large enough to be useful in trade can be easily transported.
5. The medium of exchange should be *divisible* because different goods are valued differently.

Dollar bills meet all these criteria. What determines the acceptability of dollar bills as a medium of exchange? Basically, it is through self-fulfilling expectations: You value something as money only if you believe that others will accept it from you as payment. A society's willingness to use paper dollars as money makes dollars an acceptable medium of exchange.

Commodity Money Commodity money has value independent of its use as money. Gold, for example, was a common form of money in the nineteenth century because it was a medium of exchange, a unit of account, a store of value, and a standard of deferred payment. But commodity money has a significant problem: Its value depends on its purity. Therefore, someone who wanted to cheat could mix impure metals with a precious metal. Another problem with using gold as money was that the money supply was difficult to control because it depended partly on unpredictable discoveries of new gold fields.

Bank of Canada The central bank of Canada.

Fiat money Money, such as paper currency, that is authorized by a central bank or governmental body and that does not have to be exchanged by the central bank for gold or some other commodity money.

Fiat Money It can be inefficient for an economy to rely on only gold or other precious metals for its money supply. What if you had to transport bars of gold to settle your transactions? Not only would doing so be difficult and costly, but you would run the risk of being robbed. To get around this problem, private institutions or governments began to store gold and issue paper certificates that could be redeemed for gold. In modern economies, paper currency is generally issued by a *central bank*, which is an agency of the government that regulates the money supply. The **Bank of Canada** is the central bank of Canada. Today, no government in the world issues paper currency that can be redeemed for gold. Paper currency has no value unless it is used as money, and it is therefore not a commodity money. Instead, paper currency is a **fiat money**, which has no value except as money. If paper currency has no value except as money, why do consumers and firms use it?

Canadian currency is fiat money, which means the Bank of Canada is not required to give you gold, silver, or even beaver pelts for your five dollar bills. Currency is *legal tender* in Canada, which means the federal government requires that it be accepted in payment of debts and requires that cash or cheques denominated in dollars be used in payment of taxes. Despite being legal tender, dollar bills would not be a good medium of exchange and could not serve as money if they weren't widely accepted by people. The key to this acceptance is that *households and firms have confidence that if they accept paper dollars in exchange for goods and services, the dollars will not lose much value during the time they hold them.* Without this confidence, dollar bills would not serve as a medium of exchange.

<table>
<tr><td>Making
the
Connection</td></tr>
</table>

The Pokémon Currency System

Many college and university students remember the collectable card game called Pokémon. The game was wildly popular among elementary school children in the late 1990s and early 2000s. To succeed at the game, players needed to collect cards to form decks. Some cards were harder to find than others, and some cards were more useful in the game than others. To add to the complexity, cards were sold in sealed packets, so players did not know which cards they were getting until after the purchase. This led to players trading the cards with one another or even trading parts of their lunch or favours for cards.

At a number of different schools, something remarkable began to happen. Students with no interest in playing the game began to accept Pokémon cards as payment for favours or in exchange for parts of their lunch. Why would these students accept cards for a game they did not play? Because they knew they would be able to trade them to other students for things they truly did want.

Essentially, Pokémon cards began to circulate as money. Different cards had different values attached to them, just as different bills have different values. For example, a Charizard card (below) was worth a lot more than a Rattata card, just as a Canadian bill with 100 on it is worth more than a Canadian bill with a 5 on it. Elementary school children recreated a currency system much like the system that has taken hundreds of years to evolve and is in use throughout the world today.

Warner Bros. Pictures/Getty Images

Your Turn: Test your understanding by doing related problem 1.5 on page 322 at the end of this chapter.

MyEconLab

How Is Money Measured in Canada Today?

10.2 LEARNING OBJECTIVE

Discuss the definitions of the money supply used in Canada today.

A narrow definition of *money* would include only those assets that obviously function as a medium of exchange: currency, chequing account deposits, and traveller's cheques. These assets can easily be used to buy goods and services and thus act as a medium of exchange. This strict interpretation is too narrow, however, as a measure of the money supply in the real world. Many other assets can fill the role of a medium of exchange, although they are not as liquid as chequing account deposits or cash. For example, you can convert your savings account at a bank to cash.

The Bank of Canada has conducted several studies to determine the appropriate definition of *money*. The job of defining the money supply has become more difficult

Figure 10.1

Components of the Money Supply

The Bank of Canada uses six different definitions of the money supply: M1+, M1++, M2, M2+, M2++, and M3. M1+ is the narrowest definition of the money supply and M2++ is the broadest.

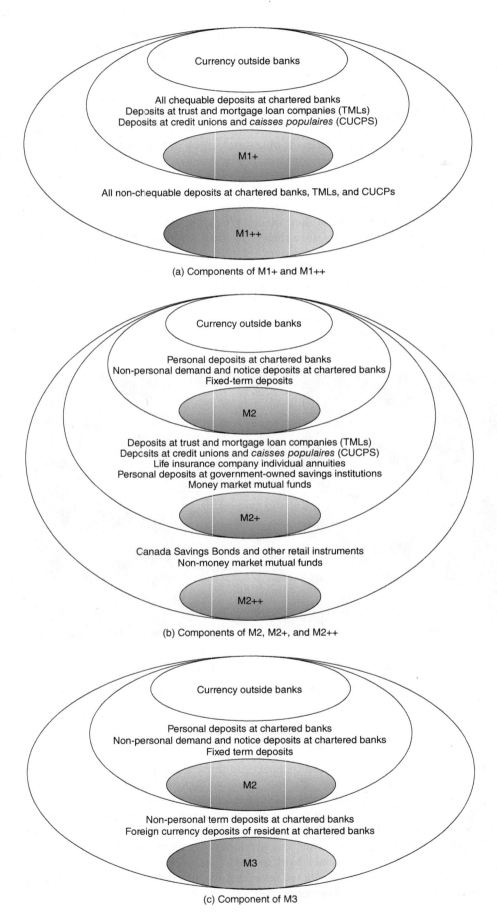

Currency outside banks

All chequable deposits at chartered banks
Deposits at trust and mortgage loan companies (TMLs)
Deposits at credit unions and *caisses populaires* (CUCPS)

M1+

All non-chequable deposits at chartered banks, TMLs, and CUCPs

M1++

(a) Components of M1+ and M1++

Currency outside banks

Personal deposits at chartered banks
Non-personal demand and notice deposits at chartered banks
Fixed-term deposits

M2

Deposits at trust and mortgage loan companies (TMLs)
Deposits at credit unions and *caisses populaires* (CUCPS)
Life insurance company individual annuities
Personal deposits at government-owned savings institutions
Money market mutual funds

M2+

Canada Savings Bonds and other retail instruments
Non-money market mutual funds

M2++

(b) Components of M2, M2+, and M2++

Currency outside banks

Personal deposits at chartered banks
Non-personal demand and notice deposits at chartered banks
Fixed term deposits

M2

Non-personal term deposits at chartered banks
Foreign currency deposits of resident at chartered banks

M3

(c) Component of M3

during the past two decades, as innovation in financial markets and institutions has created new substitutes for traditional chequing account deposits. The Bank of Canada uses six different definitions of the money supply: M1+, M1++, M2, M2+, M2++, and M3.

Next, we will look more closely at the Bank of Canada's definitions of the money supply. Central banks outside of Canada use similar measures.

The M1+ and M1++ Definitions of the Money Supply

Panel (a) of Figure 10.1 illustrates the narrow definitions of the money supply in Canada. The narrowest definition is called **M1+**. It includes the following:

1. *Currency,* which is all the paper money and coins that are in circulation, where "in circulation" means not held by banks or the government
2. The value of all chequable deposits at chartered banks, trust and mortgage loan companies (TMLs), and credit unions and *caisses populaires* (CUCPs)

These assets are all extremely liquid because they can be turned into cash quickly at very little cost. A broader definition of the money supply is **M1++**. As panel (a) of Figure 10.1 shows, M1++ includes everything that is in M1+ as well as all non-chequable deposits at chartered banks, TMLs, and CUCPs.

The M2, M2+, and M2++ Definitions of the Money Supply

As panel (b) of Figure 10.1 shows, the **M2** money supply includes currency, personal deposits at chartered banks, non-personal demand and notice deposits at chartered banks, and fixed-term deposits. The **M2+** money supply includes everything that is in M2 plus deposits at TMLs, deposits at CUCPs, life insurance company individual annuities, personal deposits at government-owned savings institutions, and money market mutual funds. **M2++** is the broadest definition of the money supply in Canada and includes everything that is in M2+ as well as Canada Savings Bonds and other retail instruments, and non-money market mutual funds.

The M3 Definition of the Money Supply

Another definition of the money supply is *M3*. As panel (c) of Figure 10.1 shows, **M3** includes everything that is in M2 plus non-personal term deposits at chartered banks, and foreign currency deposits of residents at chartered banks.

In the discussion that follows, we will use the M1+ definition of the money supply because it corresponds most closely to money as a medium of exchange. However, there are two key points to keep in mind about the money supply:

1. The money supply consists of *both* currency and chequing and non-chequing account deposits.
2. Because balances in chequing and non-chequing account deposits are included in the money supply, banks play an important role in the way the money supply increases and decreases.

We will discuss this second point further in the next section.

M1+ The narrowest definition of the money supply: It includes currency and other assets that have cheque-writing features—all chequable deposits at chartered banks, TMLs, and CUCPs.

M1++ This broader definition of the money supply includes everything that is in M1+ as well as all non-chequable deposits at chartered banks, TMLs, and CUCPs.

M2 A monetary aggregate that includes currency outside banks and personal deposits at chartered banks, non-personal demand and notice deposits at chartered banks, and fixed-term deposits.

M2+ A broader monetary aggregate that includes everything that is in M2 plus deposits at TMLs, deposits at CUCPs, life insurance company individual annuities, personal deposits at government-owned savings institutions, and money market mutual funds.

M2++ The broadest definition of the money supply: It includes everything that is in M2+ as well as Canada Savings Bonds and other retail instruments, and non-money market mutual funds.

M3 A category within the money supply that includes everything that is in M2 plus non-personal term deposits at chartered banks and foreign currency deposits of residents at chartered banks.

Making the Connection | Canada Drops the Penny

We have seen that fiat money has no value except as money. Governments actually make a profit from issuing fiat money because fiat money is usually produced using paper or low-value metals that cost far less than the face value of the money. For example, it costs only about 4 cents to manufacture a $20 bill. The government's profit from issuing fiat money—which is equal to the difference between the face value of the money and its production cost—is called *seigniorage*.

Unfortunately, these cost the government more than a penny to produce.

James L. Amos/Science Source

With small-denomination coins—like pennies or nickels—there is a possibility that the coins will cost more to produce than their face value. This was true in recent years after the rising price of copper meant that the Royal Canadian Mint was spending more than 1 cent to produce a penny. Not only does it cost more to produce a penny than it is worth, but inflation had eroded the penny's purchasing power to such an extent that some people just found it to be a nuisance. Many people would not bother to pick up a penny from the sidewalk.

Because of a growing movement to get rid of the penny, in its 2012 budget, the federal government announced that it would scrap the penny, ending 150 years of penny production. As a result, the Canadian Mint stopped distributing pennies to banks in the fall of 2012, and the government started the process of withdrawing pennies from circulation. In fact, several countries, including Great Britain, Australia, and the European countries that use the euro, have already eliminated their lowest-denomination coins.

Your Turn: Test your understanding by doing related problems 2.7 and 2.8 on page 322 at the end of this chapter.

MyEconLab

Don't Let This Happen to You

Don't Confuse Money with Income or Wealth

According to *Forbes* magazine, Bill Gates's wealth of US$56 billion makes him the second-richest person in the world. He also has a very large income, but how much money does he have? Your *wealth* is equal to the value of your assets minus the value of any debts you have. Your *income* is equal to your earnings during the year. Bill Gates's earnings as chairman of Microsoft and from his investments are very large. But his *money* is just equal to what he has in currency and in chequing accounts. Only a small proportion of Gates's US$56 billion in wealth is likely to be in currency or chequing accounts. Most of his wealth is invested in stocks and bonds and other financial assets that are not included in the definition of money.

In everyday conversation, we often describe someone who is wealthy or who has a high income as "having a lot of money." But when economists use the word *money*, they are usually referring to currency plus chequing account deposits. It is important to keep straight the differences between wealth, income, and money.

Just as money and income are not the same for a person, they are not the same for the whole economy. National income in Canada was equal to $1.7 trillion in 2011. The money supply in 2011 was $618 billion (using the M1+ measure). There is no reason national income in a country should be equal to the country's money supply, nor will an increase in a country's money supply necessarily increase the country's national income.

Source: Based on "The World's Billionaires," Forbes, March 19, 2011.

MyEconLab
Your Turn: Test your understanding by doing related problems 2.4 and 2.5 on page 322 at the end of this chapter.

Solved Problem **10.1**

The Definitions of M1+ and M1++

Suppose that you decide to withdraw $2000 from your chequing account and use the money to buy Canada Savings Bonds. Briefly explain how this will affect M1+ and M1++.

Solving the Problem

Step 1: **Review the chapter material.** This problem is about the definitions of the money supply, so you may want to review the section "How Is Money Measured in Canada Today?" which begins on page 295.

Step 2: **Use the definitions of M1+ and M1++ to answer the problem.** Funds in chequable deposit accounts are included in both M1+ and M1++. Funds in non-chequable deposit accounts are included only in M1++. It is tempting to answer this problem by saying that shifting $2000 from a chequable deposit account to a non-chequable deposit account reduces M1+ by $2000 and increases M1++ by $2000, but the $2000 in your chequable deposit account was already counted in M1++. So, the correct answer is that your action reduces M1+ by $2000 but leaves M1++ unchanged.

Your Turn: For more practice, do related problems 2.2 and 2.3 on page 322 at the end of this chapter.

MyEconLab

What about Credit Cards and Debit Cards?

Many people buy goods and services with credit cards, yet credit cards are not included in definitions of the money supply. The reason is that when you buy something with a credit card, you are in effect taking out a loan from the bank that issued the credit card. Only when you pay your credit card bill at the end of the month—often with a cheque or an electronic transfer from your chequing account—is the transaction complete. In contrast, with a debit card, the funds to make the purchase are taken directly from your chequing account. In either case, the cards themselves do not represent money.

How Do Banks Create Money?

We have seen that the most important component of the money supply is chequing accounts in banks. To understand the role money plays in the economy, we need to look more closely at how banks operate. Banks are profit-making private businesses, just like bookstores and supermarkets. Some banks are quite small, with just a few branches, and they do business in a limited area. Others are among the largest corporations in Canada, with hundreds of branches spread across many provinces. The key role that banks play in the economy is to accept deposits and make loans. By doing this, they create chequing account deposits.

10.3 LEARNING OBJECTIVE

Explain how banks create money.

Bank Balance Sheets

To understand how banks create money, we need to briefly examine a typical bank balance sheet. In a balance sheet, a firm's assets are listed on the left, and its liabilities and shareholders' equity are listed on the right. Assets are the value of anything owned by the firm, liabilities are the value of anything the firm owes, and shareholders' equity is the difference between the total value of assets and the total value of liabilities. Shareholders' equity represents the value of the firm if it had to be closed, all its assets were sold, and all its liabilities were paid off. A corporation's shareholders' equity is also referred to as its *net worth*.

Figure 10.2 shows the actual balance sheet of Royal Bank of Canada, a large bank. The key assets on a bank's balance sheet are its *reserves*, *loans*, and *securities*, such as Canada bonds.

Reserves are deposits that a bank has retained rather than loaned out or invested. Banks keep reserves either physically within the bank, as *vault cash*, or on deposit with the Bank of Canada. Banks desire to keep a fraction of their deposits as reserves: in 2011, banks kept about 5 percent of their deposits as reserves. These reserves are

Reserves Deposits that a bank keeps as cash in its vault or on deposit with the Bank of Canada.

Figure 10.2

Balance Sheet for Royal Bank, October 31, 2011

The items on a bank's balance sheet of greatest economic importance are its reserves, loans, and deposits. Notice that the difference between the value of this bank's total assets and its total liabilities is equal to its shareholders' equity. As a consequence, the left side of the balance sheet always equals the right side.

Note: Some entries have been combined to simplify the balance sheet.

Source: Data from Royal Bank Annual Report 2011, p. 37. (Accessed 21 February 2012)

Assets (in millions)		Liabilities and Stockholders' Equity (in millions)	
Reserves	$13 247	Deposits	$444 181
Loans	296 284	Borrowing	111 127
Securities	179 558	Other liabilities	154 687
Other assets	262 613		
		Total liabilities	709 995
		Shareholders' equity	41 707
Total assets	$751 702	Total liabilities and shareholders' equity	$751 702

Desired reserves Reserves that a bank desires to hold, based on its chequing account deposits.

Desired reserve ratio The minimum fraction of deposits banks desire to keep as reserves.

Excess reserves Reserves that banks hold over and above the desired amounts.

called **desired reserves**. The minimum fraction of deposits that banks desire to keep as reserves is called the **desired reserve ratio**. We can abbreviate the desired reserve ratio as r_d. Any reserves that banks hold over and above the desired amounts are called **excess reserves**. The balance sheet in Figure 10.2 shows that loans are this bank's largest asset, which is true of most banks.

Banks make *consumer loans* to households and *commercial loans* to businesses. A loan is an asset to a bank because it represents a promise by the person taking out the loan to make certain specified payments to the bank. A bank's reserves and its holdings of securities are also assets because they are things of value owned by the bank.

As with most banks, this bank's largest liability is its deposits. Deposits include chequing accounts, savings accounts, and certificates of deposit. Deposits are liabilities to banks because they are owed to the households or firms that have deposited the funds. If you deposit $100 in your chequing account, the bank owes you the $100, and you can ask for it back at any time. So, your chequing account is an asset to you, and it is a liability to the bank.

Using T-Accounts to Show How a Bank Can Create Money

It is easier to show how banks create money by using a T-account than by using a balance sheet. A T-account is a stripped-down version of a balance sheet that shows only how a transaction *changes* a bank's balance sheet. For example, suppose that you deposit $1000 in currency into an account at Bank of Montreal. This transaction raises the total deposits at Bank of Montreal by $1000 and also raises its reserves by $1000. We show this on the following T-account:

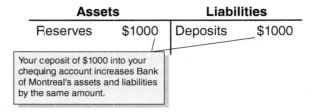

Remember that because the total value of all the entries on the right side of a balance sheet must always be equal to the total value of all the entries on the left side of a balance sheet, any transaction that increases (or decreases) one side of the balance sheet must also increase (or decrease) the other side of the balance sheet. In this case, the T-account shows that we increased both sides of the balance sheet by $1000.

Initially, this transaction does not increase the money supply. The currency component of the money supply declines by $1000 because the $1000 you deposited is no longer in circulation and, therefore, is not counted in the money supply. But the decrease in currency is offset by a $1000 increase in the chequing account deposit component of the money supply.

This initial change is not the end of the story, however. To simplify the analysis, assume that banks keep 10 percent of deposits as reserves. Because the Bank of Canada pays banks only a low rate of interest on their reserves, the bank rate less 50 basis points, banks have an incentive to loan out or buy securities with the other 90 percent. In this case, Bank of Montreal can keep $100 as desired reserves and loan out the other $900, which represents excess reserves. Suppose Bank of Montreal loans out the $900 to someone to buy a very inexpensive used car. Bank of Montreal could give the $900 to the borrower in currency, but usually banks make loans by increasing the borrower's chequing account. We can show this with another T-account:

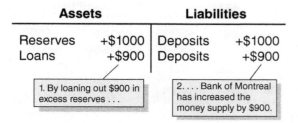

A key point to recognize is that *by making this $900 loan, Bank of Montreal has increased the money supply by $900*. The initial $1000 in currency you deposited into your chequing account has been turned into $1900 in chequing account deposits—a net increase in the money supply of $900.

But the story does not end here. The person who took out the $900 loan did so to buy a used car. To keep things simple, let's suppose he buys the car for exactly $900 and pays by writing a cheque on his account at Bank of Montreal. The seller of the used car will now deposit the cheque in her bank. That bank may also be a branch of Bank of Montreal, but in most cities, there are many banks, so let's assume that the seller of the car has her account at a branch of Royal Bank. Once she deposits the cheque, Royal Bank will send it to Bank of Montreal to *clear* the cheque and collect the $900. We show the result in the following T-accounts:

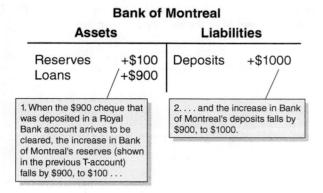

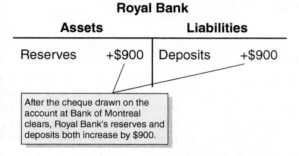

After the car buyer's cheque clears, Bank of Montreal has lost $900 in deposits—the amount loaned to the car buyer—and $900 in reserves—the amount it had to pay Royal

Bank when Royal Bank sent Bank of Montreal the car buyer's cheque. Royal Bank has an increase in chequing account deposits of $900—the deposit of the car seller—and an increase in reserves of $900—the amount it received from Bank of Montreal.

Royal Bank has 100 percent reserves against this new $900 deposit, when it needs only 10 percent reserves. The bank has an incentive to keep $90 as reserves and to loan out the other $810, which are excess reserves. If Royal Bank does this, we can show the change in its balance sheet by using another T-account:

Royal Bank

Assets		**Liabilities**	
Reserves	+$900	Deposits	+$900
Loans	+$810	Deposits	+$810

By making an $810 loan, Royal Bank has increased both its loans and its deposits by $810.

In loaning out the $810 in excess reserves, Royal Bank creates a new chequing account deposit of $810. The initial deposit of $1000 in currency into Bank of Montreal has now resulted in the creation of $1000 + $900 + $810 = $2710 in chequing account deposits. The money supply has increased by $2710 – $1000 = $1710.

The process is still not finished. The person who borrows the $810 will spend it by writing a cheque against his account. Whoever receives the $810 will deposit it in her bank, which could be a Bank of Montreal branch or a Royal Bank branch or a branch of some other bank. That new bank—if it's not Royal Bank—will send the cheque to Royal Bank and will receive $810 in new reserves. That new bank will have an incentive to loan out 90 percent of these reserves—keeping 10 percent to meet the desired reserves—and the process will go on. At each stage, the additional loans being made and the additional deposits being created are shrinking by 10 percent, as each bank wants to withhold that amount as desired reserves. We can use a table to show the total increase in chequing account deposits set off by your initial deposit of $1000. The dots in the table represent additional rounds in the money creation process:

Bank	Increase in Chequing Account Deposits
Bank of Montreal	$1000
Royal Bank	+ 900 (= 0.9 × $1000)
Third Bank	+ 810 (= 0.9 × $ 900)
Fourth Bank	+ 729 (= 0.9 × $ 810)
•	+ •
•	+ •
•	+ •
Total change in chequing account deposits	= $10 000

The Simple Deposit Multiplier

Simple deposit multiplier The ratio of the amount of deposits created by banks to the amount of new reserves.

Your initial deposit of $1000 increased the reserves of the banking system by $1000 and led to a total increase in chequing account deposits of $10 000. The ratio of the amount of deposits created by banks to the amount of new reserves is called the **simple deposit multiplier**. In this case, the simple deposit multiplier is equal to $10 000/$1000 = 10. Why 10? How do we know that your initial $1000 deposit ultimately leads to a total increase in deposits of $10 000?

There are two ways to answer this question. First, each bank in the process is keeping desired reserves equal to 10 percent of its deposits. For the banking system as a whole, the total increase in reserves is $1000—the amount of your original currency deposit. Therefore, the system as a whole will end up with $10 000 in deposits because $1000 is 10 percent of $10 000.

A second way to answer the question is by deriving an expression for the simple deposit multiplier. The total increase in deposits equals:

$$\$1000 + [0.9 \times \$1000] + [(0.9 \times 0.9) \times \$1000] + [(0.9 \times 0.9 \times 0.9) \times \$1000] + \ldots$$

or

$$\$1000 \times [0.9 \times \$1000] + [0.9^2 \times \$1000] + [0.9^3 \times \$1000] + \ldots$$

or

$$\$1000 \times (1 + 0.9 + 0.9^2 + 0.9^3 + \ldots).$$

The rules of algebra tell us that an expression like the one in the parentheses sums to

$$\frac{1}{1 - 0.9}$$

Simplifying further, we have

$$\frac{1}{0.10} = 10.$$

So

$$\text{Total increase in deposit} = \$1000 \times 10 = \$10\ 000$$

Note that 10 is equal to 1 divided by the desired reserve ratio, r_d, which in this case is 10 percent, or 0.10. This gives us another way of expressing the simple deposit multiplier:

$$\text{Simple deposit multiplier} = \frac{1}{r_d}$$

This formula makes it clear that the higher the desired reserve ratio, the smaller the simple deposit multiplier. With a desired reserve ratio of 10 percent, the simple deposit multiplier is 10. If the desired reserve ratio were 20 percent, the simple deposit multiplier would fall to 1/0.20, or 5. We can use this formula to calculate the total increase in chequing account deposits from an increase in bank reserves due to, for instance, currency being deposited in a bank:

$$\text{Change in chequing account deposits} = \text{Change in bank reserves} \times \frac{1}{r_d}$$

For example, if $100 000 in currency is deposited in a bank and the desired reserve ratio is 10 percent, then:

$$\text{Change in chequing account deposits} = \$100\ 000 \times \frac{1}{0.10}$$

$$= \$100\ 000 \times 10 = \$1\ 000\ 000$$

Don't Let This Happen to You

Don't Confuse Assets and Liabilities

Consider the following reasoning: "How can chequing account deposits be a liability to a bank? After all, they are something of value that is in the bank. Therefore, chequing account deposits should be counted as a bank *asset* rather than as a bank liability."

This statement is incorrect. The balance in a chequing account represents something the bank *owes* to the owner of the account. Therefore, it is a liability to the bank, although it is an asset to the owner of the account. Similarly, your car loan is a liability to you—because it is a debt you owe to the bank—but it is an asset to the bank.

MyEconLab

Your Turn: Test your understanding by doing related problem 3.5 on page 323 at the end of this chapter.

Solved Problem **10.2**

Showing How Banks Create Money

Suppose that you deposit $5000 in currency into your chequing account at a branch of Royal Bank, which we will assume has no excess reserves at the time you make your deposit. Also assume that the desired reserve ratio is 0.10.

a. Use a T-account to show the initial effect of this transaction on Royal Bank's balance sheet.
b. Suppose that Royal Bank makes the maximum loan it can from the funds you deposited. Use a T-account to show the initial effect on Royal Bank's balance sheet from granting the loan. Also include in this T-account the transaction from question (a).

c. Now suppose that whoever took out the loan in question (b) writes a cheque for this amount and that the person receiving the cheque deposits it in Bank of Montreal. Show the effect of these transactions on the balance sheets of Royal Bank and Bank of Montreal *after the cheque has cleared.* On the T-account for Royal Bank, include the transactions from questions (a) and (b).
d. What is the maximum increase in chequing account deposits that can result from your $5000 deposit? What is the maximum increase in the money supply that can result from your deposit? Explain.

Solving the Problem

Step 1: Review the chapter material. This problem is about how banks create chequing account deposits, so you may want to review the section "Using T-Accounts to Show How a Bank Can Create Money," which begins on page 300.

Step 2: Answer part (a) by using a T-account to show the effect of the deposit. Keeping in mind that T-accounts show only the changes in a balance sheet that result from the relevant transaction and that assets are on the left side of the account and liabilities are on the right side, we have:

Royal Bank

Assets		Liabilities	
Reserves	+$5000	Deposits	+$5000

Because the bank now has your $5000 in currency in its vault, its reserves (and, therefore, its assets) have risen by $5000. But this transaction also increases your chequing account balance by $5000. Because the bank owes you this money, the bank's liabilities have also risen by $5000.

Step 3: Answer part (b) by using a T-account to show the effect of the loan. The problem tells you to assume that Royal Bank currently has no excess reserves and that the desired reserve ratio is 10 percent. This means that if the bank's chequing account deposits go up by $5000, the bank wants to keep $500 as reserves and can loan out the remaining $4500. Remembering that new loans usually take the form of setting up, or increasing, a chequing account for the borrower, we have:

Royal Bank

Assets		Liabilities	
Reserves	+$5000	Deposits	+$5000
Loans	+$4500	Deposits	+$4500

The first line of the T-account shows the transaction from question (a). The second line shows that Royal Bank has loaned out $4500 by increasing the chequing account of the borrower by $4500. The loan is an asset to Royal Bank because it represents a promise by the borrower to make certain payments spelled out in the loan agreement.

Step 4: **Answer part (c) by using T-accounts for Royal Bank and Bank of Montreal to show the effect of the cheque clearing.** We now show the effect of the borrower having spent the $4500 he received as a loan from Royal Bank. The person who received the $4500 cheque deposits it in her account at Bank of Montreal. We need two T-accounts to show this activity:

Royal Bank

Assets		Liabilities	
Reserves	+$500	Deposits	+$5000
Loans	+$4500		

Bank of Montreal

Assets		Liabilities	
Reserves	+$4500	Deposits	+$4500

Look first at the T-account for Royal Bank. Once Bank of Montreal sends the cheque written by the borrower to Royal Bank, Royal Bank loses $4500 in reserves, and Bank of Montreal gains $4500 in reserves. The $4500 is also deducted from the account of the borrower. Royal Bank is now satisfied with the result. It received a $5000 deposit in currency from you. When that money was sitting in the bank vault, it wasn't earning any interest for Royal Bank. Now $4500 of the $5000 has been loaned out and is earning interest. These interest payments allow Royal Bank to cover its costs and earn a profit, which it has to do to remain in business.

Bank of Montreal now has an increase in deposits of $4500, resulting from the cheque being deposited, and an increase in reserves of $4500. Bank of Montreal is in the same situation as Royal Bank was in question (a): It has excess reserves as a result of this transaction and a strong incentive to lend them out.

Step 5: **Answer part (d) by using the simple deposit multiplier formula to calculate the maximum increase in chequing account deposits and the maximum increase in the money supply.** The simple deposit multiplier expression is (remember that r_d is the desired reserve ratio)

$$\text{Change in chequing account deposits} = \text{Change in bank reserves} \times \frac{1}{r_d}$$

In this case, bank reserves rose by $5000 as a result of your initial deposit, and the desired reserve ratio is 0.10, so

$$\text{Change in chequing account deposits} = \$5000 \times \frac{1}{0.10}$$

$$= \$5000 \times 10 = \$50\ 000$$

Because chequing account deposits are part of the money supply, it is tempting to say that the money supply has also increased by $50 000. Remember, though, that your $5000 in currency was counted as part of the money supply while you had it, but it is not included when it is sitting in a bank vault. Therefore:

Increase in chequing account deposits − Decline in currency in circulation = Change in the money supply

or

$$\$50\ 000 - \$5000 = \$45\ 000.$$

Your Turn: For more practice, do related problem 3.3 on page 322 at the end of the chapter.

MyEconLab

The Simple Deposit Multiplier versus the Real-World Deposit Multiplier

The story we have told about the way an increase in reserves in the banking system leads to the creation of new deposits and, therefore, an increase in the money supply has been simplified in two ways. First, we assumed that banks do not keep any excess reserves. That is, we assumed that when you deposited $1000 in currency into your chequing account at Bank of Montreal, it loaned out $900, keeping only the $100 in desired reserves. In fact, banks often, and especially during anxious times, keep some excess reserves to guard against the possibility that many depositors may simultaneously make withdrawals from their accounts. During the financial crisis that began in 2007, banks kept substantial excess reserves. The more excess reserves banks keep, the smaller the deposit multiplier. Imagine an extreme case in which Bank of Montreal keeps your entire $1000 as reserves. If Bank of Montreal does not loan out any of your deposit, the process described earlier—loans leading to the creation of new deposits, leading to the making of additional loans, and so on—will not take place. The $1000 increase in reserves will lead to a total increase of $1000 in deposits, and the deposit multiplier will be only 1, not 10.

Second, we assumed that the whole amount of every cheque is deposited in a bank; no one takes any of it out as currency. In reality, households and firms keep roughly constant the amount of currency they hold relative to the value of their chequing account balances. So, we would expect to see people increasing the amount of currency they hold as the balances in their chequing accounts rise. Once again, think of the extreme case. Suppose that when Bank of Montreal makes the initial $900 loan to the borrower who wants to buy a used car, the seller of the car cashes the cheque instead of depositing it. In that case, Royal Bank does not receive any new reserves and does not make any new loans. Once again, the $1000 increase in your chequing account at Bank of Montreal is the only increase in deposits, and the deposit multiplier is 1.

The effect of these two factors is to reduce the real-world deposit multiplier. However, the key point to bear in mind is that the most important part of the money supply is the chequing account balance component. When banks make loans, they increase chequing account balances, and the money supply expands. Banks make new loans whenever they gain reserves. The whole process can also work in reverse: If banks lose reserves, they reduce their outstanding loans and deposits, and the money supply contracts.

We can summarize these important conclusions:

1. When banks gain reserves, they make new loans, and the money supply expands.
2. When banks lose reserves, they reduce their loans, and the money supply contracts.

10.4 LEARNING OBJECTIVE

Discuss the policy tools the Bank of Canada uses to manage the money supply.

Fractional reserve banking system A banking system in which banks keep less than 100 percent of deposits as reserves.

Bank run A situation in which many depositors simultaneously decide to withdraw money from a bank.

Bank panic A situation in which many banks experience runs at the same time.

The Bank of Canada

Many people are surprised to learn that banks do not keep locked away in their vaults all the funds that are deposited in chequing accounts. Canada, like nearly all other countries, has a **fractional reserve banking system**, which means that banks keep less than 100 percent of deposits as reserves. When people deposit money in a bank, the bank loans most of the money to someone else. What happens, though, if depositors want their money back? This would seem to be a problem because banks have loaned out most of the money and can't easily get it back.

In practice, though, withdrawals are usually not a problem for banks. On a typical day, about as much money is deposited as is withdrawn. If a small amount more is withdrawn than deposited, banks can cover the difference from their excess reserves or by borrowing from other banks. Sometimes depositors lose confidence in a bank when they question the value of the bank's underlying assets, particularly its loans. Often, the reason for a loss of confidence is bad news, whether true or false. When many depositors simultaneously decide to withdraw their money from a bank, there is a **bank run**. If many banks experience runs at the same time, the result is a **bank panic**. It is possible for one bank to handle a run by borrowing from other banks, but if many banks simultaneously experience runs, the banking system may be in trouble.

A *central bank*, like the Bank of Canada, can help stop a bank panic by acting as a *lender of last resort*. In acting as a lender of last resort, a central bank makes loans to banks that can't borrow funds elsewhere. The banks can use these loans to pay off depositors. When the panic ends and the depositors put their money back in their accounts, the banks can repay the loans to the central bank.

The Establishment of the Bank of Canada

The Bank of Canada plays a central role in the Canadian economy. It conducts monetary policy, designs and issues currency, promotes a stable financial system, manages the funds of the federal government, and even engages in important economic research. Given its important role in the Canadian economy, you might be surprised to learn that the Bank of Canada is less than 100 years old. It was created after a Royal Commission in 1933 and came into being in 1934.

The overall responsibility for the operation of the Bank of Canada rests with a **board of directors**, which consists of 15 members—the governor, the senior deputy governor, the deputy minister of finance, and 12 outside directors. The board appoints the governor and senior deputy governor, with the government's approval, for a renewable term of seven years. The outside directors are appointed by the minister of finance, with Cabinet approval, for a three-year term, and they are required to come from all regions of Canada and represent a variety of occupations with the exception of banking. The governor of the Bank of Canada is the chief executive officer and chair of the board of directors. Currently, the governor of the Bank of Canada is Stephen Poloz, appointed in May 2013 for a term of seven years.

In 1994 the board of directors made some changes to the internal organization of the Bank of Canada. The most prominent change was the establishment of a new senior decision-making authority within the Bank of Canada called the **governing council**. The governing council is chaired by the governor and is composed of the senior deputy governor and four deputy governors. Since this change, the six members of the governing council collectively assume responsibility for the Bank of Canada's quarterly *Monetary Policy Report that presents the Bank of Canada's projections for inflation and growth and its assessment of risks in the Canadian economy*. This system of "collective responsibility" ensures that the Bank of Canada's governor is not personally identified with the Bank of Canada's policy.

The Bank of Canada is responsible for **monetary policy** in Canada, but the objectives of monetary policy are determined jointly by the Bank of Canada and the minister of finance, with the latter acting on behalf of the federal government. In fact, the governor of the Bank of Canada and the minister of finance consult regularly and, in the event of a serious disagreement over the conduct of monetary policy, the government has the right to override the Bank of Canada's decisions. In particular, the minister of finance can issue a directive to the Bank of Canada indicating the specific policy changes that the Bank of Canada must follow. However, the directive must be published, indicating not only the new policy that the Bank of Canada is supposed to undertake but also the period during which it is to apply.

Hence, ultimate responsibility for monetary policy rests with the democratically elected government. However, because of the consequences of issuing a directive, it is unlikely that such a directive would be issued, and none has been issued to date. (For more information on monetary policy, see Chapter 11.)

The Bank of Canada's Operating Band for the Overnight Interest Rate

The Bank of Canada signals its stance on monetary policy by announcing a target for the **overnight interest rate**. The target for the overnight interest rate, known as the **key policy rate** (or *policy rate*, for short), is the Bank of Canada's main tool for conducting monetary policy. This rate refers to **collateralized transactions** in the

Board of directors (of the Bank of Canada) A board with 15 members (including the governor) that is responsible for the management of the Bank of Canada.

Governing council (of the Bank of Canada) A council with six members (including the governor) that is responsible for the management of the Bank of Canada.

Monetary policy The actions the Bank of Canada takes to manage the money supply and interest rates to pursue macroeconomic policy objectives.

Overnight interest rate The interest rate banks charge each other for overnight loans.

Key policy rate The Bank of Canada's target for the overnight interest rate.

Collateralized transactions Transactions that involve property being pledged to the lender to guarantee payment in the event that the borrower is unable to make debt payments.

Figure 10.3

Operating Band for the Overnight Interest Rate

The upper limit of the operating band for the overnight interest rate defines the bank rate (or lending rate), and the lower limit of the operating band defines the deposit rate.

Source: From The Bank of Canada. Reprinted with permission.

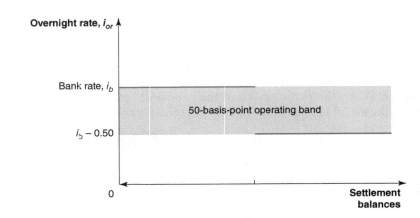

Operating band The Bank of Canada's 50-basis-point range for the overnight interest rate.

Bank rate The interest rate the Bank of Canada charges on loans (advances) to banks.

Settlement balances Deposits held by banks in their accounts at the Bank of Canada.

Advances to banks Loans the Bank of Canada makes to banks.

Standing liquidity facilities The Bank of Canada's readiness to lend to or borrow from a bank.

Open market buyback operations Agreements in which the Bank of Canada, or another party, purchase securities with the understanding that the seller will repurchase them in a short period of time, usually less than a week.

overnight interbank market. (For more information on the overnight interest rate, see Chapter 11.)

In normal times, the Bank of Canada's operational objective is to keep the overnight interest rate within an **operating band** (also known as a *channel* or *corridor*) of 50 basis points (half of 1 percent). This channel/corridor system for setting the overnight interest rate is also used by the Reserve Bank of Australia, the Bank of England, the European Central Bank, the Bank of Japan, the Reserve Bank of New Zealand, Norges Bank of Norway, and the Riksbank of Sweden.

As Figure 10.3 shows, the upper limit of the operating band defines the **bank rate**, i_b. The bank rate is the interest rate the Bank of Canada charges financial institutions that require an overdraft loan to cover negative **settlement balances** on the Bank of Canada's books at the end of the banking day. Loans that the Bank of Canada makes to banks are referred to as **advances to banks**. The lower limit of the operating band is the rate the Bank of Canada pays to financial institutions with positive settlement balances at the end of the day. The midpoint of the operating band is the Bank of Canada's target for the overnight interest rate. For example, when the operating band is from 0.75 percent to 1.25 percent, the bank rate is 1.25 percent, the rate the Bank of Canada pays on deposits to financial institutions is 0.75 percent, and the Bank of Canada's target for the overnight interest rate is 1 percent.

Since December 2000, the Bank of Canada has been operating under a system where any changes to the target and the operating band for the overnight interest rate are announced on eight "fixed" dates throughout the year, and the Bank of Canada has the option of acting between the fixed dates in "extraordinary circumstances." The Bank of Canada implements the operating band for the overnight interest rate by using its **standing liquidity facilities**, lending to and taking deposits from financial institutions. In particular, if the overnight interest rate increases toward the upper limit of the operating band, then the Bank of Canada will lend at the bank rate, i_b, to put a ceiling on the overnight interest rate, i_{or}. If the overnight interest rate declines toward the lower limit of the operating band, then the Bank of Canada will accept deposits from financial institutions at the bank rate less 50 basis points, $i_b - 0.50$, to put a floor on the overnight interest rate.

How the Bank of Canada Implements Monetary Policy

The Bank of Canada is responsible for managing interest rates and the money supply. As we will see in Chapter 11, managing interest rates and the money supply is part of monetary policy, which the Bank of Canada undertakes to pursue macroeconomic objectives (mainly price stability). To manage interest rates and the money supply, the Bank of Canada mainly uses the following two monetary policy tools:

1. Open market buyback operations
2. Lending to financial institutions

Remember that the most important component of the money supply is chequing accounts in banks. Not surprisingly, both of the Bank of Canada's monetary policy tools are aimed at influencing interest rates and bank reserves.

Open Market Buyback Operations **Open market operations** (the buying and selling of government securities) are an important monetary policy tool for many central banks around the world, because they are the primary determinants of changes in interest rates and the money supply. Open market purchases expand bank settlement balances, thereby lowering short-term interest rates and raising the money supply. Open market sales shrink bank reserves and the **monetary base**, raising short-term interest rates and lowering the money supply.

Since 1994, the Bank of Canada's most common open market operations have been repurchase transactions, a special type of open market operations. In particular, the Bank of Canada uses **Purchase and Resale Agreements (PRAs)** as a tool to reduce undesired upward pressure on the overnight interest rate, and **Sale and Repurchase Agreements (SRAs)** as a tool to reduce undesired downward pressure on the overnight interest rate. Let's see how the Bank of Canada uses PRAs and SRAs in order to reinforce the target for the overnight interest rate during the course of a day and to manage the money supply.

Assume that the operating band for the overnight interest rate is 0.75 percent to 1.25 percent and that the Bank of Canada is targeting the overnight interest rate at the midpoint of the band, at 1 percent. If overnight funds are traded at a rate higher than the target rate of 1 percent, then the Bank of Canada enters into PRAs at a price that works out to a 1 percent interest rate, the midpoint of the operating band. That is, the Bank of Canada purchases government of Canada Treasury bills and bonds, with an agreement that the sellers will repurchase those Treasury bills and bonds at a specified time in the future. When the sellers of the Canada securities deposit the funds in their banks, the settlement balance of the banks rise. This increase in reserves starts the process of increasing loans and chequing account deposits that increases the money supply.

If, on the other hand, overnight funds are traded at a rate below the target rate of 1 percent, then the Bank of Canada enters into SRAs, in which the Bank of Canada sells government securities and the buyer agrees to sell them back to the Bank of Canada a number of business days later. When the buyers pay for the securities with cheques, the reserves of their banks fall. This decrease in bank reserves starts a contraction of loans and chequing account deposits that reduces the money supply.

The Bank of Canada conducts monetary policy principally through open market buyback operations for three reasons. First, because the Bank of Canada initiates open market buyback operations, it completely controls their volume. Second, the Bank of Canada can make both large and small open market buyback operations. Third, the Bank of Canada can implement its open market buyback operations quickly, with no administrative delay or required changes in regulations. Many other central banks, including the US Federal Reserve, the European Central Bank, and the Bank of Japan, also use open market operations to conduct monetary policy.

The Bank of Canada is responsible for putting the paper currency of Canada into circulation. Recall that if you look at the top of a Canadian bill, you see the words "Bank of Canada: This Note is Legal Tender." When the Bank of Canada takes actions to increase the money supply, commentators sometimes say that it is "printing more money." The main way the Bank of Canada increases the money supply, however, is not by printing more paper dollars but by buying government securities. Similarly, to reduce the money supply, the Bank of Canada does not set fire to stacks of paper dollars. Instead, it sells government securities. We will spend more time discussing how and why the Bank of Canada manages the money supply in Chapter 11, in which we discuss monetary policy.

Lending to Financial Institutions As we have seen, the Bank of Canada is operating its standing liquidity facilities to reinforce the operating band for the overnight interest rate. When a bank borrows money from the Bank of Canada by taking out a

Open market operations The buying and selling of government securities by the Bank of Canada in order to control the money supply.

Monetary base The sum of the Bank of Canada's monetary liabilities (i.e., paper money in circulation and bank settlement balances) and the Canadian Mint's coins outstanding (i.e., coins in circulation).

Purchase and Resale Agreements (PRAs) The Bank of Canada's purchase of government securities from primary dealers (i.e., banks or securities brokers/dealers), with an agreement to resell them later.

Sale and Repurchase Agreements (SRAs) The Bank of Canada's sale of government securities to primary dealers (i.e., banks or securities brokers/dealers), with an agreement to repurchase them later.

Figure 10.4

How the Bank of Canada Keeps the Rate of Inflation from Falling Below the Target Range

If the Bank of Canada expects the economy to slow down, it lowers the target and operating band for the overnight interest rate. This reduces interest rates and the value of the dollar and leads to an increase in the supply of money, aggregate demand, and the price level, preventing the inflation rate from falling below 1 percent.

Source: From The Bank of Canada. Reprinted with permission.

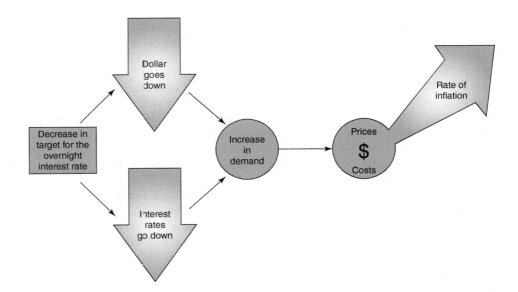

loan, the interest rate the bank pays is the bank rate, i_b, which is typically higher than the target overnight interest rate by 25 basis points. However, the bank's reserves increase, and with more reserves, the bank will make more loans to households and firms, which will increase chequing account deposits and the money supply.

In addition to its use of standing liquidity facilities to reinforce the operating band for the overnight interest rate, Bank of Canada lending is also important in preventing financial panics. In fact, one of the Bank of Canada's most important roles is to be the lender of last resort in the Canadian economy. It provides emergency lending assistance (against eligible collateral) for a maximum period of six months (which can be extended for periods of up to six months as many times as the Bank of Canada judges necessary) to solvent (but illiquid) deposit-taking institutions to prevent bank failures from spinning further out of control, thereby preventing bank and financial panics.

The Bank of Canada's Approach to Monetary Policy

The goal of the Bank of Canada's current monetary policy is to keep the inflation rate within a target range of 1 percent to 3 percent, with the midpoint of the inflation target range, 2 percent, being the most desirable outcome. The Bank of Canada implements monetary policy by changing the policy rate in order to influence other short-term interest rates, the exchange rate, and the level of economic activity.

As an example, suppose that the Bank of Canada expects the economy to slow down and wishes to ease monetary conditions. It lowers the target and operating band for the overnight interest rate. As you can see in Figure 10.4, this reduces interest rates and the value of the dollar and leads to an increase in the supply of money, aggregate demand (the total quantity of output demanded in the economy), and the price level, thereby preventing the inflation rate from falling below the target range of 1 percent to 3 percent.

In the opposite case, if the Bank of Canada expects the economy to exceed its capacity at some point in the future, it raises the operating band in order to prevent inflationary pressures from building. The consequent increase in interest rates and the value of the dollar lead to a decline in the supply of money, aggregate demand, and the inflation rate, thereby preventing the inflation rate from moving above the Bank of Canada's target range of 1 percent to 3 percent (see Figure 10.5).

The "Shadow Banking System" and the Global Financial Crisis of 2007–2009

The banks we have been discussing in this chapter are *commercial banks*, whose most important economic role is to accept funds from depositors and lend those funds to

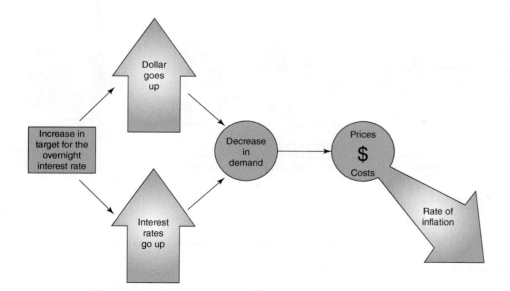

Figure 10.5

How the Bank of Canada Keeps the Rate of Inflation from Moving Above the Target Range

If the Bank of Canada expects the economy to exceed its capacity, it increases the target and operating band for the overnight interest rate. This increases interest rates and the value of the dollar and leads to a decline in the supply of money, aggregate demand, and the inflation rate, preventing the inflation rate from rising above 1 percent.

Source: From The Bank of Canada. Reprinted with permission.

borrowers. In Chapter 6, we noted that large firms can sell stocks and bonds on financial markets but that investors are typically unwilling to buy stocks and bonds from small and medium-sized firms because they lack sufficient information on the financial health of smaller firms. So, smaller firms—and households—have traditionally relied on bank loans for their credit needs. In the past 20 years, however, two important developments have occurred in the financial system: (1) Banks have begun to resell many of their loans rather than keep them until they are paid off, and (2) financial firms other than commercial banks have become sources of credit to businesses.

Securitization Comes to Banking   Traditionally, when a bank made a *residential mortgage loan* to a household to buy a home or made a commercial loan to a business, the bank would keep the loan and collect the payments until the loan was paid off. A financial asset—such as a loan or a stock or a bond—is considered a **security** if it can be bought and sold in a *financial market* as, for instance, shares of stock issued by BlackBerry can be bought and sold on the Toronto Stock Exchange. When a financial asset is first sold, the sale takes place in the *primary market*. Subsequent sales take place in the *secondary market*. Prior to 1970, most loans were not securities because they could not be resold—there was no secondary market for them. First, residential mortgages and then other loans, including car loans and commercial loans, began to be *securitized*. The process of **securitization** involves creating a secondary market in which loans that have been bundled together can be bought and sold in financial markets, just as corporate or government bonds are. Figure 10.6 outlines the securitization process. We will discuss the process of securitization further in Chapter 11, in which we discuss monetary policy.

Security A financial asset—such as a stock or a bond—that can be bought and sold in a financial market.

Securitization The process of transforming loans or other financial assets into securities.

The Shadow Banking System   In addition to the changes resulting from securitization, the financial system was transformed in the 1990s and 2000s by the increasing importance of nonbank financial firms. Investment banks, such as BMO Nesbitt Burns and CIBC World Markets in Canada, and Goldman Sachs and Morgan Stanley in the United States, differ from commercial banks in that they do not accept deposits, and they rarely lend directly to households. Instead, investment banks traditionally concentrated on providing advice to firms issuing stocks and bonds or considering mergers with other firms. In the late 1990s, investment banks expanded their buying of mortgages, bundling large numbers of them together as bonds known as *mortgage-backed securities*, and reselling them to investors. Mortgage-backed securities proved very popular with investors because they often paid higher interest rates than other securities with comparable default risk.

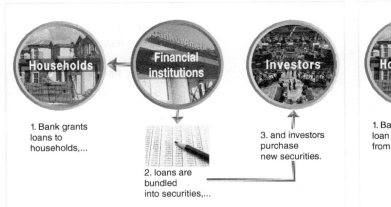

(a) Securitizing a loan

1. Bank grants loans to households,...

2. loans are bundled into securities,...

3. and investors purchase new securities.

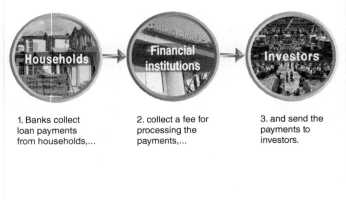

(b) The flow of payments on a securitized loan

1. Banks collect loan payments from households,...

2. collect a fee for processing the payments,...

3. and send the payments to investors.

Figure 10.6 **The Process of Securitization**

Panel (a) shows how in the securitization process banks grant loans to households and bundle the loans into securities that are then sold to investors. Panel (b) shows that banks collect payments on the original loans and, after taking a fee, send the payments to the investors who bought the securities.

Photo credits : (left to right) AP Photos/Lynne Sladky; Ezio Petersen/Landov; © EIGHTFISH / Alamy; (bottom) © imagebroker / Alamy

Money market mutual funds have also increased their importance in the financial system over time. These funds sell shares to investors and use the money to buy short-term securities such as Treasury bills and commercial paper issued by corporations. Commercial paper represents short-term borrowing corporations use to fund their day-to-day operations. Many corporations that previously met such needs by borrowing from banks began instead to sell commercial paper to money market mutual funds.

Hedge funds raise money from wealthy investors and use sophisticated investment strategies that often involve significant risk. By 2005, hedge funds had become an important source of demand for securitized loans and an important source of loans to other financial firms.

In 2008, Timothy Geithner, who was US Secretary of the Treasury during the first term of the Obama administration, referred to investment banks, money market mutual funds, hedge funds, and other financial firms engaged in similar activities as the "shadow banking system." By raising money from individual investors and providing it directly or indirectly to firms and households, these firms were carrying out a function that at one time was almost exclusively the domain of commercial banks.

The Financial Crisis of 2007–2009 The firms in the shadow banking system differed from commercial banks in two important ways: First, the government agencies—including the Office of the Superintendent of Financial Institutions Canada (OSFI) and the Bank of Canada—that regulated the commercial banking system did not regulate these firms. Second, these firms were more highly *leveraged*—that is, they relied more heavily on borrowed money to finance their operations—than were chartered banks. If a firm uses a small amount of its own money and a lot of borrowed money to make an investment, both the firm's potential profits and its potential losses are increased. For example, suppose a firm invests $100 of its own money. If the investment earns a return of $3, the firm has earned 3 percent ($3/$100) on its funds. But if the firm's investment consists of $10 of its own money and $90 it has borrowed, a return of $3 becomes a return of 30 percent ($3/$10) on the firm's $10 investment. If the investment loses $2, however, the firm's return is −20 percent (−$2/$10). Leveraged investments have a potential for both large gains and large losses.

Chartered banks have rarely experienced bank runs since the federal government established the Canada Deposit Insurance Corporation (CDIC) in 1967 to insure deposits (currently up to $100 000) with all federally chartered banks and near banks. However, beginning in 2007, firms in the shadow banking system were quite vulnerable to runs. As we will discuss further in Chapter 11, the underlying cause of the financial crisis of 2007–2009 was problems in the US housing market. As housing prices began to fall in the United States, a significant number of borrowers began to default on their mortgages, which caused mortgage-backed securities to lose value. Financial firms, including both commercial banks and many firms in the shadow banking system, that had invested in these securities suffered heavy losses. The more leveraged the firm, the larger the losses. Although deposit insurance helped commercial banks avoid runs, investment banks and other financial firms that had borrowed short term and invested the funds long term were in trouble. As lenders refused to renew their short-term loans, many of these firms had to sell their holdings of securities in an attempt to raise cash. But as the prices of these securities continued to fall, the losses to these firms increased.

In the spring of 2008, US investment bank Bear Stearns was saved from bankruptcy only when the Federal Reserve arranged for it to be acquired by JPMorgan Chase. In the fall of 2008, the Federal Reserve and the US Treasury decided not to take action to save the investment bank Lehman Brothers, which failed. The failure of Lehman Brothers reverberated throughout the financial system, setting off a panic. The process of securitization—apart from government-guaranteed residential mortgages—ground to a halt. The well-publicized difficulties of a money market mutual fund that had suffered losses on loans to Lehman Brothers led to a wave of withdrawals from these funds. In turn, the funds were no longer able to fulfill their role as buyers of corporate commercial paper. As banks and other financial firms sold assets and cut back on lending to shore up their financial positions, the flow of funds from savers to borrowers was disrupted. The resulting credit crunch significantly worsened the global recession that had begun in December 2007.

The Quantity Theory of Money

10.5 LEARNING OBJECTIVE

Explain the quantity theory of money, and use it to explain how high rates of inflation occur.

People have been aware of the connection between increases in the money supply and inflation for centuries. In the sixteenth century, the Spanish conquered Mexico and Peru and shipped large quantities of gold and silver from those countries back to Spain. The gold and silver were minted into coins and spent across Europe to further the political ambitions of the Spanish kings. Prices in Europe rose steadily during these years, and many observers discussed the relationship between this inflation and the flow of gold and silver into Europe from the Americas.

Connecting Money and Prices: The Quantity Equation

In the early twentieth century, Irving Fisher, an economist at Yale, formalized the connection between money and prices by using the *quantity equation*:

$$M \times V = P \times Y.$$

The quantity equation states that the money supply (M) multiplied by the *velocity of money* (V) equals the price level (P) multiplied by real output (Y). Fisher defined the **velocity of money**, often referred to simply as "velocity," as the average number of times each dollar of the money supply is used to purchase goods and services included in GDP. Rewriting the original equation by dividing both sides by M, we have the equation for velocity:

$$V = \frac{P \times Y}{M}$$

Velocity of money The average number of times per year each dollar in the money supply is used to purchase goods and services included in GDP.

If we use M1+ to measure the money supply, the GDP price deflator to measure the price level, and real GDP to measure real output, the value for velocity for 2012 was as follows:

$$V = \frac{1.27 \times \$1378 \text{ billion}}{\$651 \text{ billion}} = 2.7.$$

This result tells us that, on average during 2012, each dollar of M1+ was spent about 2.7 times on goods or services included in GDP.

Quantity theory of money A theory about the connection between money and prices that assumes that the velocity of money is constant.

Because velocity is defined to be equal to $(P \times Y)/M$, we know that the quantity equation must always hold true: The left side *must* be equal to the right side. A theory is a statement about the world that might possibly be false. Therefore, the quantity equation is not a theory. Irving Fisher turned the quantity equation into the **quantity theory of money** by asserting that velocity was constant. He argued that the average number of times a dollar is spent depends on how often people get paid, how often they do their grocery shopping, how often businesses mail bills, and other factors that do not change very often. Because this assertion may be true or false, the quantity theory of money is, in fact, a theory.

The Quantity Theory Explanation of Inflation

The quantity equation gives us a way of showing the relationship between changes in the money supply and changes in the price level, or inflation. To see this relationship more clearly, we can use a handy mathematical rule that states that an equation where variables are multiplied together is equal to an equation where the *growth rates* of these variables are *added* together. So, we can transform the quantity equation from

$$M \times V = P \times Y$$

to

Growth rate of the money supply + Growth rate of velocity =
Growth rate of the price level (or inflation rate) + Growth rate of real output.

This way of writing the quantity equation is more useful for investigating the effect of changes in the money supply on the inflation rate. Remember that the growth rate for any variable is the percentage change in the variable from one year to the next. The growth rate of the price level is the inflation rate, so we can rewrite the quantity equation to help understand the factors that determine inflation:

Inflation rate = Growth rate of the money supply +
Growth rate of velocity − Growth rate of real output.

If Irving Fisher was correct that velocity is constant, then the growth rate of velocity will be zero. That is, if velocity is, say, always eight, then its percentage change from one year to the next will always be zero. This assumption allows us to rewrite the equation one last time:

Inflation rate = Growth rate of the money supply − Growth rate of real output.

This equation leads to the following predictions:

1. If the money supply grows at a faster rate than real GDP, there will be inflation.
2. If the money supply grows at a slower rate than real GDP, there will be deflation. (Recall that *deflation* is a decline in the price level.)
3. If the money supply grows at the same rate as real GDP, the price level will be stable, and there will be neither inflation nor deflation.

It turns out that Irving Fisher was wrong in asserting that the velocity of money is constant. From year to year, there can be significant fluctuations in velocity. As a result, the predictions of the quantity theory of money do not hold every year, but most economists agree that the quantity theory provides useful insight into the long-run relationship between the money supply and inflation: *In the long run, inflation results from the money supply growing at a faster rate than real GDP.*

How Accurate Are Estimates of Inflation Based on the Quantity Theory?

Note that the accuracy of the quantity theory depends on whether the key assumption that velocity is constant is correct. If velocity is not constant, then there may not be a tight link between increases in the money supply and increases in the price level. For

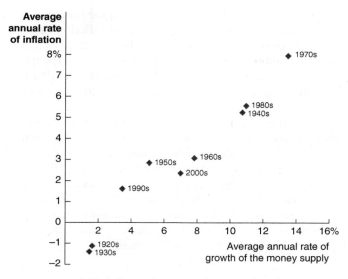

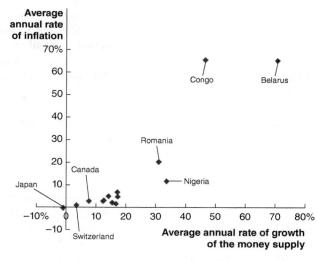

(a) Inflation and money supply growth in Canada, 1920s–2010s

(b) Inflation and money supply growth in 14 countries, 1999–2008

Figure 10.7 **The Relationship between Money Growth and Inflation over Time and around the World**

Panel (a) shows that, by and large, in Canada, the rate of inflation has been highest during the decades in which the money supply has increased most rapidly, and the rate of inflation has been lowest during the decades in which the money supply has increased least rapidly. Panel (b) shows that for the decade from 1999 to 2008, there is not an exact relationship between money supply growth and inflation, but in countries such as Canada, Japan, and Switzerland, both the growth rate of the money supply and the rate of inflation were low, while countries such

as Belarus, the Congo, and Romania had both high rates of growth of the money supply and high rates of inflation.

Sources: Panel (a): Data for 1870 to 1960, M.C. Urquhart, "Canadian Economic Growth 1870-1985," Institute for Economic Research, Queens University: Kingston, Ontario, Discussion Paper No. 734; and since 1961 Statistics Canada CANSIM II series V3860248 and V41552796; Panel (b): World Bank. (Accessed 21 February 2012)

example, an increase in the quantity of money might be offset by a decline in velocity, leaving the price level unaffected. Because velocity can move erratically in the short run, we would not expect the quantity equation to provide good forecasts of inflation in the short run. Over the long run, however, there is a strong link between changes in the money supply and inflation. Panel (a) of Figure 10.7 shows the relationship between the growth of the M2 measure of the money supply and the inflation rate by decade in Canada. (We use M2 here because data on M2 are available for a longer period of time.) There is a clear pattern that decades with higher growth rates in the money supply were also decades with higher inflation rates. In other words, most of the variation in inflation rates across decades can be explained by variation in the rates of growth of the money supply.

Panel (b) provides further evidence consistent with the quantity theory by looking at rates of growth of the money supply and rates of inflation across countries for the decade from 1999 to 2008. Although there is not an exact relationship between rates of growth of the money supply and rates of inflation across countries, panel (b) shows that countries where the money supply grew rapidly tended to have high inflation rates, while countries where the money supply grew more slowly tended to have much lower inflation rates. Not included in panel (b) are data for the African country of Zimbabwe, which we mentioned at the beginning of the chapter. Over this decade, the money supply in Zimbabwe grew by more than 7500 percent per year. The result was an accelerating rate of inflation that eventually reached 15 billion percent during 2008. Zimbabwe was suffering from hyperinflation—that is, a rate of inflation that exceeds 100 percent per year.

High Rates of Inflation

Why do governments allow high rates of inflation? The quantity theory can help us to understand the reasons for high rates of inflation, such as that experienced by Zimbabwe. Very high rates of inflation—in excess of 100 percent per year—are known as *hyperinflation*. Hyperinflation is caused by central banks increasing the money supply at a rate far in excess of the growth rate of real GDP. A high rate of inflation causes money to lose its value so rapidly that households and firms avoid holding it. If, as happened in Zimbabwe, the inflation becomes severe enough, people stop using paper currency, so it no longer serves the important functions of money discussed earlier in this chapter. Economies suffering from high inflation usually also suffer from very slow growth, if not severe recession.

Given the dire consequences that follow from high inflation, why do governments cause it by expanding the money supply so rapidly? The main reason is that governments often want to spend more than they are able to raise through taxes. Developed countries, such as Canada, can usually bridge gaps between spending and taxes by borrowing through selling bonds to the public. Developing countries, such as Zimbabwe, often have difficulty selling bonds because investors are skeptical of their ability to pay back the money. If they are unable to sell bonds to the public, governments in developing countries will force their central banks to purchase them. As we discussed previously, when a central bank buys bonds, the money supply will increase.

During the hyperinflation of the 1920s, people in Germany used paper currency to light their stoves.

Making the Connection | The German Hyperinflation of the Early 1920s

When Germany lost World War I, a revolution broke out that overthrew Kaiser Wilhelm II and installed a new government known as the Weimar Republic. In the peace treaty of 1919, the Allies—the United States, Great Britain, France, and Italy—imposed payments called *reparations* on the new German government. The reparations were meant as compensation to the Allies for the damage Germany had caused during the war. It was very difficult for the German government to use tax revenue to cover both its normal spending and the reparations.

The German government decided to pay for the difference between its spending and its tax revenues by selling bonds to the central bank, the Reichsbank. After a few years, the German government fell far behind in its reparations payments. In January 1923, the French government sent troops into the German industrial area known as the Ruhr to try to collect the payments directly. German workers in the Ruhr went on strike, and the German government decided to support them by paying their salaries. Raising the funds to do so was financed by an inflationary monetary policy: The German government sold bonds to the Reichsbank, thereby increasing the money supply.

The inflationary increase in the money supply was very large: The total number of marks—the German currency—in circulation rose from 115 million in January 1922 to 1.3 billion in January 1923 and then to 497 billion *billion*, or 497 000 000 000 000 000 000, in December 1923. Just as the quantity theory predicts, the result was a staggeringly high rate of inflation. The German price index that stood at 100 in 1914 and 1440 in January 1922 had risen to 126 160 000 000 000 in December 1923. The German mark became worthless. The German government ended the hyperinflation by (1) negotiating a new agreement with the Allies that reduced its reparations payments, (2) reducing other government expenditures and raising taxes to balance its budget, and (3) replacing the existing mark with a new mark. Each new mark was worth 1 trillion old marks. The German central bank was also limited to issuing a total of 3.2 billion new marks.

These steps were enough to bring the hyperinflation to an end—but not before the savings of anyone holding the old marks had been wiped out. Most middle-income Germans were extremely resentful of this outcome. Many historians believe that the hyperinflation greatly reduced the allegiance of many Germans to the Weimar Republic and may have helped pave the way for Adolph Hitler and the Nazis to seize power 10 years later.

Source: Based on Thomas Sargent, "The End of Four Big Hyperinflations," Rational Expectations and Inflation (New York: Harper & Row, 1986).

MyEconLab **Your Turn:** Test your understanding by doing related problem 5.5 on page 323 at the end of this chapter.

Economics in Your Life

What If Money Became Increasingly Valuable?

At the beginning of the chapter, we asked you to consider whether you would like to live in an economy in which the purchasing power of money rises every year. The first thing to consider when thinking about the advantages and disadvantages of this situation is that the only way for the purchasing power of money to increase is for the price level to fall; in other words, *deflation* must occur. Because the price level in Canada hasn't fallen for an entire year since the 1930s, most people alive today have experienced only rising price levels—and declining purchasing power of money. Would replacing rising prices with falling prices necessarily be a good thing? It might be tempting to say "yes," because if you have a job, your salary will buy more goods and services each year. But, in fact, just as a rising price level results in most wages and salaries rising each year, a falling price level is likely to mean falling wages and salaries each year. So, it is likely that, on average, people would not see the purchasing power of their incomes increase, even if the purchasing power of any currency they hold would increase. There can also be a significant downside to deflation, particularly if the transition from inflation to deflation happens suddenly. In Chapter 5, we defined the real interest rate as being equal to the nominal interest rate minus the inflation rate. If an economy experiences deflation, then the real interest rate will be greater than the nominal interest rate. A rising real interest rate can be bad news for anyone who has borrowed, including homeowners who may have substantial mortgage loans. So, you are probably better off living in an economy experiencing mild inflation than one experiencing deflation.

Conclusion

Money plays a key role in the functioning of an economy by facilitating trade in goods and services and by making specialization possible. Without specialization, no advanced economy can prosper. Households and firms, banks, and the central bank (such as the Bank of Canada) are participants in the process of creating the money supply. In Chapter 11, we will explore how the Bank of Canada uses monetary policy to promote its economic objectives.

Read *An Inside Look* on the next page for a discussion of alternative monetary policy procedures.

Price-Level Targeting versus Inflation-Rate Targeting

ECONOMIST

Level Worship: Price-Level Targeting Could Make Monetary Policy More Potent—Or Just More Confusing

Ever since Ben Bernanke, the chairman of the Federal Reserve, signalled in the summer that he stood ready to keep using unconventional monetary policy to shore up America's fragile economic recovery, expectations have been building that the Fed will launch a second programme of quantitative easing (QE)—the purchase of bonds with newly printed money. That moment is likely to come at the Fed's meeting on November 2nd-3rd. Whether QE2 can live up to the hype is another matter. QE aims to stimulate demand by lowering nominal long-term interest rates, much as conventional monetary easing works by lowering short-term nominal rates. But with short-term rates already close to zero and long-term rates also very low, the room for further reductions in nominal rates is tight.

There may in any case be another way to achieve the same stimulus. What matters for boosting demand is the real interest rate—the nominal rate minus expected inflation—since inflation reduces the burden of repaying debt. If nominal rates cannot fall any further, why not raise expected inflation? Central bankers have roundly rejected the most obvious way to do that. Raising official inflation-rate targets, they say, would destroy years of hard-won credibility.

But they are more receptive to another idea: targeting the level of prices rather than the inflation rate.

Assume that inflation of 2%, on average, is ideal. This implies that if the price level is 100 this year, it will be 102 next year and 104 (or more precisely, 104.04) in the second year. If inflation is only 1% in one year, a conventional inflation-targeting central bank would aim only to return inflation to a rate of 2% the next. This would leave the price level at 103, lower than its original implied path. In contrast, a central bank that targets the price level wants to make up any lost ground on prices. It would seek to raise inflation to 3% in the second year to get to a target of 104.

Although no central bank currently targets a price level, the concept is not a new one. Sweden's Riksbank did it from 1931 to 1937 as a way of warding off both inflation and deflation after leaving the gold standard. The Bank of Canada has conducted regular reviews on whether to replace its inflation-rate target, which was adopted in 1991, with a price-level target. The latest review will conclude next year.

In theory price-level targeting is superior to inflation-targeting because it provides more certainty about the long-term purchasing power of money. Central banks always target inflation flexibly. The Bank of Canada and the Bank of England, for example, target a rate of 2% but permit a range of 1% to 3%. That means someone making a 30-year investment must plan for cumulative inflation of as much as 143% or as little as 35%. A credible price-level target eliminates that uncertainty.

In the early 2000s academics such as Mr Bernanke (then a governor at the Fed) urged the Bank of Japan to adopt a price-level target to reverse the effect of years of deflation on Japanese inflationary expectations. The same advice is being offered to America now that it exhibits similar symptoms—namely, falling inflation and short-term interest rates at zero. Charles Evans, president of the Federal Reserve Bank of Chicago, proposed on October 16th that the Fed adopt a temporary price-level target. As with Japan the goal would be to raise expected inflation and lower real short-term interest rates at a time when nominal rates are stuck near zero. Eventually Mr Evans would have the Fed, which has no official inflation target, revert to focusing on the inflation rate.

Although elegant in theory, a price-level target has some serious practical drawbacks. It would require a central bank repeatedly to alter its goal for future inflation as prices deviated from the desired path. This could befuddle a public long accustomed to thinking in terms of inflation rather than price levels. There are questions, too, about how central bankers would deal with a one-time rise in the price level because of a new value-added tax, say, or higher oil prices. The boost to inflation would be temporary, but to the price level, permanent. In theory a central bank would have to wrestle all other prices lower no matter what the cost. It could make an exception, but too many exceptions would dent the bank's credibility. Conversely, a positive shock such as lower oil prices or higher productivity that pushes prices lower would require the central bank to raise future inflation, driving down real interest rates and maybe risking an asset bubble.

There are some decent counterarguments to these objections. Mark

Carney, the governor of the Bank of Canada, has argued that inflation-targeting can foster financial instability. A central bank that wants to tamp down excessive borrowing will not raise interest rates if it pushes inflation below target. If it targeted the price level over a period of time, it could justify a temporary decline in that level provided it later made up the lost ground.

Rate Expectations

By far the biggest question is whether price-level targeting would actually work, and that depends critically on how people form inflation expectations. The more they look ahead, basing their views on economic conditions and the central bank's policy, the more effective price-level targeting becomes, since inflation expectations would adjust more easily to the central bank's shifting target. If people look backwards, however, and base their expectations on where inflation has been in the past, price-level targeting loses effectiveness: getting inflation expectations up will rely on getting inflation itself up, a chicken-and-egg dilemma.

Research by the Bank of Canada suggests that if more than 40% of people base their expectations on rules of thumb or past inflation, price-level targeting loses its edge. "If the learning curve is too long and expectations are too slow to adjust, the present value of any shift to price-level targeting could easily turn negative," says John Murray at the Bank of Canada. Whichever course central banks set, boosting demand will not be simple.

Key Points in the Article

The article raises the question of whether targeting the price level, instead of the inflation rate, could make monetary policy more effective. In Canada, the Bank of Canada has been targeting the inflation rate since February 26, 1991, when a joint announcement by the minister of finance and the governor of the Bank of Canada established formal inflation targets. The targets were 3 percent by the end of 1992, falling to 2 percent by the end of 1995, to remain within a range of 1 percent to 3 percent thereafter. The 1 percent to 3 percent target range for inflation was renewed in December 1995, in early 1998, May 2001, November 2006, and again in November 2011 to apply until the end of 2016. The midpoint of the current inflation target range, 2 percent, is regarded as the most desirable outcome.

Currently no central bank is targeting the price level, but some central banks, including the Bank of Canada, have considered the issue of whether to replace inflation-rate targeting with price-level targeting. The advantage of price-level targeting is that it reduces the uncertainty about the long-term purchasing power of money.

Analyzing the News

a Economists recognize that the zero lower bound (i.e., the short-term nominal interest rate being zero or near zero) for the policy rate is problematic, because conventional monetary policy is ineffective at the zero lower bound. In fact, when the policy rate reaches the effective lower bound (i.e., the zero lower bound), the central bank loses its usual ability to signal policy changes via changes in the policy rate. Moreover, with short-term interest rates close to zero, the central bank also loses its ability to lower long-term interest rates by lowering short-term interest rates.

For these reasons, during the global financial crisis, many central banks around the world, including the Bank of Canada, the Bank of Japan, the US Federal Reserve, and the Bank of England, departed from the traditional interest-rate targeting approach to monetary policy and focused on their balance sheets instead, using quantitative measures of monetary policy.

b The Bank of Canada uses the nominal overnight interest rate as its operating instrument, but the effects of monetary policy on economic activity stem from how the real interest rate, rather than the nominal interest rate, affects the economy. In fact, the current interest rate targeting approach is based on the belief that it is the real long-term interest rate, and not the real short-term interest rate, that affects the level of economic activity.

c The question is whether the optimal level of the inflation rate is higher than the official inflation-rate target, which in Canada is 2 percent. The idea is that with the policy rate close to zero, a higher inflation rate target would lead to an even lower real interest rate. For example, with an overnight nominal interest rate of zero, raising the inflation target from 2 percent to 4 percent will produce a real interest rate of -4 percent, rather than -2 percent with the 2 percent inflation target.

Thinking Critically

1. The Bank of Canada uses its monetary policy tools (open market buyback operations, lending to financial institutions, and settlement balances management) to target the nominal overnight interest rate. How is it that changes in the nominal overnight interest rate affect the long-term real interest rates that affect the level of economic activity?

2. The global financial crisis has shown that monetary policy strategy needs to be modified to increase the effectiveness of monetary policy. It has been argued, for example, that inflation-targeting central banks should raise the inflation target. Should the Bank of Canada raise the official inflation-rate target from 2 percent to 4 percent?

Chapter Summary and Problems

Key Terms

Advances to banks, p. 308

Asset, p. 292

Bank of Canada, p. 294

Bank panic, p. 306

Bank rate, p. 308

Bank run, p. 306

Board of directors (of the Bank of Canada), p. 307

Collateralized transactions, p. 307

Commodity money, p. 292

Desired reserve ratio, p. 300

Desired reserves, p. 300

Excess reserves, p. 300

Fiat money, p. 294

Fractional reserve banking system, p. 306

Governing council (of the Bank of Canada), p. 307

Key policy rate, p. 307

M1+, p. 297

M1++, p. 297

M2, p. 297

M2+, p. 297

M2++, p. 297

M3, p. 297

Monetary base, p. 309

Monetary policy, p. 307

Money, p. 292

Open market buyback operations, p. 308

Open market operations, p. 309

Operating band, p. 308

Overnight interest rate, p. 307

Purchase and Resale Agreements (PRAs), p. 309

Quantity theory of money, p. 314

Reserves, p. 299

Sale and Repurchase Agreements (SRAs), p. 309

Securitization, p. 311

Security, p. 311

Settlement balances, p. 308

Simple deposit multiplier, p. 302

Standing liquidity facilities, p. 308

Velocity of money, p. 313

Summary

*LO **10.1** A *barter economy* is an economy that does not use money and in which people trade goods and services directly for other goods and services. Barter trade occurs only if there is a *double coincidence of wants*, where both parties to the trade want what the other one has. Because barter is inefficient, there is strong incentive to use *money*, which is any *asset* that people are generally willing to accept in exchange for goods or services or in payment of debts. An *asset* is anything of value owned by a person or a firm. A *commodity money* is a good used as money that also has value independent of its use as money. Money has four functions: It is a medium of exchange, a unit of account, a store of value, and a standard of deferred payment. The gold standard was a monetary system under which the government produced gold coins and paper currency that were convertible into gold. The gold standard collapsed in the early 1930s. Today, no government in the world issues paper currency that can be redeemed for gold. Instead, paper currency is *fiat money*, which has no value except as money.

LO **10.2** The narrowest definition of the money supply in Canada today is M1+, which includes currency plus all chequable deposits at chartered banks, TMLs, and CUCPs. A broader definition of the money supply is M1++, which includes everything that is in M1+ and all non-chequable deposits at chartered banks, TMLs, and CUCPs. Other definitions of the money supply are M2, M2+, M2++, and M3, with M2++ being the broadest definition of the money supply.

LO **10.3** On a bank's balance sheet, *reserves* and loans are assets, and deposits are liabilities. *Reserves* are deposits that the bank has retained rather than loaned out or invested. *Desired reserves* are reserves that banks desire to hold, based on their chequing account deposits. The fraction of deposits that banks desire to keep as reserves is called the *desired reserve ratio*. Any reserves banks hold over and above the desired reserves are called *excess reserves*. When a bank accepts a deposit, it keeps only a fraction of the funds as reserves and loans out the remainder. In making a loan, a bank increases the chequing account balance of the borrower. When the borrower uses a cheque to buy something with the funds the bank has loaned, the seller deposits the cheque in his or her bank. The seller's bank keeps part of the deposit as reserves and loans out the remainder. This process continues until no banks have excess reserves. In this way, the process of banks making new loans increases the volume of chequing account balances and the money supply. This money creation process can be illustrated with T-accounts, which are stripped-down versions of balance sheets that show only how a transaction changes a bank's balance sheet. The *simple deposit multiplier* is the ratio of the amount of deposits created by banks to the amount of new reserves. An expression for the simple deposit multiplier is $1/r_d$.

LO **10.4** Canada has a *fractional reserve banking system* in which banks keep less than 100 percent of deposits as reserves. In a *bank run*, many depositors decide simultaneously to withdraw money from a bank. In a *bank panic*, many banks experience runs at the same time. The Bank of Canada is the central bank of Canada. It was originally established in 1934. The recession of 2007–2009 put renewed emphasis on the Bank of Canada's goal of financial market stability. *Monetary policy* refers to the actions the Bank of Canada takes to manage the money supply and interest rates to pursue macroeconomic policy objectives. The Bank of Canada's main monetary policy tools are *open market buyback operations* and lending to financial institutions. *Open market operations* are the buying and selling of government securities by the Bank of Canada. The loans the Bank of Canada makes to banks are called *advances to banks*, and the interest rate the Bank of Canada charges on advances to banks is the *bank rate*. In the past 20 years, a "shadow banking system" has developed. During the financial crisis of 2007–2009, the existence of the shadow banking system

---

*'Learning Objective' is abbreviated to 'LO' in the end of chapter material.

complicated the policy response of central banks around the world. A *security* is a financial asset—such as a stock or a bond—that can be bought and sold in a financial market. The process of *securitization* involves creating a secondary market in which loans that have been bundled together can be bought and sold in financial markets just as corporate or government bonds are.

LO 10.5 The *quantity equation*, which relates the money supply to the price level, is $M \times V = P \times Y$ where M is the money supply, V is the *velocity of money*, P is the price level, and Y is real output. The *velocity of money* is the average number of times each dollar in the money supply is spent during the year. Economist Irving Fisher developed the *quantity theory of money*, which

assumes that the velocity of money is constant. If the quantity theory of money is correct, the inflation rate should equal the rate of growth of the money supply minus the rate of growth of real output. Although the quantity theory of money is not literally correct because the velocity of money is not constant, it is true that in the long run, inflation results from the money supply growing faster than real GDP. When governments attempt to raise revenue by selling large quantities of bonds to the central bank, the money supply will increase rapidly, resulting in a high rate of inflation.

MyEconLab   Log in to MyEconLab to complete these exercises and get instant feedback.

Review Questions

LO 10.1

1.1 A baseball fan with a Ricky Romero baseball card wants to trade it for a José Bautista baseball card, but everyone the fan knows who has a Bautista card doesn't want a Romero card. What do economists call the problem this fan is having?

1.2 What is the difference between commodity money and fiat money?

1.3 What are the four functions of money? Can something be considered money if it does not fulfill all four functions?

1.4 Why do businesses accept paper currency when they know that, unlike a gold coin, the paper the currency is printed on is worth very little?

LO 10.2

2.1 What is the main difference between the M1+ and M1++ definitions of the money supply?

2.2 Why does the Bank of Canada use six definitions of the money supply rather than one?

2.3 Distinguish among money, income, and wealth. Which one of the three does the central bank of a country control?

LO 10.3

3.1 What are the largest asset and the largest liability of a typical bank?

3.2 Suppose that you decide to withdraw $100 in cash from your chequing account. Draw a T-account showing the effect of this transaction on your bank's balance sheet.

3.3 What does it mean to say that banks "create money"?

3.4 Give the formula for the simple deposit multiplier. If the desired reserve ratio is 20 percent, what is the maximum increase in chequing account deposits that will result from an increase in bank reserves of $20 000?

3.5 What causes the real-world money multiplier to be smaller than the simple deposit multiplier?

LO 10.4

4.1 Why did the government decide to set up the Bank of Canada in 1934?

4.2 What policy tools does the Bank of Canada use to control the money supply? Which tool is the most important?

4.3 Why does an open market purchase of government securities by the Bank of Canada increase bank reserves? Why does an open market sale of government securities by the Bank of Canada decrease bank reserves?

4.4 What is the "shadow banking system"? Why were the financial firms of the shadow banking system more vulnerable than commercial banks to bank runs?

LO 10.5

5.1 What is the quantity theory of money? What explanation does the quantity theory provide for inflation?

5.2 Is the quantity theory of money better able to explain the inflation rate in the long run or in the short run? Briefly explain.

5.3 What is hyperinflation? Why do governments sometimes allow it to occur?

Problems and Applications

LO 10.1

1.1 English economist William Stanley Jevons described a world tour during the 1880s by a French singer, Mademoiselle Zélie. One stop on the tour was a theatre in the Society Islands, part of French Polynesia in the South Pacific. She performed for her usual fee, which was one-third of the receipts. This turned out to be three pigs, 23 turkeys, 44 chickens, 5000 coconuts, and "considerable quantities of bananas, lemons, and oranges." She estimated that all of this would have had a value in France of 4000 francs.

According to Jevons, "as Mademoiselle could not consume any considerable portion of the receipts herself, it became necessary in the meantime to feed the pigs and poultry with the fruit." Do the goods Mademoiselle Zélie received as payment fulfill the four functions of money described in the chapter? Briefly explain.

Based on W. Stanley Jevons, Money and the Mechanism of Exchange (New York: D. Appleton and Company, 1889), pp. 1–2.

1.2 [**Related to** the Chapter Opener **on page 291**] An article in the *New York Times* provides the following description of a hospital in Zimbabwe: "People lined up on the veranda of the American mission hospital here from miles around to barter for doctor visits and medicines, clutching scrawny chickens, squirming goats and buckets of maize." Why wouldn't the people buying medical services at this hospital use money to pay for the medical services they are buying?

From Celia W. Dugger, "Zimbabwe Health Care, Paid With Peanuts," New York Times, December 18, 2011.

1.3 In the late 1940s, the Communists under Mao Zedong were defeating the government of China in a civil war. The paper currency issued by the Chinese government was losing much of its value, and most businesses refused to accept it. At the same time, there was a paper shortage in Japan. During these years, Japan was still under military occupation by the United States, following its defeat in World War II. Some of the US troops in Japan realized that they could use dollars to buy up vast amounts of paper currency in China, ship it to Japan to be recycled into paper, and make a substantial profit. Under these circumstances, was the Chinese paper currency a commodity money or a fiat money? Briefly explain.

1.4 According to Peter Heather, a historian at the University of Oxford, during the Roman Empire, the German tribes east of the Rhine River produced no coins of their own but used Roman coins instead:

> Although no coinage was produced in Germania, Roman coins were in plentiful circulation and could easily have provided a medium of exchange (already in the first century, Tacitus tells us, Germani of the Rhine region were using good-quality Roman silver coins for this purpose).

a. What is a medium of exchange?

b. What does the author mean when he writes that Roman coins could have provided the German tribes with a medium of exchange?

c. Why would any member of a German tribe have been willing to accept a Roman coin from another member of the tribe in exchange for goods or services when the tribes were not part of the Roman Empire and were not governed by Roman law?

Based on Peter Heather, The Fall of the Roman Empire: A New History of Rome and the Barbarians (New York: Oxford University Press, 2006), p. 89.

1.5 [**Related to** Making the Connection **on page 295**] Suppose that the government changes the law to require all firms to accept paper currency in exchange for whatever they are selling. Briefly discuss who would gain and who would lose from this legislation.

LO 10.2

2.1 Briefly explain whether each of the following is counted in M1+.

a. The coins in your pocket

b. The funds in your chequing account

c. The funds in your savings account

d. The Canada Savings Bonds that you are holding

e. Your Bank of Montreal Platinum MasterCard

2.2 [**Related to** Solved Problem 10.1 **on page 298**] Suppose that you have $2000 in currency in a shoebox in your closet. One day, you decide to deposit the money in a chequing account. Briefly explain how doing so will affect M1+ and M1++.

2.3 [**Related to** Solved Problem 10.1 **on page 298**] Suppose that you decide to withdraw $100 in currency from your chequing account. What is the effect on M1+? Ignore any actions the bank may take as a result of your having withdrawn the $100.

2.4 [**Related to** Don't Let This Happen to You **on page 298**] Briefly explain whether you agree with the following statement: "I recently read that more than half of the money issued by the government is actually held by people in foreign countries. If that's true, then Canada is less than half as wealthy as government statistics indicate."

2.5 [**Related to** Don't Let This Happen to You **on page 298**] A newspaper article contains the statement: "Income is only one way of measuring wealth." Do you agree that income is a way of measuring wealth?

From Sam Roberts, "As the Data Show, There's a Reason the Wall Street Protesters Chose New York," New York Times, October 25, 2011.

2.6 The paper currency of Canada is technically called "Bank of Canada Notes." If you took a $20 bill to the Bank of Canada, will the Bank of Canada redeem it with some other type of money?

2.7 [**Related to** Making the Connection **on page 298**] In the nineteenth century, the Canadian government had difficulty getting banks and the public to accept the penny, which had been introduced a few years before. As a result, the government offered pennies for sale at a 20 percent discount. One account of this episode describes what the Canadian government did as "negative seigniorage." What is seigniorage? Why might the Canadian government's selling pennies at a 20 percent discount be considered "negative seigniorage"?

Based on Nicholas Kohler, "A Penny Dropped," macleans.ca, January 14, 2011.

2.8 [**Related to** Making the Connection **on page 298**] There were several billion Canadian pennies in circulation before the government scrapped the penny in its 2012 budget. Suppose that instead of scrapping the penny, the government followed the proposal of François Velde, an economist at the Federal Reserve Bank of Chicago, and made the penny worth 5 cents. What would be the effect on the value of M1+? Would that change have had much impact on the economy?

François Velde, "What's a Penny (or a Nickel) Really Worth?" Federal Reserve Bank of Chicago, Chicago Fed Letter, No. 235a, February 2007.

LO 10.3

3.1 "Most of the money supply of Canada is created by banks making loans." Briefly explain whether you agree with this statement.

3.2 Would a series of bank runs in a country decrease the total quantity of M1+? Wouldn't a bank run simply move funds in a chequing account to currency in circulation? How could that movement of funds decrease the quantity of money?

3.3 [**Related to** Solved Problem 10.2 **on page 304**] Suppose that you deposit $2000 in currency into your chequing account at a branch of Bank of Montreal, which we will assume has no excess reserves at the time you make your deposit. Also assume that the desired reserve ratio is 0.20, or 20 percent.

a. Use a T-account to show the initial impact of this transaction on Bank of Montreal's balance sheet.

b. Suppose that Bank of Montreal makes the maximum loan it can from the funds you deposited. Using a T-account, show the initial impact of granting the loan on Bank of Montreal's balance sheet. Also include on this T-account the transaction from part (a).

c. Now suppose that whoever took out the loan in part (b) writes a cheque for this amount and that the person receiving the cheque deposits it in a branch of CIBC. Show the effect of these transactions on the balance sheets of Bank of Montreal and CIBC *after the cheque has been cleared*. (On the T-account for Bank of Montreal, include the transactions from parts (a) and (b).)

d. What is the maximum increase in chequing account deposits that can result from your $2000 deposit? What is the maximum increase in the money supply? Explain.

3.4 Consider the following simplified balance sheet for a bank:

Assets		Liabilities	
Reserves	$10 000	Deposits	$70 000
Loans	$66 000	Shareholders' equity	$6000

a. If the desired reserve ratio is 0.10, or 10 percent, how much in excess reserves does the bank hold?

b. What is the maximum amount by which the bank can expand its loans?

c. If the bank makes the loans in part (b), show the *immediate* impact on the bank's balance sheet.

3.5 [**Related to** Don't Let This Happen to You **on page 303**] Briefly explain whether you agree with the following statement: "Assets are things of value that people own. Liabilities are debts. Therefore, a bank will always consider a chequing account deposit to be an asset and a car loan to be a liability."

LO 10.4

4.1 The text explains that Canada has a "fractional reserve banking system." Why do most depositors seem to be unworried that banks loan out most of the deposits they receive?

4.2 Suppose that you are a bank manager, and because of an increase in the level of uncertainty in financial markets you want to hold more reserves. You raise your desired reserve ratio from 10 percent to 12 percent. What actions would you need to take? How would your actions (and perhaps similar actions by other bank managers) end up affecting the money supply?

4.3 Suppose that the Bank of Canada makes a $10 million discount loan to First National Bank (FNB) by increasing FNB's account at the Bank of Canada.

a. Use a T-account to show the impact of this transaction on FNB's balance sheet. Remember that the funds a bank has on deposit at the Bank of Canada count as part of its reserves.

b. Assume that before receiving the loan, FNB has no excess reserves. What is the maximum amount of this $10 million that FNB can lend out?

c. What is the maximum total increase in the money supply that can result from the Bank of Canada loan? Assume that the desired reserve ratio is 10 percent.

4.4 When the Bank of Canada steps in as the lender of last resort to prevent a bank panic, does this constitute a "bail out of the banks"? Briefly explain.

LO 10.5

5.1 If the money supply is growing at a rate of 6 percent per year, real GDP is growing at a rate of 3 percent per year, and velocity is constant, what will the inflation rate be? If velocity is increasing 1 percent per year instead of remaining constant, what will the inflation rate be?

5.2 Suppose that during one period, the velocity of money is constant and during another period, it undergoes large fluctuations. During which period will the quantity theory of money be more useful in explaining changes in the inflation rate? Briefly explain.

5.3 [**Related to the** Chapter Opener **on page 291**] In April 2009, the African nation of Zimbabwe suspended the use of its own currency, the Zimbabwean dollar. According to an article from the Voice of America, "Hyperinflation in 2007 and 2008 made Zimbabwe's currency virtually worthless despite the introduction of bigger and bigger notes, including a 10 trillion dollar bill." Zimbabwe's Economic Planning Minister, Elton Mangoma, was quoted as saying the Zimbabwean dollar "will be out for at least a year," and in January 2009, the government of Zimbabwe made the US dollar the country's official currency. Why would hyperinflation make a currency "virtually worthless"? How might using the US dollar as its currency help stabilize Zimbabwe's economy?

From Voice of America News, "Zimbabwe Suspends Use of Own Currency," voanews.com, April 12, 2009.

5.4 [**Related to the** Chapter Opener **on page 291**] A *New York Times* article on Zimbabwe describes conditions in summer 2008 as follows: "Official inflation soared to 2.2 million percent in Zimbabwe—by far the highest in the world … [and] unemployment has reached 80 percent." Is there a connection between the very high inflation rate and the very high rate of unemployment? Briefly explain.

From "Inflation Soars top 2 Million Percent in Zimbabwe," New York Times, July 17, 2008.

5.5 [**Related to** Making the Connection **on page 316**] During the German hyperinflation of the 1920s, many households and firms in Germany were hurt economically. Do you think any groups in Germany benefited from the hyperinflation? Briefly explain.

Monetary Policy

Chapter Outline and Learning Objectives

11.1 What Is Monetary Policy? page 326
Define monetary policy and describe the Bank of Canada's monetary policy goals.

11.2 The Money Market and the Bank of Canada's Choice of Monetary Policy Targets, page 328
Describe the Bank of Canada's monetary policy targets and explain how expansionary and contractionary monetary policies affect the interest rate.

11.3 Monetary Policy and Economic Activity, page 333
Use aggregate demand and aggregate supply graphs to show the effects of monetary policy on real GDP and the price level.

11.4 Monetary Policy in the Dynamic Aggregate Demand and Aggregate Supply Model, page 339
Use the dynamic aggregate demand and aggregate supply model to analyze monetary policy.

11.5 A Closer Look at the Bank of Canada's Setting of Monetary Policy Targets, page 343
Discuss the Bank of Canada's setting of monetary policy targets.

11.6 Central Bank Policies during the 2007–2009 Global Financial Crisis, page 346
Discuss the policies central banks used during the 2007–2009 global financial crisis.

© Hemis / Alamy

Monetary Policy and the Canadian Housing Market

The global financial crisis was caused by excessive risk taking and credit growth in the United States. The key problem was the boom in the US housing market that turned into a "bubble." In a bubble, prices soar to levels that are not sustainable. When the housing bubble finally burst in 2006, sales of new homes and the prices of existing homes began a sharp decline. By 2007, the US economy had entered a recession and the whole world, including Canada, followed it.

As Canada entered the 2007–2009 recession, the Bank of Canada cut interest rates to record low levels to encourage building and investment. This policy was successful. However, because of the low interest rates that have been in place over the last five years, Canadian households today have a debt to after-tax income ratio of over 150 percent, meaning that for every dollar of after-tax income, the average household owes $1.50 in mortgages, car loans, credit cards, and lines of credit. This high debt ratio among Canadians has alarmed the Bank of Canada, the Depart-

ment of Finance, and the Office of the Superintendent of Financial Institutions (Canada's banking regulator), because it is almost as high as the debt-to-income ratio households in the United States had before the subprime financial crisis.

House prices in Canada have doubled since 2002, and economists and bankers are now concerned that, with historically low interest rates, already leveraged Canadians are taking on even more debt, increasing house prices above the value of the housing services that houses provide. In fact, Mark Carney, the governor of the Bank of Canada from 2008 to 2013, and Jim Flaherty, the minister of finance, have been warning Canadians that interest rates will increase in the near future, which will make paying household debts difficult.

In this chapter, we will learn how monetary policy can affect economic activity.

AN INSIDE LOOK on **page 354** discusses the Canadian housing market and the Bank of Canada's policy in response to a developing housing price bubble.

Economics in Your Life

Should You Buy a House during a Recession?

If you are like most postsecondary students, buying a house is one of the farthest things from your mind. But suppose you think forward a few years to when you might be married and maybe even (gasp!) have children. Leaving behind years of renting apartments, you are considering buying a house. But, suppose that according to an article in the *Globe and Mail*, a majority of economists are predicting that a recession is likely to begin soon. What should you do? Would this be a good time or a bad time to buy a house? As you read the chapter, see if you can answer these questions. You can check your answers against those we provide on page 353 at the end of this chapter.

I n Chapter 10, we saw that banks play an important role in providing credit to households and firms, and in creating the money supply. We also saw that the government established the Bank of Canada to stabilize the financial system and that the Bank of Canada is responsible for managing the money supply. In this chapter, we will discuss the Bank of Canada's four main policy goals: (1) price stability, (2) high employment, (3) stability of financial markets and institutions, and (4) economic growth. We will explore how the Bank of Canada decides which *monetary policy* actions to take to achieve its goals.

11.1 LEARNING OBJECTIVE

Define monetary policy and describe the Bank of Canada's monetary policy goals.

What Is Monetary Policy?

The devastation of the Great Depression was fundamentally important to the creation of the Bank of Canada. Because the depth of the Great Depression was blamed on the operation of the country's financial system, the federal Conservative government established the Royal Commission on Banking and Currency in 1933 to study the country's banking and monetary system. Based on the commission's recommendation, Parliament passed the Bank of Canada Act in 1934, and the newly founded Bank of Canada started operations on March 11, 1935. The main responsibility of the Bank of Canada is to conduct monetary policy "in the best interests of the economic life of the nation."

Monetary policy The actions the Bank of Canada takes to manage the money supply and interest rates to pursue macroeconomic policy goals.

Since World War II, the Bank of Canada has carried out an active *monetary policy*. **Monetary policy** refers to the actions the Bank of Canada takes to manage the money supply and interest rates to pursue its macroeconomic policy goals.

The Goals of Monetary Policy

The Bank of Canada has four main *monetary policy goals* that are intended to promote a well-functioning economy:

1. Price stability
2. High employment
3. Stability of financial markets and institutions
4. Economic growth

We briefly consider each of these goals.

Price Stability As we have seen in previous chapters, rising prices erode the value of money as a medium of exchange and a store of value. Especially after inflation rose dramatically and unexpectedly during the 1970s, policymakers in most industrial countries have had price stability as the main monetary policy goal. Figure 11.1 shows that for the

Figure 11.1

The Inflation Rate, January 1952–April 2013

For most of the 1950s and 1960s, the inflation rate in Canada was 4 percent or less. During the 1970s, the inflation rate increased, peaking during 1979–1981. After 1992, the inflation rate was usually below 4 percent. The effects of the 2007–2009 recession caused several months of deflation—a falling price level—during the second half of 2009.

Note: The inflation rate is measured as the percentage change in the consumer price index (CPI) from the same month in the previous year.

Source: Statistics Canada CANSIM II series V41690973 (Accessed 21 February 2012). Reproduced and distributed on an "as is" basis with the permission of Statistics Canada.

most part, from the early 1950s until 1968, the inflation rate remained below 4 percent per year. Inflation was above 4 percent for most of the 1970s. In 1974–1975 and early 1979, the inflation rate increased to more than 12 percent, where it remained until late 1982, when it began to rapidly fall back to the 4 percent range. After 1992, the inflation rate was usually below 4 percent. The effects of the recession caused several months of deflation—a falling price level—during the second half of 2009.

As we discussed in Chapter 10, the main goal of the Bank of Canada's current monetary policy is to keep the inflation rate within a target range of 1 percent to 3 percent, with the midpoint of the inflation target range, 2 percent, being the most desirable outcome. The Bank of Canada's approach to **inflation targeting** is **symmetric**, meaning that the Bank of Canada is equally concerned about inflation rising above the target as it is about inflation falling below the target. Such an approach to monetary policy guards against high inflation as well as against sustained deflation (a decline in the price level).

However, the Bank of Canada engages in **flexible inflation targeting**, in the sense that it does not rely on mechanical rules to achieve its inflation target, regardless of the shocks hitting the economy. The Bank of Canada (like most other inflation-targeting central banks) tries to meet its inflation target typically over a two-year period to minimize economic and financial volatility, which could be harmful to employment and economic growth in Canada.

High Employment In addition to price stability, high employment, or a low rate of unemployment, is also an important monetary policy goal. Unemployed workers and underused factories and office buildings reduce GDP below its potential level. Unemployment causes financial distress and decreases the self-esteem of workers who lack jobs. The goal of high employment extends beyond the Bank of Canada to other branches of the federal government.

Stability of Financial Markets and Institutions Resources are lost when financial markets and institutions are not efficient in matching savers and borrowers. Firms with the potential to produce goods and services that consumers value can't obtain the financing they need to design, develop, and market those products. Savers waste resources looking for satisfactory investments. The Bank of Canada promotes the stability of financial markets and institutions so that an efficient flow of funds from savers to borrowers will occur. As we saw in Chapter 10, the global financial crisis of 2007–2009 brought the issue of stability in financial markets to the forefront.

While the Bank of Canada doesn't regulate financial institutions, it does play a key role in providing liquidity to banks. Commercial banks can borrow from the Bank of Canada when they find themselves temporarily short of funds at the bank rate. By acting as a "lender of last resort" the Bank of Canada reduces the risk of a financial institution—that is otherwise healthy—failing because it cannot access short-term funds.

Economic Growth In Chapters 6 and 7, we discussed the importance of economic growth to raising living standards. Policymakers aim to encourage *stable* economic growth because it allows households and firms to plan accurately and encourages the long-run investment that is needed to sustain growth. Policy can spur economic growth by providing incentives for saving to ensure a large pool of investment funds, as well as by providing direct incentives for business investment. The government, however, may be better able to increase saving and investment than is the Bank of Canada. For example, the government can change the tax laws to increase the return to saving and investing. In fact, some economists question whether the Bank of Canada can play a role in promoting economic growth beyond attempting to meet its goals of price stability and financial stability.

In the next section, we will look at how the Bank of Canada attempts to attain its monetary policy goal of price stability. We also look at how the turmoil in financial markets that began in 2007 led the Bank of Canada and other central banks around the world to put new emphasis on the goal of financial market stability.

Inflation targeting Conducting monetary policy so as to commit the central bank to achieving a publicly announced level of inflation.

Symmetric inflation targeting Conducting monetary policy based on equal concern about inflation rising above its target as about inflation falling below its target.

Flexible inflation targeting Conducting monetary policy that does not rely on mechanical rules to achieve its inflation target, but tries to meet the inflation target over some time horizon (typically a two-year horizon).

11.2 LEARNING OBJECTIVE

Describe the Bank of Canada's monetary policy targets and explain how expansionary and contractionary monetary policies affect the interest rate.

The Money Market and the Bank of Canada's Choice of Monetary Policy Targets

The Bank of Canada aims to use its policy tools to achieve its monetary policy goals. Recall from Chapter 10 that the Bank of Canada's key monetary policy tools are open market buyback operations and lending to financial institutions. At times, the Bank of Canada encounters conflicts between its policy goals. For example, as we will discuss later in this chapter, the Bank of Canada can raise interest rates to reduce the inflation rate. But, as we saw in Chapter 9, higher interest rates typically reduce household and firm spending, which may result in slower growth and higher unemployment. So, a policy that is intended to achieve one monetary policy goal, such as reducing inflation, may have an adverse effect on another policy goal, such as high employment.

Monetary Policy Targets

As 2 percent is regarded as the most desirable inflation rate, the main objective of the Bank of Canada's monetary policy is to keep the inflation rate between 1 and 3 percent. In fact, the Bank of Canada can't tell firms how many people to employ or what prices to charge for their products. Instead, it uses *monetary policy targets*—that is, variables that it can directly influence and which, in turn, affect the inflation rate. The two main monetary policy targets are the money supply and the interest rate. As we will see, the Bank of Canada typically uses the *overnight interest rate* as its policy target.

It's important to bear in mind that while the Bank of Canada has typically used the interest rate as its target, this target was not central to the Bank of Canada's policy decisions during the global financial crisis. As we will discuss later in this chapter, because financial markets suffered a degree of disruption not seen since the Great Depression of the 1930s, the Bank of Canada and other central banks around the world were forced to develop new policy tools. However, it is still important to have a good grasp of how the Bank of Canada carries out policy during normal times.

The Demand for Money

The Bank of Canada's two monetary policy targets are related in an important way. To see this relationship, we first need to examine the demand and supply for money. Figure 11.2 shows the demand curve for money. The interest rate is on the vertical axis, and the quantity of money is on the horizontal axis. Here we are using the M1+ definition of money, which equals currency in circulation plus chequing account deposits. Notice that the demand curve for money is downward sloping.

To understand why the demand curve for money is downward sloping, consider that households and firms have a choice between holding money and holding other

Figure 11.2

The Demand for Money

The money demand curve slopes downward because lower interest rates cause households and firms to switch from financial assets such as Treasury bills to money. All other things being equal, a fall in the interest rate from 4 percent to 3 percent will increase the quantity of money demanded from $90 billion to $95 billion. An increase in the interest rate will decrease the quantity of money demanded.

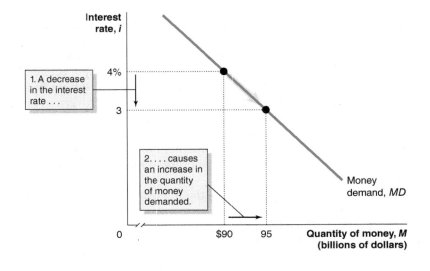

financial assets, such as Canada bonds. Money has one particularly desirable characteristic: You can use it to buy goods, services, or financial assets. Money also has one undesirable characteristic: It earns either no interest or a very low rate of interest. The currency in your wallet earns no interest, and the money in your chequing account earns either no interest or very little interest. Alternatives to money, such as Treasury bills, pay interest but have to be sold if you want to use the funds to buy something. When interest rates rise on financial assets such as Treasury bills, the amount of interest that households and firms lose by holding money increases. When interest rates fall, the amount of interest households and firms lose by holding money decreases. Remember that *opportunity cost* is what you have to forgo to engage in an activity. The interest rate is the opportunity cost of holding money.

We now have an explanation of why the demand curve for money slopes downward: When interest rates on Treasury bills and other financial assets are low, the opportunity cost of holding money is low, so the quantity of money demanded by households and firms will be high; when interest rates are high, the opportunity cost of holding money will be high, so the quantity of money demanded will be low. In Figure 11.2, a decrease in interest rates from 4 percent to 3 percent causes the quantity of money demanded by households and firms to rise from $90 billion to $95 billion.

Shifts in the Money Demand Curve

We saw in Chapter 3 that the demand curve for a good is drawn holding constant all variables, other than the price, that affect the willingness of consumers to buy the good. Changes in variables other than the price cause the demand curve to shift. Similarly, the demand curve for money is drawn holding constant all variables, other than the interest rate, that affect the willingness of households and firms to hold money. Changes in variables other than the interest rate cause the demand curve to shift. The two most important variables that cause the money demand curve to shift are real GDP and the price level.

An increase in real GDP means that the amount of buying and selling of goods and services will increase. This additional buying and selling increases the demand for money as a medium of exchange, so the quantity of money households and firms want to hold increases at each interest rate, shifting the money demand curve to the right. A decrease in real GDP decreases the quantity of money demanded at each interest rate, shifting the money demand curve to the left. A higher price level increases the quantity of money required for a given amount of buying and selling. Eighty years ago, for example, when the price level was much lower and someone could purchase a new car for $500 and a salary of $30 per week put you in the middle class, the quantity of money demanded by households and firms was much lower than today, even adjusting for the effect of the lower real GDP and smaller population of those years. An increase in the price level increases the quantity of money demanded at each interest rate, shifting the money demand curve to the right. A decrease in the price level decreases the quantity of money demanded at each interest rate, shifting the money demand curve to the left. Figure 11.3 illustrates shifts in the money demand curve.

How the Bank of Canada Manages the Money Supply: A Quick Review

Having discussed money demand, we now turn to money supply. In Chapter 10, we saw how the Bank of Canada manages the money supply. If the Bank of Canada decides to increase the money supply, it purchases government of Canada securities. The sellers of these government securities deposit the funds they receive from the Bank of Canada in banks, which increases the banks' reserves. Typically, banks loan out most of these reserves, which creates new chequing account deposits and expands the money supply. If the Bank of Canada decides to decrease the money supply, it sells Canada securities, which decreases banks' reserves and contracts the money supply.

Figure 11.3

Shifts in the Money Demand Curve

Changes in real GDP or the price level cause the money demand curve to shift. An increase in real GDP or an increase in the price level will cause the money demand curve to shift from MD_1 to MD_2. A decrease in real GDP or a decrease in the price level will cause the money demand curve to shift from MD_1 to MD_3.

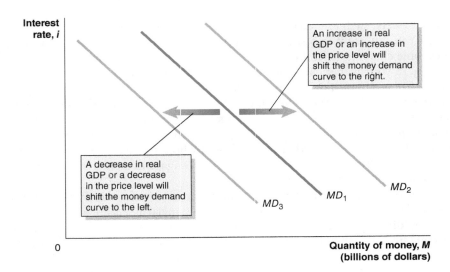

Equilibrium in the Money Market

In Figure 11.4, we include both the money demand and money supply curves. We can use this figure to see how the Bank of Canada affects both the money supply and the interest rate. For simplicity, we assume that the Bank of Canada is able to completely control the money supply. Therefore, the money supply curve is a vertical line, and changes in the interest rate have no effect on the quantity of money supplied. Just as with other markets, equilibrium in the *money market* occurs where the money demand curve crosses the money supply curve. If the Bank of Canada increases the money supply, the money supply curve will shift to the right, and the equilibrium interest rate will fall. In Figure 11.4, when the Bank of Canada increases the money supply from $90 billion to $95 billion, the money supply curve shifts from MS_1 to MS_2, and the equilibrium interest rate falls from 4 percent to 3 percent.

In the money market, the adjustment from one equilibrium to another equilibrium is a little different from the adjustment in the market for a good. In Figure 11.4, the money market is initially in equilibrium, with an interest rate of 4 percent and a money supply of $90 billion. When the Bank of Canada increases the money supply by $5 billion, households and firms have more money than they want to hold at an interest rate of

Figure 11.4

The Effect on the Interest Rate When the Bank of Canada Increases the Money Supply

When the Bank of Canada increases the money supply, households and firms will initially hold more money than they want, relative to other financial assets. Households and firms use the money they don't want to hold to buy short-term financial assets, such as Treasury bills, and make deposits in interest-paying bank accounts. This increase in demand allows banks and sellers of Treasury bills and similar securities to offer a lower interest rate. Eventually, the interest rate will fall enough that households and firms will be willing to hold the additional money the Bank of Canada has created. In the figure, an increase in the money supply from $90 billion to $95 billion causes the money supply curve to shift to the right, from MS_1 to MS_2, and causes the equilibrium interest rate to fall from 4 percent to 3 percent.

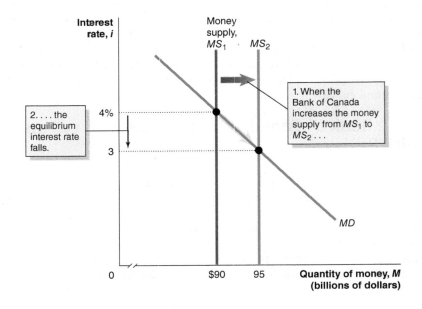

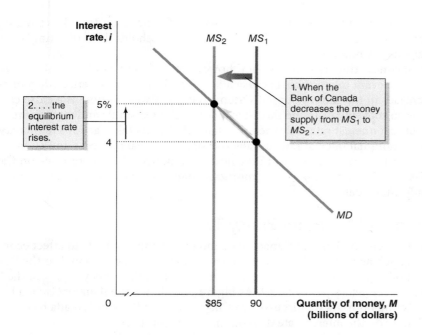

Figure 11.5

The Effect on the Interest Rate When the Bank of Canada Decreases the Money Supply

When the Bank of Canada decreases the money supply, households and firms will initially hold less money than they want, relative to other financial assets. Households and firms will sell Treasury bills and other short-term financial assets and withdraw money from interest-paying bank accounts. These actions will increase interest rates. Eventually, interest rates will rise to the point at which households and firms will be willing to hold the smaller amount of money that results from the Bank of Canada's actions. In the figure, a reduction in the money supply from $90 billion to $85 billion causes the money supply curve to shift to the left, from MS_1 to MS_2, and causes the equilibrium interest rate to rise from 4 percent to 5 percent.

4 percent. What do households and firms do with the extra $5 billion? They are most likely to use the money to buy short-term financial assets, such as Canada bonds, or to deposit the money in interest-paying bank accounts, such as certificates of deposit. This increase in demand for interest-paying bank accounts and short-term financial assets allows banks to offer lower interest rates on certificates of deposit, and it allows sellers of Canada bonds and similar assets to also offer lower interest rates. As the interest rates on certificates of deposit, Canada bonds, and other short-term assets fall, the opportunity cost of holding money also falls. Households and firms move down the money demand curve. Eventually the interest rate will have fallen enough that households and firms are willing to hold the additional $5 billion worth of money the Bank of Canada has created, and the money market will be back in equilibrium. To summarize: *When the Bank of Canada increases the money supply, the short-term interest rate must fall until it reaches a level at which households and firms are willing to hold the additional money.*

Figure 11.5 shows what happens when the Bank of Canada decreases the money supply. The money market is initially in equilibrium, at an interest rate of 4 percent and a money supply of $90 billion. If the Bank of Canada decreases the money supply to $85 billion, households and firms will be holding less money than they would like, relative to other financial assets, at an interest rate of 4 percent. To increase their money holdings, they will sell Treasury bills and other short-term financial assets and withdraw funds from certificates of deposit and other interest-paying bank accounts. Banks will have to offer higher interest rates in order to retain depositors, and sellers of Treasury bills and similar securities will have to offer higher interest rates in order to find buyers. Rising short-term interest rates increase the opportunity cost of holding money, causing households and firms to move up the money demand curve. Equilibrium is finally restored at an interest rate of 5 percent.

A Tale of Two Interest Rates

In Chapter 6, we discussed the loanable funds model of the interest rate. In that model, the equilibrium interest rate is determined by the demand and supply for loanable funds. Why do we need two models of the interest rate? The answer is that the loanable funds model is concerned with the *long-term real rate of interest*, and the money market model is concerned with the *short-term nominal rate of interest*. The long-term real rate of interest is the interest rate that is most relevant when savers consider purchasing a long-term financial investment such as a corporate bond. It is also the rate of interest that is most relevant to firms that are borrowing to finance long-term investment projects such as new factories or office buildings, or to households that are taking out mortgage loans to buy new homes.

When conducting monetary policy, however, the short-term nominal interest rate is the most relevant interest rate because it is the interest rate most affected by increases and decreases in the money supply. Often—but not always—there is a close connection between movements in the short-term nominal interest rate and movements in the long-term real interest rate. So, when the Bank of Canada takes actions to increase the short-term nominal interest rate, usually the long-term real interest rate also increases. In other words, as we will discuss in the next section, when the interest rate on Canada bonds rises, the real interest rate on mortgage loans usually also rises, although sometimes only after a delay.

Choosing a Monetary Policy Target

As we have seen, the Bank of Canada uses monetary policy targets to affect economic variables, such as real GDP or the price level, that are closely related to the Bank of Canada's policy goals. The Bank of Canada can use either the money supply or the interest rate as its monetary policy target. As Figure 11.5 shows, the Bank of Canada is capable of affecting both. As we discussed in Chapter 10, the Bank of Canada has generally focused more on the interest rate than on the money supply.

There are many different interest rates in the economy. For purposes of monetary policy, the Bank of Canada has targeted the interest rate known as the *overnight interest rate*. In the next section, we discuss the overnight interest rate before examining how targeting the interest rate can help the Bank of Canada achieve its monetary policy goals.

The Importance of the Overnight Interest Rate

Recall from Chapter 10 that every bank likes to keep a fraction of its deposits as reserves, either as currency held in the bank or as deposits (settlement balances) with the Bank of Canada. The Bank of Canada pays banks a low interest rate on their reserve deposits, which (during normal times) is the bank rate less 50 basis points, $i_b - 0.50$, so banks normally have an incentive to invest reserves above the desired amounts. As the global financial crisis that began in 2007 deepened during 2008, bank reserves soared (especially in the United States) as banks attempted to meet an increase in deposit withdrawals and as they became reluctant to lend to any borrowers except those with the most flawless credit histories. These conditions were very unusual, however. In normal times, banks keep few excess reserves, and when they need additional reserves, they borrow in the *overnight funds market* from banks that have reserves available. The **overnight interest rate** is the interest rate banks charge one another on loans in the overnight funds market. The loans in that market are usually very short term, often just overnight.

Overnight interest rate The interest rate banks charge each other for overnight loans.

Operating band The Bank of Canada's 50-basis-point range for the overnight interest rate.

The Bank of Canada does not set the overnight interest rate. Instead, it sets an **operating band** of 50 basis points wide for the overnight interest rate, and the rate is determined by the supply of reserves relative to the demand for them. Because the Bank of Canada can increase and decrease the supply of bank reserves through open buyback market operations, it can set a *target* for the overnight interest rate and usually comes very close to reaching it. The Bank of Canada operates under a system in which it announces the target for the overnight interest rate on eight "fixed" dates throughout the year. In April 2009, the Bank of Canada lowered the band for the overnight interest rate from 50 basis points to 25 basis points (from 0.50 percent to 0.25 percent) and instead of targeting the overnight interest rate at the midpoint of the band (as it does during normal times), it started targeting the overnight interest rate at the bottom of the operating band. On June 1, 2010, the Bank of Canada re-established the normal operating band of 50 basis points for the overnight interest rate, and the band currently is from 0.75 percent to 1.25 percent.

These very low overnight interest rates reflect the severity of the global financial crisis. The overnight interest rate is not directly relevant to households and firms. Only banks can borrow or lend in the overnight funds market. However, changes in the overnight interest rate usually result in changes in interest rates on other short-term financial assets, such as Canada bonds, and changes in interest rates on long-term financial assets, such as corporate bonds and mortgages. A change in the overnight interest rate has a greater effect on short-term interest rates than on long-term interest rates, and its effect on long-term interest rates may occur only after a lag in time. Although a majority of economists support the Bank of Canada's choice of the interest rate as its monetary policy target, some economists believe the Bank of Canada should concentrate on the money supply instead. We will discuss the views of these economists later in this chapter.

Monetary Policy and Economic Activity

Remember that the Bank of Canada uses the overnight interest rate as a monetary policy target because it can influence the overnight interest rate through **open market buyback operations** and because it believes that changes in the overnight interest rate will ultimately affect economic variables that are related to its monetary policy goals. It is important to consider again the distinction between the nominal interest rate and the real interest rate. Recall that we calculate the real interest rate by subtracting the inflation rate from the nominal interest rate. Ultimately, the ability of the Bank of Canada to use monetary policy to affect economic variables such as real GDP depends on its ability to affect real interest rates, such as the real interest rates on mortgages and corporate bonds. Because the overnight interest rate is a short-term nominal interest rate, the Bank of Canada sometimes has difficulty affecting long-term real interest rates. Nevertheless, for purposes of the following discussion, we will assume that the Bank of Canada is able to use open market buyback operations to affect long-term real interest rates.

How Interest Rates Affect Aggregate Demand

Changes in interest rates affect *aggregate demand*, which is the total level of spending in the economy. Recall from Chapter 9 that aggregate demand has four components: consumption, investment, government purchases, and net exports. Changes in interest rates will not affect government purchases, but they will affect the other three components of aggregate demand in the following ways:

- **Consumption.** Many households finance purchases of consumer durables, such as automobiles and furniture, by borrowing. Lower interest rates lead to increased spending on durables because they lower the total cost of these goods to consumers by lowering the interest payments on loans. Higher interest rates raise the cost of consumer durables, and households will buy fewer of them. Lower interest rates also reduce the return to saving, leading households to save less and spend more. Higher interest rates increase the return to saving, leading households to save more and spend less.

- **Investment.** Firms finance most of their spending on machinery, equipment, and factories out of their profits or by borrowing. Firms borrow either from the financial markets by issuing corporate bonds or from banks. Higher interest rates on corporate bonds or on bank loans make it more expensive for firms to borrow, so they will undertake fewer investment projects. Lower interest rates make it less expensive for firms to borrow, so they will undertake more investment projects. Lower interest rates can also increase investment through their effect on stock prices. As interest rates decline, stocks become a more attractive investment relative to bonds. The increase in demand for stocks raises their price. An increase in stock prices sends a signal to firms that the future profitability of investment projects has increased. By issuing additional shares of stocks, firms can acquire the funds they need to buy new factories and equipment, thereby increasing investment.

11.3 LEARNING OBJECTIVE

Use aggregate demand and aggregate supply graphs to show the effects of monetary policy on real GDP and the price level.

Open market buyback operations Agreements in which the Bank of Canada, or another party, purchase securities with the understanding that the seller will repurchase them in a short period of time, usually less than a week.

Finally, spending by households on new homes is also part of investment. When interest rates on mortgage loans rise, the cost of buying new homes rises, and fewer new homes will be purchased. When interest rates on mortgage loans fall, more new homes will be purchased.

- **Net exports.** Recall that net exports are equal to spending by foreign households and firms on goods and services produced in Canada minus spending by Canadian households and firms on goods and services produced in other countries. The value of net exports depends partly on the exchange rate between the Canadian dollar and foreign currencies. When the value of the dollar rises, households and firms in other countries will pay more for goods and services produced in Canada, but Canadian households and firms will pay less for goods and services produced in other countries. As a result, Canada will export less and import more, so net exports fall. When the value of the dollar falls, net exports will rise. If interest rates in Canada rise relative to interest rates in other countries, investing in Canadian financial assets will become more desirable, causing foreign investors to increase their demand for dollars, which will increase the value of the dollar. As the value of the dollar increases, net exports will fall. If interest rates in Canada decline relative to interest rates in other countries, the value of the dollar will fall, and net exports will rise.

The Effects of Monetary Policy on Real GDP and the Price Level

In Chapter 9, we developed the *aggregate demand and aggregate supply model* to explain fluctuations in real GDP and the price level. In the basic version of the model, we assume that there is no economic growth, so the long-run aggregate supply curve does not shift. In panel (a) of Figure 11.6, we assume that the economy is in short-run equilibrium at point A, where the aggregate demand (AD_1) curve intersects the short-run aggregate supply (SRAS) curve. Real GDP is below potential real GDP, as shown by the long-run aggregate supply (LRAS) curve, so the economy is in a recession, with some firms operating below normal capacity and some workers having been laid off. To reach its goal of high employment, the Bank of Canada needs to carry out an **expansionary monetary policy** by increasing the money supply and decreasing interest rates. Lower interest rates cause an increase in consumption, investment, and net exports, which shifts the aggregate demand curve to the right, from AD_1 to AD_2. Real GDP increases from $1.3 trillion to potential GDP of $1.4 trillion, and the price level rises from 98 to 100 (point B). The policy successfully returns real GDP to its potential level. Rising production leads to increasing employment, allowing the Bank of Canada to achieve its goal of high employment.

In panel (b) of Figure 11.6, the economy is in short-run equilibrium at point A, with real GDP of $1.5 trillion, which is above potential real GDP of $1.4 trillion. With some firms producing beyond their normal capacity and the unemployment rate very low, wages and prices are increasing. To reach its goal of price stability, the Bank of Canada needs to carry out a **contractionary monetary policy** by decreasing the money supply and increasing interest rates. Higher interest rates cause a decrease in consumption, investment, and net exports, which shifts the aggregate demand curve from AD_1 to AD_2. Real GDP decreases from $1.5 trillion to $1.4 trillion, and the price level falls from 102 to 100 (point B). Why would the Bank of Canada want to intentionally cause real GDP to decline? Because in the long run, real GDP can't continue to remain above potential GDP. Attempting to keep real GDP above potential GDP would result in rising inflation. As aggregate demand declines and real GDP returns to its potential level, upward pressure on wages and prices will be reduced, allowing the Bank of Canada to achieve its goal of price stability.

We can conclude that the Bank of Canada can use monetary policy to affect the price level and, in the short run, the level of real GDP, allowing it to attain its policy goals of high employment and price stability.

Expansionary monetary policy The Bank of Canada's decreasing interest rates to increase real GDP.

Contractionary monetary policy The Bank of Canada's increasing interest rates to reduce inflation.

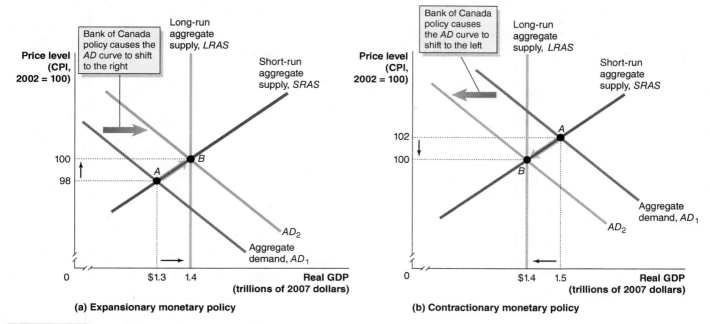

Figure 11.6 Monetary Policy

In panel (a), the economy begins in a recession at point *A*, with real GDP of $1.3 trillion and a price level of 98. An expansionary monetary policy causes aggregate demand to shift to the right, from AD_1 to AD_2, increasing real GDP from $1.3 trillion to $1.4 trillion and the price level from 98 to 100 (point *B*). With real GDP back at its potential level, the Bank of Canada can meet its goal of high employment.

In panel (b), the economy begins at point *A*, with real GDP at $1.5 trillion and the price level at 102. Because real GDP is greater than potential GDP, the economy experiences rising wages and prices. A contractionary monetary policy causes aggregate demand to shift to the left, from AD_1 to AD_2, decreasing real GDP from $1.5 trillion to $1.4 trillion and the price level from 102 to 100 (point *B*). With real GDP back at its potential level, the Bank of Canada can meet its goal of price stability.

Making
the
Connection

Too Low for Zero: Central Banks Try "Quantitative Easing"

In the aftermath of the global financial crisis and the Great Recession, policy rates such as the overnight interest rate in Canada and the federal funds rate in the United States have hardly moved at all, while central bank monetary policies have been the most volatile and extreme in their entire histories. This unpredictability has discredited policy rates as indicators of monetary policy and led central banks to look elsewhere.

In particular, the US Federal Reserve and many central banks around the world, including the Bank of Canada, have departed from the traditional interest-rate targeting approach to monetary policy and are now focusing on their balance sheet instead, using quantitative measures of monetary policy, such as credit easing and quantitative easing.

For example, in December 2008, the Federal Reserve pushed the target for the federal funds rate (the US equivalent of our overnight interest rate) to nearly zero and kept it there until now. Because the 2007–2009 recession was so severe, even this very low rate did little to stimulate the US economy. To lower the federal funds rate, the Federal Reserve buys Treasury bills through open market purchases, which increases bank reserves. Banks then lend out these reserves. As the figure below shows, however, in late 2008, many banks began piling up excess reserves rather than lending the funds out. Total bank reserves had been less than US$50 billion in August 2008, but with the deepening of the global financial crisis, they had soared to more than US$900 billion by May 2009.

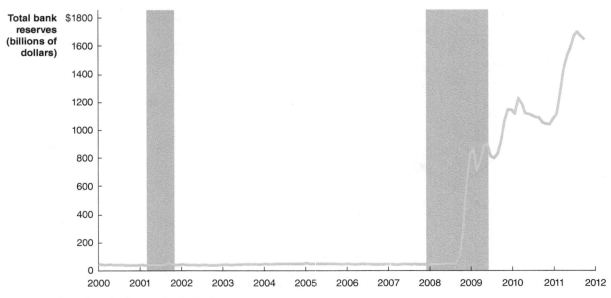

Total bank reserves (billions of dollars)

Source: Data from The Federal Reserve Bank of St. Louis.

The increase in bank reserves was partly due to the Federal Reserve's decision in October 2008 to start paying interest of 0.25 percent on bank reserves held as deposits at the Federal Reserve. Primarily, though, the increase in reserves occurred because banks were reluctant to make loans at low interest rates to households and firms whose financial positions had been damaged by the recession. Some economists believed the Federal Reserve was facing a situation known as a *liquidity trap*, in which short-term interest rates are pushed to zero, leaving the central bank unable to lower them further. Some economists believe that liquidity traps occurred in the United States during the 1930s and in Japan during the 1990s.

Not being able to push the target for the federal funds rate below zero was a problem for the Federal Reserve. Glenn Rudebusch, an economist at the Federal Reserve Bank of San Francisco, calculated that given how high the unemployment rate was, the appropriate target for the federal funds rate was −5 percent. Because the federal funds rate can't be negative, the Federal Reserve turned to other policies. In particular, it decided to embark on a policy of *quantitative easing*, which involves buying securities beyond the short-term Treasury securities that are usually involved in open market operations. The Federal Reserve began purchasing 10-year Treasury notes to keep their interest rates from rising. Interest rates on home mortgage loans typically move closely with interest rates on 10-year Treasury notes. It also purchased certain *mortgage-backed securities*. The Federal Reserve's objective was to keep interest rates on mortgages low and to keep funds flowing into the mortgage market in order to help stimulate demand for housing.

Central banks pushed interest rates to very low levels during 2008 and 2009.

Later in this chapter, we will consider other new programs the Bank of Canada and many other central banks around the world put in place to deal with the global financial crisis of 2007–2009 and the slow recovery that followed, as the traditional focus on lowering policy rates to stimulate the economy proved ineffective.

Source: Based on Glenn Rudebusch, "The Fed's Monetary Policy Response to the Current Crisis," FRBSF Economic Letter, May 22, 2009.

Your Turn: Test your understanding by doing related problems 3.8 and 3.9 on page 359 at the end of this chapter.

MyEconLab

Can the Bank of Canada Eliminate Recessions?

Panel (a) of Figure 11.6 shows an expansionary monetary policy that performs perfectly by shifting the *AD* curve to bring the economy back to potential GDP. In fact, however, this ideal is very difficult for the Bank of Canada to achieve, as the length and severity of the 2007–2009 recession indicates. In practice, the best the Bank of Canada can do is keep recessions shorter and milder than they would otherwise be.

If the Bank of Canada is to be successful in offsetting the effects of the business cycle, it needs to quickly recognize the need for a change in monetary policy. If the Bank of Canada is late in recognizing that a recession has begun or that the inflation rate is increasing, it may not be able to implement a new policy soon enough to do much good. In fact, implementing a policy too late may actually destabilize the economy. To see how this can happen, consider Figure 11.7. The straight line represents the long-run growth trend in real GDP in Canada. On average, real GDP grows about 3 percent per year. The actual path of real GDP differs from the underlying trend because of the business cycle, which is shown by the red curved line. As we saw in Chapter 6, the actual business cycle is more irregular than the stylized cycle shown here.

Suppose that a recession begins in August 2014. Because it takes months for economic statistics to be gathered by Statistics Canada and the Bank of Canada, there is a *lag*, or delay, before the Bank of Canada recognizes that a recession has begun. Then it takes time for the Bank of Canada's economists to analyze the data. Finally, in June 2015, the Bank of Canada concludes that the economy is in recession and begins an expansionary monetary policy. As it turns out, June 2015 is actually the trough of the recession, meaning that the recession has already ended, and an expansion has begun. In these circumstances, the Bank of Canada's expansionary policy is not needed to end the recession. The increase in aggregate demand caused by the Bank of Canada's lowering interest rates is likely to push the economy beyond potential real GDP and cause a significant acceleration in inflation. Real GDP ends up following the path indicated by the blue curved line. The Bank of Canada has inadvertently engaged in a *procyclical policy*, which increases the severity of the business cycle, as opposed to a *countercyclical*

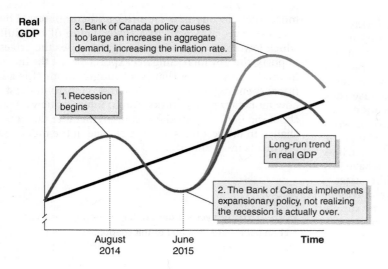

Figure 11.7

The Effect of a Poorly Timed Monetary Policy on the Economy

The upward-sloping straight line represents the long-run growth trend in real GDP. The curved red line represents the path real GDP takes because of the business cycle. If the Bank of Canada is too late in implementing a change in monetary policy, real GDP will follow the curved blue line. The Bank of Canada's expansionary monetary policy results in too great an increase in aggregate demand during the next expansion, which causes an increase in the inflation rate.

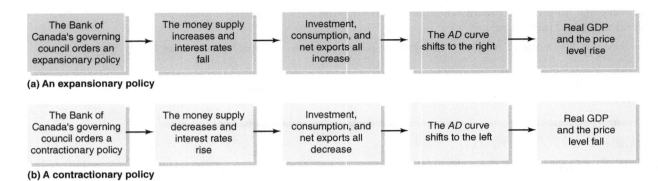

(a) An expansionary policy

(b) A contractionary policy

Table 11.1 **Expansionary and Contractionary Monetary Policies**

policy, which is meant to reduce the severity of the business cycle, and which is what the Bank of Canada intends to use.

Failing to react until well after a recession has begun (or ended) can be a serious problem for the Bank of Canada. In the case of the 2007–2009 recession, however, the Bank of Canada did promptly cut the overnight interest rate in response to the beginning of the global financial crisis, even though the recession did not actually begin until some months later.

A Summary of How Monetary Policy Works

Table 11.1 compares the steps involved in expansionary and contractionary monetary policies. We need to note an important qualification to this summary. At every point, we should add the phrase "relative to what would have happened without the policy." Table 11.1 isolates the impact of monetary policy, *holding constant all other factors affecting the variables involved*. In other words, we are invoking the *ceteris paribus* condition,

Don't Let This Happen to You

Remember that with Monetary Policy, It's the Interest Rates—Not the Money—that Counts

It is tempting to think of monetary policy working like this: If the Bank of Canada wants more spending in the economy, it increases the money supply, and people spend more because they now have more money. If the Bank of Canada wants less spending in the economy, it decreases the money supply, and people spend less because they now have less money. In fact, that is *not* how monetary policy works. Remember the important difference between money and income: The Bank of Canada increases the money supply by buying government securities, such as Canada bonds. The sellers of the Canada bonds have just exchanged one asset—Canada bonds—for another asset— a cheque from the Bank of Canada; the sellers have *not* increased their income. Even though the money supply is now larger, no one's income has increased, so no one's spending should be affected.

It is only when this increase in the money supply results in lower interest rates that spending is affected. When interest rates are lower, households are more likely to buy new homes and automobiles, and businesses are more likely to buy new factories and computers. Lower interest rates also lead to a lower value of the dollar, which lowers the prices of exports and raises the prices of imports, thereby increasing net exports. It isn't the increase in the money supply that has brought about this additional spending; *it's the lower interest rates*. To understand how monetary policy works, and to interpret news reports about the Bank of Canada's actions, remember that it is the change in interest rates, not the change in the money supply, that is most important.

MyEconLab
Your Turn: Test your understanding by doing related problem 3.11 on page 359 at the end of this chapter.

discussed in Chapter 3. This point is important because, for example, a contractionary monetary policy does not cause the price level to fall; rather, a contractionary monetary policy causes the price level *to rise by less than it would have risen without the policy*. One final note on terminology: An expansionary monetary policy is sometimes referred to as a *loose* policy, or an *easy* policy. A contractionary monetary policy is sometimes referred to as a *tight* policy.

Monetary Policy in the Dynamic Aggregate Demand and Aggregate Supply Model

11.4 LEARNING OBJECTIVE

Use the dynamic aggregate demand and aggregate supply model to analyze monetary policy.

The overview of monetary policy we just finished contains a key idea: The Bank of Canada can use monetary policy to affect aggregate demand, thereby changing the price level and the level of real GDP. The discussion of monetary policy illustrated by Figure 11.6 is simplified, however, because it ignores two important facts about the economy: (1) The economy experiences continuing inflation, with the price level rising every year, and (2) the economy experiences long-run growth, with the *LRAS* curve shifting to the right every year. In Chapter 9, we developed a *dynamic aggregate demand and aggregate supply model* that takes into account these two facts. In this section, we use the dynamic model to gain a more complete understanding of monetary policy. Let's briefly review the dynamic model. Recall from Chapter 9 that over time, the Canadian labour force and Canadian capital stock will increase. Technological change will also occur. The result will be an increase in potential real GDP, which we show by the long-run aggregate supply curve shifting to the right. These factors will also result in firms supplying more goods and services at any given price level in the short run, which we show by the short-run aggregate supply curve shifting to the right. During most years, the aggregate demand curve will also shift to the right, indicating that aggregate expenditure will be higher at every price level. Aggregate expenditure usually increases for several reasons: As population grows and incomes rise, consumption will increase over time. Also, as the economy grows, firms expand capacity, and new firms are established, increasing investment spending. Finally, an expanding population and an expanding economy require increased government services, such as more police officers and teachers, so government purchases will expand.

The Effects of Monetary Policy on Real GDP and the Price Level: A More Complete Account

During certain periods, *AD* does not increase enough during the year to keep the economy at potential GDP. This slow growth in aggregate demand may be due to households and firms becoming pessimistic about the future state of the economy, leading them to cut back their spending on consumer durables, houses, and factories. As we have seen, the collapse of the US housing bubble and the resulting global financial crisis had a negative effect on aggregate demand during the 2007–2009 recession. Other possibilities exist as well: The federal government might decide to balance the budget by cutting back its purchases, or recessions in other countries might cause a decline in Canadian exports. In the hypothetical situation shown in Figure 11.8, in the first year, the economy is in equilibrium, at potential real GDP of $1.4 trillion and a price level of 100 (point *A*). In the second year, *LRAS* increases to $1.6 trillion, but *AD* increases only to $AD_{2(\text{without policy})}$, which is not enough to keep the economy in macroeconomic equilibrium at potential GDP. If the Bank of Canada does not intervene, the short-run equilibrium will occur at $1.5 trillion (point *B*). The $100 billion gap between this level of real GDP and potential real GDP at $LRAS_2$ means that some firms are operating at less than their normal capacity. Incomes and profits will fall, firms will begin to lay off workers, and the unemployment rate will rise.

Economists at the Bank of Canada closely monitor the economy and continually update forecasts of future levels of real GDP and prices. When these economists

Figure 11.8

An Expansionary Monetary Policy

The economy begins in equilibrium at point A, with real GDP of $1.4 trillion and a price level of 100. Without monetary policy, aggregate demand will shift from AD_1 to $AD_{2(\text{without policy})}$, which is not enough to keep the economy at full employment because long-run aggregate supply has shifted from $LRAS_1$ to $LRAS_2$. The economy will be in short-run equilibrium at point B, with real GDP of $1.5 trillion and a price level of 102. By lowering interest rates, the Bank of Canada increases investment, consumption, and net exports sufficiently to shift aggregate demand to $AD_{2(\text{with policy})}$. The economy will be in equilibrium at point C, with real GDP of $1.6 trillion, which is its full employment level, and a price level of 103. The price level is higher than it would have been if the Bank of Canada had not acted to increase spending in the economy.

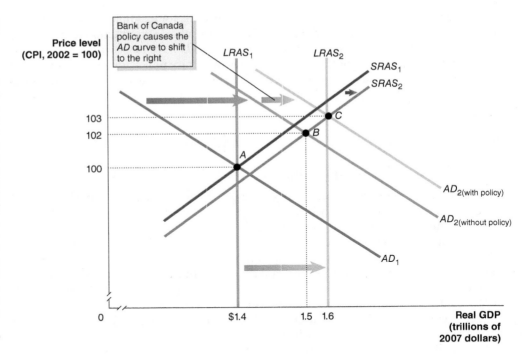

Governing council (of the Bank of Canada) A council with six members (including the governor) that is responsible for the management of the Bank of Canada.

anticipate that aggregate demand is not growing fast enough to allow the economy to remain at full employment, they present their findings to the Bank of Canada's **governing council**, which decides whether circumstances require a change in monetary policy. For example, suppose that the governing council meets and considers a forecast from the staff indicating that during the following year, a gap of $100 billion will open between equilibrium real GDP and potential real GDP. In other words, the macroeconomic equilibrium illustrated by point B in Figure 11.8 will occur. The Bank of Canada may then decide to carry out an expansionary monetary policy to lower interest rates to stimulate aggregate demand. The figure shows the results of a successful attempt to do this: AD has shifted to the right, and equilibrium occurs at potential GDP (point C). The Bank of Canada will have successfully headed off the falling incomes and rising unemployment that otherwise would have occurred. Bear in mind that we are illustrating a perfectly executed monetary policy that keeps the economy at potential GDP, which is difficult to achieve in practice for reasons already discussed.

Notice in Figure 11.8 that the expansionary monetary policy caused the inflation rate to be higher than it would have been. Without the expansionary policy, the price level would have risen from 100 to 102, so the inflation rate for the year would have been 2 percent. By shifting the aggregate demand curve, the expansionary policy caused the price level to increase from 102 to 103, raising the inflation rate from 2 percent to 3 percent.

Using Monetary Policy to Fight Inflation

In addition to using an expansionary monetary policy to reduce the severity of recessions, the Bank of Canada can also use a contractionary monetary policy to keep aggregate demand from expanding so rapidly that the inflation rate begins to increase above the upper limit of the inflation rate target band of 3 percent. Figure 11.9 shows the situation during 2006 and 2007, when the Bank of Canada faced this possibility. During 2006, the economy was at equilibrium at potential GDP, but the Bank of Canada's economists and governing council were concerned that the continuing boom in the commodities sector might lead aggregate demand to increase so rapidly that the inflation rate would begin to accelerate.

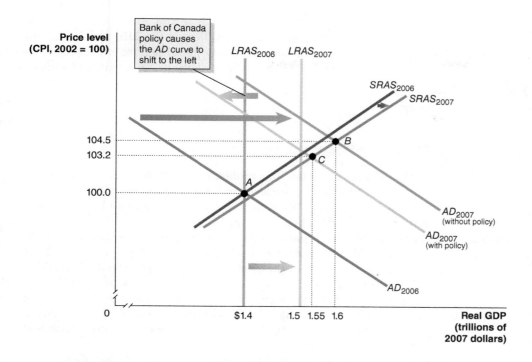

Figure 11.9

A Contractionary Monetary Policy in 2006

The economy began 2006 in equilibrium at point A, with real GDP equal to potential GDP of $1.4 trillion and a price level of 100.0. From 2006 to 2007, potential GDP increased from $1.4 trillion to $1.5 trillion, as long-run aggregate supply increased from $LRAS_{2006}$ to $LRAS_{2007}$. The Bank of Canada raised interest rates because it believed the commodities boom was causing aggregate demand to increase too rapidly. Without the increase in interest rates, aggregate demand would have shifted from AD_{2006} to $AD_{2007(without\ policy)}$, and the new short-run equilibrium would have occurred at point B. Real GDP would have been $1.6 trillion—$100 billion greater than potential GDP—and the price level would have been 104.5. The increase in interest rates resulted in aggregate demand increasing only to $AD_{2007(with\ policy)}$. Equilibrium occurred at point C, with real GDP of $1.55 trillion being only $50 billion greater than potential GDP and the price level rising only to 103.2.

Between January 2006 and July 2007, the target for the overnight interest rate rose from 3.25 percent to 4.5 percent as the Bank of Canada tried to slow the increase in prices. To see how the Bank of Canada can use this sort of monetary policy, let's work through Figure 11.9. Assume that the economy starts at point A with a real GDP of $1.4 trillion dollars and a price level of 100.0. We'll assume that the Canadian economy's potential GDP continued to grow during this period, which means that long-run aggregate supply and short-run aggregate supply both shift to the right. If the Bank of Canada takes no action, the aggregate demand curve will shift from AD_{2006} to $AD_{2007(without\ policy)}$ and the economy will be in equilibrium at point B. At point B, the economy is in a short-run equilibrium with real GDP of $1.6 trillion and a price level of 104.5.

A movement in the price level from 100.0 to 104.5 means an inflation rate of 4.5 percent, which exceeds the target range of 1 to 3 percent. The Bank of Canada used contractionary monetary policy to reduce inflation. In 2006, it began to increase its target for the overnight interest rate, which caused interest rates in the economy to rise. As a result investment, consumption, and net exports fell (or didn't increase as much as they would have), and the aggregate demand curve shifted to $AD_{2007(with\ policy)}$. As a result, the economy found equilibrium at point C, with real GDP of $1.55 trillion and a price level of 103.2. A change in price level from 100.0 to 103.2 meant that the inflation rate would be 3.2 percent, just a bit higher than the upper limit of the inflation target band.

Solved Problem **11.1**

The Effects of Monetary Policy

The hypothetical information in the following table shows what the values for real GDP and the price level will be in 2017 if the Bank of Canada does *not* use monetary policy:

Year	Potential GDP	Real GDP	Price Level
2016	$1.52 trillion	$1.52 trillion	114
2017	1.56 trillion	1.54 trillion	116

a. If the Bank of Canada wants to keep real GDP at its potential level in 2017, should it use an expansionary policy or a contractionary policy? Should the trading desk buy Canada bonds or sell them?

b. Suppose the Bank of Canada's policy is successful in keeping real GDP at its potential level in 2017. State whether each of the following will be higher or lower than if the Bank of Canada had taken no action:

i. Real GDP
ii. Potential real GDP
iii. The inflation rate
iv. The unemployment rate

c. Draw an aggregate demand and aggregate supply graph to illustrate your answer. Be sure that your graph con-

tains *LRAS* curves for 2016 and 2017; *SRAS* curves for 2016 and 2017; an *AD* curve for 2016 and 2017, with and without monetary policy action; and equilibrium real GDP and the price level in 2017, with and without policy.

Solving the Problem

Step 1: Review the chapter material. This problem is about the effects of monetary policy on real GDP and the price level, so you may want to review the section "The Effects of Monetary Policy on Real GDP and the Price Level: A More Complete Account," which begins on page 339.

Step 2: Answer the questions in part (a) by explaining how the Bank of Canada can keep real GDP at its potential level. The information in the table tells us that without monetary policy, the economy will be below potential real GDP in 2017. To keep real GDP at its potential level, the Bank of Canada must undertake an expansionary policy. To carry out an expansionary policy, the trading desk needs to buy Canada bonds. Buying Canada bonds will increase reserves in the banking system. Banks will increase their loans, which will increase the money supply and lower the interest rate.

Step 4: Answer part (b) by explaining the effect of the Bank of Canada's policy. If the Bank of Canada's policy is successful, real GDP in 2017 will increase from $1.54 trillion, as given in the table, to its potential level of $1.56 trillion. Potential real GDP is not affected by monetary policy, so its value will not change. Because the level of real GDP will be higher, the unemployment rate will be lower than it would have been without policy. The expansionary monetary policy shifts the *AD* curve to the right, so short-run equilibrium will move up the short-run aggregate supply (*SRAS*) curve, and the price level will be higher.

Step 4: Answer part (c) by drawing the graph. Your graph should look similar to Figure 11.8.

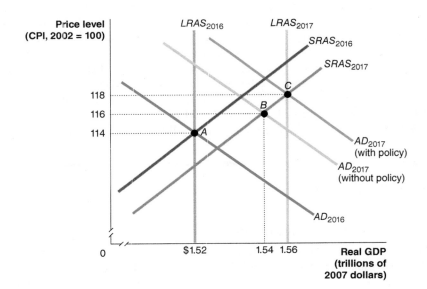

The economy starts in equilibrium in 2016 at point *A*, with the *AD* and *SRAS* curves intersecting along the *LRAS* curve. Real GDP is at its potential level of $1.52 trillion, and the price level is 114. Without monetary policy, the *AD* curve shifts to $AD_{2017(\text{without policy})}$, and the economy is in short-run equilibrium at point *B*. Because potential real GDP has increased from $1.52 trillion to $1.56 trillion, short-run equilibrium real GDP of $1.54 trillion is below the potential level. The price level has increased from 114 to 116. With policy, the *AD* curve shifts to $AD_{2017(\text{with policy})}$, and the economy is in equilibrium at point *C*. Real GDP is at its potential level of $1.56 trillion. We don't have enough information to be sure of the new equilibrium price level. We do know that it will be higher than 116. The graph shows the price level rising to 118. Therefore, without the Bank of Canada's expansionary policy, the inflation rate in 2017 would have been about 1.8 percent. With policy, it will be about 3.5 percent.

Extra credit: Bear in mind that in reality, the Bank of Canada is unable to use monetary policy to keep real GDP exactly at its potential level, as this problem suggests.

Your Turn: For more practice, do related problems 4.2 and 4.3 on pages 359–360 at the end of this chapter.   MyEconLab

A Closer Look at the Bank of Canada's Setting of Monetary Policy Targets

We have seen that in carrying out monetary policy, the Bank of Canada changes its target for the overnight interest rate, depending on the state of the economy. During times when the economy is not experiencing a financial crisis, is using the overnight interest rate as a target the best way to conduct monetary policy? If the Bank of Canada targets the overnight interest rate, how should it decide what the target level should be? In this section, we consider some important issues concerning the Bank of Canada's targeting policy.

Should the Bank of Canada Target the Money Supply?

Some economists have argued that rather than use an interest rate as its monetary policy target, the Bank of Canada should use the money supply. Many of the economists who make this argument belong to a school of thought known as *monetarism*. The leader of the monetarist school was Nobel Laureate Milton Friedman, who was skeptical that central banks would be able to correctly time changes in monetary policy.

Friedman and his followers favoured replacing *monetary policy* with a *monetary growth rule*. Ordinarily, we expect monetary policy to respond to changing economic conditions: When the economy is in recession, the central bank reduces interest rates, and when inflation is increasing, the central bank raises interest rates. A **monetary growth rule**, in contrast, is a plan for increasing the money supply at a constant rate that does not change in response to economic conditions. Friedman and his followers proposed a monetary growth rule of increasing the money supply every year at a rate equal to the long-run growth rate of real GDP, which is about 3 percent. If the Bank of Canada adopted this monetary growth rule, it would stick to it through changing economic conditions.

Monetary growth rule A plan for increasing the quantity of money at a fixed rate that does not respond to changes in economic conditions.

But what happens under a monetary growth rule if the economy moves into recession? Shouldn't the Bank of Canada abandon the rule to drive down interest rates? Friedman argued that the central bank should stick to the rule even during recessions because, he believed, active monetary policy destabilizes the economy, increasing the number of recessions and their severity. By keeping the money supply growing at a constant rate, Friedman argued, the central bank would greatly increase economic stability.

Although during the 1970s some economists and politicians pressured the Bank of Canada to adopt a monetary growth rule, most of that pressure has disappeared in recent years. A key reason is that the fairly close relationship between movements in the money supply and movements in real GDP and the price level that existed before 1980 has become much weaker. Since 1980, the growth rate of narrow money supply measures (such as M1+) has been unstable. In some years, M1+ has grown more than

Figure 11.10

The Bank of Canada Can't Target Both the Money Supply and the Interest Rate

The Bank of Canada is forced to choose between using either an interest rate or the money supply as its monetary policy target. In this figure, the Bank of Canada can set a target of $90 billion for the money supply or a target of 5 percent for the interest rate, but the Bank of Canada can't reach both targets because it can achieve only combinations of the interest rate and the money supply that represent equilibrium in the money market.

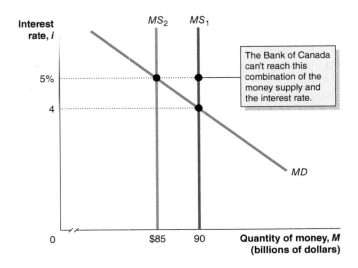

10 percent, while in other years, it has actually fallen. Yet despite these wide fluctuations in the growth of this narrow money supply measure, growth in real GDP has been fairly stable, and inflation has remained low during most years.

Why Doesn't the Bank of Canada Target Both the Money Supply and the Interest Rate?

Most economists believe that an interest rate is the best monetary policy target, but other economists believe the Bank of Canada should target the money supply. Why doesn't the Bank of Canada satisfy both groups by targeting both the money supply and the interest rate? The simple answer to this question is that the Bank of Canada can't target both at the same time. To see why, look at Figure 11.10, which shows the money market.

Remember that the Bank of Canada controls the money supply, but it does not control money demand. Money demand is determined by decisions of households and firms as they weigh the trade-off between the convenience of money and its low interest rate compared with other financial assets. Suppose the Bank of Canada is targeting the interest rate and decides, given conditions in the economy, that the interest rate should be 5 percent. Or, suppose the Bank of Canada is targeting the money supply and decides that the money supply should be $90 billion. Figure 11.10 shows that the Bank of Canada can bring about an interest rate of 5 percent or a money supply of $90 billion, but it can't bring about both. The point representing an interest rate of 5 percent and a money supply of $90 billion is not on the money demand curve, so it can't represent an equilibrium in the money market. Only combinations of the interest rate and the money supply that represent equilibrium in the money market are possible.

The Bank of Canada has to choose between targeting an interest rate and targeting the money supply. For most of the period since World War II, the Bank of Canada has chosen an interest rate target.

The Taylor Rule

Taylor rule A rule developed by John Taylor that links the central bank's target for the overnight interest rate to economic variables.

How does the Bank of Canada choose a target for the overnight interest rate? John Taylor of Stanford University has analyzed the factors involved in central bank decision making and developed the **Taylor rule** to explain overnight interest rate targeting. The Taylor rule begins with an estimate of the value of the equilibrium real overnight interest rate, which is the overnight interest rate—adjusted for inflation—that would be consistent with real GDP being equal to potential real GDP in the long run. According to the Taylor rule, the Bank of Canada should set the target for the overnight interest rate so that it is equal to the sum of the inflation rate, the equilibrium real overnight interest rate, and two additional terms. The first of these additional terms is the *inflation gap*—the difference between current inflation and a target rate; the second is the *output* *gap*—the percentage difference between real GDP and potential real GDP. The inflation gap and output gap are each given "weights" that reflect their influence on the overnight interest rate target. With weights of 1/2 for both gaps, we have the following Taylor rule:

Overnight interest rate target = Current inflation rate + Real equilibrium overnight interest rate + ((1/2) × Inflation gap) + ((1/2) × Output gap).

The Taylor rule includes expressions for the inflation gap and the output gap because the Bank of Canada is concerned about both inflation and fluctuations in real GDP. Taylor demonstrated that if the equilibrium real overnight interest rate is 2 percent and the target rate of inflation is 2 percent, the preceding expression does a good job of explaining changes in the Bank of Canada's target for the overnight interest rate during most years. Consider an example in which the current inflation rate is 1 percent, and real GDP is 1 percent below potential real GDP. In that case, the inflation gap is 1 percent − 2 percent = −1 percent and the output gap is also −1 percent. Inserting these values in the Taylor rule, we can calculate the predicted value for the overnight interest rate target:

Overnight interest rate target = 1% + 2% + ((1/2) × −1%) + ((1/2) × −1%) = 2%.

It should also be noted that in the Taylor rule, the coefficient on the inflation gap is greater than zero. This means that when the inflation rate increases by 1 percentage point, the central bank increases the overnight interest rate by more than 1 percentage point (in the case of the above equation, by 1+1/2) so that the real interest rate also rises. This is known as the **Taylor principle** and is critical to the success of monetary policy as it ensures that monetary policy is stabilizing. For example, if when the overnight interest rate increases by less than the increase in the inflation rate, then the real interest rate would decline, stimulating the level of economic activity and leading to more inflation.

Although the Taylor rule does not account for changes in the target inflation rate or the equilibrium interest rate, many economists view the rule as a convenient tool for analyzing the overnight funds target.

Taylor principle The principle that the central bank should raise the nominal interest rate by more than the increase in the inflation rate so that the real interest rate also increases.

Making the Connection	## How Does the Bank of Canada Measure Inflation?

To attain its goal of price stability, the Bank of Canada has to consider carefully the best way to measure the inflation rate. As we saw in Chapter 5, the consumer price index (CPI) is the most widely used measure of inflation. But we also saw that the CPI suffers from biases that cause it to overstate the true underlying rate of inflation. An alternative measure of changes in consumer prices can be constructed from the data gathered to calculate GDP. We saw in Chapter 4 that the GDP deflator is a broad measure of the price level that includes the price of every good or service that is in GDP. Changes in the GDP deflator are not a good measure of inflation experienced by the typical consumer, worker, or firm, however, because the deflator includes prices of goods, such as industrial equipment, that are not widely purchased.

The Bank of Canada uses the rate of change in the CPI to measure inflation because it is the most commonly used and understood price measure in Canada. The Bank of Canada's inflation targets are specified in terms of "headline CPI" (all items), but it also uses "core CPI," which excludes volatile components (such as food, energy, and the effect of indirect taxes) as a measure of the headline rate's trend. For example, prices of food and energy tend to fluctuate up and down for reasons that may not be related to the causes of general inflation and that can't easily be controlled by monetary policy. Oil prices, in particular, have moved dramatically up and down in recent years. Therefore, a price index that includes food and energy prices may not give a clear view of underlying trends in inflation.

The following graph shows movements in the CPI and the core CPI from January 1993 through December 2011. Although the two measures of inflation move

The Bank of Canada excludes food and energy prices from its main measure of inflation.

roughly together, the core CPI has been more stable than the CPI. Note in particular the period in late 2009 when the CPI was indicating that the economy was experiencing deflation, but the core CPI was still showing moderate inflation rates of about 2 percent.

If you want to know what the Bank of Canada thinks the current inflation rate is, the best idea is to look at data on the core CPI.

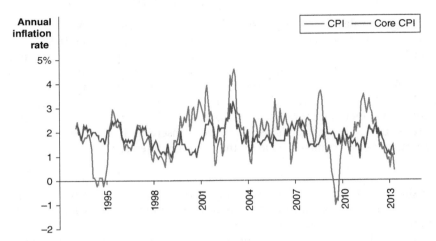

Source: Statistics Canada CANSIM II series V41690914 and V41690926. Reproduced and distributed on an "as is" basis with the permission of Statistics Canada.

MyEconLab

Your Turn: Test your understanding by doing related problems 5.3 and 5.4 on page 360 at the end of this chapter.

11.6 LEARNING OBJECTIVE

Discuss the policies central banks used during the 2007–2009 global financial crisis.

Central Bank Policies during the 2007–2009 Global Financial Crisis

As we have seen, a country's central bank traditionally responds to a recession by lowering the target for the interest rate. The severity of the recession of 2007–2009, particularly the problems in global financial markets during those years, complicated the job of the Federal Reserve in the United States, the world's largest central bank. For example, by December 2008, the US Federal Reserve had effectively lowered the target for the overnight interest rate to zero, but the zero interest rate alone did not achieve the desired expansionary effect on the economy. In this section, we will discuss some of the additional policy measures the Federal Reserve took during the 2007–2009 recession. Some of these measures were used for the first time in its history.

The Inflation and Deflation of the Housing Market Bubble in the United States

To understand the 2007–2009 global financial crisis and the difficulties in financial markets that occurred during it, we need to start by considering the housing market in the United States. The US Federal Reserve lowered the target for its federal funds rate during the 2001 recession to stimulate demand for housing. The policy was successful, and most builders experienced several years of high demand. By 2005, however, many economists argued that a "bubble" had formed in the housing market. As we discussed in Chapter 6, the price of any asset reflects the returns the owner of the asset expects to receive. For example, the price of a share of stock reflects the profitability of the firm issuing the stock because the owner of a share of stock has a claim on the firm's profits and assets. Many economists believe, however, that sometimes a *stock market bubble* can form when the prices of stocks rise above levels that can be justified by the profitability of the firms issuing the stock. Stock market bubbles end when enough investors decide

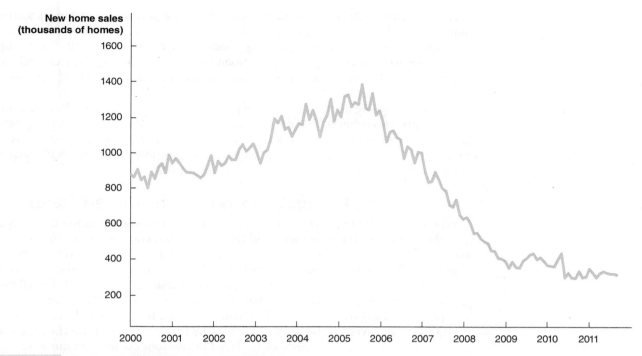

Figure 11.11 **The Housing Bubble in the United States**

Sales of new homes in the United States went on a roller-coaster ride, rising by 60 percent between January 2000 and July 2005, before falling by 80 percent between July 2005 and May 2010.

Note: The data are seasonally adjusted at an annual rate.
Source: Data from U.S. Bureau of the Census.

stocks are overvalued and begin to sell. Why would an investor be willing to pay more for a share of stock than would be justified by its underlying value? There are two main explanations: The investor may be caught up in the enthusiasm of the moment and, by failing to gather sufficient information, may overestimate the true value of the stock; or the investor may expect to profit from buying stock at inflated prices if the investor can sell the stock at an even higher price before the bubble bursts.

The price of a house should reflect the value of the housing services the house provides. We can use the rents charged for comparable houses in an area to measure the value of housing services. By 2005, in some US cities, the prices of houses had risen so much that monthly mortgage payments were far above the monthly rent on comparable houses. In addition, in some cities, there was an increase in the number of buyers who did not intend to live in the houses they purchased but were using them as investments. Like stock investors during a stock market bubble, these housing investors were expecting to make a profit by selling houses at higher prices than they had paid for them, and they were not concerned about whether the prices of the houses were above the value of the housing services provided.

During 2006 and 2007, it became clear that the air was rapidly escaping from the US housing bubble. Figure 11.11 shows new home sales for each month from January 2000 through August 2011. New home sales rose by 60 percent between January 2000 and July 2005 and then fell by 80 percent between July 2005 and May 2010; sales remained at low levels during the following year. Sales of existing homes followed a similar pattern. Prices of new and existing homes in most markets also began to decline beginning in 2006, and the inventory of unsold homes offered for sale soared. Some homebuyers began having trouble making their loan payments. When lenders foreclosed on some of these loans, the lenders sold the homes, causing housing prices to decline further. *Subprime loans* are loans granted to borrowers with flawed credit histories. Some mortgage lenders that had concentrated on making subprime loans suffered heavy losses and went out of business, and most banks and other lenders tightened the requirements for borrowers. This *credit crunch* made it more difficult for potential homebuyers to obtain mortgages, further depressing the market.

The decline in the housing market affected other markets as well. For example, with home prices falling, consumption spending on furniture, appliances, and home improvements declined as many households found it more difficult to borrow against the value of their homes.

Was the housing bubble the result of overly optimistic expectations by homebuyers and builders who believed that new residential construction and housing prices would continue to rise at rapid rates indefinitely? While overly optimistic expectations may have played some role in the housing bubble, many economists believe that changes in the market for mortgages may have played a bigger role.

The Changing Mortgage Market in the United States

Until the 1970s, the financial institutions that granted mortgages in the United States kept the loans until the borrowers paid them off. As we saw in Chapter 10, a financial asset such as a mortgage is a security only if it can be resold in a secondary market. Many politicians in the United States believed that home ownership could be increased by creating a secondary market in mortgages. If financial institutions could resell mortgages, then, in effect, individual investors would be able to provide funds for mortgages. The process would work like this: If a bank granted a mortgage and then resold the mortgage to an investor, the bank could use the funds received from the investor to grant another mortgage. In this way, financial institutions could grant more mortgage loans because they would no longer depend only on deposits for the funds needed to make the loans. One barrier to creating a secondary market in mortgages was that most investors were unwilling to buy mortgages because they were afraid of losing money if the borrower stopped making payments, or *defaulted*, on the loan.

To reassure investors, the US government used two *government-sponsored enterprises (GSEs)*: the Federal National Mortgage Association ("Fannie Mae") and the Federal Home Loan Mortgage Corporation ("Freddie Mac"), the equivalent of Canada's Canada Mortgage and Housing Corporation (CMHC). These two institutions stand between investors and banks that grant mortgages. Fannie Mae and Freddie Mac sell bonds to investors and use the funds to purchase mortgages from banks. By the 1990s, a large secondary market existed in mortgages, with funds flowing from investors through Fannie Mae and Freddie Mac to banks and, ultimately, to individuals and families borrowing money to buy houses.

The Role of Investment Banks in the United States

By the 2000s, further changes had taken place in the US mortgage market. First, investment banks became significant participants in the secondary market for mortgages. Investment banks, such as Goldman Sachs and Morgan Stanley, differ from commercial banks in that they do not take in deposits and rarely lend directly to households. Instead, investment banks concentrate on providing advice to firms issuing stocks and bonds or considering mergers with other firms. Investment banks began buying mortgages, bundling large numbers of them together as bonds known as *mortgage-backed securities*, and reselling them to investors. Mortgage-backed securities proved very popular with investors because they often paid higher interest rates than other securities with comparable default risk.

Second, by the height of the US housing bubble in 2005 and early 2006, lenders had greatly loosened the standards for obtaining a mortgage loan. Traditionally, only borrowers with good credit histories and who were willing to make a down payment equal to at least 20 percent of the value of the house they were buying would be able to receive a mortgage. By 2005, however, lenders were issuing many mortgages to subprime borrowers with flawed credit histories. In addition, "Alt-A" borrowers (those with mortgages that are riskier than prime mortgages but less risky than subprime mortgages) who stated—but did not document—their incomes and borrowers who made very small down payments found it easier to take out loans. Lenders also created new types of *adjustable-rate mortgages* that allowed borrowers to pay a very low interest rate for the first few years of the mortgage and then pay a higher rate in later years. The chance that the borrowers using these nontraditional mortgages would default was higher than for borrowers using traditional mortgages. Why would borrowers take out mortgages if they doubted that they could make the payments, and why would lenders grant these mortgages? The answer seems to be that both borrowers and lenders were anticipating that housing prices would continue to rise, which would reduce the chance that borrowers would default on the mortgages and would also make it easier for borrowers to convert to more traditional mortgages in the future.

Unfortunately, the decline in housing prices in the United States led to rising defaults among subprime and Alt-A borrowers, borrowers with adjustable-rate mortgages, and borrowers who had made only small down payments. When borrowers began defaulting on mortgages, the value of many mortgage-backed securities declined sharply. Investors feared that if they purchased these securities, they would not receive the promised payments because the payments on the securities depended on borrowers making their mortgage payments, which an increasing number were failing to do. Many commercial banks and investment banks owned these mortgage-backed securities, so the decline in the value of the securities caused these banks to suffer heavy losses. By mid-2007, the decline in the value of mortgage-backed securities and the large losses suffered by commercial banks and investment banks began to cause turmoil in the financial system. Many investors refused to buy mortgage-backed securities, and some investors would buy only bonds issued by the US Treasury.

Why Didn't Canada Have a Housing Bubble and Banking Crisis in 2008?

As already noted, during the subprime financial crisis, the value of mortgage-backed securities held by financial institutions in the United States plummeted. Moreover, the US government, as well as governments in some European countries, worked on full-scale banking bailouts and rescue packages in the trillions of dollars. Canada, however, did not have to bail out any banks, although Canadian banks also had their problems; their shares fell by almost 50 percent, and some of them experienced huge losses.

One reason the Canadian economy and banks have done much better than their US and European counterparts is that Canada's banking regulator, the Office of the Superintendent of Financial Institutions (OSFI), has been more conservative than banking regulators in other countries. As a result, Canadian banks have lower leverage and more conservative lending and acquisition practices. In fact, in the aftermath of the subprime recession, Canada's banking system has been viewed as the soundest in the world, with many countries considering Canadian-style reforms of their financial markets.

However, the low interest rates over the past five years are creating distortions in the economy, such as a household debt to after-tax income ratio of over 165 percent (as of May 2013) and an overheated housing market. These distortions have alarmed the Bank of Canada, the Department of Finance, and the Office of the Superintendent of Financial Institutions. So far, the Bank of Canada has resisted raising interest rates, but there has been some coordination between monetary policy and financial stability policy. In particular, the Minister of Finance has tightened the country's mortgage insurance rules four times so far since the global financial crisis, in an attempt to cool the housing market and address financial imbalances in the economy.

| Making the Connection | ## The Wonderful World of Leverage |

Traditionally, most people taking out a mortgage make a down payment equal to 20 percent of the price of the house and borrow the remaining 80 percent. During a housing boom, however, many people purchase houses with down payments of 5 percent or less. In this sense, borrowers are highly *leveraged*, which means that their investment in their house is made mostly with borrowed money.

© Lee Brown/Alamy

Making a very small down payment on a home mortgage leaves a buyer vulnerable to falling house prices.

To see how leverage works in the housing market, consider the following example: Suppose that you buy a $200 000 house on January 1, 2016. On January 1, 2017, the price of the house—if you decide to sell it—has risen to $220 000. What return have you earned on your investment in the house? The answer depends on how much you invested when you bought the house. For example, if you paid $200 000 in cash for the house, your return on that $200 000 investment is the $20 000 increase in the price of the house divided by your $200 000 investment, or 10 percent. Suppose that rather than paying cash, you made a down payment of 20 percent, or $40 000, and borrowed the rest by taking out a mortgage loan of $160 000. Now the return on your investment in the house is the $20 000 increase in the price of the house divided by your $40 000 investment, or 50 percent. If the down payment is less than 20 percent, your return on investment will be higher. The second column in the table below shows how the return on your investment increases as your down payment decreases:

Return on your investment from ...

Down Payment	A 10 Percent Increase in the Price of Your House	A 10 Percent Decrease in the Price of Your House
100%	10%	−10%
20	50	−50
10	100	−100
5	200	−200

An investment financed at least partly by borrowing is called a *leveraged investment*. As this example shows, the larger the fraction of an investment financed by borrowing, the greater the degree of leverage in the investment, and the greater the potential return. But as the third column in the table shows, the reverse is also true: The greater the leverage, the greater the potential loss. To see why, consider once again that you buy a house for $200 000, except that in this case, after one year the price of the house falls to $180 000. If you paid $200 000 in cash for the house—so your leverage was zero—the $20 000 decline in the price of the house represents a loss of 10 percent of your investment. But if you made a down payment of only $10 000 and borrowed the remaining $190 000, then the $20 000 decline in the price of the house represents a loss of 200 percent of your investment. In fact, the house is now worth $10 000 less than the amount of your mortgage loan. The *equity* in your house is the difference between the market price of the house and the amount you owe on a loan. If the amount you owe is greater than the price of the house, you have *negative equity*. A homeowner who has negative equity is also said to be "upside down" on his or her mortgage.

When the housing bubble burst in the United States and housing prices started to fall, many people found that they had negative equity. In that situation, some people defaulted on their loans, sometimes by simply moving out and abandoning their homes. Leverage had contributed to the housing boom and bust and the severity of the 2007–2009 recession.

MyEconLab **Your Turn:** Test your understanding by doing related problem 6.6 on page 361 at the end of this chapter.

The US Federal Reserve and the US Treasury Department Respond

Because the problems in financial markets resulting from the bursting of the housing bubble in the United States were so profound, the US Federal Reserve entered into an unusual partnership with the Treasury Department to develop suitable policies. Federal Reserve Chairman Ben Bernanke and Treasury Secretaries Henry Paulson (in the Bush administration) and Timothy Geithner (in the first Obama administration) responded to the crisis by intervening in financial markets in unprecedented ways.

Initial US Federal Reserve and Treasury Actions   The financial crisis significantly worsened following the bankruptcy of the investment bank Lehman Brothers on September 15, 2008. So it is useful to look at the actions taken by the US Federal Reserve and the Treasury before and after that date. First, although the Federal Reserve traditionally made loans only to commercial banks, in March 2008, it announced it would temporarily make discount loans to *primary dealers*—firms that participate in regular open market transactions with the Federal Reserve. This change was intended to provide short-term funds to these dealers, some of which are investment banks. Second, also in March, the Federal Reserve announced that it would loan up to US$200 billion of Treasury securities in exchange for mortgage-backed securities. This temporary program made it possible for primary dealers that owned mortgage-backed securities that were difficult or impossible to sell, to have access to Treasury securities that they could use as collateral for short-term loans. Third, once again in March, the Federal Reserve and the Treasury helped JPMorgan Chase acquire the investment bank Bear Stearns, which was on the edge of failing. The Federal Reserve agreed that if JPMorgan Chase would acquire Bear Stearns, the Federal Reserve would guarantee any losses JPMorgan Chase suffered on Bear Stearns's holdings of mortgage-backed securities, up to a limit of US$29 billion. The Federal Reserve and the Treasury were convinced that the failure of Bear Stearns had the potential of causing a financial panic, as many investors and financial firms would have stopped making short-term loans to other investment banks. Finally, in early September, the Treasury moved to have the federal government take control of Fannie Mae and Freddie Mac. Although Fannie Mae and Freddie Mac had been sponsored by the federal government, they were actually private businesses whose stock was bought and sold on the New York Stock Exchange. Under the Treasury's plan, Fannie Mae and Freddie Mac were each provided with up to US$100 billion in exchange for 80 percent ownership of the firms. The firms were placed under the supervision of the Federal Housing Finance Agency. The Treasury believed that the bankruptcy of Fannie Mae and Freddie Mac would have caused a collapse in confidence in mortgage-backed securities, further devastating this already weak housing market.

Responses to the Failure of Lehman Brothers   Some economists and policymakers criticized the decision by the US Federal Reserve and the Treasury to help arrange the sale of Bear Stearns to JPMorgan Chase. Their main concern was with what is known as the *moral hazard problem*, which is the possibility that managers of financial firms such as Bear Stearns might make riskier investments if they believe that the federal government will save them from bankruptcy. The Federal Reserve and the Treasury acted to save Bear Stearns because they believed that the failure of a large financial firm could have wider economic repercussions. As we discussed in Chapter 10, when a financial firm sells off its holdings of bonds and other assets, it causes their prices to fall, which in turn can undermine the financial position of other firms that also own these assets. In September 2008, when the investment bank Lehman Brothers was near bankruptcy, the Federal Reserve and the Treasury had to weigh the moral hazard problem against the possibility that the failure of Lehman Brothers would lead to further declines in asset prices and endanger the financial positions of other firms.

The Federal Reserve and the Treasury decided to allow Lehman Brothers to go bankrupt, which it did on September 15, 2008. The adverse reaction in financial markets was stronger than the Federal Reserve and the Treasury had expected, which led them to reverse course two days later, when the Federal Reserve agreed to provide a US$85 billion loan to the American International Group (AIG)—the largest insurance company in the United States—in exchange for an 80 percent ownership stake, effectively giving the federal government control of the company. One important result of the failure of Lehman Brothers was the heavy losses suffered by Reserve Primary Fund, a money market mutual fund that had invested in loans to Lehman Brothers. The problems at Reserve Primary Fund led many investors to withdraw their funds from it and other money market funds. These withdrawals reduced the ability of the money market funds to purchase commercial paper from corporations. Because in recent years corporations had become dependent on selling commercial paper to finance their operations, the Treasury and the Federal Reserve moved to stabilize this market and ensure that the flow of funds from investors to corporations continued. The Treasury announced a plan to provide insurance for deposits in money market mutual funds, similar to the existing insurance on bank deposits. The Federal Reserve announced that for a limited time it would lend directly to corporations by purchasing three-month commercial paper issued by non-financial corporations.

Finally, in October 2008, Congress passed the *Troubled Asset Relief Program (TARP)*, under which the Treasury attempted to stabilize the commercial banking system by providing funds to banks in exchange for stock. Taking partial ownership positions in private commercial banks was an unprecedented action for the federal government.

Clearly, the recession of 2007–2009 and the accompanying global financial crisis had led the Federal Reserve and the Treasury to implement new approaches to policy. Many of these new approaches were controversial because they involved partial government ownership of financial firms, implicit guarantees to large financial firms that they would not be allowed to go bankrupt, and unprecedented intervention in financial markets. Although the approaches were new, they were intended to achieve the traditional macroeconomic policy goals of high employment, price stability, and stability of financial markets. What remains to be seen is whether these new approaches represent a permanent increase in federal government involvement in US financial markets or whether the end of the recession will see policy return to more traditional approaches.

The US Federal Reserve Adopts Flexible Inflation Targeting

Inflation targeting has been adopted by the central banks of New Zealand (1989), Canada (1991), the United Kingdom (1992), Finland (1993), Sweden (1993), and Spain (1994), and by the European Central Bank. Inflation targeting has also been used in some newly industrializing countries, such as Chile, South Korea, Mexico, and South Africa, as well as in some transition economies in Eastern Europe, such as the Czech Republic, Hungary, and Poland. The results of inflation targeting have varied, but typically the move to inflation targeting has been accompanied by lower inflation (sometimes at the cost of temporarily higher unemployment).

Over the past decade, many economists in the United States and the current Federal Reserve chair, Ben Bernanke, had proposed using *inflation targeting* as a framework for conducting monetary policy in that country. As we have already discussed, with inflation targeting, the central bank commits to achieving a publicly announced inflation target of, for example, 2 percent. Inflation targeting does not impose an inflexible rule on the central bank. The central bank would still be free, for example, to take action in the case of a severe recession. Nevertheless, monetary policy goals and operations would focus on inflation and inflation forecasts.

Although Ben Bernanke's appointment as chair of the Federal Reserve in January 2006 signalled that the Federal Reserve would likely adopt a policy of inflation targeting, the necessity of dealing with the recession of 2007–2009 temporarily pushed the issue off the Federal Reserve's agenda. In 2011, however, the Federal Reserve adopted *flexible inflation targeting*, a strategy that has been practised for over 20 years by the Bank of Canada and a number of other central banks around the world.

Economics in Your Life

Should You Buy a House during a Recession?

At the beginning of this chapter, we asked whether buying a house during a recession is a good idea. Clearly, there are many considerations to keep in mind when buying a house, which is the largest purchase you are likely to make in your lifetime. Included among these considerations are the price of the house relative to other comparable houses in the neighbourhood, whether house prices in the neighbourhood have been rising or falling, and the location of the house relative to stores, work, and good schools. Also important is the interest rate you will have to pay on the mortgage loan you would need in order to buy the house. As we have seen in this chapter, during a recession, the Bank of Canada often takes actions to lower interest rates. So, mortgage rates are typically lower during a recession than at other times. You may want to take advantage of low interest rates to buy a house during a recession. But, recessions are also times of rising unemployment, and you would not want to make a commitment to borrow a lot of money for 15 or more years if you were in significant danger of losing your job. We can conclude, then, that if your job seems secure, buying a house during a recession may be a good idea.

Conclusion

Monetary policy is one way governments pursue goals for inflation, employment, and financial stability. Many journalists and politicians refer to the governor of the Bank of Canada as second only to the prime minister of Canada in terms of ability to affect the Canadian economy. The government and the prime minister, however, also use their power over spending and taxes to try to stabilize the economy. In Chapter 12, we discuss how *fiscal policy*—changes in government spending and taxes—affect the economy.

Read *An Inside Look* on the next page for a discussion of the Bank of Canada's new policies designed to address monetary policy issues in the aftermath of the global financial crisis and the "Great Recession."

The Bank of Canada's Response to a Developing Housing Price Bubble

ECONOMIST

Canada's Housing Market: Look Out Below

In few corners of the world would a car park squeezed between two arms of an elevated highway be seen as prime real estate. In Toronto, however, a 75-storey condominium is planned for such an awkward site, near the waterfront. The car park next door will become a pair of 70-storey towers too. In total, 173 sky-scrapers are being built in Toronto, the most in North America. New York is second with 96.

When the United States saw a vast housing bubble inflate and burst during the 2000s, many Canadians felt smug about the purported prudence of their financial and property markets. During the crash, Canadian house prices fell by just 8%, compared with more than 30% in America. They hit new record highs by 2010. "Canada was not a part of the problem," Stephen Harper, the prime minister, boasted in 2010.

Ⓐ Today the consensus is growing on Bay Street, Toronto's answer to Wall Street, that Mr Harper may have to eat his words. In response to America's slow economic recovery and uncertainty in Europe, the Bank of Canada has kept interest rates at record lows. Five-year fixed-rate mortgages now charge interest of just 2.99%. In response, Canadians have sought ever-bigger loans for ever-costlier homes. The country's house prices have doubled since 2002.

Speculators are pouring into the property markets in Toronto and Vancouver. "We have foreign investors who are purchasing two, three, four, five properties," says Michael Thompson, who heads Toronto's economic-development committee. Last month a modest Toronto home put on the market for C$380,000 ($381,500) sold for C$570,000, following a bidding war among 31 prospective buyers. According to Demographia, a consultancy, Vancouver's ratio of home prices to incomes is the highest in the English-speaking world.

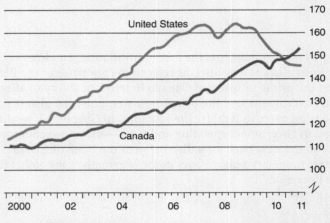

A dubious crown
Household debt* as % of personal disposable income

Sources: US Federal Reserve; Statistics Canada; Thomson Reuters

*Includes non-corporate business sector

Bankers are becoming alarmed. Mark Carney, the governor of the central bank, has been warning for years that Canadians are consuming beyond their means. The bosses of banks with big mortgage businesses, including CIBC, Royal Bank of Canada and the Bank of Montreal, have all said the housing market is at or near its peak. Canada's ratio of household debt to disposable income has risen by 40% in the past decade, recently surpassing America's (see chart). And its ratio of house prices to income is now 30% above its historical average—less than, say, Ireland's excesses (which reached 70%), but high enough to expect a drop. A recent report from Bank of America said Canada was "showing many of the signs of a classic bubble."

The consequences of such a bubble bursting are hard to predict. On the one hand, high demand for Canada's commodity exports could cushion the blow from a housing bust. And since banks have recourse to all of a borrower's assets, and Canadian lending standards are stricter than America's were, a decline in house prices would probably not wreck the banks as it did in the United States.

Ⓑ However, the Canadian economy is still dependent on the consumer. Fears about the global economy have slowed business investment, and all levels of government are bent on austerity. The Conservative government's next budget is expected to put forward a plan to close the federal deficit, now 2% of GDP, by 2015—modest austerity compared to Europe's, but still a drag on the economy. Few new jobs are being created. Assuming there is no setback in Europe's debt crunch, slowdown in America or drop in commodity prices, GDP is forecast to grow by a meagre 2% this year. If consumers start feeling less well off, Canada could slip back into recession.

The inevitable landing will probably be soft. Increases in house prices and sales volumes are slowing, and the 2015 Pan American Games in Toronto should prop up builders. "The national housing market is more like a balloon than a bubble," says a report by the Bank of Montreal. "While bubbles always burst, a balloon often deflates slowly in the absence of a 'pin.'"

Moreover, the government is trying to cool the market. The banking regulator is increasing its scrutiny of housing in response to concerns about speculators. The Canada Mortgage and Housing Corporation, a government mortgage-insurance agency, says it will have to start reducing its new coverage because of legal limits. And the finance ministry has cut the maximum term of publicly insured mortgages from 35 years to 30. Some bank managers are calling for it to be reduced to 25, the historical norm. Canada's reputation for financial sobriety is not entirely unwarranted.

However, the state has refused to use its most powerful tool. To protect business investment, the central bank has made clear that it plans to keep interest rates low. As long as money stays cheap, the balloon could get bigger—perhaps big enough to become a fully fledged bubble after all.

Source: Copyright © The Economist Newspaper Limited, London (February 4th, 2012).

Key Points in the Article

The Bank of Canada lowered its policy rate during the global financial crisis to 25 basis points (0.25 percentage points) to deal with the crisis and stimulate the level of economic activity. The policy was successful, although due to the severity of the 2007–2009 recession, this very low rate still did little to stimulate the economy.

Today, many economists argue that low interest rates are encouraging excessive risk taking and that a bubble is developing in the Canadian housing market, with house prices above levels that can be justified by the value of the housing services that houses provide.

The Bank of Canada is also concerned about the high debt to after-tax income ratio of over 150 percent, which is almost as high as the debt-to-income ratio US households had before the subprime financial crisis. If interest rates increase in the future, mortgage rates will also increase, leading to higher monthly mortgage payments and, therefore, less income to spend on other goods and services. Higher mortgage rates might also reduce house sales, and the decrease in demand may reduce housing prices.

Analyzing the News

(a) Economists and bankers are becoming alarmed that a bubble is developing in the Canadian housing market. This bubble could be driven by overly optimistic expectations, which former US Federal Reserve chairman Alan Greenspan referred to as "irrational exuberance." However, the consensus is that this is a credit-driven bubble, similar to the housing price bubble in the United States that led to the global financial crisis and a number of banking crises around the world.

(b) Due to the slow economic recovery in the United States and the economic uncertainty in Europe, the Bank of Canada is not using monetary policy to raise interest rates and constrain the credit-driven housing bubble. Because the Bank of Canada is refraining from leaning on the bubble, economists and bankers are concerned the bubble might burst and cause housing prices to decline. A burst bubble and decline in housing prices would have negative effects both on households and the balance sheets of banks, causing damage to the economy.

(c) The figure below shows the average annual interest rates for the overnight interest rate, long-term Canada bonds, and

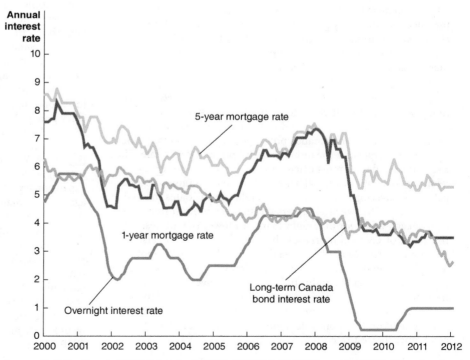

Source: Statistics Canada CANSIM II series V39079, V122520, V122521, and V122544. Reproduced and distributed on an "as is" basis with the permission of Statistics Canada.

one- and five-year mortgages from 2000 to January 2012. The overnight interest rate in 2012 was 1 percent, and the five-year mortgage rate was around 5 percent. The Bank of Canada has committed to keeping the overnight interest rate this low, and it seems that currently the only option for Canada is the use of financial stability policies, also known as *macroprudential* policies. In fact, banking regulators hope that tighter macroprudential policies will restrain excessive risk taking and credit growth, thereby promoting financial stability.

Thinking Critically

1. An increase in interest rates that are necessary to prick the housing bubble will affect not only the prices of housing, but all prices within the economy. Thus, the Bank of Canada is concerned that taking actions to prick the housing bubble could have harmful effects on the aggregate economy. Should the Bank of Canada pop the housing price bubble? Alternatively, to minimize the negative effect on the economy that will occur when the bubble bursts, should the Bank of Canada slow the bubble's growth?

2. Monetary policy and financial stability policy must be coordinated if the Bank of Canada is to achieve its objectives of price stability and financial market stability. How can coordination between monetary policy and financial stability policy be achieved, given that control of these policies rests with different government agencies?

Chapter Summary and Problems

Key Terms

Contractionary monetary policy, p. 334

Expansionary monetary policy, p. 334

Flexible inflation targeting, p. 327

Governing council (of the Bank of Canada), p. 340

Inflation targeting, p. 327

Monetary growth rule, p. 343

Monetary policy, p. 326

Open market buyback operations, p. 333

Operating band, p. 332

Overnight interest rate, p. 332

Symmetric inflation targeting, p. 327

Taylor rule, p. 344

Summary

*LO 11.1 *Monetary policy* is the actions the Bank of Canada takes to manage the money supply and interest rates to pursue its macroeconomic policy goals. The Bank of Canada has four *monetary policy goals* that are intended to promote a well-functioning economy: price stability, high employment, stability of financial markets and institutions, and economic growth.

LO 11.2 The Bank of Canada's *monetary policy targets* are economic variables that it can affect directly and that in turn affect variables such as real GDP and the price level that are closely related to the Bank of Canada's policy goals. The two main monetary policy targets are the money supply and the interest rate. The Bank of Canada has most often chosen to use the interest rate as its monetary policy target. The Bank of Canada announces a target for the *overnight interest rate* on eight "fixed" dates throughout the year. The overnight interest rate is the interest rate banks charge each other for overnight loans. To lower the interest rate, the Bank of Canada increases the money supply. To raise the interest rate, the Bank of Canada decreases the money supply. In a graphical analysis of the money market, when the money supply curve shifts to the right, the result is a movement down the money demand curve and a new equilibrium at a lower interest rate. When the money supply curve shifts to the left, the result is a movement up the money demand curve and a new equilibrium at a higher interest rate.

LO 11.3 An *expansionary monetary policy* lowers interest rates to increase consumption, investment, and net exports. This increased spending causes the aggregate demand (*AD*) curve to shift out more than it otherwise would, raising the level of real GDP and the price level. An expansionary monetary policy can help the Bank of Canada achieve its goal of high employment. A *contractionary monetary policy* raises interest rates to decrease consumption, investment, and net exports. This decreased spending causes the aggregate demand curve to shift out less than it otherwise would, reducing both the level of real GDP and the inflation rate below what they would be in the absence of monetary policy. A contractionary monetary policy can help the Bank of Canada achieve its goal of price stability.

LO 11.4 We can use the *dynamic aggregate demand and aggregate supply model* introduced in Chapter 9 to look more closely at expansionary and contractionary monetary policies. The dynamic aggregate demand and aggregate supply model takes into account that (1) the economy experiences continuing inflation, with the price level rising every year, and (2) the economy experiences long-run growth, with the *LRAS* curve shifting to the right every year. In the dynamic model, an expansionary monetary policy tries to ensure that the aggregate demand curve will shift far enough to the right to bring about macroeconomic equilibrium with real GDP equal to potential GDP. A contractionary monetary policy attempts to offset movements in aggregate demand that would cause macroeconomic equilibrium to occur at a level of real GDP that is greater than potential real GDP.

---

*'Learning Objective' is abbreviated to 'LO' in the end of chapter material.

LO **11.5** Some economists have argued that the Bank of Canada should use the money supply, rather than the interest rate, as its monetary policy target. Milton Friedman and other monetarists argued that central banks should adopt a *monetary growth rule* of increasing the money supply every year at a fixed rate. Support for this proposal declined after 1980 because the relationship between movements in the money supply and movements in real GDP and the price level weakened. John Taylor analyzed the factors involved in central bank decision making and developed the *Taylor rule* for overnight interest rate targeting. The Taylor rule links the central bank's target for the overnight interest rate to economic variables. The Bank of Canada adopted *inflation targeting*—conducting monetary policy so as to commit the central bank to achieving a publicly announced level of inflation—back in 1991, and its performance in the 1990s and 2000s generally received high marks from economists. Over the past decade, many economists and central bankers have expressed significant interest in using inflation targeting. A number of foreign central banks have adopted inflation targeting, including the US Federal Reserve.

LO **11.6** A bubble in the US housing market that began to deflate in 2006 led to the global recession of 2007–2009 and an accompanying global financial crisis. In response, central banks around the world, including the Bank of Canada, instituted a variety of policy actions to protect their economies. In a series of steps, the Bank of Canada cut the target for the overnight interest rate from 4.5 percent in July 2007 to 0.25 percent in April 2009. The US Federal Reserve also cut the target for the federal funds rate from 5.25 percent in September 2007 to effectively zero in December 2008. The decline in the US housing market caused wider problems in the global financial system, as defaults on home mortgages rose and the value of mortgage-backed securities declined. Central banks around the world implemented a series of new policies to provide liquidity and restore confidence. They expanded the types of firms eligible for loans from the central bank and began lending directly to corporations by purchasing commercial paper. In the United States, under the *Troubled Asset Relief Program*, the US Treasury provided financial support to banks and other financial firms in exchange for part ownership. The Treasury also moved to have the federal government take control of Fannie Mae and Freddie Mac, government-sponsored firms that play a central role in the US mortgage market. The failure of the investment bank Lehman Brothers in September 2008 led to a deepening of the global financial crisis and provided the motivation for some of the new monetary policies. Ultimately, the new policies stabilized the financial system, but their long-term effects remain the subject of debate.

MyEconLab   Log in to MyEconLab to complete these exercises and get instant feedback.

Review Questions

LO 11.1
1.1 When the government established the Bank of Canada in 1934, what was its main responsibility?

1.2 What are the Bank of Canada's four monetary policy goals?

1.3 How can the government of Canada influence the conduct of monetary policy?

1.4 How can investment banks be subject to liquidity problems?

LO 11.2
2.1 What is a monetary policy target? Why does the Bank of Canada use policy targets?

2.2 What do economists mean by the demand for money? What is the advantage of holding money? What is the disadvantage?

2.3 Draw a demand and supply graph showing equilibrium in the money market. Suppose the Bank of Canada wants to lower the equilibrium interest rate. Show on the graph how the Bank of Canada would accomplish this objective.

2.4 What is the overnight interest rate? What role does it play in monetary policy?

LO 11.3
3.1 How does an increase in interest rates affect aggregate demand? Briefly discuss how each component of aggregate demand is affected.

3.2 If the Bank of Canada believes the economy is about to fall into recession, what actions should it take? If the Bank of Canada believes the inflation rate is about to increase, what actions should it take?

3.3 What is "quantitative easing" and what are the central banks' objectives in using it?

LO 11.4
4.1 What are the key differences between how we illustrate an expansionary monetary policy in the basic aggregate demand and aggregate supply model and in the dynamic aggregate demand and aggregate supply model?

4.2 What are the key differences between how we illustrate a contractionary monetary policy in the basic aggregate demand and aggregate supply model and in the dynamic aggregate demand and aggregate supply model?

LO 11.5
5.1 What is a monetary rule, as opposed to a monetary policy? What monetary rule would Milton Friedman have liked central banks to follow? Why has support for a monetary rule of the kind advocated by Friedman declined since 1980?

5.2 For more than 20 years, the Bank of Canada has used the overnight interest rate as its monetary policy target. Why doesn't the Bank of Canada target the money supply at the same time?

5.3 What is the Taylor rule? What is its purpose?

LO 11.6
6.1 What is a mortgage? What were the important developments in the mortgage market during the years after 1970?

6.2 Beginning in 2008, the US Federal Reserve, the Bank of Canada, and other central banks around the world responded to the financial crisis by intervening in financial markets in unprecedented ways. Briefly summarize the actions of the Federal Reserve.

Problems and Applications

LO 11.1

1.1 What is a bank panic?

1.2 Why is price stability one of the Bank of Canada's main monetary policy goals? What problems can high inflation rates cause for the economy?

1.3 What is the difference between the Bank of Canada and commercial banks, such as CIBC, Royal Bank, TD Canada Trust, ScotiaBank, and Bank of Montreal?

1.4 Stock prices rose rapidly in 2005, as did housing prices in many parts of the country. By late 2008, both stock prices and housing prices were declining sharply. Some economists have argued that rapid increases and decreases in the prices of assets such as shares of stock or houses can damage the economy. Currently, stabilizing asset prices is not one of the Bank of Canada's policy goals. In what ways would a goal of stabilizing asset prices be different from the four goals of monetary policy listed on page 325? Do you believe that stabilizing asset prices should be added to the list of the Bank of Canada's policy goals? Briefly explain.

LO 11.2

2.1 In the graph of the money market below, what could cause the money supply curve to shift from MS_1 to MS_2? What could cause the money demand curve to shift from MD_1 to MD_2?

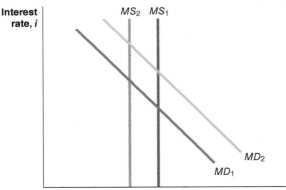

2.2 The following excerpt is from a July 2010 *Financial Post* article:

> The Bank of Canada raised its benchmark policy rate Tuesday by 25 basis points to 0.75 per cent, even though it scaled back its growth outlook on the belief budget cutting among households and governments in advanced economies will "temper" the pace of the global recovery. Many of Canada's commercial banks followed suit by raising their prime lending rates.

a. What is the name of the "benchmark policy rate" mentioned in this article?

b. Briefly explain who borrows money and who lends money at this "benchmark policy rate"?

c. What is the "prime lending rate" and what is its relationship to the "benchmark policy rate" mentioned in the article?

Paul Viera, "Bank of Canada raises key interest rate to 0.75 per cent," Financial Post, July 20, 2010.

2.3 If the Bank of Canada purchases $100 million worth of Canada bonds from the public, predict what will happen to the money supply. Explain your reasoning.

2.4 In response to problems in financial markets and a slowing economy, the Bank of Canada cut the target overnight interest rate to an all-time low. BMO Capital Markets economist Michael Gregory said that "Quantitative easing [expanding the money supply] is looming. I see printing money, high-powered money, as providing excess reserves in the banking system, so the banks will do something with that extra money." What is the relationship between the overnight interest rate falling and the money supply expanding? How does lowering the target overnight interest rate provide the banks with "extra money"?

CBC News "Bank of Canada cuts key interest rate to 0.25%": http://www.cbc.ca/news/business/story/2009/04/21/bank-canada-rate.html#ixzz14nj1WnFZ (Accessed on April 1, 2012).

LO 11.3

3.1 [**Related to the** Chapter Opener **on page 325**] An October 2010 article in the *Financial Post* said:

> Canadian households have been running a net financial deficit for 37 consecutive quarters, and [former Bank of Canada governor Mark] Carney acknowledged that the current situation in which investment in housing is outstripping total savings cannot continue. But how do you stop this when the economy continues to create jobs and home affordability remains near an all-time high? [National Bank Financial economist Stéfane] Marion says unless the Department of Finance introduces a more stringent set of rules for access to housing, the Bank of Canada may be forced to send a price signal to consumers in the form of another rate hike.

What sort of "price signal" would the Bank of Canada be sending? Why would the Bank of Canada be "forced" to send it?

Ratner, Jonathan, "Housing and jobs may still prompt Bank of Canada rate hike," Financial Post October 1 2010. Material reprinted by the express permission of: National Post, a division of Postmedia Network, Inc.

3.2 In explaining why monetary policy did not pull Japan out of a recession in the early 2000s, an official at the Bank of Japan was quoted as saying that despite "major increases in the money supply," the money "stay[ed] in banks." Explain what the official meant by saying that the money stayed in banks. Why would that be a problem? Where does the money go if an expansionary monetary policy is successful?

Based on James Brooke, "Critics Say Koizumi's Economic Medicine Is a Weak Tea," New York Times, February 27, 2002.

3.3 According to an article in the *Wall Street Journal*:

> In February... [Japan's] gauge of core consumer prices slipped 0.1% from a year earlier.... The Bank of Japan said last year it would regard prices as stable if they rose from zero to 2% a year.... The Bank of Japan's target for short-term interest rates is just 0.5%.... it will be difficult for the Bank of Japan to "raise interest rates when prices are below the range it defines as stable," says Teizo Taya, special counselor for the Daiwa Institute of Research and a former BOJ policy board member.

  a. What is the term for a falling price level?

  b. Why would the Bank of Japan, the Japanese central bank, be reluctant to raise its target for short-term interest rates if the price level is falling?

  c. Why would a country's central bank consider a falling price level to be undesirable?

  "Japan's Consumer Prices May Threaten Economy," by Yuka Hayashi from Wall Street Journal, April 25, 2007.

3.4 An article by three economists at the Federal Reserve Bank of Richmond notes that by the fall of 2011, many unemployed people in the United States had been out of work for more than six months. The economists argue that "After a long period of unemployment, affected workers may become effectively unemployable." They conclude that "Policy options [such as providing additional training] that increase the ability of unemployed workers to find work... may be more effective at reducing unemployment than additional monetary stimulus."

  a. What is a policy of monetary stimulus?

  b. If many unemployed people have been out of work for a long time, why might policies that increase their ability to find jobs be more effective in reducing unemployment than a policy of monetary stimulus?

  Andreas Hornstein, Thomas A. Lubik, and Jessie Romero, "Potential Causes and Implications of the Rise in Long-Term Unemployment," Federal Reserve Bank of Richmond, Economic Brief, September 2011.

3.5 William McChesney Martin, who was US Federal Reserve chairman from 1951 to 1970, was once quoted as saying, "The role of the Federal Reserve is to remove the punchbowl just as the party gets going." What did he mean?

  William McChesney Martin

3.6 If monetary policy is so effective at helping the economy stabilize and protecting against recessions, why does recovery take so long? And why are the monetary policy effects not always readily apparent (effects can take years to determine)?

3.7 Former US president Ronald Reagan once stated that inflation "has one cause and one cause alone: government spending more than government takes in." Briefly explain whether you agree.

  From Edward Nelson, "Budget Deficits and Interest Rates," Monetary Trends, Federal Reserve Bank of St. Louis, March 2004.

3.8 [Related to Making the Connection **on page 337**] John Maynard Keynes is said to have remarked that using an expansionary monetary policy to pull an economy out of a deep recession can be like "pushing on a string." Briefly explain what Keynes is likely to have meant.

3.9 [Related to Making the Connection **on page 337**] Martin Feldstein, an economist at Harvard University, has argued that QE2 (i.e., the second round of quantitative easing in the United States) led consumers to decrease saving and increase spending: "A likely reason for the fall in the saving rate and the resulting rise in consumer spending was the sharp increase in the stock market, which rose by 15% between August [2010] and the end of the year. That, of course, is what the Fed had been hoping for."

  a. Why might QE2, which resulted in a decline in interest rates on long-term Treasury securities, have resulted in an increase in stock prices?

  b. Why was the Bank of Canada hoping for consumers to increase their spending in late 2010?

  Martin Feldstein, "Quantitative Easing and America's Economic Rebound," www.project-syndicate.org, February 24, 2011.

3.10 [Related to Making the Connection **on page 337**] If policymakers at the Bank of Canada are aware that GDP data are sometimes subject to large revisions, how might this affect their views about how best to conduct policy?

3.11 [Related to Don't Let This Happen to You **on page 338**] Briefly explain whether you agree with the following statement: "The Bank of Canada has an easy job. Say it wants to increase real GDP by $200 billion. All it has to do is increase the money supply by that amount."

LO 11.4

4.1 Explain whether you agree with this argument:

> If the Bank of Canada actually ever carried out a contractionary monetary policy, the price level would fall. Because the price level has not fallen in Canada over an entire year since the 1930s, we can conclude that the Bank of Canada has not carried out a contractionary policy since the 1930s.

4.2 [Related to Solved Problem 11.1 **on page 342**] Use this graph to answer the following questions.

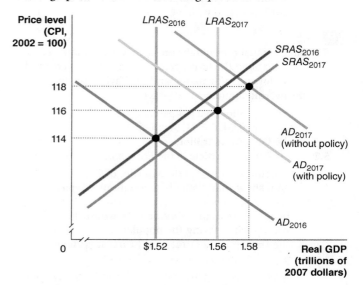

a. If the Bank of Canada does not take any policy action, what will be the level of real GDP and the price level in 2017?

b. If the Bank of Canada wants to keep real GDP at its potential level in 2017, should it use an expansionary policy or a contractionary policy? Should the Bank of Canada be buying Canada bonds or selling them?

c. If the Bank of Canada takes no policy action, what will be the inflation rate in 2017? If the Bank of Canada uses monetary policy to keep real GDP at its full-employment level, what will be the inflation rate in 2017?

4.3 [**Related to** Solved Problem 11.1 **on page 342**] The hypothetical information in the following table shows what the situation will be in 2017 if the Bank of Canada does *not* use monetary policy.

Year	Potential GDP	Real GDP	Price Level
2016	$1.52 trillion	$1.52 trillion	110.0
2017	1.56 trillion	1.58 trillion	115.5

a. If the Bank of Canada wants to keep real GDP at its potential level in 2017, should it use an expansionary policy or a contractionary policy? Should the trading desk be buying Treasury bills or selling them?

b. If the Bank of Canada's policy is successful in keeping real GDP at its potential level in 2017, state whether each of the following will be higher, lower, or the same as it would have been if the Bank of Canada had taken no action:

   i. Real GDP

   ii. Potential real GDP

   iii. The inflation rate

   iv. The unemployment rate

c. Draw an aggregate demand and aggregate supply graph to illustrate the effects of the Bank of Canada's policy. Be sure that your graph contains *LRAS* curves for 2016 and 2017; *SRAS* curves for 2016 and 2017; *AD* curves for 2016 and 2017, with and without monetary policy action; and equilibrium real GDP and the price level in 2017, with and without policy.

LO 11.5

5.1 Suppose that the equilibrium real overnight interest rate is 2 percent and the target rate of inflation is 2 percent. Use the following information and the Taylor rule to calculate the overnight interest rate target:

Current inflation rate = 4 percent

Potential real GDP = $1.4 trillion

Real GDP = $1.54 trillion

5.2 According to an article in the *Economist*:

> Calculations by David Mackie, of J.P. Morgan, show that virtually throughout the past six years, interest rates in the euro area have been lower than a Taylor rule would have prescribed, refuting the popular wisdom that the [European Central Bank] cares less about growth than do other central banks.

Why would keeping interest rates "lower than a Taylor rule would have prescribed" be an indication that the European Central Bank cared more about growth than popular wisdom held?

"The European Central Bank: Haughty Indifference, or Masterly Inactivity?" Economist, July 14, 2005.

5.3 [**Related to** Making the Connection **on page 346**] If the core CPI is a better measure of the inflation rate than is the CPI, why is the CPI more widely used? In particular, can you think of reasons the federal government uses the CPI when deciding how much to increase social security payments to retired workers to keep the purchasing power of the payments from declining?

5.4 [**Related to** Making the Connection **on page 346**] According to an article in the *Globe and Mail* in 2012, "Canada's statistics agency is refining the consumer price index, a key economic yardstick for matching pensions and salaries to the rising cost of living—and the result could mean sizable savings for governments and corporations that hike payments annually to keep pace with inflation."

Why do you think Statistics Canada would engage in this exercise? What kind of benefits do changes in the CPI affect?

Steven Chase and Tavia Grant, "Retooling of key inflation measure to influence pensions and wages," The Globe and Mail, February 13, 2012.

LO 11.6

6.1 Some economists argue that one cause of the financial problems resulting from the housing crisis in the United States was the fact that lenders who grant mortgages no longer typically hold the mortgages until they are paid off. Instead, lenders usually resell their mortgages in secondary markets. How might a lender intending to resell a mortgage act differently than a lender intending to hold a mortgage?

6.2 William A. Barnett recently wrote the book *Getting It Wrong: How Faulty Monetary Statistics Undermine the Fed, the Financial System, and the Economy* (MIT Press, 2012). This book provides evidence that low-quality money supply measures produced and supplied by the Federal Reserve may have caused the subprime financial crisis in the United States and the global recession.

We discussed the money supply measures in Chapter 10. What are the problems with the money supply measures currently produced by most central banks around the world, including the Bank of Canada, that William Barnett is concerned with?

James Pressley. "Fed's Poor Data, Not Greed, Drove Wall Street Off Cliff: Books," Bloomberg, February 16, 2012.

6.3 A recent article by leading economist Frederic S. Mishkin, "Monetary Policy Strategy: Lessons from the Crisis," concludes that

> the field of macro/monetary economics has become a hell of a lot more exciting. We are now faced with a whole new agenda for research that should keep people in the field very busy for a very long time. It has also made the work of central bankers more exciting as well. They now have to think about a much wider range of policy issues than they had to previously. This will surely be exhausting, but

central banking will be a far more stimulating profession.

What are the policy issues that economists and central bankers are concerned with in the aftermath of the global financial crisis and the Great Recession?

Frederic S. Mishkin. "Monetary Policy Strategy: Lessons from the Crisis," Graduate School of Business, Columbia University and National Bureau of Economic Research, December 2010.

6.4 Recall that *securitization* is the process of turning a loan, such as a mortgage, into a bond that can be bought and sold in secondary markets. An article in the *Economist* notes:

> That securitization caused more subprime mortgages to be written is not in doubt. By offering access to a much deeper pool of capital, securitization helped to bring down the cost of mortgages and made home-ownership more affordable for borrowers with poor credit histories.

What is a "subprime mortgage"? What is a "deeper pool of capital"? Why would securitization give mortgage borrowers access to a deeper pool of capital? Would a subprime borrower be likely to pay a higher or a lower interest rate than a borrower with a better credit history? Under what circumstances might a lender prefer to loan money to a borrower with a poor credit history rather than to a borrower with a good credit history? Briefly explain.

"Ruptured Credit," Economist, May 15, 2008.

6.5 In the fall of 2011, investors began to fear that some European governments, particularly Greece and Italy, might default on the bonds they had issued, making the prices of the bonds fall sharply. Many European banks owned these bonds, and some investors worried that these banks might also be in financial trouble. An article in the *Economist* magazine referred to the "prospect of another Lehman moment." The article noted that, "Governments are once again having to step in to support their banks." What did the article mean by another "Lehman moment"? Why might European governments have felt the need to support their banks in order to avoid another Lehman moment?

"Here We Go Again," Economist, October 8, 2011.

6.6 **[Related to** Making the Connection **on page 349]** Suppose that you buy a house for $150 000. One year later, the market price of the house has risen to $165 000. What is the return on your investment in the house if you made a down payment of 20 percent and took out a mortgage loan for the other 80 percent? What if you made a down payment of 5 percent and borrowed the other 95 percent? Be sure to show your calculations in your answer.

MyEconLab   MyEconLab is an online tool designed to help you master the concepts covered in your course. It will create an adaptive, highly personalized study plan to stimulate and measure your learning. Log in to take advantage of this powerful study aid, and to access quizzes and other valuable course-related material.

Fiscal Policy

Chapter Outline and Learning Objectives

12.1 What Is Fiscal Policy? page 364
Define fiscal policy.

12.2 The Effects of Fiscal Policy on Real GDP and the Price Level, page 369
Explain how fiscal policy affects aggregate demand and how the government can use fiscal policy to stabilize the economy.

12.3 Fiscal Policy in the Dynamic Aggregate Demand and Aggregate Supply Model, page 371
Use the dynamic aggregate demand and aggregate supply model to analyze fiscal policy.

12.4 The Government Purchases and Tax Multipliers, page 373
Explain how the government purchases and tax multipliers work.

12.5 The Limits of Fiscal Policy as a Stimulus, page 379
Discuss the difficulties that can arise in implementing fiscal policy.

12.6 Deficits, Surpluses, and Federal Government Debt, page 382
Define federal budget deficit and federal government debt and explain how the federal budget can serve as an automatic stabilizer.

12.7 The Effects of Fiscal Policy in the Long Run, page 387
Discuss the effects of fiscal policy in the long run.

Appendix E: A Closer Look at the Multiplier Formula, page 400
Apply the multiplier formula.

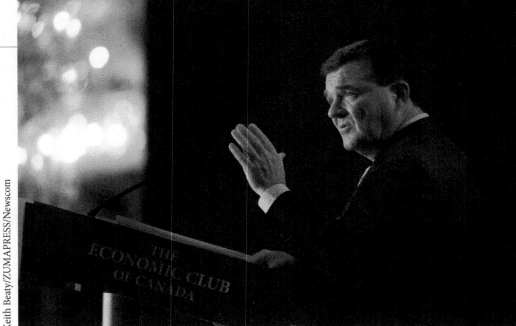

Keith Beaty/ZUMAPRESS/Newscom

Canadian Fiscal Policy during and after the 2008–2009 Recession

In December 2008, the Canadian economy was facing some very serious threats. The American economy was struggling, and so were the economies of most developed nations around the world. As a result, Canadian net exports, consumer spending, and the economy as a whole were contracting sharply. To encourage building and investment, the Bank of Canada cut interest rates to their lowest levels in 50 years. Since the room for the central bank to cut interest rates further had disappeared, the only other way to help stimulate the Canadian economy in the short term was for the government of Canada to engage in *discretionary fiscal policy*.

Many politicians and economists believe that changes in government spending and taxation can be used to manage the overall level of economic activity in a country. During 2007–2009, countries around the world used both monetary and fiscal policies to try and offset the drop in economic activity and the resulting jump in unemployment that occurred in the wake of the global financial crisis.

Fiscal policy is not only used to stabilize the economy. It is also used to encourage investment and savings. For example, the federal government gives tax breaks to businesses that invest in research and development. It also allows people to save tax-free in special savings accounts. Canada's Economic Action Plan involved increases in government spending on infrastructure (roads, airports, and water treatment) as well as tax breaks, such as the home improvement tax credit.

After the recession ended in Canada, the federal government made plans to reduce spending and return the budget to balance—effectively ending the fiscal policy stimulus—by the 2014–2015 fiscal year. These plans may not come to pass. Slow economic growth around the world and in Canada has limited the new revenue from taxation and has increased the importance of government spending in the economy. Some economists are concerned that cutting spending too quickly will cause another recession in Canada.

AN INSIDE LOOK on **page 394** discusses the Canadian federal government's fiscal policy response to the recent recession.

Sources: Paul Vieira, Financial Post · Monday, Dec. 8, 2008, Balanced budget two years behind schedule: TD Economics, Christine Dobby, Financial Post – Oct. 27, 2011.

Economics in Your Life

What Would You Do with $500 Less?

Suppose the federal government announces that it will ask every person in Canada over the age of 18 to pay an additional tax of $500 a year. You expect that this tax increase will be permanent; that is, you'll be required to pay this $500 tax every year in the future. How will you respond to this decrease in your disposable income? What effect will this tax increase likely have on equilibrium real GDP in the short run? As you read this chapter, see if you can answer these questions. You can check your answers against those we provide on page 392 at the end of this chapter.

I n Chapter 11 we discussed how the Bank of Canada uses monetary policy to pursue its main macroeconomic policy goals: (1) price stability, (2) high employment, (3) stability of financial markets and institutions, and (4) economic growth. In this chapter, we will explore how the government uses *fiscal policy*, which involves changes in taxes and government purchases, to achieve similar policy goals. As we have seen, in the short run, the price level and the level of real GDP and total employment in the economy depend on aggregate demand and short-run aggregate supply. The government can affect the levels of both aggregate demand and aggregate supply through fiscal policy. We will explore how Parliament and the prime minister decide which fiscal policy actions to take to achieve their goals. We will also discuss the disagreements among economists and policymakers over the effectiveness of fiscal policy.

12.1 LEARNING OBJECTIVE

Define fiscal policy.

Fiscal policy Changes in federal taxes and purchases that are intended to achieve macroeconomic policy objectives.

Automatic stabilizers Government spending and taxes that automatically increase or decrease along with the business cycle.

What Is Fiscal Policy?

Since the Great Depression of the 1930s, federal, provincial, and territorial governments have been actively engaged in keeping their economies stable. The Bank of Canada closely monitors the economy and meets eight times a year to decide on any changes in monetary policy. Any time Parliament is in session, government can take action to change taxes and/or spending to influence the economy. Changes in taxes and spending that are intended to achieve macroeconomic policy goals are called **fiscal policy**.

What Fiscal Policy Is and What It Isn't

In Canada, federal, provincial, territorial, and local governments all have the ability to levy taxes and spend money. Economists generally use the term *fiscal policy* to refer only to the actions of the federal government. Provincial, territorial, and local governments sometimes use their ability to tax and spend to aid their local economies, but only the federal government is focused on the economy of the whole country. The federal government also makes decisions about taxes and spending that are not related to the health of the economy. For example, a decision to tax junk food is a health policy, not a fiscal policy. Similarly, a decision to purchase new F-35 fighter jets to assert arctic sovereignty is a national security policy, not a fiscal policy.

Automatic Stabilizers versus Discretionary Fiscal Policy

There is an important distinction between *automatic stabilizers* and *discretionary fiscal policy*. Some types of government spending and taxes, which automatically increase and decrease to counter the business cycle, are referred to as **automatic stabilizers**. The word *automatic* in this case refers to the fact that changes in these types of spending and taxes happen without actions by the government. For example, when the economy is expanding and employment is increasing, government spending on Employment Insurance payments to workers who have lost their jobs will automatically decrease. During a recession, as employment declines, this type of spending will automatically increase. Similarly, when the economy is expanding and incomes are rising, the amount the government collects in taxes will increase as people pay additional taxes on their higher incomes. When the economy is in recession, the amount the government collects in taxes will fall.

With discretionary fiscal policy, the government takes actions to change spending or taxes. The increased spending and tax cut cuts for 2009–2010—along with the spending cuts of 2012—are examples of discretionary fiscal policy actions.

An Overview of Government Spending and Taxes

To provide a context for understanding fiscal policy, it's important to understand the big picture of government taxing and spending.

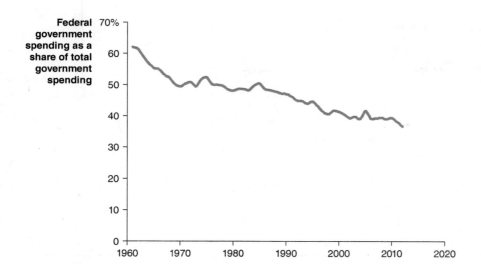

Federal government spending as a share of total government spending

Figure 12.1

The Federal Government's Share of Total Government Spending, 1961–2012

The federal government's share of government spending has been falling for the past 50-plus years.

Sources: Statistics Canada, National Economic and Financial Accounts (Table 380-0007, Series v499138 and v499183). Reproduced and distributed on an "as is" basis with the permission of Statistics Canada.

Over the past 50-plus years, the federal government's share of total government spending has been declining, as Figure 12.1 shows. There are two reasons for this decline: The federal government has been delegating the administration of certain responsibilities to provincial and territorial agencies (e.g., the regulation of interprovincial and international highway traffic, and the management of forestry and natural resources), and the importance of health care in the budgets of other levels of government has grown.

Over the past 20 years in particular, overall government spending on health care has increased significantly. Figure 12.2 shows the percentage of total government spending on health care since the late 1980s. According to the division of powers between the federal and provincial governments, health care is a provincial responsibility (it is also a territorial responsibility). However, the federal government supports health care through the Canada Health Transfer, a payment program that provides money to provincial and territorial governments to pay for health care. Even though a significant portion of health care funding comes from the federal government, provincial and territorial governments are responsible for how that funding is spent. In 2012, the Canada Health Transfer from the federal government to provincial and territorial governments accounted for approximately 10 percent of federal government spending.

Economists often measure government spending relative to the size of the economy by calculating government spending as a percentage of GDP. Remember that there is a

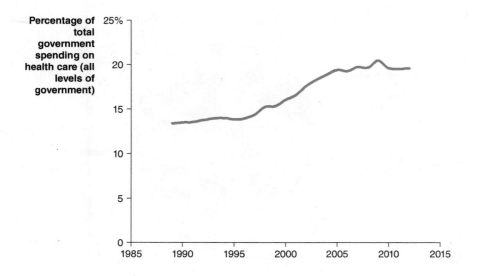

Percentage of total government spending on health care (all levels of government)

Figure 12.2

Total Government Spending on Health Care, 1989–2012

Like other levels of government, the federal government has been spending an increasing amount on health care over the past 20 years.

Sources: Statistics Canada, Consolidated federal, provincial, territorial and local government revenue and expenditures (Table 385-0001, series v156299 and v156311). Reproduced and distributed on an "as is" basis with the permission of Statistics Canada.

Figure 12.3

Federal Government Expenditures as a Percentage of GDP, 1962–2012

From the early 1960s until the mid-1990s, the government played an increasingly important role in the Canadian economy. The importance of government spending in the economy has fallen since the 1990s but still accounted for over 40 percent of all economic activity in 2012.

Sources: Statistics Canada, National Economic and Financial Accounts CANSIM Table 380-0007, Series v499183, and CANSIM Table 380-0017, Series v464937. Reproduced and distributed on an "as is" basis with the permission of Statistics Canada.

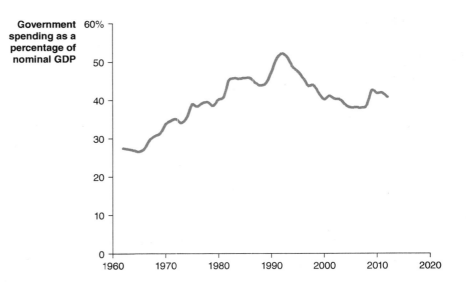

difference between government *purchases* and government *expenditures*. When the federal government purchases a new jet for the Canadian Armed Forces or hires an RCMP officer, it receives a good or service in return. Federal government expenditures include purchases plus all other forms of government spending, such as transfer payments to the provinces/territories and civil servants' paycheques. The change in the size of government spending relative to the Canadian economy is shown in Figure 12.3. The government was responsible for almost half the economic activity in Canada in 1992. From that time until 2008, the government played less of a role in the Canadian economy. In 2009, however, government spending increased in an effort to stimulate the shrinking economy, and the size of government spending relative to the Canadian economy rose significantly.

Where Does the Money Go?

The federal government spends money in a variety of areas. Figure 12.4 shows that in 2012, the largest area of federal government spending (25 percent) was transfers to persons, which accounts for approximately $1 out of every $4 spent. This spending includes the Guaranteed Annual Income Supplement (for the elderly) and the Universal Child Care Benefit. The second-largest area of federal government expenditures was government operations, which covers most federal government programs, such as Fisheries

Figure 12.4

Federal Government Spending, 2011–2012

Transfers to persons, such as elderly support programs, Employment Insurance, and support for children, accounts for 25 percent of federal government spending.

Source: Data from Department of Finance, Government of Canada, http://www.fin.gc.ca/tax-impot/2011/html-eng.asp (accessed Feb. 7, 2012.).

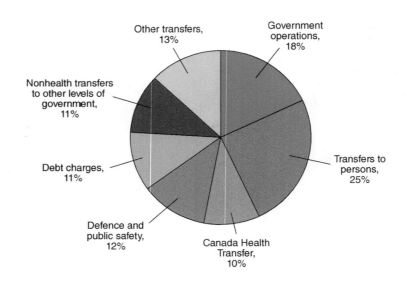

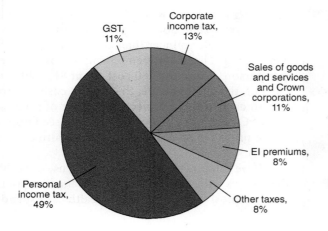

Figure 12.5

Federal Government Revenue, 2012

While all government revenue ultimately comes from people, almost half of the federal government's revenue comes from directly taxing personal income.

Source: Data from : Department of Finance, Government of Canada, http://www.fin.gc.ca/tax-impot/2011/html-eng.asp (accessed Feb. 7, 2012.)

and Oceans Canada and the Department of Justice. Spending on defence (e.g., the Royal Canadian Armed Forces) and public safety (e.g., the RCMP, prisons, and border security) accounted for 12 percent of federal government expenditures. Debt charges, which are payments made on the money the federal government has borrowed in the past, also accounted for 11 percent of federal government expenditures. The Canada Health Transfer made up 10 percent of federal government expenditures. Nonhealth transfers, such as the Canada Social Transfer, which are made to other levels of government, accounted for another 11 percent of federal government expenditures. The "other transfers" category accounted for 13 percent of federal government expenditures, and covers a wide variety of transfers from the federal government to small businesses, research groups, First Nations, farmers, and so on.

Where Does the Money Come From?

The short answer to this question is that the federal government's money comes from the people of Canada. The two main ways in which the federal government raises revenue are by taxing the population and charging for services. Figure 12.5 shows that in 2012, income taxes on individuals were the largest source of revenue for the federal government. Personal income taxes accounted for 49 percent of federal government revenue. Corporate income taxes, which are taxes on the profits of corporations before they pay their owners, generated 13 percent of federal government revenue. The Goods and Services Tax (GST) brought in 11 percent of federal government revenue. Crown corporations, which are businesses owned by the federal government and other sales of goods and services, also brought in 11 percent of federal government revenue. Employment Insurance premiums, which are paid as a portion of wages by everyone who has a job, made up another 8 percent of federal government revenue. The remaining 8 percent of federal government revenue came from consumption taxes, such as alcohol and tobacco taxes, import duties, and energy taxes.

Making the Connection | ## The Exploding Costs of Health Care

For many Canadians, public health care is central to Canadian identity. Under the current system, provincial, territorial, and federal governments collect taxes from a variety of sources (primarily people's incomes), and use the funds raised to pay for hospitals, doctors, nurses, and all other elements essential to providing health care services to the people of Canada.

While most Canadians agree that public health care is a good idea, doctors and nurses don't work for free, and drug companies don't either. Moreover, the costs of health care are increasing. The problem of paying for health care arises when we start to think about the distribution of health care spending by age. In 2009, health care

The aging population of Canada will lead to higher costs for health care.

spending in Canada was about $5500 per person. However, the health care system doesn't spend the same amount on everyone. In 2007, people younger than 64 cost an average of about $2000 per person. Those between 65 and 69 cost an average of $5589 per person. Those over 80 cost about $17 500 per person. Simply put, the older you are, the more it costs to provide you with health care, and the projected number of seniors as a percentage of Canada's population is growing (see figure (a), below), as is the projected spending on public health care (see figure (b), below).

If we combine data on the growing use of health care by older Canadians with data on the aging Canadian population, we get some explosive predictions on health care spending. Let's take

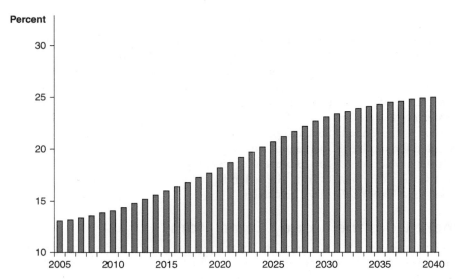

(a) Seniors as a percentage of Canada's population, 2005–2040

Source: Christopher Ragan, "Two Policy Changes Driven by Population Aging," *Options*, October 2010, p. 73, figure 2.

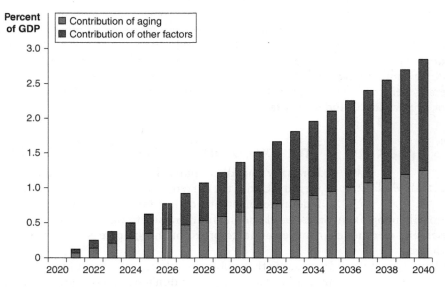

(b) Projected increase in public health care spending, 2020–2040

Source: Christopher Ragan, "Two Policy Changes Driven by Population Aging," *Options*, October 2010, p. 77, figure 7.

Quebec as an example (the other provinces and territories aren't much different in terms of health care spending). In 1980, about 31 percent of Quebec government spending went to providing health care. By 2010, health care accounted for 45 percent of Quebec government spending and is projected to reach 67 percent by 2030. That means that by 2030, $2 out of every $3 spent by the government of Quebec will be spent on providing health care.

This projected level of health care spending can be maintained by provinces and territories in three ways. First, they could cut back on spending in other areas, such as education and infrastructure significantly. However, cutting back on investment in areas such as education and infrastructure is likely to reduce the size of the economy in the future. Second, they could run a budget deficit. Provincial and territorial governments can run deficits by borrowing from investors. The problem with this approach is that future taxpayers will have to pay for today's health care costs, with interest. Finally, they could increase taxes. Doing so would also have a negative impact on the economy and inevitably make people unhappy.

The aging of Canada's population and the associated increase in health care costs will mean that different methods of delivering health care and/or paying for them will emerge. Most likely, provinces and territories will use a combination of the three options noted above and transfer more health care costs directly to patients.

Sources: Based on The health care time bomb: Our aging population will make unthinkable reforms inevitable by John Geddes on Monday, April 12, 2010; http://www2.macleans.ca/2010/04/12/the-health-care-time-bomb/; Two Policy Challenges Driven by Population Aging by Chris Ragan http://people.mcgill.ca/files/christopher.ragan/Oct2010PO.pdf

Your Turn: Test your understanding by doing related problems 1.2 and 1.3 on page 397 at the end of this chapter.

MyEconLab

The Effects of Fiscal Policy on Real GDP and the Price Level

12.2 LEARNING OBJECTIVE

Explain how fiscal policy affects aggregate demand and how the government can use fiscal policy to stabilize the economy.

The federal government uses macroeconomic policies to offset the effects of the business cycle on the economy. We saw in Chapter 11 that the Bank of Canada carries out monetary policy through changes in the money supply and interest rates. Governments carry out fiscal policy through changes in government purchases and taxes. Because changes in government purchases and taxes lead to changes in aggregate demand, they can affect the level of real GDP, employment, and the price level. When the economy is in a recession, *increases* in government purchases or *decreases* in taxes will increase aggregate demand. As we saw in Chapter 9, the inflation rate may increase when real GDP is beyond potential GDP. Decreasing government purchases or raising taxes can slow the growth of aggregate demand and reduce the inflation rate.

Expansionary and Contractionary Fiscal Policy

Expansionary fiscal policy involves increasing government purchases or decreasing taxes. An increase in government purchases will increase aggregate demand directly because government expenditures are a component of aggregate demand. A cut in taxes has an indirect effect on aggregate demand. The income households have available to spend after they have paid their taxes is called *household disposable income.* Cutting the individual income tax will increase household disposable income and consumption spending. Cutting taxes on business income can increase aggregate demand by increasing business investment.

Figure 12.6 shows the results of an expansionary fiscal policy using the basic version of the aggregate demand and aggregate supply model. In this model, there is no economic growth, so the long-run aggregate supply (*LRAS*) curve does not shift. Notice that this figure is similar to Figure 11.6, which shows the effects of monetary

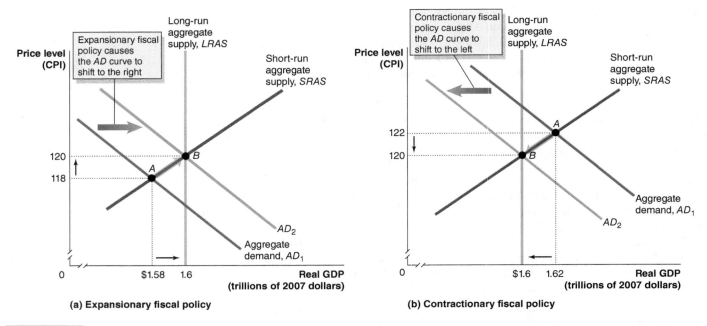

(a) Expansionary fiscal policy

(b) Contractionary fiscal policy

Figure 12.6 **Fiscal Policy**

In panel (a), the economy begins in recession at point *A*, with real GDP of $1.58 trillion and a price level of 118. An expansionary fiscal policy will cause aggregate demand to shift to the right, from AD_1 to AD_2, increasing real GDP from $1.58 trillion to $1.6 trillion and the price level from 118 to 120 (point *B*). In panel (b), the economy begins at point *A*, with real GDP at $1.62 trillion and the price level

at 122. Because real GDP is greater than potential GDP, the economy will experience rising wages and prices. A contractionary fiscal policy will cause aggregate demand to shift to the left, from AD_1 to AD_2, decreasing real GDP from $1.62 trillion to $1.6 trillion and the price level from 122 to 120 (point *B*).

policy. The goal of both expansionary fiscal and expansionary monetary policy is to increase aggregate demand relative to what it would have been without a policy intervention.

In panel (a) of Figure 12.6, we assume that the economy is in short-run equilibrium at point *A*, where the aggregate demand curve (AD_1) intersects the short-run aggregate supply curve (*SRAS*). Real GDP is below potential GDP, so the economy is in recession, with some firms operating below capacity and some workers having been laid off. To bring real GDP back to potential GDP, the government can increase government purchases or decrease taxes, which will shift the aggregate demand curve to the right, from AD_1 to AD_2. Real GDP increases from $1.58 trillion to potential GDP of $1.6 trillion, and the price level rises from 118 to 120 (point *B*). The policy has successfully returned real GDP to its potential level. Rising production will lead to increasing employment, reducing the unemployment rate.

Contractionary fiscal policy involves decreasing government purchases or increasing taxes. Policymakers use contractionary fiscal policy to reduce increases in aggregate demand that seem likely to lead to inflation. In panel (b) of Figure 12.6, the economy is in short-run equilibrium at point *A*, with real GDP of $1.62 trillion, which is above potential GDP of $1.6 trillion. With some firms producing beyond their normal capacity and the unemployment rate very low, wages and prices will be increasing. To bring real GDP back to potential GDP, the government can decrease government purchases or increase taxes, which will shift the aggregate demand curve from AD_1 to AD_2. Real GDP falls from $1.62 trillion to $1.6 trillion, and the price level falls from 122 to 120 (point *B*).

We can conclude that government can attempt to stabilize the economy by using fiscal policy to affect the price level and the level of real GDP. It is, of course, extremely difficult to get the amount of fiscal expansion or contraction to exactly offset the business cycle and keep real GDP equal to potential GDP.

Problem	Type of Policy	Action by Government	Result
Recession	Expansionary	Increase government spending or cut taxes	Real GDP and the price level rise.
Rising inflation	Contractionary	Decrease government spending or raise taxes	Real GDP and the price level fall.

Table 12.1

Countercyclical Fiscal Policy

A Summary of How Fiscal Policy Affects Aggregate Demand

Table 12.1 summarizes how fiscal policy affects aggregate demand. Just as we did with monetary policy, we must add a very important qualification to this summary of fiscal policy: The table isolates the impact of fiscal policy *by holding everything else—including monetary policy—constant.* In other words, we are again invoking the *ceteris paribus* condition we discussed in Chapter 3. This point is important because, for example, a contractionary fiscal policy doesn't cause the price level to fall. A contractionary fiscal policy causes the price level *to rise by less than it would have without the policy.*

Fiscal Policy in the Dynamic Aggregate Demand and Aggregate Supply Model

12.3 LEARNING OBJECTIVE

Use the dynamic aggregate demand and aggregate supply model to analyze fiscal policy.

The overview of fiscal policy we just finished contains a key idea: Government can use fiscal policy to affect aggregate demand, thereby changing the price level and the level of real GDP. The discussion of expansionary and contractionary fiscal policy illustrated by Figure 12.6 is simplified, however, because it ignores two important facts about the economy: (1) The economy experiences continuing inflation, with the price level rising virtually every year, and (2) the economy experiences long-run growth, with the *LRAS* curve shifting to the right every year. In Chapter 10, we developed a *dynamic aggregate demand and aggregate supply model* that took these two facts into account. In this section, we use the dynamic model to gain a more complete understanding of fiscal policy.

To briefly review the dynamic model, recall that over time, potential GDP increases, which we show by the *LRAS* curve shifting to the right. The factors that cause the *LRAS* curve to shift also cause firms to supply more goods and services at any given price level in the short run, which we show by shifting the *SRAS* curve to the right. Finally, during most years, the *AD* curve also shifts to the right, indicating that aggregate expenditure is higher at every price level.

Figure 12.7 shows the results of an expansionary fiscal policy using the dynamic aggregate demand and aggregate supply model. Notice that this figure is very similar to Figure 11.8, which shows the effects of an expansionary monetary policy. The goal of both expansionary monetary policy and expansionary fiscal policy is to increase aggregate demand relative to what it would have been without the policy.

In the hypothetical situation shown in Figure 12.7, the economy begins in equilibrium at potential GDP of $1.6 trillion and a price level of 120 (point A). In the second year, *LRAS* increases to $1.64 trillion, but *AD* increases only to $AD_{2(\text{without policy})}$, which is not enough to keep the economy in macroeconomic equilibrium at potential GDP. Let's assume that the Bank of Canada doesn't react to this situation with expansionary monetary policy. In that case, without an expansionary fiscal policy of increased government spending or tax cuts, the short-run equilibrium will occur at $1.63 trillion (point B). The $10 billion gap between this level of real GDP and the potential level means that some firms are operating at less than their normal capacity. Incomes and profits will be falling, firms will begin to lay off workers, and the unemployment rate will rise.

Increasing government purchases or cutting taxes can shift aggregate demand to $AD_{2(\text{with policy})}$. The economy will be in equilibrium at point C, with real GDP of $1.64

Figure 12.7

An Expansionary Fiscal Policy in the Dynamic Model

The economy begins in equilibrium at point A, at potential GDP of $1.6 trillion and a price level of 120. Without an expansionary policy, aggregate demand will shift from AD_1 to $AD_{2(without\ policy)}$, which is not enough to keep the economy at potential GDP because long-run aggregate supply has shifted from $LRAS_1$ to $LRAS_2$. The economy will be in short-run equilibrium at point B, with real GDP of $1.63 trillion and a price level of 121. Increasing government purchases or cutting taxes will shift aggregate demand to $AD_{2(with\ policy)}$. The economy will be in equilibrium at point C, with real GDP of $1.64 trillion, which is its potential level, and a price level of 122. The price level is higher than it would have been without an expansionary fiscal policy.

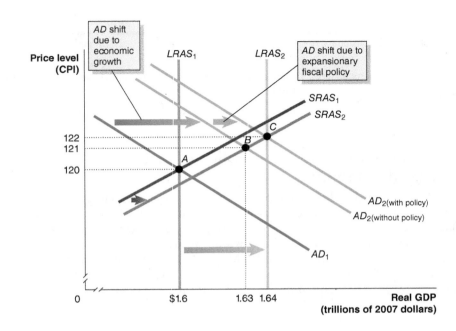

trillion, which is potential GDP, and a price level of 122. The price level is higher than it would have been if expansionary fiscal policy had not been used.

Contractionary fiscal policy involves decreasing government purchases or increasing taxes. Policymakers use contractionary fiscal policy to reduce increases in aggregate demand that seem likely to lead to inflation. In Figure 12.8, the economy again begins at potential GDP of $1.6 trillion and a price level of 120 (point A). Once again LRAS increases to $1.64 trillion in the second year. In this scenario, the shift in aggregate demand to $AD_{2(without\ policy)}$ results in a short-run macroeconomic equilibrium beyond potential GDP (point B). If we assume that the Bank of Canada does not respond to this situation with a contractionary monetary policy, the economy will experience rising inflation. Decreasing government purchases or increasing taxes can keep real GDP from moving beyond its potential level. The result, shown in Figure 12.8, is that in the new equilibrium at point C, the inflation rate is 1.7 percent rather than 3.3 percent.

Figure 12.8

A Contractionary Fiscal Policy in the Dynamic Model

The economy begins in equilibrium at point A, with real GDP of $1.6 trillion and a price level of 100. Without a contractionary policy, aggregate demand will shift from AD_1 to $AD_{2(without\ policy)}$, which results in a short-run equilibrium beyond potential GDP at point B, with real GDP $1.66 trillion and a price level of 124. Decreasing government purchases or increasing taxes can shift aggregate demand to $AD_{2(with\ policy)}$. The economy will be in equilibrium at point C, with real GDP of $1.64 trillion, which is its potential level, and a price level of 122. The inflation rate will be 1.7 percent, as opposed to the 3.3 percent it would have been without the contractionary fiscal policy.

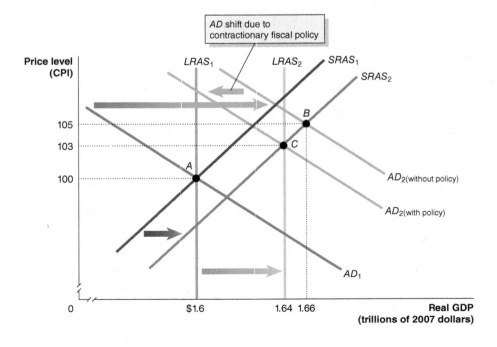

The Government Purchases and Tax Multipliers

Suppose that during a recession, the government decides to use discretionary fiscal policy to increase aggregate demand by spending $10 billion more on constructing roads and bridges in several cities. How much will equilibrium GDP increase as a result of this increase in government purchases? We might expect that the answer is greater than $10 billion because the initial increase in aggregate demand should lead to additional increases in income and therefore increases in consumer spending. To build the roads and bridges, the government hires private construction firms. These firms will hire more workers to carry out the new projects. Newly hired workers will increase their spending on cars, furniture, appliances, and other products. Sellers of these products will increase their production and hire more workers, and so on. At each step, real GDP and income will rise, thereby increasing consumption spending and aggregate demand.

Economists refer to the initial increase in government purchases as *autonomous* because it is a result of a decision by the government and does not directly depend on the level of real GDP. The increases in consumption spending that result from the initial autonomous increase in government purchases are *induced* because they are caused by the initial increase in autonomous spending. Economists refer to the series of induced increases in consumption spending that result from an initial increase in autonomous expenditures as the **multiplier effect**.

Figure 12.9 illustrates how an increase in government purchases affects the aggregate demand curve. The initial increase in government purchases causes the aggregate demand curve to shift to the right because total spending in the economy is now higher at every price level. The shift to the right from AD_1 to the dashed AD curve represents the impact of the initial increase of $10 billion in government purchases. Because this initial increase in government purchases raises incomes and leads to further increases in consumption spending, the aggregate demand curve will ultimately shift from AD_1 all the way to AD_2.

To better understand the multiplier effect, let's start with a simplified analysis in which we assume that the price level is constant. In other words, initially we will ignore the effect of an upward-sloping *SRAS*. Figure 12.10 shows how spending and real GDP increase over a number of periods, beginning with the initial increase in government purchases in the first period. The initial spending in the first period raises real GDP and therefore total income in the economy by $10 billion. How much additional consumption will result from the $10 billion increase in incomes? We know

12.4 LEARNING OBJECTIVE

Explain how the government purchases and tax multipliers work.

Multiplier effect The series of induced increases in consumption spending that results from an initial increase in autonomous expenditures.

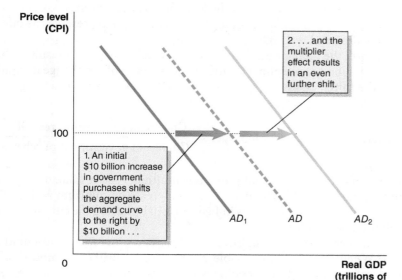

Figure 12.9

The Multiplier Effect and Aggregate Demand

An initial increase in government purchases of $10 billion causes the aggregate demand curve to shift to the right, from AD_1 to the dashed AD curve, and represents the effect of the initial increase of $10 billion in government purchases. Because this initial increase raises incomes and leads to further increases in consumption spending, the aggregate demand curve will ultimately shift further to the right, to AD_2.

Time Period	Additional Spending This Period	Cumulative Increase in Spending and Real GDP
1	$10 billion in government purchases	$10 billion
2	$5 billion in consumption spending	$15 billion
3	$2.5 billion in consumption spending	$17.5 billion
4	$1.25 billion in consumption spending	$18.75 billion
5	$0.625 billion in consumption spending	$19.375 billion
6	$0.3125 billion in consumption spending	$19.6875 billion
⋮	⋮	⋮
n	0	$20 billion

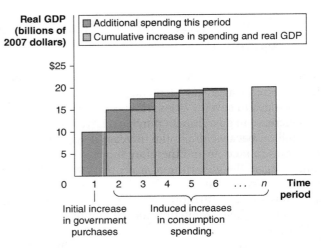

Figure 12.10 **The Multiplier Effect of an Increase in Government Purchases**

Following an initial increase in government purchases, spending and real GDP increase over a number of periods due to the multiplier effect. The new spending and increased real GDP in each period is shown in green, and the level of spending from the previous period is shown in orange. The sum of the orange and green areas represents the cumulative increase in spending and real GDP. In total, equilibrium real GDP will increase by $20 billion as a result of an initial increase of $10 billion in government purchases.

that in addition to increasing their consumption spending on domestically produced goods, households will save some of the increase in income, use some to pay income taxes, and use some to purchase imported goods, which will have no direct effect on spending and production in the Canadian economy. In Figure 12.10, we assume that in the second period, households increase their consumption spending by one-half of the increase in income from the first period on domestically produced goods and services—or by $5 billion. This spending in the second period will, in turn, increase real GDP and income by an additional $5 billion. In the third period, consumption spending will increase by $2.5 billion, or one-half of the $5 billion increase in income from the second period.

The multiplier effect will continue through a number of periods, with the additional consumption spending in each period being half of the income increase from the previous period. Eventually, the process will be complete, although we can't say precisely how many periods it will take, so we simply label the final period n rather than assign it a specific number. In the graph in Figure 12.10, the new spending and increased real GDP in each period is shown in green, and the level of spending from the previous period is shown in orange. The sum of the orange and green areas represents the cumulative increase in spending and real GDP.

How large will the total increase in equilibrium real GDP be as a result of the initial increase of $10 billion in government purchases? The ratio of the change in equilibrium real GDP to the initial change in government purchases is known as the *government purchases multiplier*:

$$\text{Government purchases multiplier} = \frac{\text{Change in equilibrium real GDP}}{\text{Change in government purchases}}$$

If, for example, the government purchases multiplier has a value of 2, an increase in government purchases of $10 billion should increase equilibrium real GDP by 2 × $10 billion = $20 billion. We show this in Figure 12.10 by having the cumulative increase in real GDP equal $20 billion.

Tax cuts also have a multiplier effect. Cutting taxes increases household disposable income. When household disposable income rises, so will consumption spending. These increases in consumption spending will set off further increases in real GDP and income, just as increases in government purchases do. Suppose we consider a change in taxes of a specific amount—say, a tax cut of $10 billion—with the tax *rate* remaining unchanged. The expression for this tax multiplier is

$$\text{Tax multiplier} = \frac{\text{Change in equilibrium real GDP}}{\text{Change in taxes}}$$

The tax multiplier is a negative number because changes in taxes and changes in real GDP move in opposite directions: An increase in taxes reduces disposable income, consumption, and real GDP, and a decrease in taxes raises disposable income, consumption, and real GDP. For example, if the tax multiplier is −1.6, a $10 billion *cut* in taxes will increase real GDP by −1.6 × −$10 billion = $16 billion. We would expect the tax multiplier to be smaller in absolute value (i.e., a smaller number) than the government purchases multiplier. To see why, think about the difference between a $10 billion increase in government purchases and a $10 billion decrease in taxes. The whole of the $10 billion increase in government purchases results in an increase in aggregate demand initially. But households will save rather than spend some portion of the $10 billion decrease in taxes, and they will spend some portion of the extra disposable income on imported goods. The fraction of the tax cut that households save or spend on imports will not increase aggregate demand. Therefore, the first period of the multiplier will lead to a smaller increase in aggregate demand than takes place after an increase in government purchases, and the total increase in equilibrium real GDP will be smaller.

The Effect of Changes in Tax Rates

A change in tax *rates* has a more complicated effect on equilibrium real GDP than does a tax cut of a fixed amount. To begin with, the value of the tax rate affects the size of the multiplier effect. The higher the tax rate, the smaller the multiplier effect. To see why, think about the size of the additional spending increases that take place in each period following an increase in government purchases. The higher the tax rate, the smaller the amount of an increase in income that households have available to spend, which reduces the size of the multiplier effect. So, a cut in tax rates affects equilibrium real GDP through two channels: (1) A cut in tax rates increases the disposable income of households, which leads them to increase their consumption spending, and (2) a cut in tax rates increases the size of the multiplier effect.

Taking into Account the Effects of Aggregate Supply

So far we've assumed that the price level didn't change when the *AD* curve shifted. However, because the *SRAS* curve is upward sloping, when the *AD* curve shifts to the right, the price level increases. As a result of the higher price level, the new equilibrium real GDP will not increase by the amount that the multiplier effect indicates. Figure 12.11 illustrates how an upward-sloping *SRAS* curve affects the size of the multiplier. To keep the graph relatively simple, we assume that the *SRAS* and *LRAS* curves do not shift. The economy starts at point *A*, with real GDP below its potential level. An increase in government purchases shifts the aggregate demand curve from AD_1 to the dashed *AD* curve. Just as in Figure 12.9, the multiplier effect causes a further shift in aggregate demand to AD_2. If the price level remained constant, real GDP would increase from $1.5 trillion at point *A* to $1.65 trillion at point *B*. However, because the *SRAS* curve is upward sloping, the price level rises from 120 to 124, reducing the total quantity of goods and services demanded in the economy. The new equilibrium occurs at point *C*, with real GDP having risen to $1.6 trillion, or by $50 billion less than if the price level had remained unchanged. We can conclude that the actual change in real GDP resulting from an increase in government purchases or a tax cut will be less than indicated by the simple multiplier effect with a constant price level.

Figure 12.11

The Multiplier Effect and Aggregate Supply

The economy is initially at point *A*. An increase in government purchases causes the aggregate demand curve to shift to the right, from AD_1 to the dashed *AD* curve. The multiplier effect results in the aggregate demand curve shifting further to the right, to AD_2 (point *B*). Because of the upward-sloping supply curve, the shift in aggregate demand results in a higher price level. In the new equilibrium at point *C*, both real GDP and the price level have increased. The increase in real GDP is less than indicated by the multiplier effect with a constant price level.

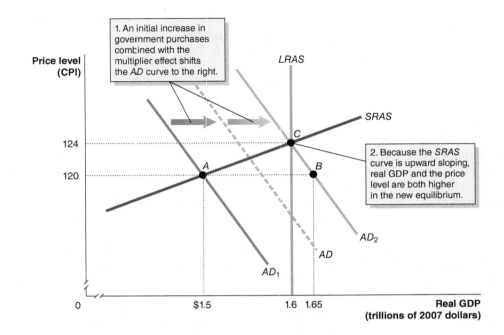

1. An initial increase in government purchases combined with the multiplier effect shifts the *AD* curve to the right.

2. Because the *SRAS* curve is upward sloping, real GDP and the price level are both higher in the new equilibrium.

The Multipliers Work in Both Directions

Increases in government spending and cuts in taxes have a positive multiplier effect on equilibrium real GDP. Decreases in government purchases and increases in taxes also have a multiplier effect on equilibrium real GDP, but in this case, the effect is negative. For example, an increase in taxes will reduce household disposable income and consumption spending. As households buy fewer cars, furniture, refrigerators, and other products, the firms that sell these products will cut back on production and begin laying off workers. Falling incomes will lead to further reductions in consumption spending. A reduction in government spending on roads would set off a similar process of decreases in real GDP and income. The cutback would be felt first by construction contractors selling their services directly to the government, and then it would spread to other firms.

We look more closely at the government purchases multiplier and the tax multiplier in the appendix to this chapter.

Don't Let This Happen to You

Don't Overestimate the Size of the Multiplier

The size of the multiplier depends on a wide variety of factors. As the income tax rate increases, the multiplier shrinks in value. As the share of new household disposable income that is saved falls, the multiplier increases in value. The more we import from other countries, the lower the value of the multiplier. Finally, as we've seen, the sensitivity of price levels to changes in demand has an impact on the multiplier—the steeper the *SRAS* curve, the lower the value of the final multiplier.

People arguing in support of specific government projects often ignore the influence of these factors when calculating the size of the multiplier for a given project in an effort to gain support for the project. In many cases,

people arguing for new sports stadiums, harbours, or other large government-funded facilities claim that the multiplier associated with these projects is well over 2 or sometimes even 3. Because Canada is an open economy with moderate income taxes, these values are not reasonable for most regions in Canada. Statistics Canada estimates the multiplier size for different types of activities for different regions. These multipliers are generally below 1.5. The next time someone promotes a large project in your community using a multiplier as part of the project's justification, ask that person how that number was determined.

MyEconLab

Your Turn: Test your understanding by doing related problem 4.3 on page 398 at the end of this chapter.

Making the Connection

Fiscal Policy in Action: The Federal Government Responds to the Global Recession of 2007–2009

As we've seen, government can increase government purchases and reduce taxes to increase aggregate demand either to avoid or at least to reduce the effects and duration of a recession. The federal government used both tax cuts and an increase in government purchases to try to offset the impact of the 2007–2009 global recession on the Canadian economy. The specific initiatives of "Canada's Economic Action Plan" are presented at the program's website: http://actionplan.gc.ca. The goal of the two-year $62-billion plan was to help offset the fall in demand caused by the global recession.

The Canadian economy started to contract in 2008. The federal government responded to this contraction in the 2009–2010 budget, dramatically increasing government purchases and reducing taxes. As a result, the government's budget deficit (i.e., the difference between the spending of the government and the revenue it takes in) rose from $5.8 billion for the 2008–2009 fiscal year to $53.8 billion in the 2009–2010 fiscal year.

What did Canadians actually get from this fiscal stimulus? The federal government delivered $33 billion in stimulus in the first fiscal year of the plan, 2009–2010. This money was spent in a variety of ways. The federal government supported a number of infrastructure projects across the country. Many cities received facilities, roads, and other improvements to existing infrastructure. This spending was intended not only to provide income for workers that might otherwise have been unemployed but also to deliver a lasting benefit to the communities in which the projects took place. The majority of spending has gone to cultural, recreational, and sports infrastructure.

The federal government didn't just spend the money on roads and buildings. It also reduced taxes. The GST was reduced from 6 percent to 5 percent, although some argue that this reduction was already planned and shouldn't count as part of the government's stimulus package. The government also introduced the Home Renovation Tax Credit, which allowed people to improve their homes and deduct some of the costs from their taxes. This program was intended to stimulate the demand for construction jobs. The package also included reductions to income tax, which were intended to increase household disposable income and household spending.

The Employment Insurance program was also expanded to provide extra support for people who lost their jobs. The length of time that people were allowed to claim benefits was extended. Extra money was also put toward skills-training initiatives. By supplementing the income of people who lost their jobs, the government was hoping to stabilize consumption spending.

Relative to GDP, Canada's stimulus package was the third largest of the G7 countries, with only Japan and the United States spending more. Of course, when money is spent by government, especially a large amount, people want to know how effective that spending was. This question is open to some debate. Those who believe that the stimulus package has been successful cite that Canada fared better than any other G7 country during the global recession, with its economy returning to growth in the fall of 2009. They also note that Canada's unemployment rate is now lower than the unemployment rate in the United States and is likely to remain lower for the next few years. Others have argued, however, that the Canadian economy would have recovered quickly without government intervention. While we're unlikely to see everyone come to agreement about how effective Canada's Economic Action Plan actually has been, we can all agree that Canada has done better than many other developed countries around the world.

The graph below shows what the federal stimulus money was spent on. Tax cuts include reductions in taxes for individuals and businesses. Unemployment includes extending the duration of Employment Insurance benefits and providing skills-training opportunities. Infrastructure spending involves the building of roads, bridges, sports facilities, and housing projects. Education and research covers spending on university and college facilities, government laboratories, and support for postgraduate students. Industry/community support covers spending on programs in targeted industries (e.g., forestry and automotive manufacturing) and for community projects.

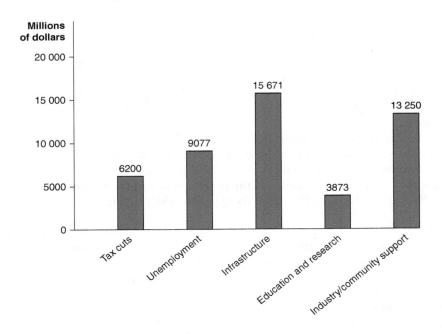

Source: Data from Canada's Economic Action Plan, Sixth Report to Canadians, Sept 27, 2010.

MyEconLab   **Your Turn:** Test your understanding by doing related problem 4.5 on page 398 at the end of this chapter.

Solved Problem **12.1**

Fiscal Policy Multipliers

Briefly explain whether you agree or disagree with the following statement: "Real GDP is currently $1.62 trillion and potential GDP is $1.64 trillion. If Parliament would increase government purchases by $20 billion ($0.02 trillion), the economy could be brought to equilibrium at potential GDP."

Solving the Problem

Step 1: Review the chapter material. This problem is about the multiplier process, so you may want to review the section "The Government Purchases and Tax Multipliers."

Step 2: Explain how the necessary increase in purchases or cut in taxes is less than $20 billion because of the multiplier effect. The statement is incorrect because it doesn't consider the multiplier effect. Because of the multiplier effect, an increase in government purchases or a decrease in taxes of less than $20 billion is necessary to increase equilibrium real GDP by $20 billion. For instance, assume that the government purchases multiplier is 2 and the tax multiplier is −1.6. We can then calculate the necessary increase in government purchases as follows:

$$\text{Government purchases multiplier} = \frac{\text{Change in equilibrium real GDP}}{\text{Change in government purchases}}$$

$$2 = \frac{\$20 \text{ billion}}{\text{Change in government purchases}}$$

$$\text{Change in government purchases} = \frac{\$20 \text{ billion}}{2} = \$10 \text{ billion}.$$

And the necessary change in taxes:

$$\text{Tax multiplier} = \frac{\text{Change in equilibrium real GDP}}{\text{Change in taxes}}$$

$$-1.6 = \frac{\$20 \text{ billion}}{\text{Change in taxes}}$$

$$\text{Change in taxes} = \frac{\$20 \text{ billion}}{-1.6} = -\$12.5 \text{ billion}.$$

Your turn: For more practice, do related problem 4.6 on page 398 at the end of this chapter.   MyEconLab

The Limits of Fiscal Policy as a Stimulus

12.5 LEARNING OBJECTIVE
Discuss the difficulties that can arise in implementing fiscal policy.

Poorly timed fiscal policy, like poorly timed monetary policy, can do more harm than good. As we discussed in Chapter 11, it takes time for policymakers to collect statistics and identify changes in the economy. If the government decides to increase spending or cut taxes to fight a recession that is about to end, the effect may be to increase the inflation rate. Similarly, cutting spending or raising taxes to slow down an economy that has actually passed the peak of the business cycle can make the recession that follows longer and deeper.

Getting the timing right can be more difficult with fiscal policy than with monetary policy for two main reasons. First, control over monetary policy is concentrated in the hands of the Bank of Canada, which can change monetary policy at any of its meetings. By contrast, the prime minister and the majority of the members of Parliament have to agree on changes in fiscal policy. The delays caused by the legislative process can be very long.

Second, even after a change in fiscal policy has been approved, it takes time to implement the policy. Suppose the federal government decides to fund the building of new roads in several cities. It will probably take at least several months to prepare detailed plans for the construction. Local government will then ask for bids from private construction companies. Once winning bidders have been selected, they will usually need several months to begin the project. Only then will significant amounts of spending actually take place. This delay may push the spending beyond the end of the recession that the spending was intended to fight. For example, while most of the stimulus announced by the federal government in 2008 was spent by 2010, not all of it was.

Does Government Spending Reduce Private Spending?

In addition to the problem of timing, using increases in government purchases to increase aggregate demand presents another potential problem. We have been assuming that when the federal government increases its purchases by $30 billion, the multiplier effect will cause the increase in aggregate demand to be greater than $30 billion. However, the size of the multiplier effect may be limited if the increase in government purchases causes one of the nongovernment, or private, components of aggregate expenditures—consumption, investment, or net exports—to fall. A decline in private expenditures as a result of an increase in government purchases is called **crowding out**.

Crowding out A decline in private expenditures as a result of an increase in government purchases.

Crowding Out in the Short Run

Consider the case of a temporary increase in government purchases. Suppose the federal government decides to fight a recession by spending $30 billion more this year on road construction. When the $30 billion has been spent, the program will end, and government spending will drop back to its previous level. As the spending takes place, income and real GDP will increase. These increases in income and real GDP will cause household and firms to increase their demand for currency and chequing account balances to accommodate the increased buying and selling. Figure 12.12 shows the result, using the money market graph introduced in Chapter 11.

At higher levels of real GDP and income, households and firms demand more money at every interest rate. When the demand for money increases, the equilibrium interest rate will rise. Higher interest rates will result in a decline in each component of private expenditures. Consumption spending and investment spending will decline because households and firms will borrow less to purchase consumer durables and to make investments. Net exports will fall as the higher interest rates will attract foreign savers. German, Japanese, and American savers will want to exchange their currencies to Canadian dollars to purchase bonds and other Canadian financial assets. This increased demand for Canadian dollars will cause the exchange rate between the dollar and other currencies to rise. When the dollar increases in value, the prices of Canadian products in foreign countries rise, causing a reduction in Canadian exports. At the same time the prices of foreign products in Canada fall causing an increase in Canadian imports. Falling exports and rising imports mean that net exports are falling.

The greater the sensitivity of consumption, investment, and net exports to changes in interest rates, the more crowding out will occur. In a deep recession, many firms may be so pessimistic about the future and have so much excess capacity that investment spending will fall to very low levels and will be unlikely to fall much further, even if interest rates rise. In this case, crowding out is unlikely to be much of a problem. If the economy is close to potential GDP, however, and firms are optimistic about the future, then an increase in interest rates may result in a significant decline in investment spending.

Figure 12.12

An Expansionary Fiscal Policy Increases Interest Rates

If the federal government increases spending, the demand for money will increase from Money demand$_1$ to Money demand$_2$ as real GDP and income rise. With the supply of money constant, at $90 billion, the result is an increase in the equilibrium interest rate from 3 percent to 4 percent, which crowds out some consumption, investment, and net exports.

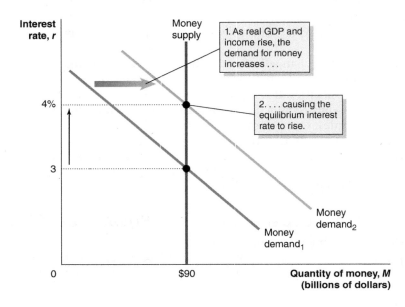

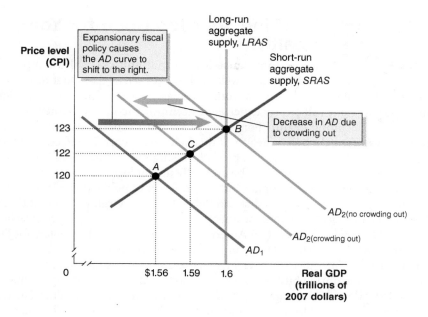

Figure 12.13

**The Effect of Crowding Out
in the Short Run**

The economy begins in a recession, with real GDP of \$1.56 trillion (point A). In the absence of crowding out, an increase in government purchases will shift aggregate demand to $AD_{2(\text{no crowding out})}$ and bring the economy to equilibrium at potential GDP of \$1.6 trillion (point B). But the higher interest rate resulting from the increased government purchases will reduce consumption, investment, and net exports, causing aggregate demand to shift to $AD_{2(\text{crowding out})}$. The result is a new short-run equilibrium at point C, with real GDP of \$1.59 trillion, which is \$10 billion short of potential GDP.

Figure 12.13 shows that crowding out may reduce the effectiveness of an expansionary fiscal policy. The economy begins in short-run equilibrium at point A, with real GDP of \$1.56 trillion. Real GDP is below potential GDP, so the economy is in recession. Suppose that the government decides to increase government purchases to bring the economy back to potential GDP. In the absence of crowding out, the increase in government purchases will shift aggregate demand to $AD_{2(\text{no crowding out})}$ and bring the economy to equilibrium at real GDP of \$1.6 trillion, which is the potential level of GDP (point B). But the higher interest rate resulting from the increased government purchases will reduce consumption, investment, and net exports, causing aggregate demand to shift back to $AD_{2(\text{crowding out})}$. The result is a new short-run equilibrium at point C, with real GDP of \$1.59 trillion, which is \$10 billion short of potential GDP.

Crowding Out in the Long Run

Most economists agree that in the short run, an increase in government spending results in partial, but not complete, crowding out. What is the long-run effect of a *permanent* increase in government spending? In this case, many economists agree that the result is complete crowding out. In the long run, the decline in investment, consumption, and net exports exactly offsets the increase in government purchases, and aggregate demand remains unchanged. To understand crowding out in the long run, recall from Chapter 9 that *in the long run, the economy returns to potential GDP.* Suppose that the economy is currently at potential GDP and that government purchases account for 35 percent of GDP. In that case, private expenditures—the sum of consumption, investment, and net exports—will make up the other 65 percent of GDP. If government purchases are increased permanently to 37 percent of GDP, in the long run, private expenditures must fall to 63 percent of GDP. There has been complete crowding out: Private expenditures have fallen by the same amount that government purchases have increased. If government spending is taking up a larger share of GDP, then private spending must take a smaller share.

An expansionary fiscal policy doesn't have to cause complete crowding out in the short run. If the economy is below potential GDP, it is possible for both government purchases and private expenditures to increase. But in the long run, a permanent increase in government purchases must come at the expense of private expenditures. Keep in mind, however, that we don't know how long it will take to arrive at this long-run outcome. It may take several—possibly many—years to arrive at the new equilibrium.

Is Losing Your Job Good for Your Health?

Recessions cause lost output and cyclical unemployment, which reduce welfare. It makes sense, then, that monetary and fiscal policies that shorten recessions would increase welfare. Someone experiencing cyclical unemployment will clearly experience declining income. Will the unemployed also suffer from declining health? For many years, most economists believed laid-off workers would suffer a decline in health. If this belief were correct, effective macroeconomic policies would improve welfare by both raising the incomes and improving the health of people who might otherwise be cyclically unemployed.

Surprisingly, however, Christopher Ruhm (professor of public policy and economics at the Frank Batten School of Leadership and Public Policy in Virginia) has found substantial evidence that during a recession, the unemployed may, on average, experience improving health. Ruhm's analysis is based on American data gathered by the Centers for Disease Control and Prevention. He found that during recessions, people tend to smoke less, drink less alcohol, eat a healthier diet, lose weight, and exercise more. As a result, death rates and sickness rates decline during business cycle recessions and increase during business cycle expansions. Why do recessions apparently have a positive impact on health? The reasons aren't completely clear, but Ruhm offers several possible explanations. The unemployed may have more time available to exercise, prepare healthy meals, and visit the doctor. Temporary joblessness may also reduce workplace stress, which some people attempt to relieve by smoking or drinking alcohol. In addition, during a recession, traffic congestion and air pollution decline, which may reduce deaths from coronary heart disease. In fact, Ruhm estimates that during business cycle expansions, a 1 percent decline in the American unemployment rate is associated with an additional 3900 deaths from heart disease.

According to Ruhm, health problems such as cancer, which tend to develop over many years, are not affected by the business cycle. In addition, unlike physical health, mental health apparently does decline during recessions and improve during expansions. It is important to understand that Ruhm's research analyzes the effects on health of temporary fluctuations in output and employment during the business cycle. Over the long run, economic research has shown that rising incomes result in better health.

The results of Ruhm's research on health and the business cycle do not mean that the federal government should abandon using monetary and fiscal policy to stabilize the economy. Although the physical health of the unemployed may, on average, increase during a recession, their incomes and their mental health may decline. No one doubts that losing one's job can be a heavy blow, as the rising suicide rate during recessions shows. So, most economists would still agree that a successful policy that reduces the severity of the business cycle will improve average well-being in the economy.

Sources: Based on Christopher J. Ruhm, "A Healthy Economy Can Break Your Heart," Demography, Vol. 44, No. 4, November 2007, pp. 829–848; Christopher J. Ruhm,"Healthy Living in Hard Times," Journal of Health Economics, Vol. 24, No. 2, March 2005, pp. 341–363; and Christopher J. Ruhm, "Are Recessions Good for Your Health?" Quarterly Journal of Economics, Vol. 115, No. 2,May 2000, pp. 617–650.

MyEconLab

Your Turn: Test your understanding by doing related problem 5.4 on page 399 at the end of this chapter.

Define federal budget deficit and federal government debt and explain how the federal budget can serve as an automatic stabilizer.

Budget deficit The situation in which the government's current expenditures are greater than its current tax revenue.

Budget surplus The situation in which the government's current expenditures are less than its current tax revenue.

Deficits, Surpluses, and Federal Government Debt

The federal government's budget shows the relationship between its expenditures and its tax revenue. When the federal government's current expenditures are greater than its current tax revenue, a **budget deficit** results. If the federal government's current expenditures are less than its current tax revenue, a **budget surplus** results. As with many other macroeconomic variables, it is useful to consider the size of the surplus or deficit relative to the size of the economy.

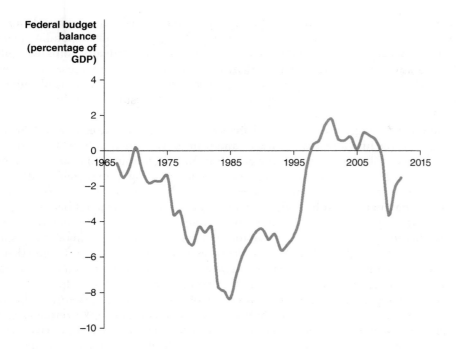

Figure 12.14

The Federal Budget Deficit, 1967–2012

The federal government has run a budget deficit for most of the past 50 years. The federal budget balance tends to be more in deficit when the economy is in recession, and the deficit tends to be smaller when the economy is doing well. You should note that the federal government changed its accounting standards in fiscal year 1983–1984, which makes comparisons between years before 1983 to later years suspect.

Note: In this graph, the years represent the end of the fiscal year. For example, fiscal year 2009–2010 is identified as "2010."

Source: Data from Department of Finance, Fiscal Reference Tables, Table 2 http://www.fin.gc.ca/frt-trf/2010/frt-trf-1001-eng.asp#tbl2

Figure 12.14 shows that the federal government has tended to run a budget deficit since the 1960s. During the 1970s and 1980s it was common for governments around the world to run large budget deficits to finance a wide variety of government spending programs. The budget balance of the federal government began to improve in the late 1980s, but it rose in the early 1990s as the Canadian economy entered a recession. In the late 1990s, the federal government began to run a surplus for the first time in decades.

You can clearly see the impact of the recent global recession and Canada's Economic Action Plan on the federal budget balance in Figure 12.14. The federal budget switches from surplus in 2008 to deficit in 2009, and the deficit grows to 3.6 percent of GDP in 2010. Remember that this increase in government spending was intended to stimulate the economy in the face of the global recession. The problem with a large deficit is that it can make funding new government initiatives difficult.

How the Federal Budget Can Serve as an Automatic Stabilizer

Discretionary fiscal policy actions can increase the federal budget deficit during recessions by increasing spending or cutting taxes to increase aggregate demand. Although the federal government delivered a fiscal stimulus package to counteract the effects of the global recession, in many milder recessions, it takes no significant fiscal policy actions. In fact, most of the increase in the federal budget deficit during a small slowdown takes place without the federal government taking any deliberate action, but is instead due to the effects of the *automatic stabilizers* we mentioned earlier in this chapter.

Deficits occur automatically during recessions for two reasons. First, during a recession, wages and profits fall, causing government tax revenues to fall. Second, the government automatically increases its spending on transfer payments when the economy moves into recession. The government's contribution to the Employment Insurance program will increase as unemployment rises. Spending will also increase on programs to aid low-income people. These spending increases take place without the government taking any action. Existing laws already specify who is eligible for Employment Insurance and other programs. As the number of eligible persons increase during a recession, so does government spending on these programs.

Because budget deficits automatically increase during recessions and decrease during expansions, economists often look at the *cyclically adjusted budget deficit or surplus*

Cyclically adjusted budget deficit or surplus The deficit or surplus in the federal government's budget if the economy were at potential GDP.

(sometimes referred to as the *structural budget balance*), which can provide a more accurate measure of the effects on the economy of the government's spending and tax policies than can the actual budget deficit or surplus. The **cyclically adjusted budget deficit or surplus** measures what the deficit or surplus would be if the economy were at potential GDP. An expansionary fiscal policy should result in a cyclically adjusted budget deficit, and a contractionary fiscal policy should result in a cyclically adjusted budget surplus.

Automatic budget surpluses and deficits can help stabilize the economy. When the economy moves into a recession, wages and profits fall, which reduces the taxes that households and firms pay to the government. In effect, households and firms have received an automatic tax cut, which keeps their spending higher than it otherwise would have been. In a recession, workers who have been laid off receive Employment Insurance payments, and households whose incomes have dropped below a certain level become eligible for government transfer programs. By receiving this extra income, households are able to spend more than they otherwise would have. This extra spending helps reduce the length and severity of the recession. Many economists argue that the absence of an employment insurance system and other government transfer programs contributed to the severity of the Great Depression of the 1930s and helps explain why the Canadian recession of 2008–2009 was not a lot worse. During the Great Depression, workers who lost their jobs saw their labour market incomes drop to zero and had to rely on their savings, what they could borrow, or what they received from private charities. As a result, many cut back their spending drastically, which made the downturn worse.

When GDP increases above its potential level, households and firms have to pay more taxes to the federal government, and the federal government makes fewer transfer payments. Higher taxes and lower transfer payments cause total spending to rise by less than it otherwise would have, which helps reduce the chance that the economy will experience high inflation.

Making the Connection

The Greek Debt Crisis and Austerity

The governments of virtually every developed economy engaged in discretionary fiscal expansion to fight the global recession of 2007–2009. Expansionary fiscal policy leads to an increase in the size of a government's budget deficit. Some countries, such as the United States, the United Kingdom, and Greece, were running budget deficits before the recession hit. In April 2010, analysts and lenders began to become particularly concerned about Greek's high government debt and whether the country would be able to repay the money it was borrowing to pay for its government spending. As a result, few people were willing to lend to the Greek government and the interest rate at which the Greek government could borrow rose to over 15 percent. Because of the high rates faced by the Greek government, the European Union and other international organizations agreed to lend to the Greek government, but only if the Greeks reduced the government deficit and changed several regulations and laws. This situation is often referred to as a *bailout*.

The bailout of the Greek government led to many protests.

In 2010, to restore the country's fiscal balance, the Greek government announced that it would follow an "austerity" plan (which has since been revised). This plan involves cutting the budget deficit to ensure that enough money is available to pay back government loans. These cuts have included a reduction in public sector pay, monthly pensions, and health spending; an increase in sales and other taxes; and the sell-off of part of the government's holdings in banks, utilities, and land.

Many people opposed to the Greek austerity program are concerned that reductions in government spending will have a negative impact on economies, just as they believe that increases in government spending will have a positive impact.

The Greeks are not alone in facing austerity plans. The governments of Portugal, Italy, Britain, and even Canada have also announced a plan for reducing their budget deficits over the medium term. Concern remains that reductions in government spending will lead the economies of these countries to shrink. Proponents of austerity measures point out that budget deficits can't be sustained forever, the crisis is over, and that a reduction in government spending may mean more opportunities for private sector job growth. We'll have to wait and see what actually happens to these economies to find out which predictions are more accurate.

Your Turn: Test your understanding by doing related problem 6.4 on page 399 at the end of this chapter.   MyEconLab

Solved Problem **12.2**

The Effect of Economic Fluctuations on the Budget Deficit

The Canadian federal government's budget deficit was $35.3 billion in 1991 and $34.4 billion in 1992. A student comments, "The government must have acted between 1991 and 1992 to raise taxes or cut spending, or possibly both." Do you agree? Briefly explain.

Solving the Problem

Step 1: **Review the chapter material.** This problem is about the federal budget as an automatic stabilizer, so you may want to review the section "How the Federal Budget Can Serve as an Automatic Stabilizer," on page 383.

Step 2: **Explain how changes in the budget deficit can occur without government action.** If government takes action to raise taxes or cut spending, the federal budget deficit will decline. But the deficit will also decline automatically when GDP increases, even if the government takes no action. When GDP increases, rising household incomes and firm profits result in higher tax revenues. Increasing GDP also usually means falling unemployment, which reduces government spending on programs for the unemployed (Employment Insurance in Canada). So, you should disagree with the comment. A falling deficit does not mean that the government *must* have acted to raise taxes or cut spending.

Extra credit: Although you don't need this detail to answer the question, Canadian GDP rose from $696.9 billion in 1991 to $713.3 billion in 1992.

Your Turn: For more practice, do related problem 6.5 on page 399 at the end of this chapter.   MyEconLab

Should the Federal Budget Always Be Balanced?

Although many economists believe that it is a good idea for the federal government to have a balanced budget when the economy is at potential GDP, few economists believe that the federal government should attempt to balance its budget every year. To see why economists take this view, consider what the government would have to do to keep the budget balanced during a recession, when the federal budget automatically moves into deficit. To bring the budget back into balance, the government would have to raise taxes or cut spending, but these actions would reduce aggregate demand, thereby making the recession worse. Similarly, when GDP increases above its potential level, the budget automatically moves into surplus. To eliminate this surplus, the government would have to cut taxes or increase government spending. But these actions would increase aggregate demand, thereby pushing GDP even further beyond potential GDP and increasing the risk of higher inflation. To balance the budget every year, the government might have to take actions that would destabilize the economy.

Some economists argue that the federal government should normally run a budget deficit, even when the economy is at potential GDP. When the federal budget is in deficit, the government sells bonds to investors to raise the funds necessary to pay the government's bills. Borrowing to pay the bills is a bad idea for a household, a firm, or a government when the bills are for current expenses, but it isn't necessarily a bad policy if the bills are for long-lived capital goods. For instance, most households pay for a home by taking a 15- to 30-year mortgage. Because houses last many years, it makes sense to pay for a house out of the income the household earns over a long period of time rather than out of the income received in the year the house is bought. Businesses often borrow the funds to buy machinery, equipment, and factories by selling long-term corporate bonds. Because these capital goods generate profits for the businesses over many years, it makes sense to pay for them over a period of years as well. By similar reasoning, when the federal government contributes to the building of a new highway, bridge, or subway, it may want to borrow funds by selling bonds. The alternative is to pay for these long-lived capital goods out of the tax revenues received in the year the goods were purchased. But that means that the taxpayers in that year have to bear the whole burden of paying for the projects, even though taxpayers for many years in the future will get to enjoy the benefits.

The Federal Government Debt

Federal government debt The total value of bonds outstanding, which is equal to the sum of past budget deficits, net of surpluses.

Every time the federal government runs a budget deficit, the government must borrow funds from investors by selling bonds. When the federal government runs a budget surplus, it pays off some existing bonds. Figure 12.14 shows that there are many more years of federal budget deficits than years of federal budget surpluses. As a result, the total number of bonds outstanding has grown over the years. The total value of bonds outstanding, which is equal to the sum of past budget deficits, is referred to as the **federal government debt**. Each year the federal budget is in deficit, the federal government debt grows. Each year the federal budget is in surplus, the debt shrinks.

Figure 12.15 shows federal government debt since 1967. The debt has been increasing over virtually the entire period. The exception is the period from 2000 to 2008, during which the debt either fell or increased very little. You can see a major increase in the debt from 1980 to 1998. While federal government debt would have naturally increased during the recessions that took place in this period, it also increased when the economy was growing. In 2000, the debt actually began to fall. This trend continued until 2009, when the debt increased dramatically. This spike in the debt was a result of Canada's Economic Action Plan. When we consider the gross federal government debt, it's important to keep a couple of points in mind. First, we haven't controlled for changes in the value of the dollar: The total debt was fewer dollars in the 1960s, but those dollars were worth more. Second, the Canadian economy has been growing at the same time that the debt has been growing.

Is Government Debt a Problem?

Debt can be a problem for a government for the same reasons that debt can be a problem for a household or a business. If a household has difficulty making the monthly mortgage payment, it will have to cut back on spending for other things. If the household is unable to make payments, it will have to default on the loan and will probably lose its house. The federal government is in no danger of defaulting on its debt. Ultimately, the government can raise the funds it needs through taxes to make the interest

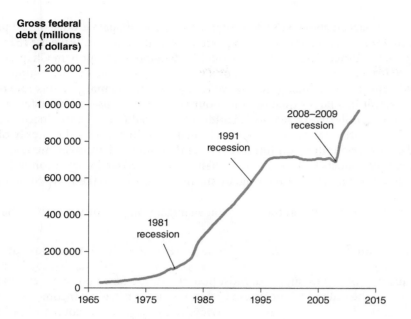

Figure 12.15

The Federal Government Debt, 1967–2012

The federal government debt increases whenever the federal government runs a budget deficit. The large deficits of the 1980s and 1990s increased the debt significantly. The debt actually began to fall in the 2000s as the federal government brought budget deficits down and began to run budget surpluses. This trend continued until 2009, when Canada's Economic Action Plan was launched.

Source: Data from Department of Finance, Fiscal Reference Tables, Table 2 http://www.fin.gc.ca/frt-trf/2010/frt-trf-1001-eng.asp#tbl2

payment on the debt. If the debt becomes very large relative to the economy, however, the government may have to raise taxes to high levels or cut back on many other types of spending to make the interest payments on the debt. Interest payments are currently about 11 percent of total federal expenditures. At this level, tax increases or significant cutbacks in other areas aren't required.

In the long run, a debt that increases in size relative to GDP, as was happening after 2009, can pose a problem. As we discussed previously, crowding out of investment spending may occur if an increasing debt drives up interest rates. Lower investment spending means a lower capital stock in the future and a lower capacity of the economy to produce goods and services. This effect is somewhat offset if some of the government debt was incurred to finance improvements in *infrastructure*, such as bridges, roads, and ports; to finance education; or to finance research and development. Improvements in infrastructure, a better-educated labour force, and additional research and development can add to the productive capacity of the economy.

The Effects of Fiscal Policy in the Long Run

12.7 LEARNING OBJECTIVE

Discuss the effects of fiscal policy in the long run.

Some fiscal policy actions are intended to meet short-run goals of stabilizing the economy. Other fiscal policy actions are intended to have long-run effects by expanding the productive capacity of the economy and increasing the rate of economic growth. Because these policy actions primarily affect aggregate supply rather than aggregate demand, they are sometimes referred to as *supply-side economics*. Most fiscal policy actions that attempt to increase aggregate supply do so by changing taxes to increase the incentives to work, save, invest, or start a business.

The Long-Run Effects of Tax Policy

The difference between the pretax and posttax return to an economic activity is known as the **tax wedge**. The tax wedge applies to the *marginal tax rate*, which is the fraction of each additional dollar of income that must be paid in taxes. For example, the Canadian income tax has several tax brackets, which are the income ranges within which a tax rate applies. In 2012, the federal tax rate on the first $42 707 of income was 5 percent. The tax rate rose for higher income brackets until it reached 29 percent

Tax wedge The difference between the pretax and posttax return to an economic activity.

on income earned above $132 406. Suppose that you are paid a wage of $20 per hour. If your marginal income tax rate is 25 percent, then the after-tax wage is $15, and the tax wedge is $5. When discussing the model of demand and supply in Chapter 3, we saw that increasing the price of a good or service increases the quantity supplied. So, we would expect that reducing the tax wedge by cutting the marginal tax rate on income would result in a larger quantity of labour supplied because the after-tax wage would be higher. Similarly, we saw in Chapter 6 that a reduction in the income tax would increase the after-tax return to saving, causing an increase in the supply of loanable funds, a lower equilibrium interest rate, and an increase in investment spending. In general, economists believe that the smaller the tax wedge for any economic activity—such as working, saving, investing, or starting a business—the more of that economic activity that will occur.

We can look briefly at the effects on aggregate supply cutting each of the following taxes:

- **Individual income tax.** As we've seen, reducing the marginal tax rates on individual income will reduce the tax wedge faced by workers, thereby increasing the quantity of labour supplied. Most households are taxed on their returns from savings at the individual income tax rates. Reducing marginal income tax rates, therefore, also increases the return to saving. Tax-free savings accounts allow households to earn small amounts of interest, tax-free.

- **Corporate income tax.** The federal government taxes the profits earned by corporations under the corporate income tax. In January 2012, the corporate income tax rate fell to 15 percent. Cutting the marginal corporate income tax rate may encourage investment spending by increasing the return corporations receive from new investments in equipment, factories, and office buildings. Because innovations are often embodied in new investment goods, cutting the corporate income tax can potentially increase the pace of technological change.

- **Taxes on dividends and capital gains.** Corporations distribute some of their profits to shareholders in the form of payments known as *dividends*. Shareholders may also benefit from higher corporate profits by receiving *capital gains*. A capital gain is the change in the price of an asset, such as a share or a stock. Rising profits usually result in rising stock prices and capital gains to shareholders. Individuals pay taxes on both dividends and capital gains (only half of dividend and capital gains are taxed, and they are taxed in the same way as other income). As a result, the same earnings are, in effect, taxed twice: once when corporations pay the corporate income tax on their profits and a second time when the profits are received by individual investors in the form of dividends or capital gains. Economists debate the cost and benefits of a separate tax on corporate profits. With the corporate income tax remaining in place, one way to reduce the "double taxation" problem is to reduce the taxes on dividends and capital gains. Lowering the tax rates on dividends and capital gains may increase the supply of loanable funds from households to firms, increasing saving and investment and lowering the equilibrium real interest rate.

Tax Simplification

In addition to the potential gains from cutting individual taxes, there are also gains from tax simplification. The complexity of the tax has created an entire industry of tax preparation services such as H&R Block. The Canadian tax system is fairly complex. François Vaillancourt, professor of economics at the University of Montreal, estimates that it costs Canadians between $4 billion and $5.8 billion annually to comply with personal income tax regulations.[1] There are costs to complying with

---

[1]François Vaillancourt, *The Cost to Canadians of Complying with Personal Income Taxes* (Vancouver: Fraser Institute, 2010).

the corporate income tax and even the GST has costs associated with collecting, calculating net tax owed, and remitting the GST. The complexity of the tax code makes it unsurprising that over half of Canadians paid someone else to prepare their income taxes.

If the tax code were greatly simplified, the economic resources currently used by the tax preparation industry would be available to produce other goods and services. In addition to wasting resources, the complexity of the tax code may also distort the decisions made by households and firms. A simplified tax code would increase economic efficiency by reducing the number of decisions households and firms make solely to reduce their tax payments.

Making the Connection	## Should Canada Adopt the "Flat Tax"?

In thinking about fundamental tax reform, some economists and policymakers have advocated simplifying the individual income tax system by adopting a "flat tax." A flat tax would replace the current individual income tax system—that includes multiple tax brackets, exemptions, and deductions—with a new system containing a single tax bracket and few, or even zero, deductions or exemptions.

In 1994, Estonia became the first country to adopt a flat tax when it began imposing a single tax rate of 26 percent on individual income. As the table below shows, a number of countries in Eastern Europe have followed Estonia's lead. Although these countries have a flat tax rate on income, they vary on the amount of annual income they allow to be exempt from the tax and on which sources of income the tax applies. For example, Estonia does not tax corporate profits directly, although it does tax dividends paid by corporations to shareholders.

Country	Flat Tax Rate	Year Flat Tax Was Introduced
Estonia	26%	1994
Lithuania	33%	1994
Latvia	25%	1995
Russia	13%	2001
Serbia	14%	2003
Ukraine	14%	2004
Slovakia	19%	2004
Georgia	12%	2005
Romania	16%	2005

Governments in Eastern Europe are attracted by the simplicity of the flat tax. It's easy for taxpayers to understand and easy for the government to administer. The result has been greater compliance with the tax code. A study of the effects of Russia moving to a flat tax found that, before tax reform, Russians whose incomes had placed them in the two highest tax brackets had, on average, been reporting only 52 percent of their income to the government. In 2001, with the new single 13 percent tax bracket in place, these high-income groups on average reported 68 percent of their income to the government.

In North America and Western Europe, proponents of the flat tax have focused on the reduction in paperwork and compliance cost and the potential increases in labour supply, saving, and investment that would result from a lower marginal tax rate. Opponents of the flat tax believe that it has two key weaknesses. First, they point out that many of the provisions that make the current tax code so complex were enacted for good reason. For example, in Canada, taxpayers are allowed to deduct tuition from their taxes, making school cheaper and thereby aiding the government's goal of increasing the skills of Canadians. Such deductions would be eliminated under most flat tax proposals, thereby reducing the ability of the government to pursue some policy goals. Second, opponents of the flat tax believe that it would make the distribution of income more unequal by reducing the marginal tax rate on high-income taxpayers. Because high-income taxpayers can now use the complexity of the tax code to shelter some of their income from taxes, it is unclear whether the amount of taxes paid by these people would actually decrease under a flat tax.

Sources: "The Case for Flat Taxes," *Economist*, April 14, 2005; and Juan Carlos Conesa and Dirk Krueger, "On the Optimal Progressivity of the Income Tax Code," *Journal of Monetary Economics* 53, no. 7 (October 2006): 1425–1450.

MyEconLab

Your Turn: Test your understanding by doing related problem 7.4 on page 399 at the end of this chapter.

The Economic Effect of Tax Reform

We can analyze the economic effects of tax reduction and simplification by using the aggregate demand and aggregate supply model. Figure 12.16 shows that without tax changes, the aggregate supply curve will shift from $LRAS_1$ to $LRAS_2$. This shift represents the increases in the labour force and the capital stock and the technological change that would occur even without tax reduction and simplification. To focus on the impact of tax changes on aggregate supply, we will ignore any shifts in the short-run aggregate supply curve, and we will assume that the aggregate demand curve remains unchanged at AD_1. In this case, equilibrium moves from point A to point B, with real GDP increasing from Y_1 to Y_2 and the price level decreasing from P_1 to P_2.

If tax reduction and simplification are effective, the economy will experience increases in labour supply, saving, investment, and the formation of new firms. Economic efficiency will also be improved. Together these factors will result in an increase in the quantity of real GDP supplied at every price level. We show the effects of the tax changes in Figure 12.16 by a shift in the long-run aggregate supply curve to $LRAS_3$. With aggregate demand remaining the same, the equilibrium in the economy moves from point A to point C (rather than to point B, which is the equilibrium without tax changes), with real GDP increasing from Y_1 to Y_3 and the price level decreasing from P_1 to P_3. An important point to notice is that compared with the equilibrium without tax

Figure 12.16

The Supply-Side Effects of a Tax Change

The economy's initial equilibrium is at point A. With no tax change, the long-run aggregate supply curve shifts to the right, from $LRAS_1$ to $LRAS_2$. Equilibrium moves to point B, with the price level falling from P_1 to P_2 and real GDP increasing from Y_1 to Y_2. With tax reductions and simplifications, the long-run aggregate supply curve shifts further to the right, to $LRAS_3$, and equilibrium moves to point C, with the price level falling to P_3 and real GDP increasing to Y_3.

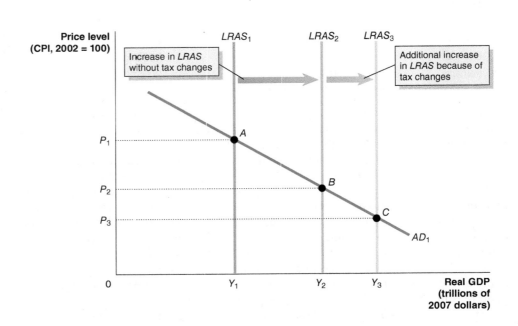

changes (point B), the equilibrium with tax changes (point C) occurs at a lower price level and a higher level of real GDP. We can conclude that the tax changes have benefited the economy by increasing output and employment while at the same time reducing the price level.

Clearly, our analysis is unrealistic because we have ignored the changes in aggregate demand and short-run aggregate supply that will occur. How would a more realistic analysis differ from the simplified one in Figure 12.16? The change in real GDP would be the same because in the long run, real GDP is equal to its potential level, which is represented by the long-run aggregate supply curve. The results for price level would be different, however, because we would expect both aggregate demand and short-run aggregate supply to shift to the right. The likeliest case is that the price level would end up higher in the new equilibrium than in the original equilibrium. However, because the position of the long-run aggregate supply curve is further to the right as a result of the tax changes, the increase in the price level will be smaller; that is, the price level at point C is likely to be lower than at point B, even if it is higher than at point A, although—as we will discuss in the next section—not all economists would agree. We can conclude that a successful policy of tax reductions and simplifications will benefit the economy by increasing output and employment, while reducing inflation (increases in the price level) at the same time.

How Big Are Supply-Side Effects?

Most economists would agree that there are supply-side effects to reducing taxes: Decreasing marginal income tax rates will increase the quantity of labour supplied, cutting the corporate income tax rates will increase the investment spending, and so on. The magnitude of the effects is the subject of ongoing debate. For example, some economists argue that the increase in the quantity of labour supplied following a tax cut will be limited because many people work a number of hours set by their employers and lack the opportunity to work additional hours. Similarly, some economists believe that tax changes have only a small effect on saving and investment. In this view, saving and investment are affected much more by changes in expectations of future profitability of new investment due to technological change or improving macroeconomic conditions than they are by tax changes.

Economists who are skeptical of the magnitude of supply-side effects believe that tax cuts have their greatest impact on aggregate demand rather than on aggregate supply. In their view, focusing on the impact of tax cuts on aggregate demand, while ignoring any impact on aggregate supply, yields accurate forecasts of future movements in real GDP and the price level, which indicates that the supply-side effects must be small. If tax changes have only small effects on aggregate supply, it is unlikely that they will reduce the size of price increases to the extent shown in the analysis in Figure 12.16.

Ultimately, the debate over the size of the supply-side effects of tax policy can be resolved only through careful study of the effects of differences in tax rates on labour supply and on saving and investment decisions. Recent US studies have arrived at conflicting conclusions. For example, a study by Edward Prescott concludes that differences between the United States and Europe with respect to the average number of hours worked per week and the average number of weeks worked per year are due to differences in taxes. The lower marginal tax rates in the United States compared with Europe increase the return to working American workers and result in a higher supply of labour. But another study by Alberto Alesina, Edward Glaeser, and Bruce Sacerdote argues that the more restrictive labour market regulations in Europe explain the shorter work weeks and longer vacations of European workers and that differences in taxes have only a small effect.

As in other areas of economics, differences among economists in their estimates of the supply-side effects of tax changes may narrow over time as additional studies are conducted.

Economics In Your Life

What Would You Do with $500 Less?

At the beginning of the chapter, we asked how you would respond to a new $500 tax and what effect this new tax would likely have on equilibrium real GDP in the short run. This chapter has shown that taxes decrease disposable income and that when there is a permanent decrease in disposable income, consumption spending decreases. So, you will likely respond to a permanent $500 decrease in your disposable income by decreasing your spending. How much your spending decreases depends in part on your overall financial situation. As mentioned in the chapter, people who are able to borrow usually try to smooth out their spending over time and don't decrease spending much in response to a one-time decrease in their income. But if you are struggling financially, your consumption may drop by the entire amount of the new tax. This chapter has also shown that tax cuts have a multiplier effect on the economy. That is, a decrease in consumption spending sets off further decreases in real GDP and income. Thus, this tax increase is likely to decrease equilibrium real GDP in the short run.

Conclusion

In this chapter, we have seen how the government uses changes in government purchases and taxes to achieve its economic policy goals. We have seen that economists debate the effectiveness of discretionary fiscal policy actions intended to stabilize the economy. Parliament and the prime minister share responsibility for economic policy with the Bank of Canada. In Chapter 13, we will discuss some the challenges that the Bank of Canada encounters as it carries out monetary policy. In Chapters 14 and 15, we will look more closely at the international economy, including how monetary and fiscal policies are affected by the linkages between economies.

Read *An Inside Look* on the next page for a discussion of Canada's stimulus package in response to the recent global recession.

FINANCIAL POST

Canada Doesn't Need to "Mindlessly Follow an Austerity Plan": BMO

The federal government may have announced this week that Canada will be late in balancing its budget, but the delay is a smart fiscal move, said BMO's chief economist.

Sherry Cooper said in a Bank of Montreal note Friday that she applauds the delay, which was announced by Finance Minister Jim Flaherty after he warned that the eurozone crisis was likely to hurt Canada's growth.

"There is no need for Canada to mindlessly follow an austerity plan that was developed when the economy was expected to grow at a relatively strong pace," Ms. Cooper said in response to the delay.

The Conservative government initially expected to balance Canada's budget deficit, which is estimated to be $33.4-billion in the latest fiscal year, by 2014–15.

But Ms. Cooper said that Canada needs to maintain "an open-minded and flexible stance on counter-cyclical monetary and fiscal policy" in the current economic environment. And she points out, Canadians live in a country that is lucky to have that luxury, at a time when many developed nations face only two options: austerity or catastrophic default. "Bank of Canada Governor Mark Carney recognized months ago that Canada's recovery is dampened by the much weaker-than-expected U.S. economy and the enlarging effects of the Euro crisis," she said.

Ms. Cooper points to Canada's history as the basis for our current leg up against other developed countries. Canada already suffered through the pain of austerity in the 1990s, when the country's massive debt could have made it an honorary PIIGS member today. Many of the fiscal reforms being enacted in Europe were implemented in Canada two decades ago (those reforms also laid the foundations for a more conservative approach to housing and banking in Canada, allowing the country to avoid the kind of mess that struck south of the border).

Given that fact, Canada now has the luxury of options when it comes to doing what's best for economic growth.

"We are lucky to be Canadian, all the more so because we are in a position to 'keep our powder dry' in the event that further countercyclical stimulus is needed," Ms. Cooper said. "Unlike most other developed economies, we have some ammo left and the good sense to know when, and if, to use it."

Source: Shmuel, John, "Canada doesn't need to 'mindlessly follow an austerity plan': BMO," Financial Post, November 11, 2011. Material reprinted by the express permission of: National Post, a division of Postmedia Network, Inc.

Key Points in the Article

After stimulating the economy using fiscal policy, governments often have to go through a painful process of cutting spending and increasing taxes to restore the budget to balance and to keep government debt from increasing. This process of cutting spending and increasing taxes is often referred to as "austerity."

In 2012, the federal government was going through the process of returning the budget to balance after engaging in expansionary fiscal policy in response to the 2008–2009 Canadian recession. The events in Europe made the process of economic recovery more difficult for Canada as firms and consumers reduced investment and consumption in response to the uncertainty around the value and the future of the euro. Many speculated that the federal government may have to engage in expansionary fiscal policy to offset the reduction in exports caused by the slowdown in Europe. Canada's relatively low debt meant that the federal government could afford more expansionary policies than some other countries.

Analyzing the News

(a) When the federal government enacted an expansionary fiscal policy response to the leftward shift in the aggregate demand curve caused by the global recession of 2007–2009, it laid out a timetable to stop spending more than it took in as revenue. Essentially, it laid out a plan to stop borrowing money. This plan involved large-scale spending cuts and increased tax revenue due to economic growth. This plan was, in part, to assure people lending money to the federal government that they would be paid back.

(b) This plan was brought into question by slow growth in the United States and the European Union, as well as the Greek debt crisis. Unlike many countries in the European Union, Canada's federal government had relatively low debt at the time and could cheaply borrow more money to engage in more expansionary fiscal policies. The countries in the European Union of most concern—Spain, Portugal, Ireland, and many others—faced interest rates so high that new borrowing wasn't in the best interest of their economies. The governments of a few European countries had to make special arrangements, including promises to change laws governing labour markets and to reduce their deficits, with other governments and international agencies because no one else would lend them money.

(c) One reason Canada was in a position to engage in further expansionary fiscal policy was because of the spending cuts and tax increases of the 1990s. These policy changes allowed the federal government to reduce its debt and to gain credibility (trust) with lenders. The PIIGS nations (Portugal, Ireland, Italy, and Spain) all had banking industries that needed government support and federal governments under severe debt burdens that made expansionary fiscal policy almost impossible.

Thinking Critically

1. Canada's Economic Action Plan was designed to stimulate the Canadian economy, primarily by providing funding for construction projects across the country. These projects were intended to provide lasting benefits to Canadians. Providing stimulus to the construction industry is likely to have the most short-run benefit to the economy, if many construction firms and workers don't currently have work. If plenty of construction is already taking place, government spending in this area is likely to crowd out private-sector construction projects and not do much to increase GDP. Do you think that the impact of stimulus spending on construction projects was the same in all regions of the country? What regions do you think were likely to benefit most?

2. Canada's Economic Action Plan resulted in a large increase in the federal budget deficit. Many inside and outside the government aren't overly worried about this deficit because it isn't as large as those in other countries and the federal government has announced plans to reduce the deficit over coming years. Briefly explain why the government would want to return to a balanced budget quickly. Why isn't the government overly worried about the impact of government borrowing on the economy?

Chapter Summary and Problems

Key Terms

Automatic stabilizers, p. 364

Budget deficit, p. 382

Budget surplus, p. 382

Crowding out, p. 380

Cyclically adjusted budget deficit or surplus, p. 384

Federal government debt, p. 386

Fiscal policy, p. 364

Multiplier effect, p. 373

Tax wedge, p. 387

Summary

*LO 12.1 *Fiscal policy* involves changes in federal taxes and purchases that are intended to achieve macroeconomic policy objectives. *Automatic stabilizers* are government spending and taxes that automatically increase or decrease along with the business cycle. Since the 1960s, the federal government's share of total government expenditures has steadily declined from above 60 percent to almost 40 percent. Federal government *expenditures* as a percentage of GDP rose from the early 1960s to the early 1990s and fell between 1992 and 2009, before rising again. The federal government's share of total government spending has declined because (1) it has been delegating the administration of certain responsibilities to provincial and territorial agencies, and (2) the importance of health care in the budgets of other levels of government has grown. The largest sources of federal government revenue are income taxes. The federal government makes large-scale transfers to provincial and territorial governments, as they have larger burdens of expenditure without reciprocal revenue-generating power.

LO 12.2 To fight recessions, the federal government can increase government purchases or cut taxes. This expansionary policy causes the aggregate demand curve to shift out more than it otherwise would, raising the level of real GDP and the price level. To fight rising inflation, the federal government can decrease government purchases or raise taxes. This contractionary policy causes the aggregate demand curve to shift out less than it otherwise would, reducing the increase in real GDP and the price level.

LO 12.3 We can use the dynamic aggregate demand and aggregate supply model introduced in Chapter 11 to look more closely at expansionary and contractionary fiscal policies. The dynamic aggregate demand and aggregate supply model takes into account that (1) the economy experiences continuing inflation, with the price level rising every year, and (2) the economy experiences long-run growth, with the LRAS curve shifting to the right every year. In the dynamic model, an expansionary fiscal policy tries to ensure that the aggregate demand curve will shift far enough to the right to bring about macroeconomic equilibrium, with real GDP equal to potential GDP. A contractionary fiscal policy attempts to offset movements in aggregate demand that would cause macroeconomic equilibrium to occur at a level of real GDP that is greater than potential GDP.

LO 12.4 Because of the *multiplier effect*, an increase in government purchases or a cut in taxes will have a multiplied effect on equilibrium real GDP. The government purchases multiplier is

equal to the change in equilibrium real GDP divided by the change in government purchases. The tax multiplier is equal to the change in equilibrium real GDP divided by the change in taxes. Increases in government purchases and cuts in taxes have a positive multiplier effect on equilibrium real GDP. Decreases in government purchases and increases in taxes have a negative multiplier effect on equilibrium real GDP.

LO 12.5 Poorly timed fiscal policy can do more harm than good. Getting the timing right with fiscal policy can be difficult because obtaining government approval for a new fiscal policy can be a very long process and because it can take months for an increase in authorized spending to take place. Because an increase in government purchases may lead to a higher interest rate, it may result in a decline in consumption, investment, and net exports. A decline in private expenditures as a result of an increase in government purchases is called *crowding out*. Crowding out may cause an expansionary fiscal policy to fail to meet its goal of keeping the economy at potential GDP.

LO 12.6 A *budget deficit* occurs when the federal government's expenditures are greater than its tax revenues. A *budget surplus* occurs when the federal government's expenditures are less than its tax revenues. A budget deficit automatically increases during recessions and tends to decrease during expansions. The automatic movements in the federal budget help stabilize the economy by cushioning the fall in spending during recessions and restraining the increase in spending during expansions. The *cyclically adjusted budget deficit or surplus* measures what the deficit or surplus would be if the economy were at potential GDP. The *federal government debt* is the total value of bonds outstanding, which is equal to the sum of past budget deficits. The national debt is a problem if interest payments on it require taxes to be raised substantially or require other federal expenditures to be cut.

LO 12.7 Some fiscal policy actions are intended to have long-run effects by expanding the productive capacity of the economy and increasing the rate of economic growth. Because these policy actions primarily affect aggregate supply rather than aggregate demand, they are sometimes referred to as *supply-side economics*. The difference between the pretax and posttax return to an economic activity is known as the *tax wedge*. Economists believe that the smaller the tax wedge for any economic activity—such as working, saving, investing, or starting a business—the more of that economic activity will occur. Economists debate the size of the supply-side effects of tax changes.

MyEconLab Log in to MyEconLab to complete these exercises and get instant feedback.

**'Learning Objective' is abbreviated to 'LO' in the end of chapter material.*

Review Questions

LO 12.1

1.1 [**Related to the** Chapter Opener **on page 363**] What is fiscal policy? Who is responsible for fiscal policy?

1.2 What is the difference between fiscal policy and monetary policy?

1.3 What is the difference between federal purchases and federal expenditures? Why have federal government expenditures as a percentage of GDP risen again since 2009?

LO 12.2

2.1 What is an expansionary fiscal policy? What is a contractionary fiscal policy?

2.2 If Parliament and the prime minster decide that an expansionary fiscal policy is necessary, what changes should they make in government spending or taxes? What changes should they make if they decide that a contractionary fiscal policy is necessary?

LO 12.3

3.1 What are the key differences between how we illustrate an expansionary fiscal policy in the basic aggregate demand and aggregate supply model and in the dynamic aggregate demand and aggregate supply model?

3.2 What are the key differences between how we illustrate a contractionary fiscal policy in the basic aggregate demand and aggregate supply model and in the dynamic aggregate demand and aggregate supply model?

LO 12.4

4.1 Why does a $1 increase in government purchases lead to more than a $1 increase in income and spending?

4.2 Define *government purchases multiplier* and *tax multiplier*.

LO 12.5

5.1 Which can be changed more quickly: monetary policy or fiscal policy? Briefly explain.

5.2 What is meant by crowding out? Explain the difference between crowding out in the short run and in the long run.

LO 12.6

6.1 In what ways does the federal budget serve as an automatic stabilizer for the economy?

6.2 What is the cyclically adjusted budget deficit or surplus? Suppose that the economy is currently at potential GDP, and the federal budget is balanced. If the economy moves into recession, what will happen to the federal budget?

6.3 Why do few economists argue that it would be a good idea to balance the federal budget every year?

6.4 What is the difference between the federal budget deficit and federal government debt?

LO 12.7

7.1 What is meant by *supply-side economics*?

7.2 What is the *tax wedge*?

Problems and Applications

LO 12.1

1.1 The BC government established the BC Scrap-It Program, which pays people between $750 and $2250 toward the purchase of a new car if they trade in older vehicles with worse fuel economy. The size of the payout is dependent on the size of the greenhouse gas benefit. Was this piece of legislation and example of fiscal policy? Does it depend on what goals the BC government had in mind when it enacted the legislation?

Based on Jeremy Cato, "Canada's cash-for-clunkers plan: Do nothing at all", CTV news, June 19, 2009, http://www.ctv.ca/CTVNews/Autos/20090618/AUTOS_cash_clunkers_090619/

1.2 [**Related to** Making the Connection **on page 367**] According to Pierre Fortin, professor of economics at the University of Québec at Montréal:

The passage of [the] large group of baby boomers into their golden years will push the percentage of senior citizens 65 and older from 13% of the total population in 2006 to 18% in 2020 . . . As a result, between now and 2020, there will be a 14% increase in annual provincial spending in health care and social services, this is above and beyond the already extremely rapid increase in spending over the past several years (on average 7% per year since 2000).

Who are the "baby boomers"? Why should their aging cause such a large increase in the growth rate of spending by the provincial governments on health care?

Pierre Fortin, "The Baby Boomers' Tab," CBC News, July 17, 2006, http://www.cbc.ca/news/background/canada2020/essay-fortin.html.

1.3 [**Related to** Making the Connection **on page 367**] According to Statistics Canada, "[b]y 2056, it is projected (based on a medium growth scenario) that there will be only 2 working-age people for every senior in Canada." Briefly explain the implications of this fact for federal government spending as a percentage of GDP in 2056.

StatsCan, Demographic change, January 14, 2010, http://www.statcan.gc.ca/pub/82-229-x/2009001/demo/int1-eng.htm

LO 12.2

2.1 Briefly explain whether you agree with the following statements: "An expansionary fiscal policy involves an increase in government purchases or an increase in taxes. A contractionary fiscal policy involves a decrease in government purchases or a decrease in taxes."

2.2 Identify each of the following as (a) part of an expansionary fiscal policy, (b) part of a contractionary fiscal policy, or (c) not part of fiscal policy.
  i. The corporate income tax rate is increased.
  ii. The Bank of Canada lowers the target for the overnight interest rate.
  iii. Individual income tax rate is decreased.
  iv. The Quebec government invests in building a new highway in an attempt to expand employment in the province.

2.3 Use an aggregate demand and aggregate supply graph to illustrate the situation where the economy begins in equilibrium at potential GDP and then the demand for housing sharply declines. What actions can the federal government take to move the economy back to potential GDP? Show the results of these actions on your graph.

2.4 A political commentator argues: "Parliament is more likely to enact an expansionary fiscal policy than a contractionary fiscal policy because expansionary policies are popular and contractionary policies are unpopular." Briefly explain whether you agree.

LO 12.3

3.1 Use the graph to answer the questions that follow.

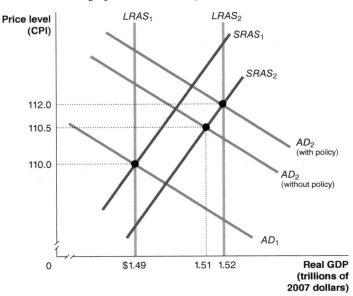

a. If the government takes no policy actions, what will be the values of real GDP and the price level in 2015 (year 2)?

b. What actions can the government take to bring real GDP to its potential level in 2015?

c. If the government takes no policy actions, what will be the inflation rate in 2015? If the government uses fiscal policy to keep real GDP at its potential level, what will be the inflation rate in 2015?

3.2 The hypothetical information in the following table shows what the situation will be in 2015 if the government does *not* use fiscal policy:

Year	Potential GDP	Real GDP	Price Level
2014	$1.50 trillion	$1.50 trillion	110.0
2015	$1.54 trillion	$1.50 trillion	111.5

a. If Parliament wants to keep real GDP at its potential level in 2015, should it use an expansionary policy or a contractionary policy? In your answer, be sure to explain whether the government should be increasing or decreasing government purchases and taxes.

b. If Parliament is successful in keeping real GDP at its potential level in 2015, state whether each of the following will be higher, lower, or the same as it would have been if they had taken no action:
  i. Real GDP
  ii. Potential GDP
  iii. The inflation rate
  iv. The unemployment rate

c. Draw an aggregate demand and aggregate supply graph to illustrate your answer. Be sure that your graph contains *LRAS* curves for 2014 and 2015; *SRAS* curves for 2014 and 2015; *AD* curves for 2014 and 2015, with and without fiscal policy action; and equilibrium real GDP and the price level in 2015, with and without fiscal policy.

LO 12.4

4.1 Why would the new bridge to the United States in Southern Ontario and similar construction projects elsewhere in the country be expected to help the economy in the short run? Proponents of government infrastructure projects often argue that government spending of this sort will have a "ripple effect" on employment. What do they mean by a *ripple effect*?

4.2 Suppose that real GDP is currently $1.31 trillion, potential GDP is $1.35 trillion, the government purchases multiplier is 2, and the tax multiplier is –1.6.
  a. Holding other factors constant, by how much will government purchases need to be increased to bring the economy to equilibrium at potential GDP?
  b. Holding other factors constant, by how much will taxes have to be cut to bring the economy to equilibrium at potential GDP?
  c. Construct an example of a combination of increased government spending and tax cuts that will bring the economy to equilibrium at potential GDP.

4.3 [**Related to** Don't Let This Happen to You **on page 376**] Consider a local politician advocating for a local government-funded project. Suppose the politician justifies the cost by stating that for each dollar spent on the project, it will generate 2.5 in economic activity.
  a. Using the simple multiplier formula, derive the marginal propensity to consume (*MPC*). Is this reasonable?
  b. Assume that, like most Canadian towns, the marginal tax rate is about 0.25 and the marginal propensity to import (*MPI*) can be conservatively estimated at 0.15. Find the *MPC*. Is this reasonable?

4.4 In many estimations of tax or expenditure multipliers, there are multiple values for different periods of time. These values generally increase as the time period gets longer. Briefly explain why a multiplier, such as the tax multiplier, might have a larger value after two years than after just one year.

4.5 [**Related to** Making the Connection **on page 377**] In their efforts to stimulate the economy during the 2007–2009 global recession, countries around the world (including Canada, China, and the United States) spent trillions of dollars on new roads and other forms of infrastructure. Why would infrastructure spending be such a popular way for government to stimulate the economy?

4.6 [**Related to** Solved Problem 12.1 **on page 378**] Briefly explain whether you agree with the following statement:

Real GDP is currently $1.65 trillion, and potential GDP is $1.64 trillion. If the federal government would decrease government purchases by $30 billion or increase taxes by $30 billion, the economy could be brought to equilibrium at potential GDP.

LO 12.5

5.1 In April 2008, the *Cape Breton Post* reported that it was widely believed that "Canada faces two lean years of slow growth, but will skirt a recession in the wake of the unfolding U.S.-centred financial crisis that is dragging down economies around the world." However, by December 2008, the *Toronto Star* reported that "Canada's economy evolved largely as expected during the summer and early autumn, it is now entering a recession as a result of the weakness in global economic activity." Does the idea that the definition of a recession comes from data released well after the fact tell us anything about the difficulty the federal government faces in implementing a fiscal policy that stabilizes rather than destabilizes the economy?

Based on Julie Beltrame, "IMF says Canada skirts recession, but growth to slow sharply to 1.3%", Cape Breton Post, April 10, 2008, http://www.capebretonpost.com/Economy/2008-04-10/article-772508/IMF-says-Canada-skirts-recession-but-growth-to-slow-sharply-to-13/1 and "Economy in recession, Bank of Canada says", Toronto Star, December 9, 2008, http://www.thestar.com/Business/article/550729

5.2 In 2011, an article in the *Economist* argued that "heavy public debt risks more than just crowding out private investment. It can, in the extreme, bring on insolvency." What does the article mean by "heavy public debts"? How might heavy public debts lead to insolvency?

"Running Out of Road," Economist, June 16, 2011.

5.3 Suppose that at the same time as Parliament pursues an expansionary fiscal policy, the Bank of Canada pursues an expansionary monetary policy. How might an expansionary monetary policy affect the extent of crowding out in the short run?

5.4 [**Related to** Making the Connection **on page 382**] Why might a recession be a reasonable time to reduce spending on health care?

LO 12.6

6.1 The federal government calculates its budget on a fiscal year that begins each year on October 1 and ends the following September 30. At the beginning of the 2003–2004 fiscal year, the Department of Finance forecast that the federal budget surplus for the fiscal year would be $4.0 billion. The actual budget surplus for the fiscal year was $9.1 billion. Federal expenditures were $1.7 billion less than the Department had forecast, and federal revenue was $1.5 billion more than the Department had forecast. The remainder of the surplus came from lower-than-forecast debt charges.

a. Is it likely that the economy grew faster or more slowly during fiscal 2003–2004 than the Department of Finance had expected? Explain your reasoning.

b. Suppose that the federal government was committed to balancing the budget each year. Does the surprise surplus during fiscal 2003–2004 provide any insight into difficulties that might arise in trying to balance the budget every year?

Data from http://www.fin.gc.ca/activty/pubs/oneil/oneil_3-eng.asp

6.2 British Columbia passed a balanced budget law in 2001, and in February 2009 the provincial government announced that it would amend the law to allow deficit spending. CBC news reported that "[then BC Finance Minister Colin] Hansen and [then] Premier Gordon Campbell announced at a joint press conference that provincial revenues have fallen prey to the worldwide economic meltdown." Do you think that nothing is more important than a balanced budget, as was stated by British Columbia's initial law, or do you think it was reasonable to amend the law for fiscal flexibility?

"BC's Balanced Budget Law to Allow 2 Years of Deficits", CBC News, February 9, 2009, http://www.cbc.ca/canada/british-columbia/story/2009/02/09/bc-legislature-budget-deficit-vote.html#ixzz18k3CFTkV

6.3 According to an article in the *Globe and Mail*, Finance Minister Jim Flaherty stated at a meeting with provincial ministers in 2010: "Canada must avoid heading in the same direction as the European Union, where many countries are in the throes of a debt crisis." He also called on provincial ministers to eliminate their deficits by 2015. How might the economy suffer from large federal deficits? How can the provincial governments rein in their budget deficits?

Karen Howlett and Bill Curry, "Rein in Deficits or Risk EU-Style Crisis, Jim Flaherty Warns Provinces," Globe and Mail, December 20, 2010, http://www.theglobeandmail.com/news/politics/rein-in-deficits-or-risk-eu-style-crisis-jim-flaherty-warns-provinces/article1844649/.

6.4 [**Related to** Making the Connection **on page 384**] What impact do you think a major reduction in US government spending would have on the Canadian economy? Explain.

6.5 [**Related to** Solved Problem 12.2 **on page 385**] The federal government's budget surplus was $14.2 billion in 1999 and $19.9 billion in 2000. What does this information tell us about fiscal policy actions that the federal government took during those years?

"Canada's Deficits and Surpluses, 1963–2012," CBC News, March 25, 2013, http://www.cbc.ca/news/interactives/canada-deficit/.

LO 12.7

7.1 It seems that both households and businesses would benefit if the federal income tax were simpler and tax forms were easier to fill out. Why then have the tax laws become increasingly complicated?

7.2 Suppose that an increase in marginal tax rates on individual income affects both aggregate demand and aggregate supply. Briefly describe the effect of the tax increase on equilibrium real GDP and the equilibrium price level. Will the changes in equilibrium real GDP and the price level be larger or smaller than they would be if the tax increase affected only aggregate demand? Briefly explain.

7.3 In a *CBC News* article on taxes, a major issue during the 2010 New Brunswick election, Craig Brett (professor of economics at Mount Allison University) stated: "There is a glimmer of hope for the supply-side myth in the case of corporate taxes. This is the only tax for which I have seen any plausible evidence that tax cuts might, I repeat might, be self-financing." Using a definition of "supply-side" tax cuts, explain how such cuts might lead to higher tax revenues and be self-financing. Why is Brett skeptical about the potential for supply-side tax cuts to be revenue generating for all types of taxes?

Craig Brett, "Talking Taxes: the Dirty Word in N.B.", CBC News, Sept 21, 2010, http://www.cbc.ca/canada/nbvotes2010/story/2010/09/20/nbvotes-analysis-craig-brett-taxes.html

7.4 [**Related to** Making the Connection **on page 389**] The majority of countries that have adopted a flat tax system of taxing individual incomes are Eastern European with historical links to the Soviet Union. Why do you think these countries might be more likely to adopt such a system than countries like Canada or the United States?

Appendix E

LO
Apply the multiplier formula.

A Closer Look at the Multiplier Formula

In this chapter, we saw that changes in government purchases and changes in taxes have a multiplied effect on equilibrium real GDP. In this appendix, we will build a simple economic model of the multiplier effect. When economists forecast the effect of a change in spending or taxes, they often rely on *econometric models*. As we saw in the appendix to Chapter 8, an econometric model is an economic model written in the form of equations, where each equation has been statistically estimated, using methods similar to those used in estimating demand curves, as briefly described in Chapter 3. In this appendix, we will start with a model similar to the one we used in the appendix to Chapter 8.

An Expression for Equilibrium Real GDP

We can write a set of equations that includes the key macroeconomic relationships we have studied in this and previous chapters. It is important to note that in this model, we will be assuming that the price level is constant. We know that this is unrealistic because an upward-sloping *SRAS* curve means that when the aggregate demand curve shifts, the price level will change. Nevertheless, our model will be approximately correct when changes in the price level are small. It also serves as an introduction to more complicated models that take into account changes in the price level. For simplicity, we also start out by assuming that taxes, T, do not depend on the level of real GDP, Y. We also assume that there are no government transfer payments to households. Finally, we assume that we have a closed economy, with no imports or exports. The numbers (with the exception of the *MPC*) represent billions of dollars:

1. $C = 100 + 0.8(Y - T)$	Consumption function
2. $I = 125$	Planned investment function
3. $G = 125$	Government purchases function
4. $T = 100$	Tax function
5. $Y = C + I + G$	Equilibrium condition

The first equation is the consumption function. The marginal propensity to consume, or *MPC*, is 0.8, and 100 is the level of autonomous consumption, which is the level of consumption that does not depend on income. We assume that consumption depends on disposable income, which is $Y - T$. The functions for planned investment spending, government spending, and taxes are very simple because we have assumed that these variables are not affected by GDP and, therefore, are constant. Economists who use this type of model to forecast GDP would, of course, use more realistic planned investment, government purchases, and tax functions.

Equation (5)—the equilibrium condition—states that equilibrium GDP equals the sum of consumption spending, planned investment spending, and government purchases. To calculate a value for equilibrium real GDP, we need to substitute equations (1) through (4) into equation (5). This substitution gives us the following:

$$Y = 100 + 0.8(Y - 100) + 125 + 125$$

$$= 100 + 0.8Y - 80 + 125 + 125.$$

We need to solve this equation for Y to find equilibrium GDP. The first step is to subtract $0.8Y$ from both sides of the equation:

$$Y - 0.8Y = 100 - 80 + 125 + 125.$$

Then, we solve for Y:

$$0.2Y = 270$$

or

$$Y = \frac{270}{0.2} = 1350.$$

To make this result more general, we can replace particular values with general values represented by letters:

$C = \overline{C} + MPC(Y - T)$	Consumption function
$I = \overline{I}$	Planned investment function
$G = \overline{G}$	Government purchases function
$T = \overline{T}$	Tax function
$Y = C + I + G$	Equilibrium condition

The letters with bars above them represent fixed, or *autonomous*, values that do not depend on the values of other variables. So, $\overline{C}$ represents autonomous consumption, which had a value of 100 in our original example. Now, solving for equilibrium, we get

$$Y = \overline{C} + MPC(Y - \overline{T}) + \overline{I} + \overline{G}$$

or

$$Y - MPC(Y) = \overline{C} - (MPC \times \overline{T}) + \overline{I} + \overline{G}$$

or

$$Y(1 - MPC) = \overline{C} - (MPC \times \overline{T}) + \overline{I} + \overline{G}$$

or

$$Y = \frac{\overline{C} - (MPC \times \overline{T}) + \overline{I} + \overline{G}}{1 - MPC}$$

A Formula for the Government Purchases Multiplier

To find a formula for the government purchases multiplier, we need to rewrite the last equation for changes in each variable rather than levels. Letting Δ stand for the change in a variable, we have:

$$\Delta Y = \frac{\Delta \overline{C} - (MPC \times \Delta \overline{T}) + \Delta \overline{I} + \Delta \overline{G}}{1 - MPC}$$

If we hold constant changes in autonomous consumption spending, planned investment spending, and taxes, we can find a formula for the government purchases multiplier, which is the ratio of the change in equilibrium real GDP to the change in government purchases:

$$\Delta Y = \frac{\Delta G}{1 - MPC}$$

or

$$\text{Government purchases multiplier} = \frac{\Delta Y}{\Delta G} = \frac{1}{1 - MPC}$$

For an MPC of 0.8, the government purchases multiplier will be

$$\frac{1}{1 - 0.8} = 5.$$

A government purchases multiplier of 5 means that an increase in government spending of $10 billion will increase equilibrium real GDP by 5 × $10 billion = $50 billion.

A Formula for the Tax Multiplier

We can also find a formula for the tax multiplier. We start again with this equation:

$$\Delta Y = \frac{\Delta \overline{C} - (MPC \times \Delta \overline{T}) + \Delta \overline{I} + \Delta \overline{G}}{1 - MPC}$$

Now we hold constant the values of autonomous consumption spending, planned investment spending, and government purchases, but we allow the value of taxes to change:

$$\Delta Y = \frac{- MPC \times \Delta T}{1 - MPC}$$

Or:

$$\text{The tax multiplier} = \frac{\Delta Y}{\Delta T} = \frac{-MPC}{1 - MPC}$$

For an *MPC* of 0.8, the tax multiplier will be:

$$\frac{-0.8}{1 - 0.8} = -4.$$

The tax multiplier is a negative number because an increase in taxes causes a decrease in equilibrium real GDP, and a decrease in taxes causes an increase in equilibrium real GDP. A tax multiplier of −4 means that a decrease in taxes of $10 billion will increase equilibrium real GDP by −4 × −$10 billion = $40 billion. In this chapter, we discussed the economic reasons for the tax multiplier being smaller than the government spending multiplier.

The "Balanced Budget" Multiplier

What will be the effect of equal increases (or decreases) in government purchases and taxes on equilibrium real GDP? At first, it might appear that the tax increase would exactly offset the government purchases increase, leaving real GDP unchanged. But we have just seen that the government purchases multiplier is larger (in absolute value) than the tax multiplier. We can use our formulas for the government purchases multiplier and the tax multiplier to calculate the net effect of increasing government purchases by $10 billion at the same time that taxes are increased by $10 billion:

$$\text{Increase in real GDP from the increase in government purchases} = \$10 \text{ billion} \times \frac{1}{1 - MPC}$$

$$\text{Decrease in real GDP from the increase in taxes} = \$10 \text{ billion} \times \frac{-MPC}{1 - MPC}$$

So, the combined effect equals

$$\$10 \text{ billion} \times \left[\left(\frac{1}{1 - MPC} \right) + \left(\frac{-MPC}{1 - MPC} \right) \right]$$

or

$$\$10 \text{ billion} \times \left(\frac{1 - MPC}{1 - MPC} \right) = \$10 \text{ billion}.$$

The balanced budget multiplier is, therefore, equal to $(1 - MPC)/(1 - MPC)$, or 1. Equal dollar increases and decreases in government purchases and in taxes lead to the same dollar increase in real GDP in the short run.

The Effects of Changes in Tax Rates on the Multiplier

We now consider the effect of a change in the tax *rate*, as opposed to a change in a fixed amount of taxes. Changing the tax rate actually changes the value of the multiplier. To see this, suppose that the tax rate is 20 percent, or 0.2. In that case, an increase in household income of \$10 billion will increase *disposable income* by only \$8 billion [or 10 billion $\times$ $(1 - 0.2)$]. In general, an increase in income can be multiplied by $(1 - t)$ to find the increase in disposable income, where t is the tax rate. So, we can rewrite the consumption function as:

$$C = \overline{C} + MPC(1 - t)Y.$$

We can use this expression for the consumption function to find an expression for the government purchases multiplier, using the same method we used previously:

$$\text{Government purchases multiplier} = \frac{\Delta Y}{\Delta G} = \frac{1}{1 - MPC(1 - t)}$$

We can see the effect of changing the tax rate on the size of the multiplier by trying some values. First, assume that $MPC = 0.8$ and $t = 0.2$. Then:

$$\text{Government purchases multiplier} = \frac{\Delta Y}{\Delta G} = \frac{1}{1 - 0.8(1 - 0.2)} = \frac{1}{1 - 0.64} = 2.77.$$

This value is smaller than the multiplier of 4 that we calculated by assuming that there was only a fixed amount of taxes (which is the same as assuming that the marginal tax *rate* was zero). This multiplier is smaller because spending in each period is now reduced by the amount of taxes households must pay on any additional income they earn. We can calculate the multiplier for an MPC of 0.8 and a lower tax rate of 0.1:

$$\text{Government purchases multiplier} = \frac{\Delta Y}{\Delta G} = \frac{1}{1 - 0.8(1 - 0.1)} = \frac{1}{1 - 0.72} = 3.57.$$

Cutting the tax rate from 20 percent to 10 percent increased the value of the multiplier from 2.77 to 3.57.

The Multiplier in an Open Economy

Up to now, we have assumed that the economy is closed, with no imports or exports. We can consider the case of an open economy by including net exports in our analysis. Recall that net exports equal exports minus imports. Exports are determined primarily by factors—such as the exchange value of the dollar and the levels of real GDP in other countries—that we do not include in our model. So, we will assume that exports are fixed, or autonomous:

$$\text{Exports} = \overline{\text{Exports}}$$

Imports will increase as real GDP increases because households will spend some portion of an increase in income on imports. We can define the *marginal propensity to import (MPI)* as the fraction of an increase in income that is spent on imports. So, our expression for imports is:

$$\text{Imports} = MPI \times Y.$$

We can substitute our expressions for exports and imports into the expression we derived earlier for equilibrium real GDP:

$$Y = \overline{C} + MPC(1 - t)Y + \overline{I} + \overline{G} + [\overline{Exports} - (MPI \times Y)],$$

where the expression $[\overline{Exports} - (MPI \times Y)]$ represents net exports. We can now find an expression for the government purchases multiplier by using the same method we used previously:

$$\text{Government purchases multiplier} = \frac{\Delta Y}{\Delta G} = \frac{1}{1 - [MPC(1 - t) + MPI]}$$

We can see the effect of changing the value of the marginal propensity to import on the size of the multiplier by trying some values of key variables. First, assume that $MPC = 0.8$, $t = 0.2$, and $MPI = 0.1$. Then:

$$\text{Government purchases multiplier} = \frac{\Delta Y}{\Delta G} = \frac{1}{1 - (0.8(1 - 0.2) - 0.1)} = \frac{1}{1 - 0.54} = 2.17.$$

This value is smaller than the multiplier of 2.5 that we calculated by assuming that there were no exports or imports (which is the same as assuming that the marginal propensity to import was zero). This multiplier is smaller because spending in each period is now reduced by the amount of imports households buy with any additional income they earn. We can calculate the multiplier with $MPC = 0.8$, $t = 0.2$, and a higher MPI of 0.2:

$$\text{Government purchases multiplier} = \frac{\Delta Y}{\Delta G} = \frac{1}{1 - (0.8(1 - 0.2) - 0.2)} = \frac{1}{1 - 0.44} = 1.79.$$

Increasing the marginal propensity to import from 0.1 to 0.2 decreases the value of the multiplier from 2.17 to 1.79. We can conclude that countries with a higher marginal propensity to import will have smaller multipliers than countries with a lower marginal propensity to import.

Bear in mind that the multiplier is a short-run effect which assumes that the economy is below the level of potential real GDP. In the long run, the economy is at potential real GDP, so an increase in government purchases causes a decline in the nongovernment components of real GDP but leaves the level of real GDP unchanged.

The analysis in this appendix is simplified compared to what would be carried out by an economist forecasting the effects of changes in government purchases or changes in taxes on equilibrium real GDP in the short run. In particular, our assumption that the price level is constant is unrealistic. However, looking more closely at the determinants of the multiplier has helped us see more clearly some important macroeconomic relationships.

LO A Closer Look at the Multiplier Formula

Problems and Applications

12A.1 Assuming a fixed amount of taxes and a closed economy, calculate the value of the government purchases multiplier, the tax multiplier, and the balanced budget multiplier if the marginal propensity to consume equals 0.6.

12A.2 Calculate the value of the government purchases multiplier if the marginal propensity to consume equals 0.8, the tax rate equals 0.25, and the marginal propensity to import equals 0.2.

12A.3 Use a graph to show the change in the aggregate demand curve resulting from an increase in government purchases if the government purchases multiplier equals 2. Now, on the same graph, show the change in the aggregate demand curve resulting from an increase in government purchases if the government purchases multiplier equals 4.

12A.4 Using your understanding of multipliers, explain why an increase in the tax rate would decrease the size of the government purchases multiplier. Similarly, explain why a decrease in the marginal propensity to import would increase the size of the government purchases multiplier.

13

Inflation, Unemployment, and Bank of Canada Policy

Chapter Outline and Learning Objectives

13.1 **The Discovery of the Short-Run Trade-off between Unemployment and Inflation,** page 408
> Describe the Phillips curve and the nature of the short-run trade-off between unemployment and inflation.

13.2 **The Short-Run and Long-Run Phillips Curves,** page 413
> Explain the relationship between the short-run and long-run Phillips curves.

13.3 **Expectations of the Inflation Rate and Monetary Policy,** page 418
> Discuss how expectations of the inflation rate affect monetary policy.

13.4 **Bank of Canada Policy from the 1970s to the Present,** page 420
> Use a Phillips curve graph to show how the Bank of Canada can permanently lower the inflation rate.

The Canadian Press

Leverage, Bubbles, Bank of Canada Policies, and Macroprudential Regulation

The Bank of Canada is continually balancing the risks of inflation against the risks of unemployment. A contractionary monetary policy that can help rein in inflation risks pushing the economy into recession. An expansionary policy that can reduce the effects of a recession risks increasing inflation.

Monetary policy is not the only tool policymakers have at their disposal to reduce risks. The Bank of Canada has indicated that monetary policy should be coordinated with sound macroprudential regulation (policies that seek to maintain system-wide financial stability) to reduce the risks that arise from the spread of leverage cycles over time and from one sector to another, and the development of asset-price bubbles. In fact, Canada has a tradition of sound macroprudential regulation that has been recognized throughout the world as having allowed it to emerge relatively unscathed from the global financial crisis of 2007–2009.

Consider the following example of the Bank of Canada's balancing act. In light of the fragile recovery and emerging global risks since the end of the global financial crisis and the "Great Recession," the Bank of Canada has kept interest rates historically low. The low interest rates have meant lower costs for consumers who borrow money to buy cars and houses. As a result, Canadians have loaded up on debt to historic levels; per capita debt is over 165 percent of disposable income, a debt-to-income ratio that is almost as high as that of households in the United States before the subprime financial crisis. According to an analysis of price-to-rent ratios by the *Economist*, Canadian housing prices were about 75 percent above their long-run "fair value" in the first quarter of 2012. It is not surprising that the Bank of Canada has called housing the most important domestic risk to financial stability in Canada. What, if anything, can be done to mitigate this risk?

In an attempt to manage leverage and the housing price bubble, on June 21, 2012, Finance Minister Jim Flaherty tightened several regulations for real-estate lending—his fourth round of tightening in four years. The most significant regulatory changes are as follows: The maximum amortization period for a mortgage will now be 25 years, down from 30; refinancing a home will be allowed only up to 80 percent of its value, down from 85 percent; and homebuyers will have to demonstrate that their housing costs are no more than 39 percent of their gross household income. In addition, Canada's banking regulator, the Office of the Superintendent of Financial Institutions (OSFI), has placed a loan-to-value limit of 65 percent on borrowing against home equity.

Undoubtedly, the Bank of Canada had a tremendous amount of influence and input into the regulatory intervention to target, or at least lean against, the forecast housing bubble to avoid future financial instability. If these regulatory changes fail to sufficiently reduce risks in the Canadian economy, the Bank of Canada can still use the blunt hammer of monetary policy.

In this chapter, we will explore the Bank of Canada's attempts to balance its goals of price stability and high employment. Because Canada has fared better economically than much of the rest of the world, **AN INSIDE LOOK** on **page 428** discusses how the US Federal Reserve attempts to reduce unemployment without causing a significant increase in inflation.

Source: Based on The Economist, June 30, 2012. http://www.economist.com/node/21557731 (Accessed on August 16, 2012).

Economics in Your Life

Is It Wise to Delay a Job Search?

Your friend was recently laid off from her entry-level job as a computer analyst. You call to console her, but she does not seem very upset. "Employment Insurance offers workers up to 45 weeks of financial assistance. I have almost one year before I have to find a new job. With my education and job experience, I should be able to find a new job by then without much trouble." Your friend did well in school, but you are not sure that waiting almost one year to find a new job is a good idea. What advice would you give someone who has decided to wait nearly one year to look for a new job? As you read this chapter, see if you can answer this question. You can check your answer against the one we provide on page 427 at the end of this chapter.

An important consideration for the Bank of Canada as it carries out monetary policy is that in the short run, there can be a trade-off between unemployment and inflation: Lower unemployment rates can result in higher inflation rates. In the long run, however, this trade-off disappears, and the unemployment rate is independent of the inflation rate. In this chapter, we will explore the relationship between inflation and unemployment in both the short run and the long run, and we will discuss what this relationship means for monetary policy. We will also provide an overview of how monetary policy has evolved over the years and conclude with a discussion of the debate over Bank of Canada policy during the 2007–2009 recession.

13.1 LEARNING OBJECTIVE

Describe the Phillips curve and the nature of the short-run trade-off between unemployment and inflation.

The Discovery of the Short-Run Trade-off between Unemployment and Inflation

Ordinarily, unemployment and inflation are the two great macroeconomic problems the Bank of Canada must deal with in the short run. As we saw in Chapter 9, when aggregate demand increases, unemployment usually falls, and inflation rises. When aggregate demand decreases, unemployment usually rises and inflation falls. As a result, there is a *short-run trade-off* between unemployment and inflation: Higher unemployment is usually accompanied by lower inflation, and lower unemployment is usually accompanied by higher inflation. As we will see later in this chapter, this trade-off exists in the short run—a period that may be as long as several years—but disappears in the long run.

Although today the short-run trade-off between unemployment and inflation plays a role in the Bank of Canada's monetary policy decisions, this trade-off was not widely recognized until the late 1950s. In 1957, New Zealand economist A. W. Phillips plotted data on the unemployment rate and the inflation rate in Great Britain and drew a curve showing their average relationship. Since that time, a graph showing the short-run relationship between the unemployment rate and the inflation rate has been called a **Phillips curve.** (Phillips actually measured inflation by the percentage change in wages rather than by the percentage change in prices. Because wages and prices usually move together, this difference is not important to our discussion.) Figure 13.1 shows a graph similar to the one Phillips prepared. Each point on the Phillips curve represents a possible combination of the unemployment rate and the inflation rate that might be observed in a given year. Point *A* represents a year in which the inflation rate is 4 percent and the unemployment rate is 5 percent, and point *B* represents a year in which the inflation rate is 2 percent and the unemployment rate is 6 percent. Phillips documented that there is usually an *inverse relationship* between unemployment and inflation. During

Phillips curve A curve showing the short-run relationship between the unemployment rate and the inflation rate.

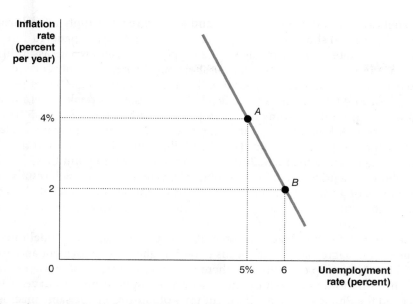

Figure 13.1

The Phillips Curve

A. W. Phillips was the first economist to show that there is usually an inverse relationship between unemployment and inflation. Here we can see this relationship at work: In the year represented by point A, the inflation rate is 4 percent and the unemployment rate is 5 percent. In the year represented by point B, the inflation rate is 2 percent and the unemployment rate is 6 percent.

years when the unemployment rate is low, the inflation rate tends to be high, and during years when the unemployment rate is high, the inflation rate tends to be low.

Explaining the Phillips Curve with Aggregate Demand and Aggregate Supply Curves

The inverse relationship between unemployment and inflation that Phillips discovered is consistent with the aggregate demand and aggregate supply analysis we developed in Chapter 9. Figure 13.2 shows why this inverse relationship exists.

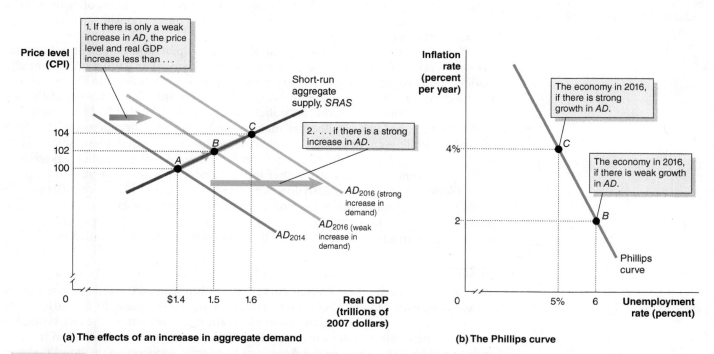

Figure 13.2   Using Aggregate Demand and Aggregate Supply to Explain the Phillips Curve

In panel (a), the economy in 2015 is at point A, with real GDP of $1.4 trillion and a price level of 100. If there is weak growth in aggregate demand, in 2016, the economy moves to point B, with real GDP of $1.5 trillion and a price level of 102. The inflation rate is 2 percent and the unemployment rate is 6 percent, which corresponds to point B on the Phillips curve in panel (b). If there is strong growth in aggregate demand, in 2016, the economy moves to point C, with real GDP of $1.6 trillion and a price level of 104. Strong aggregate demand growth results in a higher inflation rate of 4 percent but a lower unemployment rate of 5 percent. This combination of higher inflation and lower unemployment is shown as point C on the Phillips curve in panel (b).

Panel (a) shows the aggregate demand and aggregate supply model from Chapter 9, and panel (b) shows the Phillips curve. For simplicity, in panel (a), we are using the basic aggregate demand and aggregate supply model, and we are assuming that the long-run aggregate supply curve and the short-run aggregate supply curve do not shift. To take a hypothetical example, assume that the economy in 2015 is at point A, with real GDP of $1.4 trillion and a price level of 100. If there is weak growth in aggregate demand, in 2016, the economy moves to point B, with real GDP of $1.5 trillion and a price level of 102. The inflation rate is 2 percent and the unemployment rate is 6 percent, which corresponds to point B on the Phillips curve in panel (b). If there is strong growth in aggregate demand, in 2016, the economy moves to point C, with real GDP of $1.6 trillion and a price level of 104. Strong aggregate demand growth results in a higher inflation rate of 4 percent but a lower unemployment rate of 5 percent. This combination of higher inflation and lower unemployment is shown as point C on the Phillips curve in panel (b).

To summarize, the aggregate demand and aggregate supply model indicates that slow growth in aggregate demand leads to both higher unemployment and lower inflation. This relationship explains why there is a short-run trade-off between unemployment and inflation, as shown by the downward-sloping Phillips curve. The AD–AS model and the Phillips curve are different ways of illustrating the same macroeconomic events. The Phillips curve has an advantage over the aggregate demand and aggregate supply model, however, when we want to analyze explicitly *changes* in the inflation and unemployment rates.

Is the Phillips Curve a Policy Menu?

Structural relationship A relationship that depends on the basic behaviour of consumers and firms and that remains unchanged over long periods.

During the 1960s, some economists argued that the Phillips curve represented a *structural relationship* in the economy. A **structural relationship** depends on the basic behaviour of consumers and firms and remains unchanged over long periods. Structural relationships are useful in formulating economic policy because policymakers can anticipate that these relationships are constant—that is, the relationships will not change as a result of changes in policy.

If the Phillips curve were a structural relationship, it would present policymakers with a reliable menu of combinations of unemployment and inflation. Potentially, policymakers could use expansionary monetary and fiscal policies to choose a point on the curve that had lower unemployment and higher inflation. They could also use contractionary monetary and fiscal policies to choose a point that had lower inflation and higher unemployment. Because many economists and policymakers in the 1960s viewed the Phillips curve as a structural relationship, they believed it represented a *permanent trade-off between unemployment and inflation*. As long as policymakers were willing to accept a permanently higher inflation rate, they would be able to keep the unemployment rate permanently lower. Similarly, a permanently lower inflation rate could be attained at the cost of a permanently higher unemployment rate. As we discuss in the next section, however, economists came to realize that the Phillips curve did *not*, in fact, represent a permanent trade-off between unemployment and inflation.

Is the Short-Run Phillips Curve Stable?

During the 1960s, the basic Phillips curve relationship seemed to hold because a stable trade-off appeared to exist between unemployment and inflation. In the early 1960s, the inflation rate was low, and the unemployment rate was high. In the late 1960s, the unemployment rate had declined, and the inflation rate had increased. Then in 1968, in his presidential address to the American Economic Association, Milton Friedman of the University of Chicago argued that the Phillips curve did *not* represent a *permanent* trade-off between unemployment and inflation. At almost the same time, Edmund Phelps of Columbia University published an academic paper making a similar argument. Friedman and Phelps noted that economists had come to agree that the long-run aggregate supply curve was vertical (a point we discussed in Chapter 9). If this observation were true, the Phillips curve could not be downward sloping in the long run.

A critical inconsistency exists between a vertical long-run aggregate supply curve and a long-run Phillips curve that is downward sloping. Friedman and Phelps argued, in essence, that there is no trade-off between unemployment and inflation in the long run.

The Long-Run Phillips Curve

To understand the argument that there is no permanent trade-off between unemployment and inflation, first recall that the level of real GDP in the long run is also referred to as *potential GDP*. At potential GDP, firms will operate at their normal level of capacity, and everyone who wants a job will have one, except the structurally and frictionally unemployed. Friedman defined the **natural rate of unemployment** as the unemployment rate that exists when the economy is at potential GDP. The actual unemployment rate will fluctuate in the short run but will always come back to the natural rate in the long run. In the same way, the actual level of real GDP will fluctuate in the short run but will always come back to its potential level in the long run.

In the long run, a higher or lower price level has no effect on real GDP because real GDP is always at its potential level in the long run. In the same way, in the long run, a higher or lower inflation rate will have no effect on the unemployment rate because the unemployment rate is always equal to the natural rate in the long run. Figure 13.3 illustrates Friedman's conclusion that the long-run aggregate supply curve is a vertical line at the potential real GDP, and *the long-run Phillips curve is a vertical line at the natural rate of unemployment.*

Natural rate of unemployment The unemployment rate that exists when the economy is at potential GDP.

The Role of Expectations of Future Inflation

If the long-run Phillips curve is a vertical line, *no trade-off exists between unemployment and inflation in the long run.* This conclusion seemed to contradict the experience of the 1950s and 1960s, which showed a stable trade-off between unemployment and inflation. Friedman argued that the statistics from those years actually showed only a short-run trade-off between inflation and unemployment.

The short-run trade-off existed—but only because workers and firms sometimes expected the inflation rate to be either higher or lower than it turned out to be. Differences between the expected inflation rate and the actual inflation rate could lead the unemployment rate to rise above or dip below the natural rate. To see why, consider a simple case of Ford negotiating a wage contract with the Canadian Auto Workers (CAW) union. Remember that both Ford and the CAW are interested in the real wage, which is the nominal wage corrected for inflation. Suppose, for example, that Ford and the CAW agree on a wage of $31.50 per hour to be paid during 2015. Both Ford and the CAW expect that the price level will increase from 100 in 2014 to 105 in 2015, so the

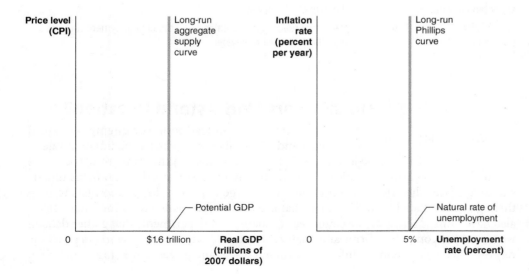

Figure 13.3

A Vertical Long-Run Aggregate Supply Curve Means a Vertical Long-Run Phillips Curve

Milton Friedman and Edmund Phelps argued that there is no trade-off between unemployment and inflation in the long run. If real GDP automatically returns to its potential level in the long run, the unemployment rate must return to the natural rate of unemployment in the long run. In this figure, we assume that potential GDP is $1.6 trillion and the natural rate of unemployment is 5 percent.

Table 13.1

The Effect of Unexpected Price Level Changes on the Real Wage

Nominal Wage	Expected Real Wage	Actual Real Wage	
	Expected $P_{2015} = 105$ Expected inflation = 5%	Actual $P_{2015} = 102$ Actual inflation = 2%	Actual $P_{2015} = 108$ Actual inflation = 8%
$31.50	$\dfrac{\$31.50}{105} \times 100 = \$30$	$\dfrac{\$31.50}{102} \times 100 = \$30.88$	$\dfrac{\$31.50}{108} \times 100 = \$29.17$

inflation rate will be 5 percent. We can calculate the real wage Ford expects to pay and the CAW expects to receive as follows:

$$\text{Real wage} = \frac{\text{Nominal wage}}{\text{Price level}} \times 100 = \frac{\$31.50}{105} \times 100 = \$30.$$

But suppose that the actual inflation rate turns out to be higher or lower than the expected inflation rate of 5 percent. Table 13.1 shows the effect on the actual real wage. If the price level rises only to 102 during 2015, the inflation rate will be 2 percent, and the actual real wage will be $30.88, which is higher than Ford and the CAW had expected. With a higher real wage, Ford will hire fewer workers than it had planned to at the expected real wage of $30. If the inflation rate is 8 percent, the actual real wage will be $29.17, and Ford will hire more workers than it had planned to hire. If Ford and the CAW expected a higher or lower inflation rate than actually occurred, other firms and workers probably made the same assumption.

If actual inflation is higher than expected inflation, actual real wages in the economy will be lower than expected real wages, and many firms will hire more workers than they had planned to hire. Therefore, the unemployment rate will fall. If actual inflation is lower than expected inflation, actual real wages will be higher than expected, many firms will hire fewer workers than they had planned to hire, and the unemployment rate will rise. Table 13.2 summarizes this argument.

Friedman and Phelps concluded that *an increase in the inflation rate increases employment (and decreases unemployment) only if the increase in the inflation rate is unexpected.* Friedman argued that in 1968, the unemployment rate in the United States was 3.6 percent rather than 5 percent only because the inflation rate of 4 percent was above the 1 percent to 2 percent inflation that workers and firms had expected: "There is always a temporary trade-off between inflation and unemployment; there is no permanent trade-off. The temporary trade-off comes not from inflation per se, but from unanticipated inflation."

Table 13.2

The Basis for the Short-Run Phillips Curve

If ...	then ...	and ...
actual inflation is greater than expected inflation,	the actual real wage is less than the expected real wage,	the unemployment rate falls.
actual inflation is less than expected inflation,	the actual real wage is greater than the expected real wage,	the unemployment rate rises.

Making the Connection | Do Workers Understand Inflation?

A higher inflation rate can lead to lower unemployment if *both* workers and firms mistakenly expect the inflation rate to be lower than it turns out to be. But this same result might be due to firms forecasting inflation more accurately than workers do or to firms understanding better the effects of inflation. Some large firms employ economists to help them gather and analyze information that is useful in forecasting inflation. Many firms also have human resources or employee compensation departments that gather data on wages paid at competing firms and analyze trends in compensation. Workers generally rely on much less systematic information about wages and prices. Workers also often fail to realize this fact: *Expected inflation increases the value of total production and the value of total income by the same amount.* Therefore, although not all wages will rise as prices rise, inflation will increase the average wage in the economy at the same time that it increases the average price.

Robert Shiller, an economist at Yale University, conducted a survey on inflation and discovered that, although most economists believe an increase in inflation will lead quickly to an increase in wages, a majority of the general public thinks otherwise. As part of the survey, Shiller asked how "the effect of general inflation on wages or salary relates to your own experience and your own job." The most popular response was: "The price increase will create extra profits for my employer, who can now sell output for more; there will be no effect on my pay. My employer will see no reason to raise my pay."

Shiller also asked the following question:

Will wage increases keep up with inflation?

Imagine that next year the inflation rate unexpectedly doubles. How long would it probably take, in these times, before your income is increased enough so that you can afford the same things as you do today? In other words, how long will it be before a full inflation correction in your income has taken place?

Eighty-one percent of the public answered either that it would take several years for the purchasing power of their income to be restored or that it would never be restored.

If workers fail to understand that rising inflation leads over time to comparable increases in wages, then when inflation increases, in the short run, firms can increase wages by less than inflation without needing to worry about workers quitting or their morale falling. Once again, we have a higher inflation rate, leading in the short run to lower real wages and lower unemployment. In other words, we have an explanation for a downward-sloping short-run Phillips curve.

Source: Robert J. Shiller, "Why Do People Dislike Inflation?" in Reducing Inflation: Motivation and Strategy by Christina D. Romer and David H. Romer, eds., (Chicago: University of Chicago Press, 1997).

Your Turn: Test your understanding by doing related problem 1.7 on page 432 at the end of this chapter.   MyEconLab

The Short-Run and Long-Run Phillips Curves

13.2 LEARNING OBJECTIVE

Explain the relationship between the short-run and long-run Phillips curves.

If there is both a short-run Phillips curve and a long-run Phillips curve, how are the two curves related? We can begin answering this question with the help of Figure 13.4, which represents macroeconomic conditions in Canada during the 1960s. In the late 1960s, workers and firms were still expecting the inflation rate to be about 1.5 percent, as it had been in the early 1960s. Expansionary monetary and fiscal policies, however, had moved the short-run equilibrium up the short-run Phillips curve to an inflation rate of 4.5 percent and an unemployment rate of about 3.5 percent. This very low unemployment rate was possible only because the real wage rate was unexpectedly low.

Once workers and firms began to expect that the inflation rate would continue to be about 4.5 percent, they changed their behaviour. Firms knew that only nominal wage increases of more than 4.5 percent would increase real wages. Workers realized that unless they received a nominal wage increase of at least 4.5 percent, their real wage would be falling. Higher expected inflation rates had an effect throughout the economy. For example, as we saw in Chapter 10, when banks make loans, they are interested in the *real interest rate* on the loan. The real interest rate is the nominal interest rate minus the inflation rate. If banks need to receive a real interest rate of 3 percent on home mortgage loans and expect the inflation rate to be 1.5 percent, they will charge a nominal interest rate of 4.5 percent. If banks revise their expectations of the inflation rate to

Figure 13.4

The Short-Run Phillips Curve of the 1960s and the Long-Run Phillips Curve

In the late 1960s, Canadian workers and firms were expecting the 1.5 percent inflation rates of the recent past to continue. However, expansionary monetary and fiscal policies moved the short-run equilibrium up the short-run Phillips curve to an inflation rate of 4.5 percent and an unemployment rate of about 3.5 percent.

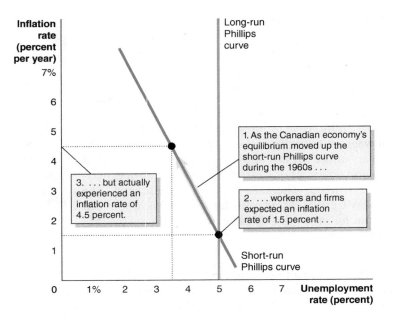

4.5 percent, they will increase the nominal interest rate they charge on mortgage loans to 7.5 percent.

Shifts in the Short-Run Phillips Curve

The new, higher expected inflation rate can become *embedded* in the economy, meaning that workers, firms, consumers, and the government all take the inflation rate into account when making decisions. The short-run trade-off between unemployment and inflation now takes place from this higher, less favourable level, as shown in Figure 13.5.

As long as workers and firms expected the inflation rate to be 1.5 percent, the short-run trade-off between unemployment and inflation was the more favourable one shown by the lower Phillips curve. Along this Phillips curve, an inflation rate of 4.5 percent was enough to drive down the unemployment rate to about 3.5 percent. Once workers

Figure 13.5

Expectations and the Short-Run Phillips Curve

By the end of the 1960s, workers and firms had revised their expectations of inflation from 1.5 percent to 4.5 percent. As a result, the short-run Phillips curve shifted up, which made the short-run trade-off between unemployment and inflation worse.

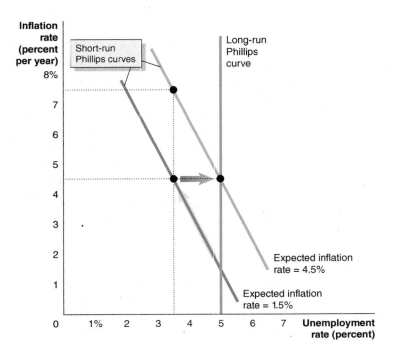

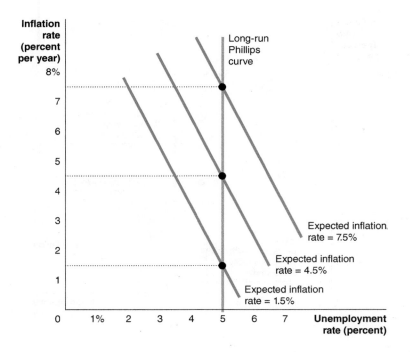

Figure 13.6

A Short-Run Phillips Curve for Every Expected Inflation Rate

There is a different short-run Phillips curve for every expected inflation rate. Each short-run Phillips curve intersects the long-run Phillips curve at the expected inflation rate.

and firms adjusted their expectations to an inflation rate of 4.5 percent, the short-run trade-off deteriorated to the one shown by the higher Phillips curve. At this higher expected inflation rate, the real wage rose, causing some workers to lose their jobs, and the economy's equilibrium returned to the natural rate of unemployment of 5 percent—but now with an inflation rate of 4.5 percent rather than 1.5 percent. On the higher short-run Phillips curve, an inflation rate of 7.5 percent would be necessary to reduce the unemployment rate to about 3.5 percent. An inflation rate of 7.5 percent would keep the unemployment rate at about 3.5 percent only until workers and firms revised their expectations of inflation up to 7.5 percent. In the long run, the economy's equilibrium would return to the 5 percent natural rate of unemployment.

As Figure 13.6 shows, there is a short-run Phillips curve for every level of expected inflation. Each short-run Phillips curve intersects the long-run Phillips curve at the expected inflation rate.

How Does a Vertical Long-Run Phillips Curve Affect Monetary Policy?

By the 1970s, most economists accepted the argument that the long-run Phillips curve is vertical. In other words, economists realized that the common view of the 1960s had been wrong: It was *not* possible to buy a permanently lower unemployment rate at the cost of a permanently higher inflation rate. The moral is that *in the long run, there is no trade-off between unemployment and inflation.* In the long run, the unemployment rate always returns to the natural rate, no matter what the inflation rate is.

Figure 13.7 shows that the inflation rate is stable only when the unemployment rate is equal to the natural rate. If the Bank of Canada were to attempt to use expansionary monetary policy to push the economy to a point such as *A*, where the unemployment rate is below the natural rate, the result would be increasing inflation as the economy moved up the short-run Phillips curve. If the economy remained below the natural rate long enough, the short-run Phillips curve would shift up as workers and firms adjusted to the new, higher inflation rate. During the 1960s and 1970s, the short-run Phillips curve did shift up, presenting the economy with a more unfavourable short-run trade-off between unemployment and inflation.

If the Bank of Canada used contractionary policy to push the economy to a point such as *B*, where the unemployment rate is above the natural rate, the inflation rate

Figure 13.7

The Inflation Rate and the Natural Rate of Unemployment in the Long Run

The inflation rate is stable only if the unemployment rate equals the natural rate of unemployment (point *C*). If the unemployment rate is below the natural rate (point *A*), the inflation rate increases, and, eventually, the short-run Phillips curve shifts up. If the unemployment rate is above the natural rate (point *B*), the inflation rate decreases, and, eventually, the short-run Phillips curve shifts down.

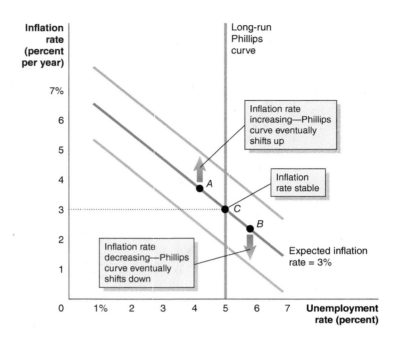

Nonaccelerating inflation rate of unemployment (NAIRU) The unemployment rate at which the inflation rate has no tendency to increase or decrease.

would decrease. If the economy remained above the natural rate long enough, the short-run Phillips curve would shift down as workers and firms adjusted to the new, lower inflation rate. Only at a point such as *C*, where the unemployment rate is equal to the natural rate, will the inflation rate be stable. As a result, the natural rate of unemployment is sometimes called the **nonaccelerating inflation rate of unemployment (NAIRU)**. We can conclude that *in the long run, the Bank of Canada can affect the inflation rate but not the unemployment rate.*

An increase in the number of younger and less skilled workers in an economy can make the natural rate of unemployment increase.

Making the Connection

Does the Natural Rate of Unemployment Ever Change?

Life would be easier for the Bank of Canada if it knew exactly what the natural rate of unemployment was and if that rate never changed. Unfortunately for the Bank of Canada, the natural rate does change over time. Remember that at the natural rate of unemployment, only frictional and structural unemployment remain. Frictional or structural unemployment can change—thereby changing the natural rate—for several reasons:

- **Demographic changes.** Younger and less skilled workers have higher unemployment rates, on average, than do older and more skilled workers. Because of the baby boom, Canada had an unusually large number of younger and less skilled workers during the 1970s and 1980s. As a result, the natural rate of unemployment rose from about 5 percent in the 1960s to about 6 percent in the 1970s and 8 percent in the 1980s and 1990s. As the number of younger and less skilled workers declined as a fraction of the labour force during the 2000s, the natural rate declined to about 6 percent.
- **Labour market institutions.** Labour market institutions such as the employment insurance system, labour unions, and legal barriers to firing workers can increase the economy's unemployment rate. Because many European countries have generous employment insurance systems, strong labour unions, and restrictive policies on firing workers, the natural rate of unemployment in most European countries has been well above the rate in Canada.
- **Past high rates of unemployment.** Evidence indicates that if high unemployment persists for a period of years, the natural rate of unemployment may increase. When workers have been unemployed for longer than a year or two, their skills deteriorate, they may

lose confidence that they can find and hold a job, and they may become dependent on government payments to survive. It has been argued that in the mid-1930s, so many Canadian workers had been out of work for so long that the natural rate of unemployment may have risen to close to 15 percent. However, even though the unemployment rate in Canada was over 19 percent in 1933, the inflation rate did not change. Similarly, many economists have argued that the high unemployment rates experienced by European countries during the 1970s increased their natural rates of unemployment. As high rates of unemployment persisted more than two and a half years after the end of the 2007–2009 recession, some economists and policymakers were concerned that the natural rate of unemployment might eventually rise.

Sources: Based on Congressional Budget Office, "The Budget and Economic Outlook: Fiscal Years 2011 to 2021," January 2011; and "Damage Assessment," Economist, May 14, 2009.

Your Turn: Test your understanding by doing related problem 2.4 on page 432 at the end of this chapter.   MyEconLab

Solved Problem **13.1**

Changing Views of the Phillips Curve

Writing in a US Federal Reserve publication, Bennett McCallum, an economist at Carnegie Mellon University, argues that during the 1970s, the Federal Reserve was "acting under the influence of 1960s academic ideas that posited the existence of a long-run and exploitable Phillips-type tradeoff between inflation and unemployment rates." What does McCallum mean by a "long-run and exploitable Phillips-type tradeoff"? How would the Federal Reserve have attempted to exploit this long-run trade-off? What would be the consequences for the inflation rate?

Solving the Problem

Step 1: **Review the chapter material.** This problem is about the relationship between the short-run and long-run Phillips curves, so you may want to review the section "The Short-Run and Long-Run Phillips Curves," which begins on page 413.

Step 2: **Explain what a "long-run exploitable Phillips-type tradeoff" means.** A "long-run exploitable Phillips-type tradeoff" means a Phillips curve that in the long run is downward sloping rather than vertical. An "exploitable" tradeoff is one that the Bank of Canada could take advantage of to *permanently* reduce unemployment, at the expense of higher inflation, or to permanently reduce inflation, at the expense of higher unemployment.

Step 3: **Explain how the inflation rate will accelerate if the Federal Reserve tries to exploit a long-run trade-off between unemployment and inflation.** As we have seen, during the 1960s, the Federal Reserve conducted expansionary monetary policies to move up what it thought was a stationary short-run Phillips curve. By the late 1960s, these policies resulted in very low unemployment rates. In the long run, there is no stable trade-off between unemployment and inflation. Attempting to permanently keep the unemployment rate at very low levels leads to a rising inflation rate, which is what happened in the late 1960s and early 1970s.

Source: Based on Bennett T. McCallum, "Recent Developments in Monetary Policy Analysis: The Roles of Theory and Evidence," Federal Reserve Bank of Richmond, Economic Quarterly, Winter 2002, p. 73.

13.3 LEARNING OBJECTIVE

Discuss how expectations of the inflation rate affect monetary policy.

Expectations of the Inflation Rate and Monetary Policy

How long can the economy remain at a point that is on the short-run Phillips curve but not on the long-run Phillips curve? It depends on how quickly workers and firms adjust their expectations of future inflation to changes in current inflation. The experience in Canada over the past 60 years indicates that how workers and firms adjust their expectations of inflation depends on how high the inflation rate is. There are three possibilities:

- **Low inflation.** When the inflation rate is low, as it was during most of the 1950s, the early 1960s, the 1990s, and the 2000s, workers and firms tend to ignore it. For example, if the inflation rate is low, a restaurant may not want to pay for printing new menus that would show slightly higher prices.

- **Moderate but stable inflation.** For the four-year period from 1968 to 1971, the inflation rate in Canada stayed in the narrow range between 4 percent and 5 percent. This rate was high enough that workers and firms could not ignore it without seeing their real wages and profits decline. It was also likely that the next year's inflation rate would be very close to the current year's inflation rate. In fact, workers and firms during the 1960s acted as if they expected changes in the inflation rate during one year to continue into the following year. People are said to have *adaptive expectations* of inflation if they assume that future rates of inflation will follow the pattern of rates of inflation in the recent past.

- **High and unstable inflation.** Inflation rates above 5 percent have been rare in Canadian history, but the inflation rate was above 5 percent every year from 1973 through 1982. Not only was the inflation rate high during these years, it was also unstable—rising from 6 percent in 1973 to about 13 percent in 1974, before falling below 6 percent in 1976 and rising again to above 11 percent in 1980. In the mid-1970s, Nobel Laureates Robert Lucas of the University of Chicago and Thomas Sargent of New York University argued that the gains to accurately forecasting inflation had dramatically increased. Workers and firms that failed to correctly anticipate the fluctuations in inflation during these years could experience substantial declines in real wages and profits. Therefore, Lucas and Sargent argued, people should use all available information when forming their expectations of future inflation. Expectations formed by using all available information about an economic variable are called **rational expectations**.

Rational expectations Expectations formed by using all available information about an economic variable.

The Effect of Rational Expectations on Monetary Policy

Lucas and Sargent pointed out an important consequence of rational expectations: An expansionary monetary policy would not work. In other words, there might not be a trade-off between unemployment and inflation, even in the short run. By the mid-1970s, most economists had accepted the idea that an expansionary monetary policy could cause the actual inflation rate to be higher than the expected inflation rate. This gap between actual and expected inflation would cause the actual real wage to fall below the expected real wage, and the unemployment rate would be pushed below the natural rate. The economy's short-run equilibrium would move up the short-run Phillips curve.

Lucas and Sargent argued that this explanation of the Phillips curve assumed that workers and firms either ignored inflation or used adaptive expectations in making their forecasts of inflation. If workers and firms have rational expectations, they will use all available information, *including knowledge of the effects of central bank policy*. If workers and firms know that an expansionary monetary policy will raise the inflation rate, they should use this information in their forecasts of inflation. If they do, an expansionary monetary policy will not cause the actual inflation rate to be above the expected inflation rate. Instead, the actual inflation rate will equal the expected inflation rate, the actual real wage will equal the expected real wage, and the unemployment rate will not fall below the natural rate.

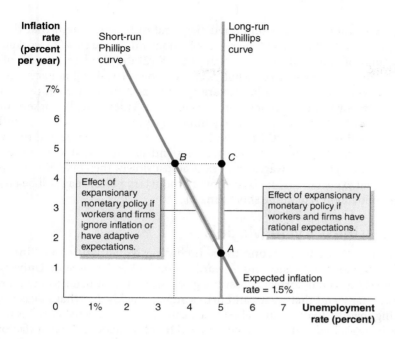

Figure 13.8

Rational Expectations and the Phillips Curve

If workers and firms ignore inflation, or if they have adaptive expectations, an expansionary monetary policy will cause the short-run equilibrium to move from point *A* on the short-run Phillips curve to point *B*; inflation will rise, and unemployment will fall. If workers and firms have rational expectations, an expansionary monetary policy will cause the short-run equilibrium to move up the long-run Phillips curve from point *A* to point *C*. Inflation will still rise, but there will be no change in unemployment.

Figure 13.8 illustrates this argument. Suppose the economy begins at point *A*, where the short-run Phillips curve intersects the long-run Phillips curve. The actual and expected inflation rates are both equal to 1.5 percent, and the unemployment rate equals the natural rate of 5 percent. Then suppose the Bank of Canada engages in an expansionary monetary policy. If workers ignore inflation or if they form their expectations adaptively, the expansionary monetary policy will cause the actual inflation rate to be higher than the expected inflation rate, and the short-run equilibrium will move from point *A* on the short-run Phillips curve to point *B*. The inflation rate will rise to 4.5 percent, and the unemployment rate will fall to 3.5 percent. The decline in unemployment will be only temporary, however. Eventually, workers and firms will adjust to the fact that the actual inflation rate is 4.5 percent, not the 1.5 percent they had expected. The short-run Phillips curve will shift up, and the unemployment rate will return to 5 percent at point *C*.

Lucas and Sargent argued that if workers and firms have rational expectations, they will realize that the central bank's expansionary policy will result in an inflation rate of 4.5 percent. Therefore, as soon as the central bank announces its new policy, workers and firms should adjust their expectations of inflation from 1.5 percent to 4.5 percent. There will be no temporary decrease in the real wage, leading to a temporary increase in employment and real GDP. Instead, the short-run equilibrium will move immediately from point *A* to point *C* on the long-run Phillips curve. The unemployment rate will never drop below 5 percent, and the *short-run* Phillips curve will be vertical.

Is the Short-Run Phillips Curve Really Vertical?

The claim by Lucas and Sargent that the short-run Phillips curve is vertical and that an expansionary monetary policy can't reduce the unemployment rate below the natural rate surprised many economists. An obvious objection to the argument of Lucas and Sargent was that the record of the 1950s and 1960s seemed to show that there was a short-run trade-off between unemployment and inflation and that, therefore, the short-run Phillips curve was downward sloping and not vertical. Lucas and Sargent argued that the apparent short-run trade-off was actually the result of *unexpected* changes in monetary policy. During those years, central banks did not announce changes in policy, so workers, firms, and financial markets had to *guess* when the central bank had begun using a new policy. In that case, an expansionary monetary policy might cause the unemployment rate to fall because workers and firms would be taken by surprise, and their expectations of inflation would be too low. Lucas and Sargent argued that a policy that was announced ahead of time would not cause a change in unemployment.

Many economists have remained skeptical of the argument that the short-run Phillips curve is vertical. The two main objections raised are that (1) workers and firms actually may not have rational expectations, and (2) the rapid adjustment of wages and prices needed for the short-run Phillips curve to be vertical will not actually take place. Many economists doubt that people are able to use information on the central bank's monetary policy to make reliable forecasts of the inflation rate. If workers and firms do not know what effect an expansionary monetary policy will have on the inflation rate, the actual real wage may still end up being lower than the expected real wage. Also, firms may have contracts with their workers and suppliers that keep wages and prices from adjusting quickly. If wages and prices adjust slowly, then even if workers and firms have rational expectations, an expansionary monetary policy may still be able to reduce the unemployment rate in the short run.

Real Business Cycle Models

During the 1980s, some economists, including Nobel Laureates Finn Kydland of Carnegie Mellon University and Edward Prescott of Arizona State University, argued that Robert Lucas was correct in assuming that workers and firms formed their expectations rationally and that wages and prices adjust quickly, but that Lucas was wrong in assuming that fluctuations in real GDP are caused by unexpected changes in the money supply. Instead, Kydland and Prescott argued that fluctuations in "real" factors, particularly *technology shocks*, explain deviations of real GDP from its potential level. Technology shocks are changes to the economy that make it possible to produce either more output—a positive shock—or less output—a negative shock—with the same number of workers, machines, and other inputs. Real GDP will be above its previous potential level following a positive technology shock and below its previous potential level following a negative technology shock. Because these models focus on real factors—rather than on changes in the money supply—to explain fluctuations in real GDP, they are known as **real business cycle models**.

Real business cycle models Models that focus on real rather than monetary explanations of fluctuations in real GDP.

The approach of Lucas and Sargent and the real business cycle models are sometimes grouped together under the label *the new classical macroeconomics* because these approaches share the assumptions that people have rational expectations and that wages and prices adjust rapidly. Some of the assumptions of the new classical macroeconomics are similar to those held by economists before the Great Depression of the 1930s. John Maynard Keynes, in his 1936 book *The General Theory of Employment, Interest, and Money*, referred to these earlier economists as "classical economists." Like the classical economists, the new classical macroeconomists believe that the economy will normally be at its potential level.

Economists who find the assumptions of rational expectations and rapid adjustment of wages and prices appealing are likely to accept the real business cycle model approach. Other economists are skeptical of these models because the models explain recessions as being caused by negative technology shocks. Negative technology shocks are uncommon and, apart from the oil price increases of the 1970s, real business cycle theorists have had difficulty identifying shocks that would have been large enough to cause recessions. Some economists have begun to develop real business cycle models that allow for the possibility that changes in the money supply may affect the level of real GDP. If real business cycle models continue to develop along these lines, they may eventually converge with the approaches central banks use.

13.4 LEARNING OBJECTIVE

Use a Phillips curve graph to show how the Bank of Canada can permanently lower the inflation rate.

Bank of Canada Policy from the 1970s to the Present

Like the United States, Canada experienced high inflation rates in the late 1960s and early 1970s due in part to the Bank of Canada's attempts to keep the unemployment rate below the natural rate. By the mid-1970s, the Bank of Canada also had to deal with the inflationary impact of the Organization of the Petroleum Exporting Countries (OPEC) oil price increases. By the late 1970s, as the Bank of Canada attempted to deal with the problem of high and worsening inflation rates, it received conflicting policy advice. Many economists argued that the inflation rate could be reduced only at the cost of a temporary increase in the unemployment rate. Followers of the Lucas–Sargent rational expectations approach, however, argued that a painless reduction in the inflation rate was possible. Before analyzing the actual policies used by the Bank of Canada, we can look at why the oil price increases of the mid-1970s made the inflation rate worse.

The Effect of a Supply Shock on the Phillips Curve

The increases in oil prices in 1974 resulting from actions by OPEC caused the short-run aggregate supply curve to shift to the left. This shift is shown in panel (a) of Figure 13.9. (For simplicity, in this panel, we use the basic rather than dynamic *AD–AS* model.) The result was a higher price level and a lower level of real GDP. On a Phillips curve graph— panel (b) of Figure 13.9—we can shift the short-run Phillips curve up to show that the inflation rate and unemployment rate both increased.

As the Phillips curve shifted up, the economy moved from an unemployment rate of about 5.6 percent and an inflation rate of about 7.8 percent in 1973 to an unemployment rate of 6.9 percent and an inflation rate of about 10.7 percent in 1975. This combination of rising unemployment and rising inflation placed the Bank of Canada in a difficult position. If the Bank of Canada used an expansionary monetary policy to fight the high unemployment rate, the *AD* curve would shift to the right, and the economy's equilibrium would move up the short-run Phillips curve. Real GDP would increase, and the unemployment rate would fall—but at the cost of higher inflation. If the Bank of Canada used a contractionary monetary policy to fight the high inflation rate, the *AD* curve would shift to the left, and the economy's equilibrium would move down the short-run Phillips curve. As a result, real GDP would fall, and the inflation rate would be reduced—but at the cost of higher unemployment. In the end, the Bank of Canada chose to fight high unemployment with an expansionary monetary policy, even though that decision worsened the inflation rate.

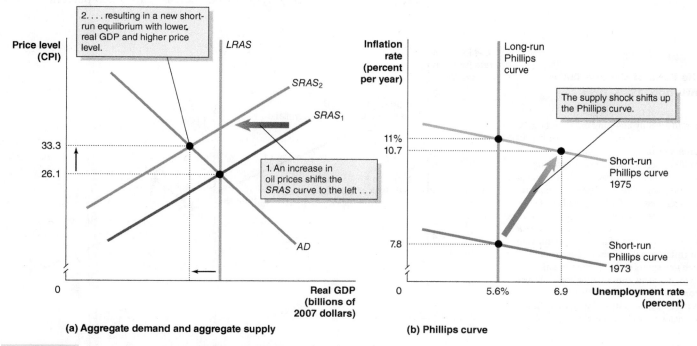

(a) Aggregate demand and aggregate supply

(b) Phillips curve

Figure 13.9   A Supply Shock Shifts the Short-Run Phillips Curve

When OPEC increased the price of a barrel of oil from less than $3 to more than $10, in panel (a), the *SRAS* curve shifted to the left. Panel (b) shows that the supply shock shifted up the Phillips curve. In 1973, the Canadian economy had an inflation rate of about 7.8 percent and an unemployment rate of about 5.6 percent. By 1975, the inflation rate had risen to about 10.7 percent and the unemployment rate to about 6.9 percent.

The Canadian Disinflation, 1989–1993

By the late 1980s, the Bank of Canada had gone through two decades of continually increasing the rate of growth of the money supply. The Bank of Canada began fighting inflation in 1989 by adopting inflation targets, after a three-year public campaign to promote price stability as the long-term goal of monetary policy. During the Hanson Lecture at the University of Alberta in January 1988, newly appointed Bank of Canada Governor John Crow announced that the Bank of Canada would subsequently pursue an objective of price stability or zero inflation; "zero inflation" should be interpreted as a small positive rate of measured inflation.

In this attempt at lowering inflation, the Bank of Canada followed a different strategy, by announcing explicit targets for its ultimate goal—the inflation rate—rather than for an intermediate variable such as money growth. In particular, in February 1991, the Bank of Canada's governor and the minister of finance jointly announced a series of declining inflation targets, with a band of plus and minus one percentage point around them. The targets were 3 percent by the end of 1992, falling to 2 percent by the end of 1995, to remain within a range of 1 percent to 3 percent thereafter.

Figure 13.10 uses the Phillips curve model to analyze the movements in unemployment and inflation from 1989 to 1993. The Bank of Canada's contractionary monetary policy shifted the economy's short-run equilibrium down the short-run Phillips curve, lowering the inflation rate from 5 percent in 1989 to less than 2 percent in 1993—but at a cost of raising the unemployment rate from 7.5 percent to 11.4 percent. As workers and firms lowered their expectations of future inflation, the short-run Phillips curve shifted down, improving the short-run trade-off between unemployment and inflation. This adjustment in expectations allowed the Bank of Canada to switch to an expansionary monetary policy. By the late 1990s, the economy was back to the natural rate of unemployment, which during these years was about 8 percent. The blue line in Figure 13.10 shows the actual combinations of unemployment and inflation for each year from 1989 to 1993.

Disinflation A significant reduction in the inflation rate.

A significant reduction in the inflation rate is called **disinflation**. In fact, this episode is often referred to as the "Canadian disinflation." The disinflation had come at a very high price, however. The unemployment rate increased from 7.5 percent in 1989

Figure 13.10

The Bank of Canada Tames Inflation, 1989–1993

The Bank of Canada began fighting inflation in 1989 by adopting inflation targets. As workers and firms lowered their expectations of future inflation, the short-run Phillips curve shifted down, improving the short-run trade-off between unemployment and inflation. This adjustment in expectations allowed the Bank of Canada to switch to an expansionary monetary policy, which by the late 1990s brought the economy back to the natural rate of unemployment, with an inflation rate of about 2 percent. The blue line shows the actual combinations of unemployment and inflation for each year from 1989 to 1993. Note that during these years, the natural rate of unemployment was estimated to be about 8 percent.

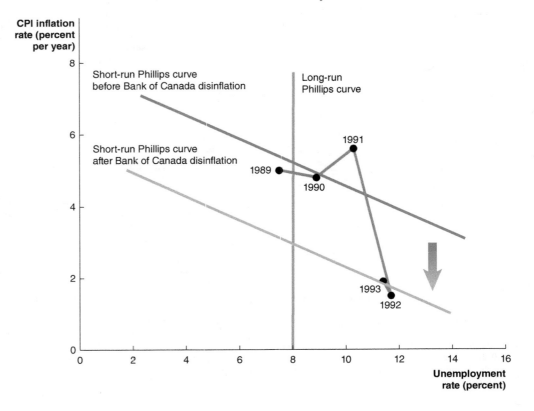

Don't Let This Happen to You

Don't Confuse Disinflation with Deflation

Disinflation refers to a decline in the *inflation rate*. *Deflation* refers to a decline in the *price level*. The Bank of Canada brought about a substantial disinflation in Canada during the years from 1989 to 1993. The inflation rate fell from over 5 percent in 1989 to below 2 percent in 1993. Yet even in 1994, there was no deflation: The price level was still rising—but at a slower rate.

The last period of significant deflation in Canada was in the early 1930s, during the Great Depression. The following table shows the consumer price index for each of those years.

Because the price level fell each year from 1929 to 1933, there was deflation.

Year	Consumer Price Index	Deflation Rate
1929	9.2	—
1930	9.1	−1.1%
1931	8.2	−9.9
1932	7.5	−8.5
1933	7.1	−5.3

MyEconLab

Your Turn: Test your understanding by doing related problem 4.2 on page 433 at the end of this chapter.

to above 11 percent in 1993, the first time this had happened since the end of the Great Depression of the 1930s and the severe 1981–1982 recession.

Inflation Targeting, 1989–Present

The Bank of Canada was successful in achieving its inflation targets during the 1989–1993 disinflation. In fact, it renewed its 1 percent to 3 percent target range for inflation in December 1995, in early 1998, May 2001, November 2006, and again in November 2011 to apply until the end of 2016. It is also to be noted that the 1995 and 1998 inflation-control agreements between the Bank of Canada and the government had a three-year horizon. However, the 2011 agreement, like the 2006 and 2001 agreements, has a five-year horizon, reflecting the wide acceptance of the targets after over 20 years of operation. The midpoint of the current inflation target range, 2 percent, is regarded as the most desirable inflation outcome.

What are the results of Canada's inflation-targeting monetary policy? Figure 13.11 plots the Canadian inflation rate for each year since 1980 and shows the Bank of Canada's target range since 1996. Clearly, inflation has fallen dramatically since the adoption of inflation targets, from above the 5 percent level in 1991 to a 1 percent rate in 1998, most of the time staying in the lower half of the target range. However, as already noted, this decline was not without cost: Unemployment soared to above the 10 percent level from 1991 until 1993, but has since fallen.

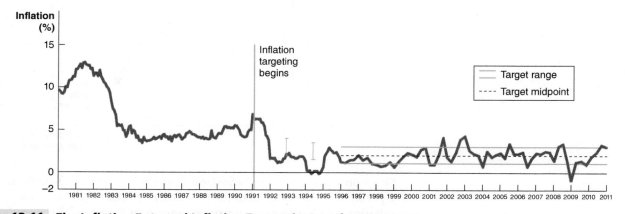

Figure 13.11 **The Inflation Rate and Inflation Targets in Canada, 1980–2011**

Canada has significantly reduced the rate of inflation and eventually achieved its inflation target.

Solved Problem **13.2**

Using Monetary Policy to Lower the Inflation Rate

Consider the following hypothetical situation: The economy is currently at the natural rate of unemployment of 5 percent. The actual inflation rate is 6 percent, and, because it has remained at 6 percent for several years, this is also the rate that workers and firms expect to see in the future. The

Bank of Canada decides to reduce the inflation rate permanently to 2 percent. How can the Bank of Canada use monetary policy to achieve this objective? Be sure to use a Phillips curve graph in your answer.

Solving the Problem

Step 1: **Review the chapter material.** This problem is about using a Phillips curve graph to show how the Bank of Canada can fight inflation, so you may want to review the section "The Canadian Disinflation, 1989–1993," which begins on page 422.

Step 2: **Explain how the Bank of Canada can use monetary policy to reduce the inflation rate.** To reduce the inflation rate significantly, the Bank of Canada will have to raise the target for the overnight interest rate. Higher interest rates will reduce aggregate demand, raise unemployment, and move the economy's equilibrium down the short-run Phillips curve.

Step 3: **Illustrate your argument with a Phillips curve graph.** How much the unemployment rate would have to rise to drive down the inflation rate from 6 percent to 2 percent depends on the steepness of the short-run Phillips curve. Here we have assumed that the unemployment rate would have to rise from 5 percent to 7 percent.

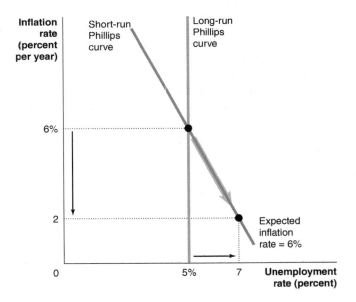

Step 4: **Show on your graph the reduction in the inflation rate from 6 percent to 2 percent.** For the decline in the inflation rate to be permanent, the expected inflation rate has to decline from 6 percent to 2 percent. We can show this decline on our graph:

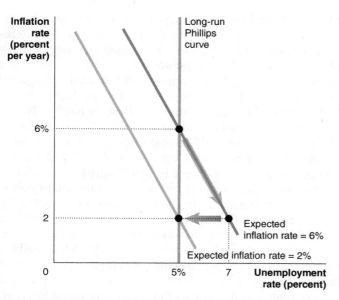

Once the short-run Phillips curve has shifted down, the Bank of Canada can use an expansionary monetary policy to push the economy back to the natural rate of unemployment. This policy is similar to the one carried out by the Bank of Canada in 1989 and the US Federal Reserve after Paul Volcker became chairman in 1979. The downside to these policies of disinflation is that they lead to significant increases in unemployment. In the United States, for example, the unemployment rate was above 10 percent from September 1982 through June 1983, the first time that this had happened since the Great Depression.

Extra credit: A follower of the new classical macroeconomics approach would have a more optimistic view of the consequences of using monetary policy to lower the inflation rate from 6 percent to 2 percent. According to this approach, the Bank of Canada's policy announcement should cause people to immediately revise downward their expectations of future inflation from 6 percent to 2 percent. The economy's short-run equilibrium would move directly down the long-run Phillips curve from an inflation rate of 6 percent to an inflation rate of 2 percent, while keeping the unemployment rate constant at 5 percent. For the reasons discussed in this chapter, many economists are skeptical that disinflation can be brought about so painlessly.

Your Turn: For more practice, do related problem 4.4 on page 433 at the end of this chapter.

MyEconLab

The 2007–2009 Global Recession and the Crisis in Monetary Policy

Around the world, the 2007–2009 recession led many central banks (including the Bank of Canada) to move well beyond the short-term nominal interest rate as the focus of monetary policy. With the target overnight interest rate having been driven to the zero lower bound (the short-term nominal interest rate being zero or near zero) without much expansionary effect on the economy, some observers began to speak of a "crisis in monetary policy." We reviewed the Bank of Canada's new policy initiatives in Chapter 11. At this point, we can discuss some issues regarding the current approach to monetary policy.

The current approach to monetary policy is based on the new Keynesian model and is expressed in terms of the short-term nominal interest rate, such as the overnight interest rate in Canada and the federal funds rate in the United States. In recent years the New Keynesian model has also been extended to allow for interest rate channels (or corridors), and many central banks have changed the institutional structure within which monetary policy is conducted and now use a corridor system of monetary policy implementation such as the one we discussed for Canada in Chapter 11. For example, such systems are also used by the Reserve Bank of Australia, the Bank of England, the European Central Bank, the Bank of Japan, the Reserve Bank of New Zealand, Norges Bank (the central bank of Norway), and the Riksbank (the central bank of Sweden).

However, in the aftermath of the global financial crisis and the Great Recession, short-term nominal interest rates have hardly moved at all, while central bank policies have been the most volatile and extreme in their entire histories. This has discredited the short-term nominal interest rate as an indicator of monetary policy and led central banks to look elsewhere. For example, the US Federal Reserve, the European Central Bank, and many other central banks have departed from the traditional interest-rate targeting approach to monetary policy and are now focusing on their balance sheet instead, using quantitative measures of monetary policy, such as credit easing and quantitative easing. Because of these unconventional monetary policies, there is uncertainty about the future path of money growth and inflation. This uncertainty can be especially damaging to the economy, as it amplifies the negative response of the economy to unfavourable shocks and dampens the positive response to favourable shocks.

In fact, one problem with the current approach to monetary policy is that it ignores the role of money measures, known as *monetary aggregates*, that we discussed in Chapter 10. It is to be noted, however, that although current monetary policy is not expressed in terms of monetary aggregates, the central bank's adjustments of the short-term nominal interest rate translate into changes in the monetary aggregates. For example, when the Bank of Canada conducts open-market buyback operations to achieve the desired target for the overnight interest rate, it exchanges the monetary base (the monetary aggregate directly affected by the Bank of Canada's open-market operations) for government securities. The question then that arises is whether there is a useful role for monetary aggregates in today's approach to monetary policy, in the aftermath of the global financial crisis.

Another problem with the current approach to monetary policy is that it ignores the role of **leverage** (or collateral rates). Leverage, l, is defined as

$$l = \frac{A}{A - L}$$

Leverage A measure of how much debt an investor assumes in making an investment.

where A denotes total assets and L liabilities other than net worth (equivalently, capital). Thus, leverage is the ratio of assets to capital and is a measure of how much debt an investor assumes in making an investment; the reciprocal of leverage, $1/l$, is known as the *leverage ratio*.

To explore the leverage concept further, let's assume that you use $10 of your own funds to buy a house that is worth $100 by issuing a mortgage for the remaining $90 using the house as collateral. In that case, the down payment (also known as the *margin* or *haircut*) is 10 percent, the loan to value ratio is $90/$100 = 90 percent, and the collateral rate is $100/$90 = 111 percent. Leverage is the reciprocal of the margin, or the ratio of the asset value to the funds needed to purchase it, $100/$10 = 10. Clearly, when leverage is high, economic agents can buy many assets with very little money down, and asset prices increase. When leverage is low, they must have all (or nearly all) of the money in hand to purchase the same assets, and asset prices decline.

In the aftermath of the global financial crisis, leverage attracted a great deal of attention and it has been argued that leverage on Wall Street increased to 35 to 1 prior to the global financial crisis, but never in the history of the United States had leverage exceeded 30 to 1. For example, in early 2007, Bear Stearns had a record-high leverage ratio of 35 to 1. Around the same time, (then) major Wall Street investment banks (Goldman Sachs, Morgan Stanley, Merrill Lynch, and Lehman Brothers) together averaged leverage ratios of 30 to 1, up from 20 to 1 in 2003. In fact, it is now widely recognized that leverage cycles (fluctuations in collateral rates) can have important effects on the level of economic activity.

With many central banks around the world implementing unconventional monetary policies in a zero lower-bound environment, having a level of excess reserves in the trillions of dollars, and having unusually high leverage ratios, no one is sure how things will unfold.

Economics in Your Life

Is It Wise to Delay a Job Search?

At the beginning of the chapter, we posed this question: What advice would you give someone who has decided to wait nearly one year to look for a new job? As we discussed in the chapter, evidence shows that many of those who are unemployed for longer than a year or two find it more difficult to find new employment than if they searched for a new job soon after they were laid off. The longer workers are unemployed, especially in a high-technology field, the more their skills deteriorate. By delaying her job search, your friend risks being unemployed for longer than one year. Eventually, she may have to be retrained or take additional courses in a different field in order to find a job. Tell your friend to start her job search right away!

Conclusion

The workings of the contemporary economy are complex. The attempts by the Bank of Canada to keep the Canadian economy near the natural rate of unemployment with a low rate of inflation have not always been successful. Economists continue to debate the best way for the Bank of Canada to proceed.

An Inside Look on the next page discusses the challenges the US Federal Reserve faces in trying to reduce unemployment without increasing inflation in the United States.

Can the Federal Reserve Balance the Trade-off between Unemployment and Inflation in the United States?

WASHINGTON POST

Ben Bernanke's Bet on Jobs and Inflation

Federal Reserve Chairman Ben Bernanke glided smoothly through his first regular news conference the other day—an event both remarkable and unremarkable. It was remarkable for symbolizing the Fed's ongoing transformation from a citadel of secrecy into an agency that tries to explain itself to the public. "The original attitude ... was that it was no one's business what they did—and if you wanted to figure it out, do so yourself," says economist Allan Meltzer, author of a history of the Fed. Until now, there had been no news conferences, a legacy of the tight-lipped past.

What was unremarkable is that reporters' questions focused on an old issue: How much can the Fed reduce unemployment without stoking inflation? Bernanke's bet is: a lot. He's embraced super-easy credit to cut the appalling 8.8 percent jobless rate; that's 13.5 million people, nearly half out of work for six months or more. Since late 2008, the Fed has held short-term interest rates near zero. To cut long-term rates, the Fed is buying gobs of Treasury bonds and mortgage securities: $1.725 trillion from late 2008 to March 2010; an additional $600 billion from last November through June. These purchases are known as QE1 and QE2, for "quantitative easing."

But there's a growing debate about whether all the pump-priming is helping recovery or simply fostering inflation. The economy's fate may hang on who's right. Studies by Fed economists are, not surprisingly, supportive. One estimated that QE1 and QE2 lowered long-term interest rates by about 0.5 percentage points and saved nearly 3 million jobs; the jobless rate otherwise could have approached 11 percent. Many private economists are less impressed; they suspect the benefits of QE1 faded with QE2....

Meanwhile, inflation creeps up. Over the past year, the consumer price index rose 2.7 percent; six months earlier, the year-over-year gain was only 1.2 percent. Bernanke blames higher oil and food prices, reflecting temporary factors (the war in Libya, poor harvests) that may be reversed. The danger of an inflationary wage-price spiral, goes this argument, is negligible because unemployment is high and pay is stagnant.

Maybe. But inflation's dynamics might be changing. Here's why. The recession caused enormous factory and business closures; now, there's less capacity to meet rising demand. Companies have more power to raise prices; a depreciating dollar compounds the effect by making imports more expensive....

The problem might become more widespread. The Fed regularly measures manufacturers' production capacity. From 2007 to 2010, it fell 5.4 percent. That's the largest drop since the statistics began being kept in 1948; the only other annual decline occurred in 2003 and was a scant 0.25 percent.

The Fed is attacked from both the left (for doing too little to create jobs) and the right (for doing too much and tempting inflation), notes former Fed vice chairman Donald Kohn. Bernanke aims for a middle course. One argument for a less secretive Fed is this: Investors, managers and workers who better understand the Fed's goals won't futilely try to defy them. The Fed's very commitment to low inflation will restrain wages and prices. Up to a point, this may be true. But public relations alone won't control behavior. Actions outrank intentions.

The lesson of the 1970s' great inflation (13 percent in 1980) is that once prices begin to rise consistently, they feed on themselves. The fallout is disastrous. People and companies can't plan for the future; recessions become more frequent. Unexpectedly high inflation would probably doom today's cheap credit policy. The Fed would have to raise rates. Criticism from both left and right would intensify. So, much is riding on Bernanke's bet: If he loses, we all lose.

Key Points in the Article

In an effort to reduce the unemployment rate and increase real GDP, the US Federal Reserve held its target for the federal funds rate close to zero for three years beginning in late 2008. The Federal Reserve also successfully lowered long-term interest rates with its quantitative easing programs. While Federal Reserve economists argue that the Federal Reserve's policies helped save nearly 3 million jobs, some economists are concerned that these policies did more to increase inflation than to assist the recovery. From mid-2010 to mid-2011, the consumer price index rose 2.7 percent, with the largest increase coming in the last six months. Some observers criticized Federal Reserve Chairman Ben Bernanke for not doing enough to lower unemployment, while others criticized him for doing too much and fanning the flames of inflation. Bernanke argues, however, that the Federal Reserve's recent policy actions will help reduce the unemployment rate without causing a significant increase in the inflation rate.

Analyzing the News

(a) US Federal Reserve Chairman Ben Bernanke argues that Federal Reserve policies that have reduced both short-term and long-term interest rates will be successful in lowering the high unemployment rate while keeping inflation in check. But some economists are convinced that monetary policy actions are doing less to improve the job situation and more to generate inflation. As you read in this chapter, A. W. Phillips discovered an inverse short-run relationship between the unemployment rate and the inflation rate. The figure below shows the short-run Phillips curve relationship from July 2008 through July 2011. For the months from July 2008 to July 2009, the Phillips curve relationship appears to fit the data well, as the unemployment rate rose from 5.8 percent to 9.5 percent while the inflation rate, measured by the percent change of the consumer price index, fell from 5.6 percent to −2.10 percent.

(b) The figure below also shows that from July 2009 to July 2011, the short-run Phillips curve relationship is less clear, as the unemployment rate remained between 9 and 10 percent, while the inflation rate rose from −2.10 percent to 3.63 percent. The article states that the dynamics of inflation may be changing and prices may rise due to reduced capacity coupled with increasing demand. As you learned in this chapter, if a higher inflation rate becomes expected in the economy, the short-run Phillips curve will shift up, and the short-run trade-off between unemployment and inflation will take place at a higher inflation rate. In the figure, the data from July 2010 to July 2011 could be indicating that workers and firms are expecting the inflation rate to increase.

(c) Some critics argue that the Federal Reserve has not done enough to create jobs and others claim that the Federal Reserve's actions will generate inflation. However, Bernanke is sticking with the policy decisions he believes will boost employment while keeping inflation under control. By announcing these policies and moving forward with them, the Federal Reserve maintains its credibility and therefore has a better chance of meeting its goals.

Thinking Critically

1. Suppose that the unemployment rate in mid-2011 was the same as it actually was, but the inflation rate during those months averaged 10 percent rather than the rate shown in the figure. What effect might the higher inflation rates have had on the Federal Reserve's monetary policy?

2. Suppose the unemployment rate is currently equal to the nonaccelerating inflation rate of unemployment (NAIRU) of 5 percent, and the inflation rate is 0 percent. If the Federal Reserve wants to raise the inflation rate permanently to 2 percent, what should it do? Explain your answer using a Phillips curve graph.

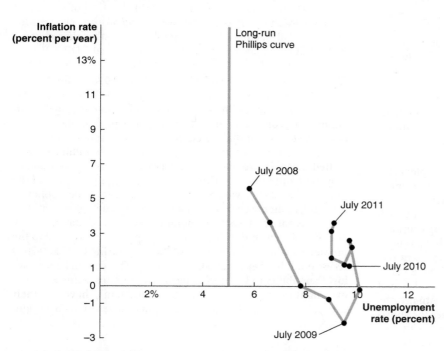

The short-run Phillips curve can be seen in the data for the period from July 2008 to July 2011.

Chapter Summary and Problems

Key Terms

Disinflation, p. 422

Leverage, p. 426

Natural rate of unemployment, p. 411

Nonaccelerating inflation rate of unemployment (NAIRU), p. 416

Phillips curve, p. 408

Rational expectations, p. 418

Real business cycle models, p. 420

Structural relationship, p. 410

Summary

*LO 13.1 The *Phillips curve* illustrates the short-run trade-off between the unemployment rate and the inflation rate. The inverse relationship between unemployment and inflation shown by the Phillips curve is consistent with the aggregate demand and aggregate supply analysis developed in Chapter 8. The aggregate demand and aggregate supply (*AD–AS*) model indicates that slow growth in aggregate demand leads to both higher unemployment and lower inflation, and rapid growth in aggregate demand leads to both lower unemployment and higher inflation. This relationship explains why there is a short-run trade-off between unemployment and inflation. Many economists initially believed that the Phillips curve was a *structural relationship* that depended on the basic behaviour of consumers and firms and that remained unchanged over time. If the Phillips curve were a stable relationship, it would present policymakers with a menu of combinations of unemployment and inflation from which they could choose. Nobel Laureate Milton Friedman argued that there is a *natural rate of unemployment*, which is the unemployment rate that exists when the economy is at potential GDP and to which the economy always returns. As a result, there is no trade-off between unemployment and inflation in the long run, and the long-run Phillips curve is a vertical line at the natural rate of unemployment.

LO 13.2 There is a short-run trade-off between unemployment and inflation only if the actual inflation rate differs from the inflation rate that workers and firms had expected. There is a different short-run Phillips curve for every expected inflation rate. Each short-run Phillips curve intersects the long-run Phillips curve at the expected inflation rate. With a vertical long-run Phillips curve, it is not possible to buy a permanently lower unemployment rate at the cost of a permanently higher inflation rate. If the Bank of Canada attempts to keep the economy below the natural rate of unemployment, the inflation rate will increase. Eventually, the expected inflation rate will also increase, which causes the short-run Phillips curve to shift up and pushes the economy back to the natural rate of unemployment. The reverse happens if the Bank of Canada attempts to keep the economy above the natural rate of unemployment. In the long run, the Bank of Canada can affect the inflation rate but not the unemployment rate.

LO 13.3 When the inflation rate is moderate and stable, workers and firms tend to have *adaptive expectations*. That is, they form their expectations under the assumption that future inflation rates will follow the pattern of inflation rates in the recent past. During the high and unstable inflation rates of the mid to late 1970s, Robert Lucas and Thomas Sargent argued that workers and firms would have rational expectations. *Rational expectations* are formed by using all the available information about an economic variable, including the effect of the policy being used by the central bank. Lucas and Sargent argued that if people have rational expectations, expansionary monetary policy will not work. If workers and firms know that an expansionary monetary policy is going to raise the inflation rate, the actual inflation rate will be the same as the expected inflation rate. Therefore, the unemployment rate won't fall. Many economists remain skeptical of Lucas and Sargent's argument in its strictest form. *Real business cycle models* focus on "real" factors—technology shocks—rather than changes in the money supply to explain fluctuations in real GDP.

LO 13.4 Inflation worsened through the 1970s. The Bank of Canada used contractionary monetary policy to reduce inflation. A significant reduction in the inflation rate is called *disinflation*. This contractionary monetary policy pushed the economy down the short-run Phillips curve. As workers and firms lowered their expectations of future inflation, the short-run Phillips curve shifted down, improving the short-run trade-off between unemployment and inflation. This change in expectations allowed the Bank of Canada to switch to an expansionary monetary policy to bring the economy back to the natural rate of unemployment.

In recent years, some economists have argued that monetary policy decisions in the United States may have contributed to the problems the financial system experienced during the 2007–2009 recession. It has been argued, for example, that central banks have lost their ability to lower long-term interest rates by lowering the overnight interest rate. Moreover, central banks have lost their usual ability to signal policy changes via changes in the overnight interest rate.

MyEconLab   Log in to MyEconLab to complete these exercises and get instant feedback.

---

*'Learning Objective' is abbreviated to 'LO' in the end of chapter material.

Review Questions

LO 13.1

1.1 What is the Phillips curve? Draw a graph of a short-run Phillips curve.

1.2 What actions should the Bank of Canada take if it wants to move from a point on the short-run Phillips curve representing high unemployment and low inflation to a point representing lower unemployment and higher inflation?

1.3 Why did economists during the early 1960s think of the Phillips curve as a "policy menu"? Were they correct to think of it in this way? Briefly explain.

1.4 Why did Milton Friedman argue that the Phillips curve did not represent a permanent trade-off between unemployment and inflation? In your answer, be sure to explain what Friedman meant by the "natural rate of unemployment."

LO 13.2

2.1 Suppose that the expected inflation rate increases from 4 percent to 6 percent. What will happen to the short-run Phillips curve?

2.2 What is the relationship between the short-run Phillips curve and the long-run Phillips curve?

2.3 Why is it inconsistent to believe that the long-run aggregate supply curve is vertical and the long-run Phillips curve is downward sloping?

LO 13.3

3.1 Why do workers, firms, banks, and investors in financial markets care about the future rate of inflation? How do they form their expectations of future inflation? Do current conditions in the economy have any bearing on how they form their expectations?

3.2 What does it mean to say that workers and firms have rational expectations?

3.3 Why did Robert Lucas and Thomas Sargent argue that the Phillips curve might be vertical in the short run? What difference would it make for monetary policy if they were right?

LO 13.4

4.1 What was the "Canadian disinflation"? What happened to the unemployment rate during the period of the Canadian disinflation?

4.2 Why is the credibility of the Bank of Canada's policy announcements particularly important?

4.3 Why do most economists believe that it is important for a country's central bank to be independent of the rest of the country's central government?

Problems and Applications

LO 13.1

1.1 Use these two graphs to answer the following questions:

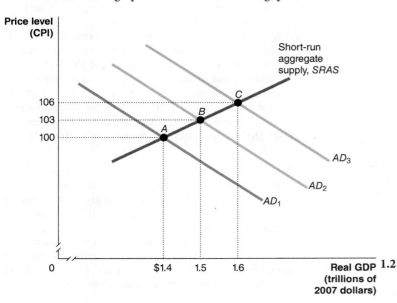

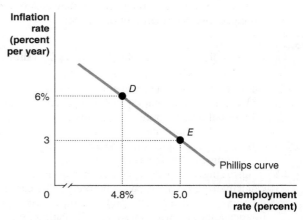

a. Briefly explain which point on the Phillips curve graph represents the same economic situation as point *B* on the aggregate demand and aggregate supply graph.

b. Briefly explain which point on the Phillips curve graph represents the same economic situation as point *C* on the aggregate demand and aggregate supply graph.

1.2 Given that the Phillips curve is derived from the aggregate demand and aggregate supply model, why do we use the Phillips curve analysis? What benefits does the Phillips curve analysis offer compared to the aggregate demand and aggregate supply model?

1.3 Briefly explain whether you agree with the following statement: "Any economic relationship that changes as economic policy changes is not a structural relationship."

1.4 General Juan Perón, the former dictator of Argentina, once said of the labour market in his country, "Prices have gone up the elevator, and wages have had to use the stairs." In this situation, what was happening to real wages in Argentina? Was unemployment likely to have been relatively high or relatively low?

Robert J. Shiller, "Why Do People Dislike Inflation?" in Christina D. Romer and David H. Romer, eds., Reducing Inflation: Motivation and Strategy, (Chicago: University of Chicago Press, 1997).

1.5 This chapter argues that if the price level increases over time, the average wage should increase by the same amount. Why is this true?

1.6 [**Related to the** Chapter Opener **on page 407**] Why might leverage cycles, which we discussed in the Chapter Opener, have an effect on the level of economic activity? In other words, why are movements in collateral rates particularly important to economic activity in actual economies?

1.7 [**Related to** Making the Connection **on page 413**] Robert Shiller asked a sample of the general public and a sample of economists the following question: "Do you agree that preventing high inflation is an important national priority, as important as preventing drug abuse or preventing deterioration in the quality of our schools?" Fifty-two percent of the general public, but only 18 percent of economists, fully agreed. Why does the general public believe inflation is a bigger problem than economists do?

LO 13.2

2.1 Use the following information to draw a graph showing the short-run and long-run Phillips curves:

Natural rate of unemployment = 5 percent
Current rate of unemployment = 4 percent
Expected inflation rate = 4 percent
Current inflation rate = 6 percent
Be sure your graph shows the point where the short-run and long-run Phillips curves intersect.

2.2 In testifying before Congress, former US Federal Reserve Chairman Alan Greenspan remarked, "The challenge of monetary policy is to interpret data on the economy and financial markets with an eye to anticipating future inflationary forces and to countering them by taking action in advance." Why should the Federal Reserve take action in anticipation of inflation becoming worse? Why not just wait until the increase in the inflation rate has occurred?

Nicoletta Batini and Andrew G. Haldane, "Forward-Looking Rules for Monetary Policy," in John B. Taylor, ed., Monetary Policy Rules, (Chicago: University of Chicago Press, 1999), p. 157.

2.3 In Congressional testimony, Federal Reserve Chairman Ben Bernanke said:

Another significant factor influencing medium-term trends in inflation is the public's expectations of inflation. These expectations have an important bearing on whether transitory influences on prices, such as changes in

energy costs, become embedded in wage and price decisions and so leave a lasting imprint on the rate of inflation.

What did Bernanke mean when he said that the public's expectations of inflation could "become embedded in wage and price decisions"? What would be the effect on the short-run Phillips curve of the public coming to expect a higher inflation rate?

"Testimony of Chairman Ben S. Bernanke before the Joint Economic Committee, U.S. Congress," March 28, 2007.

2.4 [**Related to** Making the Connection **on page 417**] In 2011, an article in the *Economist* magazine argued that the natural rate of unemployment in the United States may have risen as high as 7.5 percent. The article suggested,

Lowering this new natural rate of unemployment will require structural reforms, such as changing education to ensure that people enter work equipped with the sort of skills firms are willing to fight over, adjusting the tax system and modernising the welfare safety net, and more broadly creating a climate conducive to entrepreneurship and innovation.

Why should policymakers be concerned with lowering the natural rate of unemployment? How would the "structural reforms" listed in the article contribute to lowering the natural rate of unemployment? Would the Federal Reserve be able to implement any of these reforms? Briefly explain.

"The Great Mismatch," Economist, September 10, 2011.

LO 13.3

3.1 During a time when the inflation rate is increasing each year for a number of years, are adaptive expectations or rational expectations likely to give the more accurate forecasts? Briefly explain.

3.2 An article in the *Economist* magazine contains the following: "Robert Lucas ... showed how incorporating expectations into macroeconomic models muddled the framework economists prior to the 'rational expectations revolution' thought they saw so clearly." What economic framework did economists change as the result of Lucas's arguments? Do all economists agree with Lucas's main conclusions about the effectiveness of monetary policy? Briefly explain.

"How to Know What Causes What," Economist, October 10, 2011.

3.3 Would a monetary policy intended to bring about disinflation cause a greater increase in unemployment if workers and firms have adaptive expectations or if they have rational expectations? Briefly explain.

3.4 If both the short-run and long-run Phillips curves are vertical, what will be the effect on the inflation rate and the unemployment rate of an expansionary monetary policy? Use a Phillips curve graph to illustrate your answer.

LO 13.4

4.1 According to an article in *BusinessWeek*, many workers who retired in the year 2000 expected to live off the interest they would receive from bank certificates of deposit or money market mutual funds. "Then came disinflation—and a steep fall in interest rates." What is disinflation, and why should it lead to a fall in interest rates?

Peter Coy, "The Surprise Threat to Nest Eggs," BusinessWeek, July 28, 2003.

4.2 **[Related to** Don't Let This Happen to You **on page 423]** Look again at the table on prices during the early 1930s on page 423. Was there disinflation during 1933? Briefly explain.

4.3 Suppose the current inflation rate and the expected inflation rate are both 4 percent. The current unemployment rate and the natural rate of unemployment are both 5 percent. Use a Phillips curve graph to show the effect on the economy of a severe supply shock. If the Bank of Canada keeps monetary policy unchanged, what will happen eventually to the unemployment rate? Show this on your Phillips curve graph.

4.4 **[Related to** Solved Problem 13.2 **on page 425]** Suppose the inflation rate has been 15 percent for the past four years.

The unemployment rate is currently at the natural rate of unemployment of 5 percent. The Bank of Canada decides that it wants to permanently reduce the inflation rate to 5 percent. How can the Bank of Canada use monetary policy to achieve this objective? Be sure to use a Phillips curve graph in your answer.

4.5 Robert Lucas has been quoted as saying: "In practice, it is much more painful to put a modern economy through a deflation than the monetary theory we have would lead us to expect. I take this to mean that we have 'price stickiness.'" What does Lucas mean by "the monetary theory we have"? What events may have led Lucas to conclude that it is more painful to reduce the inflation rate than theory would predict? Why does he conclude that the economy apparently has "price stickiness"?

Paul A. Samuelson and William A. Barnett, eds., Inside Economist's Mind: Conversations with Eminent Economists, (Malden, MA: Blackwell Publishing, 2007).

MyEconLab   MyEconLab is an online tool designed to help you master the concepts covered in your course. It will create an adaptive, highly personalized study plan to stimulate and measure your learning. Log in to take advantage of this powerful study aid, and to access quizzes and other valuable course-related material.

14

Macroeconomics in an Open Economy

Chapter Outline and Learning Objectives

14.1 The Balance of Payments: Linking Canada to the International Economy, page 436

Explain how the balance of payments is calculated.

14.2 The Foreign Exchange Market and Exchange Rates, page 440

Explain how exchange rates are determined and how changes in exchange rates affect the prices of imports and exports.

14.3 The International Sector and National Saving and Investment, page 448

Explain the saving and investment equation.

14.4 The Effect of a Government Budget Deficit on Investment, page 451

Explain the effect of a government budget deficit on investment in an open economy.

14.5 Monetary Policy and Fiscal Policy in an Open Economy, page 453

Compare the effectiveness of monetary policy and fiscal policy in an open economy and in a closed economy.

Corbis

A Strong US Dollar Hurts McDonald's Profits

The McDonald's Big Mac is one of the most widely available products in the world. McDonald's has 32 000 outlets in 118 countries, serving 60 million customers per day. The company's stock was one of only two in the Dow Jones Industrial Average to post a gain in 2008, which was a bad year for most US firms. During the recession of 2007–2009, McDonald's prospered as many consumers switched to eating out at fast-food restaurants rather than at restaurants that provide table service. The success of McDonald's continued into 2010, with the company's stock price increasing 22.5 percent, more than double the 11 percent gain in the Dow Jones Industrial Average.

With expansion in the US market limited, McDonald's has grown in recent years mostly by expanding in foreign markets. About 34 percent of its sales come from the United States; 40 percent from Europe; 20 percent from the Middle East, Asia, and Africa; and about 6 percent from Canada and Latin America. Because McDonald's has restaurants in so many different countries, it receives revenue in many different currencies. As a result, the company's revenue and profits are affected by fluctuations in the value of the US dollar in exchange for other currencies. In some years, converting revenue from foreign currencies yields more US dollars than in other years. For example, in August 2011, global revenues for McDonald's increased by 11.3 percent from the previous year when measured in local currency—pounds in Great Britain, euros in France, yen in Japan. But when measured in terms of US dollars, the company's revenues rose by only 5.4 percent. Why the discrepancy? The value of the US dollar had increased relative to most other currencies. So, converting pounds, euros, and yen into US dollars yielded fewer US dollars for McDonald's.

Canadian companies that sell their products abroad are also exposed to foreign exchange risk. For example, when the Canadian dollar increases in value relative to other currencies, BlackBerry's Canadian dollar revenue from its smartphone sales in foreign markets declines. What explains fluctuations in the exchange rate between the dollar and other currencies? In this chapter and the next, we will look more closely at how exchange rates are determined and at other important issues involving the international financial system. Read **AN INSIDE LOOK** on **page 456** for a discussion of the effects of changes in the value of the Canadian dollar relative to other currencies.

Sources: Based on Dimitra Defotis, "McDonald's Shares Hit New High; Sales Strong in EU," Barron's, July 22, 2011; and McDonald's, "Financial Press Release," September 9, 2011.

Economics in Your Life

The South Korean Central Bank and Your Car Loan

Suppose that you are shopping for a new car, which you plan to finance with a loan from a local bank. One morning, as you head out the door to visit another automobile dealership, you hear the following newsflash on the radio: "The Bank of Korea, South Korea's central bank, announces it will sell its large holdings of Canada bonds." What effect will the Bank of Korea's decision to sell its Canada bonds likely have on the interest rate you pay on your car loan? As you read this chapter, see if you can answer this question. You can check your answer against the one we provide on page 454 at the end of this chapter.

I n this chapter, we look closely at the linkages among countries at the macroeconomic level. Countries are linked by trade in goods and services and by flows of financial investment. We will see how policymakers in all countries take these linkages into account when conducting monetary policy and fiscal policy.

Explain how the balance of payments is calculated.

Open economy An economy that has interactions in trade or finance with other countries.

Closed economy An economy that has no interactions in trade or finance with other countries.

Balance of payments The record of a country's trade with other countries in goods, services, and assets.

The Balance of Payments: Linking Canada to the International Economy

Today, consumers, firms, and investors routinely interact with consumers, firms, and investors in other economies. A consumer in France may use computer software produced in Canada, watch a television made in South Korea, and wear a sweater made in Italy. A firm in Canada may sell its products in dozens of countries around the world. An investor in London, England, may sell a Canada bond to an investor in Mexico City. Nearly all economies are **open economies** and have extensive interactions in trade or finance with other countries. Open economies interact by trading goods and services and by making investments in each other's economies. A **closed economy** has no interactions in trade or finance with other countries. No economy today is completely closed, although a few countries, such as North Korea, have very limited economic interactions with other countries.

A good way to understand the interactions between one economy and other economies is through the **balance of payments**, which is a record of a country's trade with other countries in goods, services, and assets. Just as Statistics Canada is responsible for collecting data on the GDP, it is also responsible for collecting data on the balance of payments. Table 14.1 shows the balance of payments for Canada in 2011. Notice that the table contains three "accounts": the *current account*, the *financial account*, and the *capital account*.

Table 14.1

The Canadian Balance of Payments, 2011 (millions of dollars)

CURRENT ACCOUNT		
Exports of goods	$457 548	
Imports of goods	−456 129	
Balance of trade		1419
Exports of services	74 845	
Imports of services	−99 465	
Balance of services		−24 620
Income received on investments	66 640	
Income payments on investments	−87 724	
Net income on investments		−21 084
Net transfers		−4018
Balance on current account		−48 303
FINANCIAL ACCOUNT		
Increase of foreign holdings of assets in Canada	159 115	
Increase in Canadian holdings of assets in foreign countries	−108 412	
Balance on financial account		50 703
BALANCE ON CAPITAL ACCOUNT		**4813**
Statistical discrepancy		−7213
Balance of payments		0

Source: Data from Statistics Canada CANSIM II Tables 376-0001 and 376-0002 (Accessed 1 May 2012).

The Current Account

The **current account** records *current*, or short-term, flows of funds into and out of a country. The current account for Canada includes exports and imports of goods and services (recall from Chapter 4 that the difference between exports and imports of goods and services is called *net exports*); income received by Canadian residents from investments in other countries; income paid on investments in Canada owned by residents of other countries (the difference between investment income received and investment income paid is called *net income on investments*); and the difference between transfers made to residents of other countries and transfers received by Canadian residents from other countries (called *net transfers*). If you make a donation to a charity caring for orphans in Afghanistan, it would be included in net transfers. Any payments received by Canadian residents are positive numbers in the current account, and any payments made by Canadian residents are negative numbers in the current account.

Current account The part of the balance of payments that records a country's net exports, net income on investments, and net transfers.

The Balance of Trade Part of the current account is the **balance of trade**, which is the difference between the value of the goods a country exports and the value of the goods a country imports. The balance of trade is the largest item in the current account and is often a topic that politicians and the media discuss. If a country exports more goods than it imports, it has a *trade surplus*. If a country exports less than it imports, it has a *trade deficit*. In 2011, Canada had a trade surplus of $1419 million (see Table 14.1). Figure 14.1 shows imports and exports of goods between Canada and its major trading partners and between the United States and its major trading partners. The data show that Canada ran a trade surplus in 2011 with the United States and the United Kingdom, but a trade deficit with its other major trading partners. The United States ran a trade deficit in 2011 with all its major trading partners and with every region of the world. (Note that exports from Canada to the United States in panel (a) of Figure 14.1 should equal imports by the United States from Canada in panel (b). These two numbers are different because international trade statistics are not measured exactly.)

Balance of trade The difference between the value of the goods a country exports and the value of the goods a country imports.

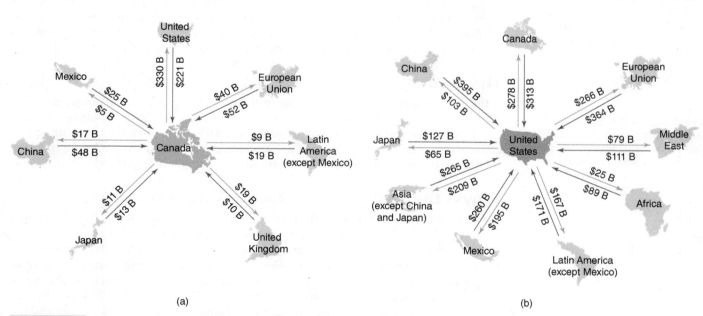

(a)   (b)

Figure 14.1   **Trade Flows for Canada and the United States, 2011**

Panel (a) shows that in 2011, Canada ran a trade surplus with the United States and United Kingdom and trade deficits with its other major trading partners. Panel (b) shows that the United States ran a trade deficit with all its major trading partners and with every region of the world. In each panel, the green arrows represent exports from Canada or the United States, and the red arrows represent imports.

Source: Data from http://www.ic.gc.ca/eic/site/tdo-dcd.nsf/eng/Home (Accessed 4 May 2012).

Net Exports Equals the Sum of the Balance of Trade and the Balance of Services In previous chapters, we saw that *net exports* is a component of aggregate expenditures. Net exports is not explicitly shown in Table 14.1, but we can calculate it by adding together the balance of trade and the balance of services. The *balance of services* is the difference between the value of the services a country exports and the value of the services a country imports. Notice that, technically, net exports is *not* equal to the current account balance because this account also includes net income on investments and net transfers. But these other two items are relatively small, so, as we will see later in this chapter, it is often a convenient simplification to think of net exports as being equal to the current account balance.

The Financial Account

Financial account The part of the balance of payments that records purchases of assets a country has made abroad and foreign purchases of assets in the country.

The **financial account** records purchases of assets a country has made abroad and foreign purchases of assets in the country. The financial account records long-term flows of funds into and out of a country. There is a *capital outflow* from Canada when an investor in Canada buys a bond issued by a foreign company or government or when a Canadian firm builds a factory in another country. There is a *capital inflow* into Canada when a foreign investor buys a bond issued by a Canadian firm or by the government or when a foreign firm builds a factory in Canada. Notice that we are using the word *capital* here to apply not just to physical assets, such as factories, but also to financial assets, such as shares of stock. When firms build or buy facilities in foreign countries, they are engaging in *foreign direct investment*. When investors buy stocks or bonds issued in another country, they are engaging in *foreign portfolio investment*.

Net foreign investment The difference between capital outflows from a country and capital inflows, also equal to net foreign direct investment plus net foreign portfolio investment.

Another way of thinking of the balance on the financial account is as a measure of *net capital flows*, or the difference between capital inflows and capital outflows. (Here we are omitting a few transactions included in the capital account, as discussed in the next section.) A concept closely related to net capital flows is **net foreign investment**, which is equal to capital outflows minus capital inflows. Net capital flows and net foreign investment are always equal but have opposite signs: When net capital flows are positive, net foreign investment is negative, and when net capital flows are negative, net foreign investment is positive. Net foreign investment is also equal to net foreign direct investment plus net foreign portfolio investment. Later in this chapter, we will use the relationship between the balance on the financial account and net foreign investment to understand an important aspect of the international economic system.

The Capital Account

Capital account The part of the balance of payments that records relatively minor transactions, such as migrants' transfers and sales and purchases of nonproduced, nonfinancial assets.

A third, less important, part of the balance of payments is called the *capital account*. The **capital account** records relatively minor transactions, such as migrants' transfers—which consist of goods and financial assets people take with them when they leave or enter a country—and sales and purchases of nonproduced, nonfinancial assets. A nonproduced, nonfinancial asset is a copyright, patent, trademark, or right to natural resources.

Why Is the Balance of Payments Always Zero?

The sum of the current account balance, the financial account balance, and the capital account balance equals the balance of payments. Table 14.1 shows that the balance of payments for Canada in 2011 was zero. It's not just by chance that this balance was zero; *the balance of payments is always zero*. Notice that the balance on the current account in 2011 was −$48 303 million. The balance on the financial account (which has the opposite sign to the balance on the current account) was $50 703 million. To make the balance on the current account equal the sum of the balance on the capital account and the balance on the financial account, the balance on capital account includes an entry called the *statistical discrepancy*.

Why does Statistics Canada include the statistical discrepancy entry to force the balance of payments to equal zero? If the sum of the current account balance and the financial account balance does not equal zero, some imports or exports of goods and services or some capital inflows or capital outflows were not measured accurately.

To better understand why the balance of payments must equal zero every year, consider the following: In 2011, Canada spent $48 303 million more on goods, services, and other items in the current account than it received. What happened to that $48 303 million? We know that every dollar of that $48 303 million was used by foreign individuals or firms to invest in Canada or was added to foreign holdings of dollars. We know this because logically there is nowhere else for the dollars to go: If the dollars weren't spent on Canadian goods and services—and we know they weren't because in that case they would have shown up in the current account—they must have been spent on investments in Canada or not spent at all. Dollars that aren't spent are added to foreign holdings of dollars. Changes in foreign holdings of dollars are known as *official reserve transactions*. Foreign investment in Canada and additions to foreign holdings of dollars both show up as positive entries in the Canadian financial account. Therefore, a current account deficit must be exactly offset by a financial account surplus, leaving the balance of payments equal to zero. Similarly, a country that runs a current account surplus, such as China or Japan, must run a financial account deficit of exactly the same size. If a country's current account surplus is not exactly equal to its financial account deficit, or if a country's current account deficit is not exactly equal to its financial account surplus, some transactions must not have been accounted for. The statistical discrepancy is included in the balance of payments to compensate for these uncounted transactions.

Don't Let This Happen to You

Don't Confuse the Balance of Trade, the Current Account Balance, and the Balance of Payments

The terminology of international economics can be tricky. Remember that the *balance of trade* includes only trade in goods; it does not include services. This observation is important because Canada, for example, usually imports more *goods* than it exports, but it usually exports more *services* than it imports. As a result, the Canadian trade deficit is almost always larger than the current account deficit. The *current account balance* includes the balance of trade, the balance of services, net income on investments, and net transfers. Net income on investments and net transfers are much smaller than the balance of trade and the balance of services.

Even though the *balance of payments* is equal to the sum of the current account balance and the financial account balance—and must equal zero—you may sometimes see references to a balance of payments "surplus" or "deficit."

These references have two explanations. The first is that the person making the reference has confused the balance of payments with either the balance of trade or the current account balance. This is a very common mistake. The second explanation is that the person is not including official reserve transactions in the financial account. If we separate changes in Canadian holdings of foreign currencies and changes in foreign holdings of Canadian dollars from other financial account entries, the current account balance and the financial account balance do not have to sum to zero, and there can be a balance of payments surplus or deficit. This may sound complicated—and it is! But don't worry. How official reserve transactions are accounted for is not crucial to understanding the basic ideas behind the balance of payments.

MyEconLab
Your Turn: Test your understanding by doing related problem 1.2 on page 459 at the end of this chapter.

Solved Problem **14.1**

Understanding the Arithmetic of Open Economies

Test your understanding of the relationship between the current account and the financial account by evaluating the following assertion by a political commentator:

The industrial countries are committing economic suicide. Every year, they invest more and more in developing countries. Every year, more US, Japanese, and European manufacturing firms move their factories to developing countries. With extensive new factories and low wages, developing countries now export far more to the industrial countries than they import.

Solving the Problem

Step 1: **Review the chapter material.** This problem is about the relationship between the current account and the financial account, so you may want to review the section "Why Is the Balance of Payments Always Zero?" which begins on page 438.

Step 2: **Explain the errors in the commentator's argument.** The argument sounds plausible. It would be easy to find statements similar to this one in recent books and articles by well-known political commentators. But the argument contains an important error: The commentator has failed to understand the relationship between the current account and the financial account. The commentator asserts that developing countries are receiving large capital inflows from industrial countries. In other words, developing countries are running financial account surpluses. The commentator also asserts that developing countries are exporting more than they are importing. In other words, they are running current account surpluses. As we have seen in this section, it is impossible to run a current account surplus *and* a financial account surplus simultaneously. A country that runs a current account surplus *must* run a financial account deficit and vice versa.

Extra credit: Most emerging economies that have received large inflows of foreign investment during the past two decades, such as South Korea, Thailand, and Malaysia, have run current account deficits: They import more goods and services than they export. Emerging economies, such as Singapore, that run current account surpluses also run financial account deficits: They invest more abroad than other countries invest in them.

The point here is not obvious; if the point was obvious, it wouldn't confuse so many intelligent politicians, journalists, and political commentators. Unless you understand the relationship between the current account and the financial account, you won't be able to understand a key aspect of the international economy.

MyEconLab **Your Turn:** For more practice, do related problem 1.3 on page 459 at the end of this chapter.

Explain how exchange rates are determined and how changes in exchange rates affect the prices of imports and exports.

The Foreign Exchange Market and Exchange Rates

A firm that operates entirely within Canada will price its products in Canadian dollars and will use Canadian dollars to pay its suppliers' bills, wages and salaries to its workers, interest to its bondholders, and dividends to its shareholders. A multinational corporation such as BlackBerry, in contrast, may sell its products in many different countries and receive payments in many different currencies. Its suppliers and workers may also be spread around the world and may have to be paid in local currencies. Corporations may also use the international financial system to borrow in a foreign currency. For example, during a period of rapid expansion in East Asian countries such as Thailand and South Korea during the late 1990s, many large firms received US dollar loans from foreign banks. When firms make extensive use of foreign currencies, they must deal with fluctuations in the exchange rate.

Nominal exchange rate The value of one country's currency in terms of another country's currency.

The **nominal exchange rate** is the value of one country's currency in terms of another country's currency. Economists also calculate the *real exchange rate*, which corrects the nominal exchange rate for changes in prices of goods and services. We discuss the real exchange rate later in this chapter. The nominal exchange rate determines how many units of a foreign currency you can purchase with $1. For example, the exchange rate between the Canadian dollar and the Japanese yen can be expressed as ¥100 = $1. (This exchange rate can also be expressed as how many Canadian dollars are required to buy 1 Japanese yen: $0.01 = ¥1.) The market for foreign exchange is very active. Every day, the equivalent of more than $3 trillion worth of currency is traded in the foreign exchange market. The exchange rates that result from this trading are reported on a number of online sites devoted to economic news and in the business or financial sections of most newspapers.

Banks and other financial institutions around the world employ currency traders, who are linked together by computer. Rather than exchange large amounts of paper currency, they buy and sell deposits in banks. A bank buying or selling dollars will actually be buying or selling dollar bank deposits. Dollar bank deposits exist not just in banks in Canada but also in banks around the world. Suppose that the Crédit Agricole bank in France wants to sell Canadian dollars and buy Japanese yen. The bank may exchange Canadian dollar deposits that it owns for Japanese yen deposits owned by the Deutsche Bank in Germany. Businesses and individuals usually obtain foreign currency from banks in their own country.

| Making the Connection | ## Exchange Rate Listings |

Many websites, such as bankofcanada.ca, wsj.com, and ca.finance.yahoo.com, as well as the financial pages of most newspapers list the exchange rates between the Canadian dollar and other important currencies. The exchange rates in the following table are for May 28, 2013. The euro is the common currency used by 17 European Union member countries, including France, Germany, and Italy.

Exchange Rate between the Canadian Dollar and the Indicated Currency		
Currency	Units of Foreign Currency per Canadian Dollar	Canadian Dollars per Unit of Foreign Currency
US dollar	1.037	0.964
Japanese yen	98.425	0.010
Mexican peso	12.091	0.082
British pound	0.640	1.562
Euro	0.749	1.334

You can find information on exchange rates on many online sites that report economic news and in the financial pages of most newspapers.

Notice that the expression for the exchange rate stated as units of foreign currency per Canadian dollar is the *reciprocal* of the exchange rate stated as Canadian dollars per unit of foreign currency. So, the exchange rate between the Canadian dollar and the British pound can be stated as either 0.640 British pounds per Canadian dollar or 1/0.640 = 1.562 Canadian dollars per British pound.

Banks are the most active participants in the market for foreign exchange. Typically, banks buy currency for slightly less than the amount for which they sell it. This spread between the buying and selling prices allows banks to cover their expenses from currency trading and to make a profit. Therefore, when most businesses and individuals buy foreign currency from a bank, they receive fewer units of foreign currency per dollar than would be indicated by the exchange rate shown on online business sites or printed in the newspaper.

Source: Based on Wall Street Journal, April 21, 2012.

Your Turn: Test your understanding by doing related problem 2.1 on page 459 at the end of this chapter.

The market exchange rate is determined by the interaction of demand and supply, just as other prices are. Let's consider the demand for Canadian dollars in exchange for Japanese yen. There are three sources of foreign currency demand for the Canadian dollar:

1. Foreign firms and households that want to buy goods and services produced in Canada.

2. Foreign firms and households that want to invest in Canada either through foreign direct investment—buying or building factories or other facilities in Canada—or through foreign portfolio investment—buying stocks and bonds issued in Canada.
3. Currency traders who believe that the value of the dollar in the future will be greater than its value today.

Equilibrium in the Market for Foreign Exchange

Figure 14.2 shows the demand and supply of Canadian dollars for Japanese yen. Notice that as we move up the vertical axis in Figure 14.2, the value of the dollar increases relative to the value of the yen. When the exchange rate is ¥150 = $1, the dollar is worth 1.5 times as much relative to the yen as when the exchange rate is ¥100 = $1. Consider, first, the demand curve for dollars in exchange for yen. The demand curve has the normal downward slope. When the value of the dollar is high, the quantity of dollars demanded will be low. A Japanese investor will be more likely to buy a $1000 bond issued by the Canadian government when the exchange rate is ¥100 = $1 and the investor pays only ¥100 000 to buy $1000 than when the exchange rate is ¥150 = $1 and the investor must pay ¥150 000. Similarly, a Japanese firm is more likely to buy $150 million worth of BlackBerrys when the exchange rate is ¥100 = $1 and the BlackBerrys can be purchased for ¥15 billion than when the exchange rate is ¥150 = $1 and the BlackBerrys cost ¥22.5 billion.

Consider, now, the supply curve of dollars in exchange for yen. The supply curve has the normal upward slope. When the value of the dollar is high, the quantity of dollars supplied in exchange for yen will be high. A Canadian investor will be more likely to buy a ¥200 000 bond issued by the Japanese government when the exchange rate is ¥200 = $1 and the investor needs to pay only $1000 to buy ¥200 000 than when the exchange rate is ¥100 = $1 and the investor must pay $2000. The owner of a Canadian electronics store is more likely to buy ¥20 million worth of television sets from Sony Corporation when the exchange rate is ¥200 = $1 and she only needs to pay $100 000 to purchase the televisions than when the exchange rate is ¥100 = $1 and she must pay $200 000.

As in any other market, equilibrium occurs in the foreign exchange market where the quantity supplied equals the quantity demanded. In Figure 14.2, ¥120 = $1 is the equilibrium exchange rate. At exchange rates above ¥120 = $1, there will be a surplus of dollars and downward pressure on the exchange rate. The surplus and the downward pressure will not be eliminated until the exchange rate falls to ¥120 = $1. If the exchange rate is below ¥120 = $1, there will be a shortage of dollars and upward pressure on the

Figure 14.2

Equilibrium in the Foreign Exchange Market

When the exchange rate is ¥150 to the dollar, it is above its equilibrium level, and there will be a surplus of dollars. When the exchange rate is ¥100 to the dollar, it is below its equilibrium level, and there will be a shortage of dollars. At an exchange rate of ¥120 to the dollar, the foreign exchange market is in equilibrium.

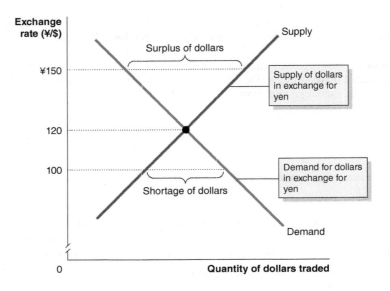

exchange rate. The shortage and the upward pressure will not be eliminated until the exchange rate rises to ¥120 = $1. Surpluses and shortages in the foreign exchange market are eliminated very quickly because the volume of trading in major currencies such as the dollar and the yen is very large, and currency traders are linked together by computer.

Currency appreciation occurs when the market value of a country's currency increases relative to the value of another country's currency. **Currency depreciation** occurs when the market value of a country's currency decreases relative to the value of another country's currency.

Currency appreciation An increase in the market value of one currency relative to another currency.

Currency depreciation A decrease in the market value of one currency relative to another currency.

How Do Shifts in Demand and Supply Affect the Exchange Rate?

Shifts in the demand and supply curves cause the equilibrium exchange rate to change. Three main factors cause the demand and supply curves in the foreign exchange market to shift:

1. Changes in the demand for Canadian-produced goods and services and changes in the demand for foreign-produced goods and services
2. Changes in the desire to invest in Canada and changes in the desire to invest in foreign countries
3. Changes in the expectations of currency traders about the likely future value of the dollar and the likely future value of foreign currencies

Shifts in the Demand for Foreign Exchange Consider how the three factors listed above will affect the demand for Canadian dollars in exchange for Japanese yen. During an economic expansion in Japan, the incomes of Japanese households will rise, and the demand by Japanese consumers and firms for Canadian goods will increase. At any given exchange rate, the demand for Canadian dollars will increase, and the demand curve will shift to the right. Similarly, if interest rates rise in Canada, the desirability of investing in Canadian financial assets will increase, and the demand curve for dollars will also shift to the right. **Speculators** are currency traders who buy and sell foreign exchange in an attempt to profit from changes in exchange rates. If a speculator becomes convinced that the value of the dollar is going to rise relative to the value of the yen, the speculator will sell yen and buy dollars. If the current exchange rate is ¥120 = $1, and the speculator is convinced that it will soon rise to ¥140 = $1, the speculator could sell ¥600 000 000 and receive $5 000 000 (= ¥600 000 000/¥120) in return. If the speculator is correct and the value of the dollar rises against the yen to ¥140 = $1, the speculator will be able to exchange $5 000 000 for ¥700 000 000 (= $5 000 000 × ¥140), for a profit of ¥100 000 000.

Speculators Currency traders who buy and sell foreign exchange in an attempt to profit from changes in exchange rates.

To summarize, the demand curve for dollars shifts to the right when incomes in Japan rise, when interest rates in Canada rise, or when speculators decide that the value of the dollar will rise relative to the value of the yen.

During a recession in Japan, Japanese incomes will fall, reducing the demand for Canadian-produced goods and services and shifting the demand curve for dollars to the left. Similarly, if interest rates in Canada fall, the desirability of investing in Canadian financial assets will decrease, and the demand curve for dollars will shift to the left. Finally, if speculators become convinced that the future value of the dollar will be lower than its current value, the demand for dollars will fall, and the demand curve will shift to the left.

Shifts in the Supply of Foreign Exchange The factors that affect the supply curve for dollars are similar to those that affect the demand curve for dollars. An economic expansion in Canada increases the incomes of Canadians and increases their demand for goods and services, including goods and services made in Japan. As Canadian consumers and firms increase their spending on Japanese products, they must supply dollars in exchange for yen, which causes the supply curve for dollars to shift to the right. Similarly, an increase in interest rates in Japan will make financial investments in Japan more attractive to Canadian investors. These higher Japanese interest rates will

Figure 14.3

Shifts in the Demand and Supply Curve Resulting in a Higher Exchange Rate

Holding other factors constant, an increase in the supply of dollars will decrease the equilibrium exchange rate. An increase in the demand for dollars will increase the equilibrium exchange rate. In the case shown in this figure, the demand curve and the supply curve have both shifted to the right. Because the demand curve has shifted to the right by more than the supply curve, the equilibrium exchange rate has increased from ¥120 to $1 at point A to ¥130 to $1 at point B.

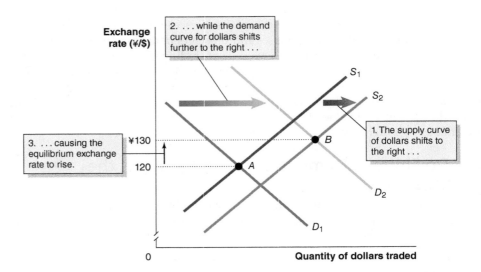

cause the supply of dollars to shift to the right, as Canadian investors exchange dollars for yen. Finally, if speculators become convinced that the future value of the yen will be higher relative to the dollar than it is today, the supply curve of dollars will shift to the right as traders attempt to exchange dollars for yen.

A recession in Canada will decrease the demand for Japanese products and cause the supply curve for dollars to shift to the left. Similarly, a decrease in interest rates in Japan will make financial investments in Japan less attractive and cause the supply curve of dollars to shift to the left. If traders become convinced that the future value of the yen will be lower relative to the dollar, the supply curve will also shift to the left.

Adjustment to a New Equilibrium The factors that affect the demand and supply for currencies are constantly changing. Whether the exchange rate increases or decreases depends on the direction and size of the shifts in the demand curve and supply curve. For example, as Figure 14.3 shows, if the demand curve for dollars in exchange for Japanese yen shifts to the right by more than the supply curve shifts, the equilibrium exchange rate will increase.

Making the Connection	**What Explains the Fall and Rise and Fall of the Canadian Dollar?**

A Canadian vacationing in New York during the spring of 2002 could have bought a meal for US$50 and paid the equivalent of Can$80 for it. In October 2007, that same US$50 meal would have cost the equivalent of Can$47. A year later, in November 2008, it would have cost Can$62. In the spring of 2012, it would have cost Can$50. Clearly, during these years, the value of the Canadian dollar in exchange for the US dollar went through substantial fluctuations. And it wasn't just against the US dollar that the Canadian dollar was gaining value, then losing some of it, and then regaining it again. The graph below shows fluctuations for the period from 1981 to early 2012 in the Canadian-dollar effective exchange rate index (CERI). This is a weighted average of bilateral exchange rates for the Canadian dollar against the currencies of Canada's six major trading partners, the United States, the European Union, Japan, the United Kingdom, China, and Mexico. The index is based to 1992 = 100, and an increase in the index represents an appreciation of the Canadian dollar, while a decrease represents a depreciation of the Canadian dollar. The shaded areas indicate recessions.

The graph indicates that although the dollar lost value against other currencies for a brief period during the early 1980s and in the 1990s, and again in 2008, overall it has gained value since 1981. What explains the increase in the value of the dollar? We have just seen that an increase in the demand by foreign investors for Canadian financial assets can increase the value of the dollar, and a decrease in the demand for Canadian financial assets can decrease the value of the dollar. The increase in the value of the dollar in the early 2000s, as shown in the graph, was driven by strong demand from foreign investors for Canadian stocks and bonds. This increase in demand was not primarily due to higher Canadian interest rates but to problems in the international financial system that we will discuss in Chapter 15.

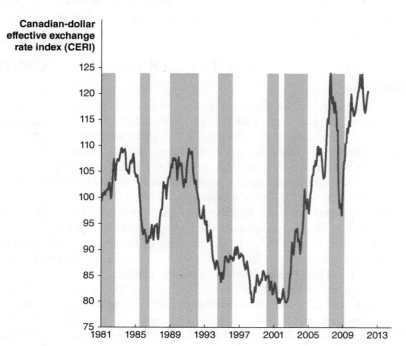

Source: Data from Statistics Canada CANSIM II series V41498903. (Accessed 1 May 2012).

What explains the fall in the value of the Canadian dollar in the 1990s? Many investors and some central banks became convinced that the value of the dollar was too high in the late 1980s and that it was likely to decline in the future. As we will see later in this chapter, Canada ran large budget deficits and current account deficits in the 1990s. Many investors believed that the substantial increase in the supply of dollars in exchange for foreign currencies that resulted from these deficits would ultimately result in a significant decline in the value of the dollar. Once investors become convinced that the value of a country's currency will decline, they become reluctant to hold that country's financial assets. A decreased willingness by foreign investors to buy Canadian financial assets decreases the demand for dollars and lowers the exchange value of the dollar.

What explains the increase in the value of the Canadian dollar since 2009? The increase has largely been the result of the good performance of the Canadian economy during the global financial crisis and the healthy and vibrant Canadian banking system that has become the envy of the world. Many investors saw Canadian securities as a safe haven and demanded dollars in order to invest in them. Also, worries that some European governments—particularly Greece— might default on their government bonds caused an increase in the value of the dollar since 2009.

The rise in the value of the dollar over the long run has been bad news for Canadian tourists travelling abroad and for anyone in Canada buying foreign goods and services. It has been bad news, however, for Canadian firms exporting goods and services to other countries.

Your Turn: Test your understanding by doing related problems 2.3 and 2.4 on page 460 at the end of this chapter.

MyEconLab

Some Exchange Rates Are Not Determined by the Market

To this point, we have assumed that exchange rates are determined in the market. This assumption is a good one for many currencies, including the Canadian dollar, the US dollar, the euro, the Japanese yen, and the British pound. Some currencies, however, have *fixed exchange rates* that do not change over long periods. For example, for more than 10 years, the value of the Chinese yuan was fixed against the US dollar at a rate of 8.28 yuan to the US dollar. As we will discuss in more detail in Chapter 15, a country's central bank has to intervene in the foreign exchange market to buy and sell its currency to keep the exchange rate fixed.

How Movements in the Exchange Rate Affect Exports and Imports

When the market value of the dollar increases, the foreign currency price of Canadian exports rises, and the dollar price of foreign imports falls. For example, suppose that initially the market exchange rate between the Canadian dollar and the euro is $1 = €1. In that case, a BlackBerry that has a price of $200 in Canada will have a price of €200 in France. A bottle of French wine that has a price of €50 in France will have a price of $50 in Canada. Now suppose the market exchange rate between the Canadian dollar and the euro changes to $1.20 = €1. Because it now takes more dollars to buy a euro, the dollar has *depreciated* against the euro, and the euro has *appreciated* against the dollar. The depreciation of the dollar has decreased the euro price of the BlackBerry from €200 to $200/(1.20 dollars/euro) = €167. The dollar price of the French wine has risen from $50 to €50 × 1.20 dollars/euro = $60. As a result, we would expect more BlackBerrys to be sold in France and less French wine to be sold in Canada.

To generalize, we can conclude that a depreciation in the domestic currency will increase exports and decrease imports, thereby increasing net exports. As we saw in previous chapters, net exports is a component of aggregate demand. If real GDP is currently below potential GDP, then, holding all other factors constant, a depreciation in the domestic currency should increase net exports, aggregate demand, and real GDP. An appreciation in the domestic currency should have the opposite effect: Exports should fall, and imports should rise, which will reduce net exports, aggregate demand, and real GDP.

Don't Let This Happen to You

Don't Confuse What Happens When a Currency Appreciates with What Happens When It Depreciates

One of the most confusing aspects of exchange rates is that they can be expressed in two ways. We can express the exchange rate between the dollar and the yen either as how many yen can be purchased with $1 or as how many dollars can be purchased with ¥1. That is, we can express the exchange rate as ¥100 = $1 or as $0.01 = ¥1. When a currency appreciates, it increases in value relative to another currency. When it depreciates, it decreases in value relative to another currency.

If the exchange rate changes from ¥100 = $1 to ¥120 = $1, the dollar has appreciated and the yen has depreciated because it now takes more yen to buy $1. If the exchange rate changes from $0.01 = ¥1 to $0.015 = ¥1, however, the dollar has depreciated and the yen has appreciated because it now takes more dollars to buy ¥1. This situation can appear somewhat confusing because the exchange rate seems to have "increased" in both cases. To determine which currency has appreciated and which has depreciated, it is important to remember that an appreciation of the domestic currency means that it now takes *more* units of the foreign currency to buy one unit of the domestic currency. A depreciation of the domestic currency means it takes *fewer* units of the foreign currency to buy one unit of the domestic currency. This observation holds no matter which way we express the exchange rate.

MyEconLab

Your Turn: Test your understanding by doing related problem 2.5 on page 460 at the end of the chapter.

Solved Problem **14.2**

The Effect of Changing Exchange Rates on the Prices of Imports and Exports

In June 2011, the average price of goods imported into the United States from Canada fell 2.1 percent. Is it likely that the value of the US dollar appreciated or depreciated versus the Canadian dollar during this period? Is it likely that the average price in Canadian dollars of goods exported from the United States to Canada during June 2011 rose or fell?

Solving the Problem

Step 1: Review the chapter material. This problem is about changes in the value of a currency, so you may want to review the section "How Movements in the Exchange Rate Affect Exports and Imports" on page 446.

Step 2: Explain whether the value of the US dollar appreciated or depreciated against the Canadian dollar. We know that if the US dollar appreciates against the Canadian dollar, it will take more Canadian dollars to purchase 1 US dollar, and, equivalently, fewer US dollars will be required to purchase 1 Canadian dollar. A Canadian consumer or business will need to pay more Canadian dollars to buy products imported from the United States: A good or service that had been selling for Can$100 will now sell for more than US$100. A US consumer or business will have to pay fewer US dollars to buy products imported from Canada: A good or service that had been selling for US$100 will now sell for fewer than US$100. We can conclude that if the price of goods imported into the United States from Canada fell, the value of the US dollar must have appreciated versus the Canadian dollar.

Step 3: Explain what happened to the average price in Canadian dollars of goods exported from the United States to Canada. If the US dollar appreciated relative to the Canadian dollar, the average price in Canadian dollars of goods exported from the United States to Canada will have risen.

Your Turn: For more practice, do related problem 2.6 on page 460 at the end of this chapter.

MyEconLab

The Real Exchange Rate

We have seen that an important factor in determining the level of a country's exports to and imports from another country is the relative prices of each country's goods. The relative prices of two countries' goods are determined by two factors: the relative price levels in the two countries and the nominal exchange rate between the two countries' currencies. Economists combine these two factors in the **real exchange rate**, which is the price of domestic goods in terms of foreign goods. Recall that the price level is a measure of the average prices of goods and services in an economy. We can calculate the real exchange rate between two currencies as

Real exchange rate The price of domestic goods in terms of foreign goods.

$$\text{Real exchange rate} = \text{Nominal rate} \times \left(\frac{\text{Domestic price level}}{\text{Foreign price level}} \right)$$

Notice that changes in the real exchange rate reflect both changes in the nominal exchange rate and changes in the relative price levels. For example, suppose that the exchange rate between the Canadian dollar and the British pound is £1, the price level in Canada is 100, and the price level in the United Kingdom is also 100. Then the real exchange rate between the dollar and the pound is

$$\text{Real exchange rate} = 1 \text{ pound/dollar} \times \left(\frac{100}{100} \right) = 1.00.$$

Now suppose that the nominal exchange rate increases to 1.1 pounds per dollar, while the price level in Canada rises to 105 and the price level in the United Kingdom remains 100. In this case, the real exchange rate will be

$$\text{Real exchange rate} = 1.1 \text{ pound/dollar} \times \left(\frac{105}{100}\right) = 1.15.$$

The increase in the real exchange rate from 1.00 to 1.15 tells us that the prices of Canadian goods and services are now 15 percent higher than they were relative to British goods and services.

Real exchange rates are reported as index numbers, with one year chosen as the base year. As with the consumer price index, the main value of the real exchange rate is in tracking changes over time—in this case, changes in the relative prices of domestic goods in terms of foreign goods.

14.3 LEARNING OBJECTIVE

Explain the saving and investment equation.

The International Sector and National Saving and Investment

Having studied what determines the exchange rate, we are now ready to explore further the linkages between the Canadian economy and foreign economies. Until 1970, Canadian imports and exports were a small fraction of GDP. Imports and exports are now two to three times as large a fraction of Canadian GDP. Imports have also consistently been larger than exports, meaning that net exports have been negative.

Net Exports Equal Net Foreign Investment

If your spending is greater than your income, what can you do? You can sell some assets—maybe those 20 shares of stock in Rogers Communications that your grandparents gave you—or you can borrow money. A firm can be in the same situation: If a firm's costs are greater than its revenues, it has to make up the difference by selling assets or by borrowing. A country is in the same situation when it imports more than it exports: The country must finance the difference by selling assets—such as land, office buildings, or factories—or by borrowing.

In other words, for any country, a current account deficit must be exactly offset by a financial account surplus. When a country sells more assets to foreigners than it buys from foreigners, or when it borrows more from foreigners than it lends to foreigners—as it must if it is running a current account deficit—the country experiences a net capital inflow and a financial account surplus. Remember that net exports is roughly equal to the current account balance. Remember also that the financial account balance is roughly equal to net capital flows, which are in turn equal to net foreign investment but with the opposite sign. To review these two points, look again at Table 14.1, which shows that the current account balance is determined mainly by the balance of trade and the balance of services, and the financial account is equal to net capital flows. Also, remember the definition of *net foreign investment*.

When imports are greater than exports, net exports are negative, and there will be a net capital inflow as people in Canada sell assets and borrow to pay for the surplus of imports over exports. Therefore, net capital flows will be equal to net exports (but with the opposite sign), and net foreign investment will also be equal to net exports (and with the same sign). Because net exports were negative for Canada during the 2009 to 2011 period, Canada was a net borrower from abroad, and Canadian net foreign investment was negative.

We can summarize this discussion with the following equations:

$$\text{Current account balance} + \text{Financial account balance} = 0$$

or

$$\text{Current account balance} = -\text{Financial account balance}$$

or

$$\text{Net exports } = \text{ Net foreign investment.}$$

This equation tells us that countries such as Canada, Japan, and China that usually export more than they import must lend abroad more than they borrow from abroad: If net exports are positive, net foreign investment will also be positive by the same amount. Countries such as the United States that import more than they export must borrow more from abroad than they lend abroad: If net exports are negative, net foreign investment will also be negative by the same amount.

Domestic Saving, Domestic Investment, and Net Foreign Investment

As we saw in Chapter 6, the total saving in any economy is equal to saving by the private sector plus saving by the government sector, which we called *public saving*. When the government runs a budget surplus by spending less than it receives in taxes, it is saving. When the government runs a budget deficit, public saving is negative. Negative saving is also known as *dissaving*. We can write the following expression for the level of saving in the economy:

$$\text{National saving } = \text{ Private saving } + \text{ Public saving}$$

or

$$S = S_{\text{private}} + S_{\text{public}}.$$

Private saving is equal to what households have left of their income after spending on consumption goods and paying taxes (for simplicity, we assume that transfer payments are zero):

$$\text{Private saving } = \text{ National income } - \text{ Consumption } - \text{ Taxes}$$

or

$$S_{\text{private}} = Y - C - T.$$

Public saving is equal to the difference between government spending and taxes:

$$\text{Government saving } = \text{ Taxes } - \text{ Government spending}$$

or

$$S_{\text{public}} = T - G.$$

Finally, remember the basic macroeconomic equation for GDP or national income:

$$Y = C + I + G + NX.$$

We can use this last equation, our definitions of private and public saving, and the fact that net exports equal net foreign investment to arrive at an important relationship, known as the **saving and investment equation**:

$$\text{National saving } = \text{ Domestic investment } + \text{ Net foreign investment}$$

or

$$S = I + NFI.$$

This equation is an *identity* because it must always be true, given the definitions we have used.

The saving and investment equation tells us that a country's saving will be invested either domestically or overseas. If you save $1000 and use the funds to buy a bond issued

Saving and investment equation An equation that shows that national saving is equal to domestic investment plus net foreign investment.

Solved Problem 14.3

Arriving at the Saving and Investment Equation

Use the definitions of private and public saving, the equation for GDP or national income, and the fact that net exports must equal net foreign investment to arrive at the saving and investment equation.

Solving the Problem

Step 1: Review the chapter material. This problem is about the saving and investment equation, so you may want to review the section "Domestic Saving, Domestic Investment, and Net Foreign Investment," which begins on page 449.

Step 2: Derive an expression for national saving (S) in terms of national income (Y), consumption (C), and government purchases (G). We can bring together the four equations we need to use:

1. $S_{private} = Y - C - T$

2. $S_{public} = T - G$

3. $Y = C + I + G + NX$

4. $NX = NFI$

Because national saving (S) appears in the saving and investment equation, we need to find an equation for it in terms of the other variables. Adding equation 1 plus equation 2 yields national saving:

$$S = S_{private} + S_{public} = (Y - C - T) + (T - G) = Y - C - G.$$

Step 3: Use the result from Step 2 to derive an expression for national saving in terms of investment (I) and net exports (NX). Because GDP (Y) does not appear in the saving and investment equation, we need to substitute the expression for it given in equation (3):

$$S = (C + I + G + NX) - C - G$$

and simplify:

$$S = I + NX.$$

Step 4: Use the results of Steps 2 and 3 to derive the saving and investment equation. Finally, substitute net foreign investment for net exports:

$$S = I + NFI.$$

MyEconLab **Your Turn:** For more practice, do related problem 3.4 on page 460 at the end of this chapter.

by BlackBerry, the company may use the $1000 to renovate a factory in Canada (I) or to build a factory in China (NFI) as a joint venture with a Chinese firm.

A country such as Canada that has positive net foreign investment must be saving more than it is investing domestically. To see this, rewrite the saving and investment equation by moving domestic investment to the left side:

If net foreign investment is positive—as it is for Canada nearly every year—domestic investment (I) must be less than national saving (S).

The level of saving in Japan has also been well above domestic investment. The result has been high levels of Japanese net foreign investment. For example, Japanese automobile companies Toyota, Honda, and Nissan have all constructed factories in Canada and the United States. Sony purchased the Columbia Pictures film studio. Japan has made many similar investments in countries around the world, which has sometimes caused resentment in those countries. There were some protests in the United States in the 1980s, for example, when Japanese investors purchased the Pebble Beach golf course in California and the Rockefeller Center complex in New York City.

Japan needs a high level of net exports to help offset a low level of domestic investment. When exports of a product begin to decline and imports begin to increase, governments are often tempted to impose tariffs or quotas to reduce imports. In fact, many Japanese firms have been urging the Japanese government to impose trade restrictions on imports from China.

The Effect of a Government Budget Deficit on Investment

14.4 LEARNING OBJECTIVE

Explain the effect of a government budget deficit on investment in an open economy.

The link we have just developed among saving, investment, and net foreign investment can help us understand some of the effects of changes in a government's budget deficit. When the government runs a budget deficit, national saving will decline unless private saving increases by the amount of the budget deficit, which is unlikely. As the saving and investment equation ($S = I + NFI$) shows, the result of a decline in national saving must be a decline in either domestic investment or net foreign investment. Why, though, does an increase in the government budget deficit cause a fall in domestic investment or net foreign investment?

To understand the answer to this question, remember that if the federal government runs a budget deficit, the government must raise an amount equal to the deficit by selling bonds. To attract investors, the government may have to raise the interest rates on its bonds. As interest rates on government bonds rise, other interest rates, including those on corporate bonds and bank loans, will also rise. Higher interest rates will discourage some firms from borrowing funds to build new factories or to buy new equipment or computers. Higher interest rates on financial assets in Canada will attract foreign investors. Investors in the United States, Japan, or China will have to buy Canadian dollars to be able to purchase bonds in Canada. This greater demand for dollars will increase their value relative to foreign currencies. As the value of the dollar rises, exports from Canada will fall, and imports to Canada will rise. Net exports and, therefore, net foreign investment will fall.

When a government budget deficit leads to a decline in net exports, the result is sometimes referred to as the *twin deficits*, which refers to the possibility that a government budget deficit will also lead to a current account deficit. The twin deficits idea first became widely discussed in Canada during the early 1980s, when the federal

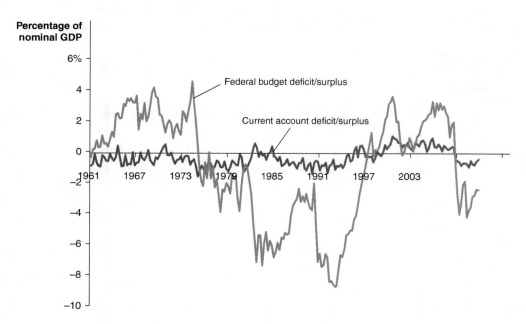

Figure 14.4

The Twin Canadian Deficits, 1961–2011

From the mid-1970s, to the mid-1990s, large federal budget deficits occurred at the same time as large current account deficits, but twin deficits did not occur in most other periods during these years, except for the 2008–2011 period, in the aftermath of the "Great Recession."

Sources: Data from Statistics Canada CANSIM II series V49086, V498316, and V114532. (Accessed 1 May 2012)

government ran a large budget deficit that resulted in high interest rates, a high exchange value of the dollar, and a current account deficit.

Although there appears a tendency for twin deficits to occur in Canada, the experience of other countries shows only mixed support for the twin deficits idea. For example, in the early 1980s, the United States had large federal budget deficits and large current account deficits. However, the twin deficits idea does not reflect the experience of the United States after 1990. The large federal budget deficits of the early 1990s occurred at a time of relatively small current account deficits, and the budget surpluses of the late 1990s occurred at a time of then-record current account deficits. Both the current account deficit and the federal budget deficit increased in the early 2000s, but the federal budget deficit declined in the mid-2000s much more than did the current account deficit. Beginning in 2008, the US federal budget deficit soared, more than doubling as a percentage of GDP, while the current account deficit declined.

Also, Germany ran large budget deficits and large current account deficits during the early 1990s, but Italy ran large budget deficits during the 1980s without running current account deficits. The saving and investment equation shows that an increase in the government budget deficit will not lead to an increase in the current account deficit, provided that either private saving increases or domestic investment declines. According to the twin deficits idea, when the federal government ran budget surpluses in the late 1990s, the current account should also have been in surplus, or at least the current account deficit should have been small. In fact, the increase in national saving due to the budget surpluses was more than offset by a sharp decline in private saving, and the United States ran very large current account deficits.

Making the Connection

Why Is the United States Called the "World's Largest Debtor"?

The following graph shows the current account balance as a percentage of GDP for the United States for the period 1950–2010. The United States has had a current account deficit every year since 1982, with the exception of 1991. Between 1950 and 1975, the United States ran a current account deficit in only five years. Many economists believe that the current account deficits of the 1980s were closely related to the federal budget deficits of those years. High interest rates attracted foreign investors to US bonds, which raised the exchange rate between the US dollar and foreign currencies. The high exchange rate reduced US exports and increased imports, leading to current account deficits.

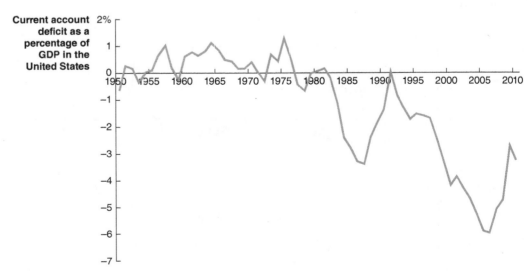

Source: Data from U.S. Bureau of Economic Analysis.

As the federal budget deficit in the United States narrowed in the mid-1990s and disappeared in the late 1990s, the foreign exchange value of the US dollar remained high—and large current account deficits continued—because foreign investors persisted in investing in the United States, despite low interest rates. In the late 1990s, a number of countries around the world, such as South Korea, Indonesia, Brazil, and Russia, suffered severe economic problems. In a process known as a *flight to quality*, many investors sold their investments in those countries and bought investments in the United States. In addition, the strong performance of the US stock market through the spring of 2000 attracted many investors. Finally, the sharp decline in private saving in the United States that began during the late 1990s also contributed to the US current account deficit. The fall in the value of the US dollar after 2008 helped reduce the size of the current account deficit, although the deficit still remained substantial.

Do persistent current account deficits represent a problem for the United States? Current account deficits result in US net foreign investment being negative. Each year, foreign investors accumulate many more US assets than US investors accumulate foreign assets. At the end of 2010, foreign investors owned about $2.5 trillion more of US assets—such as stocks, bonds, and factories—than US investors owned of foreign assets, which is why the United States is sometimes called "the world's largest debtor." But the continued willingness of foreign investors to buy US stocks and bonds and of foreign companies to build factories in the United States can be seen as a vote of confidence in the strength of the US economy and the buying power of US consumers. When private saving rates declined in the United States to historically low levels in the mid-2000s, only the continued flow of funds from foreign investors made it possible for the United States to maintain the high levels of domestic investment required for economic growth. Beginning in 2009, private saving rates increased, but public saving turned sharply negative as the federal budget deficit soared. Domestic investment in the United States remains reliant on funds from foreign investment.

Your Turn: Test your understanding by doing related problem 4.3 on page 461 at the end of this chapter.

MyEconLab

Monetary Policy and Fiscal Policy in an Open Economy

14.5 LEARNING OBJECTIVE

Compare the effectiveness of monetary policy and fiscal policy in an open economy and in a closed economy.

When we discussed monetary policy and fiscal policy in Chapters 11 and 12, we did not emphasize that Canada is an open economy. Now that we have explored some of the links among economies, we can look at the difference between how monetary policy and fiscal policy work in an open economy as opposed to in a closed economy. Economists refer to the ways in which monetary policy and fiscal policy affect the domestic economy as *policy channels*. An open economy has more policy channels than does a closed economy.

Monetary Policy in an Open Economy

When the Bank of Canada engages in an expansionary monetary policy, it buys government securities to lower interest rates and stimulate aggregate demand. In a closed economy, the main effect of lower interest rates is on domestic investment spending and purchases of consumer durables. In an open economy, lower interest rates will also affect the exchange rate between the dollar and foreign currencies. Lower interest rates will cause some investors in Canada and abroad to switch from investing in Canadian financial assets to investing in foreign financial assets. This switch will lower the demand for the dollar relative to foreign currencies and cause its value to decline. A lower exchange rate will decrease the price of Canadian products in foreign markets and increase the price of foreign products in Canada. As a result, net exports will increase. This additional policy channel will increase the ability of an expansionary monetary policy to affect aggregate demand.

When the Bank of Canada wants to reduce aggregate demand to reduce inflation, it engages in a contractionary monetary policy. The Bank of Canada sells government securities to increase interest rates and reduce aggregate demand. In a closed economy, the main effect is once again on domestic investment spending and purchases of consumer durables. In an open economy, higher interest rates will lead to a higher foreign exchange value of the dollar. The prices of Canadian products in foreign markets will increase, and the prices of foreign products in Canada will fall. As a result, net exports will fall. The contractionary policy will have a larger effect on aggregate demand, and therefore it will be more effective in slowing down the growth in economic activity. To summarize: *Monetary policy has a greater effect on aggregate demand in an open economy than in a closed economy.*

Fiscal Policy in an Open Economy

To engage in an expansionary fiscal policy, the federal government increases its purchases or cuts taxes. Increases in government purchases directly increase aggregate demand. Tax cuts increase aggregate demand by increasing household disposable income and business income, which results in increased consumption spending and investment spending. An expansionary fiscal policy may result in higher interest rates. In a closed economy, the main effect of higher interest rates is to reduce domestic investment spending and purchases of consumer durables. In an open economy, higher interest rates will also lead to an increase in the foreign exchange value of the dollar and a decrease in net exports. Therefore, in an open economy, an expansionary fiscal policy may be less effective because the *crowding out effect* may be larger. In a closed economy, only consumption and investment are crowded out by an expansionary fiscal policy. In an open economy, net exports may also be crowded out.

The government can fight inflation by using a contractionary fiscal policy to slow the growth of aggregate demand. A contractionary fiscal policy cuts government purchases or raises taxes to reduce household disposable income and consumption spending. It also reduces the federal budget deficit (or increases the budget surplus), which may lower interest rates. Lower interest rates will increase domestic investment and purchases of consumer durables, thereby offsetting some of the reduction in government spending and increases in taxes. In an open economy, lower interest rates will also reduce the foreign exchange value of the dollar and increase net exports. Therefore, in an open economy, a contractionary fiscal policy will have a smaller effect on aggregate demand and therefore will be less effective in slowing down an economy. In summary: *Fiscal policy has a smaller effect on aggregate demand in an open economy than in a closed economy.*

Economics in Your Life

The South Korean Central Bank and Your Car Loan

At the beginning of the chapter, we posed this question: What effect will the Bank of Korea's decision to sell its Canada bonds likely have on the interest rate that you pay on your car loan? To sell its holdings of Canada bonds, South Korea's central bank may have to offer them at a lower price. When the prices of bonds fall, the interest rates on them rise. As the interest rates on Canada bonds increase, the interest rates on corporate bonds and bank loans, including car loans, may also increase. So, the decision of the Bank of Korea has the potential to increase the interest rate you pay on your car loan. In practice, the interest rate on your car loan is likely to be affected only if the Bank of Korea sells a very large number of bonds and if investors consider it likely that other foreign central banks may soon do the same thing. The basic point is important, however: Economies are interdependent, and interest rates in Canada are not determined entirely by the actions of people in Canada.

Conclusion

At one time, Canadian policymakers—and economics textbooks—ignored the linkages between Canada and other economies. In the modern world, these linkages have become increasingly important, and economists and policymakers must take them into account when analyzing the economy. In Chapter 15, we will discuss further how the international financial system operates.

Read *An Inside Look* on the next page for a discussion of the changing value of the Canadian dollar against major foreign currencies.

The Canadian Dollar and the Effects of Economic Interdependence

ECONOMIST

Canada's Economy: Still Safe and Sound?

The last time the global economy cooled off in a hurry, frigid Canada proved the best place to take shelter. Its tightly regulated banks had avoided subprime mortgages entirely, its housing market was reasonably valued and its sound public finances gave the government ample room for stimulus. Moreover, strong Asian demand for Canadian commodity exports had tied the country's fortunes to the world's fastest-growing economies. While the United States and Europe plunged deep into recession in 2008, Canada's GDP barely shrunk at all. And when the recovery began the following year, Canada quickly returned to growth.

The events of the past few weeks have sharply increased fears of a double-dip recession elsewhere in the developed world. With worries about Europe's sovereign debt threatening Spain and Italy (and even possibly France); America's economy stagnating and its credit rating downgraded; and central banks in the developing world applying the brakes to control inflation, investors are frantically searching for safe havens. Will Canada prove as sturdy this time as it did in 2008?

Most of Canada's economic advantages remain intact. Employment is higher now than it was when the current Conservative government took office in 2006. Its battle-tested financial system is a source of strength. The government has been cutting the budget deficit since the recovery began in an effort to return it to balance by 2015, making Canada one of the only rich countries capable of further Keynesian pump-priming.

Moreover, Canada's highly diversified economy automatically gives it some cushioning from external shocks. Because the country exports so many natural resources like oil, minerals and timber, its currency tends to track commodity prices. The boom of the last decade has propelled Canada's dollar to parity with America's, forcing its manufacturers to become highly efficient to survive. If commodity prices fall and the loonie, as the currency is known, takes a tumble, Canadian producers of cars and machinery will gain competitiveness and should be able to expand their output. "In relative terms [to the rest of the world], Canada could hardly be positioned better," says Finn Poschmann, an economist at the C.D. Howe Institute, a think tank in Toronto.

Some economists express concern that Canada has followed a similar trajectory in recent years to that of the United States leading up to its financial collapse in 2008. Canada's trade surpluses have turned to deficits. Housing prices have soared since the economy started its rebound in 2009. And household debt, at 147% of GDP, is among the highest in the OECD. But Canada's balance of payments will improve if its dollar weakens. And with low interest rates and plain-vanilla mortgages, a full-blown Canadian credit crunch seems unlikely.

The biggest threat to Canada's economy is its intrinsic vulnerability to the outside world. With a population of 30m, the country does not consume enough on its own to maintain output if foreign demand dries up: exports make up one-third of its GDP. "Canada is not an island," Jim Flaherty, the finance minister, said earlier this week. "We are a trading nation." The world's rising economic tide has lifted Canada higher than most rich countries over the past decade. A falling one could pull it down nearly as far.

Source: Copyright © The Economist Newspaper Limited, London (August 10th, 2011).

Key Points in the Article

Due to a properly regulated financial sector and strong foreign demand for commodities, Canada emerged relatively unscathed from the Great Recession of 2007–2009. As a small open economy, Canada trades a large portion of its national output. In a typical year, Canada exports and imports around a third of its GDP.

Canada is a diversified economy made up of significant contributions from the commodity sectors (i.e., agriculture, energy, mining, and forestry) and the manufacturing sector. In recent years, rising commodity prices have caused Canada's currency to appreciate in value to near parity with the US dollar. Consequently, the value of Canadian imports recently exceeded that of Canadian exports.

Canadian consumers, in the face of historically low interest rates have loaded up with debt to a point where their obligations (relative to income) now exceed those of their OECD counterparts. However, the largest risks to Canada's economic prosperity are external due to its reliance on trade. Canada's future economic outlook is heavily dependent on global economic activity and events that occur outside its borders.

Analyzing the News

(a) As the saying goes, "I would rather be lucky than good." Canada has been both. Where has Canada been good? For years the federal government has been criticized by many market observers for not allowing Canada's largest banks to merge so that they could compete better in the global market of financial services. Talking heads in the media have described the Canadian financial system as boring and overregulated. The global financial crisis of 2008 saw much of the US and European banking systems decimated by improper lending standards, excessive risk taking, and too much leverage. In order to prevent the entire global financial system from collapsing, governments and central banks were required to step in and bail out their national banks that were deemed too big to fail. In the wake of the crisis, Canada's regulation policy, once derided, is now being held up as a model for other countries to follow.

Where has Canada been lucky? In the aftermath of the 2007–2009 Great Recession, global demand and growth have been weak as financial markets remain impaired and Western consumers' historically high debt levels have held back growth in consumption. Furthermore, many of the European nations are approaching unsustainable national debt levels and are responding by cutting spending and raising taxes. In the United States, consumer leverage remains high and so does unemployment. The one bright spot in global demand has been commodities, particularly energy. Canada, a nation replete with natural resources, has been a beneficiary of the commodity price and demand boom.

(b) The Canadian currency has appreciated in recent years because the relative demand for Canadian commodities and their prices have strengthened. In particular, the Canadian currency is often referred to in the media as a "petro currency," given the observation that strong daily increases in the price of oil are often accompanied by an appreciation of the Canadian dollar against the US dollar and other currencies. The article obliquely suggests that as a result of changes in global demand and currency appreciation, the relative composition of Canada's trade has shifted away from manufacturing toward commodities.

Thinking Critically

1. Why might Canada be borrowing internationally at this time, despite being a mature economy? Do you think this trend might continue? When might such borrowing be good for Canada's future? When might it not be so good? Mark Carney, the former governor of the Bank of Canada, has said that Canadians should be using Canada's current macroeconomic environment to invest in equipment, not houses. Why?

2. Do you think consumer debt levels in Canada have been influenced by the value of the Canadian currency? What is the likely impact the appreciation of the currency has had on inflationary pressures in Canada? How would that influence Bank of Canada policy? Why are interest rates so low in Canada despite its relative economic strength?

3. Have the benefits to the commodity price and currency appreciation been felt equally across all of Canada? Are there any sectors and regions of the economy that have been hurt by these events, and if so, which ones and where? Which provinces have the lowest unemployment rates in Canada? Why? What structural changes do we expect to see in the Canadian economy over time if recent trends persist?

Chapter Summary and Problems

Key Terms

Balance of payments, p. 436

Balance of trade, p. 437

Capital account, p. 438

Closed economy, p. 436

Currency appreciation, p. 443

Currency depreciation, p. 443

Current account, p. 437

Financial account, p. 438

Net foreign investment, p. 438

Nominal exchange rate, p. 440

Open economy, p. 436

Real exchange rate, p. 447

Saving and investment equation, p. 449

Speculators, p. 443

Summary

*LO **14.1** Nearly all economies are *open economies* that trade with and invest in other economies. A *closed economy* has no transactions in trade or finance with other economies. The *balance of payments* is the record of a country's trade with other countries in goods, services, and assets. The *current account* records a country's net exports, net investment income, and net transfers. The *financial account* shows investments a country has made abroad and foreign investments received by the country. The *balance of trade* is the difference between the value of the goods a country exports and the value of the goods a country imports. *Net foreign investment* is the difference between capital outflows from a country and capital inflows. The *capital account* is a part of the balance of payments that records relatively minor transactions. Apart from measurement errors, the sum of the current account balance and the financial account balance must equal zero. Therefore, the balance of payments must also equal zero.

LO **14.2** The *nominal exchange rate* is the value of one country's currency in terms of another country's currency. The exchange rate is determined in the foreign exchange market by the demand and supply of a country's currency. Changes in the exchange rate are caused by shifts in demand or supply. The three main sets of factors that cause the supply and demand curves in the foreign exchange market to shift are (1) changes in the demand for Canadian-produced goods and services and changes in the demand for foreign-produced goods and services, (2) changes in the desire to invest in Canada and changes in the desire to invest in foreign countries, and (3) changes in the expectations of currency traders—particularly *speculators*—concerning the likely future value of the dollar and the likely future value of foreign currencies. *Currency appreciation* occurs when a currency's market value increases relative to another currency. *Currency depreciation* occurs when a currency's market value decreases relative to another currency. The *real exchange rate* is the price of domestic goods in terms of foreign goods. The real exchange rate is calculated by multiplying the nominal exchange rate by the ratio of the domestic price level to the foreign price level.

LO **14.3** A current account deficit must be exactly offset by a financial account surplus. The financial account is equal to net capital flows, which is equal to net foreign investment but with the opposite sign. Because the current account balance is roughly equal to net exports, we can conclude that net exports will equal net foreign investment. National saving is equal to private saving plus government saving. Private saving is equal to national

income minus consumption and minus taxes. Government saving is the difference between taxes and government spending. As we saw in previous chapters, GDP (or national income) is equal to the sum of consumption, investment, government spending, and net exports. We can use this fact, our definitions of private and government saving, and the fact that net exports equal net foreign investment to arrive at an important relationship known as the *saving and investment equation*: $S = I + NFI$.

LO **14.4** When the government runs a budget deficit, national saving will decline unless private saving increases by the full amount of the budget deficit, which is unlikely. As the saving and investment equation ($S = I + NFI$) shows, the result of a decline in national saving must be a decline in either domestic investment or net foreign investment.

LO **14.5** When the Bank of Canada engages in an expansionary monetary policy, it buys government bonds to lower interest rates and increase aggregate demand. In a closed economy, the main effect of lower interest rates is on domestic investment spending and purchases of consumer durables. In an open economy, lower interest rates will also cause an increase in net exports. When the Bank of Canada wants to slow the rate of economic growth to reduce inflation, it engages in a contractionary monetary policy. With a contractionary policy, the Bank of Canada sells government securities to increase interest rates and reduce aggregate demand. In a closed economy, the main effect is once again on domestic investment and purchases of consumer durables. In an open economy, higher interest rates will also reduce net exports. We can conclude that monetary policy has a greater impact on aggregate demand in an open economy than in a closed economy. To engage in an expansionary fiscal policy, the government increases government spending or cuts taxes. An expansionary fiscal policy can lead to higher interest rates. In a closed economy, the main effect of higher interest rates is on domestic investment spending and spending on consumer durables. In an open economy, higher interest rates will also reduce net exports. A contractionary fiscal policy will reduce the budget deficit and may lower interest rates. In a closed economy, lower interest rates increase domestic investment and spending on consumer durables. In an open economy, lower interest rates also increase net exports. We can conclude that fiscal policy has a smaller impact on aggregate demand in an open economy than in a closed economy.

MyEconLab   Log in to MyEconLab to complete these exercises and get instant feedback.

*'Learning Objective' is abbreviated to 'LO' in the end of chapter material.

Review Questions

LO 14.1

1.1 What is the relationship among the current account, the financial account, and the balance of payments?

1.2 What is the difference between net exports and the current account balance?

1.3 Explain whether you agree with the following statement: "Canadian net foreign investment was negative in 2009, 2010, and 2011."

LO 14.2

2.1 Suppose that the current exchange rate between the dollar and the euro is €0.7 = $1. If the exchange rate changes to €0.8 = $1 has the euro appreciated or depreciated against the dollar?

2.2 Why do foreign households and foreign firms demand Canadian dollars in exchange for foreign currency? Why do Canadian households and Canadian firms supply Canadian dollars in exchange for foreign currency?

2.3 What are the three main sets of factors that cause the supply and demand curves in the foreign exchange market to shift?

LO 14.3

3.1 Explain the relationship between net exports and net foreign investment.

3.2 What is the saving and investment equation? If national saving declines, what will happen to domestic investment and net foreign investment?

3.3 If a country saves more than it invests domestically, what must be true of its net foreign investment?

LO 14.4

4.1 What happens to national saving when the government runs a budget surplus? What is the twin deficits idea? Did it hold for Canada in the 1990s? Briefly explain.

4.2 Why were the early 2010s particularly difficult times for Canadian exporters?

4.3 Why is the United States sometimes called the "world's largest debtor"?

LO 14.5

5.1 What is meant by a "policy channel"?

5.2 Why does monetary policy have a greater effect on aggregate demand in an open economy than in a closed economy?

5.3 Why does fiscal policy have a smaller effect on aggregate demand in an open economy than in a closed economy?

Problems and Applications

LO 14.1

1.1 Use the (hypothetical) information in the following table to prepare a balance of payments account, like the one shown in Table 14.1 on page 436. Assume that the balance on the capital account is zero.

Increase in foreign holdings of assets in Canada	$1181
Exports of goods	856
Imports of services	−256
Statistical discrepancy	?
Net transfers	−60
Exports of services	325
Income received on investments	392
Imports of goods	−1108
Increase in Canadian holdings of assets in foreign countries	−1040
Income payments on investments	−315

1.2 [**Related to** Don't Let This Happen to You **on page 439**] In 2010, Germany had a trade surplus of $204 billion and a current account balance of $188 billion. Explain how Germany's current account surplus could be smaller than its trade surplus. In 2010, would we expect that Germany's balance on financial account would have been −$188 billion? Briefly explain.

1.3 [**Related to** Solved Problem 14.1 **on page 439**] Suppose we know that a country has been receiving large inflows of foreign investment. What can we say about the country's current account balance?

1.4 An article in the *New York Times* observes that "China is quickly shifting from being a country known for exports to one capable of making huge investments in global financial markets, analysts say." Is there a connection between China's exports and its financial investments in other countries? Your answer should mention China's current account and its financial account.

From David Barboza, "China's Growing Overseas Portfolio," New York Times, May 9, 2011.

LO 14.2

2.1 [**Related to** Making the Connection **on page 441**] On January 1, 2002, the European Union comprised 15 member countries. Twelve of those countries eliminated their own individual currencies and began using a new common currency, the euro. For a three-year period from January 1, 1999, through December 31, 2001, these 12 countries priced goods and services in terms of both their own currencies and the euro. During that period, the value of their currencies was fixed against each other and against the euro. So during that time, the US dollar had an exchange rate against each of these currencies and against the euro. The information in the following table shows the fixed exchange rates of four European currencies against the euro and their exchange rates against the US dollar on March 2, 2001. Use the information below to calculate the exchange rate between the US dollar and the euro (in euros per US dollar) on March 2, 2001.

Currency	Units per Euro (Fixed)	Units per US Dollar (as of March 2, 2001)
German mark	1.9558	2.0938
French franc	6.5596	7.0223
Italian lira	1936.2700	2072.8700
Portuguese escudo	200.4820	214.6300

2.2 Use the graph to answer the following questions.

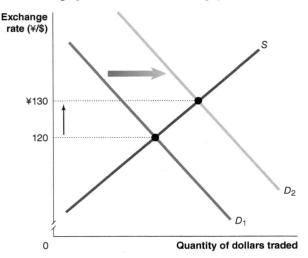

a. Briefly explain whether the dollar appreciated or depreciated against the yen.
b. Which of the following events could have caused the shift in demand shown in the graph?
   i. Interest rates in Canada decline.
   ii. Income rises in Japan.
   iii. Speculators begin to believe the value of the Canadian dollar will be higher in the future.

2.3 [**Related to** Making the Connection **on page 444**] According to an article in the *Economist*: "[T]he combination of commodity revenues and investors seeking safety in Canadian assets has caused the currency to take off. After falling as low as 77 American cents during the recession, the Canadian dollar has now returned to rough parity with the greenback."
Why did the Canadian dollar lose value against the US dollar during the global economic crisis of 2007–2009?
The Economist, 6 May 2010. http://www.economist.com/node/16060113 (Accessed on May 1, 2012).

2.4 [**Related to** Making the Connection **on page 444**] According to an article in the *Financial Post*: "If there's still any doubt whether the Canadian dollar is a commodity currency, it can be put to rest: the venerable loonie is right up there with the Aussie and New Zealand dollars as currencies driven largely by the trade of unfinished materials."
What does it mean to say that "the Canadian dollar is a commodity currency"?
Financial Post, 20 April 2012. http://business.financialpost.com/2012/04/20/yes-the-loonie-is-a-commodity-currency-heres-proof (Accessed on May 1, 2012).

2.5 [**Related to** Don't Let This Happen to You **on page 446**] If we know the exchange rate between Country A's currency and Country B's currency and we know the exchange rate between Country B's currency and Country C's currency, then we can compute the exchange rate between Country A's currency and Country C's currency.
a. Suppose the exchange rate between the Japanese yen and the Canadian dollar is currently ¥75 = $1 and the exchange rate between the British pound and the Canadian dollar is £0.62 = $1. What is the exchange rate between the yen and the pound?
b. Suppose the exchange rate between the yen and dollar changes to ¥85 = $1 and the exchange rate between the pound and dollar changes to £0.55 = $1. Has the dollar appreciated or depreciated against the yen? Has the dollar appreciated or depreciated against the pound? Has the yen appreciated or depreciated against the pound?

2.6 [**Related to** Solved Problem 14.2 **on page 447**] When a country's currency appreciates, is this generally good news or bad news for the country's consumers? Is it generally good news or bad news for the country's businesses? Explain your reasoning.

LO 14.3

3.1 According to an article in the *Financial Post*: "'It is reasonable to expect that Canada will attract for the next decade or so sizeable foreign capital . . . and the question is what are we going to do with that capital,' [Mark] Carney told a business audience in Ottawa. 'Are we going to build houses . . . or are we going to invest in our businesses and retool our competitiveness?'"
What did then Bank of Canada governor Mark Carney mean by "Are we going to build houses . . . or are we going to invest in our businesses and retool our competitiveness?"
Financial Post, 27 April 2012. http://business.financialpost.com/2012/04/27/use-foreign-funds-to-boost-canadian-business-not-housing-carney-warns (Accessed on May 1, 2012).

3.2 In 2010, domestic investment in Japan was 20.6 percent of GDP, and Japanese net foreign investment was 1.3 percent of GDP. What percentage of GDP was Japanese national saving?

3.3 In 2010, France's net foreign investment was negative. Which was larger in France in 2010: national saving or domestic investment? Briefly explain.

3.4 [**Related to** Solved Problem 14.3 **on page 450**] Look again at *Solved Problem 14.3*, in which we derived the saving and investment equation $S = I + NX$. In deriving this equation, we assumed that national income was equal to Y. But Y only includes income *earned* by households. In the modern Canadian economy, households receive substantial transfer payments—such as social security payments and Employment Insurance payments—from the government. Suppose that we define *national income* as being equal to $Y + TR$, where TR equals government transfer payments, and we also define government spending as being equal to $G + TR$. Show that after making these adjustments, we end up with the same saving and investment equation.

LO 14.4

4.1 Tim Condon, an economist at the European bank ING, was quoted in the *Wall Street Journal* in 2011 as predicting that "China's current account or saving-investment surplus [will be in] the 1–2% of GDP range. . . ." Is he correct in referring to China's current account as being the same as its saving-investment surplus? Briefly explain. If the Chinese government runs a large budget deficit, what will be the likely effect on its current account?

Josh Chin, "Economists React: Chinese Imports Way Up in August," Wall Street Journal, September 12, 2011.

4.2 According to an article in the *Wall Street Journal*:

> Economists at China International Capital Corp., or CICC, say the companies that will suffer most from a stronger yuan are textile and apparel makers and office equipment producers. . . . That could also mean a sting for clothing retailers such as Wal-Mart Stores Inc. that buy a lot from China. . . .

a. Does a "stronger yuan" mean that the yuan will exchange for more or fewer dollars?

b. How can both Chinese companies, such as apparel makers, and foreign companies, such as Wal-Mart Stores and Carrefour, be hurt by a stronger yuan?

c. What effect will a stronger yuan be likely to have on the Chinese current account? What effect is it likely to have on the US current account?

Jason Dean, Norihiko Shirouzu, Clare Ansberry and Kersten Zhang, "Yuan Impact: General Manufacturing," Wall Street Journal, June 21, 2010.

4.3 [**Related to** Making the Connection **on page 452**] Why might "the continued willingness of foreign investors to buy Canadian stocks and bonds and foreign companies to build factories in Canada" result in Canada running a current account deficit?

LO 14.5

5.1 An article in the *Economist* magazine describes Ireland as "an extraordinarily open economy." Is fiscal policy in Ireland likely to be more or less effective than it would be in a less open economy? Briefly explain.

"Celtic Cross," Economist, May 26, 2011.

5.2 Suppose that Bank of Canada policy leads to higher interest rates in Canada.

a. How will this policy affect real GDP in the short run if Canada is a closed economy?

b. How will this policy affect real GDP in the short run if Canada is an open economy?

c. How will your answer to part (b) change if interest rates also rise in the countries that are the major trading partners of Canada?

5.3 Suppose the federal government increases spending without also increasing taxes. In the short run, how will this action affect real GDP and the price level in a closed economy? How will the effects of this action differ in an open economy?

MyEconLab   MyEconLab is an online tool designed to help you master the concepts covered in your course. It will create an adaptive, highly personalized study plan to stimulate and measure your learning. Log in to take advantage of this powerful study aid, and to access quizzes and other valuable course-related material.

The International Financial System

Chapter Outline and Learning Objectives

15.1 Exchange Rate Systems, page 464
   Understand how different exchange rate systems operate.

15.2 The Current Exchange Rate System, page 465
   Discuss the three key features of the current exchange rate system.

15.3 International Capital Markets, page 478
   Discuss the growth of international capital markets.

AP Photos/MEIGNEUX

Airbus Deals with Fluctuating Exchange Rates

In 1967, France, Germany, and the United Kingdom formed Airbus as a firm to develop and manufacture passenger aircraft. The new firm was formally organized as a manufacturing subsidiary of the European Aeronautic Defence and Space Company (EADS), located in France. The first Airbus plane, the A300, was introduced at the Paris Air Show in 1969. Over the following decades, Airbus manufactured more than 6000 passenger aircraft and sold them to airlines around the world.

In October 2009, Airbus delivered its first A380 super-jumbo jetliner to Air France. Although the sale was cause for celebration among Airbus executives, it had a downside. Even though Airbus is a European firm and Air France is a European airline, the worldwide aerospace industry conducts business in US dollars. Because Airbus received dollars from Air France rather than euros, Airbus had to convert the dollars it received into euros. Between 2001, when Air France agreed to buy 10 A380 jetliners from Airbus, and 2009, the exchange value of the euro increased by about 60 percent against the US dollar—or, in other words, the value of the dollar had decreased against the euro. Therefore, when Airbus converted the dollars it received from Air France into euros, it received many fewer euros than it would have if the value of the dollar hadn't declined against the euro.

Airbus's main competitor is Boeing, a US multinational aerospace and defence corporation founded in 1916, which conducts its buying and selling in US dollars. As a result, Boeing is not subject to losses resulting from fluctuations in exchange rates. Unlike Airbus, Air France has suffered less from exchange rate changes because it receives much of its revenue in euros, while the costs of planes, fuel, and other inputs purchased by Air France are priced in US dollars. So, an increase in the value of the euro against the US dollar increases Air France's profits.

In 2011, EADS announced that its first-half profits decreased by 41 percent due to the appreciation of the euro relative to the US dollar. As a result, Airbus announced that it was considering pricing its aircraft in euros.

In this chapter, we will look more closely at the international financial system and at what determines fluctuations in exchange rates, **AN INSIDE LOOK** on **page 482** discusses a bill that the US Senate passed to raise tariffs on Chinese imports in response to claims that the Chinese yuan was undervalued.

Sources: Based on Daniel Michaels, "Strong Euro Weighs on Airbus, Suppliers," Wall Street Journal, October 30, 2009; and David Pearson, "EADS Hit By Currency Swings," Wall Street Journal, July 29, 2011.

Economics in Your Life

Exchange Rate Risk in Your Life

Suppose that you decide to take a job in Spain. You plan to work there for the next 10 years, build up some savings, and then return to Canada. As you prepare for your move, you read that economists expect the average productivity of Spanish firms to grow faster than the average productivity of Canadian firms over the next 10 years. If economists are correct, then, all else being equal, will the savings that you accumulate (in euros) be worth more or less in Canadian dollars than they would have been worth without the relative gains in Spanish productivity? As you read this chapter, see if you can answer this question. You can check your answer against the one we provide on page 480 at the end of this chapter.

A key fact about the international economy is that exchange rates among the major currencies fluctuate. These fluctuations have important consequences for firms, consumers, and governments. In Chapter 14, we discussed the basics of how exchange rates are determined. We also looked at the relationship between a country's imports and exports, as well as at capital flows into and out of a country. In this chapter, we will look further at the international financial system and at the role central banks play in the system.

Understand how different exchange rate systems operate.

Floating currency The outcome of a country allowing its currency's exchange rate to be determined by demand and supply.

Exchange rate system An agreement among countries about how exchange rates should be determined.

Managed float exchange rate system The current exchange rate system, under which the value of most currencies is determined by demand and supply, with occasional government intervention.

Fixed exchange rate system A system under which countries agree to keep the exchange rates among their currencies fixed for long periods.

Bretton Woods system An exchange rate system that lasted from 1944 to 1973, under which countries pledged to buy and sell their currencies at a fixed rate against the dollar.

Exchange Rate Systems

A country's exchange rate can be determined in several ways. Some countries simply allow the exchange rate to be determined by demand and supply, just as other prices are. A country that allows demand and supply to determine the value of its currency is said to have a **floating currency**. Some countries attempt to keep the exchange rate between their currency and another currency constant. For example, China kept the exchange rate constant between its currency, the yuan, and the US dollar, from 1994 until 2005, when it announced it would allow greater exchange rate flexibility. When countries can agree on how exchange rates should be determined, economists say that there is an **exchange rate system**. Currently, many countries, including Canada and the United States, allow their currencies to float most of the time, although they occasionally intervene to buy and sell their currency or other currencies to affect exchange rates. In other words, many countries attempt to *manage* the float of their currencies. As a result, the current exchange rate system is a **managed float exchange rate system**.

Historically, the two most important alternatives to the managed float exchange rate system were the *gold standard* and the *Bretton Woods system*. These were both **fixed exchange rate systems**, where exchange rates remained constant for long periods. Under the gold standard, a country's currency consisted of gold coins and paper currency that the government was committed to redeem for gold. When countries agree to keep the value of their currencies constant, there is a fixed exchange rate system. The gold standard was a fixed exchange rate system that lasted from the nineteenth century until the 1930s.

Under the gold standard, exchange rates were determined by the relative amounts of gold in each country's currency, and the size of a country's money supply was determined by the amount of gold available. To rapidly expand its money supply during a war or an economic depression, a country would need to abandon the gold standard. In response to the Great Depression, by the mid-1930s, most countries, including Canada and the United States, had abandoned the gold standard. Although during the following decades there were occasional discussions about restoring the gold standard, no serious attempt to do so occurred.

A conference held in Bretton Woods, New Hampshire, in 1944 set up an exchange rate system in which the United States pledged to buy or sell gold at a fixed price of $35 per ounce. The central banks of all other members of the new **Bretton Woods system** pledged to buy and sell their currencies at a fixed rate against the US dollar. By fixing their exchange rates against the US dollar, these countries were fixing the exchange rates among their currencies as well. Unlike under the gold standard, neither the United States nor any other country was willing to redeem its paper currency for gold domestically. The United States would redeem dollars for gold only if they were presented by a foreign central bank. Fixed exchange rate regimes can run into difficulties because exchange rates are not free to adjust quickly to changes in demand and supply for currencies. As we will see in the next section, central banks often encounter difficulty if they are required to keep an exchange rate fixed over a period of years. By the early 1970s, the difficulty of keeping exchange rates fixed led to the end of the Bretton Woods system.

Don't Let This Happen to You

Remember That Modern Currencies Are Fiat Money

Although Canada has not been on the gold standard since the beginning of World War I, many people still believe that somehow gold continues to "back" Canadian currency. Although the Canadian government still owns billions of dollars worth of gold bars, this gold no longer has any connection to the amount of paper money issued by the Bank of Canada.

As we saw in Chapter 10, Canadian currency—like the currencies of other countries—is *fiat money*, which means that it has no value except as money. The link between gold and money that existed for centuries has been broken in modern economies.

MyEconLab

Your Turn: Test your understanding by doing related problem 1.1 on page 485 at the end of this chapter.

The Current Exchange Rate System

The current exchange rate system has three important aspects:

1. Canada allows the dollar to float against other major currencies.
2. Seventeen countries in Europe have adopted a single currency, the **euro**.
3. Some countries have attempted to keep their currencies' exchange rates fixed against the US dollar or another major currency.

We begin our discussion of the current exchange rate system by looking at the changing value of the dollar over time. In discussing the value of the dollar, we can look further at what determines exchange rates in the short run and in the long run.

15.2 LEARNING OBJECTIVE

Discuss the three key features of the current exchange rate system.

Euro The common currency of many European countries.

The Floating Canadian Dollar

Since 1973, the value of the Canadian dollar has fluctuated widely against other major currencies. Panel (a) of Figure 15.1 shows the exchange rate between the Canadian dollar and the US dollar between January 1974 and January 2013, and panel (b) shows the

(a) The exchange rate between the Canadian dollar and the US dollar

(b) The exchange rate between the Canadian dollar and the Japanese yen

Figure 15.1   **US Dollar–Canadian Dollar and Yen–Canadian Dollar Exchange Rates, 1974–2013**

Panel (a) shows that from the end of the Bretton Woods system through January 2013, there have been a number of long swings in the US dollar per Canadian dollar exchange rate, but that overall the Canadian dollar did not lose value against the US dollar. Panel (b) shows that during the same period, the Canadian dollar lost value against the Japanese yen.

Source: Data from Statistics Canada CANSIM II series V37426 and V37456 (Accessed 21 April 2012).

exchange rate between the Canadian dollar and the Japanese yen for the same period. Remember that the dollar increases in value when it takes more units of foreign currency to buy $1, and it falls in value when it takes fewer units of foreign currency to buy $1. From January 1974 to January 2013, the Canadian dollar lost about 75 percent in value against the yen, and there have been a number of long swings in the US dollar per Canadian dollar exchange rate. Overall, however, the Canadian dollar did not lose much value against the US dollar over this period.

Making the Connection | The Canadian Province of . . . Arizona?

In 2011, there seemed to be a lot of Canadians buying houses in Phoenix and other cities in Arizona. For many years, some Canadians have found buying a second home in Arizona or Florida a good way to avoid the harsh Canadian winters. As panel (a) of Figure 15.1 shows, the value of the US dollar has been declining relative to the Canadian dollar for most of the period since 2000. Although the value of the US dollar soared by more than 30 percent relative to the Canadian dollar during the height of the financial crisis in 2008, it continued to decline during most of the period after the crisis had ended. The falling value of the US dollar was a great help to Canadian buyers of US homes.

In late 2001, it took 1.60 Canadian dollars to purchase 1 US dollar. So, a Canadian purchasing a house in Phoenix priced at US$125 000 would have had to pay Can$200 000. In the summer of 2011, it took only 0.95 Canadian dollars to purchase 1 US dollar. The stronger Canadian dollar meant that a Canadian could now purchase a house in Phoenix priced at US$125 000 for only Can$118 750. In other words, the decline in the value of the US dollar resulted in a more than 40 percent reduction in the price of the house in Canadian dollars. As one Canadian who was buying a vacation home in Desert Ridge, Arizona, put it: "It's purchasing power, plain and simple. In the days when our dollar was 60 or 65 [US] cents, I wouldn't even be talking to you. The strong Canadian dollar has created a lot of opportunities for Canadians." In addition to the decline in the value of the US dollar, many Canadians found Arizona to be an ideal place to buy a second home because overbuilding in the state during the housing bubble had resulted in many property owners being willing to accept sharply lower prices (in US dollars). Little wonder that by 2011, restaurants and bars in Arizona began staging Canada Day celebrations to attract the growing Canadian population.

In addition to individual Canadians looking to buy second homes in Arizona, some Canadian investors bought multiple properties, hoping to resell them for a profit in the future after local housing prices had risen and after the value of the US dollar had increased relative to the Canadian dollar. Some Canadian manufacturers have also shifted operations to the United States. For example, E.H. Price, a firm that produces ventilation systems for commercial buildings and is headquartered in Winnipeg, Manitoba, doubled the size of its operations in the United States, where nearly half of its sales were. The rising value of the Canadian dollar would have priced its products out of the US market if it had continued manufacturing the products in Canada.

Of course, further fluctuations in the value of the Canadian dollar could pose problems for Canadians buying and investing in the United States. For example, if the value of the US dollar were to continue to decline, then Canadians who bought second homes in the United States or Canadian investors buying multiple US homes would take a loss in terms of Canadian dollars should they decide to sell. An increase in the value of the US dollar would be good news for Canadian owners of US houses but bad news for

Thomas Barwick/Getty Images

In 2011, many individual Canadians purchased second homes in Arizona, thanks to the favourable exchange rate.

Canadian manufacturers if they intended to export goods to Canada from their US plants.

Sources: Based on Chana R. Schoenberger, "Canadians Warm to Phoenix," Wall Street Journal, October 8, 2011; Julie Schmit, "Foreign Buyers Lifting U.S. Home Sales," USA Today, July 14, 2011; and Barrie McKenna, "For Canadian Manufacturers, Foreign Assets Tantalizingly Cheap," (Toronto) Globe and Mail, June 12, 2011.

Your Turn: Test your understanding by doing related problem 2.1 on page 485 at the end of this chapter.

MyEconLab

What Determines Exchange Rates in the Long Run?

Over the past 40 years, why has the value of the Canadian dollar fallen against the Japanese yen and fluctuated wildly against the US dollar? In the short run, the two most important causes of exchange rate movements are changes in interest rates—which cause investors to change their views of which countries' financial investments will yield the highest returns—and changes in investors' expectations about the future values of currencies. Over the long run, other factors are also important in explaining movements in exchange rates.

The Theory of Purchasing Power Parity It seems reasonable that, in the long run, exchange rates should be at a level that makes it possible to buy the same amount of goods and services with the equivalent amount of any country's currency. In other words, the purchasing power of every country's currency should be the same. The idea that in the long run, exchange rates move to equalize the purchasing powers of different currencies is referred to as the theory of **purchasing power parity**.

To make the theory of purchasing power parity clearer, consider a simple example. Suppose that a Hershey candy bar has a price of $1 in Canada and £1 in the United Kingdom and that the exchange rate is £1 = $1. In that case, at least with respect to candy bars, the dollar and the pound have equivalent purchasing power. If the price of a Hershey bar increases to £2 in the United Kingdom but stays at $1 in Canada, the exchange rate will have to change to £2 per $1 in order for the pound to maintain its relative purchasing power. As long as exchange rates adjust to reflect purchasing power, it will be possible to buy a Hershey bar for $1 in Canada or to exchange $1 for £2 and buy the candy bar in the United Kingdom.

If exchange rates are not at the values indicated by purchasing power parity, it appears that there are opportunities to make profits. For example, suppose a Hershey candy bar sells for £2 in the United Kingdom and $1 in Canada and the exchange rate between the dollar and the pound is £1 = $1. In this case, it would be possible to exchange £1 million for $1 million and use the dollars to buy 1 million Hershey bars in Canada. The Hershey bars could then be shipped to the United Kingdom, where they could be sold for £2 million. The result of these transactions would be a profit of £1 million (minus any shipping costs). In fact, if the dollar–pound exchange rate does not reflect the purchasing power for many products—not just Hershey bars—this process could be repeated until extremely large profits were made. In practice, though, as people attempted to make these profits by exchanging pounds for dollars, they would bid up the value of the dollar until it reached the purchasing power exchange rate of £2 = $1. Once the exchange rate reflected the purchasing power of the two currencies, there would be no further opportunities for profit. This mechanism appears to guarantee that exchange rates will be at the levels determined by purchasing power parity.

Three real-world complications, though, keep purchasing power parity from being a complete explanation of exchange rates, even in the long run:

1. **Not all products can be traded internationally.** Where goods are traded internationally, profits can be made whenever exchange rates do not reflect their purchasing power parity values. However, more than half of all goods and services produced in Canada and most other countries are not traded internationally. When goods are

Purchasing power parity The theory that in the long run, exchange rates move to equalize the purchasing powers of different currencies.

not traded internationally, their prices will not be the same in every country. For instance, suppose that the exchange rate is £1 for $1, but the price for having a cavity filled by a dentist is twice as high in Canada as it is in the United Kingdom. In this case, there is no way to buy up the low-priced British service and resell it in Canada. Because many goods and services are not traded internationally, exchange rates will not reflect exactly the relative purchasing powers of currencies.

2. **Products and consumer preferences are different across countries.** We expect the same product to sell for the same price around the world, but if a product is similar but not identical to another product, their prices might be different. For example, a 3-ounce Hershey candy bar may sell for a different price in Canada than does a 3-ounce Cadbury candy bar in the United Kingdom. Prices of the same product may also differ across countries if consumer preferences differ. If consumers in the United Kingdom like candy bars more than do consumers in Canada, a Hershey candy bar may sell for more in the United Kingdom than in Canada.

3. **Countries impose barriers to trade.** Most countries, including Canada and the United States, impose *tariffs* and *quotas* on imported goods. A **tariff** is a tax imposed by a government on imports. A **quota** is a government-imposed limit on the quantity of a good that can be imported. For example, Canada has a quota on imports of milk. As a result, the price of milk in Canada is much higher than the price of milk in other countries. Because of the quota, there is no legal way to buy up the cheap foreign milk and resell it in Canada.

Tariff A tax imposed by a government on imports.

Quota A numerical limit that a government imposes on the quantity of a good that can be imported into the country.

Making the Connection | **The Big Mac Theory of Exchange Rates**

In a lighthearted attempt to test the accuracy of the theory of purchasing power parity, the *Economist* magazine regularly compares the prices of Big Macs in different countries. If purchasing power parity holds, you should be able to take the dollars required to buy a Big Mac in the United States and exchange them for the amount of foreign currency needed to buy a Big Mac in any other country. The following table is for July 2011, when Big Macs were selling for an average price of $4.07 in the United States. The "implied exchange rate" shows what the exchange rate would be if purchasing power parity held for Big Macs. For example, a Big Mac sold for 20.0 pesos in Argentina and $4.07 in the United States, so for purchasing power parity to hold, the exchange rate should have been 20.0 pesos/US$4.07, or 4.91 pesos = 1 US dollar. The actual exchange rate in July 2011 was 4.13 pesos = 1 US dollar. So, on Big Mac purchasing power parity grounds, the Argentine peso was *overvalued*

No es un sueño hecho realidad. Son tres.

Getty Images

Is the price of a Big Mac in Buenos Aires the same as the price of a Big Mac in New York?

against the US dollar by 19 percent (((4.91 − 4.13)/4.13) × 100 = 19 percent). That is, if Big Mac purchasing power parity held, it would have taken 19 percent more Argentine pesos to buy a US dollar than it actually did.

Could you take advantage of this difference between the purchasing power parity exchange rate and the actual exchange rate to become fabulously wealthy by buying up low-priced Big Macs in New York and reselling them at a higher price in Buenos Aires? Unfortunately, the low-priced US Big Macs would be a soggy mess by the time you got them to Buenos Aires. The fact that Big Mac prices are not the same around the world illustrates one reason purchasing power parity does not hold exactly: Many goods are not traded internationally.

Country	Big Mac Price	Implied Exchange Rate	Actual Exchange Rate
Mexico	32.0 pesos	7.86 pesos per US dollar	11.70 pesos per US dollar
Japan	320 yen	78.62 yen per US dollar	78.40 yen per US dollar
United Kingdom	2.39 pounds	0.59 pound per US dollar	0.61 pound per US dollar
Switzerland	6.50 Swiss francs	1.60 Swiss francs per US dollar	0.81 Swiss franc per US dollar
Indonesia	22,534 rupiahs	5,537 rupiahs per US dollar	8,523 rupiahs per US dollar
Canada	4.73 Canadian dollars	1.16 Canadian dollars per US dollar	0.95 Canadian dollar per US dollar
China	14.7 yuan	3.61 yuan per US dollar	6.45 yuan per US dollar

Source: Data from "Currency Comparisons, to Go," Economist, July 28, 2011.

Your Turn: Test your understanding by doing related problem 2.4 on page 485 at the end of this chapter.

MyEconLab

Solved Problem **15.1**

Calculating Purchasing Power Parity Exchange Rates Using Big Macs

Fill in the missing values in the following table. Remember that the implied exchange rate shows what the exchange rate would be if purchasing power parity held for Big Macs. Assume that the Big Mac is selling for $4.07 in the United States. Explain whether the US dollar is overvalued or undervalued relative to each currency and predict what will happen in the future to each exchange rate. Finally, calculate the implied exchange rate between the Polish zloty and the Brazilian real (plural: reais) and explain which currency is undervalued in terms of Big Mac purchasing power parity.

Country	Big Mac Price	Implied Exchange Rate	Actual Exchange Rate
Brazil	9.50 reais		1.54 reais per US dollar
Poland	8.63 zlotys		2.80 zlotys per US dollar
South Korea	3700 won		1056 won per US dollar
Malaysia	7.20 ringgits		2.97 ringgits per US dollar

Solving the Problem

Step 1: Review the chapter material. This problem is about the theory of purchasing power parity, as illustrated by prices of Big Macs, so you may want to review the sections "The Theory of Purchasing Power Parity," which begins on page 467, and *Making the Connection* "The Big Mac Theory of Exchange Rates" on page 468.

Step 2: Fill in the table. To calculate the purchasing power parity exchange rate, divide the foreign currency price of a Big Mac by the US price. For example, the implied exchange rate between the Brazilian real and the US dollar is 9.50 reais/$4.07, or 2.33 reais per US dollar.

Country	Big Mac Price	Implied Exchange Rate	Actual Exchange Rate
Brazil	9.50 reais	2.33 reais per US dollar	1.54 reais per US dollar
Poland	8.63 zlotys	2.12 zlotys per US dollar	2.80 zlotys per US dollar
South Korea	3700 won	909 won per US dollar	1056 won per US dollar
Malaysia	7.20 ringgits	1.77 ringgits per US dollar	2.97 ringgits per US dollar

Step 3: Explain whether the US dollar is overvalued or undervalued against the other currencies. The US dollar is overvalued if the actual exchange rate is greater than the implied exchange rate, and it is undervalued if the actual exchange rate is less than the implied exchange rate. In this case, the US dollar is overvalued against the zloty, the won, and the ringgit, but it is undervalued against the real. So, we would predict that in the future the value of the US dollar should rise against the real but fall against the zloty, the won, and the ringgit.

Step 4: Calculate the implied exchange rate between the zloty and the real. The implied exchange rate between the zloty and the real is 8.63 zlotys/9.50 reais, or 0.91 zlotys per real. We can calculate the actual exchange rate by taking the ratio of zlotys per dollar to reais per dollar: 2.80 zlotys/1.54 reais, or 1.82 zlotys per real. Therefore, the zloty is undervalued relative to the real because our Big Mac purchasing power parity calculation tells us that it should take fewer zlotys to buy a real than it actually does.

Source: Data from "Currency Comparisons, to Go," Economist, July 28, 2011.

MyEconLab **Your Turn:** For more practice, do related problem 2.5 on page 485 at the end of this chapter.

The Four Determinants of Exchange Rates in the Long Run

We can take into account the shortcomings of the theory of purchasing power parity to develop a more complete explanation of how exchange rates are determined in the long run. There are four main determinants of exchange rates in the long run:

1. **Relative price levels.** The purchasing power parity theory is correct in arguing that in the long run, the most important determinant of exchange rates between two countries' currencies is their relative price levels. If prices of goods and services rise faster in Canada than in the United States, the value of the Canadian dollar has to decline to maintain demand for Canadian products. Over the past 30 years, prices in Canada have risen slightly faster than average prices in the United States. The relationship among inflation rates helps explain why the US dollar has increased slightly in value against the Canadian dollar.

2. **Relative rates of productivity growth.** When the productivity of a firm increases, the firm is able to produce more goods and services using fewer workers, machines, or other inputs. The firm's costs of production fall, and usually so do the prices of its products. If the average productivity of Japanese firms increases faster than

the average productivity of Canadian firms, Japanese products will have relatively lower prices than Canadian products, which increases the quantity demanded of Japanese products relative to Canadian products. As a result, the value of the yen should rise against the dollar. For most of the period from the early 1970s to the early 1990s, Japanese productivity increased faster than Canadian productivity, which contributed to the fall in the value of the Canadian dollar versus the yen.

3. **Preferences for domestic and foreign goods.** If consumers in the United States increase their preferences for Canadian products, the demand for Canadian dollars will increase relative to the demand for US dollars, and the Canadian dollar will increase in value relative to the US dollar. During the 1970s and 1980s, many Canadian consumers increased their preferences for Japanese products, particularly automobiles and consumer electronics. This greater preference for Japanese products helped to increase the value of the yen relative to the Canadian dollar.

4. **Tariffs and quotas.** The Canadian milk quota forces Canadian firms to buy expensive Canadian milk rather than less expensive foreign milk. The quota increases the demand for Canadian dollars relative to the currencies of foreign milk producers and, therefore, leads to a higher exchange rate. Changes in tariffs and quotas have not been a significant factor in explaining trends in the US dollar–Canadian dollar or yen–Canadian dollar exchange rates.

Because these four factors change over time, the value of one country's currency can increase or decrease by substantial amounts in the long run. These changes in exchange rates can create problems for firms. A decline in the value of a country's currency lowers the foreign currency prices of the country's exports and increases the prices of imports. An increase in the value of a country's currency has the reverse effect. Firms can be both helped and hurt by exchange rate fluctuations.

The Euro

A second key aspect of the current exchange rate system is that most Western European countries have adopted a single currency. After World War II, many of the countries of Western Europe wanted to more closely integrate their economies. In 1957, Belgium, France, West Germany, Italy, Luxembourg, and the Netherlands signed the Treaty of Rome, which established the European Economic Community, often referred to as the *European Common Market*. Tariffs and quotas on products being shipped within the European Common Market were greatly reduced. Over the years, Britain, Sweden, Denmark, Finland, Austria, Greece, Ireland, Spain, and Portugal joined the European Economic Community, which was renamed the European Union (EU) in 1991. By 2013, 27 countries were members of the EU.

EU members decided to move to a common currency beginning in 1999. Three of the 15 countries that were then members of the EU—the United Kingdom, Denmark, and Sweden—decided to retain their domestic currencies. The move to a common currency took place in several stages. On January 1, 1999, the exchange rates of the 12 participating countries (risen to 17 in 2013) were permanently fixed against each other and against the common currency, the *euro*. At first the euro was a pure *unit of account*. No euro currency was actually in circulation, although firms began quoting prices in both the domestic currency and euros. On January 1, 2002, euro coins and paper currency were introduced, and on June 1, 2002, the old domestic currencies were withdrawn from circulation. Figure 15.2 shows the countries in the EU that had adopted the euro as of 2011. These countries are sometimes referred to as the "eurozone."

A new European Central Bank (ECB) was also established. Although the central banks of the member countries continue to exist, the ECB has assumed responsibility for monetary policy and for issuing currency. The ECB is run by a governing council that consists of a six-member executive board—appointed by the participating governments—and the governors of the central banks of the 17 member countries that have adopted the euro. The ECB represents a unique experiment in allowing a multinational organization to control the domestic monetary policies of independent countries.

Figure 15.2

Countries Adopting the Euro

The 17 member countries of the European Union that have adopted the euro as their common currency as of 2013 are shaded with red hash marks. The members of the EU that have not adopted the euro are coloured tan. Countries in white are not members of the EU.

Making the Connection

Can the Euro Survive?

The euro was first introduced as a currency at the beginning of 2002. The period from then until the beginning of the global economic downturn at the end of 2007 was one of relative economic stability in most of Europe. With low interest rates, low inflation rates, and expanding employment and production, the advantages of the euro seemed obvious. The countries using the euro no longer had to deal with problems caused by fluctuating exchange rates. Having a common currency also makes it easier for consumers and firms to buy and sell across borders. It is no longer necessary for someone in France to exchange francs for marks in order to do business in Germany. Having a single currency reduces costs and increases competition. Some of the lower-income European countries seemed to particularly prosper under the euro. The Spanish economy grew at a rate of 3.9 percent between 1999 and 2007. The unemployment rate in Spain had been nearly 20 percent in the mid-1990s, but it had dropped to 7.9 percent in 2007. Ireland and Greece also experienced rapid growth during these years.

German Chancellor Angela Merkel, then Greek Prime Minister George Papandreou, left, and then French President Nicolas Sarkozy debated how to handle Greece's financial rescue.

But by 2008, with the global recession gathering force, some economists and policymakers were starting to question whether the euro was making the economic crisis worse. The countries using the euro are not able to pursue independent monetary policies, which are instead determined by the ECB from its headquarters in Frankfurt, Germany. Countries that were particularly hard hit by the recession—for example, Spain, where the unemployment rate had more than doubled to 18 percent by 2009 and was over 26 percent in 2013—were unable to pursue a more expansionary policy than the ECB was willing to implement for the eurozone as a whole. Similarly, countries could not attempt to revive their exports by allowing their exchange rates to depreciate because (1) most of their exports were to other eurozone countries, and (2) the value of the euro was determined by factors affecting the eurozone as a whole.

Problems in the eurozone were made worse by a *sovereign debt* crisis that developed in 2010. Sovereign debt refers to bonds issued by a government. The recession of 2007–2009 caused large increases in government spending and reductions in tax revenues in a number of European countries, particularly Greece, Ireland, Spain, Portugal, and Italy. The resulting government budget deficits were paid for by issuing government bonds. By the spring of 2010, many investors had come to doubt the ability of Greece, in particular, to make the interest payments on the bonds. If Greece defaulted and stopped making interest payments on its bonds, investors would be likely to stop buying bonds issued by several other European governments, and the continuation of the euro would be called into question. The European Central Bank helped Greece avoid a default by directly buying its bonds. The bank extended similar help to Spain, Ireland, and Italy. The International Monetary Fund and the European Union put together aid packages meant to keep Greece and other countries from defaulting. In exchange for the aid, these countries were required to cut government spending and raise taxes, even though doing so resulted in significant protests from unions, students, and other groups. The bank extended similar help to Spain, Ireland, Italy, and Cyprus. In the case of Cyprus, the bailout deal (in early 2013) also required a bail-in of the creditors of its banks (bondholders and depositors), forcing them to take a hit. In mid-2013, it seemed that the actions the European Union had taken would be sufficient to keep Greece and possibly other countries from defaulting on their bonds.

During the years of the gold standard, countries couldn't run expansionary monetary policies and were unable to have their exchange rates depreciate. During the Great Depression of the 1930s, these drawbacks to remaining on the gold standard led one country after another to abandon it, and by the mid-1930s, the gold standard had collapsed. In 2012, some economists and policymakers were predicting a similar abandonment of the euro. There were significant reasons, though, that no government had yet been willing to consider reverting from the euro to its own currency. Because many eurozone countries export a significant fraction of GDP to other eurozone countries, exchange rate stability has been important to their economic stability, making these countries reluctant to abandon the euro. In addition, some of the European countries hit hardest by the recession, particularly Spain and Ireland, were suffering from the bursting of housing bubbles. More expansionary monetary policies or depreciating exchange rates were unlikely to result in economic recovery until the effects of the collapse in residential construction had run its course. So, it was unclear that the constraints imposed by the euro were holding back recovery in Europe. Finally, because so many contracts and agreements among households, firms, and governments in Europe were written in euros, abandoning the euro was likely to be disruptive to the financial system and to trade.

However, the euro crisis is continually unfolding, with the recession spreading to core countries. The ultimate fate of the eurozone will help to answer the question of whether independent countries with diverse economies can successfully maintain a joint monetary policy and a single currency.

Sources: Based on Jack Ewing, Stephen Castle, and Liz Alderman, "Debt Plan Is Delayed in Europe," New York Times, October 20, 2011; Terence Roth, "Setting Up the Greek Default," Wall Street Journal, October 11, 2011; and "Solving the Euro-Zone Crisis," Economist, October 6, 2011.

Pegging against Another Currency

A final key aspect of the current exchange rate system is that some countries have attempted to keep their exchange rates fixed against the US dollar or another major currency. Having a fixed exchange rate can provide important advantages for a country that has extensive trade with another country. When the exchange rate is fixed, business planning becomes much easier. For instance, if the South Korean won increases in value relative to the Canadian dollar, Hyundai, the Korean car manufacturer, may have to raise the Canadian dollar price of cars it exports to Canada, thereby reducing sales. If the exchange rate between the Korean won and the Canadian dollar is fixed, Hyundai's planning is much easier.

In the 1980s and 1990s, an additional reason developed for having fixed exchange rates. During those decades, the flow of foreign investment funds to developing countries, particularly those in East Asia, increased substantially. It became possible for firms in countries such as South Korea, Thailand, Malaysia, and Indonesia to borrow US dollars directly from foreign investors or indirectly from foreign banks. For example, a Thai firm might borrow US dollars from a Japanese bank. If the Thai firm wants to build a new factory in Thailand with the borrowed US dollars, it has to exchange the US dollars for the equivalent amount of Thai currency, the baht. When the factory opens and production begins, the Thai firm will be earning the additional baht it needs to exchange for US dollars to make the interest payments on the loan. A problem arises if the value of the baht falls against the US dollar. Suppose that the exchange rate is 25 baht per US dollar when the firm takes out the loan. A Thai firm making an interest payment of US$100 000 per month on a US dollar loan could buy the necessary US dollars for 2.5 million baht. But if the value of the baht declines to 50 baht to the US dollar, it would take 5 million baht to buy the US dollars necessary to make the interest payment. These increased payments might be a crushing burden for the Thai firm. The government of Thailand would have a strong incentive to avoid this problem by keeping the exchange rate between the baht and the US dollar fixed.

Finally, in the 1980s and 1990s, some countries feared the inflationary consequences of a floating exchange rate. When the value of a currency falls, the prices of imports rise. If imports are a significant fraction of the goods consumers buy, a fall in the value of the currency may significantly increase the inflation rate. During the 1990s, an important part of Brazil's and Argentina's anti-inflation policies was a fixed exchange rate against the US dollar. (As we will see, though, there are difficulties with following a fixed exchange rate policy, and, ultimately, both Brazil and Argentina abandoned fixed exchange rates.)

The East Asian Exchange Rate Crisis of the Late 1990s When a country keeps its currency's exchange rate fixed against another country's currency, it is **pegging** its currency. It is not necessary for both countries involved in a peg to agree to it. When a country has pegged the value of its currency against the US dollar, the responsibility for maintaining the peg has been entirely with the pegging country.

Countries attempting to maintain a peg can run into problems, however. As we saw in Chapter 4, when the government fixes the price of a good or service, the result can be persistent surpluses or shortages. Figure 15.3 shows the exchange rate between the US dollar and the Thai baht. The figure is drawn from the Thai point of view, so we measure the exchange rate on the vertical axis as US dollars per baht. The figure represents the situation in the 1990s, when the government of Thailand pegged the exchange rate between the US dollar and the baht above the equilibrium exchange rate, as determined by demand and supply. A currency pegged at a value above the market equilibrium exchange rate is said to be *overvalued*. A currency pegged at a value below the market equilibrium exchange rate is said to be *undervalued*.

Pegging made it easier for Thai firms to export products to the United States and protected Thai firms that had taken out US dollar loans. The pegged exchange

Pegging The decision by a country to keep the exchange rate fixed between its currency and another country's currency.

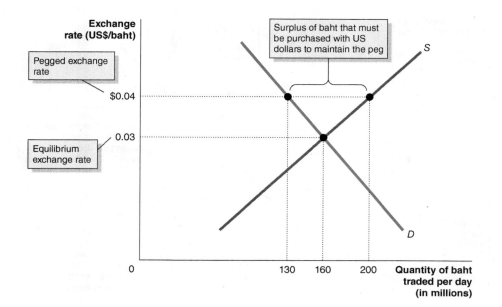

Exchange rate (US$/baht)

Pegged exchange rate

$0.04

0.03

Equilibrium exchange rate

Surplus of baht that must be purchased with US dollars to maintain the peg

S

D

0   130   160   200   Quantity of baht traded per day (in millions)

Figure 15.3

By 1997, the Thai Baht Was Overvalued against the US Dollar

The government of Thailand pegged the value of the baht against the US dollar to make it easier for Thai firms to export to the United States and to protect Thai firms that had taken out US dollar loans. The pegged exchange rate of US$0.04 per baht was well above the equilibrium exchange rate of US$0.03 per baht. In the example in this figure, the overvalued exchange rate created a surplus of 70 million baht, which the Thai central bank had to purchase with US dollars.

rate was 25.19 baht to the US dollar, or about US$0.04 to the baht. By 1997, this exchange rate was well above the market equilibrium exchange rate of 35 baht to the US dollar, or about US$0.03 to the baht. The result was a surplus of baht on the foreign exchange market. To keep the exchange rate at the pegged level, the Thai central bank, the Bank of Thailand, had to buy these baht with US dollars. In doing so, the Bank of Thailand gradually used up its holdings of US dollars, or its *US dollar reserves*. To continue supporting the pegged exchange rate, the Bank of Thailand borrowed additional US dollar reserves from the **International Monetary Fund (IMF)**. The Bank of Thailand also raised interest rates to attract more foreign investors to investments in Thailand, thereby increasing the demand for the baht. The Bank of Thailand took these actions even though allowing the value of the baht to decline against the US dollar would have helped Thai firms exporting to the United States by reducing the US dollar prices of their goods. The Thai government was afraid of the negative consequences of abandoning the peg even though the peg had led to the baht being overvalued.

International Monetary Fund (IMF) An international organization that provides foreign currency loans to central banks and oversees the operation of the international monetary system.

Although higher domestic interest rates helped attract foreign investors, they made it more difficult for Thai firms and households to borrow the funds they needed to finance their spending. As a consequence, domestic investment and consumption declined, pushing the Thai economy into recession. International investors realized that there were limits to how high the Bank of Thailand would be willing to push interest rates and how many US dollar loans the IMF would be willing to extend to Thailand. These investors began to speculate against the baht by exchanging baht for US dollars at the official, pegged exchange rate. If, as they expected, Thailand was forced to abandon the peg, they would be able to buy back the baht at a much lower exchange rate, making a substantial profit. Because these actions by investors make it more difficult to maintain a fixed exchange rate, they are referred to as *destabilizing speculation*. Figure 15.4 shows the results of this destabilizing speculation. The decreased demand for baht shifted the demand curve for baht from D_1 to D_2, increasing the quantity of baht the Bank of Thailand needed to buy in exchange for US dollars.

Foreign investors also began to sell off their investments in Thailand and exchange the baht they received for US dollars. This *capital flight* forced the Bank of Thailand to run through its US dollar reserves. US dollar loans from the IMF temporarily allowed Thailand to defend the pegged exchange rate. Finally, on July 2, 1997, Thailand abandoned its pegged exchange rate against the US dollar and allowed the baht to float. Thai firms that had borrowed US dollars were now faced with interest payments that were

Figure 15.4

Destabilizing Speculation against the Thai Baht

In 1997, the pegged exchange rate of US$0.04 = 1 baht was above the equilibrium exchange rate of US$0.03 = 1 baht. As investors became convinced that Thailand would have to abandon its pegged exchange rate against the US dollar and allow the value of the baht to fall, they decreased their demand for baht, causing the demand curve to shift from D_1 to D_2. The new equilibrium exchange rate became US$0.02 = 1 baht. To defend the pegged exchange rate, the Bank of Thailand had to increase the quantity of baht it purchased in exchange for US dollars from 70 million per day to 140 million. The *destabilizing speculation* by investors caused Thailand to abandon its pegged exchange rate in July 1997.

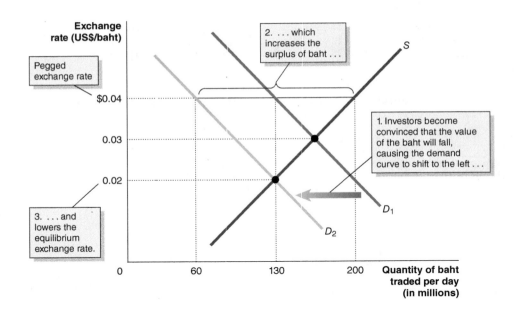

much higher than they had planned. Many firms were forced into bankruptcy, and the Thai economy plunged into a deep recession.

Many currency traders became convinced that other East Asian countries, such as South Korea, Indonesia, and Malaysia, would have to follow Thailand and abandon their pegged exchange rates. The result was a wave of speculative selling of these countries' currencies. These waves of selling—sometimes referred to as *speculative attacks*—were difficult for countries to fight off. Even if a country's currency was not initially overvalued at the pegged exchange rate, the speculative attacks would cause a large reduction in the demand for the country's currency. The demand curve for the currency would shift to the left, which would force the country's central bank to quickly run through its US dollar reserves. Within a few months, South Korea, Indonesia, the Philippines, and Malaysia abandoned their pegged currencies. All these countries also plunged into recession.

The Decline in Pegging Following the disastrous events experienced by the East Asian countries, the number of countries with pegged exchange rates declined sharply. Most countries that continue to use pegged exchange rates are small and trade primarily with a single, much larger, country. So, for instance, several Caribbean countries continue to peg against the US dollar, and several former French colonies in Africa that formerly pegged against the French franc now peg against the euro. Overall, the trend has been toward replacing pegged exchange rates with managed floating exchange rates.

The Chinese Experience with Pegging As we discussed in Chapter 7, in 1978, China began to move away from central planning and toward a market system. The result was a sharp acceleration in economic growth. Real GDP per capita grew at a rate of 6.5 percent per year between 1979 and 1995 and at the very rapid rate of more than 9 percent per year between 1996 and 2010. An important part of Chinese economic policy was the decision in 1994 to peg the value of the Chinese currency, the yuan, to the US dollar at a fixed rate of 8.28 yuan to the US dollar. Pegging against the US dollar ensured that Chinese exporters would face stable US dollar prices for the goods they sold in the United States. By the early 2000s, many economists argued that the yuan was undervalued against the US dollar, possibly significantly so. Many US firms claimed that the undervaluation of the yuan gave Chinese firms an unfair advantage in competing with US firms.

To support the undervalued exchange rate, the Chinese central bank had to buy large amounts of US dollars with yuan. By 2005, the Chinese government had accumulated more than US$700 billion, a good portion of which it had used to buy US Treasury bonds. In addition, China was coming under pressure from its trading partners to allow the yuan to increase in value. Chinese exports of textile products were driving some textile producers out of business in Japan, the United States, and Europe. China had also begun to export more sophisticated products, including televisions, personal computers, and cellphones. Politicians in other countries were anxious to protect their domestic industries from Chinese competition, even if the result was higher prices for domestic consumers. The Chinese government was reluctant to revalue the yuan, however, because it believed high levels of exports were needed to maintain rapid economic growth. The Chinese economy needs to create as many as 20 million new nonagricultural jobs per year to keep up with population growth and the shift of workers from rural areas to cities. Because of China's large holdings of US dollars, it would also incur significant losses if the yuan increases in value.

By July 2005, the pressure on China to revalue the yuan had become too great. The government announced that it would switch from pegging the yuan against the US dollar to linking the value of the yuan to the average value of a basket of currencies—the US dollar, the Japanese yen, the euro, the Korean won, and several other currencies. The immediate effect was a fairly small increase in the value of the yuan from 8.28 to the US dollar to 8.11 to the US dollar. The Chinese central bank declared that it had switched from a peg to a managed floating exchange rate. Some economists and policymakers were skeptical, however, that much had actually changed because the initial increase in the value of the yuan had been small and because the Chinese central bank did not explain the details of how the yuan would be linked to the basket of other currencies. By mid-2013, the value of the yuan had slowly increased to 6.18 to the US dollar. Despite this increase, some economists and policymakers still believed that the yuan was overvalued and urged the Chinese government to allow its currency to become more responsive to changes in demand and supply in the foreign exchange markets.

Making the Connection | Crisis and Recovery in South Korea

Korea spent the first part of the twentieth century as a colony of Japan. In 1945, at the end of World War II, Korea was divided into Communist North Korea and democratic South Korea. North Korea's invasion of South Korea in June 1950 set off the Korean War, which devastated South Korea, before ending in 1953. Despite these difficult beginnings, by the 1960s, the South Korean economy was growing rapidly. As one of the *newly industrializing countries*, South Korea was a model for other developing countries.

To make it easier for firms such as Hyundai to export to the United States and to protect firms that had taken out US dollar loans, the South Korean government pegged the value of its currency, the won, to the US dollar. Following Thailand's decision in July 1997 to abandon its peg, large-scale destabilizing speculation took place against the won. Foreign investors scrambled to sell their investments in Korea and to convert their won into US dollars. South Korea was unable to defend the peg and allowed the won to float in October 1997.

Like other countries that underwent exchange rate crises, South Korea had attempted to maintain the value of the won by raising domestic interest rates. The result was a sharp decline in aggregate demand and a severe recession. However, unlike other East Asian countries—particularly Thailand and Indonesia—that made only slow progress in recovering from exchange rate crises, South Korea bounced back rapidly. The figure below shows that after experiencing falling real GDP through 1999, South Korea quickly returned to high rates of growth.

Why was the performance of South Korea so much better than that of other East Asian countries? Jahyeong Koo and Sherry L. Kiser, economists at the Federal Reserve Bank of Dallas, cite several factors:

- South Korea benefited from a US$21 billion loan from the IMF in December 1997. This loan helped stabilize the value of the won.

- Even though South Korean banks were badly hurt in the crisis and cut back their loans, South Korean firms were able to obtain financing for investment projects from the stock and bond markets.

- The South Korean labour market was flexible enough to allow wage reductions, which offset some of the negative effect of the crisis on corporate profits.

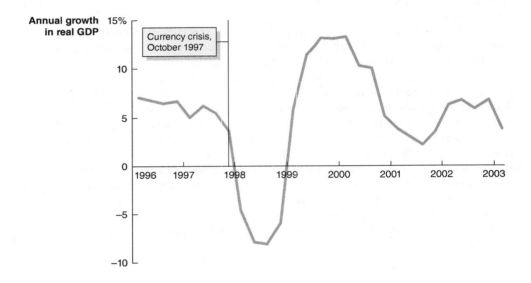

In 2011, some South Korean firms were still paying off debts originally incurred in the late 1990s, and the Korean banking system had yet to fully recover. But South Korea was able to emerge from its exchange rate crisis without suffering the political and social upheavals that occurred in countries such as Indonesia.

Source: Based on Korea National Statistical Office; and Jahyeong Koo and Sherry L. Kiser, "Recovery from a Financial Crisis: The Case of South Korea." Federal Reserve Bank of Dallas, Economic and Financial Review, Fourth Quarter 2001.

MyEconLab

Your Turn: Test your understanding by doing related problem 2.14 on page 486 at the end of this chapter.

15.3 LEARNING OBJECTIVE

Discuss the growth of international capital markets.

International Capital Markets

One important reason exchange rates fluctuate is that investors seek out the best investments they can find anywhere in the world. For instance, if Chinese investors increase their demand for Canada bonds, the demand for Canadian dollars will increase, and the value of the Canadian dollar will rise. But if interest rates in Canada decline, foreign investors may sell Canadian investments, and the value of the Canadian dollar will fall.

Shares of stock and long-term debt, including corporate and government bonds and bank loans, are bought and sold on *capital markets*. Before 1980, most Canadian corporations raised funds only in Canadian stock and bond markets or from Canadian banks. Canadian investors rarely invested in foreign capital markets. In the 1980s and 1990s, European governments removed many restrictions on foreign investments in their financial markets. It became possible for Canadian and other foreign investors to freely invest in Europe and for European investors to freely invest in foreign markets. Improvements in communications and computer technology made it possible for Canadian investors to receive better and more timely information about foreign firms and for foreign investors to receive better information about Canadian firms. The growth in economies around the world also made more savings available to be invested.

Today there are large capital markets in the United States, Europe, and Japan, and there are smaller markets in Latin America and East Asia. The three most important international financial centres today are New York, London, and Tokyo. Each day, the *Globe and Mail* and the *Financial Post* provide data not just on the S&P/TSX Composite Index of Canadian stocks but also on the Dow Jones Industrial Average and the Standard & Poor's 500 stock indexes of US stocks, the Nikkei 225 average of Japanese stocks, the FTSE 100 index of stocks on the London Stock Exchange, and the Dow Jones STOXX 50 index of European stocks.

Beginning in the 1990s, the flow of foreign funds into Canadian stocks and bonds— or *portfolio investments*—increased substantially. As Figure 15.5 shows, foreign purchases of stocks and bonds issued by corporations increased dramatically between 1995 and 2007. Foreign purchases of Canadian securities soared again in 2011, as fears that some European governments might default on their bonds led investors to a *flight to safety*, in which they sold other investments to buy Canadian securities. The fact that Canada ran current account deficits also fuelled some of the demand for Canadian government bonds. These current account deficits led to an accumulation of dollars by foreign central banks and foreign investors who used the dollars to purchase Canadian securities.

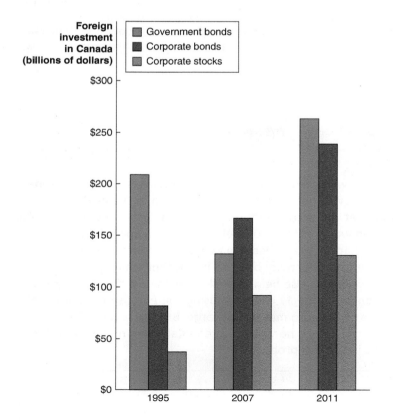

Figure 15.5

Growth of Foreign Portfolio Investment in Canada

Between 1995 and 2011, there was a large increase in foreign purchases of stocks and bonds issued by Canadian corporations and of bonds issued by the federal government.

Source: Data from Statistics Canada CANSIM II Table 3760037. (Accessed 21 April 2012).

Figure 15.6

The Distribution of Foreign Purchases of Canadian Stocks and Bonds by Country, 2011

Investors in the United States accounted for 60 percent of all foreign purchases of Canadian stocks and bonds, while investors in the United Kingdom accounted for 16 percent, and investors in Japan accounted for 7 percent.

Source: Data from Statistics Canada CANSIM II Table 3760063. (Accessed 21 April 2012).

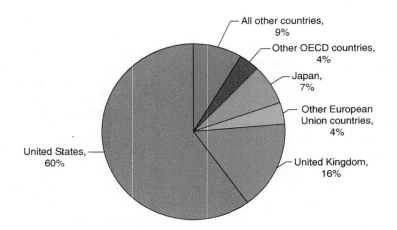

Figure 15.6 shows the distribution during 2011 of foreign portfolio investment in Canada by country. Investors in the United States accounted for 60 percent of all foreign purchases of Canadian stocks and bonds. The two other countries with the largest shares of foreign purchases were the United Kingdom, with 16 percent, and Japan, with 7 percent.

The globalization of financial markets has helped increase growth and efficiency in the world economy. Now it is possible for the savings of households around the world to be channelled to the best investments available. It is also possible for firms in nearly every country to tap the savings of foreign households to gain the funds needed for expansion. No longer are firms forced to rely only on the savings of domestic households to finance investment.

But the globalization of financial markets also has a downside, as the events of 2007–2009 showed. Because financial securities issued in one country are held by investors and firms in many other countries, if those securities decline in value, the financial pain will be widely distributed. For example, the sharp decline in the value of mortgage-backed securities issued in the United States hurt not only US investors and financial firms but investors and financial firms in many other countries as well, including Canada.

Economics in Your Life

Exchange Rate Risk in Your Life

At the beginning of the chapter, we posed this question: If economists are correct about the relative rates of average productivity growth between Spain and Canada in the next decade, then, all else being equal, will the savings that you accumulate (in euros) be worth more or less in Canadian dollars than they would have been worth without the relative gains in Spanish productivity? To answer this question, we saw in this chapter that when the average productivity of firms in one country increases faster than the average productivity of firms in another country, the value of the faster-growing country's currency should—all else being equal—rise against the slower-growing country's currency. Of course, Spain is only 1 of the 17 countries using the euro, so the impact of productivity increases in Spain on the value of the euro may not be large. But the savings that you accumulate in euros while you are in Spain are likely to be worth more in Canadian dollars than they would have been worth without the gains in Spanish productivity.

Conclusion

Fluctuations in exchange rates continue to cause difficulties for firms and governments. From the gold standard to the Bretton Woods system to currency pegging, governments have attempted to find a workable system of fixed exchange rates. Fixing exchange rates runs into the same problems as fixing any other price: As demand and supply shift, surpluses and shortages will occur unless the price adjusts. Seventeen countries in Europe are attempting to avoid this problem by using a single currency. Economists are looking closely at the results of that experiment.

Read *An Inside Look* on the next page for a discussion of a US Senate bill aimed at raising tariffs on goods from China in response to claims that the Chinese yuan was undervalued.

Can Tariffs Offset the Effect of Overvaluation?

ASSOCIATED PRESS

China Slams US Currency Bill as Threat to Trade

(a) China criticized an American currency bill as a threat to a shaky global economic recovery and warned Wednesday that trade ties will be "severely damaged" if it becomes law.

Beijing rejected the measure passed Tuesday by the Senate as a form of damaging protectionism at a time when other nations are trying to sustain free trade. The bill would allow Washington to raise tariffs on Chinese imports that critics say are unfairly cheap due to Beijing's exchange-rate controls and are destroying U.S. jobs.

"It is completely harmful and unbeneficial," said Foreign Ministry spokesman Ma Zhaoxu in a statement. Ma said it would do nothing to reduce U.S. unemployment and would disrupt global efforts to revive economic growth.

Tuesday's 63–35 Senate vote showed a bipartisan consensus in favor of tougher action against Beijing after years of diplomatic pressure and a gradual rise in China's currency, the yuan, that critics say is inadequate.

Still, the bill is unlikely to become law because it lacks the support of the majority Republican leadership in the lower House of Representatives, who are reluctant to take up the measure. The White House and President Barack Obama have not come out against the bill but have shown they are uncomfortable with it.

(b) U.S. manufacturers complain that Beijing's controls keep the yuan undervalued by up to 40 percent. They say that gives China's exporters an unfair price advantage and hurts foreign competitors, eroding American employment. The currency bill's supporters say it would support creation of 1 million jobs in the United States.

American critics of the bill have warned Beijing might retaliate, hurting U.S. companies in China's relatively robust markets, which are a rare bright spot for exporters amid weak demand elsewhere.

If it becomes law, "Sino–U.S. economic and trade relations will inevitably be severely damaged," Commerce Ministry spokesman Shen Dayang said in a statement.

Some opponents of the measure argue that currency sanctions would do little to help the U.S. job market because Chinese goods would simply be replaced by goods from other low-wage countries such as Vietnam and Bangladesh.

Ma, the Foreign Ministry spokesman, said the measure violates World Trade Organization rules.

"It not only cannot solve the problems in the U.S. economy or unemployment, but will seriously impede Sino–U.S. economic and trade ties and impede the joint efforts that China, the U.S. and the international community have made to enable a strong recovery and the growth of the global economy," Ma said.

The officials gave no details of a possible response but have warned in the past that unilateral trade action could damage the full array of U.S.–Chinese cooperation. That ranges from efforts to protect U.S. intellectual property rights in China to assuring the security of Taiwan and keeping the Korean Peninsula peaceful. . . .

(c) The currency legislation would set in motion the imposition of higher tariffs on a country if the U.S. Treasury Department decides its currency is "misaligned" and the country does not act to correct it. Currently, Treasury must resolve that a country is willfully manipulating its currency, a higher bar to reach, before sanctions can be considered.

The bill also makes it easier for specific industries to petition the Commerce Department for redress if they believe an exchange rate is giving a foreign competitor the equivalent of an export subsidy.

Beijing has said repeatedly it is pushing ahead reforms of its exchange rate controls but says it will set the pace. Chinese leaders have warned that an abrupt rise in the yuan could lead to job losses and fuel unrest.

The yuan's value has been allowed to rise by about 5 percent against the dollar over the past year in tightly controlled trading. The rise has quickened in recent weeks.

On Wednesday, China's central bank issued a statement defending its currency controls as an "important contribution" to international financial stability.

Source: McDonald, Joe, "China Slams U.S. Currency Bill as Threat to Trade," from the Associated Press, October 12, 2011. Reprinted by permission of the YGS Group.

Key Points in the Article

China was the main target of a US Senate bill to raise tariffs. Many politicians in the United States claimed that China had manipulated its currency to give Chinese exporters an unfair advantage over US companies. Politicians and US manufacturers supporting the bill argued that the Chinese yuan was undervalued by up to 40 percent, leading to job losses in the United States. Some opponents of the bill claimed that the sanctions would do little to help employment in the United States because the targeted Chinese products would just be replaced by goods from other countries. China said that the bill violates World Trade Organization rules and might retaliate should the bill become law. However, the bill was not expected to pass in the US House of Representatives, nor did it get support from the Obama White House.

Analyzing the News

a In October 2011, the US Senate passed a bill that would allow US companies to apply for tariffs on imports from countries that deliberately undervalued their currencies in order to become more competitive. As you read in this chapter, a currency is said to be *undervalued* if it is pegged at a value below the market equilibrium exchange rate. Many politicians claimed that China kept its currency undervalued in order to keep the prices of its exports low. The figure below shows the value of the yuan against the US dollar. After 2005, the appreciation of the yuan against the US dollar was relatively modest in comparison with the growing US trade deficits with China. As you read in this chapter, the Chinese central bank has managed to keep the yuan at relatively low levels by buying large amounts of US dollars with yuan. An increase in the US trade deficit with China caused an increase in the supply of US dollars in the foreign exchange market. Without any government intervention, the exchange rate between the US dollar and the yuan might have dropped below 6 yuan per US dollar. By increasing the demand for US dollars in exchange for yuan, the Chinese government was able to keep the exchange rate between 6 and 7 yuan per US dollar.

b US manufacturers supporting the tariff bill claim that the Chinese yuan is undervalued by up to 40 percent, and this has given Chinese exporters an unfair advantage in competing with US firms, leading to job losses. Supporters of the bill claim it would help create 1 million jobs in the United States. Critics have warned that Chinese retaliation could hurt US companies that currently export to China and lead to unemployment in those exporting industries.

c The US Treasury is required by law to investigate whether any country unfairly manipulates its currency. If it became law, the Senate bill would impose higher tariffs on countries if the Treasury Department determined that a currency is "misaligned" and the country took no corrective action. The bill also would make it easier for manufacturing firms to petition for sanctions if they believe a country is undervaluing its currency and giving foreign manufacturers what amounts to an export subsidy. China is the largest creditor of the United States, with holdings of more than US$1.25 trillion in US Treasury securities as of March 2013.

Thinking Critically

1. Supporters of the tariff bill discussed in this article claim that the yuan is undervalued, and tariffs on Chinese products would save jobs in the United States. Would passage of the bill hurt anyone in the United States? Briefly explain.

2. China is currently the largest creditor of the United States, with holdings of more than US$1.25 trillion in US Treasury securities as of March 2013. Suppose the Senate tariff bill were signed into law and China retaliated by selling all of its holdings of US Treasury securities. How would interest rates in the United States be affected? How would the exchange rate of the US dollar be affected? Briefly explain.

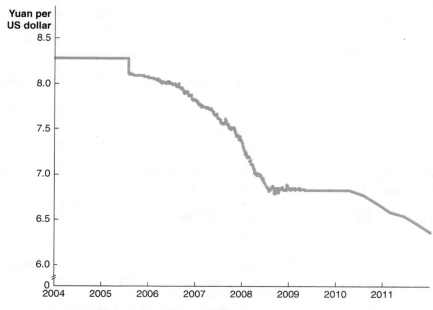

Historically, the exchange rate between the yuan and the US dollar has been stable.

Source: Data from the Federal Reserve Bank of St. Louis.

Chapter Summary and Problems

Key Terms

Bretton Woods system, p. 464

Euro, p. 465

Exchange rate system, p. 464

Fixed exchange rate system, p. 464

Floating currency, p. 464

International Monetary Fund (IMF), p. 475

Managed float exchange rate system, p. 464

Pegging, p. 474

Purchasing power parity, p. 467

Quota, p. 468

Tariff, p. 468

Summary

*LO 15.1 When countries agree on how exchange rates should be determined, economists say that there is an *exchange rate system*. A *floating currency* is the outcome of a country allowing its currency's exchange rate to be determined by demand and supply. The current exchange rate system is a *managed float exchange rate system*, under which the value of most currencies is determined by demand and supply, with occasional government intervention. A *fixed exchange rate system* is a system under which countries agree to keep the exchange rates among their currencies fixed. Under the gold standard, the exchange rate between two currencies was automatically determined by the quantity of gold in each currency. By the end of the Great Depression of the 1930s, every country had abandoned the gold standard. Under the Bretton Woods system, which was in place between 1944 and the early 1970s, the United States agreed to exchange US dollars for gold at a price of $35 per ounce. The central banks of all other members of the system pledged to buy and sell their currencies at a fixed rate against the dollar.

LO 15.2 The current exchange rate system has three key aspects: (1) The Canadian dollar floats against other major currencies, (2) seventeen countries in Europe have adopted a single currency, and (3) some countries have attempted to keep their currencies' exchange rates fixed against the US dollar or another major currency. Since 1973, the value of the Canadian dollar has fluctuated widely against other major currencies. The theory of *purchasing power parity* states that in the long run, exchange rates move to equalize the purchasing power of different currencies. This theory helps to explain some of the long-run movements in the value of the Canadian dollar relative to other currencies. Purchasing power parity does not provide a complete explanation of movements in exchange rates for several reasons, including the existence of *tariffs* and quotas. A *tariff* is a tax imposed by a government on imports. A *quota* is a government-imposed limit on the quantity of a good that can be imported. Currently, 17 European Union member countries use a common currency, known as the *euro*. The experience of the countries using the euro will provide economists with information on the costs and benefits to countries of using the same currency.

When a country keeps its currency's exchange rate fixed against another country's currency, it is *pegging* its currency. Pegging can result in problems similar to the problems countries encountered with fixed exchange rates under the Bretton Woods system. If investors become convinced that a country pegging its exchange rate will eventually allow the exchange rate to decline to a lower level, the demand curve for the currency will shift to the left. This illustrates the difficulty of maintaining a fixed exchange rate in the face of destabilizing speculation.

LO 15.3 A key reason exchange rates fluctuate is that investors seek out the best investments they can find anywhere in the world. Since 1980, the markets for stocks and bonds have become global. Foreign purchases of Canadian corporate bonds and stocks and Canadian government bonds have increased greatly in the period since 1995. As a result, firms around the world are no longer forced to rely only on the savings of domestic households for funds.

MyEconLab   Log in to MyEconLab to complete these exercises and get instant feedback.

Review Questions

LO 15.1

1.1 What is an exchange rate system? What is the difference between a fixed exchange rate system and a managed float exchange rate system?

1.2 How were exchange rates determined under the gold standard? How did the Bretton Woods system differ from the gold standard?

LO 15.2

2.1 What is the theory of purchasing power parity? Does the theory give a complete explanation for movements in exchange rates in the long run? Briefly explain.

2.2 Briefly describe the four determinants of exchange rates in the long run.

2.3 Which European countries currently use the euro as their currency? Why did these countries agree to replace their previous currencies with the euro?

2.4 What does it mean when one currency is "pegged" against another currency? Why do countries peg their currencies? What problems can result from pegging?

2.5 Briefly describe the Chinese experience with pegging the yuan.

LO 15.3

3.1 What were the main factors behind the globalization of capital markets in the 1980s and 1990s?

3.2 Briefly describe the pattern of foreign investment in Canadian securities between 1995 and 2010.

---

*'Learning Objective' is abbreviated to 'LO' in the end of chapter material.

Problems and Applications

LO 15.1

1.1 [**Related to** Don't Let This Happen to You **on page 465**] Briefly explain whether you agree with the following statement: "The Bank of Canada is limited in its ability to issue paper currency by the amount of gold the federal government has. To issue more paper currency, the government first has to buy more gold."

1.2 Canada and most other countries abandoned the gold standard during the 1930s. Why would the 1930s have been a particularly difficult time for countries to have remained on the gold standard? (*Hint:* Think about the macroeconomic events of the 1930s and about the possible problems with carrying out an expansionary monetary policy while remaining on the gold standard.)

1.3 If a country is using the gold standard, what is likely to happen to the country's money supply if new gold deposits are discovered in the country? Is this change in the money supply desirable? Briefly explain.

1.4 After World War II, why might countries have preferred the Bretton Woods system to reestablishing the gold standard? In your answer, be sure to note the important ways in which the Bretton Woods system differed from the gold standard.

LO 15.2

2.1 [**Related to** Making the Connection **on page 466**] In the *Toronto Sun*, columnist Bob Elliot wrote: "Is there an advantage to playing for the [Toronto] Blue Jays over the Boston Red Sox or New York Yankees? . . . The exchange numbers say it's better to play for the Jays—as long as you are paid in Canadian funds." Why would it be better for a baseball player on a Canadian team to be paid in Canadian dollars rather than US dollars? What do the "exchange numbers" have to do with your answer? Does it matter whether the player lives in Canada or in the United States? Briefly explain.

Bob Elliott, "Jays Wishing They Signed for Canadian Coin?" Toronto Sun, May 11, 2011.

2.2 Consider this statement:

> It usually takes about 98 yen to buy 1 Canadian dollar and more than 1.5 Canadian dollars to buy 1 British pound. These values show that Canada must be a much wealthier country than Japan and that the United Kingdom must be wealthier than Canada.
>
> Do you agree with this reasoning? Briefly explain.

2.3 According to the theory of purchasing power parity, if the inflation rate in Australia is higher than the inflation rate in New Zealand, what should happen to the exchange rate between the Australian dollar and the New Zealand dollar? Briefly explain.

2.4 [**Related to** Making the Connection **on page 468**] Look again at the table on page 469 that shows the prices of Big Macs and the implied and actual exchange rates. Indicate which countries listed in the table have undervalued currencies versus the US dollar and which have overvalued currencies.

2.5 [**Related to** Solved Problem 15.1 **on page 469**] Fill in the missing values in the following table. Assume that the Big Mac is selling for $4.07 in the United States. Explain whether the US dollar is overvalued or undervalued relative to each of the other currencies and predict what will happen in the future to each exchange rate. Finally, calculate the implied exchange rate between the Russian ruble and the New Zealand dollar and explain which currency is overvalued in terms of Big Mac purchasing power parity.

Country	Big Mac Price	Implied Exchange Rate	Actual Exchange Rate
Chile	1850 pesos		463 pesos per US dollar
Israel	15.9 shekels		3.40 shekels per US dollar
Russia	75.0 rubles		27.8 rubles per US dollar
New Zealand	5.10 New Zealand dollars		1.16 New Zealand dollars per US dollar

Data from "The Big Mac Index: Currency Comparisons, to Go," Economist, July 28, 2011.

2.6 Britain decided not to join other European Union countries in using the euro as its currency. One British opponent of adopting the euro argued, "It comes down to economics. We just don't believe that it's possible to manage the entire economy of Europe with just one interest rate policy. How do you alleviate recession in Germany and curb inflation in Ireland?" What interest-rate policy would be used to alleviate recession in Germany? What interest-rate policy would be used to curb inflation in Ireland? What does adopting the euro have to do with interest-rate policy?

Alan Cowell, "Nuanced Conflict over Euro in Britain," New York Times, June 22, 2001.

2.7 When the euro was introduced in January 1999, the exchange rate was Can$1.72 per euro. In May 2013, the exchange rate was Can$1.32 per euro. Was this change in the dollar–euro exchange rate good news or bad news for Canadian firms exporting goods and services to Europe? Was it good news or bad news for European consumers buying goods and services imported from Canada? Briefly explain.

2.8 [**Related to the** Chapter Opener **on page 463**] When Airbus, a subsidiary of a company located in France, sold A380 super-jumbo jetliners to Air France, the transaction was made in US dollars, rather than euros. What advantages are there to aerospace firms in different countries in agreeing to carry out all transactions in a single currency? What disadvantages are there?

2.9 Use the graph to answer the following questions.

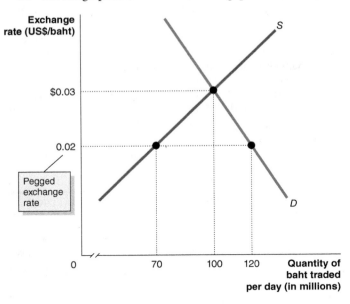

a. According to the graph, is there a surplus or a shortage of baht in exchange for US dollars? Briefly explain.

b. To maintain the pegged exchange rate, will the Thai central bank need to buy baht in exchange for US dollars or sell baht in exchange for US dollars? How many baht will the Thai central bank need to buy or sell?

2.10 For many years, Argentina suffered from high rates of inflation. As part of its program to fight inflation, in the 1990s, the Argentine government pegged the value of the Argentine peso to the US dollar at a rate of one peso per US dollar. In January 2002, the government decided to abandon the peg and allow the peso to float. Just before the peg was abandoned, firms in Buenos Aires posted signs urging customers to come in and shop and take advantage of the "Last 72 Hours of One to One." What was likely to happen to the exchange rate between the US dollar and the peso when Argentina abandoned the peg? Why would customers find it better to shop before the peg ended than after?

Based on Larry Rohter, "Argentina Unlinks Peso from Dollar, Bracing for Devaluation," *New York Times*, January 7, 2002.

2.11 The *Economist* observed the following: "In Argentina, many loans were taken out in [US] dollars: this had catastrophic consequences for borrowers once the peg collapsed." What does it mean that Argentina's "peg collapsed"? Why was the end of the peg catastrophic for borrowers in Argentina who had taken loans in US dollars?

"Spoilt for Choice," *Economist*, June 3, 2002.

2.12 In a column in the *New York Times*, by Christina Romer, former chair of President Barack Obama's Council of Economic Advisers, made the following observations:

a. "Our exchange rate is just a price—the price of the dollar in terms of other currencies. It is not controlled by anyone."

b. ". . . a high price for the dollar, which is what we mean by a strong dollar, is not always desirable."

Briefly explain whether you agree with these two observations.

Christina D. Romer, "Needed: Plain Talk about the Dollar," New York Times, May 21, 2011.

2.13 Graph the demand and supply of Chinese yuan for US dollars and label each axis. To maintain its pegged exchange rate, the Chinese central bank used yuan to buy large quantities of US dollars. Indicate whether the pegged exchange rate was above or below the market equilibrium exchange rate and show on the graph the quantity of yuan the Chinese central bank would have to supply each trading period.

2.14 [**Related to** Making the Connection **on page 477**] The following is from an article in the *Wall Street Journal* on changes in the Korean economy:

> The biggest is a change in where Korean companies are finding growth. It is no longer just the US and Europe, markets where Samsung, Hyundai and other big exporters have long focused on. Instead, it is in places like China, central Asia and the Middle East. . . . The broader trend is that global economic growth is less tied to the US, a phenomenon that has been called "decoupling."

If the trend identified in this article is correct, what are the implications for the policy of the Korean government with respect to the US dollar–won exchange rate?

"Korean Stock Rally Shows a Different Picture," Wall Street Journal, June 19, 2007, p. C3.

LO 15.3

3.1 Why are foreign investors more likely to invest in Canadian government bonds than in Canadian corporate stocks and bonds?

3.2 The text states that "the globalization of financial markets has helped increase growth and efficiency in the world economy." Briefly explain which aspects of globalization help to increase growth in the world economy.

3.3 The global financial crisis of 2007–2009 led some economists and policymakers to propose the reinstitution of capital controls—or limits on the flow of foreign exchange and financial investments across countries—which existed in many European countries prior to the 1960s. Why would a financial crisis lead to a reconsideration of using capital controls? What problems might result from reinstituting capital controls?

GLOSSARY

A

Absolute advantage The ability of an individual, a firm, or a country to produce more of a good or service than potential trading partners, using the same amount of resources.

Advances to banks Loans the Bank of Canada makes to banks.

Aggregate demand (AD) curve A curve that shows the relationship between the price level and the quantity of real GDP demanded by households, firms, and the government. It also shows the relationship between the price level and the level of planned aggregate expenditure in the economy, holding constant all other factors that affect aggregate expenditure.

Aggregate demand and aggregate supply model A model that explains short-run fluctuations in real GDP and the price level.

Aggregate expenditure (AE) Total spending in the economy: the sum of consumption, planned investment, government purchases, and net exports.

Aggregate expenditure model A macroeconomic model that focuses on the short-run relationship between total spending and real GDP, assuming that the price level is constant.

Allocative efficiency A state of the economy in which production is in accordance with consumer preferences; in particular, every good or service is produced up to the point where the last unit provides a marginal benefit to society equal to the marginal cost of producing it.

Asset Anything of value owned by a person or a firm.

Automatic stabilizers Government spending and taxes that automatically increase or decrease along with the business cycle.

Autonomous expenditure An expenditure that does not depend on the level of GDP.

B

Balance of payments The record of a country's trade with other countries in goods, services, and assets.

Balance of trade The difference between the value of the goods a country exports and the value of the goods a country imports.

Bank of Canada The central bank of Canada.

Bank panic A situation in which many banks experience runs at the same time.

Bank rate The interest rate the Bank of Canada charges on loans (advances) to banks.

Bank run A situation in which many depositors simultaneously decide to withdraw money from a bank.

Board of directors (of the Bank of Canada) A board with 15 members (including the governor) that is responsible for the management of the Bank of Canada.

Bretton Woods system An exchange rate system that lasted from 1944 to 1973, under which countries pledged to buy and sell their currencies at a fixed rate against the dollar.

Budget deficit The situation in which the government's current expenditures are greater than its current tax revenue.

Budget surplus The situation in which the current government's expenditures are less than its current tax revenue.

Business cycle Alternating periods of economic expansion and economic recession.

C

Capital Manufactured goods that are used to produce other goods and services.

Capital account The part of the balance of payments that records relatively minor transactions, such as migrants' transfers and sales and purchases of nonproduced, nonfinancial assets.

Capital controls Limits on the flow of foreign exchange and financial investment across countries.

Cash flow The difference between the cash revenues received by a firm and the cash spending by the firm.

Catch-up The prediction that the level of GDP per capita (or income per capita) in poor countries will grow faster than in rich countries.

Centrally planned economy An economy in which the government decides how economic resources will be allocated.

***Ceteris paribus* ("all else equal") condition** The requirement that when analyzing the relationship between two variables—such as price and quantity demanded—other variables must be held constant.

Circular-flow diagram A model that illustrates how participants in markets are linked.

Closed economy An economy that has no interactions in trade or finance with other countries.

Collateralized transactions Transactions that involve property being pledged to the lender to guarantee payment in the event that the borrower is unable to make debt payments.

Commodity money A good used as money that also has value independent of its use as money.

Comparative advantage The ability of an individual, a firm, or a country to produce a good or service at a lower opportunity cost than potential trading partners.

Competitive market equilibrium A market equilibrium with many buyers and many sellers.

Complements Goods and services that are used together.

Consumer price index (CPI) An average of the prices of the goods and services purchased by a typical household.

Consumption Spending by households on goods and services, not including spending on new houses.

Consumption function The relationship between consumption spending and disposable income.

Contractionary monetary policy The Bank of Canada's increasing interest rates to reduce inflation.

Crowding out A decline in private expenditures as a result of an increase in government purchases.

Currency appreciation An increase in the market value of one currency relative to another currency.

Currency depreciation A decrease in the market value of one currency relative to another currency.

Current account The part of the balance of payments that records a country's net exports, net income on investments, and net transfers.

Cyclical unemployment Unemployment caused by a business cycle recession.

Cyclically adjusted budget deficit or surplus The deficit or surplus in the federal government's budget if the economy were at potential GDP.

D

Demand curve A curve that shows the relationship between the price of a product and the quantity of the product demanded.

Demand schedule A table that shows the relationship between the price of a product and the quantity of the product demanded.

Demographics The characteristics of a population with respect to age, race, and gender.

Desired reserve ratio The minimum fraction of deposits banks desire to keep as reserves.

Desired reserves Reserves that a bank desires to hold, based on its chequing account deposits.

Devaluation A reduction in a fixed exchange rate.

Discouraged workers People who are available for work but have not looked for a job during the previous four weeks because they believe no jobs are available for them.

Disinflation A significant reduction in the inflation rate.

E

Economic growth The ability of an economy to produce increasing quantities of goods and services.

Economic growth model A model that explains growth rates in real GDP per capita over the long run.

Economic model A simplified version of reality used to analyze real-world economic situations.

Economic variable Something measurable that can have different values, such as the price of coffee.

Economics The study of the choices people make to attain their goals, given their scarce resources.

Efficiency wage A higher-than-market wage that a firm pays to increase worker productivity.

Employment–population ratio A measure of the portion of the population engaged in paid work.

Entrepreneur Someone who operates a business, bringing together factors of production—labour, capital, and natural resources—to produce goods and services.

Equity The fair distribution of economic benefits.

Euro The common currency of many European countries.

Excess reserves Reserves that banks hold over and above the desired amounts.

Exchange rate system An agreement among countries about how exchange rates should be determined.

Expansion The period of a business cycle during which total production and total employment are increasing.

Expansionary monetary policy The Bank of Canada's decreasing interest rates to increase real GDP.

Exports Goods and services produced domestically but sold to foreign households or firms.

F

Factor market A market for the factors of production, such as labour, capital, natural resources, and entrepreneurial ability.

Factors of production The inputs used to make goods and services.

Federal government debt The total value of bonds outstanding, which is equal to the sum of past budget deficits.

Fiat money Money, such as paper currency, that is authorized by a central bank or governmental body and that does not have to be exchanged by the central bank for gold or some other commodity money.

Final good or service A good or service purchased by a final user.

Financial account The part of the balance of payments that records purchases of assets a country has made abroad and foreign purchases of assets in the country.

Financial intermediaries Firms, such as banks, mutual funds, pension funds, and insurance companies, that borrow funds from savers and lend them to borrowers.

Financial markets Markets where financial securities, such as stocks and bonds, are bought and sold.

Financial system The system of financial markets and financial intermediaries through which firms acquire funds from households.

Fiscal policy Changes in federal taxes and purchases that are intended to achieve macroeconomic policy objectives.

Fixed exchange rate system A system under which countries agree to keep the exchange rates among their currencies fixed for long periods.

Flexible inflation targeting Conducting monetary policy that does not rely on mechanical rules to achieve its inflation target, but tries to meet the inflation target over some time horizon (typically a two-year horizon).

Floating currency The outcome of a country allowing its currency's exchange rate to be determined by demand and supply.

Foreign direct investment (FDI) The purchase or building by a corporation of a facility in a foreign country.

Foreign portfolio investment The purchase by an individual or a firm of stocks or bonds issued in another country.

Fractional reserve banking system A banking system in which banks keep less than 100 percent of deposits as reserves.

Free market A market with few government restrictions on how goods or services can be produced or sold, on who can buy or sell goods or services, or on how factors of production can be employed.

Frictional unemployment Short-term unemployment that arises from the process of matching workers with jobs.

G

GDP deflator A measure of the price level, calculated by dividing nominal GDP by real GDP and multiplying by 100.

Globalization The process of countries becoming more open to foreign trade and investment.

Governing council (of the Bank of Canada) A council with six members (including the governor) that is responsible for the management of the Bank of Canada.

Government purchases Spending by federal, provincial, and local governments on goods and services.

Gross domestic product (GDP) The market value of all final goods and services produced in a geographic area (country) during a period of time, typically one year.

H

Household production Goods and services people produce for themselves.

Human capital The accumulated knowledge and skills that workers acquire from education and training or from their life experiences.

I

Imports Goods and services bought domestically but produced in other countries.

Income effect The change in the quantity demanded of a good that results from the effect of a change in the good's price on consumers' purchasing power.

Industrial Revolution The application of mechanical power to the production of goods, beginning in England around 1750.

Inferior good A good for which the demand increases as income falls and decreases as income rises.

Inflation A general increase in the prices of goods and services over time.

Inflation rate The percentage increase in the price level from one year to the next.

Inflation targeting Conducting monetary policy so as to commit the central bank to achieving a publicly announced level of inflation.

Intermediate good or service A good or service that is an input into another good or service, such as car seats.

Inventories Goods that have been produced but not yet sold.

Investment Spending by firms on new factories, office buildings, machinery, and additions to inventories, plus spending by households and firms on new houses.

K

Key policy rate The Bank of Canada's target for the overnight interest rate.

L

Labour force The sum of employed and unemployed workers in the economy.

Labour force participation rate The percentage of the working-age population in the labour force.

Labour productivity The quantity of goods and services that can be produced by one worker or by one hour of work.

Law of demand The rule that, holding everything else constant, when the price of a product falls, the quantity demanded of the product will increase, and when the price of a product rises, the quantity demanded of the product will decrease.

Law of supply The rule that, holding everything else constant, increases in price cause increases in the quantity supplied, and decreases in price cause decreases in the quantity supplied.

Leverage A measure of how much debt an investor assumes in making an investment.

Liability Anything owed by a person or a firm.

Long-run aggregate supply (LRAS) curve A curve that shows the relationship in the long run between the price level and the quantity of real GDP supplied.

Long-run economic growth The process by which rising productivity increases the average standard of living.

M

M1+ The narrowest definition of the money supply: It includes currency and other assets that have cheque-writing features—all chequable deposits at chartered banks, TMLs, and CUCPs.

M1++ This broader definition of the money supply includes everything that is in M1+ as well as all non-chequable deposits at chartered banks, TMLs, and CUCPs.

M2 A monetary aggregate that includes currency outside banks and personal deposits at chartered banks, non-personal demand and notice deposits at chartered banks, and fixed-term deposits.

M2+ A broader monetary aggregate that includes everything that is in M2 plus deposits at TMLs, deposits at CUCPs, life insurance company individual annuities, personal deposits at government-owned savings institutions, and money market mutual funds.

M2++ The broadest definition of the money supply: It includes everything that is in M2+ as well as Canada Savings Bonds and other retail instruments, and non-money market mutual funds.

M3 A category within the money supply that includes everything that is in M2 plus non-personal term deposits at chartered banks, and foreign currency deposits of residents at chartered banks.

Macroeconomics The study of the economy as a whole, including topics such as inflation, unemployment, and economic growth.

Managed float exchange rate system The current exchange rate system, under which the value of most currencies is determined by demand and supply, with occasional government intervention.

Marginal analysis Analysis that involves comparing marginal benefits and marginal costs.

Marginal propensity to consume (MPC) The slope of the consumption function: The amount by which consumption spending changes when disposable income changes.

Marginal propensity to save (MPS) The amount by which saving changes when disposable income changes.

Market A group of buyers and sellers of a good or service and the institutions or arrangements by which they come together to trade.

Market demand The demand by all the consumers of a given good or service.

Market economy An economy in which the decisions of households and firms interacting in markets allocate economic resources.

Market equilibrium A situation in which quantity demanded equals quantity supplied.

Market for loanable funds The interaction of borrowers and lenders that determines the market interest rate and the quantity of loanable funds exchanged.

Menu costs The costs to firms of changing prices.

Microeconomics The study of how households and firms make choices, how they interact in markets, and how the government attempts to influence their choices.

Mixed economy An economy in which most economic decisions result from the interaction of buyers and sellers in markets, but in which the government plays a significant role in the allocation of resources.

Monetary base The sum of the Bank of Canada's monetary liabilities (i.e., paper money in circulation and bank settlement balances) and the Canadian Mint's coins outstanding (i.e., coins in circulation).

Monetary growth rule A plan for increasing the quantity of money at a fixed rate that does not respond to changes in economic conditions.

Monetary policy The actions the Bank of Canada takes to manage the money supply and interest rates to pursue macroeconomic policy goals.

Money Assets that people are generally willing to accept in exchange for goods and services or for payment of debts.

Multiplier The increase in equilibrium real GDP divided by the increase in autonomous expenditure.

Multiplier effect The series of induced increases in consumption spending that results from an initial increase in autonomous expenditures.

N

Natural rate of unemployment The normal rate of unemployment, consisting of frictional unemployment plus structural unemployment, that exists when the economy is at potential GDP.

Net exports The value of a country's total exports minus the value of a country's total imports.

Net foreign investment The difference between capital outflows from a country and capital inflows, also equal to net foreign direct investment plus net foreign portfolio investment.

New growth theory A model of long-run economic growth that emphasizes that technological change is influenced by economic incentives and so is determined by the working of the market system.

Nominal exchange rate The value of one country's currency in terms of another country's currency.

Nominal GDP The value of final goods and services evaluated at current-year prices.

Nominal interest rate The stated interest rate on a loan.

Nonaccelerating inflation rate of unemployment (NAIRU) The unemployment rate at which the inflation rate has no tendency to increase or decrease.

Normal good A good for which the demand increases as income rises and decreases as income falls.

Normative analysis Analysis concerned with what ought to be.

O

Open economy An economy that has interactions in trade or finance with other countries.

Open market buyback operations Agreements in which the Bank of Canada, or another party, purchase securities with the understanding that the seller will repurchase them in a short period of time, usually less than a week.

Open market operations The buying and selling of government securities by the Bank of Canada in order to control the money supply.

Operating band The Bank of Canada's 50-basis-point range for the overnight interest rate.

Opportunity cost The highest-valued alternative that must be given up to engage in an activity.

Overnight interest rate The interest rate banks charge each other for overnight loans.

P

Patent The exclusive right to produce a product for a period of 20 years from the date the patent is applied for.

Pegging The decision by a country to keep the exchange rate fixed between its currency and another country's currency.

Perfectly competitive market A market that meets the conditions of (1) many buyers and sellers, (2) all firms selling identical products, and (3) no barriers to new firms entering the market.

Per-worker production function The relationship between real GDP per hour worked and capital per hour worked, holding the level of technology constant.

Phillips curve A curve showing the short-run relationship between the unemployment rate and the inflation rate.

Positive analysis Analysis concerned with what is.

Potential GDP The level of real GDP attained when all firms are producing at capacity.

Price level A measure of the average prices of goods and services in the economy.

Producer price index (PPI) An average of the prices received by producers of goods and services at all stages of production.

Product market A market for goods—such as computers—or services—such as haircuts.

Production possibilities frontier (PPF) A curve showing the maximum attainable combinations of two products that may be produced with available resources and current technology.

Productive efficiency A situation in which a good or service is produced at the lowest possible cost.

Property rights The rights individuals or firms have to the exclusive use of their property, including the right to buy or sell it.

Purchase and Resale Agreements (PRAs) The Bank of Canada's purchase of government securities from primary dealers (i.e., banks or securities brokers/dealers), with an agreement to resell them later.

Purchasing power parity The theory that in the long run, exchange rates move to equalize the purchasing powers of different currencies.

Q

Quantity demanded The amount of a good or service that a consumer is willing and able to purchase at a given price.

Quantity supplied The amount of a good or service that a firm is willing and able to supply at a given price.

Quantity theory of money A theory about the connection between money and prices that assumes that the velocity of money is constant.

Quota A numerical limit that a government imposes on the quantity of a good that can be imported into the country.

R

Rational expectations Expectations formed by using all available information about an economic variable.

Real business cycle models Models that focus on real rather than monetary explanations of fluctuations in real GDP.

Real exchange rate The price of domestic goods in terms of foreign goods.

Real GDP The value of final goods and services evaluated at base-year prices.

Real interest rate The nominal interest rate minus the inflation rate.

Recession The period of a business cycle during which total production and total employment are decreasing.

Reserves Deposits that a bank keeps as cash in its vault or on deposit with the Bank of Canada.

Revaluation An increase in a fixed exchange rate.

Rule of law The ability of a government to enforce the laws of the country, particularly with respect to protecting private property and enforcing contracts.

S

Sale and Repurchase Agreements (SRAs) The Bank of Canada's sale of government securities to primary dealers (i.e., banks or securities brokers/dealers), with an agreement to repurchase them later.

Saving and investment equation An equation that shows that national saving is equal to domestic investment plus net foreign investment.

Scarcity A situation in which unlimited wants exceed the limited resources available to fulfill those wants.

Seasonal unemployment Unemployment that is due to seasonal factors, such as weather or the fluctuation in demand for some products during different times of the year.

Securitization The process of transforming loans or other financial assets into securities.

Security A financial asset—such as a stock or a bond—that can be bought and sold in a financial market.

Settlement balances Deposits held by banks in their accounts at the Bank of Canada.

Shortage A situation in which the quantity demanded is greater than the quantity supplied.

Short-run aggregate supply (SRAS) curve A curve that shows the relationship in the short run between the price level and the quantity of real GDP supplied by firms.

Simple deposit multiplier The ratio of the amount of deposits created by banks to the amount of new reserves.

Speculators Currency traders who buy and sell foreign exchange in an attempt to profit from changes in exchange rates.

Stagflation A combination of inflation and recession, usually resulting from a supply shock.

Standing liquidity facilities The Bank of Canada's readiness to lend to or borrow from a bank.

Structural relationship A relationship that depends on the basic behaviour of consumers and firms and that remains unchanged over long periods.

Structural unemployment Unemployment that arises from a persistent mismatch between the skills and attributes of workers and the requirements of jobs.

Substitutes Goods and services that can be used for the same purpose.

Substitution effect The change in the quantity demanded of a good that results from a change in price making the good more or less expensive relative to other goods, holding constant the effect of the price change on consumer purchasing power.

Supply curve A curve that shows the relationship between the price of a product and the quantity of the product supplied.

Supply schedule A table that shows the relationship between the price of a product and the quantity of the product supplied.

Supply shock An unexpected event that causes the short-run aggregate supply curve to shift.

Surplus A situation in which the quantity supplied is greater than the quantity demanded.

Symmetric inflation targeting Conducting monetary policy based on equal concern about inflation rising above its target as about inflation falling below its target.

T

Tariff A tax imposed by a government on imports.

Tax wedge The difference between the pretax and posttax return to an economic activity.

Taylor rule A rule developed by John Taylor that links the central bank's target for the overnight interest rate to economic variables.

Technological change A change in the quantity of output a firm can produce using a given quantity of inputs.

Trade The act of buying and selling.

Trade-off The idea that because of scarcity, producing more of one good or service means producing less of another good or service.

Transfer payments Payments by the government to households for which the government does not receive a new good or service in return.

U

Underground economy Buying and selling of goods and services that is concealed from the government to avoid taxes or regulations or because the goods and services are illegal.

Unemployment rate The percentage of the labour force that is unemployed.

V

Value added The market value a firm adds to a product.

Velocity of money The average number of times each dollar in the money supply is used to purchase goods and services included in GDP.

Voluntary exchange A situation that occurs in markets when both the buyer and seller of a product are made better off by the transaction.

W

Working age population People 15 years of age and older who are legally entitled to work in Canada.

COMPANY INDEX

Airbus, 463
Air Canada, 98
Air France, 463
Alcool NB Liquor, 65
American International Group (AIG), 351
Apple, 29, 98, 138
AU Optronics, 78

Bear Stearns, 313, 351
Beaver Buzz Energy, 61, 62, 66, 82
Bell Canada, 155, 156
Best Buy, 137
BlackBerry, 50, 52, 311, 435, 440, 446, 450
BMO Financial Group, 114
Boeing, 463
Bombardier Inc., 147, 154, 168, 227–228

Canada Post, 128–129
Canadian National Railway (CN), 253, 280
Caterpillar Inc., 127
Chapters, 215
Chrysler, 23, 127
Coca-Cola Co., 61, 77, 291
Columbia Pictures, 450
Corning, 78
Costco, 131

DD Beverage Company, 61, 69
Demographia, 354
Diavik Diamond Mine, 103
Dreamworks, 127

Edward Jones, 280
E.H. Price, 466
Estée Lauder, 262

Fannie Mae (Federal National Mortgage Association), 348, 351
Federal Home Loan Mortgage Corporation (Freddie Mac), 348, 351
Federal National Mortgage Association (Fannie Mae), 348, 351
Ford Motor Company, 23, 411–412
Foxcomm, 138
Freddie Mac (Federal Home Loan Mortgage Corporation), 348, 351
Future Shop, 98

General Motors, 23
Goldman Sachs, 311, 348, 426
Google, 175

Hershey Food Company, 467
Honda, 450

H&R Block, 388
Hyundai, 474, 477

IHS Global Insight, 114
IKEA, 101

JPMorgan Chase, 313, 351

L'Auto-Neige Bombardier Limitée, 147
Lehman Brothers, 313, 351, 426
LG Phillips, 78

MacDougall, MacDougall and MacTier, 280
Matsushita, 78
McCain Foods, 6–7
McDonald's, 435
Merrill Lynch, 426
Microsoft, 100, 298
Monster Beverage Corp., 61, 66, 69
Monster.ca, 129
Morgan Stanley, 311, 348, 426

Nissan, 450

Pebble Beach golf course, 450
PepsiCo, 61, 84–85
Porsche, 55
Purolator Courier, 263–264

Quanta Computer, 50

Red Bull, 61, 62, 66, 69, 82
Rockefeller Center, 450
Rockstar Energy Drink, 61
Rogers Communications, 448
Rona, 158
Royal Bank, 140

Samsung Electronics, 78
SanDisk, 50
Sharp Corporation, 78
Sony, 450
Standard & Poor's Corporation, 156, 479

TD Economics, 114
Teamsters Canada, 263–264
Texas Instruments, 50, 52
Tim Hortons Inc., 213, 215, 244–245
Toyota Motor Corporation, 35, 36–37, 54–55, 97, 182, 450

Vizio, 78

Walmart, 131
Walt Disney Pictures, 127

Key terms and the page on which they are defined appear in **boldface**.

45°-line diagram, 230–234

absolute advantage
comparative advantage, confusion with, 46
defined, **45**
vs. comparative advantage, 44–45
accounting profit, 14
actual investment *vs.* planned investment, 215
adjustable-rate mortgages, 349
advances to banks, 308
Afghanistan, 198
Africa, 148, 153
aggregate demand
and fiscal policy, 365, 371
and interest rates, 333–334
and multiplier effect, 373–375
aggregate demand and aggregate supply model
defined, **254**–255
and Phillips curve, 409–410
and tax reform, 390–391
aggregate demand (AD) curve
consumption, 255, 333
defined, **242**, 254
described, 241–243
downward sloping nature of, 254–256
and expansion, 269–270
and exports, 258–259
and investments, 333
and net exports, 334
and recession, 267–268
shift prediction, 261–262
shifts in, *versus* movements along, 256, 259–261
variables shifting, 256–257, 260–261
aggregate expenditure (AE), 214
aggregate expenditure model
components of, 214–215, 217
consumption, 214, 218–222
defined, **214**–215
equations, 250–251
government purchases, 214, 228–229
graphing, 230–235
macroeconomic equilibrium, 215–217, 230–235, 250–251
and national income, 222–223
net exports, 215, 228–230
planned and actual investment, 215

planned investment, 214, 225–227
and saving, 223–225
Tim Hortons example, 213, 244–245
aggregate supply, 262–267
and multiplier effect, 375–376
aging of population, and health care costs, 367–369
AIDS, 198–199
Alesina, Alberto, 391
allocative efficiency, 9, 37
Alt-A borrowers, 348
American Economic Association, 410
An Essay on the Principle of Population (Malthus), 188
Angola, 198
An Inquiry into the Nature and Causes of the Wealth of Nations (Smith), 50
anticipated inflation, 137–138
areas of a rectangle formulas, 31
areas of a triangle formulas, 31–32
Argentina, 176
economic growth failure, 178–179
pegging against US dollar, 474
assets
defined, **218–219**, 292
vs. liabilities, 303
austerity program, 384–385, 394
Australia, 106–107
automakers, 35, 54–55
automatic mechanism, 268
automatic stabilizers
defined, **364**
federal budget as, 383–384
vs. discretionary fiscal policy, **364**
automobile purchase trade-offs, 35, 52
autonomous expenditure, 236
autonomous government purchases, 373
average annual growth rate, 151
average annual growth rates in real GDP in Canada, 189
average annual percentage change *vs.* total percentage change, 179
average people, 138

baby boomers, 66–67
baht, 474–476
bailout, 384

balanced budget, 157
multiplier, 402–403
balance of payments
balance of trade, confusion with, 439
Canadian, 436
capital account, 438
current account, 436–438
current account balance, confusion with, 439
defined, **436**
financial account, 438
sum as zero, 438–439
balance of trade
balance of payments, confusion with, 439
current account balance, confusion with, 439
defined, **437**
balance sheets, bank, 299–300
banking crisis, 349
Bank of America, 354
Bank of Canada
balance sheets, 335
and bank rate, 136
bankofcanada.ca, 441
board of directors (of the Bank of Canada), 307
as central bank, 307
credit easing, 335
defined, **294**
establishment of, 307
flexible inflation targeting, 352
governing council (of the Bank of Canada), 307
inflation measurement, 345–346
lending to financial institutions, 309–310
monetary policy, choice of, 328–333
monetary policy, goals, 326–327
monetary policy, implementation by, 308–310, 337–339
monetary policy in open economy, 453–454
monetary policy targets, 328, 332, 343–346
money supply, 295–299, 329–331, 343–344
operating band, 308, 332–333
operating band for overnight interest rate, 307–308
and output gap, 154–155
policies from 1970s to the present, 420–427

price-level *vs.* inflation-rate targeting, 318–319
quantitative easing, 335–336
rate of inflation below target range, 310, 311
and recessions, 277, 337–339
target both money supply and interest rates, 344
Taylor rule, 344–345
Bank of England, 318, 426
Bank of Japan, 318, 426
Bank of Korea, 435, 454
Bank of Montreal, 301–302, 306, 354, 355, 394
Bank of Thailand, 475–476
bank panic, 306
bank rate, 136, 308
bank run, 306
banks
See also shadow banking system
balance sheets, 299–300, 335, 426
layoffs in, 121
money creation, 299–306
real-world deposit multiplier, 306
securitization, 311
simple deposit multiplier, 302–303, 306
T-accounts, 300–302
bar graphs, 23
Barro, Robert, 288
barter economies, 292
beer, as inferior good, 65
behavioural assumptions, 10
Bernanke, Ben, 318–319, 350, 352, 428
Big Mac theory of exchange rates, 468–470
Blue-ray players, falling price of, 9
BMO Nesbitt Burns, 311
board of directors (of the Bank of Canada), 307
Bombardier, Joseph-Armand, 147
bonds, 155, 331, 478
Botswana, and economic growth, 153–154
brain drain, 202
Bretton Woods system, 464
Brin, Sergey, 175
budget deficit, 157, 382, 382–383, 385
budget surplus, 158, 382
Buenos Aires, 468

business, 14
business cycle
    defined, **96, 148**
    expansion phase, 162
    and inflation rate, 164
    peak, 162
    and recessions, 163–165
    trough, 162
    unemployment rate, 165
business gross fixed capital
        formation, 100
business investment, 100
business taxes, and aggregate
        demand (AD) curve shift,
        260

ca.finance.yahoo.com, 441
Canada
    balance of payments, 436
    catch-up, 194–196
    consumption as percentage of
        GDP, 102–103
    disinflation, 1989-1993,
        422–423
    economic growth, 42
    economic growth since 1950,
        189–190
    economic health of, 95,
        114–115
    Employment Insurance (EI),
        129–130
    environmental protection, 105
    exports, and global recession,
        258
    financial crisis of 2007–2009,
        312–313
    and flat tax, 389–390
    foreign portfolio investment,
        479
    foreign purchases of stocks and
        bonds by country, 2011,
        480
    free market system, 50
    global recession (2007–2009),
        168–169, 325, 425–427
    graduates, and recession, 95
    gross national product (GNP),
        110
    health care spending trade-offs
        in, 40
    housing bubble, 349, 354–355,
        407
    inflation targeting,
        1989–present, 423
    life expectancy, 150
    long-run economic growth in,
        177, 189–190
    manufacturing sector, 121
    minimum wage, 11–13, 130
    modern mixed economy,
        9, 42
    money, measurement of, in,
        295–299
    and net exports to US,
        229–230

OECD Better Life Index,
        106–107
penny is dropped, 297–298
PMI (Purchasing Managers'
        Index), 140–141
productivity slowdown from
        1973–1994, 190
property rights, 51
real GDP per capita,
        1961–2012, 148–149
recession of 2008-2009,
        275–277, 363
recessions in, 154–155,
        162–165, 269
social program payments, 99
standard of living, 148,
        200–201
trade flows, 2011, 437
twin deficits, 1961–2011,
        451–452
unemployment rate, 126
Canada Health Transfer, 40, 365,
        367
Canadair Regional Jet (CRJ), 147,
        168
Canada Mortgage and Housing
        Corporation (CMHC),
        348, 355
Canada Social Transfer, 367
Canadian Auto Workers (CAW),
        411–412
Canadian-dollar effective
        exchange rate index
        (CERI), 444–445
capital
    defined, **15, 152**
    as factor of production, 14
    and long-run economic
        growth, 183
capital account, 438
capital flight, 475
capital inflow, 438
capital markets, 478–480
capital outflow, 438
capital per hour worked, 152
capital stock, 152
    shifts in short-run aggregate
        supply (SRAS) curve,
        265–266
Carney, Mark, 318–319, 325, 354,
        394
cash flow, 227
catch-up
    among high-income countries,
        192
    defined, **191**
    and economic growth model,
        191–194
    prediction of, 192–193
    and the world, 193
causal relationship, 11
cause and effect, on graphs,
        26–28
Central African Republic, 198
central banks, 307

inflation targeting, 352
policies during global financial
        crisis (2007–2009),
        346–352
policies during global recession
        (2007–2009), 425–427
centrally planned economy, 8–9,
        175
    in China, 175, 203
    in Soviet Union, 184–185
Centres for Disease Control and
        Prevention, 382
ceteris paribus ("**all else equal**"),
        64, 69, 158, 371
Chad, 150
chain-weighted prices, 107
Chile
    inflation targeting, 352
    OECD Better Life Index,
        106–107
China
    centrally planned economy,
        175, 203
    Communism, 201
    currency bill (US), 482–483
    economic growth in, 175
    environmental protection, 105
    exports, and global recession,
        258
    GDP, 95, 112
    intellectual property, 175
    Internet regulation, 175
    and investment as economic
        growth, 204–205
    low birthrate, 201
    modern mixed economy, 9
    pegging against US dollar,
        476–477
    PMI (Purchasing Managers'
        Index), 140–141
    pollution, 105
    real GDP growth, 175
    standard of living, 200–201
Chrétien, Jean, 228
CIBC, 354
CIBC World Markets, 311
circular-flow diagram, 49
    and gross domestic product
        (GDP), 98–100
circular flow of income,
        48–**49**
classical economists, 288, 420
closed economy, 157, 436
Club of Rome, 202
CMHC (Canada Mortgage and
        Housing Corporation), 348
coffee, 3, 15, 16–17
collateralized transactions,
        307–308
college students, and
        employment, 95, 121
commercial loans, 300
commodity money, 292, 294
company, 14
comparative advantage

absolute advantage, confusion
        with, 46
    defined, **45**
    and trade, 42–47
    vs. absolute advantage, 44–45
**competitive market
        equilibrium, 74**
complements, 66
Composite Index of Leading
        Indicators, 261
compounding rates, 178
Conference Board of Canada, 261
consumer confidence, 213, 243
consumer confidence index,
        219–220
consumer expectations, and
        demand, 67
consumer loans, 300
consumer price index (CPI)
    basket, 133
    defined, **132–133**
    and inflation, 133–134,
        345–346
consumer savings, 147, 166
consumer spending, 147, 166
consumer tastes, and demand, 66
consumption
    aggregate demand (AD) curve
        shift, 260
    aggregate expenditure
        component, 214
    Canadian, 102–103
    current disposable income, 218
    defined, **100**
    expected future income, 219
    of fixed capital, 110
    household wealth, 218–219
    and income, 221
    interest rates, 220–221, 333
    and national income, 222–224
    price level, 220
    and saving, 223–225
    United Kingdom, 102
    United States, 102
    variables of, 218–221
    wealth effect, 255
consumption function, 221–222
consumption taxes, 161–162, 367
contractionary fiscal policy
    described, 369–370
    in the dynamic model, 372
contractionary monetary policy,
        341
    defined, **334–335, 338**
contracts, enforcement of,
        51–52
conventional mortgage rate, 136
convergence. *See* catch-up
Cooper, Sherry, 114, 394
copyright protection, 187
corporate income tax, 226, 388
corruption, and rule of law,
        197–198, 200–201
Cotsomitis, John, 220
countercyclical fiscal policy, 371

creative destruction (Schumpeter's theory), 188
credit cards, 299
credit crunch, 348
credit easing, 335
crime, and GDP, 105, 149
Crow, John, 422
crowding out
    defined, **161, 380**
    in the long run, 381
    in the short run, 380–381
crowding out effect, 454
Cuba, 8, 50
currency appreciation, 443, 446
currency depreciation, 443, 446
current account
    balance of payments, confusion with, 439
    balance of trade, confusion with, 439
    defined, **437–438**
current disposable income, 218
current production, and gross domestic product (GDP), 97
cyclically adjusted budget deficit or surplus, 383–384
cyclical unemployment, 127, 128, 382
Czech Republic, 352

Das Kapital (Marx), 289
Dayang, Shen, 482
debit cards, 299
debt charges, 367
deflation
    disinflation, confusion with, 423
    and housing bubble (US), 346–348
DeLong, Bradford, 176
demand
    See also market demand
    ceteris paribus ("all else equal") condition, 64
    change in, *vs.* change in quantity demand, 68–69
    curves, 62–63
    equations, 90–92
    health care demand, example, 66–67
    high demand and low prices example, 80–81
    income effect, 63–64
    law of demand, 63
    in loanable funds market, 158–161
    schedules, 62–63
    shifts in, effect on market equilibrium, 78–79
    shifts in, effect on market equilibrium over time, 79–80

substitution effect, 63
    variables that shift, 64–68
demand curve, 24, 26
    defined, **62**
    shifting, 64, 81–82
    vs. movements along a curve, 82
demand schedule, 62
Democratic Republic of the Congo, 179, 198
demographics
    baby boomers, 66–67
    defined, **66**
    and demand, 66–67
    and unemployment, 416
Department of Finance, 325, 349
Department of Justice, 367
depreciation, 110
desired reserve ratio, 300
desired reserves, 300
developing countries, 179
    and catch-up, 192
diagrams, 49
discouraged workers, 123–124
discretionary fiscal policy, 363
    vs. automatic stabilizers, 364
disinflation
    Canadian disinflation, 1989–1993, 422–423
    defined, **422**
    deflation, confusion with, 423
dissaving, 157–158, 449
distribution of income, and inflation, 138
division of income, 111–112
Doerksen, Cameron, 168
dollar (Canadian)
    and economic interdependence, 456–457
    floating, 465–466
    fluctuating, 444–445
    strong, 466
    and US dollar exchange rates, 1974-2013, 465–466
    and yen-dollar exchange rates, 1974-2013, 465–466
domestic saving, 449–451
double coincidence of wants, 292
Dow Jones Industrial Average, 435, 479
Dow Jones STOXX 50 index, 479
dynamic aggregate demand and aggregate supply model
    and Canadian recession (2008-2009), 275–277
    described, 272–275
    and fiscal policy, 371–372
    millennium economic boom, 277–278
    and monetary policy, 339–343

East Asian exchange rate crisis, 474–476
Easterly, William, 181
Eastern Europe, 389

econometric models, 250, 400–404
Economic Action Plan, 271, 363, 383, 386
economic activity, and monetary policy, 333–339
economic growth, 41–42
    See also long-run economic growth
    in Botswana, 153–154
    calculation of, 150–151
    consumer tax, 161–162
    defined, **96**
    and health, 149–150
    and monetary policy goal, 327
    and property rights, 153
    rule of 70, 150–151
    technological change, 152–153
economic growth model
    catch-up, predicted, 192–194
    catch-up predicted by, 191
    defined, **181**
    long-run economic growth, speed of, 181
    Soviet Union, failure of, 184–186
economic incentives, 5
economic interdependence, and Canadian dollar, 456–457
economic models, 4
    assumptions, role of, 10
    circular flow of income, 48–49
    hypotheses, 10–11
    normative analysis, 11–12
    positive analysis, 11–12
economic problems, 7–10
economic profit, 14
economic resources, 14
economics, 4
    as a social science, 12–13
economic variables, 10–11
Economist, 407, 456, 468
education, 188
    poor education as barrier to economic growth, 201–202
efficiency, 9–10
efficiency wages, 130–131
employment, 95, 112
Employment Insurance (EI), 129–130
employment insurance premiums, 367
employment-population ratio, 123
endogenous population growth (Malthus theory), 188–189
energy drinks, 61, 82, 84–85
England, and Industrial Revolution, 177
entrepreneurs, 14, 48, 152, 185
environment
    and GDP, 105, 149

and long-run economic growth, 203
equations
    demand, 90–92
    gross domestic product (GDP), 101–102
    macroeconomic equilibrium, 250–251
    multipliers, 400–404
    net exports, 448–449
    net foreign investment, 448–449
    quantity theory of money, 313–314
    real exchange rate, 447–448
    saving and investment equation, 449–450
    supply, 90–92
equilibrium, and foreign exchange market and exchange rates, 442–443
equilibrium in the money market, 330–331
equilibrium wage, 129
equity, 9–10, 350
Estonia, 389
Ethiopia, 198
euro
    countries adopting, 472–473
    defined, **465**
    establishment of, 471
    exchange rates and market, 446
    exchange rate system, 471
    sovereign debt crisis, 472–473
    survival of, 472–473
European Aeronautic Defence and Space Company (EADS), 463
European Central Bank (ECB), 352, 426, 471
European Common Market, 471
European Economic Community, 471
European Union (EU), 384, 471
Evans, Charles, 318
excess reserves, 300
exchange rates
    aggregate demand curve shift, 261
    Canadian-dollar effective exchange rate index (CERI), 444–445
    and exports, 446–447
    fixed, 446
    fluctuating, Airbus example, 463
    and imports, 446–447
    listings, 441
    in long run, 467–471
    and net exports, 230
    nominal, 440
    real, 440
    real exchange rate, 447–448
    systems, defined, 464

exchange rate systems
Big Mac theory of exchange rates, 468–470
currency, pegging against, 474–477
defined, **464**
domestic and foreign goods, preferences for, 471
euro, 471–473
floating dollar, 465–466
purchasing power parity, 467–470
quotas, 471
relative price levels, 470
relative rates of productivity growth, 470–471
tariffs, 471
expansion
defined, **96, 148**
short-run and long-run effect in aggregate demand, 269–270
expansionary fiscal policy
described, 369–370
in the dynamic model, 372
and interest rates, 380
expansionary monetary policy, 334–335, 338, 340
expansion phase of business cycle, 162
expectations
aggregate demand curve shift, 257, 261
and demand, 67
of future inflation, and unemployment, 411–412
of the inflation rate and monetary policy, 418–420
rational, 288, 418–419
shifts in short-run aggregate supply (SRAS) curve, 265–266
expected future income, as consumption variable, 219
expected future prices, 72
exports
and aggregate demand, 258–259
defined, **101**
and exchange rates, 446–447
expropriation, 51

factor markets, 48
factors of production, 14, 36
Farag, John-Paul, 54
federal funds rate (U.S.), 335
federal government debt, 386–387
Federal Reserve.
See US Federal Reserve
Federal Reserve Bank of Dallas, 478
fiat money
defined, **294**
vs. gold, 465

final good or service, 97
financial account, 438
financial intermediaries, 155–156
financial markets, 155
Financial Post, 479
financial security, 155
financial system, 100, 148, **155**–156
Finland, 352
firms, 14, 48
expectations, shifts in aggregate demand curve, 257, 261
expectations, shifts in aggregate supply curve, 265–266
expectations of inflation, 418
and inflation, understanding, 412–413
manufacturing, 121
and rational expectations, 288
and supply, 71–72
wage adjustments, and SRAS curve, 264
fiscal policy
and aggregate demand, 365, 371, 373–375
automatic stabilizers vs. discretionary fiscal policy, 364
balanced federal budget, 385–386
contractionary, 369–370, 372
countercyclical, 371
deficits, surpluses, and federal government debt, 382–387
defined, **257, 364**
discretionary, 363
and dynamic aggregate demand and aggregate supply model, 371–372
expansionary, 369–370, 372
global recession (2007–2009), 377–378
government purchases and tax multipliers, 373–379
government spending and taxes, 364–369
Great Depression, 384
limits of, as a stimulus, 379–381
long-run crowding out, 381
long-run effects of tax policy, 387–388
multiplier formula, 400–404
and open economy, 454
private spending reduction, 379–380
and real GDP and price level, 369–371
recession (2008–2009), 363

and recessions, 271
short-run crowding out, 380–381
supply-side effects, size of, 391
tax reform, 390–391
and tax reforms, 390–391
tax simplification, 388–389
Fisher, Irving, 314
Fisheries and Oceans Canada, 367
Fisman, Raymond, 197
fixed exchange rates, 446
fixed exchange rate system, 464
Flaherty, Jim, 114, 325, 394, 407, 456
flat tax, 389–390
flexible inflation targeting
adopted by US Federal Reserve, 352
defined, **327**
flight to quality, 453
flight to safety, 479
floating currency, 464, 465–466
Fogel, Robert, 149, 201
Forbes magazine, 298
Ford, Henry, 131
foreign direct investment (FDI), 199, 438
foreign exchange market and exchange rates
demand shifts, 443
described, 440–442
equilibrium, 442–444
exports and imports, 446
listings, 441
McDonald's example, 435
non-market exchange rates, 446
real exchange rate, 447–448
supply shifts, 443–444
foreign portfolio investment, 199, 438, 479
foreign variables, aggregate demand curve shifts, 257
formulas
area of a rectangle, 31
area of a triangle, 31–32
balanced budget multiplier, 402–403
for government purchases multiplier, 401–402
for a percentage change, 30–31
for the tax multiplier, 402
fractional reserve banking system, 306
France, 177
free markets, 50
frictional unemployment, 126–127, 128, 416
Friedman, Milton, 287, 343, 410, 412
FTSE 100 index, 479
full employment, 128
full-employment GDP, 262

gains from trade, 42–44, 45–47
Gates, Bill, 4, 298
GDP. *See* gross domestic product (GDP)
GDP deflator, 109–110
Geithner, Timothy, 312, 350
General Theory of Employment, Interest, and Money (Keynes), 214, 420
Germany
exports, and global recession, 258–259
federal budget deficit, 452
hyperinflation of early 1920s, 316
long-run economic growth in, 177
Glaeser, Edward, 391
global financial crisis (2007–2009)
Canada unscathed, 407
central bank policies during, 346–352
euro, 472–473
exports and aggregate demand, 258–259
and shadow banking system, 311–312
unemployment, 121, 125, 312–313
globalization
benefits to long-run economic growth, 199–200, 203
defined, **199**
of financial markets, 480
global recession (2007–2009), 168–169, 258–259, 325, 377–378, 425–427, 472–473
Globe and Mail, 108, 325, 479
Glorious Revolution, 177 cd
gold standard, 464, 473
goods, 7–8, **14**
Goods and Services Tax (GST), 161, 367
governing council (of the Bank of Canada), 307, 340
government
balanced federal budget, 385–386
budgets, 157–158
and corruption, 200–201
federal budget deficit, 1967-2012, 382–383
federal government debt, 386–387
and property rights, 153
public saving, 157
recessions, and intervention by, 271–272
and scarcity, 40
government budget deficit, 451–453
government policies
aggregate demand curve shift, 256–257

education subsidies, 188
fiscal policy. *See* fiscal policy
and growth, 187–188, 200–203
and knowledge capital, 187–188
protection of intellectual property, 187
research and development subsidies, 187–188
and saving and investment, 202
and technological change, 202
and unemployment rate, 129–130
government purchases
See also government spending
aggregate demand (AD) curve shift, 260
aggregate expenditure component, 214, 228–229
autonomous, 373
defined, **100–101**
and GDP, 100–101
and tax multipliers, 373–379
and tax rates, 375
and transfer payments to households, 99
government purchases multiplier, 374, 379, 401–402
government saving, 449–451
government spending, 364–369
See also government purchases
Canada Social Transfer, 367
debt charges, 367
federal government spending, 2011-2012, 366–367
on government operations, 366–367
Guaranteed Income Supplement, 366
on health care, 365
as a percentage of GDP, 1962-2012, 366
and private spending reduction, 379–380
Universal Child Care Benefit, 366
government sponsored enterprises (GSEs), 348
graduates
and GDP, 95
and recession, 121
graphs/graphing, 22–30
aggregate supply graph, 277–278
cause and effect determination, 26–28
demand equations, 91–92
economic growth, 42
income and consumption, 27
macroeconomic equilibrium, 230–235
more than two variables, 25–26, 27

one variable, 23–24
positive and negative relationships, 26
price and quantity points, 25
production possibilities frontier (PPF), 36–41
slopes of lines, 24–25, 26
slopes of nonlinear curves, 29–30
straight lines, 29
supply equations, 91–92
total revenue, 31
two variables, 24
Great Depression, 125, 199, 214, 287–288, 328, 384, 464, 473
Great Recession, 353, 407, 426, 451, 457
Greece, 384–385
gross domestic income, 111
gross domestic product (GDP)
aggregate demand curve shift, 261
calculating, 97–98
and current production, 97
defined, **96–97**
equation, 101–102
GDP deflator, 109–110
government consumption and gross investment, 100–101
government spending as a percentage of GDP, 1962-2012, 366
gross private domestic investment, 100
and happiness, 106–107, 149
and macroeconomic equilibrium, 235
market value as measurement of, 97
measurement of total production, 96–97
as measure of employment, 95
net exports, and growth of, 230
net exports of goods and services, 101
per capita in the world, 179–180
personal consumption expenditures, 100
and planned aggregate expenditure, 217, 235
potential GDP, 154
and production, income, and circular-flow diagram, 98–100
real GDP forecasting, 235
real GDP *vs.* nominal GDP, 107–109
shortcomings of, 105–106
total production and total income other than, 110–112

value-added method, 103–104
gross national product (GNP), 110
gross private domestic investment, 100
GST (Goods and Services Tax), 161, 367
Guaranteed Income Supplement, 99, 366
guild system, 51

Hachey, Guy, 168
happiness, and gross domestic product (GDP), 106–107, 149
Harmonized Sales Tax (HST), 161
Harper, Stephen, 354
Harrison, Hunter, 280
health
and economic prosperity, 149–150
and job loss, 382
low-income countries, 198–199
poor health as barrier to economic growth, 201–202
health care spending
costs of health care, 367–369
federal government's share of total government spending, 365
total government spending, 1989-2012, 365
trade-offs in, 40
hedge funds, 312
high-income countries, 179
and catch-up, 192
Hobbes, Thomas, 176
hockey cards, 75–77
home equity, 350
hourly wages, 135–136
House, Paul, 244
household disposable income, 369
household production, 104
households
in circular-flow diagram, 49
defined, **14, 48**
disposable income, 111
expectations, shifts in aggregate demand curve, 257, 261
income, 111
transfer payments to, 99
household wealth, as consumption variable, 218–219
housing bubble (U.S.), 269, 276, 325, 346–348, 466
housing market, Canadian housing bubble, 349, 354–355, 407

and leverage, 349–350
and monetary policy, 325, 349
HST (Harmonized Sales Tax), 161
human capital, 15, 152, **182,** 201
Hungary, 352
hyperinflation
defined, 315–316
in Germany, early 1920s, 316
in Zimbabwe, 291, 315
hypotheses, 10–11

imports, 99
defined, **101**
and exchange rates, 446–447
and tariffs, 482–483
income
and consumption, 221
defined, **65**
distribution of, and inflation, 138
and gross domestic product (GDP), 98–100, 105–106
and long-run economic growth, 180–181
and standard of living, 180–181
vs. money, 298
income effect, 63–64
increase in quality bias, 134
Index of Consumer Confidence, 261
individual income tax, 388
industrial countries, 179
Industrial Revolution, 177
inferior good, 65
inflation
anticipated inflation, 137–138
consumer price index (CPI), 132–134
costs on economy, 137–139
defined, **131**
distribution of income, 138
dynamic aggregate demand and aggregate supply model, 275
flexible inflation targeting, 327
future, role of expectations of, 411–412
high rates of, 315–316
and housing bubble (US), 346–348
measurement by Bank of Canada, 345–346
and monetary policy, 340–341
and money growth, 315
price indexes, 135
producer price index (PPI), 134
quantity theory of money, 314–315
rate, 1952-2013, 326

symmetric inflation targeting, 327
unanticipated inflation, 139
unemployment, short-run trade off between, 408–412
workers' understanding of, 412–413
inflation gap, 344
inflation rate
   and business cycle, 164
   defined, **96, 132**
   miscalculation, 134
   and monetary policy, 418–420
   and monetary policy to lower, 424–425
   and natural rate of unemployment in the long run, 416
   rational expectations on monetary policy, 418–419
   short-run Phillips curve for expected, 415
   vs. price level, 165
inflation targeting
   adopted by central banks, 352
   in Canada, 1989-present, 423
   defined, **327**
information, of financial system, 156
infrastructure, 387
innovation, 14
input, 71
Institute for Supply Management, 140
intellectual property rights, 51, 187
interest rate effect on investment, 255
interest rates, 136–137
   and aggregate demand (AD), 333–334
   aggregate demand (AD) curve shift, 260
   consumer tax, 161–162
   as consumption variable, 220–221
   loanable funds, 158–162, 331–332
   long-term real rate of interest, 331
   monetary policy, 338
   and money supply decreases, 331
   and money supply increase, 330
   and money supply target by Bank of Canada, 344
   overnight interest rate, 307–308
   planned investment, 226
   real *vs.* nominal, 136–137
   short-term nominal rate of interest, 331
intermediate good or service, 97

international capital markets, 478–480
international financial system
   Big Mac theory of exchange rates, 468–470
   currency, pegging against, 474–477
   euro, 471–473
   exchange rate systems. *See* exchange rate systems
   floating dollar, 465–466
   gold standard, 464
   long-run determinants, 470–471
   purchasing power parity, 467–470
   South Korea, crisis and recovery in, 477–478
International Monetary Fund (IMF), 95, 475
international-trade effect, 256
invention, 14
inventories
   defined, **215**
   and planned aggregate expenditure, 234–235
investment
   as China's economic growth, 204–205
   consumer tax, 161–162
   defined, **100**
   economists' definition, 100
   government budget deficit, effect on, 451–453
   interest-rate effect on, 255, 333
   low-income countries, 199
   market for loanable funds, 158–161
   savings and, 199, 202
investment banks, 348–349
investment tax credits, 202
investment tax incentive, 226
iPad, 98
iPod, 137
Ivey Business School, 261
Ivey Purchasing Managers Index, 261

Japan
   catch-up, 194–196
   exchange rate, 443–444, 446
   foreign exchange, 443
   free market system, 50
   national saving, 450–451
   standard of living, 148
job creation and job destruction over time, 125–126
job loss, and health, 382
job search, 126–127
just-in-time system, 182

Kenny, Charles, 180
Keynes, John Maynard, 214, 241, 420

Keynesian revolution, 287
key policy rate, 307
Kiser, Sherry L., 478
knowledge capital, 186–187
Koo, Jahyeong, 478
Krushchev, Nikita, 184
Kwan, Andy, 220
Kydland, Finn, 288, 420

labour
   as factor of production, 14
   natural rate of unemployment, 128
labour force
   defined, **123**
   shifts in short-run aggregate supply (SRAS) curve, 265
labour force participation rate
   defined, **123**
   measuring, 122–126
   trends, 124–125
Labour Force Survey (LFS), 122–123
labour income, 111
labour productivity
   capital per hour worked, 152
   defined, **151–152, 181**
   long-run economic growth, speed of, 181
labour theory of value, 289
labour unions, 130
Lammam, Charles, 271
Lauder, Leonard, 262
law of demand, 63
   See also demand
law of diminishing return, 183
law of supply, 70
legal issues
   contracts, enforcement of, 51–52
   of market system, 51–52
   property rights, 51
leisure, and GDP, 105
leverage
   defined, **426**
   in housing market, 349–350
leverage ratio, 426
Levesque, Leslie, 114
liabilities
   defined, **219**
   vs. assets, 303
life expectancy, and economic growth, 149–150, 179
Limits to Growth, The (Club of Rome), 202
Lipstick Index, 262
liquidity, 156, 195
liquidity trap, 336
living standards. *See* standard of living
loanable funds market, 148, 158–162, 331–332
lobster industry, prices in, 80–81
London Stock Exchange, 479

long-run aggregate supply (LRAS) curve
   defined, **262**–263
   and long-run Phillips curve, 411
long-run economic growth
   See also economic growth
   average annual growth rates for the World Economy, 178
   average annual percentage change *vs.* total percentage change, 179
   barriers to, 201–202
   in Canada, 177, 189–190
   and capital, 183
   and catch-up, 191–196
   creative destruction (Schumpeter's theory), 188
   defined, **148**
   endogenous population growth (Malthus theory), 188–189
   and environment, 203
   globalization, benefits to, 199–200
   good and bad, 202–203
   and government policies, 187–188, 200–203
   growth rates, importance of, 178–179
   high-income *vs.* developing countries, 178–179
   importance of small differences in rates, 178
   and income, 180–181
   low-income countries slow growth, 196–199
   new growth theory, 186–188
   from one million B.C. to present, 176–177
   per-worker production function, 182–183
   and pollution, 203
   and poor education as barrier to, 201–202
   and poor health as barrier to, 201–202
   potential GDP, 154
   rate of, 151–152
   real GDP per capita, 1961-2012, 148–149
   Soviet Union, failure of, 184–186
   speed of growth, 181–182
   and technological change, 183–184
long-run macroeconomic equilibrium, 267–272
long-run Phillips curve
   and monetary policy, 415–416
   natural rate of unemployment, 411

and short-run Phillips curve of
    1960s, 413–414
long-term real rate of interest,
    331
low-income countries, barriers
    to economic growth,
    196–199
LRAS. *See* long-run aggregate
    supply (LRAS) curve
Lucas, Robert, 201, 288, 418–419,
    420

M1+, 297–299
M1++, 297–299
M2, 297
M2+, 297
M2++, 297
M3, 297
MacDonald-Laurier Institute, 261
macroeconomic equilibrium
    aggregate expenditure model,
        215–217, 230–233
    algebra of, 250–251
    graphs/graphing, 230–235
    long run, 267–272
    numerical example of, 235
    short run, 267–272
macroeconomics, 13
    defined, 96
    of investment, 158–162
    Keynesian revolution, 287
    monetarist model, 287–288
    new classical model, 288
    real business cycle model, 288
    of saving, 156–158
Malthus, Thomas, 188–189
managed float exchange rate
    system, 464
manufacturing sector, 121, 125,
    140–141
maps, 22–23
marginal analysis, 6
marginal benefit (MB), 6
marginal cost (MC), 6
marginal opportunity costs,
    increasing, 40–41
marginal propensity to consume
    (MPC)
    calculation, 224–225
    defined, 221–222
marginal propensity to save
    (MPS)
    calculation, 224–225
    defined, 224
marginal science, 6
marginal tax rate, 387
market demand
    See also demand
    defined, 62
    variables that shift, 64–68
market economy, 8–9
market equilibrium
    defined, 73–74
    demand and supply
        interaction, 73–74, 74–77

elimination of surpluses and
    shortages, 74–75
    example, 75–77
    increase in supply on, 77
    shifts in demand, effect on,
        78–79
    shifts in demand over time,
        effect on, 79–80
    shifts in supply, effect on, 77–78
    shifts in supply over time,
        effect on, 79–80
market for loanable funds, 148
    defined, 158
    demand and supply, 158–161
    movements in saving,
        investment, and interest
        rates, 159–161
markets, 4, 48
market supply curve, 70
market system
    circular flow of income, 48–49
    factor markets, 48
    factors of production, 14, 36
    gains from trade, 42–44, 45–47
    legal basis of, 51–52
    product markets, 48
market value, as measurement of
    GDP, 97
Marx, Karl, 289
medium of exchange, 293–294
Meltzer, Allan, 428
menu costs
    defined, 138, 264
    price levels, and SRAS curve,
        264
Merkel, Angela, 472
Mexico
    inflation targeting, 352
    OECD Better Life Index,
        106–107
microeconomics, 13, 96
Miguel, Edward, 197
Mill, John Stuart, 289
minimum wage, 11–13, 130
misery index, 122
Mittelstand, 258
mixed economy, 9
mixed income, 112
MLI Leading Economic
    Indicator, 261, 269
monetarism, 288, 343
monetarist model, 287–288
monetary aggregates, 426
monetary base, 309
monetary growth rule,
    287, 343
monetary policy
    choice of, 328–333
    contractionary, 334–335, 338,
        341
    defined, 257, 307, 326
    demand for money, 328–329
    and dynamic aggregate
        demand and aggregate
        supply model, 339–343

and economic activity,
    333–339
economic growth goal, 327
    effects of, 341–343
    expansionary, 334–335, 338
    goals of, 326–327
    high employment goal, 327
    implementation of, 308–310,
        337–339
    and inflation, 340–341
    and inflation rate, 418–420
    and inflation rate, lowered,
        424–425
    interest rates, 338
    and long-run Phillips curve,
        415–416
    money demand curve, shifts,
        329–330
    and open economy, 453–454
    and price levels, 339–340
    and price-level targeting,
        318–319
    price stability goal, 326–327
    rational expectations, effect on,
        418–419
    and real gross domestic
        product (GDP), 334–336,
        339–340
    and recessions, 271, 337–339,
        425–427
    stability of financial markets
        and institutions goal, 327
    summary of, 338–339
    targets, 328, 332, 343–346
money
    See also banks
    defined, 292
    demand curve, shifts,
        329–330
    demand for, 328–329
    fiat money, 294, 465
    functions of, 293–294
    growth and inflation, 315
    invention of, 292–293
    measurement of, 295–299
    quantity theory of money,
        313–316
    velocity of, 313–314
    vs. income or wealth, 298
money market, equilibrium in,
    330–331
money market mutual funds, 312
money supply, 295–299, 329–331,
    343–344
Mongeau, Claude, 280
moral hazard problem, 351
mortgage-backed securities, 311,
    336, 348
mortgages, 139, 348
Mozambique, 198
multiplier
    balanced budget, 402–403
    defined, 236
    and open economy,
        403–404

size of, 376
    tax formula, 402
    tax rates, 403
multiplier effect
    and aggregate demand,
        373–375
    and aggregate supply,
        375–376
    defined, 237, 373
    described, 235–236
    on equilibrium real GDP, 376,
        400–401
    fiscal policy, 400–404
    formula, 237–240, 400–404
    key points, 239
mutual funds, 156

National Economic Accounts,
    110
national income
    and consumption, 222–225
    measure of total production
        and income, 110–111
    and saving, 223–225
national income accounting, 110,
    156–157
national saving, 449–451
natural rate of unemployment,
    128, 411
natural resources
    depletion of, 203
    as factor of production, 14
    prices, 269
    shifts in short-run aggregate
        supply (SRAS) curve,
        265–266
negative equity, 350
neo-Quantity Theory of Money
    model, 287–288
net capital flows, 438
net exports
    aggregate demand curve shift,
        257
    aggregate expenditure
        component, 214, 228–230
    and current account, 437
    defined, 101
    equals the sum of the balance
        of trade and services, 438
    and interest rates, 334
    and net foreign investment,
        448–449
    price level, 256
    and tariffs, 240–241
    variables, 230
net foreign investment
    defined, 438
    and net exports, 448–449
net income on investments,
    437
net transfers, 437
new classical macroeconomics,
    288, 420
new classical model, 288
new growth theory, 186–188

newly industrializing countries, 179, 477
new product bias, 134
New Zealand, 106–107, 352
Nikkei 225 index, 479
nominal exchange rate, 440
nominal gross domestic product (GDP)
    compared to real GDP, 108–109
    defined, **107**
    vs. real GDP, 107–108
nominal interest rates, 136–137, 158, **220**
nonaccelerating inflation rate of unemployment (NAIRU), 416
nonlinear curves, slope of, 29–30
nonlinear relationship, 29
Norges Bank, 426
normal good, 65
normative analysis, 11–12
North, Douglass, 177
North Korea, 8, 50

Obama, Barack, 482
OECD.
    See Organisation for Economic Cooperation and Development (OECD)
OECD Better Life Index, 106–107
Office of the Superintendent of Financial Institutions (OSFI), 325, 349, 407
official reserve transactions, 439
Okun, Arthur, 122
Old Age Security, 99
omitted variable, 28
open economy, 157
    arithmetic of, 439–440
    defined, **436**
    and fiscal policy, 454
    and monetary policy, 453–454
    and multiplier, 403–404
open market buyback operations, 308–309, **333**
open market operations, 309
operating band, 308, 332**–333**
opportunity costs, 45, 129
    defined, 7, **37**
    increasing marginal, 40–41
    production possibilities frontier (PPF), 36–42
optimal decisions at margin, 4, 6
Organisation for Economic Cooperation and Development (OECD), 102, 106, 456
Organization of the Petroleum Exporting Countries (OPEC), 420
origin, 23
outlet bias, 134
output gap, 154–155

output per hour worked, and technological change, 184
overnight interest rate, 307–308, 328, **332**
overnight rate, 136

Page, Larry, 175
Papandreou, George, 472
paradox of thrift, 241
parking ticket example, of rule of law, 197–198
patents, 187
Paulson, Henry, 350
pegging
    Chinese experience with, 476–477
    decline in, 476
    defined, **474**
    East Asian exchange rate crisis, 474–476
pennies, 297–298
percentage change formulas, 30–31
perfectly competitive market, 62
personal income taxes and, aggregate demand (AD) curve shift, 260
Peru, 104
per-worker production function, 182
Petramala, Diana, 114
Phelps, Edmund, 410–412
Phillips, A.W., 408
Phillips curve
    and aggregate demand and aggregate supply curves, 409–410
    changing views of, 417
    defined, **408**–409
    long-run, 411, 413–417
    and long-run aggregate supply (LRAS) curve, 411
    and rational expectations, 418–419
    short-run, 410–411, 412, 413–417
    stability of short-run, 410–411
    and structural relationship, 410
    supply shock, effect on, 421
physical capital, 15, 182
pie charts, 23
planned aggregate expenditure, 215
    and GDP relationship, 217
    and inventories, 234–235
planned investment
    actual investment, difference between, 215
    aggregate expenditure component, 214
    cash flow, 227
    expectations of future profits, 226
    interest rates, 226
    and real investment spending, 225–226

taxes, 226
    variables of, 226–227
Playbook, 50
plotting price and quantity points, 25
PMI (Purchasing Managers' Index), 121, 140–141
Pokémon currency system, 295
Poland, 352
policy channels, 453
pollution
    and GDP, 105, 149
    and long-run economic growth, 203
population
    and demand, 66–67
    endogenous population growth (Malthus theory), 188–189
    increase, as incentive, 5
portfolio investments, 479
positive analysis, 11–12
potential GDP, 411
    defined, **154, 262**
    and expansion, 270
    and recession, 268
    and supply shock, 270–271
Prescott, Edward, 288, 391, 420
price levels
    business cycle, 164
    changes on real wage, 412
    consumption, 255
    as consumption variable, 220
    defined, **109, 132, 254**
    and fiscal policy, 369–371
    investment, 255
    and monetary policy, 339–340
    and net exports, 230, 256
    and short-run aggregate supply (SRAS) curve, 263–266
    sticky, 263–264
    vs. inflation rate, 165
price-level targeting and, monetary policy, 318–319
prices
    high demand and low prices example, 80–81
    of inputs, 71
    of related goods, and demand, 65–66
    of substitutes in production, 71
prime rate, 136
private saving, 157, 449–451
producer price index (PPI), 134–135
production
    defined, **14**
    and gross domestic product (GDP), 98–100
production possibilities frontier (PPF)
    defined, **36**
    example, 38–39
    graphing, 36–41

and opportunity costs, 36–42
productive efficiency, 9
productivity
    shifts in short-run aggregate supply (SRAS) curve, 266
    technological change, 71
product markets, 48
profit, 14, 226
property rights
    defined, **51, 196**
    and economic growth, 153, 200–201
    enforcement of, 51–52
    and low-income countries, 196–197
    protection of private property, 51
public education, low-income countries, 198–199
public saving, 157, 449
Purchase and Resale Agreements (PRAs), 309
Purchasing Managers' Index (PMI), 121
purchasing power, 63, 107
purchasing power parity, 467–470

quality bias, 134
quantitative easing, 335–336
quantity demanded
    change in, *vs.* change in demand, 68–69
    defined, **62**
    and supply analysis, 90–92
quantity supplied
    change in, *vs.* change in supply, 72–73
    defined, **69**
quantity theory of money, 288
    defined, 313–**314**
    equation, 313–314
    inflation, 314–315
quota, 468

rational expectations
    defined, **418**
    and the Phillips curve, 418–419
    and workers and firms, 288
rational thought, 4–5
real business cycle model, 288, 420
real exchange rate, 440, 447–448
real gross domestic product (GDP)
    in Botswana, 153–154
    calculating, 107–108
    compared to nominal GDP, 108–109
    defined, **107**
    and fiscal policy, 369–371
    monetary policy effect on, 334–336, 339–340

and multiplier effect, 376, 400–401
per capita, 1961–2012, 148–149
real interest rates, 136–137, 158, **220–221**
real variable, 135
real wage, 412
real-world deposit multiplier *vs.* simple deposit multiplier, 306
recessions
  on the 45°-line diagram, 233–234
  and aggregate demand (AD) curve, 267–268
  and Bombardier example, 168–169, 227–228
  and business cycle, 163–165
  in Canada, 154–155, 162–165, 269, 275–277, 363
  Canadian National Railway recovery, 280–281
  defined, **96, 148**
  effect of, on inflation rate, 164–165
  global recession (2007–2009), 168–169, 258–259, 325, 377–378, 425–427, 472–473
  and graduates, 121, 139
  in Greece, 384–385
  imported recessions, 269
  and monetary policies, 337–339
  and net exports, 229–230
  pay cuts, 253, 278
  potential GDP in long run, 268
  short-run and long-run effects on aggregate demand, 267–268
  in Spain, 472–473
  unemployment rate length, 125
  in United States, 269
  in Zimbabwe, 291
rectangle, area of, 31
Registered Retirement Savings Plans (RRSPs), 202
research and development, 187–188
Reserve Bank of Australia, 426
Reserve Bank of New Zealand, 426
Reserve Primary Fund, 351
reserves, 299
residential construction, 226
residential mortgage loan, 311
residential structures, 100
resources, 14
retained earnings, 155
revenue, 14
reverse causality, 28
Ricardo, David, 289
Riksbank, 426
risk, 156
Romer, Paul, 186, 201
Roubini, Nouriel, 201

Royal Bank of Canada, 300, 301–302, 354
Royal Canadian Mint, 298
Rudebusch, Glenn, 336
Ruhm, Christopher, 382
rule of 70, 150–151
rule of law
  and corruption, 197–198, 200–201
  defined, **196**–197
Russia, 389

Sacerdote, Bruce, 391
Sale and Repurchase Agreements (SRAs), 309
Sargent, Thomas, 288, 418–419
Sarkozy, Nicolas, 472
saving and investment equation, 449–450
savings
  consumer tax, 161–162
  income, and consumption, 223–225
  and investments, 199, 202
  low-income countries, 199
  market for loanable funds, 159–161
scarcity
  defined, **4, 36**
  governments and, 40
Schumpeter, Joseph, 188
Schwartz, Anna Jacobson, 287
scientific method, 11
Sears, Chris, 280
seasonal unemployment, 127
securitization, 311–312
security, 311
seigniorage, 297
services, 7–8, **14**
settlement balances, 308
shadow banking system, 310–313
Shiller, Robert, 413
shortage, 74
short-run aggregate supply (SRAS) curve
  defined, **254**
  and labour contracts, 263–264
  shifts in, *vs.* movements along, 264
  variables shifting, 264–267
short-run macroeconomic equilibrium, 267–272
short-run Phillips curve
  of 1960s, and long-run Phillips curve, 413–414
  basis for, 412
  for expected inflation rate, 415
  shifts in, 414–415
  stability of, 410–411
  vertical, 419–420
short-run trade-off, between unemployment and inflation, 408–412
short-term nominal rate of interest, 331

simple circular-flow diagram, 49
simple deposit multiplier
  defined, **302**–303
  vs. real-world deposit multiplier, 306
Singapore, 152–153
Ski-Doo, 147
Skinny Tie Width indicator, 262
slopes
  calculation of, 26
  of lines, in graphs, 24–25
  of nonlinear curves, in graphs, 29–30
small business income, 112
Smith, Adam, 50–51, 289
Smoot Hawley Tariff Act, 241
snowmobile purchases, 227
social problems, and GDP, 105
social program payments, 99
social science, economics as, 12–13
Solow, Robert, 186
South Africa, 352
South Korea, 352
  pegging against US dollar, 477–478
sovereign debt crisis, 472–473
Soviet Union
  as centrally planned economy, 8
  economic growth failure, 184–186
Spain, 352
  global recession, 472–473
specialization from trade, 42–44
speculative attacks, 476
speculators, 443
S&P/TSX Composite Index of Canadian stocks, 479
SRAS.
  See short-run aggregate supply (SRAS) curve
stagflation, 270
standard of deferred payment, 293–294
standard of living, 148
  China, compared to Canada, 200–201
  and income, 180–181
standing liquidity facilities, 308
Statistics Canada, 337, 438
sticky price levels, 263–264
sticky wages, 263–264
stocks, 155, 478–480
store of value, 293
structural relationship, 410
structural unemployment, 127, 129, 416
subprime loans, 347
sub-Saharan Africa, 148, 153
substitutes
  defined, **65**
  price of, in production, 71
substitution bias, 134
substitution effect, 63
supply

change in, *vs.* change in quantity supplied, 72–73
  curve, and change in good's price, 81–82
  curves, 69–70
  equations, 90–92
  expected future prices, 72
  law of, 70–71
  in loanable funds market, 158–161
  of the market, 69–73
  number of firms in the market, 71–72
  price of inputs, 71
  prices of substitutes in production, 71
  quantity supplied, 69
  schedules, 69–70
  shifts in, effect on market equilibrium, 77–78
  shifts in, effect on market equilibrium over time, 79–80
  technological change, 71
  variables that shift, 71–72
supply analysis, and quantity demanded, 90–92
supply curve
  defined, **69**–70
  vs. movements along a curve, 82
supply schedule, 69
supply shock
  defined, **266**
  effect on Phillips curve, 421
  and potential GDP, 270–271
  short-run and long-run effect, 270–271
supply-side economics, 387
supply-side effects, 391
surplus, 74
Sutton, Camilla, 140
Sweden
  inflation targeting, 352
  life expectancy, and real CDP per capita, 150
  monetary policy, 426
Switzerland, 150
symmetric inflation targeting, 327

T-accounts, 300–302
tangent line, 30
Tanzania, 153
tariffs
  defined, **468**
  on goods from China, 482–483
  and multiplier, 240–241
tastes, and demand, 66
taxes
  consumption taxes, 161–162, 367
  corporate income tax, 388
  on dividends and capital gains, 388

flat tax, 389–390
Goods and Services Tax (GST), 161, 367
and government spending, 367
Harmonized Sales Tax (HST), 161
individual income tax, 388
investment tax credits, 202
long-run effects of tax policy, 387–388
planned investment, 226
reforms, 390–391
and tariffs, 240–241
tax simplification, 388–389
tax wedge, 387
tax multipliers, 375, 379
formula, 402
and government purchases, 373–379
tax rates
and government purchases, 375
multiplier, effect on changes in, 403
tax wedge, 387
Taylor, George, 262
Taylor, John, 344
Taylor principle, 345
Taylor rule, 344–345
Taylor's Hemline Index, 262
technological change, 71, 152–153
defined, **181**
and government policies, 202
long-run economic growth, 181, 183–184
output per hour worked and, 184
shifts in short-run aggregate supply (SRAS) curve, 265
technology, 14, 129, 152
technology shocks, 420
Thailand
destabilizing speculation, 476
pegging, 474–476
Thompson, Michael, 354
thrift, paradox of, 241
time-series graphs, 24
Togo, 150
Toronto, 22, 90–92
Toronto Stock Exchange (TSX), 156, 280, 311
total income, 110–112
total production
and gross domestic product (GDP), 96–97
measures of, 110–112
shortcomings of GDP as a measure, 104–105

trade
and comparative advantage, 42–47
comparative advantage and, 45–47
defined, **36, 42**
gains from, 42–44
specialization from, 42–44
trade deficit, 437
trade flows, Canada and US, 2011, 437
trade-offs
automobile purchase, 35, 52
defined, **7**
in health care spending, 40
trade secrets, 187
trade surplus, 437
trade war, 241
transfer payments, 99, 111, 218
triangle, area of, 31–32
Troubled Asset Relief Program (TARP), 352
twin deficits in Canada, 1961–2011, 451–452

unanticipated inflation, 139
underground economy, 104–105
unemployment
efficiency wages, 130–131
government policies and unemployment rate, 129–130
inflation, short-run trade off between, 408–412
job creation and job destruction over time, 125–126
and labour unions, 130
length of time unemployed, 125
in the long run, and inflation rate, 416
natural rate of, 416–417
types of, 126–128
unemployment rate
business cycle, 165
defined, **122**
measuring, 122–126
and recession, 165
United Kingdom
consumption as percentage of GDP, 102
GDP, 95, 112
graduates, and recession, 95
inflation targeting, 352
United States
and Canada's catch-up to, 194–196

China, pegging against US dollar, 476–477
consumption as percentage of GDP, 102
credit easing, 335
currency bill, and China, 482–483
dollar and Canadian dollar exchange rates, 465–466
economic recovery, 318–319
environmental protection, 105
exports, and global recession, 258
federal budget deficit, 452
federal funds rate, 335
financial crisis of 2007–2009, 312–313, 346–352
flexible inflation targeting, 352
free market system, 50
housing bubble, 269, 276, 325, 346–348, 350–352
investment banks, role in, 348–349
and Japan's catch-up to, 194–196
long-run economic growth in, 177
modern mixed economy, 9
mortgage market, 348
and net exports, 229–230
OECD Better Life Index, 106–107
quantitative easing, 335–336
recessions, 269, 275–276, 352
standard of living, 148
trade flows, 2011, 437
unemployment and inflation tradeoff, 428–429
and Western Europe's catch-up to, 194–196
as world's largest debtor, 452–453
unit of account, 293
Universal Child Care Benefit, 366
university students, and employment, 95, 121
US Federal Reserve
and financial crisis of 2007–2009, 313, 335, 350–352
flexible inflation targeting, 352
monetary policy, 426
unemployment and inflation tradeoff, 428–429
US Treasury Department, 313, 350–352

Vaillancourt, François, 388
value, 97

value-added method, 103–104
variables
economic variables, 10–11
graphs, more than two variables, 25–26
graphs, one variable, 23–24
graphs, two variables, 24
omitted, 28
that shift market demand, 64–68
that shift supply, 71–72
Veldhuis, Niels, 271
velocity of money, 313–314
venture capital firms, 196
voluntary exchange, 9

wages
efficiency wages, 130–131
equilibrium wage, 129
hourly wages, 135–136
minimum wage, 11–13, 130
and short-run aggregate supply (SRAS) curve, 263–264
Wall Street Journal, 78
wars, low-income countries, 198
wealth effect, 255
wealth *vs.* money, 298
Western Europe
catch-up, 194–196
free market system, 50
standard of living, 148
won, 477
workers
expectations of inflation, 418
have rational expectations, 288
and inflation, understanding, 412–413
working age population, 122
wsj.com, 441

x-axis, 24

Yap, Laurance, 54
Yarbrough, Brian, 280
y-axis, 24
yen, 446, 465–466
Young, Alwyn, 152
yuan, 446, 476–477

zero inflation, 422
Zhaoxu, Ma, 482
Zimbabwe
hyperinflation in, 291, 315
life expectancy, and real CDP per capita, 150
underground economy in, 104